OBSERVATIONS

ON

THE GOSPEL of JOHN

Based Upon
The Jonathan Mitchell New Testament

Together With
An Expanded Translation
of
The Epistle of Barnabas

by
JONATHAN MITCHELL, M.A.

DEDICATION

This book is dedicated to my sister, Rebecca Ruth Mitchell, in appreciation for her years of careful and faithful proofing of all the books that we have published. Her work has gone throughout all the world. Our Father has seen, and will reward her, accordingly.

ACKNOWLEDGEMENTS

I am indebted to Dan Kaplan for his many insightful additions to this book, and I am blessed by our son, Joshua Mitchell, for his commitment to this ministry and for his technical support in IT, as well as for being the technical creator of our book covers, our webmaster and our publisher. I am thankful for support in this work by my wife, Lynda, and for her participation in the creation of the all the book covers – and for her tasteful input on those projects. I am also grateful that she has stood with me for 49+ years, even during times of pushback from the establishment. It has not been easy, as you might imagine.

I am happy to have been able to include linguistic insights from my friend, Arthur Eedle, and I want to express my appreciation for his many decades of service to our Lord.

We are also grateful for those who have financially supported our work, thus making it all possible.

Jonathan Mitchell
Surprise AZ, USA, 2020

TABLE of CONTENTS

DEDICATION and ACKNOWLEDGEMENTS
CONTENTS
INTRODUCTION
ABBREVIATIONS and APPARATUS

Cover Photo: I-Stock

New Testament text:
The New Testament, God's Message of Goodness, Ease and Well-Being, Which Brings God's Gifts of His Spirit, His Life, His Grace, His Power, His Fairness, His Peace and His Love, translated by Jonathan Mitchell; Copyright 2009, 2015 and 2019, all rights reserved; ISBN 978-1-4507-0505-9

Front Cover design and creation: Lynda Mitchell, Joshua Mitchell and Mishara Cruz
Cover productions: Joshua Mitchell, Volcano Studios LLC

INTRODUCTION

According to the critical analysis of John A.T. Robinson (*Redating the New Testament*, The Westmister Press, 1976 pp 254-311), this work was originally written circa A.D. 40-65. It has been more commonly dated at some time after A.D. 80, but for us, Robinson's extensive arguments are more convincing, and recent archaeological discoveries seem to corroborate this Gospel's awareness of details about Jerusalem, such as the Pool of Siloam (9:7) and Solomon's Porch (10:23), that point to a period prior to Jerusalem's destruction. In a study shared with us, our friend, Arthur Eedle, has astutely argued that it would have been illogical for our author to have waited decades before sharing these things, especially considering the purpose, cited below, which the author gave for composing this Gospel. It is only logical that he would have been familiar with the other Gospels that were also written during this same period, and, "undoubtedly he would have spent time gathering all his journal entries and composing the Gospel. To leave it until some later date would have been unthinkable" (Eedle).

The author has traditionally been considered to be John, but there is scholarly debate about this. From the internal evidence, during the writing of these *Observations*, we have come to suspect that it may have been someone else – as will be considered, later in the text. However, neither the date nor authorship are primary concerns of this work. Our purpose is to be a catalyst for our readers to give greater pause in reading this Gospel, and to pay attention to the particular details that its author shares, and the nuances and allusions that populate the work. This Gospel is foundational to Christianity, and its focus is critical to those who sense a call to be a follower of Jesus Christ. The author's purpose is given in 20:31,

> **"Yet these things have been written to the end that you folks can** (or: may; would) **continue trusting and keep on believing** [other MSS: should come to trust and believe] **that** (or: should progressively be faithful, because) **Jesus is the Christ** (Anointed One), **God's Son** (or: the Son of The God and from God), **and so that in continually trusting, believing and being loyal, you can continuously hold** (would progressively have) **Life** [other MSS: eonian life (or: life from, and in the realm of, the Age; age-lasting life)] **within, in the midst of, in union with, and centered in, His Name."**

Understanding the genre of the particular literature that a person begins reading will affect the strategy of interpretation that the reader will employ. A Gospel is a unique genre of ancient literature. It is based upon history, but it tells a story. The story is about Jesus Christ: Who He was, His life, His message and the Work that God gave Him to do. There are many stories, within this Story, and what was written was crafted to proclaim what was really going on in the overarching story (i.e., what God was doing in history, and why) within the midst of what was historically happening during the Incarnation of the Logos, the Word which was God and which was manifested in Jesus of Nazareth. We get a glimpse of how His followers came to understand "what was going on" within the "history" of the death of Jesus in Peter's first sermon:

> **"Men! Israelites! Continue listening and hear these words! Jesus the Nazarene, a mature Man having been fully pointed out unto you and continuing publicly exhibited and demonstrated [to be] from God – in powers and by abilities, together with miracles and signs which God did and performs through Him within your midst – just as you yourselves have seen, and thus are aware and know. This Man, given forth** (or: lent out; provided out of the Midst [of God]; given out [as in marriage]; given from the midst [of one's house]; issued forth [in birth]; or: surrendered; or: **This Fully-given, Emerged and Emptied One) in and by the specific, determined, bounded plan** (intended purpose, design and counsel) **and foreknowledge** (intimate knowledge which was experienced beforehand) **of God, you folks – through the hand of people not bound by the Law – took up and assassinated by fastening [Him] to a cross, Whom God resurrected, after loosing the birth-pangs of the death – corresponding to the fact that it was not possible for Him to be held fast by it"** (Acts. 2:22-24).

This presented God as being very much a part of the entire story. We will see this corroborated in 3:16-17, below. Later, when Paul wrote to Corinth he would encapsulate what he saw as the main point of this entire story, by saying, "**For you see, I decided not to see, perceive or know anything within or among you folks, except Jesus Christ – and this One being one having been crucified**" (1 Cor. 2:2). And then, in 2 Cor. 5:14b he gives the following conclusion:

> "**[We are] deciding** (discerning and concluding; judging) **this: that** [some MSS add: since] **One Person** (or: Man) **died over [the situation of] all people** (or: for the sake of all humans); **consequently all people died** (or: accordingly, then, all humans died)."

With these thoughts in mind, let us turn to a short description of how our author arranged this Gospel.

His work begins with a clear allusion to Gen. 1:1 in his opening verse. This is the Good News about the New Creation. There is a Prologue (1:1-18) and an Epilogue (chapter 21). Signs, some of which are designated as such by the author and others that can be observed from the text, appear from chapter 2, and on throughout, including in the Epilogue. Topics of focus will be the Logos, Light, Life, Bread, Water, Truth, Path (Way; Road), Resurrection and Love, which paint Jesus in a much larger picture and context than the traditional messianic categories presented in the OT. His story does not begin with His birth as a human, or with His appearance as a Jewish rabbi. As the Logos, He is connected to God's creative power, to the created universe, and at the same time, to the Hellenistic world of philosophy. It reaches back to the entire corpus of the OT. Jesus will speak of a new Temple, a new Birth, and a new realm of worship. The metaphors of shepherds and sheep, of a Vine and its branches, and the theme of Life of the Age of the Messiah, will also be highlighted. The human side of the story of Jesus is seen first of all as Him being "the Logos made flesh," and then "taking up residence among the People" (1:14). The social side of His life is presented as Him "being in the world" (1:10), attending a wedding (2:1ff), and striking up a conversation with a woman who was a stranger (4:3ff). The period of His public ministry is mostly covered from chapters 2-12. Chapters 13-17 record His upper room experience in intimate fellowship, and His final meal with His disciples, and then chapters 14-16 offer continuous teaching given to them (including the announcement of the coming Paraclete) which carries on through chapter 17 – an intimate view of His relationship with both His Father and His apprentices, in His long prayer for them. Chapters 18-20 involve His arrest, His trial, His crucifixion and then His resurrection. In 1:41 Andrew terms Him the Messiah, and in 1:49, Nathanael proclaims Him to be "the Son of God... the King of Israel," then in 6:69, Simon Peter will acclaim, "**we by personal, intimate experience have come to know that You, Yourself, are God's Holy One**."

Our work will spend considerable time on the various ways that the first sentence of the Prologue can be rendered, and the implications that are associated with each potential rendering. There will be an extensive investigation of the Greek word *Logos*, which dominates the theme of Jn. 1:1-14, and we will point out its use elsewhere in this Gospel. This Gospel contains numerous iconic verses for the "Christian Faith," such as these:

> "**Within the midst of a beginning** (or: In [the] Origin, in union with Headship and centered in Sovereignty) **there was, and continued being, the Logos** (the Word; the Thought; the collection of thoughts; the Idea; the Reason; the discourse; the speech and communication; the verbal expression; the Message; the reasoned, laid-out and ordered arrangement).
> **And the Logos** (the idea; the thought; the expression; the Word) **was, and continued being, facing, [directed, and moving] toward**, (or: continued being face to face with) **God**" (1:1)

> "**It was** (or: He was, and continued being) **the True and Genuine Light which** (or: Who) **is continuously** (repeatedly; progressively) **enlightening** (giving light to) **every person** (or: all humanity) **continuously** (repeatedly; progressively; constantly; one after another) **coming into the world** (or: the ordered system of culture, religion, economics and government; aggregate of humans; or: the universe)" (1:9)

"**Yet, as many as grasp, receive or accept It** (or: took Him in hand; seized to possess Him) – **to, for and among the ones habitually trusting into Its** (or: believing and being faithful unto His) **Name – It gives** (or: He gave) **to them** (or: for them; in them; among them) **authority** ([the] right; or: privilege from out of the midst of Being) **to be birthed God's children**" (1:12)

"**You should not be amazed** (or: begin to marvel; at some point be filled with wonder; suddenly be astonished; or: Don't be surprised) **that I said to you, 'It is necessary and binding for you folks to be born back up again to a higher place** (or: for you people to be given birth from above).'" (3:7)

"**And so, just as** (or: correspondingly as) **Moses lifted up** (elevated; raised up high) **the serpent, within the wilderness** (desert; desolate place) [Num. 21:7ff], **thus it is necessary and binding for the Son of Mankind** (Humanity's Son; the Human Being) **to be lifted up** (elevated; raised up high; exalted), **with the result and end that all – this progressively believing and successively** (one-after-another) **trusting humanity – in union with Him** (or: in order that all humanity, who being constantly loyal, centered in and within the midst of Him), **would continuously have eonian Life For thus God loves** (or: You see God, in this manner, fully gives Himself to and urges toward reunion with) **the aggregate of humanity** (universe; ordered arrangement; organized System [of life and society]; the world), **so that He gives His** [other MSS: the] **only-born** (or: only-kin; unique-class) **Son, to the end that all humanity, which** (or: everyone, who) **– when progressively trusting and successively believing into Him and thus being constantly faithful to Him – would not lose or destroy itself, or cause itself to fall into ruin, but rather can continuously have** (or: would habitually possess and hold) **eonian life. You see, God does not send forth His** [other MSS: the] **Son as a Representative or Emissary into the world** (or: System; aggregate of humanity) **to the end that He should continuously separate and make decisions about the world** (or: would at some point sift and judge the System, or the aggregate of humanity), **but to the contrary, to the end that the world would be delivered**
> (or: for the result that the System could be healed and made whole; so that the ordered arrangement should be restored to health; to the end that the aggregate of mankind may be saved – rescued and re-established in its original state): **through Him!**" (3:14-17)

In this passage, we want to point to the present participles, "**progressively believing and successively** (one-after-another) **trusting**…. **progressively trusting and successively believing**… **being constantly faithful**." This Gospel does not use the noun "faith; trust; faithfulness," but rather different forms of the verb, and usually in a durative tense that signifies continual and/or progressive action. These imply a dynamic interpersonal relationship with the object of the verb: Jesus, His words, and the Scriptures (2:22). We suggest that the stories in this Gospel are purposely symbolic; look for layers of meanings.

"**No one is able** (or: is presently having power) **to come toward Me unless the Father – the One sending Me – should drag him [as with a net]** (or: draw him [as drawing water in a bucket or a sword from its sheath])…" (6:44a)

"**It exists having been written within the Prophets: 'And all humans** (all people) **will continue existing being God's taught-ones** (or: folks having had instruction from God).' [Isa. 54:13] **All humanity – which, in hearing from the Father** (or: the person listening at the Father's side), **and learning** [D and others read: progressively learning] **– is progressively coming toward Me!**" (6:45)

"**I, Myself, am** (or: continuously exist being) **the continuously living Bread – the One stepping down** (or: descending) **from out of the midst of the atmosphere** (or: heaven). **If anyone should eat from out of this Bread, he will continue living on into the Age. Now also, the**

Bread which I, Myself, will continue giving, over (or: for the sake of; on behalf of) the life of the world (the ordered system; or: the aggregate of humanity), is My flesh!" (6:51)

"I Myself AM the Door for the sheep (or: the sheep's Gate and Entrance).... I, Myself, AM the Ideal Shepherd (the Beautiful Protector of, and Provider for, the sheep). The Ideal (Fine; Beautiful) Shepherd continually places His soul over the sheep" (10:7, 11)

"Jesus said to her, "I AM the Resurrection (or: I exist Being the standing back up again: the Arising), and (or: that is to say,) the Life. The one progressively believing and habitually putting trust into Me, even if he may die-off (or: die-away), will continue Living (or: will proceed being alive)!" (11:25)

"And thus I Myself: if (when) I should be lifted up from out of the earth (or: can be exalted from the midst of this Land), I will progressively (or: one after another) drag [note: drag as with, or in, a net; or: draw, as drawing water with a bucket, or a sword its sheath] all humans (or: everyone) to Myself" (12:32)

"I, Myself, AM (exist being) the Way (or: Path), the Truth (the Reality) and the Life (or: = I am the way to really live). No one is presently going to, or progressively coming toward, the Father, except through Me (through means of Me, or, through the midst of Me)." (14:6)

"I, Myself, AM the Grapevine; you folks [are] the tender branches (shoots or twigs that can be easily broken). The person continuously remaining (dwelling; abiding) within the midst of Me – and I within the midst of and in union with him – this one is repeatedly bearing (bringing forth; = producing) much fruit. [It is the case] that apart from (or: Because separated from) Me you folks continue having ability and power to do (make; construct; create; form; perform; produce) nothing!" (15:5)

"I am not now making a request about these only, but further about those habitually trusting and progressively believing into Me through their word (or: logos; message; what they lay out), to the end that all humans would (or: all people can and should) continuously exist being one, correspondingly as You, O Father [other MSS: Father], [are] within the midst of Me, and I [am] within the midst of You – so that they, themselves, may and would also continuously exist being within the midst of Us, to the end that the aggregate of humanity (the System: world of culture, religion and government; or: secular society) can (may; could) continuously trust and progressively believe that (would continue faithful because) YOU sent Me forth as an Emissary with a mission." (17:20-21)

"Correspondingly (or: Accordingly; On the same level; In the same sphere; In line with) as the Father has sent Me forth with a mission and as an Emissary (Representative), I Myself also am progressively (or: repeatedly; or: one after another) sending (dispatching) you folks" (20:21)

This is indeed a message of Goodness, Ease and Wellbeing (The Good News). There is no mention of The Unseen (*hades*) nor of Gehenna (the Valley of Hinnom, the city dump outside Jerusalem) in this Gospel. It is a Gospel about continuously having and holding Life.

Jonathan Mitchell
Surprise AZ, USA, 2020

ABBREVIATIONS and TEXTUAL APPARATUS

ABBREVIATIONS:
CVOT: *Concordant Version of the Old Testament*
CLNT: *Concordant Literal New Testament*
JM: translations of the LXX by the author
LXX: The Septuagint – Greek version of the Old Testament
MS: manuscript; MSS: manuscripts
NETS: *A New English Translation of the Septuagint*, A. Pietersma, B. Wright, Oxford Univ. Press, 2007
n: note
OT, NT: Old Testament, New Testament
Gen., Ex., Mat., Rom., etc.: commonly accepted indicators of the books of the Bible
Aleph, A, B, C, D, Ψ, etc.: indicate an individual codex or MS
p: signifies that the MS is a papyrus MS
TR: *Textus Receptus* (the "Received Text;" the "Majority Text")
cf: confer or compare
TDNT: *Theological Dictionary of the New Testament*, Ed. Gerhard Kittle, W.B. Eerdmans, 1977

APPARATUS:
Brackets, [ ]'s, have been used for the following situations:
to give a reading based upon other MSS
to insert notes or comments into the text
to insert words to aid in the reading of the English version
to indicate the reference of a quote from the Old Testament
to insert explanations
Parentheses, ( )'s, have been used for the following situations:
to give other possible meanings of a Greek word
to give alternate renderings of phrases or verses
to give a potential idiomatic translation
"=" has been placed before words for the following situations:
    to signify that the following is a potential idiomatic translation, or paraphrase; to give another
    spelling of a name or a suggested equivalent name; to give a Hebrew equivalent of a word or
    name; to give an explanatory note

OTHER PUBLISHED WORKS BY THE AUTHOR

THE NEW TESTAMENT, Expanded, Amplified and with Multiple Renderings
PETER, PAUL & JACOB, Comments on First Peter, Philippians, Colossians, First Thessalonians, Second Thessalonians, First Timothy, Second Timothy, Titus, Jacob (James)
JOHN, JUDAH, PAUL & ?, Comments on First John, Second John, Third John, Judah (Jude), Hebrews, Galatians
JUST PAUL, Comments on Romans
PETER'S ENCORE & LATER PAUL, Comments on Second Peter & Ephesians
THE END of the OLD and the BEGINNING of the NEW, Comments on Revelation
PAUL to CORINTH, Comments on First Corinthians and Second Corinthians
ζ Available from Harper Brown Publishing, www.jonathanmitchellnewtestament.com ζ

Other Translations Cited in This Work
A New English Translation of the Septuagint; Concordant Version of the Old Testament; Concordant Literal New Testament; The Emphasized Bible (J.B. Rotherham); *The Septuagint Bible; The New English Bible* (1970); *OT Pseudepigrapha, Vol. 2*

THE GOSPEL of JOHN

Chapter 1

In the Jonathan Mitchell New Testament, on offer are multiple renderings of verse 1. We will begin our Observation on this Gospel by investigating the implications and interpretations of each of these translations. May the Spirit lead us into all layers of the Truth offered therein. We will discuss a fair amount of grammar and word meanings, along the way. We will observe different paradigms that emerge. Let us read with an open mind and an enquiring spirit. Let us now look at the beginning...

"**Within the midst of a beginning** (or: In [the] Origin, in union with Headship and centered in Sovereignty) **there was, and continued being, the Logos** (the Word; the Thought; the collection of thoughts; the Idea; the Reason; the discourse; the speech and communication; the verbal expression; the Message; the reasoned, laid-out and ordered arrangement).
And the Logos (the idea; the thought; the expression; the Word) **was, and continued being, facing, [directed, and moving] toward,** (or: continued being face to face with) **God.**
And the Logos (the Word; the thought; the idea; the reason; the expression) **continued being God.**"

This verse begins with the preposition *en*, and this first translation offers four ways to render it:
> a) "Within the midst of" which presents us with the sense of location; what follows is located "within the midst of a beginning." Notice that there is no definite article before the noun "beginning." The subject of the first statement is in reference to "a beginning," not "the beginning."
> b) In the parenthetical expansion, on offer is the simple rendering "in" which is broader, and more ambiguous. Because of the semantic range of this preposition, any of the other meanings could be nuanced from the phrase "in [the] Origin." The definite article "the" is inserted, bracketed, since it is not in the Greek text but this is a possible rendering into English, even though it would not carry the sense of the definite article, were it in the text. Notice the alternate rending of *archē* as "Origin," rather than the first rendering, "beginning." This would emphasize the nuance of "source," rather than the sense of the "start" of something.
> c) Next is the emphasis of the preposition in relationship, as well as location: "in union with Headship," offering another meaning of the noun. Here *archē* also has the sense of relationship – as with that of a "head" to its "body." The context could also refer to the position of the leader, or progenitor, of a tribe or other social organization.
> d) Finally, in this first expanded rendering of the verse, we have "centered in Sovereignty." This rendering of the noun is similar to "Headship," but suggests a political or governmental context, such as a "reign" or a "kingdom." Here, the statement which follows has its center in Sovereignty.

We will consider other renderings of this opening phrase, below.

Before moving on in this verse, let us briefly look at a couple other places where we find the term *archē*. The foremost, where we find it in the same Greek phrase, is in Gen. 1:1 (LXX):
> "**Within the midst of beginning** (or: In union with Headship and centered in Sovereignty), **God produced** (or: formed; constructed) **the atmosphere** (or: sky; heaven) **and the land** (territory; ground; soil)." (JM)

We can observe how closely these two verses are connected when we read Jn. 1:3,
> "**All things suddenly happened and came to be** (or: occur and come to be; were birthed) **by means of It, or Him** (or: He at some point gives birth to all humanity through It), **and apart from It** (or: Him) **not even one thing comes into being** (occurs; was birthed; came into being; happens) **which has come into being** (which has occurred; which has happened)."

The subject of John's prologue (Jn. 1:1-18) fleshes out the topic of the first verse, but this first study will be focused on 1:1. Now John later records Jesus as referring to Himself as the *archē*, in Jn. 8:25,

> "**They then began saying to Him, "YOU! – what** (or: who) **ARE you?" Jesus says to them, 'That which I am even habitually telling you: the Beginning, the Origin, the Source and the Chief One** (or: The *Archē*).'"

We find more instruction in Rev. 21:6b,

> "**I am the Alpha and the Omega: The Beginning** (Origin; Source; Headship; First Principle) **and The End** (The Goal; Consummation; The Final Act; The Finished Product; The Destiny; The Purpose)."

In his booklet, *Hidden Gems*, Arthur Eedle instructs us concerning the Hebrew particle, *eth*, which is used in the Hebrew version of Gen. 1:1.

> "The Hebrew Bible is literally peppered with *eth*. It is a grammatical word that needs no translation, but it consists of two Hebrew letters, *Aleph* and *Tau*, the **first** and the **last** letters of the [Hebrew] alphabet. 'Thus says the LORD, the King of Israel, and his Redeemer, the LORD of hosts; I am the FIRST, and I am the LAST; and beside Me there is no God' (Isa. 44:6). In the Revelation, Jesus declared, 'I am the Alpha and the Omega, the Beginning and the End, the First and the Last' (Rev. 22:13). *Eth* is therefore the *Logos*, and the first time it occurs in the Bible it is **right next to** Elohim, God. So the Logos is **with** GOD and the Logos **IS** GOD" (ibid pp 13-14, emphasis original; brackets added).

We will now move on to the rest of the first clause of 1:1.

"**there was, and continued being, the Logos** (the Word; the Thought; the collection of thoughts; the Idea; the Reason; the discourse; the speech and communication; the verbal expression; the Message; the reasoned, laid-out and ordered arrangement)."

The verb of this clause is the imperfect tense of the verb "to be; to exist." This tense indicates continued action that began in the past and may continue on to the present time. Thus, the verb is given as "**was, and continued being**." In this rendering, the subject of the verb is "**there**," and the predicate is "**the Logos** (etc.)." This same verb, in the same tense, is also used in the next two statements of this verse.

The term "Logos" has become a common loan word from the Greek, and is a transliteration of the Greek noun. In the next two declarative statement, "**Logos**" is set as the subject of those sentences, and is the primary subject of vss. 1-14. However, in all these verses, we realize that the Logos also is incarnated (made flesh) in Jesus Christ, but we will not develop that thought here. So our next step is to examine the semantic range of this Greek term, as given in the first rendering of vs. 1. Other meanings will be presented, below.

As we observe, in the parenthetical expansion, the term Logos has a very broad semantic range. It comes from the verb *legō*, which begins with the core idea of laying something out in a particular arranged order. It can also signify gathering things together to present a thought or an idea. The most common rendering of this verb is "to say; to make a verbal expression; to speak a message; to make a declaration; etc." Therefore, what is said is "a word; a thought; etc." The definite article is present, so the offered renderings are: "the Word; the Thought; the collection of thoughts; the Idea; the Reason; the discourse; the speech and communication; the verbal expression; the Message; the reasoned, laid-out and ordered arrangement." That's a mouthful.

A word usually begins with a thought. Messages usually involve reason, and by extension, the reason usually has purpose. This term can also signify a collection of thoughts, or, an idea. It can refer to discourse, a speech or communication, such as "a message." All of this was "in union with a beginning," and it was "the reasoned, laid-out and ordered arrangement" that was "centered in" a particular beginning.

All these terms are easily understood, but meditating upon each of these options (substituting one, after another, into this opening clause) can really color our world. But on to the next statement…

"**And the Logos** (the idea; the thought; the expression; the Word) **was, and continued being, facing, [directed, and moving] toward**, (or: continued being face to face with) **God.**"

We just discussed the subject, Logos (etc.), and the verb in the previous section (they are repeated here) and so let us move on to the prepositional phrase that ends this statement, serving as a predicate. The preposition is *pros*, and, like all Greek prepositions, can serve different functions. The basic idea of this preposition is movement toward something, and by implication, "facing" the object of this preposition. Here I inserted "**[directed, and moving]**" to aid the reader in getting a mental picture of what is being described. The expanded rendering, including the verb, is "continued being face to face with." And this brings us to the object of this facing, moving toward, and being face to face with: **God.**

Now the phrase is commonly rendered "with God," which is grammatically correct, but leaves a lot out of what John could have been saying about the relationship between the Logos and God. If we consider the idea of directed motion, we see that God is the destiny of this directed motion. If we ponder what it means to be "face-to-face" with God, this gives much more to consider. Focus on God, moving toward God, and being present with God is what this statement is telling us about "the Logos." Now before rushing on, alternatively read this statement while one-after-another substituting each semantic meaning of Logos as the subject. Below we get to do this in a number of different ways. But now, to the next sentence…

"**And the Logos** (the Word; the thought; the idea; the reason; the expression) **continued being God.**"

Now the only difference in this statement from the last is that the predicate is "**God.**" It is common in English translations to omit the definite article, "the," before a proper name, and the term God is often classified as a proper name, as in the second statement of this verse. There, the Greek has "toward the God." But in our present statement, John did not put the definite article before "God." We mention this because theological debate has arisen where some have claimed that the term God, without the article, is not saying that the Logos was "the God" of the previous statement, and of the virtual conflation of the first two statements in the following verse (1:2): "**This** (or: This One) [i.e., the Logos] **was continuing in existence, within a power of beginning and in union with Headship and Sovereign principle, facing [directed, and moving] toward** (or: staying with) **[the] God.**" Here, for clarity of my point, I added the definite article that is in the Greek text, before the word "God."

We suggest that this final statement of vs. 1, above, is defining the essence, being, character and source of the Logos. The Logos is the subject of the sentence, since it has the definite article. The term God is the predicate of the sentence: it gives us information about the Logos. We might compare this to the statement that "God is Spirit" (4:24, below). Here we could simply say "The Logos is God."

Let us now give attention to the first alternate rendering of verse 1:

"Originally, within the midst of the first principle, the Word, a Patterned Design, was existing and continued to be; and then the Word, or Patterned Design, was being [projected] toward God. And this Word, or Patterned Design… It continued existing actually and essentially being God."

On offer here are two renderings of the opening prepositional phrase. The first one gives us the whole phrase in one word: "Originally." The second one modifies "Originally," adding the information that this origin was "within the midst of the 'first principle' (*archē*)." I joined the first and second clauses into a compound sentence while instead of rendering the conjunction between them as "and," rendering it as "and then." This reading of the Greek suggests a dynamic: a movement from beginning to development.

Thus we have: "the Word, a Patterned Design, was existing and continued to be; and then the Word, or Patterned Design, was being [projected] toward God." Take note of the expanded rendering of "the Word" as being "a Patterned Design." This second meaning of Logos was taken from the theological discussions of *logos* in *Information and the Nature of Reality*, Paul Davies & Niels Henrik Gregersen, Editors, Cambridge Univ. Press 2010. I draw from this work once again in the final rendering, below.

In the final clause I rendered the definite article as a demonstrative, "this," which, according to A.T. Robertson, was the original function of the article. It was like a finger, pointing: "this Word, or Patterned Design." The three dots that follow suggest a pause in John's thoughts, and then he continues, "It continued existing actually and essentially being God. Here, "continued existing actually and essentially being" is an expanded rendering of the verb, offering the nuances inherent in the verb "to be; to exist." This Word was an essential aspect – dare we say infusing ingredient (?) – of Who and What God is. This Word was within the midst of the First Principle, which is God, Himself. The idea of a Patterned Design can be seen in language, in DNA, in fractals, to mention just a few, and it is a characteristic of *logos*. Next:

"In command was Reason {the ontological "structure of the mind which enables the mind to grasp and transform reality" [Paul Tillich]}, and Reason was staying with God, for Reason {this ontological mental structure} was just what God was."

A cognate of *archē* is the noun *archōn*: one invested with power; a chief; a ruler; a prince; a magistrate; a high official; a lord; the one in first place. This person was normally "in command." Then on offer is one of the central meanings of *logos*: **reason**. I inserted Paul Tillich's definition of reason in brackets: "the ontological structure... etc." The enabling of "the mind to grasp and transform reality" fits well with the idea of "creating." Reason guided the creation (Jn. 1:3). In the next clause I rendered the verb and the preposition, "was staying with," since the verb is in the imperfect tense, and "being with" is one of the meanings of the preposition. The final clause ends in a paraphrase, "was just what God was," which is a more emphatic way of reading the Greek.

Now **reason** may be thought of as involving "words" and "thoughts," but it holds for us a more purposed, even patterned, way of thinking or communicating. Should we read John's prologue with this as the meaning of *logos*, we might arrive at a different picture from this passage. I recommend doing this.

Then, another rendering:

"The Thought, or The Concept, was in the midst of [the] Source. The Thought, or The Concept, was oriented toward the Deity. And the Thought, or The Concept, was Deity."

Here I focused on "thought" and "concept," from among our choices for *logos*. "Source" views "the beginning" as the environment from which the thought or the concept emerged. Rearranging the order, placing Thought/Concept where normal English subjects stand in a sentence, takes our emphasis away from "in the beginning" to the main topic of the Prologue: the Logos. The Logos was within the midst of, in union with, and centered in God (the Source). The Logos (Thought/Concept) "was oriented toward the Deity (an alternate rendering of *theos*). "And the Thought, or The Concept, was Deity." Using different terms can be a catalyst for new thinking. Such famous verses, as Jn. 1:1, can often be passed over without our letting them speak deeper into us. Since John equates the Concept with Deity, can we see in a new way how it was Deity that did the work of creation (vs. 3)? That is not a new idea, but it might enable us to see the Deity in all that He created from out of Himself.

And then:

"In beginning, the collected and put side by side Thoughts continued in progressive existence, and the collected and put side by side Thoughts continued being a progression to God, and God {"the Divine Mystery" – Paul Tillich's definition of *theos*} was in continued existence being those collected and put side by side Thoughts."

I now rendered the opening phrase (rendered literally, here) as functioning as a participle that sets the stage for the action that will be following, in subsequent verses. But in this beginning the Actor (Thoughts) is described and identified. "The collected and put side by side Thoughts" is an expansion of *logos*, drawing from the basic idea of *legō*, cited above. The verb, being in the imperfect tense, can indicate progressive action – or in this case, progressive being or existence. As Paul said in Rom. 11:36, all things are from out of the midst of God, pass through the midst of God, and return into the midst of God (my translation). There is a dynamic, a progression, and as Paul instructs us, it is a progression "to God."

In the final clause, some will object that since here God does not have the definite article that it cannot be the subject of the clause. However, I chose to break with that rule and simply follow the order of the words in the text, reading this whole verse as one sentence. In the text, we have "a progression to [the] God, and God... was in continued existence being... Thoughts." It seems reasonable that if we don't insert a break between "the God" and "and God" (there was no punctuation in the oldest manuscripts), that the term God is the same in both cases. The final "the *logos*" has the article, not because it is the subject of the clause, but because throughout this verse it has been indicated as "the Word/this Word" – in its various renderings. "God was in continued existence being those collected and put side by side Thoughts." Notice that because *logos* can mean "thoughts," and not just "a thought," or an "idea," that I translated a singular noun into a plural. We have the same thing in the rendering "message."

And now:

"In union with [the] beginning there was the continued existence of the laid-out Idea {the blueprint – Rohr}, and the laid-out Idea {blueprint} was continued existence face to face with God, and the laid-out Idea {blueprint} continued in existence being "the Divine Mystery."

The emphasis, here, is on the preposition being rendered "in union with," and on the expanded rendering of *logos* as "the laid-out idea (the blueprint)." As indicated, I follow Richard Rohr with translating the *logos* as "the blueprint." This is a brilliant and insightful capturing of a central idea inherent in this word. It corresponds to Yahweh telling Moses to construct the tabernacle "according to the pattern" – and that was during the time of the creation of Israel as a People of God. The Logos is the Pattern; the Blueprint. The Blueprint involved Reason; it was God's Idea – and that Idea is Christ!

This Idea/Blueprint is constantly "face to face with God." This Blueprint continued in existence being "the Divine Mystery" (Tillich), the Mystery (Secret) of which Paul has expounded in his letters.

Next:

"At a starting point, the Word continued Being. Then the Word was Being [directed] toward God. And then {or: yet} the Word was Being God {essential Deity; Divine Essence}."

Now we have the *archē* phrase as: "At the starting point." This simply provides the picture using different words. By rendering the verb, "continued Being," we indicate that the Word had "being" before the "starting point" of creation, and by capitalizing "Being," we indicate its participation in, or essential existence as, God – as the rest of the verse goes on to explain. The Word continued existing as "Being." Also, it was "Being [directed] toward God." It has a focus, a destiny, a purpose. It would take all that It created (1:3) into the midst of God.

The conjunction opening the final clause is offered in two ways: "And then," or, "And yet." Now possibly the simple rendering "And," would be better, but in that case our readers might not ponder these possibilities. "And then," suggests a progression, based upon the "toward" of the previous clause. "And yet," as the rendering, might have John affirming that even though the Word was being "[directed] toward God," It was, in fact, "Being God {essential Deity; Divine Essence}." Choices in translating the smallest word can make a difference.

And another:

"Within the power of beginning – which is the controlling principle and power of the entire process – there existed the Idea {the creative and unifying principle of the cosmos}, and the Idea was aimed at and moving toward God. Also, the Idea existed being God."

The opening phrase combines the idea of the power of one who leads, with the project which he is beginning. Next is the qualifier that explains this power: "the controlling principle and power of the entire process." This expansion, which is derived from the root concepts of *arché*, presents the ideas of process (implied from "at the start" or "in a beginning) along with the principle of position (leadership; headship) combined with the power of the position that is held. So "within the power of beginning, there existed the Idea." This idea can be seen as "the creative and unifying principle of the cosmos" ("**All things [that] suddenly happened and came to be**" – Jn. 1:3a). This Idea (that existed in a beginning) "was aimed at and moving toward God." God is the target; God is the goal; God is the destiny toward which this Idea (Logos) is moving. The Logos is pointing to God. And then we see that "the Idea existed being God." It is God from beginning to end; from the Alpha to the Omega. God was the Power of this beginning, and of the process that followed, and which continues moving forward into the midst of God.

Next is an expanded rendering, including paraphrases, based upon the insights of Jean-Yves Leloup:

"The Logos continued being within Arché (Source; = The Son was in the midst of [the] Father; [note: I owe to Jean-Yves Leloup the connecting of Arché with the Father]), and the Logos continued being in a movement toward God (= The Son existed in a movement toward the Father), and the Logos continued being God (= The Son was [part of? Within?] the Father)."

We begin with transliterations of the Greek words that are now familiar to our readers. In the parenthetical expansion, I offer *arché* as "Source," followed by a paraphrase, "The Son was in the midst of [the] Father." Then we have "the Logos continued being in a movement toward (Greek: *pros*) God. I followed this with another paraphrase: "The Son existed in a movement toward the Father." The Son, the Logos, is the Way to union with God. The Son (Logos) is the Pattern and the Path. The last clause is, "the Logos continued being God." Paraphrasing this clause we have "The Son was…" But here the analogy may break down, so I inserted potential qualifiers, "[part of? Within?]," before the predicate, "the Father." Now Leloup did not equate the term "God" with "the Father," in this verse, but assigning the Son and the Father as being identities in the verse seems to lead to the interpretation of God being the Father, in this scene. This rendering was included in my NT to cause the reader to think. May His Reason shed light on it.

Finally, a full paraphrase:

"Centered in, and in union with, a starting of a Beginning, there was existing, and continued being, the transfer and input of Information that was conveying Meaning [= the Word and Will], and this transfer and input of Information that conveyed [purposed, causal] Meaning continued being projected with God as its Aim, and God continued in existence in this transfer and conveyance of Meaning-bearing Information (or: this 'Flow of Information that is a Pattern-forming Influence;' = 'God's self-expression in a creation')."

14

I owe the concepts of these interpretive renderings in this final option to an essay, "The science of complexity: a new theological resource?" by Arthur Peacocke, citing John Macquarrie, in *Information and the Nature of Reality*, cited above.

Here I conflated both the preposition (Centered in, and in union with) and the noun (a starting of a Beginning). The renderings of *logos* are drawn from the authors cited: "the transfer and input of Information that was conveying Meaning [= the Word and Will], and this transfer and input of Information that conveyed [purposed, causal] Meaning…" These expanded renderings were based upon interpreting the *logos* in terms of Quantum Physics/Mechanics. This connection between science and Scripture is very logical. What the scientists who offered essays in this book perceived in terms of Quantum theory, the theologians identified as the Logos.

The "conveyed [purposed, causal] Meaning (of the universe) continued being projected (*pros*) with God as its Aim." This is the plan of the Ages.

"And God continued in existence in this transfer and conveyance of Meaning-bearing Information," or, this rendering of *logos* said another way: "this 'Flow of Information that is a Pattern-forming Influence.'" And a last interpretation: "= 'God's self-expression in a creation.'"

Scripture is here for our meditating on, and our pondering of, ideas that the Spirit causes to rise within us. Our speculating on layers of interpretation that come to us, while holding them loosely to see if the Spirit either confirms or adjusts what we see, brings an inflow of the Life of Christ. A flat reading of Scripture will leave us with a flat earth, and a heaven that is far, far away. The Logos came to be here with us; to become flesh (1:14) and set up Its tent among us; and then to join itself to us and lead us on the heavenly circuit, through the midst of God. So let us look at…

THE LOGOS

This section will focus on the context of Jn 1:1ff in its connection with its antecedent context of Gen. 1:1ff. Jn. 1:1-3 can be seen as both a synopsis of, and a commentary on, Gen. 1:1-2:4, while shedding further light on the construction of "the heaven and the earth" that is narrated in this Genesis passage. Since the Septuagint (LXX) opens with the identical Greek phrase that opens the Gospel of John, *en archē* (In a beginning; etc.), we will use this version of the OT.

In the "creation/construction/production" of the "sky and the Land (or: the heaven and the earth)" as recorded in Gen. 1:1, we observe that the Actor (the One doing the action) is God (*ho theos*). In the synopsis given in Jn. 1:1-3, we observe that the Actor (the One doing the action) is The *Logos*. Let us now read these two opening statements, first considering Gen. 1:1,

> "**Within the midst of a beginning** (or: In [the] Origin, in union with Headship and centered in Sovereignty), **God produced** (or: formed; constructed) **the heaven and the earth** (the sky and atmosphere as well as the land, territory, ground and soil)" (LXX, JM).

And now, Jn. 1:1-3,

1. **Within the midst of a beginning** (or: In [the] Origin, in union with Headship and centered in Sovereignty) **there was, and continued being, the Logos** (the Word; the Thought; the collection of thoughts; the Idea; the Reason; the discourse; the speech and communication; the verbal expression; the Message; the reasoned, laid-out and ordered arrangement).
And the Logos (the idea; the thought; the expression; the Word) **was, and continued being, facing, [directed, and moving] toward**, (or: continued being face to face with) **God.**
And the Logos (the Word; the thought; the idea; the reason; the expression) **continued being God.**

2. **This** (or: This One) **was continuing in existence, within a power of beginning and in union with Headship and Sovereign principle, facing [directed, and moving] toward** (or: staying with) **God.**
> (or: This [situation?] was existing {or: continued being} within the midst of Archē (Source; = Father), [aimed; progressing; being; moving] toward, and thus [to be] face-to-face with, God.)

3. **All things happened and came to be** (or: occur and come to be; were birthed) **by means of It, or Him** (or: He at some point gives birth to all humanity through It), **and apart from It** (or: Him) **not even one thing comes into being** (occurs; was birthed; came into being; happens) **which has come into being** (which has occurred; which has happened)."

Verse 2 is virtually a restatement of the first two statements of vs. 1, the third statement of vs. 1 identifying the Logos as "**being God**." The parenthetical expansion of vs. 2 gives the transliteration, *Archē*, while offering the meaning "Source" and the suggested implication (a metaphorical reading) "= Father." Next this expansion inserts "[aimed; progressing; being; moving]," which express the nuances of the preposition *pros*, which is primarily a directional, and secondarily implies association within the presence of another "face-to-face with." Thus, joining this with vs. 14b, below, presents us with a picture of "Family."

Verse 3 identifies the Logos as the Creator God: the means of the "birthing" of the cosmos, humanity, and then Israel as His special project, where the Logos is the Alpha (Source; Beginning; First Expression) and the Omega (the goal; the finished project; the termination – of the first "metaphorical creation," Israel). The last statement of this verse is astounding, and calls us to meditate upon its implications: "**apart from It** (or: Him) **not even one thing comes into being** (occurs; was birthed; came into being; happens) **which has come into being** (which has occurred; which has happened)." Think beyond birds and squirrels, rocks and trees. Think beyond the physical creation, as important and foundational as it is. Think of the history of Israel and of all that has "come into being" from the first Adam to the Last Adam. All of history and humanity has not come into being "**apart from the Logos**." The Logos is both intertwined with and infused into all of existence. Paul refers to this as "the plan of the ages" (Eph. 3:11).

In John's explanation, vs. 1 gives us the subject of 1:1-14, the Logos. Verse 3 explains that the Logos is the One that "produced, formed and constructed" everything – i.e., "the heavens and the earth (or: the land and the sky)." Following this correlation, we can understand why Jn. 1:1 ends with the Logos being identified as God, since Gen. 1:1 informs us that it was God that brought this all about.

Although Gen. 1 does not use the term Logos, if we consider the parenthetical expansion of this term in Jn. 1:1, above, we can see its connection with Gen. 1:3, so let us bring to mind some verses from that opening passage in Gen, following the LXX (JM):
> 2. **yet the land was invisible and unprepared** (not commensurately prepared, fitted well together, thoroughly adjusted, directed in accord, correspondingly made ready [as for giving birth] and not completely united [for ripeness]; down-supplied to fully establish), **and darkness [was] back up upon** (or: above, on) **the Deep. And so God's Breath-effect was continuously imposed back up upon the water.**
> > (or: Originally God made the heaven/sky and the earth, but the earth was continuing in existence being unseen, and not ready. Later, a darkness [spread] back upon the abyss. And then a spirit of, and which was, God progressively brought experiences upon the water again.)
>
> 3. **Later on God said, "Light, be born** (or: Let light come into existence)**!" And so light was birthed** (or: at once came into existence).
>
> 4. **Then God saw the light, that [it was] fine, ideal and beautiful. So God passed** (or: excreted) **through the midst again and divided back between the light and the darkness.**
>
> 5. **And God called the light "day," and He called the darkness "night." And so evening was birthed** (or: at once came to be), **and later morning was birthed** (or: came to be)**: a first** (or: one) **day.**

Notice: "**God said…**" We find this again in vs. 6, 9, 11, 14, 20, 24, 26, 29, and then in 2:3 we read that "**God spoke words of goodness, ease and well-being to** (or: blessed)…" So, throughout this narration of creation (forming; constructing; producing), God's Word was involved, even though the term *logos* was not used in this passage. But we do find the participle *legōn*, "proceeding in saying," in vs. 28, when God blesses the male and the female that He had "produced; formed; constructed."

Before moving on, let me explain my use of the term "**It**," in reference to the Logos, in Jn. 1:3 (and on through Jn. 1:4-14): the Greek pronoun is masculine because it corresponds to the term *logos*, which is masculine; however, translated into English, the term "Word" does not have a gender associated with it. I also offer the pronoun, "Him," in vs. 3 and in the rest of the passage, but that is a theological interpretation, based upon vs. 14, below, where we read:

> 14. **And so That Which had been Laid Out as a transfer of Information, i.e., The Word**
>> (the Idea; the Thought; the Reason; the Discourse; the Message; The Collected Expression of Rational Logic; *The Logos*; = the meaning, plan and rational purpose of the ordered universe),
> **births Itself flesh**
>> (or: became flesh; came to be [in] flesh; came into existence being flesh; = God's thought, the ground of all real existence, became projected into creation as an immanent power within the world of mankind, inhabiting flesh),
> **and lives in a tent, within us** (or: set up a tent and tabernacled among us), **and we view** (attentively gaze at; looked at so as to contemplate) **Its** (or: His) **glory and assumed appearance**
>> (Its manifestation which calls forth praise; Its appearance which creates and effects opinions in regard to the whole of human experience; His imagination; = His manifest presence): **a glory** (= prestige and importance; reputation and opinion-forming appearance) **as of an only-begotten person** (or: like One that is an only kin, of a solitary race, in a by-itself-class) **at a father's side** (or: in the presence of, and next to, [the] Father), **full of grace and truth** (filled and replete with joy-producing favor, as well as reality and genuineness).

That being said, the subject of this entire passage, in Jn. 1, is "The Logos," as we clearly see, in vs. 14. While accepting the traditional interpretation that vs. 14 refers to the "incarnation (enfleshment)" of the Logos as Jesus, our focus will continue on the topic of the term and concept of the Logos, as such.

Returning to Gen. 1, it seems logical to conclude that each time that "**God said…**" we perceive the Logos in whatever it was that He was saying. Those "sayings" WERE the Logos: "the Word; the Thought; the collection of thoughts; the Idea; the Reason; the discourse; the speech and communication; the verbal expression; the Message; the reasoned, laid-out and ordered arrangement."

> "**Because, forth from out of the midst of Him, then through the midst of Him** (or: through means of Him), **and [finally] into the midst of Him, [is; will be] the whole** (everything; [are] all things)! **By Him** (In Him; To Him; For Him; With Him) **[is] the glory** (the assumed appearance; the manifestation of that which calls forth praise; the reputation; the notion; the opinion; the imagination; the credit; the splendor) **on into the ages**" (Rom. 11:36).

The Subject (the Him) of Rom. 11:32-35 is God, the LORD (Yahweh). Everything came from out of the midst of Him (no creation *ex nihilo*, "out of nothing," here) by means of the Logos. This entire journey of all things is by means of, and through the midst of, the Logos. It (He) is the Alpha and the Omega; the Beginning and the End (Goal; Finished Product). This is why our author said that the Logos "**was, and continued being, facing, [directed, and moving] toward God**" (Jn. 1:1), because God was the Destiny of all that God spoke. Isa. 55:11 affirmed,

> "**Thus, in this way, will continue being My gush-effect** (the result of the flow from Me; My spoken words and utterances), **which would at any point issue forth from My mouth: It can**

by no means be turned back (or: return) **until as much as** (or: whatever) **I would will** (intend; desire) **would be accomplished** (fulfilled; finished; brought to its goal)…" (LXX, JM).

The "Idea" (creation, and all that this implies) was spoken forth toward God. Everything that exists came to be via the Logos. The Logos was, and is, an expression of God. The creation is the embodiment of the Logos, and is thus the embodiment of God. J. Preston Eby has said regarding the creation, "God expressed out of Himself a different form of Himself" (paraphrased, as best as I can remember hearing him). "**And the Logos became flesh**…"

In Gen. 2:7 we read a more detailed account about the origin of the humans:
> "**Then** (or: And so) God formed (molded and fashioned) **the human being** (or: humanity) – **soil** (loose, moist earth) **from the ground** (earth; land; territory; dirt) – **and then He breathed into his face a breath of life** (or: a wind from Life), **and the human being** (or: humanity) **was birthed into a living soul** (or: came to exist being a living person)" (LXX, JM).

No wonder Jesus said to Philip,
> "**The person having discerned and seen Me has seen, and now perceives, the Father!**" (Jn. 14:9).

Adam had God's Life breathed into Him. As the Second Humanity (the Last Adam; 1 Cor. 15:45-47), Jesus had the Father's Life breathed into Him. "**He Whom God sends forth with a mission… God is habitually** (or: continuously) **giving the Spirit** (Breath-effect) **[and] not from out of a measure** (= not by a measured portion or limit; = without measure and without limitation)" (Jn. 3:34). In Lu. 24:49, Jesus told His followers:
> "**And so, look and take note: I Myself am now progressively sending forth the Promise from out of the midst of, and from, My Father** (or: am out from within repeatedly sending forth My Father's promise, as an Emissary; [with other MSS: From where I now am, I now continuously send off the Promise, **which is My Father**]) **upon you people**…"

Then is Acts 1:8a, He said to them:
> "**you folks will progressively receive power and will continue taking to yourselves ability: a sudden** (point of time) **added, full coming [= Parousia] of the Set-apart Breath-effect** (the Holy Spirit and Sacred Attitude) **upon you folks**…"

John 6:63 records Jesus saying:
> "**The Spirit** (or: Breath-effect; or: spirit; Breath) **is** (or: continues being) **the One continuously creating Life** (or: repeatedly making alive; habitually forming life)… **The declarations** (gush-effects; spoken words; sayings; results of the Flow) **which I, Myself, have spoken to you folks are** (or: continue to be) **Spirit** (or: spirit; Breath-effect) **and they are** (or: continue being) **Life.**"

There seem to be "dots" that can be connected here. In Acts 4:4 we read:
> "**many of the folks presently hearing the word** (message; information; the *LOGOS*) **trusted and believed.**"

A new creation was happening…

In Acts 4:31 we are instructed concerning Christ's followers:
> "**Later they kept on speaking God's *Logos*** (the message and information from God; the Word of, and which is, God) **with a citizen's right of complete freedom from constraint.**"

God spoke – and His speaking took the form of the Logos. The Directives that He spoke were, in fact, the Logos. And thus, in Jn. 1:3, we read that all things came into being through the Logos. Then, in Jn. 1:14, we are instructed that the Logos "became flesh." So we ask, "What did the Logos become as a result of the Declarations in Gen. 1?"

> "**The skies** (heavens; atmospheres) **constantly set out, and continue fully describing in detail, an assumed appearance which is God** (or: repeatedly relate, progressively tell, and keep on thoroughly declaring a glory of, and a reputation from, God), **but** (or: and yet) **the effect**

of firmness and the result of solidity (or: the firmament) **continuously recounts** (proclaims again; reports back) **a production of** (or: a performing, a doing, a creating, a working, and a doing, from) **His hands.**

Day to (or: by) **day continuously discharges** (spews forth) **a result of the Flow** (or: repeatedly utters an effect of a gush of what is, or was, spoken; habitually bubbles up a saying), **and then night to** (or: by) **night continuously recounts** (proclaims again; reports back) *Gnosis* (intimate, experiential Knowledge and Insight).

Are there (or: they) **not continual conversations** (or: Do not chats and speeches continuously exist) **and not also [are they/there] words** (expressed thoughts; reasons; ideas; patterned messages, blueprints), **from which, are not their voices** (or: sounds; articulations) **constantly heard** (normally listened to and obeyed)?

Their sound (tone; voice) **goes forth** (or: went out) **into the midst of all the earth – and the results of the Flow** (effects of the gush of utterances) **into limits** (boundaries) **of the habitable earth** (or: inhabited land)" (Ps. 19:1-4; 18:1-4 in the LXX, JM).

Gen. 1 is echoed in Ps. 33:6,

"**By** (With; In) **the Logos** (Word; patterned communication; reasoned thought; idea) **of, and from, the LORD [Yahweh] the heavens** (skies; atmospheres) **were established** (fixed; made firm and solid), **and their every power** (or: all the ability of, and from, them) **by** (with; in) **the Breath-effect** (Spirit) **of, and from, His mouth**" (32:6, LXX, JM).

Here the Logos is set as parallel to the Breath-effect. The Word is the Spirit, or the Spirit coveys and gives existence to the Word.

Ps. 119:89 proclaims:

"**Unto the age [of Messiah], O LORD [Yahweh], the** *Logos,* **which is You** (or: Your Word; the Blueprint from You; the pattern-forming Message, pertaining to You; Your thought, reason and idea; the flow and transfer for input of Information that was conveying Meaning concerning You) **continues remaining-throughout, within the midst of the Atmosphere** (in union with the heaven; centered in the sky)" (LXX, 118:89; JM).

The Logos, from the time of "the Beginning," "continued remaining-throughout, within the midst of the Atmosphere (in union with the heaven; centered in the sky)." The Atmosphere that blankets the earth continued with "the flow and transfer for input of Information that was conveying Meaning concerning [God]." God's presence drenched the earth, but folks continued sitting in darkness, and lived unaware of Him (Jn. 1:5). We find a beautiful proclamation in Ps. 119:160 (118:160, LXX):

"**A beginning of Your Words [is] Truth** (An origin of Your blueprints [is] reality; a first cause and rule from the thoughts, reasons, ideas and patterned messages from You [is] reality of Truth), **and on into the midst of the Age [of Messiah]** (the indefinite time of [the Anointing]) **[continue] all the effects of the decisions of Your eschatological deliverance** (all the results from the evaluations and judgments which are the rightwised relationships in covenant participation of the Way pointed out)!" (JM).

It would seem that all of creation is infused with the Logos, the flow of God's speech, in Gen. 1. But we see that the Logos interacted with the life of Israel. The book of Jeremiah opens with:

"**The Gush-effect from God** (or: The result of the flow of God; The thing spoken, which was God), **which came to be upon Jeremiah... A Logos of God** (or: God's Logos) **came to be face-to-face with him** (or: [The] Word from God was birthed into existence [directed] toward him)..." (Jer. 1:1-2a, LXX; JM)

In Ezk. 1:3a, 4a, and 5, we read:

"**And then [the] Logos of [the] LORD came to be face-to-face with Ezekiel** (or: a Word, or a patterned message from [Yahweh] was birthed into existence [directed] toward Ezekiel).... **And [the] Hand of [the] LORD [= Yahweh] came to be upon me. And then I looked, and –**

consider this – a Breath-effect (Spirit; Wind), **continuously lifting up from out of the midst, was progressively coming from the north, and a great cloud [was] within** (centered in) **it**…. **And within the midst [there was] a likeness of four living beings, and this [was] the appearance of them: a likeness of a human being [was] upon them**" (LXX, JM).

Those four living beings appear once more, in Rev. 4:6-9, and can be seen as, among other things, both representations of God's Life within all of creation, and of the new-creation humanity, because Ezk. 1:5 instructs us that "they had the **likeness of a human**." Verse 1:8 tells us that they had "**the hands of a human**," indicating their ability to work and do tasks. Ezekiel sees these four symbolic beings again, in Ezk. 10, where they are termed "**cherubim**." This term takes us back to those watching and guarding the Way of the Garden, in Gen. 3:24, and which we also find embroidered onto the inner Veil of the Tabernacle (noted in Heb. 10:20 as a symbol of Christ's flesh), which was the entrance and Way into the Holy of Holies, the place of God's manifest presence, His throne room. Cherubim were also of one piece with the Mercy Seat (God's throne) that covered over the Law written in stone, and Aaron's priestly leadership rod. They were two witnesses of God's presence, and they faced God there. In Ezk. 1:9a, the Hebrew reads: "Their wings joined a woman to a sister." In Ezk. 3:13 he tells us that "the noise of the wings of the living creatures touching (or: brushing; kissing) a woman and a sister, and the noise of the wheels with them, [was] also a sound of a great rushing (or: quaking)." These beings were visionary symbols of the activities of God through humans who "walk in the Spirit," as Paul says in Gal. 5:25,

> "**Since we continue living in and by spirit** (or: for [the] Spirit; to Breath-effect; or: with Attitude), **we also can habitually advance orderly in line in regard to, or amidst, elementary principles in and by spirit** (or: for [the] Spirit; by Breath-effect; with Attitude; or: = walk in rank following [the footsteps] behind the Spirit)," [*cf* Ezk. 1:9b]

This calls to mind Rom. 8:14, where he speaks of those who are led by the Spirit, being **sons of God**. But we digress, and this broad topic is for another study.

Mal. 1:1 opens with:

> "**A theme, or matter, received from [the] LORD's Logos, laid upon Israel, within [the] hand of His agent: place [it; this], then, upon your hearts**"
>> (or: "You folks, at this point, at once lay upon your hearts a burden from a premise of [the] Logos of [Yahweh] that is laid upon Israel, centered in [the] hand of His messenger")
>> (LXX, JM).

The Logos (both in the singular, and in the plural) is found throughout the LXX of the OT. It does not suddenly appear in Jn. 1:1. Most of the time it is associated with Yahweh, and can be read in the text as being Yahweh's Logos, or the Logos which was Yahweh – i.e., Yahweh coming in the form (or, expression, or appearance and manifestation) of, and as, the Logos. We should not jump to premature conclusions, for as we have seen, the word *logos* has a wide semantic range. Here is where we must listen to the Breath-effect as we read the Scriptures. Context must be attended. Throughout the NT, the word *logos* is used by many people and with a variety of significances. When God first spoke in Gen. 1, the Logos could be "face-to-face with" only God, for there was nothing else to face, until the effect of that Pattern-laden Breath took shape and assumed a form. Was this the situation of the Beginning of which John spoke in Jn. 1:1? The orientation of the Logos could only be toward God, for God was all there was, until the Logos brought everything else into being (Jn. 1:3).

Before continuing in Jn. 1, and focusing on the term *logos*, let us take a short detour to Prov. 8, where some interesting statements were made about the word "Wisdom," which is personified in this passage. Both Wisdom and Logos are functions of the mind of God. In this Proverbs passage, the context is "the beginning," and "creation," and "being face-to-face with God." So, in having this picture of another aspect of God's Spirit in mind, it can temper our understanding of this Prologue, here in Jn. 1. Now for some selected verses from Prov. 8:

> 12. **I Myself, Wisdom, at one point pitched a tent and settled down to dwell** [note: *cf* Jn. 1:14]. **I Myself, called upon counsel, purpose and determined design, as well as intimate,**

experiential knowledge (insight) **and centered-thinking** (inner use of the mind in thought – in union with reflection, conception and cognition), **within Myself**....

22. **[The] LORD** (= Yahweh) **at one point framed and founded** (created) **Me [Wisdom] a BEGINNING** (starting; leader; source) **of His Paths** (Ways) **unto His works, deeds and courses of action.**

23. **He at one point laid Me as a Foundation, piled Me up and founded Me, before the Age – within** (in union with) **a BEGINNING of the [situation] to construct** (make; produce; create) **the earth –**

24. **even before the [situation] to construct** (make; produce; create) **the Abyss** (Deep) **– and before the [situation for] the fountains of the waters to go in advance and come forth** (proceed)....

27. **At the time when He was progressively preparing the atmosphere, making ready the sky and equipping the heaven, I continued being present, together with Him – even when** (or: while) **He was progressively marking off boundaries for His own throne upon [the] winds**....

30. **I continued being beside Him, continuously adapting, progressively suiting and repeatedly tuning [everything] – I, Myself, continued being that wherein He continued taking joy and delight** [cf Jn. 1:14]. **Now I continued daily in a good frame of mind and with a healthy attitude, constantly enjoying myself in His presence** (centered in front of Him; in union with His Face) **within every season** (at and on every fitting situation; in union with every fertile moment). (LXX, JM)

The Wisdom of Solomon adds another voice to what we just read in Prov. 8, above. In Wis. 9, we read interesting perspectives, from that author:

1. **O God of [the] fathers and Lord of Mercy** (or: even [Yahweh], Who is the Mercy), **the One forming** (making; constructing; producing) **all things** (the whole of creation) **centered in Your Logos** (in union with the Blueprint which is You; within Your Word)

2. **and then preparing, furnishing, equipping and making humanity ready by and with Your Wisdom** (in the Wisdom which is You)....

9. **What is more, this Wisdom [is] with You, which has perceived and thus knows Your works and actions, and continued present alongside** (constantly existed being at the side) **when You were progressively forming** (making, constructing, producing) **the cosmos** (or: the aggregate of humanity)... (LXX, JM)

The 2nd century BC book in the LXX, Ben Sirach, presents more thoughts on Wisdom, in chapter 24. Here are some brief excerpts from this chapter:

3. **I [Wisdom], Myself, came** (or: went) **forth from out of the mouth of the Most High, and as** (or: like) **a mist** (or: fog; cloud-like darkness) **I covered [the] earth** (or: Land)....

8. **Then the Creator of** (the One who founds and establishes) **all implanted a destiny in Me** (imparted a goal to Me; gave an inner directive for an end in view for Me), **and the One creating, founding and establishing Me caused My tabernacle** (tent) **to rest down, and said, "Pitch Your tent and take up quarters within the midst of Jacob, and in union with Israel, be made heir and then receive and enjoy an allotted inheritance as a possession**....

9. **He created, founded and established Me, from [the; a] Beginning, before the Age, and until an Age I will by no means leave from out of the midst of it or forsake it.**

10. **Within a set-apart tabernacle** (holy tent) **I gave public service in His presence** (before His Face), **and thus** (in this manner) **I was set in position, established, supported and made to stand fast.**

11. **Likewise, He caused Me to rest down within a beloved city, and centered in** (in union with) **Jerusalem was My right and privilege from out of Being** (My authority).

12. **Then I took root within a People having been glorified and now existing with a reputation and an assumed appearance – within** (in union with; centered in) **a portion** (a piece; a share; a part) **of [the] LORD, [as] His allotted portion** (inheritance)....

16. **I, Myself, like a terebinth** (or: turpentine), **stretch and spread out My branches, and My branches [are] branches of glory and grace** (or: [are] from an assumed appearance and joyous favor).

17. **I, Myself, as a Vine** (a grapevine; a vineyard) **budded forth grace and joyous favor, My buds and flowers [were; are] fruit of glory** (a manifestation which calls forth praise) **and of wealth** (or: fruit from an assumed appearance and from riches). (JM)

Let us now proceed in John's Prologue, taking it up in 1:4ff, reading the pronoun as "**It**," since our author is still speaking of **the Logos**:

4. **Within It life was continuing and progressively existing**

(or: In It was life [as a source]; [Aleph, D and other witnesses read present tense: In union with it there continues being life; Life progressively exists within the midst of It]). **And the life was continuing being, and began progressively existing as, the Light of the humans**

(or: Furthermore, the Light progressively came to be the life known as {or: which was} the humans, and was for the human beings; or: Then later the life was existing being the light from the humans).

LIFE continuously exists within, and in union with, the Logos. In 6:63, below, Jesus informs us:

"**The Spirit** (or: Breath-effect; or: spirit; Breath; Attitude) **is** (or: continues being) **the One continuously creating Life** (or: repeatedly making alive; habitually forming life)... **The declarations** (gush-effects; spoken words; sayings; results of the Flow) **which I, Myself, have spoken to you folks are** (or: continue to be) **Spirit** (or: spirit; Breath-effect; attitude) **and they are** (or: continue being) **Life**."

The association of the Spirit with the Logos (which is often the result of the gush of spoken words) is hard to miss. In the last rendering of 1:1, above, we saw that the Logos was "Flow of Information that is a Pattern-forming Influence." The science of genetics observes that this is true within a living organism. Within the same scientific-theological paraphrase, in 1:1, we also see that the Logos (and now, here, **life**) was "the transfer and input of Information that was conveying Meaning." And now, here in vs. 4, we are instructed that the **life** that was centered within the **Logos** was, and is, existing as "**the Light of the humans**." In nature we realize the connection between light and life. But in the Gospels, Light is a metaphor for understanding and the ability to make things flow together.

Let us pause to examine the nuances of the imperfect tense of the verb that expresses the action of **the life** in its existential relationship to **the Light**:

a) **the life was continuing being, and began progressively existing as, the Light of the humans** – the Logos had Life within It, and this Life gives humans understanding (or, "the Light") of Reality (14:6, below);

b) the Light progressively came to be the life known as (or: which was) the humans, and was for the human beings – "**you all are** (or: exist being) **sons of** (from; associated with and having the qualities of; or: which are) **Light and sons of** (from; associated with and having qualities of; or: which are [the; this; a]) **Day**" (1 Thes. 5:5); Eph. 5:8-9a,

"**you folks were once existing being darkness, yet now [you are] Light, within and in union with [the] Lord. Be constantly walking about** (= Habitually conduct yourselves) **as children of Light**..."

c) Then later the life was existing being the light from the humans – once they are birthed from the Light.

These variations of the final phrase come from the potential functions of the genitive form of the noun, **"the humans."** The 1st century BC collection of Jewish psalms, The Psalms of Solomon, contain an interesting pronouncement, in 3:12b,

> **"Yet the folks habitually respecting** (having reverence for; fearing) **the LORD will, one after another, stand back up again** (or: rise up) **into the midst of eonian Life** (Life corresponding to the Age of Messiah), **with their Life centered in** (in union with; within the midst of) **[the] LIGHT of [the] Lord** (a Light which is [the] Lord; Light from [the] Lord; [the] LORD'S Light), **and it will no longer cease or come to an end** (or: and He will no longer abandon or leave from out of the midst)" (LXX, JM).

5. **And the Light is constantly shining in the dim and shadowed places, and keeps on progressively giving light within the gloomy darkness where there is no light**
>   (or: within the midst of the obscurity of The Darkness where there is no light of The Day;
>   or: = in the ignorant condition or system).

And yet the darkness does not grasp or receive It on the same level
>   (or: Furthermore, the Darkness did not take It down, so as to overcome It or put It out; or:
>   = the ignorant condition or system would have none of It, nor receive It down into itself [in order to perceive It]; But that darkness does not correspondingly accept It nor commensurately take It in hand so as to follow the pattern or be in line with Its bidding).

So what are "**the dim and shadowed places**" and "**the gloomy darkness where there is no light**"? This is figurative language. Consider the clause just quoted from Eph. 5:8, "**you folks were once existing being darkness**." In Eph. 2:1 Paul spoke of folks who had been "DEAD, in trespasses and sins…" The **Light** came into the "death" of Adam, and shines into our shadowy inner selves and our gloomy moods, and our darkness (metaphor for ignorance; inability to see). Jesus was manifested within the **shadowed places** of the Law (Heb. 10:1). There was only The Darkness, until the coming of The Day. As noted under vs. 4, "darkness" is a metaphor for "the ignorant condition or system."

The second half of this verse can be understood in a number of ways:
>   a) "**does not grasp or receive It on the same level**" – this is the verb "to grasp or receive or take" with the prefix *kata-* whose main idea is "down," but also means "to the same degree, or on the same level" – as the Pharisees, or sometimes the disciples, not grasping the spiritual significance of what Jesus said; it could mean "missing the point" of His teachings;
>   b) "the Darkness did not take It down, so as to overcome It or put It out" – this is a core idea of the verb; it signifies that even though they resisted the Light, they could not stop it from shining;
>   c) "the ignorant condition or system would have none of It, nor receive It down into itself [in order to perceive It]" – this emphasizes both their resistance and their not taking the Message to heart;
>   d) "But that darkness does not correspondingly accept It nor commensurately take It in hand so as to follow the pattern or be in line with Its bidding" – this variation emphasizes the meanings of *kata-* as corresponding; being commensurate; and, following the pattern or being in line with the Light of the Logos.

Notice the switch from the Logos (It) to the Light: the Logos is now:
>   "**the Light of this ordered world** (or: of the aggregate of humanity; for the System of domination; of the cultural, political, and religious arrangements; from the cosmos; of 'the theater of history' – Walter Wink)" (8:12, below).

And thus, the Light and Logos of Christ "**keeps on progressively giving light within the gloomy darkness**" of the whole world, as well as within the aggregate of humanity.

6. **A man came to be** (was birthed), **being one having been sent forth with a mission, as a representative, from God's side** (or: having been commissioned as an emissary and sent forth from

beside God; having been sent forth to the side, as an envoy, whose source was God); **a name for him: John.**

7. **This one came into a testimony** (or: went unto evidence, a witness), **to the end that he may give testimony** (be a witness; show evidence) **about The Light, so that all humans** (or: everyone) **would at some point come to believe and trust through It** (or: by means of Him; or: through him).

Observe the purpose of John's ministry: **so that all humans** (or: everyone) **would at some point come to believe and trust through [the Light]** (or: by means of Him; or: through him). The transition into the new Age, and the move of a New Covenant (or: Arrangement) now being for "all humans" (not just Israel), and the beginning of a New Creation was a turning point in human history – and John was the first witness that would announce its advent. His testimony would, as we will see below, point to Jesus.

8. **That person** (= He) **was not The Light, but rather [he came] so that he could give testimony** (would be a witness; should present evidence) **about The Light.**

Take note: baptism and repentance was NOT the Light; it was to prepare folks FOR the Light. A change in thinking (*metanoia*) – away from custom, legalism and religion – is necessary; but it is NOT the Good News. It did not open the (spiritual) eyes of the blind. John spoke within the midst of the darkness, and told folks that the Light of the Day was at hand. But the old saying holds true, "the darkest hour is just before the Dawn." Our author is setting the record straight: John, and his ministry, was not The Light.

9. **It was the True and Genuine Light which is continuously** (repeatedly; progressively) **enlightening** (giving light to) **every person** (or: all humanity) **continuously** (repeatedly; progressively; constantly; one after another) **coming into the world** (or: the ordered system of culture, religion, economics and government; aggregate of humans; or: the universe)
> (or: It was the real Light, progressively coming into the world {organized system and aggregate of humanity}, which is progressively illuminating {or: shedding light on} every human).

In 8:12, below, Jesus makes a definitive statement:
> "I, **Myself, am** (or: continuously exist being) **the Light of this ordered world. The one habitually and progressively following Me can by no means walk around** (= under no circumstances live his or her life) **within, or in union with, the Darkness [of the old order] but, to the contrary, he will progressively possess** (constantly have and hold) **the Light of 'the Life!'** (or: the light which is life; or: the Light from the Life.)."

Our author clarifies the fact that John was not the One to whom all the OT pointed – and John was the final witness that pointed to "**the True and Genuine Light**" (Mat. 11:11; Lu. 7:28). But now let sink-in the profound statement by our author:
> "**the True and Genuine Light which is continuously** (repeatedly; progressively) **enlightening** (giving light to) **every person** (or: all humanity) **continuously** (repeatedly; progressively; constantly; one after another) **coming into the world** (or: aggregate of humanity)."

The alternate rendering proclaims the same Truth:
> "It was the real Light, progressively coming into the world (organized system and aggregate of humanity), which is progressively illuminating (or: shedding light on) every human."

The idea of a progressive coming can be pictured as the dawning of the New Day (*cf* Prov. 4:18). It also speaks of the progressive conveyance of this True and Genuine Light being carried into all the earth, and on into every generation that would follow.

10. **It was** (and continued existing being) **within the world** (or: centered in the ordered system; in the midst of the aggregate of humanity), **and the world** (ordered system; etc.; or: cosmos) **came to be** (or:

was birthed) **through It and the world** (ordered system; etc.) **did not have intimate, experiential knowledge of It** (or: had no insight into It).

Observe the allusion to creation, here in vs. 10: "**the world** (ordered system; etc.; or: cosmos) **came to be** (or: was birthed) **through It**," once again joining the Light to the Logos. Also notice that the Logos and the Light "continued existing, being **within the world**" – you see, it provided the "order" for the ordered system of the universe, and for the ordered system of the nation and cultus of Israel. Both the creation of the universe, and the creation of Israel as a nation (at Mt. Sinai) "**came to be** (or: was birthed) **through [the Logos and the Light]**." Nonetheless, those systems "**did not have intimate, experiential knowledge of It** (or: had no insight into It)" – and this especially applied to Israel, as vs. 11 explains.
"My People are destroyed (or: cut off) for lack of knowledge…" (Hos. 4:6a).

Let us ponder what Paul wrote concerning this situation, in Rom. 1:

18. **But you see, God's personal emotion** (or: mental bent; natural impulse; teeming desire and swelling passion; temperament; disposition; or: anger; wrath; or: an inherent fervor, which is God,) **is continuously and progressively being unveiled** (revealed; disclosed) **from heaven upon every irreverence** (lack of awe or absence of pious fear; disrespect) **and injustice** (wrongdoing; unrighteousness; situation or behaving that is contrary to the Way pointed out) **of people** (or: that arises from humans) – **the folks continuously holding down** (restraining; stopping while possessing) **the Truth** (or: reality) **in the sphere of** (or: within the midst of) **injustice** (unrighteousness; that which is not right; unfairness and inequality) –
19. **simply because the thing experientially known** (or: personally knowable; able to be gained by insight) **pertaining to God** (or: from, and which has its origin in, God; which is God) **is continuously made visible** (made apparent; manifested by light) **within** (or: among) **them, for God at one point made** (or: makes) **it visible** (manifests it) **to them** (or: for them; in them; by them; among them).
20. **For you see, from [the] creation** (framing; founding of order out of chaos; settling) **of [the] ordered System** (cosmos; universe; or: world of culture, religion and government) **His invisible things** (unseen [qualities and attributes]) – **both His imperceptible** (unobservable, but effecting-all) **power, ability and capacity, as well as divinity** (Godship; God-state) – **are habitually seen down the line** (or: are normally correspondingly perceived), **being continually apprehended** (grasped by the mind; mentally conceived) **in the results and by the effects of things which are made or done, in order for them to be continuously defenseless** (without an excuse),
21. **simply because, although at one point experientially knowing God with insight, they did** (or: do) **not glorify** (imagine; esteem; suppose; fancy; conjecture about; hold an opinion of; repute) **[Him] as God, or even thank [Him]** (or: give thanks in joyously expressing the goodness and well-being inherent in [His] grace and favor). **And so in contrast, they were made futile** (vain; fruitless; without profit; empty; useless; worthless; subject to a process of meaningless frustration; subject to exercises in futility) **in their reasonings** (or: thought processes; dialogues; ideas that went throughout in every direction), **and their [collective] unintelligent** (stupid; unable-to-put-things-together) **heart was darkened** (= the core of their being was made to experience an absence of light in a dim, shadowy gloom of obscurity [= ignorance]).

For comments on this passage, cf *Just Paul, comments on Romans*, Harper Brown Pub., 2014.

11. **It came into Its own things** (possessions, realms, or people), **and yet Its own people did not grasp, receive or accept It or take It to their side.**

Dan Kaplan reads in this verse an allusion to the Paraclete, of which Jesus will speak in 14:16, below. The Paraclete is One who comes to our "**side**" to help us – just as the Logos did, here, in the advent of the Christ.

12. Yet, as many as grasp, receive or accept It – to, for and among the ones habitually trusting into Its Name – It gives to them (or: for them; in them; among them) **authority** ([the] right; or: privilege from out of the midst of Being) **to be birthed God's children** (or: to become born-ones from God),

It is both the Logos and the Light that implant the privilege to be born as God's children. The terms, "authority, right and privilege" offer a semantic range of the Greek, *exousia*. This is the present participle *ousia* (being; existing) prefixed by the preposition *ek-* (from out of). So a literal rendering of the term is "from out of the midst of Being." I capitalized "Being," since the contextual reference is to God.

The ability to "**grasp, receive or accept**" is something that is given by God (the Father of the child), as Jesus said in Mat. 13:11,

> "**To** (or: For; With) **you folks it has been given to intimately experience and insightfully know the secrets** (mysteries) **of the reign and dominion of the heavens**..."

When the Logos and the Light are implanted with folks, they become "**ones habitually trusting into Its** (or: His) **Name**." We suggest that the ability to trust and believe falls into the same category as what Paul described in Eph. 2:8,

> "**For you see, by** (or: to; in; for; with) **the grace and joyous favor you are** (you continuously exist being) **folks having been delivered** (rescued; kept safe; saved; made whole; restored to your original state and condition) **so as to now be enjoying salvation through** [some MSS add: the] **faithfulness** (or: loyalty; trust; faith; confidence), **and even this not forth from out of you folks, [it is] the gift of and from God** (or: the gift which is God; or: the gift pertains to God)."

Put in terms of a natural analogy, a child is given life at conception because of the actions of its parents. The "just" LIVE by faith and trust. Faith and trust are qualities and ingredients of the Life of the Spirit. Adam began to breathe when God breathed into him the breath of Life. No one "decides" to become a child – of God, or of anyone. Trusting and believing are the "pulse" of one who has "become a born-one from God."

13. who are born (or: were given birth) **not out of bloods** (or: [flows] of blood; or: blood [lines]), **neither forth from the will of flesh** (or: from the intent of a flesh [ceremony]), **nor yet out of the will** (purpose; intent) **of an adult male, but to the contrary and in contrast, from out of the midst of God!**

Born "**from out of the midst of God**" is the only thing that makes a person "**God's child**," but here we must understand that this is referring to a particular relationship to God, just as Yahweh declared, "Israel is My son, My firstborn" (Ex. 4:22). This is speaking of what we will read in 3::3, below:

> "**unless anyone may** (or: someone would) **be born back up again to a higher place** (or: can be brought to birth again; or: would be given birth from above), **he continues having no power** (or: remains unable) **to see or perceive God's reign**."

What our author speaks of here, and what Jesus explains to Nicodemus in chapter 3, are what Paul was referring to in 1 Cor. 15:22b-23a, "**within the Christ, all humans will keep on being made alive** (or: in union with the Anointed One, everyone will one-after-another be created and produced with Life) [*cf* Rom. 5:18] **– yet each person within the result of his or her own set position [in line]**."

The last phrase joins God to the topics of Logos and Light. God is both of these manifestations of Himself.

14. And so That Which had been Laid Out as a transfer of Information, i.e., The Word
> (the Idea; the Thought; the Reason; the Discourse; the Message; The Collected Expression of Rational Logic; *The Logos*; = the meaning, plan and rational purpose of the ordered universe; The Blueprint),

births Itself flesh

(or: became flesh; came to be [in] flesh; came into existence being flesh; = God's thought, the ground of all real existence, became projected into creation as an immanent power within the world of mankind, inhabiting flesh),

and lives in a tent, within us (or: set up a tent and tabernacled among us), **and we view** (attentively gaze at; looked at so as to contemplate) **Its glory and assumed appearance**

(Its manifestation which calls forth praise; Its appearance which creates and effects opinions in regard to the whole of human experience; His imagination; = His manifest presence): **a glory** (= prestige and importance; reputation and opinion-forming appearance) **as of an only-begotten person** (or: like One that is an only kin, of a solitary race, in a by-itself-class) **at a father's side** (or: in the presence of, and next to, [the] Father), **full of grace and truth** (filled and replete with joy-producing favor, as well as reality and genuineness).

Verse 14 is one of the foundational verses for "the Incarnation," and Jn. 8:12, cited above, affirms its truth. But we should ponder the fact that vs. 14 follows directly out of vss. 12-13, where the subject is us humans. The "**glory**" of the Logos' "assumed appearance" is, in vs. 14, COMPARED to "an only-begotten person at a father's side." John does not say that the Logos WAS "an only-begotten person." Our common reading of the text has made this latter assumption. Consider what Paul said of God's glory, in 1 Cor. 11:7, which speaks of:

"**a husband** (or: a mature Male)... **being inherently** (or: constantly being under the rule and headship of) **God's image** (resemblance; likeness; portrait) **and glory**."

Also, observe the reading in vs. 14, above, "*The Logos* **births Itself flesh and lives in a tent, within us**." The term "tent" (a temporary and moveable residence) was used metaphorically of a person's body. Might we take the term "flesh" (which is used in more than one way, in Scripture) in the sense of "matter"? God appeared as a Pillar of Smoke mingled with Fire during Israel's Exodus. Then He "tabernacled" (took up residence) among them, in the Tabernacle. So the language of this verse is an allusion to God dwelling in a tent when He traveled with Israel in the wilderness. The language of a **tent**, that the Logos "tabernacled" among them, coupled with the language of **glory**, are clear allusions to Ex. 40:34,

"The cloud covered the tent of appointment, then the glory of Yahweh filled the tabernacle."

Therefore, thus it is with the Logos (God) "tabernacling" within Jesus. And speaking of "appearing," the word "**glory**" has a wide semantic range, as seen in the parenthetical expansions of this verse, with "assumed appearance" being one of those meanings. Also, consider Mk. 16:12,

"**Yet after these things, He was displayed in clear light and manifested – in a different form – to two of their group, when they continued walking along, being on their way journeying into [the] country**."

We wonder if tradition has taken too limited an understanding of Jn. 1:14, above.

In 1 Jn. 1 we get another picture:

1. **The One who was continuously existing from a beginning** (or: He Who was progressively being parted away from [the] Source, Headship and Rule). **The One whom we have listened to, and still hear; the One whom we have discerningly seen, and now yet perceive with our eyes** (or: in our eyes); **the One whom we contemplatively gazed upon as a public spectacle** (as an exhibit in a theater) **and our hands handled in investigation** (felt about for and touched) **– groping around the Word of the Life** [cf Lu. 24:39]

(or: the Logos, which is the Life; the thought which pertains to life; the Information and Idea from the Life; the message with the character and qualities of the Life; the Reason which belongs to the Life; [note: I have treated *ho* as the definite article in the first four phrases here and in vs. 3; many treat it as a neuter relative and render it: That which]),

2. **and the Life was manifested** (or: is brought into the clear light and made visible)! **And so we have discerningly seen, and still perceptively observe, and are repeatedly testifying** (bearing witness; giving evidence) **and in a message are constantly reporting to you folks the**

Life which has the character and qualities of the Age (or: the life of, for and pertaining to the age [of the Messiah]; eonian life) **which Certain [Life] was continuously existing [oriented and proceeding] toward** (or: was face to face with) **the Father, and was manifested** (or: is made visible; appeared) **to us, in us, by us, among us and for us.** [*cf* Jn. 14:26]
3. **The One whom we have seen, and still now see, and we have heard, and now continue listening to and hearing, we are also constantly reporting to you, to the end that you, too, may be continuously having common being and existence** (or: would be progressively holding partnership and participation) **with us. And yet, our common being and existence** (or: participation; fellowship; partnership; sharing) **[is] with the Father, even with His Son** (or: as well as with the Son from Him; or, in apposition: and with the Son which is Him), **Jesus Christ.**

Here, "the Logos, which is the Life," is identified as Jesus Christ. But notice what vs. 3 says about us: "**our common being and existence [is] with the Father, even with His Son.**" We should just pause and meditate on that clause. We have a common existence with the Father; we have a common existence with His Son (as in Rom. 8:29). We are His Family (Acts 17:28-29a).

Now let us consider Col. 1:12-20 and note the correlations between Gen. 1, John 1 and this passage:

12**. [We are folks who are] constantly giving thanks to the Father: the One calling you** [other MSS: us] **– as well as making [you; us] competent** (sufficient; qualified; fit; suitable) **– into the divided share of the lot of the inheritance** (or: into the part and portion of the allotted possession) **of the set-apart folks** (or: pertaining to the holy ones; belonging to the saints; from the sacred people; which is the different-from-the-ordinary folks) **within the Light;**

In both Gen. 1, and Jn. 1, the first act of the Logos is the creation/existence of the Light. Here, in vs. 12, the "calling" is a function of the Father's Logos, and the inheritance of the set-apart folks is that of being "**within the Light**." Then 1 Jn. 1:7a informs us,
"**Yet if we keep on walking about** (= continue living our life) **within the midst of and in union with the Light, as He exists** (or: is) **within the Light, we constantly have common being and existence** (or: hold common fellowship, participation and enjoy partnership) **with one another…**"
And back to Col. 1:
13. **He who drags us out of danger** (or: rescued us) **forth from out of the midst of the authority of the Darkness** (from Darkness's jurisdiction and right; from existing out of gloomy shadows and obscure dimness; = the privilege of ignorance), **and changes [our] position** (or: transported [us], thus, giving [us] a change of standing, and transferred [us]) **into the midst of the kingdom and reign of the Son of His love**
(or: into the midst of the sovereign influence of the Son Who has the characteristics and qualities of His accepting love; into union with the sovereign activities of the Son Whose origin is His love; or: into the sphere of the reign of the Son of the Love which is Him; into the center of **the kingdom** of the Son, **which is His love and drive toward union**),

Observe "the Darkness," here, and recall Gen. 1:2, and take note of "**the Son**" being introduced into this context.

14. **in Whom** (or: in union with [which Son]) **we continuously have and hold the release into freedom from slavery or imprisonment** (the liberation from our predicament) **[which results in] the sending away of the failures** (or: the dismissal of the errors pertaining to falling short and straying to the side of the target; the flowing away of the sins; the divorce from mistakes).
15. **It is [this Son] Who is the Image** (portrait; the Exact Formed Likeness; the Figure and Representation; visible likeness and manifestation) **of the not-seen God** (or: the unable to be seen God; the invisible God), **the Firstborn of all creation**

28

(or: of every creature; or: of every framing and founding; of every act of settling from a state of disorder and wildness; or: pertaining to the whole creation; or: = the Inheritor of all creation Who will also assume authority over and responsibility for every creature [note: this is the duty of the firstborn]),

Note the reference to "**the Image of God**," and to "**creation**," in this verse. But continuing on…

16. **because within Him was created the whole** (or: in union with Him everything is founded and settled, is built and planted, is brought into being, is produced and established; or: within the midst of Him all things were brought from chaos into order) – **the things within the skies and atmospheres, and the things upon the earth** (or: those [situations, conditions and/or people] in the heavens and on the land); **the visible things, and the unseen** (or: unable to be seen; invisible) **things: whether thrones** (seats of power) **or lordships** (ownership systems) **or governments** (rulers; leadership systems; sovereignties) **or authorities – the whole has been created and all things continue founded, put in order and stand framed through means of Him, and [proceeds, or were placed] into Him** (or: = He is the agent and goal of all creation).
17. **And He is before** (prior to; or: maintains precedence of) **all things and all people, and the whole has** (or: all things have) **been placed together and now continues to jointly-stand** (stands cohesively; is made to have a co-standing) **within the midst of and in union with Him,**
18. **and so He is the Head** (or: Source) **of the body – which is the called-out community** (the ecclesia; the summoned congregation) – **Who is the Beginning** (or: the Source, Origin and Ruling Principle; the Beginning Power and Ability of the process), **a Firstborn forth from out of the midst of dead folks, to the end that He would be birthed** (may come into existence; or: could come to be) **within all things and in all people: He continuously holding first place**
       (or: constantly being preeminent; or: habitually being the First One; or: continuing being the First Man),

Verses 16-18 of Col. 1 continue on the subject of "the Son," and vs. 18 points us to "**the Beginning**," and "**a Firstborn**," which can be construed as pointing back to Adam (humanity), and then to Israel, and ultimately to Jesus, and then to the Family of sons (Rom. 8:29).

19. **because WITHIN Him all – the entire contents** (the result of that which fills everything; all the effect of the full measure [of things]) – **delights to settle down and dwell as in a house** (or: because He approved all the fullness [of all existence] to permanently reside within Him) [cf 2:9]

Verses 16 and 19 give rise to the philosophical concept of "the cosmic Christ" that we find in current theology. But we may be on more solid ground by relating these verses to the Logos, in all that we've considered about It, along with the corporate, many-membered Son/body which composes the Anointed.

20. **and THROUGH Him at once to transfer the all** (the whole; = all of existential creation), **away from a certain state to the level of another which is quite different**
       (or: to change all things, bringing movement away from being down; to reconcile all things; to change everything from estrangement and alienation to friendship and harmony and move all), **INTO Him – making** (constructing; forming; creating) **peace** (harmonious joining) **through the blood of His cross** (execution stake/pole): **through Him, whether the things upon the earth** (or: land) **or the things within the atmospheres and heavens!**

And that last clause of Col. 1:20 takes us back to Gen. 1:1, so let us consider another version of this same topic, in Heb. 1:
1. **Long ago** (or: In the old days), **in many parts** (or: with fragments; by divided portions; = bit by bit) **and in** (or: with; by) **much-traveled ways consisting of many turns and directions, God,**

having spoken to (or: in talking with; when discoursing by; making vocal utterances for) **the fathers – in** (in union with; centered in; = through; in [the words of]) **the prophets –**

2. **upon [the] last of these days spoke to** (or: speaks for and concerning; discourses in; makes conversation with) **us in a Son whom He placed** (or: sets) **[as; to be] Heir of all** (or: One who receives all humanity as an allotment; or: One who received everything as His allotted inheritance) **through Whom He also made the ages**

> (or: forms and constructs the various designated periods of time [which compose existence, as well as God's influence and activities]; produces the life-times);

3. **Who, continuously being an effect of the radiance from**

> (or: a result from a dawning and breaking forth of the bright light of the Day which is; a result of the outshining which is; an effulgence from; an effect of an off-shining [light]-beam belonging to; or: a result of a reflection of) **the Glory and Splendor as well as an exact impress** (or: exact likeness as from a stamp or a die; or: a carving) **of His substructure**

> (or: of His substance [that is] standing under as a foundation; which is the underlying support of His outward form and properties; from His sub-placing; or: from His assumed groundwork of the full expression [of His idea]) **– besides continuously bearing** (or: and while progressively carrying; and then repeatedly bringing) **the whole** (all things; everything and all existence) **by the gush-effect which is His power**

> (or: in the result of the flow from the power which is Him; or: with the saying pertaining to His ability; in the spoken declaration of, and which has the character of and its source in, His power and ability) **through and by means of Himself – in producing a cleansing of** (or: after making a ritual purification in regard to) **the failures** (the misses of the target; the mistakes and errors; or: a clearing by pruning which pertains to the sins) **He at once seated Himself within [the] right part** (or: hand; = in union with the receiving aspect, honored position and place of power) **of the Greatness centered and resident within high places.**

This passage can be viewed as an expansion of Rom. 11:36, cited above. Verse 2b echoes Gen 1, as well as Jn. 1:3. Although the term *logos* is not used in these verses, the topic of "speaking" is prominent in vss. 1-2, and vs. 3 uses the word *rhēma* ("**the gush-effect which is His power,**" etc., in the parenthetical expansion).

Heb. 4:2 alludes to Israel's history, and the interaction of the Logos with them: "**But the Word** (or: message; thought; idea; **Logos**) **which they heard did not profit** (or: benefit) **those folks.**" And now let us ponder two verses in this same chapter that shed light on our investigation:

12. **You see, the Word of God** (or: God's thought, idea and message; or: the expressed *Logos* from God; or: the Word which is God) **[is] living** (or: alive), **and active** (working; operative; energetic; at work; productive) **and more cutting above every two-mouthed sword, even passing through** (penetrating) **as far as a dividing** (or: parting; partitioning) **of soul and spirit** (or: of inner self-life/consciousness and breath-effect), **both of joints and marrows, even able to discern** (separate; judge; decide) **concerning thoughts** (ponderings; reflections; in-rushings; passions) **and intentions** (notions; purposes) **of a heart** (= core of the being).

13. **And no creature** (thing formed, framed or created) **is** (or: exists being) **out of sight** (not manifest; concealed) **in Its** (i.e., the Word's; or: His) **presence, but all things [are] naked and have been gripped and bent back at the neck** [thus, exposing the face and throat] **to** (or: in; by) **Its** (or: His) **eyes, face to face with Which** (or: Whom) **in us** (or: to us; for us; with us) **[is] this Word** (or: with a view to Whom by us [is] the message and the account; or: toward which, for us and among us, [comes] the Logos: the Idea and the Reason).

So, without discounting the connection of the Son, and of Jesus, with the Logos, we can discern the pervasiveness and imminence of the Logos, from the Alpha to the Omega; from the Beginning on through to the End (*telos*: Goal; Finished Product). The Logos is both the Creator, and the creation. Paul put it this way, in 1 Cor. 15:28,

"**Now when the whole** (or: all things) **would be completely supportively-aligned in Him** (or: attached and appended to Him; subordinately sheltered and arranged by and for Him), **then the Son Himself will also continue being supportively aligned to, fully subjoined for and humbly attached under as an arranged shelter in, the One subjecting, appending and sheltering the whole in Him** (or: attaching all things to Him), **to the end that God can be all things within the midst of and in union with all humans** (or: may be everything in all things; or: should exist being **All in all**; or: would exist being everything, within the midst of everyone)."

Can we not see an almost interchangeability, as well as union, expressed in Jn. 14:10?

"**it is continuously** (it constantly exists being) **I, Myself, within the midst of the Father, and the Father within the midst of Me** (or: I Myself centered in union with the Father, and the Father centered in union with Me). **The gush-effects** (results of the flow; or: utterances, declarations, words spoken) **which I, Myself, am constantly saying to you men, I am not constantly saying from Myself. But the Father, continuously dwelling and remaining** (abiding; staying) **within the midst of Me, is habitually** (constantly) **doing** (making; constructing; creating; forming; performing; producing) **His works** (actions; deeds)."

Here it is not stated as the Logos doing the work, but the Father, yet the gush-effects come through the Son. If we focus on the idea of "union" that is expressed by Jesus, in this verse, we may encounter less confusion than by trying to make from it a theological statement about the Being of God.

In Jn. 14:18 Jesus says, "**I am repeatedly** (or: habitually) **and now progressively coming to** (or: face to face with; toward) **you people**." The Logos is now face-to-face with us. This is the result of It bringing into existence the creation – both the old, and now the new. Reminiscent of Gen. 2:7, Jn. 20:22 reports that Jesus "**suddenly blows on, and says to, them** (or: He breathes within [them], so as to inflate them [note: same verb as used in Gen. 2:7, LXX], and is saying to them), '**Receive a set-apart spirit!** (or: Get [the] Holy Spirit!; take the Sacred Breath-effect!; or: Receive a sacred attitude).'"

Before moving on, let us observe that, "**That Which had been Laid Out as a transfer of Information, i.e., The Word** (The Blueprint)," is "**full of grace and truth** (filled and replete with joy-producing favor, as well as reality and genuineness)." The incarnated Logos, Jesus, and the message that It/He brings (i.e., the Good News, the Gospel) is Full of **grace and truth**. It is NOT full of the Law. It is "replete with joy-producing favor." If anyone proclaims something that does not have these ingredients or characteristics, it is NOT the Gospel; it is not a message of goodness, ease or wellbeing. You see,

"**For you see, by** (or: to; in; for; with) **the grace and joyous favor you are** (you continuously exist being) **folks having been delivered** (rescued; kept safe; saved; made whole; restored to your original state and condition) **so as to now be enjoying salvation through** [some MSS add: the] **faithfulness** (or: loyalty; trust; faith; confidence), **and even this not forth from out of you folks, [it is] the gift of and from God** (or: the gift which is God; or: the gift pertains to God)" (Eph. 2:8; cf 14:6, below).

We will now take a detour, from Jn. 1:14, and will select verses or passages in the NT that seem to use the term *logos* in ways that are significant for this study. Our investigation will look for aspects of the word's uses that might shed Light on "the Logos," within these texts, where it can be discerned as possibly inferring something more than the everyday use of the word. So, let us begin...

Mat. 8:16 may reflect more than one level of interpretation:

"**Now with it becoming evening, people brought many folks being habitually affected by demons** [a Hellenistic word and concept: = animistic influences] **and He cast out the spirits** (breath-effects; attitudes) **with a word** (a *Logos*; by a message; in a thought), **and He served, cured and restored to health** (or: gave attentive care or prescribed therapy or instigated ongoing treatment for) **all those continuously having it badly** (= those habitually with illness)."

As an aside, notice the apparent equivalence between the word *demon* and "spirit (breath-effect; attitude)," in this verse. But now to our investigation: was Matthew describing this act of deliverance from a spirit in terms of just "speaking something," as suggested by the centurion, in Mat. 8:8? Or, is there an allusion, here, to Gen. 1:2-3, where God's Logos brings the Light from out of the midst of the Darkness (2 Cor. 4:6a)? Was Jesus performing as the creative Logos in those practical situations with people? Was it something He said, out loud, or was it just a thought (a projection of well-being from the Logos within Him that was mentally or spiritually activated)? The main word that is commonly rendered "prayer," in the NT, is *proseuchē*: a thought, word or action that is focused or directed toward (*pros-*) having (*chē*) goodness, ease and well-being (*-eu-*). This is the *logos* in action.

Paul, in Rom. 10:8, quoted a statement from the Law, which might be appropriate here:
> "**But rather, what is He** (or: it) **saying?**
>> '**The result of the flow** (the gush-effect; or: the saying; the declaration; that which is spoken; the speech) **is** (or: exists) **near you – within your mouth and within your heart!**'" [Deut. 30:11-14]

Recall, from our previous sections of this series, the relationship between *rhēma*, used here, and *logos*, used above.

Next, let us consider Jesus' explanation of *logos* used in a parable, in Mat. 13:
> 19. "**Concerning everyone constantly listening to and hearing the Word of the sovereign reign and activities** (or: the *Logos* – the thought, idea and message – of the kingdom) **and yet continuing in not understanding** (being unable to have things flow together unto comprehension)**: the worthless person or the disadvantageous circumstance** (or: the one who brings pain and misery through hard labor; the malevolent and wicked man; the evil one; or: the difficult and wearisome situation) **is repeatedly coming and is habitually snatching up what has been sown** (scattered as seed) **within his heart – this is the one sown alongside the path or road.**
> 20. "**Now [as to] the one being sown** (scattered) **upon the rocky places, this one is the person continuing in hearing the Word** (*Logos*; thought; idea; message), **and at once, set for success, progressively receiving it with joy!**

Here, the Logos is put symbolically as a Seed that is planted in the soil. The topic of "Seed" could take us in a number of symbolic directions. But just note that the Seed has Life within it! Does Jesus' parable foreshadow the new creation that comes within the kingdom of God? The new creation is basically the Christ-Life that transforms humanity. In 1 Cor. 15:35-49, Paul uses the metaphor of "a seed" that is planted and then sprouts to speak of "the resurrection." Consider the two elements in both of these passages: the Seed, and the soil into which it is sown.

Christ's Logos is associated with "creation," in Mat. 24:35,
> "**The heaven and the earth** (i.e.: This Atmosphere and this Territory) **WILL progressively pass on by. Now in contrast, My thoughts and words** (or: messages; patterned declarations; transfers and conveyances of Meaning-bearing Blueprints) **can by no means pass on by.**"

Here we should understand that "heaven and earth" had become a code phrase for the creation of Israel as a nation, at Mt. Sinai. The temple was a symbol of "heaven (the home of God, and His throne – in the Holy of Holies)," while the people of Israel were indicated by the term "the earth," or, "the Land." The old "heaven and earth" did indeed pass away, in AD 70, with the destruction of the temple and of Jerusalem (which represented the Judean expression of the People). The "Meaning-bearing Blueprints" spoken by Jesus held the designs of the new creation, also termed, "the reign of God." Also, consider that when God blew His breath into Adam (that prior to this act was simply formed soil, or earth) He was blowing "the heaven" into him.

The "parable of the Sower," as given by Mark 4:3ff, explains that:

"**The one habitually sowing** (The sower) **is continually sowing the Word** (the *Logos*; the idea; the thought; the meaning and reason; the message; the patterned or blueprint Information)."

The Logos is continually entering into the soil, or, the earth – both of these being figures of "people." Mk. 4:33 instructs us, that:

"**So by means of many parables** (illustrative comparisons) **of this kind He continued speaking the message** (Word; *Logos*) **to them** (or: kept on conveying a flow of the information for them and progressively declared the Thought and Idea among them) **– according as they continued able to continue hearing** (or: continued having power to be repeatedly listening)."

Now, can the creation be distorted? Of course it can – we see this every day, both in the physical world, and in the new creation, as represented by the institutional church, in many times and situations. This had happened in the previous age, the age that was ending with the Advent of the Messiah. Mk. 7:12-13 offers the statement by Jesus, in regard to the Judean leadership of His day:

12. **"You continue allowing him to no longer do a single thing** (or: And so you people still continue releasing him to do nothing) **for father or mother!**

13. **"This is habitually invalidating** (depriving of lordship; making void of authority) **the Word of God** (God's thought and idea; the message from God; the *Logos* which is God) **by** (or: in; with) **your tradition which you folks deliver and pass along** (or: handed down) **– and you are constantly doing many such things of this kind** (or: repeatedly performing many such similar [rituals] along this line).**"

Consider how the institutional traditions of Second Temple Judaism invalidated Christ, the Logos made flesh; they crucified Him.

We find a disturbing effect of the Logos recorded in Mk. 10:24,

"**Now the disciples began being affected by an emotion of astonishment in which awe is mixed with fear, upon [hearing] His words which expressed His thoughts and reasoning** (the ideas and blueprints of the Logos from Him)."

Jesus used the plural of *logos* in Lu. 24:

44. **Now He says to them, "These [were] My words** (thoughts; ideas; laid-out transmissions of information; or =: This [is] My message) **– which I spoke to you folks, while yet being together with you – That it continues binding and necessary for all the things having been written within the Law of Moses, and in the Prophets and Psalms, concerning Me, to be fulfilled."**

45. **At that time He fully OPENED back up again their minds to be habitually making the Scriptures flow together** (or: to continue putting the Scriptures together so as to comprehend [them]).

Prior to what is stated in vs. 45, we can assume that their minds had been closed. We suggest that what happened to the disciples, here, is the same thing that happened to Jesus, in Lu. 3:21b-22a,

"**with Jesus also having been immersed** (baptized) **and then continuing in prayer** (or: thinking with a view toward having goodness, ease and well-being), **[the time and situation] had come to be** (or: was birthed; occurred; happened) **[for] the heaven to be OPENED back up again, and [for] the Set-apart Breath-effect** (or: the Holy Spirit; the Sacred Attitude) **to descend** (step down)… **upon Him.**"

Jn. 10:34-35a echoes OT situations that involved the Logos:

"**Jesus judiciously replies to them, 'Is it not standing written within your Law** [other MSS: the Law; = the Torah] **that "I say, you people are** (or: exist being) **gods"?** [Ps. 82:6] **Since He said "gods"** [= *elohim*] **to whom God's *Logos*** (the Word which was laid out from God) **came to be** (or: toward whom the Idea, whose source and origin is God, was birthed; toward whom God's message proceeded and was directed into existence)…'"

The verb used here, in 35a, means "to come to be, or exist; to be birthed." The final expanded, parenthetical rendering is revealing of the potential human experience: "toward whom God's message

(Logos) proceeded and was directed into existence." Therein were incarnations of the Logos. "The Logos birthed Itself flesh…"

In Jn. 17:17 Jesus instructs us: "**Set them apart** (or: Make them different from the norm) **within the midst of the Truth** (or: in union with, and centered in, reality). **Your *Logos*** (Word; blueprint; patterned idea) **exists being Truth**." This was why He could proclaim, in Jn. 14:6, "**I, Myself, AM** (exist being)**… the Truth** (the Reality) **and the Life**," because He was the Logos living in a Tent (Tabernacle) among them.

In Acts 6:7, Luke recorded that, "**the *Logos* of God** (or: God's idea, message; the Word from God, which was God) **kept on progressively growing and increasing** (also: = God's Reason was spreading out like a growing Vine)," and then, in Acts 12:24, we learned that, "**But the *Logos* of God kept on growing** (increasing) **and continued being multiplied**." The Logos was being incarnated in more and more people. Jesus was gaining more and more brothers and sisters. This was God's Family "being multiplied." The Logos was, and continues, bringing about the new creation – as well as inhabiting it all.

The Logos had interacted with Abraham, for we read in Rom. 9:9,
> "**For the Word** (or: message; *Logos*) **of Promise [is] this:**
>> '**Corresponding to** (or: At; In line with) **this season** (or: In accord with this fitting situation and fertile moment) **I will be coming, and then a son will be existing for Sarah** (or: shall progressively be by Sarah and will be existing in Sarah).'" [Gen. 18:14]

It was the Logos that revived both Abraham and Sarah, and that created their son. Take note of the dative case functions: for Sarah; by Sarah; in Sarah. But this was by the Logos of Promise, within her.

Paul explained, in 2 Cor. 5:19, that:
> "**God was existing within Christ** (God was and continued being centered in, and in union with [the] Anointed One) **progressively and completely transforming [the] aggregate of humanity** (or: world) **to be other [than it is] in Himself, to Himself, for Himself, by Himself and with Himself, not accounting to them** (not putting to their account; not logically considering for them; not reasoning in them) **the results and effects of their falls to the side** (their trespasses and offenses), **even placing within us the Word** (the *Logos*; the Idea; the Reason; the message; the pattern-forming information) **of the corresponding transformation to otherness** (or: the full alteration; the change from enmity to friendship; the conciliation)."

This same Logos (God) has been placed within US, just as It was "within Christ." What He did has made it possible for us to continue doing what He placed within us: to be speaking the Logos of "transformation to otherness (the full alteration)."

Paul declared of himself and his associates:
> "**[We have served and dispensed] with pureness** (or: centered in [a life of] purity); **in personally experienced knowledge; with forbearing patience** (in taking a long time before becoming emotional or rushing with passion); **with useful kindness; in a set-apart** (holy) **spirit** (or: within the midst of [the] Holy Spirit; within a hallowed breath-effect; in a set-apart attitude); **centered in, and with, uncritical love** (or: acceptance that is free from prejudice and from a separating for evaluation; love that is not based on making distinctions, fault-finding or judging) **with a *Logos* and in a message of Truth** (or: centered in a thought, idea and Word of Reality; in union with pattern-forming information from Reality); **within God's power and ability; through means of the tools and instruments** (or: weapons; utensils; implements) **of and from the liberating deliverance, rightwised relationships and with the justice and equity of the Way pointed out in new covenant participation – on the right hand and on the left**" (2 Cor. 6:6-7).

Writing to the Province of Galatia, Paul said, in chapter 5:

14. **for you see, the entire Law has been fulfilled and stands filled up within one word** (or: centered in one thought or idea; in union with one *Logos* and blueprint-message) – **within this: "You will continue loving** [*agapaō*] **your near-one** (your associate; your neighbor; the one close by your position), **as** (in the same way as; or: as he/she were) **yourself."** [Lev. 19:18; comment: this one "expressed thought" is the idea and purpose of the Word]

Col. 3:16a offers this beautiful admonition:
"**Let Christ's Word** (or: the *Logos*, which is the Christ; the Idea which is the Anointing; or: the message of and from the Christ [other MSS: of God; of {the} Lord]) **be continuously making its home within you folks** (or: progressively indwelling and residing – centered in and in union with you) **richly, within the midst of and in union with all wisdom…**"

Jacob gave us understanding, in Jas. 1:18,
"**Being purposed** (intended; willed; resolved), **from being pregnant He gave birth to us** (brought us forth; prolifically produced us) **by a Word** (in a collected thought and blueprint; for an expressed idea; with a message; into a *Logos*) **of Truth and from Reality – into the [situation for] us to be** (or: to continuously exist being) **a specific** (or: a certain; some) **firstfruit** (first portion) **of, and from among, His created beings** (or: of the effects of His act of creating; or: from the results of the founding and creation which is Himself; [other MSS: of the Himself-creatures])."

Then Peter affirms this, in 1 Pet. 1:23,
"**being folks having been born again** (been regenerated; been given birth back up again), **not from out of a corruptible** (or: perishable) **seed that was sown, but rather from an incorruptible** (imperishable; undecayable) **one: through God's continually living and permanently remaining** *Logos.*"

In 2 Pet. 3:5, we are brought back, full circle, to another description of Gen. 1,
"**skies** (or: atmospheres; heavens) **and land were continuously existing from long ago** (or: = from ancient times) – **from out of the midst of water, and through water – being made to stand together** (being placed or put together) **by** (or: in; with) **the Word** (*Logos*; thought and idea; reason; patterned information) **of God** (or: which is God)."

We will end this tour of NT Logos verses by visiting the Unveiling (Rev.):
12:11a,
"**And they at once overcame** (or: at some point conquer) **him** (or: it) **because of and through the blood of the little Lamb, and because of the word** (*Logos*) **of their witness, as well as through the message from their testimony** (that reason laid-out from the evidence, which is them)…"
19:11-13,
"**Then I saw the atmosphere** (or: sky; heaven), **having been opened – and consider! A bright, white horse. And the One continually sitting upon it being constantly called "Faithful** (Full of Faith; To Be Trusted; Trustworthy; Loyal) **and True** (or: Real)," **and He is continuously judging** (making decisions and evaluations) **and battling** (making war) **in eschatological deliverance** (within equitable dealings; in justice, fairness and righted relations which accord with the covenantal Way pointed out). **And His eyes [are]** [other MSS add: as] **a flame of fire; and upon His head [are] many diadems** (kingly bands), **having a name having been written** [other MSS: having names written, and a name] **which no one knows except Himself, and having been clothed** (or: cast around) **with a garment having been dipped in** (immersed; [other MSS: sprinkled with]) **blood** (or: dyed with blood), **and His Name is being called 'The Word of God** (God's Logos; The Message from God; The Idea which is God; The Expression about God)." [*cf* Rev. 1:13-16]

So there we have it: samplings of the Logos, from Genesis through Revelation. May these meditations expand our perception of God's Logos. We are convinced that It is much more than we ever suspected. We will now return to our text, at 1:15...

15. **John is continuing witnessing about It** (or: Him) **and has cried out, repeatedly saying, "This** (or: This One) **was That** (or: the One) **of Which** (or: Whom) **I said, 'That** (or: The One) **progressively coming behind me has come to be in front of me** (or: has taken precedence of me),**' because It** (or: He) **was existing first, before me** (or: 'that It, or He, was first [in place and station] in regard to me'),**"**

John was either referring to the pre-existence of the Logos (or, Jesus) – since John was born six months before Jesus (Lu. 1:36) – or it is as the parenthetical rendering offers: "that It, or He, was first [in place and station] in regard to me." We have ended John's statement, here, and read vs. 16 as beginning a narrative, giving information on through vs. 20a, and not resuming John's words until vs. 20b, below...

16. **because we all at some point receive** (take with our hands) **from out of the result of Its** (or: His) **filling** (or: the effect of Its full contents; that which fills Him up)**: even grace in the place of grace** (or: favor corresponding to and facing favor; a [new fresh] gracious favor in the place of and replacing [the previous] gracious favor; [one] joyous favor after and exchanged for [another] joyous favor),

Notice our author's declaration, in vs. 16: "**we all at some point receive** (take with our hands) **from out of the result of Its** (or: His) **filling** (or: the effect of Its full contents; that which fills Him up)**: even grace in the place of grace**!" What a proclamation, and a promise! The final phrase, "grace in the place of grace," forecasts the new covenant in place of the old covenant; the new creation in place of the old creation; the new age in place of the old age.

The alternate renderings of that last phrase are noteworthy:
a) favor corresponding to and facing favor – this is the grace and favor that we enjoy when we face the Father, when we face the grace of God;
b) a [new fresh] gracious favor in the place of and replacing [the previous] gracious favor;
c) [one] joyous favor after and exchanged for [another] joyous favor – a never-ending succession.

17. **because the Law was given through Moses, yet grace and truth are birthed** (or: joyous favor and reality came to be and exists) **through Jesus Christ** [= Messiah Yahshua].

This simply contrasts the former with the (present) latter. The old has passed on by (2 Cor. 5:17), and new things have come into existence: **through Jesus Christ**. Jesus is the new Moses, in the ongoing story of the Ages.

18. **No one at any time has seen God. The only-begotten** (solitary-race, one of a kind) **God** [other MSS: Son] **– the One continuously Existing – THAT** (or: that One) **ruled and led the Way forth into the Father's safe place of honored intimacy** (or: unto the midst of the breast and garment fold of the Father)**: [It; He] interprets** (explains) **[Him] by unfolding and bringing Itself** (or: Himself) **forth, out of the midst.**

Conventional interpretation of these verses has rendered the personal pronoun in the predicate of the first clause of vs. 15, and in the clauses following, as "Him" – referring specifically to Jesus. I include this rendering, in parentheses. It is not an incorrect reading to see verses 15-16 as referring to Jesus Christ, who is specifically named in vs. 17b.

So why did I choose to render the prepositional phrase, in vs. 15a, as "**about It**"? Because the opening topic, and subject, of vs. 14 is "**the Logos**." Reading from Jn. 1:1 straight through vss. 14-15, the topic has continued being the Logos. The first word that John cried out is the word, "**This**," which is a demonstrative pronoun whose antecedent was the Logos of vs. 14. The closest referent of "**This**," is either the Logos, or Its glory, in vs. 14, where this glory is compared to being "**AS of an only-begotten person** (or: like One that is an only kin, of a solitary race, in a by-itself-class) **at a father's side** (or: in the presence of, and next to, [the] Father)." Now notice the location of the Logos: it is the same as that described in Jn. 1:1, where the phrase is often rendered "with God." Now we can apply this to Jesus Christ, introduced in the text in vs. 17, but thus far the topic of the passage is still, "the Logos."

Jumping ahead to vs. 18b we find another demonstrative, "**THAT** (or: that One)," and this whole verse is echoing the situation described in Jn. 1:1-2. Our point is that John is still talking about the Logos (that was incarnated in Jesus). In 18b, the subject of the verb, "**interprets** (explains) **[Him] by unfolding and bringing Itself** (or: Himself) **forth, out of the midst**," can be either the Logos, "**It**," or Jesus, "**He**," both supplied in brackets, which in turn refers back to either rendering of the demonstrative: "**THAT** (or: that One)" which begins the sentence. Our purpose is to uncover the reading of Jn. 1:1-18 (the Prologue of the Gospel of John) as primarily being a discussion about the Logos. We, of course, find this implied in vs. 17, for Jesus was the Agent and Carrier of "**grace and truth**." But grace/favor and truth/reality comes to us via the Logos, just as well. The Logos is the vehicle that inhabits Jesus, the Anointed One.

Why did our author contrast the Law, and Moses, to grace and truth that came through Jesus? If we look back to the account of Moses being the agent and vehicle of the Law (Mt. Sinai), we observe that the Law was also a production of God's Logos. Of course, the author is announcing the new creation of what will become the resurrected Israel – which now is a joining of Jew and Gentile (Eph. 2:15).

With this overview of our present passage, let us now move to some particulars. In vs. 15b:
> "'**That** (or: The One) **progressively coming behind me has come to be in front of me** (or: has taken precedence of me),' **because It** (or: He) **was existing first, before me** (or: 'that It, or He, was first [in place and station] in regard to me')."

The verb "was existing" is the same verb used of the Logos, in 1:1-2. If we take the reading that "**It was existing first, before me**," we see that this could not apply to Jesus, because John was six months older than Jesus. If we take the reading, "that It, or He, was first [in place and station] in regard to me," then it can refer either to the Logos, or, to Jesus. Likewise, the first clause, "**progressively coming behind me has come to be in front of me** (or: has taken precedence of me)," can be applied to either the Logos, or to Jesus. Both the Message (Word; Logos) and Jesus Himself came after John, but took precedence of him. We can easily see that Jesus was a manifestation of the Logos, or, existentially was the Logos. But if we keep in mind both the flow of John's Prologue and the topic of the Logos, they will add to our vision and to our comprehension of what John was saying.

Now, to vs. 16: "**because we all at some point receive** (take with our hands) **from out of the result of Its** (or: His) **filling** (or: the effect of Its full contents; that which fills Him up)**: even grace in the place of grace**." Once again, the Greek text is ambiguous. We thus translate it according to the lens with which we read the text. I have given both options. Yes, we do receive from out of the result of His filling, but in reality this happens to us through the Logos: the Word about Him, the Patterned Information that IS Him, and the Message from Him. So, you see, the Logos (and recall that the effects of the flows of words from Jesus ARE Spirit, and they are Life) is critically and essentially involved in our receiving **grace** from the Logos, and Jesus, being filled with grace.

Another thing to observe in this verse, is that it does not say "grace in the place of the Law." The Law was grace (a favor which created them as a nation with probably the best ethics of that day) to Israel, and we read of repeated favor to them, in their story. But now comes a new expression of grace: "a [new fresh] gracious favor in the place of and replacing [the previous] gracious favor; or: [one] joyous favor after and exchanged for [another] joyous favor." Consider the provision given to Israel in their wilderness wanderings. Paul instructs us that,

> "they all drank the same spiritual drink, for they kept on drinking from out of a spiritual bedrock (or: cliff rock; rock mass) – one continually following along behind (or: progressively accompanying [them]). Now the bedrock (or: cliff rock) was the Christ (or: the rock mass was existing being the Anointing)" (1 Cor. 10:4).

We have two different verbs that John used in vs. 17: "the Law was given through Moses, yet grace and truth are birthed (or: joyous favor and reality came to be and exists) through Jesus Christ." Law was GIVEN; grace and truth are BIRTHED. This latter takes us back to Jn. 1:12-13, where it speaks of being birthed as God's children. It was the Law, GIVEN at Sinai, that made Israel the People of God, or, God's corporate Son (Ex. 4:22). Notice that in that verse of the Torah, Yahweh pronounced this Son as His Firstborn. Ponder that, in regard to Jn. 1:14. As noted above, both the Law and Grace-Truth were embodiments of the Logos. The author's point, here in vs. 17, may be pointing to what we find in Heb. 8:

> 6. **But now He has hit the mark of a thoroughly carried-through public service, even by as much as He continues being a Medium** (an agency; an intervening substance; a middle state; one in a middle position; a go-between; an umpire; a Mediator) **of a superior** (stronger and better) **arrangement** (covenant; settlement; disposition) **which has been instituted** (set by custom; legally [= by/as Torah] established) **upon superior** (stronger and better) **promises!**
> 7. **For if that first one was being unblamable** (without ground for faultfinding; beyond criticism; satisfying), **a place of a second one would not have continued to be sought** (looked for).
> 8. **For continuously blaming** (finding fault and being dissatisfied with) **them, He is saying, "'Consider! Days are progressively coming,' says the Lord** [=Yahweh], **'and I shall progressively bring an end together** (a conclusion of its destiny; or: a joint-goal) **upon the house of Israel and upon the house of Judah with a new arrangement** (a different covenant; an innovative disposition),
> 9.   **"'not down from nor in accord with the arrangement** (covenant) **which I made with their fathers, in a day of My taking hold upon their hand to lead them out of the land of Egypt, because they did not remain** (abide; dwell) **in My arrangement** (covenant) **and, for my part, I paid no attention to and gave no care for** (or: was unconcerned about; neglected) **them,' says the Lord** [= Yahweh].
> 10.   **"'Because this is the arrangement** (covenant; disposition) **which I shall continue arranging for the house of Israel, after those days,' says the Lord: 'progressively giving My Laws into their thought** (into that which goes through their mind; into their perception and comprehension), **and I shall progressively imprint them** (write or inscribe marks) **upon their hearts, and I shall continue being in and among them** ([in relation] to them; for them), **into [the position of] a God, and they shall continue being** (exist being) **in Me** ([in relation] to Me; for Me), **into [the position of] a people.**
> 11.   **"'And they may by no means teach each one his fellow-citizen, and each one his brother, saying, "Know the Lord** (or: You must be intimate with [Yahweh])," **because everyone** (all) **shall progressively perceive and thus understand and be acquainted with Me, from a little one even to a large one of them,**
> 12.   **"'because I shall continue being** (existing) **merciful with a cleansing covering for their injustices** (behaviors contrary to the Way pointed out; inequities) **and acts of lawlessness, and then I would by no means be reminded further of their mistakes and failures** (errors and falling short of the target; sins).'" [Jer. 31:30-33]
> 13. **In thus to be saying "new: different in kind and quality," He has made the first** (or: former) **"old," and that [which is] progressively growing old** (or: obsolete) **and decrepit** (failing of age; ageing into decay), **[is] near its disappearing** (vanishing away). [cf 2 Cor. 3:7-13]

The "grace and truth" that came through Jesus Christ was the new arrangement (covenant) prophesied by Jeremiah. This was the fulfilling of the Law (Mat. 5:17: Lu. 21:22). The new arrangement is a blueprint (Logos) for the new creation, and for the new Temple.

In light of Jn. 1:17, Dan Kaplan has pointed us to Heb. 3:

1. **Wherefore** (From which situation), **O set-apart and sacred brothers** (= consecrated fellow members from the same womb) – **common-holders** (partners; sharing possessors; joint-participants; associates; partaking members) **of an imposed-heavenly calling – consider** (ponder; focus your thoughts down upon and think carefully about) **Jesus, the Sent-off Emissary** (or: Representative; [*cf* 1 Jn. 4:14]) **and Chief and Ruling Priest of our agreed message** (or: our like-reasoned idea; our saying of the same word; our unanimous consent and avowal; or: our binding association-agreement; the like-*logos* which is US),

2. **[and His] continuously being faithful by and loyal to and in the One forming** (making; creating; constructing; establishing; producing; [in LXX the same word as Gen. 1:1]) **Him, even as "Moses [was loyal] within His** (or: his) **whole house."** [Num. 12:7]

3. **For this [reason] He** (or: You see, this One) **has been esteemed worthy of more glory and a greater reputation than Moses, proportionally to the degree that He who constructs** (or: prepares; fully implements) **it has more value** (honor; worth) **than the house itself.**

4. **For every house is constructed, prepared and fully implemented by someone, but the One constructing all humanity** (or: all [situations; circumstances]; = everything) **[is] God!**

5. **And so on the one hand, Moses [was] faithful and loyal in the midst of His** (or: centered in his) **whole house, as an attending therapeutic and medical care-provider** (or: trainer; cultivator; or: valet; squire; companion in arms) – **[which leads] unto a testimony** (or: witness) **of the things going to be spoken** (or: into evidence from those [future] sayings being said) –

6. **Yet on the other hand, Christ [is faithful and loyal] as a Son upon His house – whose** [*p*46, D* read: which] **house** (or: household) **we, ourselves, are** (or: continuously exist being)!...

This passage expands the thoughts of John, in Jn. 1:17. Observe the appositional reading of the last phrase of Heb. 3:1, "the like-*logos* which is US!" Consider allusion to the creation passage of Gen. 1, and to the "beginning" statement of Jn. 1:1 that we see in Heb. 3:2a. And then the metaphor of "houses" that we read in Heb. 3:2b-6, which sheds light on the contrast between Land and Grace/Truth in Jn. 1:17. The Logos created a replica of Itself, a "like-*logos*" which is the "house" of the Son, Who "**has been esteemed worthy of more glory and a greater reputation than Moses**" (Heb. 3:3). Jn. 1:3 is echoed in Heb. 3:4, where we are informed that, "**but the One constructing all humanity** (or: all [situations; circumstances]; = everything) **[is] God!**" Heb. 3:6a explains that we are Christ's house, just as we are the like-*logos*.

Dan also pointed us to what is given in 2 Pet. 1:19,

"**And so, we continue having** (or: constantly hold) **the Idea which was spoken ahead of time in and as Light** (or: the prior-enlightening *Logos*, Blueprint, Thought and Reason; or: the Prophetic Word) **more confirmed** (validated; established; certain), **by which** (or: in which) **you folks continue doing beautifully** (performing ideally; producing finely), **while continuously holding toward** (= paying close attention to) **[it] as to a lamp continually shining within a parched place – until which [time or occasion] the Day may shine through and a light bearer** [= a morning star] **may rise within your hearts**

(or: constantly heeding, as to a lamp progressively making things appear in a dark, dingy or dirty place, until that Day can dawn, and a light-bringer can arise in union with your core and innermost being)."

In this verse, Peter speaks of "**continuously holding toward** (= paying close attention to)" the prophetic Logos, and this calls to mind Jesus' admonition to His followers in Jn. 15:5.

"**I, Myself, AM the Grapevine; you folks [are] the tender branches. The person continuously remaining** (dwelling; abiding) **within the midst of Me – and I within the midst of and in union with him – this one is repeatedly bearing** (bringing forth; = producing) **much fruit. [It is the case] that apart from** (or: Because separated from) **Me you folks continue having ability and power to do** (make; construct; create; form; perform; produce) **nothing!**'

This in turn enlightens the admonition in Heb. 3:

12. **Exercise sight** (Be continuously observing), **brothers, [so] there shall not once be** (or: exist) **in any of you folks a bad, useless or misery-gushed heart** (a heart causing labor, sorrow or pain) **of unfaithfulness** (or: from disloyalty, disbelief or distrust; or: the source and character of which is an absence of faith and trust), **in withdrawing** (or: standing away and aloof; separating or revolting) **from the living God.**

13. **But rather, be habitually calling yourselves alongside – entreating, admonishing, encouraging, bringing relief and helping each other – daily, concerning** (or: in accord with) **each day, until** (or: as long as; during) **that which continues being called "Today"** [with A, C and other MSS: while you folks continue inviting this present Day,] **so that not any one from the midst of you folks may be hardened by a deception of failure** (or: in treachery from a miss of the target; with seduction of sin; by cunning in regard to error; by deceit relating to a mistake).

14. **For we have been born partners of the Christ** (or: we have come to be associates and participants who partake of the Anointed One and commonly hold the Anointing) **with the result that we are now in a binding partnership with Him, since surely we can fully hold in our possession – so as to retain firm and steadfast – the Origin of the substructure to the point of completion of the intended goal**

> (or: if indeed, unto [the condition or state of] maturity, we would fully hold in our possession, so as to retain firm and steadfast, the beginning [position] with regard to the substance, essential nature and basis [of the new reality] – as well as the rule of that [which was] put under, as a standing for support)."

Now even though the Prologue of this Gospel begins Good News about Jesus, this Gospel was written after the life, death and resurrection of Jesus. So why does John open 1:18, here, with, "**No one at any time has seen God**"? It would seem that John is using this verb for "seeing" in the sense of perceiving, or understanding, or seeing with the mind or with spiritual discernment. Recall Jn. 14:9b, where Jesus told His disciples, "**The person having discerned and seen Me has seen, and now perceives, the Father!**" But taking 1:18a at face value, was John saying that before Jesus no one had really perceived or understood Who God is? They observed the results of His works and experienced His presence, but apparently did not really know Who He is, until: "**The only-begotten** (solitary-race, one of a kind) **God**… **ruled and led the Way forth into the Father's safe place of honored intimacy** [cf Jn. 1:1-2] **[and] interprets** (explains) **[Him] by unfolding and bringing Itself** (or: Himself) **forth, out of the midst.**"

There are other MSS which read "Son" instead of "God" following "only-begotten." Some MSS, which have the word "God," do not have the definite article "The" before "only-begotten," and thus it could read, "An only-begotten God." We will not attempt to sort this out, but rather commend our readers to the Spirit of Truth for understanding.

The MS variations, and the awkward syntax of vs. 18b, has made translation of the text a bit difficult. As noted above, my decision was to set off in dashes the subordinate clause, "**the One continuously Existing**," which directly follows," **The only-begotten God**," thus rendering this clause as describing the noun "God." By doing this, we have "The only-begotten God" as the referent of the final clause:

> "**THAT** (or: that One) **ruled and led the Way forth into the Father's safe place of honored intimacy** (or: unto the midst of the breast and garment fold of the Father): **[It; He] interprets** (explains) **[Him] by unfolding and bringing Itself** (or: Himself) **forth, out of the midst.**"

This can, of course, be read as referring to Jesus (and is probably why some MSS changed the word God to Son). But John's ambiguous language can give rise to the consideration that this "only-begotten God" phrase is speaking of the Logos, which originated in the Mind of God as the Thought, the Idea and the Blueprint of the plan of the ages, and which was given birth by the Breath-effect when God spoke the Logos into Being – both as creation, in its beginning, and as fulfillment throughout the ages. The Alpha and the Omega; the Beginning and the End. It was this Logos (from Gen. through Rev.) that explains and interprets God – forth from out of the midst of Himself (cf Rom. 11:36).

The intimacy implied by the phrase, "unto the midst of the breast and garment fold of the Father," is another allusion of Jn. 1:1 – the implied face-to-face intimacy of the Logos with God. An expressed *logos* comes forth via a breath-effect, or life-spirit. The Blueprint (Logos) "explains" what God has been, and continues, doing. But back to Jn. 1:

19. **And this is** (or: continues being) **the testimony of John** (the witness from John), **when the [Sanhedrin, or religious authorities, of the] Judeans** (or: Jews) **sent forth the priests and the Levites** [note: thus, these may have included some Sadducees] **as emissaries out of Jerusalem toward** (or: to; to face) **him – to the end that they may ask him, "You, who are you?"** –

The Jerusalem leadership was concerned that John might be starting a movement that would in one way or another be a problem for them. They would later have this same concern about Jesus. They asked an open-ended question, but John's response in the next verse shows that he understood what this rather ambiguous question was really asking.

20. **and he confessed and did not contradict or deny, and even agreed that, "I am not the Christ** (the Anointed One; = the Messiah)**."**

Well, they must have breathed a sigh of relief, but since he had answered so directly, they wanted to make sure that he was not a pretender of being a fulfillment of some other prophecy, so they pointedly ask two more questions:

21. **And so they asked him, "What, then? Are you Elijah?" And then he continues saying, "I am not." "Are you The Prophet?" Then he distinctly replied, "No!"**

The first question was in reference to Mal. 4:5-6a,
    "Behold, I will send to you Elijah, the prophet, before the coming of the great and advent Day of Yahweh, and he will restore the heart of the fathers to the sons and the heart of the sons to their fathers…" (CVOT).
The second question was an allusion to Deut. 18:15 (quoted about Jesus, in Acts 3:22),
    "**The LORD (= Yahweh) your God will progressively raise up for** (or: proceed to make to stand back up, again, to and with) **you a Prophet like me from among your brothers; you folks will continue listening to Him** (or: keep on hearing from Him)." (LXX, JM)
Cf 6:14b and 7:40, below

22. **Therefore they said to him, "Who are you, so that we may give a decided reply to the ones sending us – what are you in the habit of saying about yourself?"**

The "authorities" always want to know what is going on, so that they can maintain control.

23. **He affirmed, "I am a voice** (or: [the] sound) **of one repeatedly calling out loudly** (crying out; exclaiming; imploring) **within the desolate place** (the wilderness; the uninhabited region; the lonely place), **'Straighten the Way of [the] LORD** (the Lord's Road; the Path pertaining to [the] Lord [= Yahweh or Christ, the Messiah])
    (or: habitually shouting, 'Make straight in the wilderness the way from [the] Owner [= Yahweh or Christ], the Way which is the Lord')**!'** [Isa. 40:3]
just as Isaiah, the prophet, said."

In 14:6, below, Jesus will instruct folks that He embodies this Way, this Path. It refers to a Way of Life, and the Path to the Father. It is the Road of following Jesus (21:19, 22b, below). It is the cruciform Life (Mat. 16:24-25).

24. Now [some] folks having been sent as emissaries were from among the Pharisees.
25. And then they asked him, and said to him, "Why, then, are you continuously immersing (or: baptizing), **since** (or: if) **you are not the Christ nor Elijah nor The Prophet?"**

By immersing folks, either John was treating the Jews as non-Jewish proselytes, or else it should be the Messiah, or His representative, initiating Israel into the new Age – if all the Jews were now supposed to be immersed.

26. John replies distinctly to them, saying, "I am repeatedly immersing (baptizing) **within water. He, Whom you men have not seen or perceived, and have no knowledge of or acquaintance with, has stood in your midst** [other MSS: continues presently standing in your midst].
27. "He is the very One, Who, progressively coming behind me, has come to be in front of me, of Whom I am not worthy (equal of value) **that I should loose the lace** (strap; thong) **of His sandal."**

This is a second witness that John gives about Jesus. It is similar to what he had said, in vs. 15, above. John had an understanding of the sense of his ministry, and of the scope of his calling. He knew that he was not the Messiah, but rather was called to prepare the People of Israel for their Messiah – to make them aware that the season, the fertile moment, was upon them. Lu. 3:7-14 reports some of the content of John's message. Mat. 3:8-12 offers more, where John spoke of the need for, "**a change in thinking, attitude and state of consciousness**." This Gospel does not focus on what the people of Judea needed to do, in preparation for receiving their Messiah, but rather, it focuses primarily upon who Jesus is, and what He and His Father will do. Even the need to be born back up, from above, again (3:7, below) implies a work and action of our Parents. He will offer Living Water (4:10, 13-14) or speak a word and a boy is healed (4:50, below). He will provide food (6:5-13), etc.

28. These things occurred (or: came into being) **in Bethany, on the other side of the Jordan, where John was living his life** (or: was existing), **repeatedly immersing.**

This account suggests that the location of John's ministry (**on the other side of the Jordan**) is outside of the places where Jesus will minister. The narrative now will move away from John, and fully focus on Jesus, and His ministry as the Anointed One, as we read in the following verses, although vss. 29-36 will be filled with John giving further witness to Jesus, and pointing his disciples to Him. Jesus is clearly the main character of this Gospel.

29. The next day he is looking at and observing Jesus progressively coming toward him, and he begins saying, "Look! (Pay attention, see and perceive)! **God's Lamb** (or: the Lamb from God; the Lamb having the character and qualities of God; or, in apposition: **the Lamb** which is **God**), **the One continuously lifting up and progressively carrying away the Sin of the world, and removing the sin which belongs to and is a part of the System**
> (or: habitually picking up and taking away the failure and error brought on by the system and in the cosmos; progressively removing the falling short and the missing of the goal from the world of culture, religion, economy, government, society, and from the aggregate of humanity)!

Here in the first chapter, John designates Jesus as **God's Lamb**. This was fitting for Him to be sacrificed by the Judean leadership in association with Passover, which also associates Him as being the new Moses (the Prophet, as noted above) that would free humanity from its bondage to sin and failure (8:34, below; Rom. 7:23) – so that:
> "**now** (at the present time), **we** [= Israel] **are** (or: were instantly) **rendered inactive** (brought down to living without labor, released from employment, made unproductive; discharged) **away from the Law** (= the Torah; [some MSS add: of Death]), **dying within that in which we were constantly being held down** (held in possession and detained), **so that it is [for] us to be**

42

habitually performing as slaves within newness of spirit and not in oldness (obsoleteness; outdatedness) **of Letter.**" (Rom. 7:6).

However, it was not just deliverance that John saw in Jesus, but also, "**carrying away the Sin of the world**." Sin was not the issue in Israel's Exodus, and the Passover. What John refers to as, "**removing the sin which belongs to and is a part of the System**," was accomplished on the Day of Atonement (Lev. 16), which was the ceremony of purification where the scapegoat figuratively carried "the iniquities of the sons of Israel" out of the camp and into the wilderness. The author of Hebrews describes how Christ did this, in Heb. 9 and 10.

The parenthetical alternate-renderings of the last clause are noteworthy:
  a) habitually picking up and taking away the failure and error brought on by the system and in the cosmos;
  b) progressively removing the falling short and the missing of the goal from the world of culture, religion, economy, government, society, and from the aggregate of humanity.
When Jesus said, "**It has been finished** (or: It has been brought to its goal and end), **and now stands complete** (having been accomplished, perfected, ended and now is at its destiny)!**," in 19:30, below, He meant that there was nothing more that needed to be done.

We want to point out the parenthetical expansion of "**God's Lamb**," since the alternatives add potential depth to John's words:
  a) the Lamb from God – this was not a lamb that some Israelite brought to be offered, but this Lamb came from God – and this is an allusion to Gen. 22:8, where Abraham told Isaac, "God will provide Himself, the Lamb"; cf 3:16, below;
  b) the Lamb having the character and qualities of God;
  c) reading as a genitive of apposition: **the Lamb** which is **God** – this could mean that Jesus was God incarnate, or that God was within the Christ (2 Cor. 5:19), or that Jesus as the Lamb was God's plan, i.e., a work of God.

30. "**This One is He over whose situation** [other MSS: concerning Whom] **I said, 'An adult male is progressively coming behind me Who has come to be in front of me,' because he was existing before me** (or: was continuously being first in rank and importance in regard to me).

Observe the added description, beyond vs. 15, "An adult male." The description, "**progressively coming behind me Who has come to be in front of me**," points to the fact that John was a part of the old covenant, and Jesus was coming "after" John's was already in full swing. Jesus' ministry and work would take precedence over John – i.e., "come to be in front of" John.

The last phrase, "**he was existing before me**," may be an allusion to 1:1, above, since He was the incarnate Logos. The parenthetical expansion is another way of reading this phrase.

31. "**And I myself had not seen Him to know, recognize or be aware of Him, but nevertheless, to the end that He may be brought to light in** (or: for; by) **Israel** (or: be manifested to Israel) – **because of this – I came continuously immersing** (or: baptizing) **in water.**"

Here, John is saying that Jesus was the purpose of John's ministry. His work pointed ahead, to Jesus, as we saw in vss. 15 and 30, above. Jesus was "**the LORD**," whose "**Way**" John instructed his listeners to "**prepare**" (vs. 23, above). His mission was to bring Jesus to light, **in Israel**. The option "for Israel" meant "for Israel to see this Lamb which is God." The option "by Israel" will be seen in 4:22b, where Jesus instructs the woman from Samaria that, "**the deliverance** (the rescue and being restored; the health and wholeness; the salvation) **continues being** (habitually is; constantly exists being) **from out of the Judeans** (or: from among those of Judah {or: from the Jews})."

The ceremony of "**immersing** (or: baptizing) **in water**" symbolized ritual cleansing, but also a death and resurrection. It foretold the end of the old, and the beginning of the new. It may have also been seen as what was needed for Israel, as Jesus said in 3:5, below: the need to be "**born forth from out of water and spirit.**" John's immersion typified the ceremonial washing of Israel's Torah (the old covenant); those "birthed" them into being ceremonially clean, and new – separated from their past failure, etc. The birth of which Jesus spoke, in 3:7, was a birth from out of the Spirit, within which they could perceive the kingdom (3:3), and enter its realm (3:5).

32. **John also testified, repeatedly saying that, "I have viewed and continued gazing at, so that I can now visualize, the Spirit progressively stepping down** (or: the Breath-effect continuously descending), **as a dove, forth from out of [the] atmosphere** (or: as a pigeon out of the sky, or from heaven), **and It remains and dwells upon Him** (or: It abode [= nested] upon Him).

Our author does not specify when John viewed this, but we read the account of it in Mat. 3:16b and Lu. 3:22. Notice that **the Spirit** was with their **atmosphere** (the "first" heaven). The **Spirit** (Breath-effect) "**remains and dwells upon Him.**" That means that He was Anointed by the Spirit – He was their Messiah. John was like Moses: he could not enter the kingdom, but he was enabled to see it.

33. **"And yet, I had not seen Him to know or be aware of Him! But further, the One sending me to be habitually immersing in water, that One said to me, 'Upon whomever you may see the Spirit progressively stepping down** (or: the Breath-effect continuously descending) **and then continuously remaining** (dwelling; abiding) **upon Him, this One is the One progressively** (or: habitually) **immersing** (or: baptizing) **within a set-apart spirit** (or: in the midst of [the] Holy Spirit; in union with the Sacred Breath-effect and Attitude).'**

We will see this clause, "**the One sending me**" used of Jesus, in reference to the Father having sent Him. So both John (here, and vs. 6, above) and Jesus were sent by God. They were both part of the same plan. John had heard from God, as would Jesus – all through His ministry. Jesus' ministry would not focus on water immersion (likewise with Paul – 1 Cor. 1:14-17). Jesus would be "**progressively** (or: habitually) **immersing** (or: baptizing) **within a set-apart spirit** (or: in the midst of [the] Holy Spirit; in union with the Sacred Breath-effect and Attitude)." He would primarily do this through His Word, the Logos that would cleanse and transform folks. He would wash them so that they would be,
> "**clean** (cleansed), **cleared and pruned ones through and because of the word** (*Logos*; laid-out message; thought; idea; pattern-conveying information; blueprint) **which I have spoken to you** (in you; for you; among you) **folks**" (15:3, below).

34. **"And so I myself have seen and given witness, and thus now bear testimony, that this One is God's Son** (or: continuously exists being **the Son which is God**; or: the son having the character and qualities of God; or: the Son from God; The Son [other MSS: Chosen One] of The God).**"

In this passage we have some specific things said about Jesus:
> a) He is God's Lamb, who is continuously lifting up and progressively carrying away the Sin of the world;
> b) the Spirit (Breath-effect) descended upon Jesus, and nested there;
> c) Jesus would also progressively (or: habitually) immerse folks within a set-apart spirit (Holy Spirit; Sacred Breath-effect);
> d) Jesus is **God's Son** (etc., as in text, above; [note: some early MSS read "The Chosen One of God;" – The New English Bible, 1970 follows these MSS])

Isa. 42:1 proclaims:

"Here is My Servant, whom I uphold, My Chosen One, in whom I delight. I have bestowed My Spirit upon Him and He will make justice shine on the nations" (NEB; upper case added). **The Logos** (Who is God) **became flesh**...

35. **The next day** (or: On the morrow) **John, and two from among his disciples, again had taken a stand and now stood [there].**

The predicate, "**again had taken a stand and now stood [there]**," depicts their habit and form of ministry. They probably simply waited for folks to arrive, so as to be immersed and hear John speak. That these two disciples took a stand with John tells us that they were serious about John's ministry, and about what God was obviously doing at that time

36. **Later, gazing upon Jesus** [= Yahshua] **progressively walking around, he is saying, "Look** (Pay attention and perceive; See and consider)**! God's Lamb** (or: The Lamb from, and whose origin is, God; or: the Lamb which is God)**."**

John gives a second witness, a shortened version of vs. 29, above. What is important is that this time it is said in the presence to two of John's disciples. John sees Jesus out in the open (on the other side of the Jordan River?), "**progressively walking around.**" Was He (being full of the set-apart Breath-effect – Lu. 4:1) in process of returning to Galilee, after being tested in the wilderness (Lu. 4:14)? Our author does not cover that episode. Emblematic of John's ministry, he points his disciples toward the next "move of God." He does not try to hold on to those in his own group, but points them to Jesus. In all of what we have observed about John the immerser, in this Gospel, we find that his primary function is to be a witness who testifies about who Jesus is. He does not function as a prophet, as in Mat. 3:11b-12, Mk. 1:8, or Lu. 3:16b-17, nor as a teacher, as in Lu. 3:7b-14. Our author and John the immerser are two witnesses about who Jesus was, and is. John was drawing crowds, and his appearance on the scene was an announcement, and the start, of something new in Israel: the advent of Israel's Messiah, and the Savior of the world – he proclaimed the Christ Event...

37. **And his two disciples hear** (or: heard; listen) **as he is speaking, and then they follow** (or: followed with) **Jesus.**

They took the cue: they had evidently been really listening to what John had been saying about the One who was to come after him...

38. **Now Jesus, being suddenly turned and then viewing** (or: gazing at) **them following, is saying to them, "What are you seeking** (or: What do you habitually look for)**?" Yet they said to Him, "Rabbi," – which, being translated and explained, is normally being called** (or: termed) **"Teacher" – "where are you presently staying** (or: habitually remaining and dwelling)**?"**

We see "the divine passive" in the words, "**being suddenly turned.**" The Spirit was active upon Jesus. So Jesus enquires of them as to what they want, and they reply by first acknowledging that they perceive Him to be a "**Teacher**," thus both showing respect and implying that they want to be His learners. The question that they proceed in asking implies that they intend to stay with Him. They have left one teacher, being now **prepared** for moving forward to the Teacher of the next Level.

39. **He replies to them, "Be coming, and you will proceed seeing for yourselves** [other MSS: Come and see (or: perceive)]**." They went** (or: came)**, then, and saw** (or: perceived) **where He is presently staying** (habitually remaining and dwelling)**, then stayed at His side** (or: remained with Him) **that day. It was about the tenth hour.**

He calls them to be His disciples by saying, "**Be coming, and you will proceed seeing for yourselves**." They accept the invitation, and accompany Him for the rest of that day. Take note that our author offers what might seem to be an insignificant detail, "**about the tenth hour**." Why should his listeners need to know this? He had just informed them that these two "**stayed at His side** (or: remained with Him) **that day**." We will find that numbers are important in this Gospel. In the next chapter he will specify that Jesus has the servants fill **six** water jars. In gematria, the number 10 has been determined to mean "fullness." Was our author indicating that Jesus is beginning His ministry by inviting His first two disciples "in the fullness of time"? Was this the beginning of His "governmental body"? Some students of numbers in the Bible assert that: "Ten is also viewed as a complete and perfect number, as are 3, 7 and 12. It is made up of 4, the number of the physical creation, and 6, the number of man. As such, 10 signifies testimony, law, responsibility and the completeness of order." (https://www.biblestudy.org/bibleref/meaning-of-numbers-in-bible/introduction.html)

40. **Now Andrew, the brother of Simon Peter, was one of the two hearing at John's side, and following Him.**
41. **This one** [i.e., Andrew] **is first finding his own brother, Simon, and is saying to him, "We have found the Messiah!" – which is presently being translated with explanation, 'Christ** ([the] Anointed One)' **– "so we now know Who and where He is!"**

In that Andrew says, "**We have found the Messiah**," it appears (together with the teachings of John, above) that Andrew and his fellows were "looking for," or "expecting" the Messiah. We are not told what else Jesus may have said to them, so we might assume that John's witness was effective. But also, Jesus will explain (6:44, below) that the Father had been dragging them toward Jesus (just like the fish, in 21:8). Also, not only had they found the Messiah, since the verb that Andrew used is in the perfect tense, this meant that they knew Who He was, and where He was.

42. **And so he led him toward Jesus. Looking within** (or: to; on; centered on; in union with) **him, Jesus said, "You are Simon, the son of John** [other MSS: Jonah]. **You will be called Cephas" – which is presently being translated and interpreted, "Peter** (a stone).**"**

The dative case of "**him**," in the second statement, offers a range of functions: Jesus may have been discerningly looking "within" Simon, or simply looking to, and then on, him. Making an assessment of him and then renaming him can tell us that He was "centered on" Simon, and perhaps (spirit-to-spirit) joining with him to be "in union with him" (which is what Love seeks). Knowing that he was the son of John (or, Jonah) shows us that Jesus had the grace-effect of a word of knowledge. We are not told why Jesus changed his name, or exactly what He meant by the new name. Rev. 3:12 speaks of overcomers receiving a new name. Perhaps Jesus is indicating that this "ordinary stone" will be turned into a gem stone, from all the pressure and fire that he will endure (cf 21:23, below; Rev. 21:14, 19, 20).

43. **The next day** (or: On the morrow), **He decided** (or: He wants) **to go out into Galilee. And then Jesus is finding Philip and proceeds saying to him, "Be constantly following Me!"**

Now Jesus is "**finding Philip**" and calls him to be His follower. It was the next day, so it must have been close to where they had been staying with Jesus.

44. **Now Philip was from** (= had been living in) **Bethsaida, the city of Andrew and Peter.**

This town was north of the Sea of Galilee, and east of the Jordan River, close to the area where John had been immersing folks. Both Philip and Andrew are Greek names, a sign of Hellenization. So there are at least three from the same city, and in the next verse, Philip finds a fourth one from the same place.

45. Philip proceeds finding Nathaniel [note: probably also called Bartholomew] **and says to him, "We have found the One of Whom Moses wrote within the Law and the Prophets: Jesus – Joseph's son** (or: a son of Joseph) **– the one from Nazareth!"**

Philip ties Jesus to "the Prophet" whom we saw referenced in vs. 21 and 23, above. Notice that he gives specific identification: Joseph's son, from Nazareth. We will find Him identified by this town at His arrest, in the Garden (18:7), and then Pilate will so designate Him on the placard attached to His cross (19:19).

46. Then Nathaniel said to him, "Can anything good be (or: Is anything virtuous normally able to exist) **from out of Nazareth?" Philip continues, saying to him, "Come and see."**

How typical of most all people is a response of this kind! We will not trace out the reasons for Nathaniel's attitude toward, and assessment of, Nazareth, but need only take to heart both the surprise that awaited him, and the words of Paul,

"**Hence** (or: And so), **do not be constantly evaluating** (or: stop judging, making decisions about or critiquing) **anything before [its] season** (before a fitting, due or appointed situation; prior to a fertile moment): **until the Lord** [= Yahweh or Christ] **would come – Who will continue giving light to** (or: shine upon and illuminate) **the hidden things of the Darkness** (or: the hiding things which are things in the shadows and dimness of obscurity), **and will progressively set in clear light** (or: keep on manifesting) **the intentions and purposes** (designs, dispositions, motives and counsels) **of the hearts – and then the praise and applause from God will repeatedly be birthed** (happen; come into being) **in each human** (or: for every person)!" (1 Cor. 4:5)

47. Jesus saw Nathaniel progressively coming toward Him, and He begins saying about him, "Look, and pay attention: truly an Israelite, within whom exists (or: there continues being) **no deceit** (bait or contrivance for entrapping; fraud; guile)!"

In 2:24, below, we will be specifically informed that,

"**Jesus, Himself, was not habitually entrusting Himself to them because of the [situation for] Him to be continuously** (habitually; progressively) **knowing all people by intimate experience and through insight.**"

Notice Jesus' association of being "**truly an Israelite**" with the characterization "**within whom exists** (or: there continues being) **no deceit** (bait or contrivance for entrapping; fraud; guile)." This calls to mind Paul's characterization in Rom. 2:

28. **for you see, the Jew is not the one in the visibly apparent or outwardly manifest** (or: For not he in the outward appearance is a Jew), **neither [is] circumcision that [which is] visibly apparent** (outwardly manifest) **in flesh** (= in body),
29. **but rather, a Jew [is] the one within the hidden [place]** (or: [that which is] in the concealed [realm]) **and circumcision [is] of [the] heart** (= core of our being) **– in union with Breath-effect** (or: within [the] spirit; in attitude), **not in letter – whose praise** (applause; full recommendation; [note play on words: Jew is a derivative of "Judah," which means "praise"]) **[is] not from out of mankind** (humanity), **but rather from out of God.**

There may also be seen in these verses an allusion to 1 Sam. 16:7,

"A human sees the visible appearance, yet Yahweh sees into the heart."

48. Nathaniel says to Him, "From where (or: what place) **are you having an intimate knowledge of me?** (or: Where do you know me from?)" **Jesus decidedly answers, and said to him, "Before Philip made a sound to call out to you, [you] being under** (beneath) **the fig tree, I saw you."**

How did Jesus see him? Perhaps it was because immediately following His immersion in the Jordan River, by John, "**now look and consider! – the heavens at once opened back up again! [or, with other**

MSS: the atmospheres were opened up to Him!] **Then He saw God's Spirit**... **progressively coming upon Him.**" It would seem that, with the Anointing of the Spirit, Jesus had become what was called "a Seer."

49. Nathaniel considered and replied to Him, "Rabbi, You – You are the Son of God! You – You are Israel's King!"

Observe the equivalence of the appellations, in Nathaniel's view. Although this was not a public act, by Jesus, it was definitely a SIGN to Nathaniel, as confirmation to what Philip had told him (vs.45, above). Although Nathaniel apparently did not become one of "the Twelve," our author records his experience of Jesus as an early witness to Who Jesus was, and in what societal role He had come. When Jesus later asked His disciples who they were normally saying Him to be, Peter, "**making a discerning and decided reply, said, 'You, Yourself, continue being the Anointed One** (the Christ; = the Messiah), **the living God's Son!'**" So then Jesus,
> "**making a considered response, said to him, 'You continue being a happy and blessed person, Simon, son of Jonah, because "flesh and blood" did not uncover [this] for you, nor disclose [this] so as to reveal [it] to you. To the contrary, [it was] My Father – the One within the heavens** (or: centered in the atmospheres)!'" (Mat. 16:16-17)

50. Jesus decidedly answers, and said to him, "Because I said to you that I saw you down under the fig tree, you proceed believing (or: are you now trusting with allegiance)? **You will continue seeing greater things than these."**

Jesus seems to downplay both His visionary ability and the significance of what He had seen. But He presents a contrast to what had amazed Nathaniel by saying, "**You will continue seeing greater things than these.**" This should give us a clue as to what we will continue reading, in this Gospel. As a preview, let us quote 14:12, from below:
> "**I am saying to you folks, the person habitually trusting and progressively believing into Me, the works which I Myself am constantly doing that person also will proceed doing and he will progressively be doing and producing greater than these, because I Myself am progressively journeying toward** (or: facing; face-to-face with) **the Father.**"

51. And He is further saying to him, "It is certainly true (or: Amen, amen; Most truly; Count on it). **I am presently laying it out, saying to you folks, you will proceed seeing the heaven** (or: sky; atmosphere) **being one that is opened back up again, and 'God's agents** (the folks with a message from God) **repeatedly** (progressively; continuously) **ascending** (stepping back up again) **and habitually** (progressively; continuously; repeatedly) **descending** (stepping down)' [Gen. 28:12] **upon the Son of the Man** (or: Mankind's Son; = the Son of Adam; the Human Son; = the Human Being; = the eschatological Messianic figure).**"**

Now what are WE to expect, in our day? Was this an allusion to 1:32, above? Was "the Son of the Man (the Human Being)" figurative language for more than just Jesus, and also inclusive of the whole of "the Second Man/Humanity" (1 Cor. 15:47)? Were the apprentices of Jesus going to experience the same thing as He did, when John immersed Him (Lu. 3:21b)? Here, Jesus told Nathaniel, regarding him and the other apprentices, "**you folks will proceed seeing the heaven** (or: sky; atmosphere) **being one that is opened back up again.**" But He continues: "**and God's agents** (the folks with a message from God) **repeatedly** (progressively; continuously) **ascending** (stepping back up again) **and habitually** (repeatedly; progressively; continuously) **descending** (stepping down)' **upon the Son of the Man.**" Take note of, in this verse, the reference to Jacob's dream, in Gen. 28:12-13,
> "a stairway, stationed (or: planted) earthward, and with its top reaching towards and touching the heavenwards [LXX: unto the sky], and look: agents of (or: folks with a message from) God were

going up and coming down upon it (or: him). And then look: Yahweh was standing up, poised over him, and He said, 'I AM Yahweh, God of Abraham your father, and God of Isaac...'"
Observe the connection: Jacob became Israel, and Jesus calls Nathaniel a paradigmatic Israelite. Jacob called the location of his dream the House of God (Bethel). Israel became the portable House of God, via the Tabernacle within its midst. This House (Tent/Temple) gave access to Yahweh, during the Mosaic covenant, and the Veils of the Tabernacle were the gates of the heavens (Gen. 28:17). In 2:16-21, below, Jesus will speak of His body being His Father's House, the Temple of God – He was now the One who gave access to the atmospheres and the heavens. Reading the Hebrew pronoun of Gen. 28:12 as "**upon him** (i.e., upon Jacob)" aligns with Jesus' statement, here in vs. 51. Also, in 3:13-14, below, we see another reference to "**the Son of Man**" who will be attached to a pole (which was "planted in the earth") as a figure of the One who gives humanity access to the upper realm of living (aionian Life – 3:15b).

With this in mind, consider a literal rendering of 1 Tim. 3:13,
> "**You see, those giving supporting service and dispensing [goods] in a fine, beautiful, excellent and ideal manner continue in** (or: by; for; among) **themselves building around themselves a beautiful** (fine; excellent; ideal) **circular staircase** (that which enables folks to step up to a higher place) **and much freedom of speech** (confident outspokenness and boldness which is the right of citizens) **resident within faith, trust and loyalty – that which is resident within, and in union with, Christ Jesus**."

This verse describes that of which Jesus spoke to Nathaniel: we, as the body of the Son of Man, become the means of transport from realm to realm; from the earth (humanity) to the heavens (realm of spirit)

So who are "**God's agents** (the folks with a message from God)"? They are those who are a part of the Logos, and who function in bringing the Logos to humanity. Paul listed some of these functions in Eph. 4:11-13. In that passage, notice the "ascending and descending" language in Eph. 4:8-10. His apprentices are called to do the works that Jesus did (Jn. 14:12). In Rev. 21:2 we see God's people descending (taking a low position, as Christ did – Phil. 2:5-9):
> "**Next I saw the set-apart** (or: holy) **city, a new Jerusalem** (or: an innovative, different Jerusalem that is new in character and quality), **progressively descending from out of the atmosphere** (or: presently stepping down out of the midst of the sky; or: steadily stepping in accord, forth from heaven), **[coming] from God, being prepared** (having been made ready)..."

In Rev. 22:17, we see one of the reasons for the Bride to descend (Eph. 2:6 tells us from where we descend, and Heb. 12:22-24 describes the location of the City):
> "**And now the Spirit and the Bride are continuously saying, 'Be repeatedly coming!' Then let the one continuing to listen and hear say, 'Be continuously coming!' And so let the person constantly thirsting continuously come; let the one habitually willing at once receive Water of Life freely**"
>> (or: "And so the Breath-effect and the Bride are constantly laying it out: 'Be progressively going!' Also, let the person now hearing say, 'Be progressively going!' Then, let the one repeatedly being thirsty habitually come and go. The person desiring and intending must at once take the Water from, and which is, Life for a free gift [to others]"). [Cf Jn. 4:14]

Moses ascended into Sinai to receive the pattern (the Blueprint; the Logos) for the first tabernacle, and then he descended to share this with the people, and then they built the tabernacle. In 1 Cor. 3:9ff, Paul, who had seen things in the third heaven (2 Cor. 12:1-5), was expecting the people to be building God's Temple, following the new Blueprint (Logos). This is what we, being filled with the Logos (the Blueprint), are about.

In Mk. 1:10, right after Jesus was immersed by John (vs. 9), "**He saw** (perceived and became aware of) **the atmosphere and sky** (or: the heavens) **being progressively split and torn apart, so as to be divided**..." Later, after forty days of being examined and tested in the wilderness, "**agents** (messengers)

had kept on giving attending service and support for, as well as dispensing provision to, and in, Him" (Mk. 1:13).

> "**But to the contrary, you folks have approached so that you are now at Mount Zion – even in a city of a continuously living God; in "Jerusalem upon heaven" – also among ten-thousands** (or: myriads) **of agents and messengers** (people with a/the message)**: [that is] in an assembly of an entire people** (or: an assembly of all; a universal convocation) **and in a summoning forth** (or: a called-out and gathered community) **of firstborn folks**…" (Heb. 12:22-23a).

That, in Heb. 12, is a picture of, "**every family** (lineage; kindred; descent; paternal group) **within heaven and upon earth** (or: in [the] sky or atmosphere, and on [the] land)…" (Eph. 3:15). Heaven and earth are joined together by the "staircase," which is the Lord, and the incarnated Logos has produced a new creation in which the two realms are now joined together to be One. The entire new creation (heaven and earth) was joined to the Lord, by the Lord, and this new sphere of existence is called "Jerusalem upon heaven," being situated, in spirit (1 Cor. 6:17), upon His Holy Mountain (Isa. 11:9; Ezk. 20:40; Obad. 21; *cf* Eph. 2:6).

We would like to suggest, for your consideration, a different version of the picture that Jesus described, here in vs. 51, as well as another version of the vision that Jacob saw (Gen. 28:12), and this is the vision that Ezekiel saw in Ezk. 1:4-28 (which is echoed in the vision that John saw, in Rev. 4:6b-8). In Ezekiel's vision, there is a key, vs. 5b, that unlocks the identity of this figurative vision. There (5b), it informs the readers that "And this was their appearance: they had the likeness of a human." We find these same "living beings" again, in Ezk. 10, where now one of the faces is described as "the face of a cherub" (vs. 14), along with the face of a human. Cherubim were a part of the mercy seat (the cover of the ark, in the holy of holies); they were also part of the design of the veil (Ex. 36:35; Heb. 10:20), which was the entrance to the holy of holies – the place of the intimate presence of Yahweh. Now connect the dots: the Tabernacle (and its successor, the Temple), was a symbol of the body of Christ (2:21, below; 2 Cor. 6:16). We suggest that all these visions are about humans, when they are anointed by God's Spirit, and reflect His glory (2 Cor. 3:18; *cf* Ezk. 1:28b; 10:4, 8b).

Chapter 2

Following the incident of what the Synoptic Gospels record of Jesus' immersion by John, and then His testing in the wilderness, we find John, here, giving a witness that Jesus is the Son of God (1:34). After this, three days are pointed out: "**The next day**" (1:35), then, "**The next day** (or: On the morrow)" (1:43), and then chapter two begins with:

1. **And on the third day a wedding occurred** (or: a marriage and wedding feast took place) **within Cana of Galilee, and the mother of Jesus was there.**

Numbers are significant in this Gospel. Why did our author specify that the event that he will describe, below, happened "on **the third day**"? We suggest that this sequence was set up to give the readers a code for interpreting the underlying theme of the "first SIGN" (vs. 11, below) which will be recorded in this incident. The called-out folks would have been aware of the tradition associated with "the third day." Matthew recorded Jesus informing His disciples,

> "**and then they will kill Him off, and later, on** (or: in; during) **the third day, He will be aroused and raised up**" (Mat. 17:23; *cf* Mat. 27:64; Mk. 9:31; Lu.. 13:32; 24:21, 46; Acts 10:40).

The Sign which will be detailed, below, involves the transformation of one substance into another substance, with the former substance being incorporated into the latter. On the third day of creation, the Land (a figure for Israel) was separated from the seas (a figure of the non-Israelite nations), and then the Land brought forth trees and vegetation that bear fruit (and the SIGN, below, relates to the fruit of the vine). This SIGN would point to a new Israel (embodied in their Messiah) and a new Vine (15:1ff, below). It was in the third month when Israel first reached Sinai (Ex. 19:1), and in Ex. 19:11, after two days of

Moses sanctifying the People and having them wash their clothes (a figure of the immersion by John), they were instructed that on "the third day Yahweh will come down in the sight of all the People, upon Mount Sinai." And so Moses told the People, "Prepare for the third day…" (19:15). The symbology of "the third day" is a study all in its own, but we suggest that in our present verse (2:1), it may have been a "sign" that our author intended to point to a relationship between water being transformed into wine, and the resurrection of Jesus. Paul emphasized "the third day" in 1 Cor. 15:3-4a,

> "**that Christ died over [the situation and circumstances of] our failures** (on behalf of our mistakes, deviations and sins) **– corresponding to the Scriptures – and that He was buried, and that He has been awakened and raised in** (or: on) **the third day**."

There is another allusion in how the narrative has been crafted: on the third day, "**a wedding occurred**." Paul will later pick up this key when he associates marriage to the relationship between Christ and the called-out communities (Eph. 5:25-32). In 3:28, below, John will use the metaphor of the bride, the bridegroom, and the friend of the bridegroom to speak of Jesus and himself. The beginning of chapter 4 will speak of a woman and her husbands. So let us read about the wedding in Cana…

2. **Now Jesus – along with His disciples – was also called into the wedding** (or: invited unto the marriage feast).
3. **Then later, there being a lack of** (a need of; a failing of sufficient) **wine, the mother of Jesus proceeds saying to Him, "They are not continuing to have** (= they're running out of) **wine."**

We are not told any reason for there being "**a lack of** (a need of; a failing of sufficient) **wine**." Was it because more guests had come than were planned on? Did Jesus and His disciples add to this drain on the homeowner's supply? Was this why Jesus' mother would bring the problem to Him? We are not told anything about the economic status of the host, or even about how many were attending. There is only a problem in the area of hospitality and need. It may be that the host of the wedding was poor. Whatever the reason, the episode presents Jesus as One who can take control, in the case of need, and can provide for the need. In chapter 6 Jesus will feed five thousand by multiplying bread and fish. Here, Jesus' mother and the wedding guests may be an allusion to Moses in the desert, when the people of Israel ran out of food and were hungry. So Yahweh told Moses that He would rain food from the sky for them (Ex. 16). We will come across the themes quenching the thirst and of "the Bread of God from the sky" in 6:32-58, below. This Gospel ends with Jesus providing breakfast for some of the disciples, in the Epilogue, and then admonishes Peter to feed His flock.

4. **So Jesus is replying to her, "What [is it] to Me and to you, madam** (or: What [is that] for Me and for you, O woman; or: = My lady, what has this got to do with us)**? My hour is not yet** (or: is still not) **arriving."**

The New English Bible (1970) paraphrases Jesus' reply, "Your concern, mother, is not mine." Is this what Jesus meant? The KJV has Jesus addressing her as, "Woman…" First of all, the term in that time and culture could be very respectful, as suggested by the rendering, "My lady," or, "**madam**." Had He said it as "O woman," we cannot hear the tone in His voice or sense the mood in which He spoke to her. Such ambiguity provides us with a seed for contemplation, and for listening to the Spirit's voice within.

Viewing this symbolically, was He responding to her as representing Israel, who wanted physical food and deliverance from her oppressors? Was He intimating that His mission was for more than sustenance for the physical body? He includes her (or: Israel) in this question – not just Himself. Israel had been given the mission of being the vehicle for blessings all the families of the earth – fulfilling the promise given to Abraham. He would tell the Samaritan woman that, "**the deliverance** (the rescue and being restored; the health and wholeness; the salvation) **continues being** (habitually is; constantly exists being) **from out of the Judeans**" (4:22, below). But as for Him, at that moment, His "**hour [was] not yet** (or: [was] still not) **arriving**." Was He referring to the cross, here, and the "cup" which His Father had given

Him to drink (18:11)? Notice that He said "**hour**" (a segment within a day) and not "**day**" (a season that could be farther off).

5. **His mother proceeds speaking, saying to the attending servants, "Do at once whatever** (or: anything which) **He may be telling** (or: should be laying out for, or saying to) **you."**

She knows that He is in control, and that He can facilitate supplying the need. Here the author is speaking to his listeners (and to us): "**Do whatever He may tell you to do**." She takes the role of the prophets, anticipating Jesus later expressly telling His apprentices,
> "**If anyone continues** (or: may be habitually) **loving, accepting, fully giving himself to, and urging toward union with, Me, he WILL continue constantly watching over so as to observe, guard, preserve keep and maintain My word** (*logos*: thought, idea; blueprint; message; laid-out, patterned information)…" (14:23a, below).

Next, we should notice that here it was "**attending servants**" that actually performed the act which gave rise to the SIGN and the miracle. That term, *diakonos* and its cognates, was how Paul frequently referred to himself and to his associates in their supportive work of the called-out communities. Jesus gave the directions to them about what to do, and they carried out His implanted goals.

6. **Now there were six stone water pots** (or: jars) **habitually lying there – corresponding to the cleansing** (or: purifying) **practice pertaining to the Jewish customs** (or: ritual and ceremony of washing, originating from the Judeans) **– having capacities for up to two or three liquid measures** (= 15 to 27 gallons).

That it is specified that they were "**stone**" water posts reminds us of what Paul said of Israel in the wilderness (Ex. 17:6; Nu. 20:11):
> "**they all drank the same spiritual drink, for they kept on drinking from out of a spiritual bedrock** (or: cliff rock; rock mass) **– one continually following along behind** (or: progressively accompanying [them]). **Now the bedrock** (or: cliff rock) **was the Christ** (or: the rock mass was existing being the Anointing)" (1 Cor. 10:3).

That it gives the number of pots is significant: **six stone water pots** (or: jars). Six is often a reference to humanity, created on the 6th Day (Gen. 1:26-31). This theme of people and water will be echoed, during a corporate party of the Judeans, in 7:37-39a, below:
> "**Now within the last day – the great one – of the Feast** (or: festival), **Jesus, after having taken a stand, stood and then suddenly cries out, saying, "If ever anyone may continue being thirsty, let him be habitually coming toward** (or: face-to-face with) **Me, and then let the person continuously trusting and progressively believing into Me be constantly** (habitually; repeatedly) **drinking!** [*cf* Isa. 12:3; 55:1]
> > (or: let him be progressively coming to Me and keep on drinking. The person habitually being   faithful unto Me,)
> **Just as the Scripture says, 'Rivers** (or: Floods; Torrents) **of living water will continuously flow** (or: gush; flood) **from out of the midst of His cavity** (or: his innermost being or part; or: the hollow of his belly; [used of the womb])."'** [*cf* Isa. 58:11; Ezk. 47:1; Joel 3:18; Zech. 13:1; 14:8]
> **Now this He said about** (or: with regard to) **the Breath-effect** (or: Spirit; Attitude; [other MSS: Holy, or set-apart Spirit; Sacred Wind]) **of which** (or: of Whom as a source; [other MSS simple read: which]) **they – those trusting and believing into Him – were about to be continuously and progressively receiving**."

The capacity of the jars, "**two or three liquid measures**," can echo this "third day" event, or be an allusion to the second and third sections of the temple: the holy place, and the holy of holies, which Heb. 9 articulates and which Paul connects to the body of Christ, as being God's Temple (1 Cor. 6:19; 2 Cor.

6:16). The extreme volume of wine (15 to 27 gallons) speaks to the superabundance of supply in God's reign, and from the work of Christ. This overflow is echoed in the twelve baskets of fragments that were left over after feeding the five thousand (6:13, below). These pots that were used for "**cleansing** (or: purifying) **practice**" involved in Jewish customs. He could have had them fill just one of those pots and it would have been more than enough wine for the celebration. Jesus provided for an abundance of "**cleansing and purifying**" by instructing six pots to be filled.

7. **Jesus says to them, "Fill the water pots** (or: jars) **full, with water." And so they filled them up to the upper part** (back up to the top, or, brim).

Humanity is to be filled with the Water of Life. They are filled "**up to the upper part**," signifying from the earth to the heavens – completely filled to the very tops.

8. **So then He continues speaking, saying to them, "Now bale out** (or: draw off) **[some] and proceed carrying** (bearing; bringing) **[it] to the head man (or: chief) of the dining room** (= the master or director of the festivities)." **And so then they brought [it].**

Notice that it is the attending servants who are being "led by the Spirit" (Rom. 8:14), and who executed the Lord's directives. There is order in this act, as was appropriate in this situation: they carried the "liquid" to "**the head man** (or: chief) **of the dining room**."

9. **Now as the head man** (chief) **of the dining room sipped and tastes the water existing having been made to be wine** (or: the water [which] had been birthed being [now] wine) – **now he had not seen to know from where it is, yet the attending servants, the ones having baled** (or: drawn) **out the water, had seen and thus knew – this director of the feast begins calling out** (continues shrieking; or: insistently summons) **the bridegroom**

It was appropriate for the man who was in charge of the dinner to taste it before it was served to the guests. Just "tasting" of the NEW is enough to know its character and value. We recall Ps. 34:8, "Taste and see that Yahweh is good." Now the head man did not know the source of this new wine, but the attending servants knew what they had done: they had filled the pots with water, and then had baled out wine. It appears that only those of the servant class knew about the miracle of this SIGN. We are not told anything about what Jesus' mother may have thought or concluded about Jesus having provided the solution to this need. Did our author purposely leave her in the background of the incident? It seems to be so. Was His mother serving the story by being blended into the "leadership" of those sponsoring the wedding (once again, figures of Israel)? The bridegroom is also left anonymous. The focus is on the miracle, which was a SIGN. For those who heard what had happened, and for we who read the story, the wedding was simply a setting, a backdrop, to highlight the new creation that was in process of coming.

However, this SIGN may point to another wedding, in Mat. 22, which was a parable given to show aspects to which the reign of the heavens could be compared, which was like, "**a king** (or: secular ruler), **who made arrangements and prepared wedding festivities** (things associated with a celebration, feast or banquet) **for his son**" (Lu. 22:2). Therefore, the setting of this first SIGN may be an allusion to the presence of God's reign, in Jesus.

10. **and proceeds, saying to him, "Every man habitually places the fine** (the beautiful; the ideal) **wine first, and whenever they may have been made drunk, then the inferior. You – you have guarded and kept the fine** (ideal) **wine until now** (the present moment)!"

This wine was better than what had come by normal means. My wife, Lynda, has pointed out that the normal process (watering and growing a vine, harvesting the fruit, crushing the grapes, fermenting the wine) had been skipped over. Water put into purification jars became immediately transformed. This is a picture of the work of the "Spirit" in us: we are purified by His water of Life, and now our inner being is filled with the wine of rightwisedness, peace and joy in the Holy Spirit (Rom. 14:17). It thus came about that God "**guarded and kept the fine** (ideal) **wine until now** (that present moment)" – the time of His kingdom. The time of "**the inferior**" (the old covenant) had run its course and had passed away (2 Cor. 5:17).

11. **This beginning of the SIGNS Jesus performed** (did; made; constructed; accomplished; produced) **within Cana, of the Galilee [district], and set His glory in clear light** (or: manifested His splendor so as to create a reputation; gave light in a manifestation which calls forth praise and has its source in Him; manifested His assumed appearance), **and His disciples trusted, had faith and believed into Him.**

The word "sign" (*sēmeion*) means, basically, something that serves as a pointer to aid perception or insight: a sign; a mark; a distinguishing characteristic; a token. It can also serve as a confirmation. It is often used with *teras*: a wonder; a miracle; a portent; something so unusual it arouses close observation.

A feast, or a banquet, was one of the metaphors for the arrival of the Jewish Messiah and the restoration of Israel, with the Anointed One as its king (e.g., Isa. 25:6-8; 49:9-10; Mat. 8:11; 22:2-13; 25:1-13). We find the symbol of the marriage of the Lamb and His Wife in Rev. 19:7-9, and right after this (Rev. 19:11) John "**saw the atmosphere** (or: sky; heaven), **having been opened back up again.**" Recall that this happened to Jesus, at His immersion in the Jordan River (Lu. 3:21). So in the Gospel of John, the setting for His first "sign" was a lived-out eschatological symbol for the coming of the Messiah, and this is very likely why the incident was recorded.

John is the only Gospel to record this incident, and to designate what Jesus did as being a "**sign.**" There is no introductory remark about what the signs were meant to point to, except that it "**set His glory in clear light.**" Our author had mentioned beholding His glory (the glory of the Logos) in 1:14, above. In 17:5, below, Jesus spoke to the Father about,

> "**the glory** (recognition; good reputation; manifestation which calls forth praise) **which I was having** (or: used to hold) **and continued holding at Your side and in Your presence, before the universe** (or: system; world of culture, religion and government) **is continuing to have being.**"

In that same conversation, 17:22 records that Jesus said that He had,

> "**given to them** (or: in them), **and they now possess, the glory** (the notion; the opinion; the imagination; the reputation; the manifestation which calls forth praise) **which You have given to Me, and which I now possess, to the end that they can continuously exist being one correspondingly as** (just as; according as; to the same level as; in the same sphere as) **We are one.**"

Notice that the reason for His giving them His own glory was so that "**they can continuously exist being one correspondingly as** (just as; according as; to the same level as; in the same sphere as) **WE are one.**" "**Being one**" seems to be the aim, and expression, of "**the glory.**" And here, following His first "**sign,**" we see that His disciples trusted, had faith and believed INTO Him. There was a joining that took place because of the trust that the miracle of turning water into wine had imparted into them. And then, in 17:24, He explains the reason for giving them His glory (etc.) was so that they,

> "**would continuously exist being with Me where I, Myself, AM, so that they can** (or: would) **constantly look upon and keep on contemplatively watching My own glory** (assumed appearance; manifested Presence which incites praise), **which You have given to Me as a possession because You loved Me before [the; a] casting-down of [the; a] universe**
> > (or: tossing down of a world; or: [the] founding of an organized system; a sowing [as seed] or [impregnating] of [the] aggregate of humanity; founding of [the] system of culture and society; or: a casting corresponding to and in agreement with an ordered disposition of [the] Dominating System)."

This was the same "**glory**" of the Logos, incarnated, of which we read in 1:14. They were given the, "**glory** (= prestige and importance; reputation and opinion-forming appearance) **as of an only-begotten person** (or: like One that is an only kin, of a solitary race, in a by-itself-class) **at a father's side** (or: in the presence of, and next to, [the] Father), **full of grace and truth** (filled and replete with joy-producing favor, as well as reality and genuineness)."

And thus He and they became a band of brothers, a new family (Rom. 8:29). It was also thus, that Paul went on to say,

"**Now [in fact, consider this]: those whom He at one point before-marked-out** (or: designates beforehand; [A reads: knew from prior intimate experience; note: may refer to Israel]), **these He also at once called** (or: calls; invited), **and whom He called** (or: calls; invites), **these He also in one stroke rightwised by an eschatological deliverance** (or: makes and sets right, frees from guilt and liberates from bondage, while making them fair and placing them in [covenant] relationships in the Way pointed out). **Now further, those whom He rightwised** (or: liberates and turns in the right direction; or: = included in covenant), **these He also instantly glorified** (or: makes of reputation which calls forth praise; gives a splendid appearance; gives honorable thoughts and imaginations; clothes with splendor)" (Rom. 8:30).

Jesus chose His disciples, and then glorified them with His own glory. We see this glory manifested with Peter and John, when on their way to the temple, and they encountered the cripple:

"**Peter said, 'Silver and gold [coin] is not normally a subsistence for me** (or: is not a possession with me), **yet what I do continuously have** [comment: he had God's glory], **this I am presently giving to you: Within, and in union with, the Name of Jesus Christ the Nazarene, start walking, and then keep on walking about** (around)!'" (Acts 3:6).

Peter was doing there what Jesus had done – with a word imparted to the lame man. This topic of "glory" is a study all on its own, but here we will just meditate on the purpose of this "**beginning sign**," and the effect that it had on His apprentices.

We will not address the symbolism of the "wine" in this study, but we will return, for the moment, to Rev. 19 and vs. 15b where it symbolically pictures the triumphant Christ, where,

"**He is continually treading, [as on a path],** (or: trampling) **the tub** (the wine vat) **of the wine of the strong passion of the internal swelling fervor** (natural impulse; mental bent; personal emotion; or: indignation; wrath) **of the All-Strong** (Almighty) **God.**"

We will discuss "**the internal swelling fervor**" when we offer thoughts on chapter 3, below, and specifically vs. 36b. But here, keep in mind that John does not specifically refer to this event as a miracle (although we can see that it was), but rather, he noted that "**This beginning of the SIGNS Jesus performed** (did; made; constructed; accomplished; produced)." Observe that the author did not term this "the first sign," but rather he used the word "**beginning**," carrying through his theme from Jn. 1:1.

Before continuing on in chapter 2, let us focus on some the other signs in this Gospel and observe this particular thread of the overall picture of Jesus' story. The Gospel of John is not laid out in a chronological order. In 2:23, when Jesus was in Jerusalem for the Passover, "**many believed and put their trust into His Name, constantly gazing upon and critically contemplating His SIGNS.**" And then in 3:2, Nicodemus speaks to Jesus regarding, "**these signs which You are constantly doing** (performing; producing)." But it is not until 4:54, below, that the author reports, "**Now this, again, [is; was] a second SIGN [which] Jesus makes** (or: did; performed; produces), **upon coming from out of Judea into the Galilee [district].**" So, what is the "second sign"?

49. **The royal officer** (courtier; king's attendant or relative) **continues, saying to Him, "Lord** (or: Sir; Master), **walk down** (or: descend) **at once, before my little boy dies!"**

50. **Jesus then says to him, "Be proceeding on your way** (or: Depart and continue traveling). **Your son continues living"....**

53. **Then the father knew by this experience that [it was] in that hour within which Jesus said to him, "Your son continues living." And so, he himself believes** (or: experiences trust; or: held conviction; or: was loyal, with faith) **and, later, his whole household.**

Now in vs. 48, Jesus had said,

> "**Unless you folks see SIGNS and unusual events** (wonders; portents; omens; miracles), **you people can in no way** (or: would under no circumstances) **trust, have confidence, believe or faith-it**."

This second sign was comprised of, once again, Jesus saying something to someone. He told the father, "**Your son continues living**." Our author does not tell us which was Jesus' "third sign," and in 12:37 he speaks of Jesus having performed "so many signs." So why does he specify that this, in 4:50, was Jesus' "second sign" (vs. 54)? Was this just to establish the truth that these two were "two witnesses" of Jesus being the Messiah?

In Jn. 6:2 we read the next occurrence of the word "sign,"

> "**Now a large crowd kept following Him, because they had been attentively viewing the SIGNS which He had been doing** (making; constructing; creating; performing; producing) **upon those who were sick** (without strength; infirm; ill)."

In this same context of Jn. 6, the author reports the people's reaction to Jesus multiplying the bread and the fish for the 5000 men,

> 14. **Then the people, seeing the signs which Jesus did, began to say** (or: kept on saying), **"This One is truly** (or: really) **The Prophet – the One periodically** (or: presently) **coming into the organized system** (or: the world of culture, religion and government; or: the aggregate of humanity).**"**
> 15. **Jesus, therefore – experientially and intimately knowing** (or: coming to perceive) **that they are presently about to be coming and to proceed snatching Him away** (seizing and forcefully taking Him away) **to the end that they may make [Him] king – withdrew Himself, alone, back up** (or: retires; leaves the area and goes back up) **again into the mountain** (or: hill country).

We read, in 6:11, that "**Jesus took the loaves and, expressing gratitude He distributes [it] to those presently lying back. Likewise, also from out of the small cooked fishes – as much as they wanted**." Afterwards He had the disciples collect the remaining fragments. It is presumed that He also distributed the food via His disciples (Mat. 14:19b), but the "sign" was accomplished simply by "**expressing gratitude**," and then others fulfilled the "multiplication." Once again, the Logos in action, this time just saying, "Thank You."

Next, it is Jesus that uses this word, in 6:26,

> "**Jesus decidedly answered them, and says, "It is certainly true** (Amen, amen), **I am saying to you folks, you people continue seeking Me not because you saw SIGNS, but rather because you ate from out of the loaves, and you were fed until satisfied**."

Now at the end of chapter 10 we find this narrative of Jesus leaving Judea:

> 40. **So He went off** (or: away), **again, to the other side of the Jordan [River], into the place where John had been habitually immersing [folks] the first time** (or: formerly), **and continued remaining** (abiding; dwelling) **there.**
> 41. **Then many came to Him, and they began saying, "John, indeed, did not perform a single** (or: one) **SIGN, yet all – whatever John said about this one – was true."**
> 42. **And so many believed and put convinced trust into Him** (or: were loyal unto Him) **there.**

It does not say that Jesus performed signs there. It only records that fact that they had apparently heard that He had performed signs, and in comparing Him to John, they became convinced about John's testimony concerning Jesus.

In 11:47,

"**the chief** (or: ranking) **priests and the Pharisees gathered [the] Sanhedrin** (= convoked a council of the leaders of the Jewish religious and political culture), **and they began to say, 'What are we presently doing, seeing that this man is repeatedly doing many SIGNS?'**"

We find the word "sign" next used in chapter 12:

17. **Accordingly, the crowd of common folks – the one constantly being with Him when He summoned Lazarus forth from out of the memorial tomb and raised him out of the midst of dead ones – kept on bearing witness and giving testimony.**
18. **[It was] on account of this, [that] the [other] crowd also came to meet with Him, because they heard [that] He had performed** (done; made; produced) **this SIGN.**
19. **So the Pharisees said among themselves** (to one another), **"You are observing** (noticing; or, as an imperative: Be watching and considering) **that your efforts are futile** (that you men are benefiting nothing; = that you are getting nowhere). **Look and consider! The world** (or: The mass of society; or: The system of our culture; or: The inhabitants of our organized society; or: This aggregate of humans) **went off after** (or: goes away behind) **him!**

The next place that we find this term is in 12:37, where it referred to an unbelieving crowd:

"**Yet, [even with] His having performed** (done; made; produced) **so many SIGNS in front of them, they were not proceeding to believe or place their trust into** (or: not continuing loyal unto) **Him.**"

The final place where John speaks of Jesus' "signs" is in 20:30,

"**To be sure** (Indeed), **then, Jesus also performed** (made; did) **many other SIGNS in the sight and presence of the disciples – which things are not written within this scroll.**"

So we can see the logic of our author not numbering all of Jesus' signs. We should recall the meaning of this term: something that serves as a pointer to aid perception or insight: a sign; a mark; a distinguishing characteristic; a token. It pointed to the new Reality of the new Creation with its new Arrangement (covenant). It pointed to the deliverance and rescue of all humanity. But before all this would happen,

"**Look and consider! This One continues lying down into the midst of a fall, and then a standing back up again, of many people within Israel – and into a SIGN being constantly spoken in opposition to, and being repeatedly contradicted!**" (Lu. 2:34)

It is evident, from the texts that we have cited, that, for our author, a "sign" was an important witness and concrete evidence that Jesus was the Christ, Israel's Messiah, God's Anointed One. The people had wanted to see signs, but Jesus did not do them just to prove who He was. In 6:30-31, folks asked Him for a sign – something physical or material:

30. **So then they say to Him, "Then what SIGN are you yourself doing** (making; performing; producing), **so that we can see and believe in** (or: trust and have faith by; be loyal to) **you? What are you, yourself, presently accomplishing** (or: actively working; habitually practicing)**?**
31. **"Our fathers ate manna within the wilderness** (in the desolate place of the desert), **according as it stands written, 'He gave to them bread from out of the atmosphere** (or: the sky; heaven) **to habitually eat.'**" [Ps. 78:24]

Jesus did not give them what they asked for, but rather, a few verses later, made a statement to them:

35. **Jesus said to them, "I, Myself, am** (or: exist being) **the Bread of 'the Life'** (or: the bread which is the Life, and which imparts the Life). **The person progressively coming toward** (or: to; or: face to face with) **Me may by no means at any point hunger** (or: would under no circumstances be hungry), **and the one constantly trusting and believing into** (or being habitually allegiant and loyal unto) **Me will by no means continue thirsting** (under no circumstances be repeatedly thirsty) **at any time**....
38. **"because I have stepped down to this level, away from the atmosphere** (or: descended, separating off from the heaven), **not to the end that I should continue doing My will** (purpose; intent), **but to the contrary, the will** (intent; purpose) **of the One sending Me.**"

Matthew, in 16:4, records another refusal to give a sign, in a particular situation, but then Jesus speaks of a sign that would be given to all:

> "'**A worthless, wicked and adulterous** (or: immoral; [note: an OT word and figure for Israel's idolatry, e.g. Ezk. 16:32]) **generation is habitually searching for and thoroughly seeking a sign, and yet a sign will not proceed in being given to it, except the SIGN of Jonah!'** **Then He went away, leaving them down behind** (or, perhaps: = Then turning His back on them, He walked away)." [comment: Jonah was sent to a Gentile nation]

Matthew, in 12:40 had explained this sign:

> "**You see, just as Jonah was within the midst of the belly of the huge fish** (or: sea monster) **[for] three days and three nights** [Jonah 1:17], **thus in this way will the Son of the Man** (humanity's son; = Adam's son) **continue being within the heart of the earth [for] three days and three nights**" [comment: then the message went to the Gentiles; see vs. 41]

Jesus' signs pointed to, and displayed, the function that He had come to perform and what role He had come to play, for humanity. To those not acquainted with the OT or Second Temple Jewish traditions, He might be seen only as a healer, miracle worker, or a wisdom teacher. To understand the significance of the SIGNS we need that basic, background information: the setting of Jesus' ministry, and the history into which He stepped. Comprehending these are necessary as light for our Path. So now, back to chapter 2...

12. **After this, He and His mother – also His brothers and disciples – went down into Capernaum, but they did not remain** (stay; abide) **there many days.**

This verse serves as a transition (it is time for a scene change on the stage) to the next act of the Play.

13. **Now the [annual observance of the] Passover [Feast; festival], which originated with and pertained to the Jews** (the Jewish people, religion and culture) **was near, so Jesus went up into Jerusalem.**

It has been observed that in the other Gospels Jesus makes only one visit to Jerusalem, following the beginning of His ministry. The Gospel of John records multiple journeys to Jerusalem. In Lu. 4:16 it mentions Jesus having a custom of attending synagogue meetings. If Jesus' ministry lasted up to three years, He would have likely followed the "custom" of attending the annual Feasts, in Jerusalem.

14. **Then within the Temple grounds** [probably the court of the Gentiles], **He found those habitually selling cattle, sheep and doves** (or: pigeons), **and those who [for a fee] exchanged foreign coins for acceptable Judean money** (money brokers) **continuously sitting [at their stations, or tables].**

Notice, in vs. 16, below, that even this area was considered to be a part of His "**Father's House.**" It was sacred ground, which recalls Israel at Sinai, and Moses at the Burning Bush.

15. **And so, after constructing a kind of whip out of small rush-fiber cords** (or: making like a lash of twisted rush-ropes), **He casts** (or: ejected) **them all out of the Temple grounds: both the sheep and the cattle** (or: He drove them all, both the sheep and the cattle, forth from the midst of the temple's outer courts). **And then He pours out the coins** (change; small pieces of money) **of the money changers** (= bankers for currency exchange), **and overturns the tables.**

Notice that the cords, or ropes, were for herding the sheep and cattle out. In the next verse, He has the salesmen remove the birds. His actions were measured and intentional. With the sheep He was a Shepherd, delivering them from the temple cultus of animal sacrifice (this applied to the cattle, as well):

this would all be soon ended. Observe the detail: "**He pours out the coins**" – He took control of their finances: they would be poured away.

16. **Next He said to the ones habitually selling doves** (or: pigeons), **"You folks at once take these things from this place! Stop making** (or: Do not habitually make) **My Father's House a house of merchandise** (a merchant's store; a market place; a house of business)!"

This verse has been seen as an allusion to Zechariah's prophecy, in chapter 14, concerning deliverance for Jerusalem when Yahweh will become king over the Land (or: earth – vs. 9). That chapter repeats the refrain "in that Day," which is "a Day pertaining to Yahweh" (vs. 1), and ends in vss. 20-21 speaking about everything in the city being "set-apart (holy) unto Yahweh." The prophecy ends by saying,
    "Neither shall there be a merchant, any more, in the House of Yahweh of hosts, in that Day."

We find this account of Jesus ejecting the sheep and the cattle out of the Temple grounds as being the first thing that He did, in Jerusalem. He instructs the dove-sellers to take the doves away, and tells them to, "**Stop making [His] Father's House a house of merchandise.**" We read about those who traded with these folks, in Rev. 18:3b, "**the merchants of the Land** (territory; earth) **are** (or: became) **rich from out of the power** (or: ability) **of her headstrong pride and wanton luxury** (or: reveling)." Then, in Rev. 18:9-13, we read the prophecy that they,
    "**will proceed weeping and lamenting upon** (over) **her when they may be observing the smoke of her burning, while standing away, at a distance, on account of the fear of her examination** (testing) **by the touchstone, repeatedly saying, 'Woe, tragic is the fate of the Great City! Babylon, the strong city! Because in one hour your evaluating and judging came!' And the merchants of the Land** (or: territory; earth) **[are] continually weeping and mourning upon** (over) **her, because no one continues buying their cargo** (merchandise) **any longer.... wine and olive oil, and the finest flour, and grain and cattle and sheep... even bodies and souls of people.**"
We suggest that this judgment foretold the destruction of Jerusalem, in AD 70, and that what Jesus did, as described above, were a prophetic act that pointed to the end of their business ventures. The overturning of the tables pointed to a destruction of their system. Recall Jesus' prediction in Mat. 24:2,
    "**Truly** (or: Count on it; or: Assuredly), **I am now saying to you folks, there can under no circumstances be a stone left or allowed to be upon [another] stone which will not be progressively loosed down to bring utter destruction.**"

Now our author does not record this as a "**sign**," but His actions evoke a request, from the Jews present, for a "sign" to be given to them (vs.18, below), as a demonstration of His authority to do what He had just done.

17. **Now His disciples are** (or: were) **reminded that it is standing written that**
    "**the zeal** (passion; the boiling jealousy) **of Your House** (or: from Your House; or: for Your House) **will 'completely consume Me'** (or: 'eat Me down and devour Me')." [Ps. 69:9]

His disciples are beginning to think about His actions, and their minds return to their Scriptures.

18. **Then the [religious authorities of the] Judeans made a decision to respond to Him. And so they say, "What SIGN** (authenticating token or distinguishing signal) **are you presently showing** (pointing out; exhibiting) **to us, [seeing] that you are proceeding to do these things?"**

His reply to them, below, was prophetic of the greatest "**sign**" that He would later perform.

19. **Jesus considered then responds to them, and says, "Loosen** (or: Undo, and thus, destroy or demolish) **this Sanctuary** (Shrine; Divine Habitation; = the Temple consisting of the holy place and the holy of holies), **and within three days I will proceed to be raising it up."**

As the listeners to this Gospel being read would likely understand, Jesus was speaking prophetically about His death and resurrection – and our author explains His metaphorical language in vs. 21, below. Here, He was declaring Himself to be the Divine Habitation of Yahweh. He was God's Sanctuary. Take note that He used the phrase "**within three days**."

20. **Then the Judeans** (= Jewish religious authorities) **say, "This Sanctuary was built** (constructed to be the House) **and erected in** (or: over a period of) **forty-six years – and now you... you will proceed to be raising it up within three days?!"**

Jesus had spoken metaphorically, figuratively; they took His words literally, for as Paul would later instruct the folks at Corinth,
> "**A soulish person** (one dominated by, or living focused on, his breath [= the transient life], or by those things which characterize the soul [emotions; will; intellect; physical life; internal welfare; the self; the ego] or psyche) **does not normally accept** (or: habitually get or welcomingly receive the offer of) **the things of God's Breath-effect** (or: which have the character and quality of the Spirit of God), **for they are stupidity to him** (foolishness for him; nonsense in him), **and he continues unable and habitually has no power to intimately and experientially know [them] or get insight, because they continue being sifted and held up for close spiritual examination**
>> (are normally evaluated spiritually above; are constantly brought back for spiritual separation and attitudinal discernment; are progressively re-evaluated through means of the Breath-effect and comparison to the Attitude; or: are pneumatically interpreted)"
>> (1 Cor. 2:14).

And in Rom. 8:7 we read:
> "**the result of the thinking** (disposition; thought processes; mind-set, outlook) **of the flesh** (= attention to Torah boundary-markers, custom and cultus; or: = from the human condition) **[is; brings] enmity, alienation and discord [streaming] into God** (or: hostility unto, or active hatred with a view to, God), **for it continues not being humbly aligned and supportive** (habitually placed under and submitted; or, as a middle: subjecting, humbly arranging or marshaling itself) **to the principle and law which is God** (or: in God's principle; by the Law from God), **for neither is it able nor does it have power.**"

But furthermore, by recording that the Judeans took Jesus literally, it alerts the readers to think deeper, and look for a hidden message in Jesus' words. This author is writing about more than what first seems to be the case. But he doesn't want his audience to miss Jesus' point, so he explains…

21. **Yet that One** (= He) **had been laying [things] out concerning, and speaking about, the Sanctuary which is His body** (or: the Divine habitation of the body belonging to, and which is, Him; the inner Temple pertaining to His whole corporeal and material substance).

Our author explains that, "**He had been laying [things] out concerning, and speaking about, the Sanctuary which is His body**." Here, I conflated the root idea of the verb (*legō*), "**laying [things] out**" and the normal rendering of the verb as "**speaking**." He was doing more than just "talking." From this same verb we get *logos*; He was giving a picture of the Blueprint.   Consider the term "**Sanctuary**" (and the parenthetical explanations for what this term means), and meditate on the fact that He was applying all of this to "**His body**." And then later, Paul would instruct us that WE are His body (1 Cor. 12:27). Simply amazing! The final phrase, "**which is His body**," is a classic example of the genitive case of the noun, being rendered as "apposition," or, definition, explanation. The genitive case is used throughout the NT, but seldom do translators opt for this function of the genitive. The KJV renders this "of his body," which is technically correct, but in this context it is ambiguous, and does not fully communicate the important point which the author was making.

The Father's "House" was actually Jesus' body. He was where the Father lived; the physical Sanctuary in Jerusalem was a symbol of the "Father's [actual] House," and for the old covenant of types (Rom. 5:14; 1 Cor. 10:6, 11) and shadows (Col. 2:17; Heb. 10:1), that stone Temple was the Father's House, for those Jews who had the Mosaic covenant. But in the new covenant, our bodies (both individually and corporately) are "the Father's House," i.e., where the Father lives.

22. **Then, when He was awakened, aroused and raised up forth from out of the midst of dead ones, His disciples were reminded that He had been repeatedly saying this, and they believed by the Scripture and put trust in the word** (Logos; Blueprint; message; idea) **which Jesus said** (proposed; had recited and laid out).

Here, our author informs us that Jesus was referring to His resurrection, when in vs. 19 He said, "**within three days I will proceed to be raising it up**." Notice the passive voice, "**were reminded**," which scholars have called "the divine passive": where the Actor (God) is not expressed, but is assumed. The Spirit had brought this saying to their minds – and notice the imperfect tense (repeated action) of the verb *legō*, "**He had been repeatedly saying**." That His resurrection was to be on the third day was not a one-time announcement. With this recollection, "**they believed by the Scripture and put trust in the Logos**." Recall Lu. 24:27 where the resurrected Jesus used the OT Scriptures in His explanation to the two disciples about how those Scriptures spoke about Him. Dan Kaplan remarks, "This is why we examine the Tabernacle in the Torah: to see Him, and thus also, ourselves, so as to understand how all the details and parts of its structure relates to His body, and how its furniture applies to us." Recall Rev. 1:20, and how the "**lampstands**" in that first vision represented the called-out communities.

23. **Now as He was continuing being within Jerusalem during the Passover** [note: the feast of unleavened bread followed for seven days right after the Passover], **in the midst of the festival** (celebration; Feast) **many believed, gave their allegiance, and put their trust into His Name, constantly gazing upon and critically contemplating His SIGNS** (or: the authenticating tokens and distinguishing signals originating in Him), **which He was continuing to perform** (or: had been one-after-another progressively doing).

Jesus was busy, publicly, during this celebration of the Passover. Our author does not give any details about what these signs were. When we compare this narrative to those of Jesus' "triumphal entry" visit to Jerusalem as recorded in the Synoptic Gospels, while here it speaks of the "**SIGNS which He was continuing to perform**," in those other Gospels we do not find this to be the case – but rather, there we find mostly teachings through many parables, and (in Mat. 23) denunciation of the Pharisees. We conclude that what is reported here is not His final Passover visit, but an earlier one.

Observe the rendering of the verb "**believed**," as also meaning "**gave their allegiance**." This latter would suppose more than a "mental decision about Him." It implies a commitment to Him – either as a Teacher from God, or as the awaited Messiah. The meaning "**put their trust into His Name**" (Name signifying Him and His mission/position) signifies that a relationship has been established – they trusted what He said and who He was.

As observed in the bracketed note inserted into the text, this was not just a one or two-day Festival. He "**was continuing being within Jerusalem**," which suggests that He may have been there for the full seven days. In contrast, on His last Passover celebration, He was soon arrested and killed. On that one, His triumphal caused the Judean leadership to challenge Him, so the Synoptic Gospels focus on dialogues, during that final visit. If we are correct in these conclusions, then Jesus drove out the animals and disrupted their business (vss. 15-16, above) more than once.

24. **Yet Jesus, Himself, was not habitually entrusting Himself to them** (or: had not been adhering Himself to them, or committing Himself for them; or: kept on refusing to trust Himself to them), **because of the [situation for] Him to be continuously** (habitually; progressively) **knowing all people by intimate experience and through insight,**

Especially since this may have been early in His ministry, He was not openly proclaiming Himself or telling people the role that He would play in their society: He "**was not habitually entrusting Himself to them.**" Recall the times in the Synoptics, where after healing someone, He told those that were healed not to tell anyone about it. As He had told His mother (2:2), His "**hour is not yet** (or: is still not) **arriving.**"

There are three other options for rendering the first clause:
a) He had not been adhering Himself to them – He was not joining any party or Jewish faction;
b) He was not committing Himself for them – He would not be their king, as they might want it;
c) He kept on refusing to trust Himself to them – He was not sharing His mission with them.
All this was because He knew them, in fact, because of being the Anointed One, He was "**continuously** (habitually; progressively) **knowing all people by intimate experience and through insight**." Recall what He said to Nathaniel, in 1:48, above.

25. **and because He was not having** (had not been continually holding) **a need requiring that anyone should bear witness** (or: give testimony or evidence) **about mankind** (or: humanity; the [corporate] Man), **for He Himself was constantly** (had been habitually) **knowing by intimate experience what was continuing to be within mankind** (the human; the [corporate] Man).

This verse repeats and expands what the author just said in the last line of vs. 24. When information is repeated it means that it is important. He needed no "intel" team to give Him the lay of the land or the composition of His audiences. He was Anointed with the Spirit – the heavens (atmospheres) were opened to Him and He saw the hearts of people and, "**was constantly** (had been habitually) **knowing by intimate experience what was continuing to be within mankind** (the human; the [corporate] Man)."

Chapter 3

1. **Now there was a man from out of the Pharisees, Nicodemus by name, a ruler** (leader; chief; head man) **of the Judeans** (those of the Jewish culture, political organization and religion, in Judea).
2. **This one comes** (or: goes; came; went) **to Him by night, and says** (or: said) **to Him, "Rabbi, we have seen and thus know that You are a Teacher having come, and are here, from God, for no one is able** (or: continues having power) **to constantly be doing** (making; producing) **these signs** (or: habitually performing these authenticating tokens and attesting signals), **which You are constantly doing** (performing; producing), **unless God would continue being with him** (or: if God should not continue being existentially with him).**"

Aside from the literal understanding that Nicodemus came to Jesus "**by night**" (presuming that his reason was that he did not want to be seen coming to speak with Jesus), does the fact that John mentioned this have figurative significance? Is our author suggesting that Nicodemus' environment was a part of "**the darkness [that] does not grasp or receive [the Logos], on the same level**" (1:5b, above)? Is the scene that he is describing in this passage setting forth Jesus, as the Logos made Flesh, being a manifestation of "**the Light [that] is constantly shining in the dim and shadowed places, and keeps on progressively giving light within the gloomy darkness where there is no light**" (1:5a, above)? Keep in mind that he instructs us about Jesus' "signs," and figurative symbols (as we find within this Gospel). Nic represented the Judean leadership during Jesus' ministry, and many of that group were

"the humans [who] loved the darkness rather than the Light" (3:19b, below). Nic seems to be an exception; he has come seeking Light. The Seed is planted within the darkness of the earth/soil/humanity, so that it would sprout and grow back up, taking the plant to a higher place.

3. **Jesus considered, and replies to him, saying, "Certainly it is so, I am saying** (= I now point out) **to you, unless anyone may** (or: someone would) **be born back up again to a higher place** (or: can be brought to birth again; or: would be given birth from above), **he continues having no power** (or: remains unable) **to see or perceive God's reign, sovereign influence, activity, or kingdom."**

Could this be why the author has given no birth or infancy narrative about Jesus? All of that and His life up to the point of beginning His ministry is compacted into 1:14a, above, "And the Logos was incarnated and lived among us…"

It is interesting that Nicodemus does not say why he has come to see Jesus. He merely acknowledges, by referencing the "signs" that Jesus had been performing, that He is a Teacher that has come from God (meaning that God had sent Him to the People of Israel), and because folks had seen what Jesus was constantly doing, they had concluded that God must continue being with Him. So Nicodemus greets Jesus with an affirmation and a recognition of Him as being a rabbi. We will see, in vs. 10, below, that Jesus knew who he was, and that he has a position among the leadership in Jerusalem. So Jesus just skips the formalities and, here in vs. 3, begins speaking with him.

Thus, Jesus ignores what Nicodemus had said, and begins with a teaching about being "**born back up again to a higher place**" in order to be able to "**see or perceive God's reign, sovereign influence, activity, or kingdom.**" We will read in the next verse that Nicodemus has no idea of what Jesus is talking about. In vss. 5-8, Jesus will more fully develop this impromptu teaching, but in vs. 9 we will see that Nic does not understand how these things can occur, and then, in vs. 10, Jesus chides him for not knowing or being familiar with these things – since Nic is "**the teacher of Israel.**" Having set this background of Nic's position among the Judeans, along with Jesus' expectations for Nic to be able to comprehend spiritual issues, John proceeds recording the rest of the teaching which Jesus shares with Nic, from vs. 11 through vs. 21. With this synopsis of the passage at hand, we will now consider Jesus' teaching, verse by verse.

Nic's reference to "signs" points back to what was said about signs, in ch. 2. Jesus' reference to being "**born,**" in a way that is different from a natural birth, echoes Jn. 1:12-13 where the topic was brought up, but not developed. We suggest that when Jesus speaks of being "**born back up again to a higher place** (or: can be brought to birth again; or: would be given birth from above)," he is speaking about what John had said in 1:13, born "**from out of the midst of God.**" God is the "higher place," or, the "above" place, to which Jesus here refers. I have given three renderings of one term, *anōthen*, following what the lexicons offer. My first, most literal, rendering conflates the semantic range of the particle, *an-*, which means "back; again; or, up." It seemed best to offer all three of these concepts, since Jesus is speaking of "**spiritual things**" (vss. 5, 6 and 8), or as He says in vs. 12, "**the things** (or: situations; ones) **upon the heavens.**" We suggest that Jesus was speaking of an existential reality, but he was using a metaphor of natural birth to give Nic, and us, an analogy of "spiritual," or, "heavenly," birth.

Notice the reason for this special birth: to be able to "**see or perceive God's reign, sovereign influence and activity** (or: kingdom)." Please note that He did not say, "so that you can go to heaven." This being able to see and perceive God's realm and activities continues to be the purpose for Jesus' teachings which follow, on through vs. 21. In 5b, below, He expands what He means about "seeing and perceiving" as speaking of being able "**to enter into God's realm** (or: reign; kingdom; sovereign activity and influence)." And all of this is tied to being "**born back up again to a higher place.**" One must experience this "again" birth, this being born from out of the midst of God, in order to see, perceive and enter into God's sovereign activities – right here on earth, in this life. Jesus elsewhere taught folks the

God's kingdom was close by, at hand, close enough to touch, and was accessible. If we can see God's sovereign activities, it means that we have entered His kingdom – in the sense in which He presented it to them. One must be "born" into this Realm.

4. **Nicodemus says to Him, "How does a man continue being able to be born, being an old man? He is not able** (or: remains powerless) **to enter into his mother's womb** (cavity; belly) **a second [time] and be born!"**

Nic misses the metaphor, and (like so many, today) interprets Jesus' words literally. Paul uses this same metaphor in Gal. 4:19,

"**O my little children** (born ones), **with whom I am progressing, again, in childbirth labor** (travail; labor pains) **until Christ may be suddenly formed within you folks** (or: = until the Anointing would at some point come full term and be birthed, centered and in union with you)!"

Having Christ formed within us is what Jesus was talking about. It equates to being born from above. It means that – in the realm of Spirit – God is our Father/Mother. God is "**the Father of the spirits**" (Heb. 12:9).

What Paul goes on to allegorize, in Gal. 4, sheds light on "being born from above," and just who is the mother that gives us birth:

22. **For it has been, and stands, written that, Abraham had two sons: one forth from out of the servant girl** (the maid; the female slave), **and one from out of the freewoman.**
23. **But, on the one hand, the one from out of the servant girl** (the maid) **had been born** (generated and birthed) **down from** (in accord with; on the level of; in the sphere of) **flesh** (= by human means); **on the other hand, the one from out of the freewoman [was] through Promise** (or: a promise)
24. **– which things are habitually being allegorized** (or: are normally being expressed in an allegory; are commonly spoken of as something other [than what the language means]) **– for these women are** (= represent) **two settled arrangements** (covenants; contracts; wills)**: one, on the one hand, from Mount Sinai, habitually** (repeatedly; continuously) **giving birth into slavery** (or: bondage) **– which is Hagar.** [cf Ex. 19:17 (LXX)]
25. **Now this Hagar is** (= represents) **Mount Sinai, within Arabia, and she continuously stands in the same line** (or: keeps step in the same rank; marches in a column; walks or stands in a parallel row; or: is habitually rudimentary together; or: = corresponds to) **with the present Jerusalem, for she continues in slavery** (or: functioning in bondage) **with her children.**
26. **Yet, on the other hand, the Jerusalem above is** (continues being) **free, who is** (or: which particular one continues being) **our mother.**…
28. **Now we [other MSS: you folks], brothers** (= fellow believers; = my family), **down from** (or: corresponding to; in the sphere and manner of) **Isaac, are** (continuously exist being) **children of Promise** (or: ones-born from [the] Promise).
29. **But nevertheless, just as then, the one being born down from** (in accordance with; corresponding to; on the level of; in the sphere of) **flesh** (= human efforts) **was constantly pursuing and persecuting the one down from** (in accordance with; corresponding to; in the sphere of) **spirit** (or: Breath-effect), **so also now.**
30. **Still, what does the Scripture yet say?**
"**Cast out** (or: At once expel) **the servant girl** (the slave-girl; the maid) **and her son, for by no means will the son of the servant girl** (the slave-girl; the maid) **be an heir** (take possession of and enjoy the distributed allotment) **with the son of the freewoman.**" [Gen. 21:10]
31. **Wherefore, brothers** (= fellow believers; family), **we are not** (we do not exist being) **children of a slave-girl** (a servant girl; a maid), **but, to the contrary, of the freewoman.**

We submit that what Paul shared with the folks in Galatia, above, is the same thing to which Jesus is referring, here in Jn. 3. Being **born back up again to a higher place** makes one a "child **of Promise**"

(Gal. 4:23, 28, above), a person "born from out of God" (Jn. 1:13b), and a participant of the second of the **two covenants** (Gal. 4:24), who has "**the Jerusalem above**" as a mother (Paul being a citizen of this city, and thus a person giving birth to those in Galatia – Gal. 4:19, above). Such a birth is, "**the one down from** (in accordance with; corresponding to; in the sphere of) **spirit** (or: Breath-effect)" – Gal. 4:29, above. Put another way, with a different metaphor, we have Paul saying:

> "**Now since you folks belong to Christ** (or: have [the] Anointing as your source and origin; or: So since you people have the qualities and character of Christ, and [are] that which is Christ), **you are straightway and consequently Abraham's Seed: heirs** (possessors and enjoyers of the distributed allotment), **down from, corresponding to and in the sphere of Promise!**" (Gal. 3:29).

Notice how Paul brought Israel's story into his explanations about this "new birth" into the "new covenant." In this, we can see where Jesus had expected Nic to understand these things (Jn. 3:10), and showed surprise that he did not.

Union with God produces His Son in us. Intimacy with God brings conception, and then growth, and at some point the birth of Christ within us. And then our journey begins…

5. **Jesus decisively replies, "Certainly that is so. I am now saying** (laying it out; = pointing out) **to you, unless anyone may** (or: someone would) **be born forth from out of water and spirit** (or: – as well as Breath-effect and attitude –) **he continues being unable** (remains having no power) **to enter into God's realm** (or: reign; kingdom; sovereign activity and influence).

6. **"The thing being birthed, having been born forth from out of the flesh, is flesh** (or: from the estranged human nature, continues being the estranged human nature; or: = from out of a flesh system is a flesh system), **and the thing being birthed, having been born forth from out of the Spirit, is spirit** (or: what is birthed out of the Breath-effect continues being Breath-effect; or: what is born from the Attitude is an attitude).

Jesus did not explain what He meant by the term, "**water**," in vs. 5, and many have suggested that He was speaking of the water in the womb of a woman that is associated with a natural birth. This would, indeed, be a "flesh birth" (vs. 6). Others have interpreted this to refer to John the immerser's baptism (immersion), or to the cleansing rituals of the Jewish religion, or even to Israel passing through the Red Sea just prior to their becoming a nation. Recall Paul in 1 Cor. 10:2, speaking figuratively of that historical event: "**they all immersed themselves into Moses** (or: got themselves baptized [other MSS: were baptized] unto Moses), **within the cloud and within the sea.**" So it is possible that Jesus was alluding to Israel's first birth, and their current state of existence: living in the Mosaic covenant. Jesus refers to the Jews in vs. 7, using the plural pronoun, "**you folks.**" He was speaking corporately, about the entire nation. Water can be traced out from Gen. 1, through Israel's history, to John the immerser, to the Living Water that Jesus offers the Samaritan woman in Jn. 4, on through to the River of Life in the new Jerusalem.

In Rom. 6:3-4a, Paul uses the implied metaphor of water as the experience of death:

> "**as many as are immersed** (or: were at one point soaked or baptized) **into Christ Jesus are immersed** (or: were then baptized) **into His death? We, then** (or: consequently), **were buried together** (entombed together with funeral rites) **in Him** (or: by Him; with Him), **through the immersion** (baptism) **into the death**…"

So being "**born forth from out of water**" may refer to the first, or old, creation coming into being. And this could be speaking of the Gen. 1 account, or the Red Sea and Sinai account. On whatever layer we read Jesus' words about water, in vs. 5, He was setting it in contrast to "**having been born forth from out of the Spirit**," in vs. 6. You see, the term "**spirit**" is a symbol for "**the above place**" – where we encounter the "Breath-effect." It is the new arrangement (or, covenant) and the realm of the new creation – what Matthew frequently termed "the kingdom of the HEAVENS (atmospheres)." It is the realm in which

God's sons (the mature children from God) are continuously led by God's Breath-effect (Rom. 8:14) and where:

> "**you received a spirit of being placed as a son** (or: a Breath-effect which set you in the position of a son), **within which** (or: in union with Whom) **we are habitually crying out, "Abba, O Father!" The same Spirit** (or: spirit; or: The Breath-effect Himself) **is constantly witnessing together with our spirit that we are, and continuously exist being, God's children** (ones born of God). **Now since children** (or: Yet if ones born by natural descent), **also heirs** (possessors and enjoyers of an allotted inheritance; those who hold sway over the allotted portion): **on the one hand, God's heirs, on the other, Christ's joint-heirs**.... **because** (or: that) **even the creation** [note: can = Israel and the Law] **itself will continue being progressively set free** (will be habitually liberated and constantly made free) **from the slavery of, and from, decay – even the bondage of deterioration which leads to fraying and ruin – [and released] into the freedom of the glory and splendor of God's children**.... **we ourselves – constantly holding** (or: having; possessing) **the firstfruit of, and which is, the Spirit** (or: the Firstfruit from the Breath-effect; or: the first offering, or first portion, which is spirit and breath, and is from the Attitude) **– we ourselves also continually sigh and groan within** (in the center of) **ourselves, continuously accepting and with our hands taking away from out of** (or: fully receiving) **a placing in the condition of a son** (or: [the] deposit of the Son; a setting in place which is the Son; a constituting as a son; a placing in the Son): **the process of the release of our body from slavery**" (Rom. 8:15b-23).

Paul simply expanded Jesus' words that we read in vss. 5-6, above.

"**To enter into God's realm**" (vs. 5b) comes via "**having been born forth from out of the Spirit**," and the realm (and new existence) into which we are born, "**is spirit**" (vs. 6b). Therefore, in Gal. 5:25 Paul informs us:

> "**Since we continue living in and by spirit** (or: for [the] Spirit; to Breath-effect; or: with Attitude), **we also can habitually advance orderly in line in regard to, or amidst, elementary principles** (or: [observing] rudimentary elements), **in and by spirit** (or: for [the] Spirit; by Breath-effect; with Attitude; or: = walk in rank following [the footsteps] behind the Spirit)."

In contrast to this spirit existence, 6a instructs us that "**The thing being birthed, having been born forth from out of the flesh, is flesh.**" The old covenant was a "flesh system" that was centered around animal sacrifices or literal grain offerings. What was born from that flesh covenant was flesh. This is one reason why the Logos became flesh – in order to fulfill the Law of the flesh covenant (that was symbolized by a circumcision of "the flesh." The priests of the Mosaic covenant ate the flesh of those sacrifices. This may be why (still being in the age of the old covenant) Jesus told folks,

> "**The person habitually eating** (constantly chewing [on]) **My flesh and repeatedly drinking My blood is continuously remaining** (abiding; dwelling) **within, and in union with, Me – and I Myself within, and in union with, him**" (6:56, below).

In 15:1ff, below, He used the metaphor of a Vine, into which His disciples were to be "**remaining** (abiding; dwelling) **within, and in union with, [Him]**."

However, metaphors aside, Paul informs us that we no longer know Christ after (or: according to; on the level of) the flesh (2 Cor. 5:16). You see:

> "**[there is] a new creation** (or: [it is] a framing and founding of an essentially different kind; [he or she is] an act of creation having a fresh character, a new quality): **the original things** (the beginning [situations]; the archaic and primitive [arrangements]) **passed by** (or: went to the side). **Consider! New, essentially different things have come into existence**" (2 Cor. 5:17).

Is it not wonderful, how Paul builds upon, and expands upon, the Gospels?

7. **"You should not be amazed** (or: begin to marvel; at some point be filled with wonder; suddenly be astonished; or: Don't be surprised) **that I said to you, 'It is necessary and binding for you folks to be born back up again to a higher place** (or: for you people to be given birth from above).'

A teacher of Israel should not have been amazed about what Jesus was teaching Nic. The higher place (Paul referred to this as a high, or upward, call – Phil. 3:14) was Israel's destiny, and therefore it was "**necessary and binding**" for them to be born back up to that place from which Adam had been evicted. They needed to get back to the Garden (which was typified by the Tabernacle/Temple) which became a City (Rev. 21 and 22), which now is a People (Rev. 21:9b) that follows the Path (Way) set forth by Jesus, and thus is "**the set-apart** (or: holy; sacred) **city, Jerusalem, progressively** (or: habitually; or: presently) **descending out of the atmosphere** (or: heaven), **from God**" (Rev. 21:10b). They descend in order to be the Light of the world (Rev. 21:24), and to heal the ethnic multitudes (Rev. 22:2). We see this City also described in Heb. 12:22-24. There it is described as being in, and on, an above place.

8. **"The Spirit** (or: Breath-effect, or, exhaled Breath; Attitude) **habitually breathes or blows where It** (or: He) **is presently intending** (willing; purposing), **and you continually hear Its** (or: His) **voice, but yet you have not seen, and thus do not know, from what source It continuously comes, and where It progressively goes and habitually brings [things and folks] under [Its] control.**
> (or: The wind constantly blows where it presently sets its will, and you constantly hear its sound, but yet you have not seen and do not know from where it is coming, nor where it is going; or: = The wind continuously blows and the Spirit normally breathes {respires} – in the place that each has purpose. And so you are often hearing the sound that either makes, although you have not perceived from what place it is presently coming, as well as to what place it is presently leading, under [its influence or control].)

Thus is everyone (or: does everyone constantly exist being) – **the person** (or: the [corporate] Person [= the Second Humanity]) **being birthed, having been born forth from out of the midst of the Spirit**
> (or: In this manner exists all mankind, which is in the state of being born from the Breath-effect)."

This verse is an expansion upon what Jesus said about the Judeans ("you folks," in vs. 7b, implying all of the "lost sheep" of the house of Israel to whom Jesus had been sent – Mat. 10:6; 15:24) being "**born back up again to a higher place**." This is the "place" where "**The Spirit** (or: Breath-effect, or, exhaled Breath; Wind) **habitually breathes or blows**" – the atmosphere, and the sky (figuratively called "heaven;" and referring to the realm of the activities of God). The atmosphere, and lower sky, is where the winds blow. Of course in our day, we read of solar winds in "space." But Jesus was speaking of both the winds that blow upon the earth/land, and the Spirit/Breath-effect of God that breathes wherever It intends, and goes in accord with Its purpose.

The parenthetical expansion gives Jesus' analogy to nature, rendering *pneuma* as "wind." As with all of nature, we can gain spiritual insights from contemplating God's creation. But Jesus had been teaching Nic about a spiritual birth, and having this insight, it is best to read this Greek word as "Spirit," or, "Breath-effect."

Notice that vs. 8b begins with "**Thus is**…" Therefore, He is saying that "**the person** (or: the [corporate] Person [= the Second Humanity]) **being birthed, having been born forth from out of the midst of the Spirit**" actually "**habitually breathes or blows where It** (or: He) **is presently intending** (willing; purposing)…" This is what Paul was speaking of, in Rom. 8:14, when he described God's sons (i.e., those having been born from out of the Spirit) as being those who are "led by the Spirit." But we can also read of our own freedom (Gal. 5:1) in this, because we, too, can also "breathe" (or, live) where the Spirit of Life, within us, blows us over the land. The Spirit's freedom is now our freedom, because we are now "one Spirit" (1 Cor. 6:17). But this freedom is to be sons who do only the things we see our Father doing. This verse is a great expansion of 1:13b, above.

The Spirit (and we who are born of this Spirit) "**progressively goes and habitually brings [things and folks] under [Its] control**." Does this remind you of Gen. 1:26?

9. **Nicodemus considered in reply, and says to Him, "How is it possible for these things to occur** (or: How can these things come to be; How is it repeatedly able [for] these to come to birth)**?"**

Nic is still one of the blind who had been leading the blind (Mat. 15:14; Lu. 6:39). But His eyes are being healed, and he will begin to see (as can be observed in 7:50 and 19:39, below).

10. **Jesus decisively responded and says to him, "You yourself are the teacher of Israel, and yet you continue not knowing and being intimately familiar with these things!**

Recall 3:1, above, where John describes Nic as "**a ruler** (leader; chief; head man) **of the Judeans** (those of the Jewish culture, political organization and religion, in Judea)." A person in this position should have had spiritual insight, and also be familiar with metaphorical teaching.

11. **"Certainly it is so, I am now saying to you, that which we have seen and thus know** (or: perceive), **we are constantly speaking** (or: telling; chattering [about]), **and what we have caught sight of and seen we repeatedly bear witness of** (constantly give testimony to), **and you folks continue not receiving** (or: none of you are laying hold of) **our witness** (or: testimony; evidence).

Notice the plural pronoun that Jesus uses: "**we**." That means that their witness is true. Was Jesus referring to John the immerser, and to Himself? Or was He referring to Himself and the Father (Jn. 5:31-36). Remember, the heavens were opened back up again (Mat. 3:16; Lu. 3:21). They were open to the immerser, too (Jn. 1:33). Those proclaiming the kingdom had actually seen it being manifested. They spoke about that of which they had "**caught sight of and seen**." We read another witness of this in 1 Jn. 1:1,

> "**The One who was continuously existing from a beginning** (or: He Who was progressively being parted away from [the] Source, Headship and Rule). **The One whom we have listened to, and still hear; the One whom we have discerningly seen, and now yet perceive with our eyes** (or: in our eyes); **the One whom we contemplatively gazed upon as a public spectacle** (as an exhibit in a theater) **and our hands handled in investigation** (felt about for and touched) **– groping around the Word of the Life** [cf Lu. 24:39]
> > (or: the Logos, which is the Life; the thought which pertains to life; the Information and Idea from the Life; the message with the character and qualities of the Life; the Reason which belongs to the Life)."

But the Judean leadership did not receive the witness of John or Jesus, nor of the Father (through the works that Jesus was doing).

12. **"Since I tell** (or: If I told) **you folks the earthly things** (or: ones; situations), **and you folks are not continuing in belief** (do not presently believe; are not proceeding to trust), **how will you continue to believe or trust if I should speak to you the things** (or: situations; ones) **upon the heavens**
> (or: the super-heavenly occurrences; the fully-atmospheric things [taking place]; the things or folks being in a position of control upon the atmospheres)**?**

What Jesus had just told Nic was about the Spirit (Breath-effect), and about being born from out of the Spirit (vs. 8, above). These were things that were both present on earth (from Gen. 1:2, on through the Scriptures) and which happened to people, here on earth (Jn. 1:13). Thus, these are "**the earthly things** (or: ones; situations)." Notice that in His speaking to Nic, He uses the plural pronoun, "**you folks**." In vs. 2, above, Nic had spoken on behalf of his fellow Judeans, and Judaism, in general, where he had used the personal pronoun, "**we**," when he had addressed Jesus.

But now Jesus makes reference to another layer of teachings, which neither Nic nor the Judean leadership were at that point prepared to believe: "**the things** (or: situations; ones) **upon the heavens** (or: the super-heavenly occurrences; the fully-atmospheric things [taking place]; the things or folks being in a position of control upon the atmospheres)." Jesus uses the word for "heaven" that has the prefix, "**upon**," added. The things that pertain to our atmospheres are ruled by "**the things**" that are "**upon**" our atmosphere – the realm of God's Spirit and His reign. The word could also be rendered "the super-heavenly occurrences," or, "the full-atmospheric situations," or, Jesus may have been referring to "the things or folks being in a position of control upon the atmospheres."

In 16:12-13, below, Jesus even told His disciples that:

> "**I still have** (or: hold) **many things to be progressively telling** (laying out for; informing) **you folks, but yet, you continue not yet being able** (or: having no power) **to habitually or progressively pick it up and carry** (or: bear) **it right now** (at present). **Yet, whenever that One – the Spirit of the Truth** (or: the Breath-effect from Reality; the attitude which is genuineness) **– would come** (or: Nonetheless, at the time when that spirit which is truth and reality should come), **It** (or: He) **will constantly be a Guide and will progressively lead you on the Path** (or: it will continue leading the way for you) **directed toward and proceeding on into all Truth and Reality…**"

These were revelations and disclosures that were given to Paul and other NT writers (e.g., Heb. 12:22-24) after Jesus' resurrection and His sending the Breath-effect into them at Pentecost (Acts 2:1ff).

From here through vs. 21, Nicodemus fades from view and Jesus continues on a monologue, continuing His teaching in this passage.

13. "**Furthermore, no one has ascended** (or: stepped up) **into the heaven** (or: atmosphere) **except the One descending** (or: stepping down) **from out of the midst of the atmosphere** (or: heaven): **the Son of Mankind** (the Son of the human [= Adam]; Humanity's Son; the Son of man) **– Who is continuously being** (or: constantly existing) **within the midst of the heaven** (or: atmosphere).
> [with p66 & p75, Aleph, B and others: And yet not even one person climbed up into heaven (or: the sky), if not that person at one point descending from out of the midst of heaven (or: the sky) – the Human Being.]

The ascent (stepping up) into the heaven (the atmosphere of the kingdom) comes with the Anointing of the Breath-effect (Spirit). When Jesus said this to Nic, at that point He was the only one who was "**continuously being** (or: constantly existing) **within the midst of the heaven** (or: atmosphere)," but His followers would enter God's realm at Pentecost, and thereafter. Keep in mind that, in the natural realm of this earth, the atmosphere (or, the sky; heaven) comes all the way down to the ground. We breathe in this atmosphere – and in the spiritual realm, we actually breathe in the Breath-effect of God. We are right now "Jerusalem upon the heavens" (Heb. 12:22) and we "walk in the Spirit," being continuously immersed in the Spirit (Acts 1:5). We are those of whom Jesus spoke in 1:51, above – ascending and descending upon Him and His cross. He led the Way (14:6, below), and He speaks of this in the next verse…

14. "**And so, just as** (or: correspondingly as) **Moses lifted up** (elevated; raised up high) **the serpent, within the wilderness** (desert; desolate place) [Num. 21:7ff], **thus it is necessary and binding for the Son of Mankind** (Humanity's Son; the Human Being) **to be lifted up** (elevated; raised up high; exalted),
15. "**with the result and end that all – this progressively believing and successively** (one-after-another) **trusting humanity – in union with Him** (or: in order that all humanity, who being constantly loyal, centered in and within the midst of Him), **would continuously have eonian Life** (life having the state of being, qualities and characteristics of the sphere pertaining to the Age [of the Messiah]; age-quality and eon-lasting life; Life in this lifetime and for a lifetime, or for an indefinite period of time)!

[with other MSS: so that all, while continuously trusting into Him {others: on Him}, may not lose or destroy themselves, but rather may continuously hold age-abiding life (eonian life; life that continues on through the ages).]

The cross was, and is, "the stairway to heaven" for all of humanity. We ascend upon Him (1:51, above), and then we descend bearing our own cross (Mat. 16:24) as we "lay down our souls and lives for our friends" (15:13, below) and follow His Path. Those who were bitten by the fiery serpents (Num. 21) needed only to look at the serpent on the pole – even if there was still rebellion in their hearts – and they were healed. But the result of Jesus being lifted up on the cross has a greater and deeper effect, as Paul instructs us in Phil. 2:9-11,

> "**For this reason, God also lifts Him up above** (or: highly exalted Him; elevates Him over) **and by grace gives to Him the Name – the one over and above every name! – to the end that within The Name: Jesus!** (or: in union with the name of Jesus) **every knee** (= person) **– of the folks upon the heaven** (of those belonging to an imposed heaven, or [situated] upon the atmosphere) **and of the people existing upon the earth and of the folks dwelling down under the ground** (or: on the level of or pertaining to subterranean ones; [comment: note the ancient science of the day – a three-tiered universe]) **– may bend** (or: would bow) **in prayer, submission and allegiance, and then every tongue** (= person) **may speak out the same thing** (or: would openly, and joyfully agree; can confess, avow and with praise acclaim) **that Jesus Christ [is] Lord** (Master; Owner) **– [leading] into [the] glory of Father God** (or: unto Father God's good reputation; into the midst of a praise-inducing manifestation and assumed appearance which is God: a Father)!"

So it was God who lifted up Jesus upon the pole. The Judeans and the Romans were just the instruments that He used (Acts 2:23). But it was also the case that:

> "**God was existing within Christ** (God was and continued being centered in, and in union with [the] Anointed One) **progressively and completely transforming [the] aggregate of humanity** (or: world) **to be other [than it is] in Himself, to Himself, for Himself, by Himself and with Himself, not accounting to them** (not putting to their account; not logically considering for them; not reasoning in them) **the results and effects of their falls to the side** (their trespasses and offenses)" (2 Cor. 5:19).

The cross and the resurrection were parts one and two of His being "**lifted up**," i.e., "ascending." But look at **the result**, in vs. 15:

> "**that ALL – this progressively believing and successively** (one-after-another) **trusting humanity – in union with Him** (or: in order that all humanity, who being constantly loyal, centered in and within the midst of Him), **would continuously have eonian Life** (life having the state of being, qualities and characteristics of the sphere pertaining to the Age [of the Messiah] (etc.)."

In regard to the bracketed alternative MS traditions, note that just as "losing or destroying themselves" were existential situations in this life (like the lost sheep that Jesus came to find), so also the "continuously hold age-abiding life" pertains first of all to this same life, here and now – but is not limited to the here and now: in 11:25b, below, Jesus told Martha,

> "**The one progressively believing and habitually putting trust into Me, even if he may die-off** (or: die-away), **will continue Living** (or: will proceed being alive)!"

16. **"For thus God loves** (or: You see God, in this manner, fully gives Himself to and urges toward reunion with) **the aggregate of humanity** (universe; ordered arrangement; organized System [of life and society]; the world), **so that He gives His** [other MSS: the] **only-born** (or: only-kin; unique-class) **Son,**
> (or, reading ōste as an adverb: You see, in this manner God loves the sum total of created beings as being the Son: He gives the solitary-race One; or: reading ōs te: For you see, [it is] in this way [that] God loves the aggregate of humanity – even as it were His Son: He gives the

by-itself-in-kind-One), **to the end that all humanity, which** (or: everyone, who) – **when progressively trusting and successively believing into Him and thus being constantly faithful to Him – would not lose or destroy itself, or cause itself to fall into ruin, but rather can continuously have** (or: would habitually possess and hold) **eonian life** (age-durative life with qualities derived from the Age [of the Messiah]; living existence of and for the ages).

[note 1): I have here given the "fact" sense of the *aorist* tense of the verbs "love" and "give" rather than the simple past tense. The statement by Jesus is a "timeless" fact of God; it signifies that the object of His love and His gift (that object being the cosmos, the universe, the world of men and created beings) is in view as a whole, and both the love and the gift are presented as fact, as one complete whole (punctiliar) which exists apart from any sense of time (i.e., coming from the realm or sphere of the "eternal," or, "the Being of God;"

note 2): Paul Tillich defines "love" (*agapē*): the whole being's drive and movement toward reunion with another, to overcome existential separation; an ecstatic manifestation of the Spiritual Presence; acceptance of the object of love without restriction, in spite of the estranged, profanized and demonized state of the object; – *Systematic Theology III*, pp 134-138; Richard Rohr: Love; a drive to give yourself totally to something or someone] *Cf* Rom. 8:3

The primary clause of vs. 16a is an astounding proclamation by Jesus: "**God loves the aggregate of humanity** (the world; etc.)." This is the primary theme from Gen. to Rev. This is the foundation for all theology. God loves us, because, "**God continuously exists being Love** (or: for God is Love and Acceptance)" (1 Jn. 4:8b). But not only this, 1 Jn. 4 also informs us:

7. **Beloved ones, we are** (or: can and should be) **continuously loving one another, because love** (or: the urge toward reunion and acceptance) **exists continuously** (or: is) **from out of the midst of God**....

9. **Within this, God's Love is instantly manifested** (or: was at one point made visible; is made apparent and clear) **within us** (or: among us), **in that** (or: because) **God has sent** (dispatched) **His uniquely-born** (or: only-begotten) **Son as a Representative** (Envoy; Emissary) **into the ordered System** (world of society, culture, religion and government; or: the cosmos; or: = the aggregate of humanity), **to the end that we would live** (or: can experience life) **through Him.**

10. **Within this exists** (or: is) **the Love, not that we ourselves have loved** [other MSS: not that we ourselves love or accept] **God, but in contrast, that He Himself loves us and sends** (or: urged toward reunion with us and sent) **His Son as a Representative** (Emissary)**: a cleansing, sheltering covering around our sins** (failures to hit the target, errors, mistakes, deviations).

This passage in 1 Jn. supports and expands the subordinate clause of vs. 16a, above: "**so that He gives His** [other MSS: the] **only-born** (or: only-kin; unique-class) **Son.**" Added to this, we have another verse from 1 Jn. 4:14b,

"**the Father has sent forth** (dispatched as a Representative) **the Son – [the] Savior of the world** (or: Deliverer of the ordered and controlling System of religion and secular society; Restorer of the universe; or: = the Rescuer and Healer of all humanity)."

Returning to 16b, above, we have the purpose statement for the giving of His Son to us: "**to the end that all humanity, which** (or: everyone, who) – **when progressively trusting and successively believing into Him and thus being constantly faithful to Him – would not lose or destroy itself, or cause itself to fall into ruin, but rather can continuously have** (or: would habitually possess and hold) **eonian life** (age-durative life with qualities derived from the Age [of the Messiah]; living existence of and for the ages)." Within this purpose statement is an attributive, dependent, participial clause which I have expanded and set off with dashes: "**when progressively trusting and successively believing into Him and thus being constantly faithful to Him.**" Notice the present tense of the participle (indicated by the auxiliary adverbs, to indicate the tense of the verb: progressively; successively; constantly). Also observe the subject of the main clause: the singular, masculine "**all,**" which means "all humanity." Thus, with this reading he is speaking corporately, meaning the whole of mankind. On offer, parenthetically, is another reading of this adjective, as "everyone," thus allowing for a singular reading. John uses this construction

71

to explain the state of being, and the existential circumstance in which, it happens that "**all humanity**" (and every person, successively) "**can continuously have** (or: would habitually possess and hold) **eonian life**." This is the gist of the main clause, and the core statement of God's purpose. It describes people who are already a part of the new creation (2 Cor. 5:17), and are described in Eph. 2:10a,

> "**for the fact is, we are** (continually exist being) **the effect of what He did** (or: His creation; the thing He has constructed; the result of His work; His achievement; His opus; the effect of His Deed)**: people being founded from a state of disorder and wildness** (being framed, built, settled and created; being changed from chaos to order), **within and in union with Christ Jesus**."

This is the purpose and the work of God, through Christ (2 Cor. 5:19). *Cf* vs. 35, below.

1 Jn. 2:2 helps us to understand how all this works:

> "**And He Himself exists continually being a cleansing, sheltering cover around our mistakes and errors, sheltering us from their effects so that we can be in peaceful and rightwised relationships** (or: being the act by which our sins and failures are cleansed and made ineffective, effecting conciliation [to us]), **yet not only around those pertaining to us** (or: having their source in us), **but further, even around the whole ordered System** (secular realm and dominating world of culture, economy, religion and government; or: universe; or: the whole aggregate of mankind)!"

Can we wrap our minds around this? Only the Love which IS God could accomplish this through His gift to the whole aggregate of humanity. Christ is "the cleansing, sheltering cover" that comes upon everyone.

Let us pause and consider the word *agapē*. Returning to the first clause of the verse, the parenthetical alternative gives two other meanings of "love": "You see God, in this manner, **fully gives Himself to** and **urges toward reunion with**... the aggregate of humanity." Wow! Let that sink in. This is our God. He is bent on union with us! On offer, in note 2, are other meanings of this word, which I gleaned from the writings of the theologian, Paul Tillich. Let us point these out, lest our readers read over the notes too quickly:

> a) the whole being's drive and movement toward reunion with another, to overcome existential separation;
> b) acceptance of the object of love without restriction, in spite of the estranged, profanized and demonized state of the object;
> c) participation in the other one
> d) the power of reunion with the other person as one standing on the same ultimate ground;
> e) unambiguous, accepting reunion;
> f) an ecstatic manifestation of the Spiritual Presence.

The definitions in c, d and e are on offer in 1 Cor. 13, where I again give more of Tillich's definitions. Now meditate on each one as expressing a part of Who and What God is. Make each one a verb, and substitute that meaning in the first clause, above: "**For thus God** employs His whole being's drive and movement toward reunion with the aggregate of humanity (etc.)." How deep and expansive, and how far reaching, is God's Love for everyone! We might be tempted to think that this is beyond our comprehension – and, humanly thinking, it is – but we are blessed with Paul's words, which can apply here:

> "**God unveils in us** (reveals to us; uncovers for us; discloses among us) **through the spirit** (or: the Spirit; the Breath-effect); **for you see, the spirit** (or: the Spirit; the Breath-effect) **constantly and progressively searches, examines and investigates all humanity, and everything – even the depths of, from, which pertain to, and which are, God!**" (1 Cor. 2:10).

I also appreciate how Richard Rohr renders *agapē*: a drive to give yourself totally to something or someone.

It is for all these reasons that God does not want the aggregate of humanity (the world) to "**lose or destroy itself, or cause itself to fall into ruin, but rather [to] continuously have** (or: would habitually possess and hold) **eonian life** (age-durative life with qualities derived from the Age [of the Messiah]; living existence of and for the ages)."

17. **"You see, God does not send forth His** [other MSS: the] **Son as a Representative or Emissary into the world** (or: System; aggregate of humanity) **to the end that He should continuously separate and make decisions about the world** (or: would at some point sift and judge the System, or the aggregate of humanity), **but to the contrary, to the end that the world would be delivered**
> (or: for the result that the System could be healed and made whole; so that the ordered arrangement should be restored to health; to the end that the aggregate of mankind may be saved – rescued and re-established in its original state): **through Him!**

The Son's mission is always Deliverance, Healing, Restoration to Wholeness, Health, Rescue and Salvation. And this is for "the aggregate of mankind;" for "the world." This is always the purpose for which He comes to us, and "**Jesus Christ [is] the same yesterday and today and on into the ages**" (Heb. 13:8).

As the parenthetical expansion offers: Christ's sending-forth is "for the result that the System could be healed and made whole; so that the ordered arrangement should be restored to health" – so that it will no longer be a domination system, but a living body of Life that gives Life; a corporate Tree of Life. The Son, and His Life are the means that bring this about: **through Him!**

18. **"The person habitually believing and progressively placing trust into Him is not being continuously sifted or evaluated** (is not habitually being separated for decisions or being judged), **yet the person not habitually trusting and believing has already been sifted and evaluated** (separated for a decision; judged) **and that decision yet exists, because he or she has not believed so that he trusts into** (or: had not been faithful and loyal unto) **the Name** [note: "name" is a Semitism for the person, or his authority, or his qualities] **of the only-born Son of God** (or: into the Name of God's Son – the only-kin and unique-class One, or the by-itself-in-kind One, or, the solitary-race One).

Why is the one not trusting or believing not being habitually judged (or: separated, through "**being continuously sifted or evaluated**"? Because this one is already serving time in prison; he or she is in the state or condition that resulted from the judgment on Adam (evicted from the Garden environment; restricted from the Tree of Life). John states this plainly, in vs. 36, below:
> "**the person now continuing being unpersuaded by the Son** (or: presently being constantly incompliant, disobedient or disbelieving to the Son; being repeatedly stubborn toward the Son) **will not be catching sight of** (seeing; observing; perceiving) **[this] Life. To the contrary** (or: Yet, nevertheless), **God's personal emotion and inherent fervor**
>> (or: the teeming passion and **swelling desire, which is God**; the mental bent, natural impulse, propensity and disposition **from God**; or: the ire, anger, wrath or indignation **having the quality and character of God**)
> **presently continues remaining** (keeps on resting, dwelling and abiding) **upon him.**"

Existing under the decision by God, for humanity, was the judgment that humanity was destined to experience – called by theologians as being "the human predicament." Paul described this in Rom. 7. So there is no more need for those who are "dead in trespasses and sins (failures)" (Eph. 2:1) to be continuously sifted or evaluated. That was done in the Garden, and "**that decision yet exists**" (this clause reflects the perfect tense of the verb "sifted and evaluated {etc.}").

Now to what does the subordinate clause refer? It says, "**because he or she has not believed so that he trusts into** (or: had not been faithful and loyal unto) **the Name** [note: "name" is a Semitism for the person, or his authority, or his qualities] **of the only-born Son of God**." On the first level of understanding, this would mean that this person has not believed that Jesus was, or is, the Christ, or, that He is Lord. But why did Jesus use this somewhat ambiguous phrase to refer to Himself? In 9:35-37, below, Jesus asked the man who had been born blind (and who Jesus had just healed):

> "**"Are you yourself now trusting or believing or putting faith into the Son of man**
> (or: = the son of Adam; = the Human Being; or: = the eschatological messianic figure [A, L and others read: Son of God])**?"**
> **And in considered response, that one says, "And who is he, sir** (or: my lord; master), **so that I can believe** (or, as a future: to the end that I will believe and progressively put trust) **into him?"**
> **Jesus said to him, "You have both seen Him, and the One presently talking** (speaking) **with you, that One is He."**

So, it is evident that not everyone would know what either "**the Name**" meant, nor, perhaps, to what the phrase, "**the only-born Son of God**," would refer. But we should keep in mind that our text does not say the Nicodemus had left this meeting with Jesus, and it is most reasonable to assume that he is still there, listening to Jesus' monologue. Nicodemus would recognize the import of both phrases. John the immerser would have known what "Son of God" meant (1:34, above). Nathaniel had assumed Jesus to be "the Son of God" because of the apparent "spiritual sight" that Jesus disclosed (1:49, above). Now Nathaniel, in that same verse, equated this title to the title, "the King of Israel," and thus Nathaniel apparently understood these titles as signifying "the Messiah." In 1:51, above, Jesus affirms Nathaniel's conclusion by using the eschatological phrase "the Son of man" (an allusion to Dan. 7:13ff). Jesus will use this term frequently in John's Gospel.

As noted in the inserted brackets in this verse, the term "name" often was used to refer to the person or personage (depending on the context) that was under discussion. It would seem that since Jesus did NOT say "**believed so that he trusts into ME**" (but rather used a third person reference), that He felt, or was teaching, that belief was to be into the "office" or "position" (such as the "Messiah"). They were supposed to put their faith and trust into whoever was God's Anointed One. This would mitigate against people making an idol of a personality (such as we observe in our day and culture); it would keep the focus on God – which Jesus always did. Jesus would not always be with them, as the Adamic man to whom they were now listening. Paul would later instruct us that we no longer know Jesus this way:

> "**if even we have intimately, by experience, known Christ** ([the] Anointed One) **on the level of flesh** (or: = in the sphere of estranged humanity; or: = in correspondence to a self that is oriented to the System; = according to the old covenant), **nevertheless we now** (in the present moment) **no longer continue [thus] knowing [Him or anyone]**" (2 Cor. 5:16b).

So, in this case, perhaps the phrase, "the Name," refers to the title and reputation, and thus to the fact that the kingdom, God's reign, had now come. This comports with His use of the term "Son of man" in chapter 9, cited above. Jesus was not beginning a personality cult, but rather, He was inaugurating the Reign of God. That said, the movement that grew out of His disciples did keep the identity of Jesus, through the repeated use of His Name (see the book of Acts). But in this eschatological context, let us keep in mind that in Rev. 3:12 the risen Jesus addresses the called-out community in Philadelphia, and there He refers to "My NEW Name." This, along with the Name of His God and the Name of the New Jerusalem, are all to be written upon "**the one habitually conquering** (repeatedly overcoming so as to be the victor)." A name could also signify ownership or authority. This latter may have been one of Jesus' main points. But holding in mind Rev. 3:12, "believing into the Name" may signify assuming a new identity, which corresponds to this new birth to which He had referred.

19. "**Now this continues being the** (or: So there continues being the same) **process of the sifting, the separating and the deciding** (the evaluating; the judging), **because the Light has come** (or: that the Light has gone) **into the world** (the aggregate of humanity; the ordered system and arrangement of religion, culture and government; or: the system of control and regulation; or: the cosmos), **and yet the humans love the darkness** (or: the men [= the leadership] love and fully give themselves to the dimness of obscurity and gloom; or: mankind loved and moved toward union with the shadow-realm) **rather than**

the Light, for their works (deeds; actions) **were continuing to be bad ones** (unsound ones; wicked, wrongful ones; laborious ones; unprofitable and disadvantageous ones; malicious ones),

The meaning of the first two clauses is somewhat ambiguous because of the demonstrative adjective, "**this**," which opens the first clause, and because of the conjunction that joins the clauses: this conjunction can be rendered either "**because**," or "**that**." With the first clause, "**this**" can point back to what was just said in vs. 18, or forward, with the second clause defining what "**the process of the sifting, the separating and the deciding** (the evaluating; the judging)" exists being. With "**this**" pointing forward, rendering the conjunction "**because**" means that what follows this conjunction is the "reason" for the sifting, evaluating, etc. Rendering the conjunction "**that**" gives the definition of the sifting and evaluation: "**the Light has come** (or: the Light has gone) **into the world**." The Light is doing the sifting, deciding (what's what, e.g.) and the judging (of the situation, etc.). The demonstrative adjective can also be rendered "the same." Thus the first clause can read, "So there continues being the same..." This would indicate that the first clause is pointing back to vs. 18.

With ambiguous readings, it is always best to give serious consideration to all possible readings. But in all of these options, we have a definite association between the separating (evaluating; judging; deciding) and the Light having come, or gone, into the aggregate of humanity. But even with the advent of the Light, Jesus states that "**the humans love the darkness rather than the Light**." This is an allusion to the Logos, in 1:4-5, above. And we should remember that this Light was, "**the True and Genuine Light which** (or: Who) **is continuously** (repeatedly; progressively) **enlightening** (giving light to) **every person** (or: all humanity) **continuously** (repeatedly; progressively; constantly; one after another) **coming into the world**" (1:9, above). And because His own people loved the darkness that they were in, "**Its own** (or: His own) **people did not grasp, receive or accept It** (or: Him) **or take It** (or: Him) **to their side**" (1:11b, above).

Now the last clause of this verse gives us the reason for these people loving their darkness, rather than the Light: it was because "**their works** (deeds; actions) **were continuing to be bad ones** (unsound ones; wicked, wrongful ones; laborious ones; unprofitable and disadvantageous ones; malicious ones)." Who, specifically, was Jesus referring to? It was not the outcasts, those considered "sinners" by the religious leadership. Those folks loved the Light. When we read of Jesus ministry, and of those who resisted Him (and then ultimately had him killed), we observe that those who loved the darkness were the religious folks of the Judean leadership. What do you think Nic was thinking when Jesus said this?

So what were these "bad works," or, "unsound actions," or, "malicious deeds" – etc.? Perhaps,
> "**O Jerusalem, Jerusalem! The one repeatedly killing the prophets, and habitually stoning the people sent off with a mission to her**..." (Mat. 23:37a).
> "**they are habitually 'saying,' and yet they are not doing or performing**" (Mat. 23:3b).
> "**So they habitually tie up and bind heavy loads** (or: burdensome cargos), **and then constantly place [these] as an addition upon the shoulders of the People** (or: belonging to persons) **– yet they, themselves, are not willing to budge or put them in motion with their finger** (or: = to 'lift a finger' to help carry them)!" (Mat. 23:4).

These are just a sample of Mat. 23. Jesus, the Light, did not draw back from critiquing wrong behavior or unprofitable living. The Light continued shining in the darkness of domination systems. He continues this exposition in the next verse...

20. "**for it follows that everyone who is habitually practicing** (or: performing) **worthless things** (base, mean, common, careless, cheap, slight, paltry, sorry, vile things or refuse) **is continuously hating** (regarding with ill-will; radically detaching from) **the light, and is not coming** (or: going) **to the light** (or: the Light), **so that his or her works** (deeds; actions) **may not be tested and put to the proof** (and thus, exposed and perhaps reproved).

Here Jesus extends His critique of "**habitually practicing** (or: performing) **worthless things**" with words that go beyond the realm of the strictly "religious," into all kinds of behavior or work that could be termed "base, mean, common, careless, cheap, slight, paltry, sorry, vile things or refuse."

Perhaps Jesus' teaching in Mat. 6 may add to our understanding of Jesus' reference to Light in this disclosure to Nicodemus:

> 22. **"The eye is the lamp of the body. If, then, your eye may continue being single-fold** (or: clear, simple and uncompounded; perhaps: single-focused, suggesting being straightforward; may = healthy; may suggest generosity), **your whole body will continue being** (will continuously exist being) **illuminated** (enlightened; or: lustrous; luminous; radiant; shining).
> 23. **"Yet if your eye should continue being in a bad condition** (useless; unsound; gushed with misery and labor; or: wicked; perhaps = diseased or clouded; may suggest stinginess or being grudging), **your whole body will continue being** (will continuously exist being) **dark** (or: in the dark; full of darkness). **If, then, the light [which is] within the midst of you is darkness** (or: continually exists being dimness and lack of Light), **how thick [is] the darkness** (or: how great and extensive [will be] the obscurity and gloom of that area of shadows)!

If the eye is the body's lamp, then the eye would give light to one's environment or shine on the path. It would also illuminate the dark places within the body (both individually, and corporately). The eye also is the place of vision and focus. If the corporate body's vision is in a bad condition, the whole corporate body will be in darkness. This was the case of the Judean leadership, of which Nic was a part.

21. **"Yet the person habitually doing the truth** (constantly constructing the real; repeatedly making the genuine; progressively producing the non-concealed, actual state) **is constantly coming** (or: moving) **toward the light** (or: the Light), **so that his or her works** (deeds; actions) **may be set in clear light and manifested, because they exist being ones having been worked, accomplished or performed within God** (or: that it is in union with God [that they are] ones having been acted out)."

Jesus' message, which began in speaking about being born back up again to a higher place, ends with a strong focus on how we live our lives, here and now. If we are "**habitually doing the truth** (constantly constructing the real; repeatedly making the genuine; progressively producing the non-concealed, actual state)," it is because we have been working, accomplishing and performing "**within God** (or: in union with God)." We are born into the "heavens" of God's Spirit in order to produce reality here on earth. If our works are in union with God, then they will be works of Love.

Our author does not comment on Nicodemus' response to this teaching. It is noteworthy that Jesus did not ask him to become His disciple. It is also noteworthy that Jesus did not say that folks need to be born from above so that they could go to heaven. Those who are thus born back up again are "**constantly coming** (or: moving) **toward the light** (or: the Light)." The Logos progressively brings them closer, to be continuously face-to-face with God.

22. **After these things, Jesus and the disciples went** (or: came) **into the Judean territory** (land; country; region), **and He was wearing away the time there with them. He was also periodically immersing** (or: baptizing).
23. **Now John was continuing repeatedly immersing** (baptizing) **in Enon** (or: Ainon), **near Salim, because much water was** (or: many waters were) **there, and [folks] kept showing up alongside and were being immersed** (baptized),
24. **for not yet was John one having been cast into the guardhouse** (jail; prison).
25. **Then there arose** (came to be) **from out of John's disciples, thereupon, a discussion** (an inquiry; a seeking question) **with a Jew** (or: a Judean) **about cleansing** (ceremonial purification).

Notice that the topic of discussion was ritual cleansing, or, ceremonial purification. Then, in the next verse, John's disciples ask him about the topic of immersion (baptism). This latter shines a light on the purpose of John immersing folks: it was a figure of cleansing; it was for spiritual purification.

26. **So they went to** (or: come toward) **John, and said** (or: say) **to him, "Rabbi, he who was with you across** (on the other side of) **the Jordan [River], to whom you have borne witness** (or: for whom you have testified), **look** (see; consider), **this one is continually immersing** (baptizing), **and everyone is** (or: all are) **constantly coming toward** (or: going to) **him."**
27. **John deliberated in reply and says, "Man continues without ability** (or: Humanity remains unable) **to be receiving anything, unless it may have been existing being having been given to him** (or: it) **from out of the heaven**

> (or: A person is continually powerless to lay hold of and take anything, unless he was possibly being one having been given [ability] from out of the atmosphere and heaven in him).

This presents at least one worldview that was held in the Palestine area, in the 1st century, AD. This concurs with a similar worldview that can be observed in the OT writings. Heaven, i.e., God, rules, and directs the affairs of humanity. Spiritual gifts and abilities originate in God. Paul affirms this, in 1 Cor. 12:11,

> "**Now the One and the same Spirit** (or: Breath-effect; Attitude) **is habitually working within** (energizing, activating and operating) **all these things, constantly dividing, apportioning and distributing in** (to; for) **each person his own [effect of grace], correspondingly as He** (She; It) **progressively intends** (is habitually willing; continuously purposes; keeps on pleasing [to do])."

28. **"You folks, yourselves, repeatedly bear me witness** (or: habitually testify for me) **that I myself said, 'I am not the Christ** (the Anointed One)!' **But rather that, 'I am one having been sent forth as an emissary** (one sent forth with a mission as a representative) **in front of That One.'**

Here John the immerser distinguishes himself, and his ministry, from that of the Christ (Anointed One; = the Messiah), and proclaims himself as a precursor to the Christ.

29. **"The One continually holding** (or: constantly having) **the bride is** (exists being) **a Bridegroom** (or: [the] Bridegroom). **Yet the friend of the Bridegroom – the man having taken a stand, and continuing standing, and continuously listening and hearing from Him in joy – is constantly rejoicing because of the Bridegroom's voice! This joy – the one [that is] mine – has therefore been fulfilled** (or: This, then, my joy, has been made full).

John is simply saying that Jesus is God's main event. John, himself, is the friend of the One who is the main event (using marriage as a metaphor for the coming of Israel's Messiah), and realizing the historical significance of Israel's Bridegroom coming on the scene, he rejoices to hear His voice. Remember that Yahweh and Israel had experienced a metaphorical marriage relationship. That is why His prophets charged Israel with adultery, when in her history she turned to the worship of idols. But in this verse, John is speaking prophetically, for "**the bride**" of Christ had not yet been resurrected to sit with Him, in the heavenly atmospheres (Eph. 2:6). She had not yet, historically, been brought to Mount Zion, the Jerusalem upon the heavens (Heb. 12:22). This would happen following Christ's resurrection, and His sending the Gift to the bride – the set-apart Spirit of God. John refers to Jesus doing this, in Mat. 3:11,

> "**I myself, on the one hand, continue immersing you folks in water, [which proceeds] into the midst of a change in thinking** (a change of perception, attitude, frame of mind, way of thinking, mode of thought, in state of consciousness, as well as a turning back [to Yahweh]). **On the other hand, the One progressively coming close after me is** (exists being) **stronger than I, Whose sandals I am not competent** (or: adequate) **to lift up and carry off. He, Himself, will proceed immersing** (baptizing) **you folks within the midst of a set-apart Breath-effect and**

Fire (or: will repeatedly submerge you to the point of saturation, in union with [the] Holy Spirit, even to the permeation of a Sacred Attitude, as well as with [the] Fire)."

So now there is a new arrangement – a new marriage covenant – and God has incarnated Himself to be the Bridegroom, as, through Jesus, He joins anew with Israel (and then with all nations) as Bridegroom and Lord. In Rev. 21:9, John is shown the Lamb's wife, and in the next verse it turns out to be:

"**the set-apart** (or: holy; sacred) **city, Jerusalem, progressively** (or: habitually; or: presently) **descending out of the atmosphere** (or: heaven), **from God – continuously having** (holding; or: = bringing with it) **the glory of God** (God's glory; God's reputation; or: God's appearance; or: the opinion from God; the manifest presence, which is God), **her illuminator** (that which gives her Light; the cause of her light)" (Rev. 21:10-11).

Paul is another witness to this new reality, when in 2 Cor. 11:2 he informs them:

"**I myself joined you folks in marriage to one Husband** (or: Man), **to make** (place) **a pure virgin** (= unmarried girl) **to stand alongside in and with the Christ** (or: by the Anointed One)."

30. **"It is necessary and binding for That One to be progressively growing and increasing, yet for me to be progressively less** (or: continually made inferior and decrease).

There was a Plan that was coming together, and John the immerser played his role in the unfolding story of humanity. John had his place in the Blueprint (the Logos that arranged God's intent on building humanity as God's new Temple – cf 1 Cor. 3:9-17). But John's role in the story was destined to fade away as the Christ took center stage.

31. **"The One repeatedly coming back again from above** (or: habitually going again to a higher place) **is above upon all people** (or: constantly exists being up over upon all things). **The person continuously being forth from out of the earth [as a source] is** (or: constantly exists being) **from out of the earth, and is habitually speaking forth from out of the earth. The One continuously coming** (or: habitually going; repeatedly coming and progressively going) **forth from out of the midst of the heaven** (or: the atmosphere) **is, and constantly exists being, above upon** (= has authority and dominion over) **all people** (or: up over upon all things).

It is uncertain who the speaker is, from vss. 31-36. The Greek text gives no indication whether John the immerser is still speaking, or whether his words ended with vs. 30, and now the author of this Gospel takes up the narrative. My rendering kept the quotation marks, reading these verses as though the immerser is still speaking – there being no indication that someone else is now speaking. However, the depth of the theological insights expressed here has caused many to see these verses as being from the pen of the Gospel's author. So our job is to just listen to the Spirit, within, to speak from this passage.

The first clause of vs. 31 opens with ambiguity. The present participle can be rendered as either "coming" or "going." Since it is in the present tense, it can refer to repeated action, or be expressed as habitual action. The adverb, *anōthen*, which modifies the participle is the same one that we found in vss. 3 and 7, above, where Jesus was speaking about birth. Putting this subordinate clause together, we have: "**repeatedly coming back again from above** (or: habitually going again to a higher place)." Is this "ladder language" (my wife Lynda's term) that can subtly allude to Jn. 1:51? Perhaps. Now this clause modifies the subject of the main clause: "**The One.**" This One "**is above upon all people** (or: constantly exists being up over upon all things)." This is clearly a functional reference to the Christ. He is the One repeatedly coming and going. We find the risen Christ symbolically referring to Himself in Rev. 1:8,

""**I am continuously** (or: repeatedly) **the Alpha and the Omega,**" says the Lord [= Christ or Yahweh] **God, "the One continuously being, even the One Who was and continued being, and the One presently and continuously** (or: progressively) **coming and going, the Almighty.**"

(or: The Owner is laying out these thoughts: "I Myself exist being the Alpha and the Omega – the continuously existing God, even the One Who continued existing [as] Being, as well as the One habitually being on the go and repeatedly moving about – the All-Strong.")

Everywhere in this Gospel where our author uses the participle of "coming/going" it is in the present tense. Why did he do this? He did not have to use a "present" participle, he could have used an aorist or a future tense – if that was what he meant to say. So did our author understand that this One had come before? Paul speaks apocalyptically in 1 Cor. 10:4, speaking of Israel's wilderness journeys, and instructs us that "**they all drank the same spiritual drink, for they kept on drinking from out of a spiritual bedrock** (or: cliff rock; rock mass) **– one continually following along behind** (or: progressively accompanying [them]). **Now the bedrock** (or: cliff rock) **was the Christ**."

Also, 1 Pet. 1:11 gives us more to think about, speaking of the prophets of earlier times, that they were:
"**constantly searching into which season or what kind of situation the Spirit of Christ** (or: Christ's spirit; or: the Breath-effect which is the Anointed One), **resident within them, was continuing to point to, making [it] evident and clearly visible, repeatedly testifying** (witnessing; giving evidence) **beforehand about the effects of the experiences and results of the sufferings [projected] into Christ**...."
We will not pursue this subject, in this study, but the topic is worth investigating.

In contrast to this One, our author next gives what is opposite: "**The person continuously being forth from out of the earth [as a source] is** (or: constantly exists being) **from out of the earth, and is habitually speaking forth from out of the earth**." The opening participial clause is followed directly by a regular clause that seems redundant, with both clauses even using the identical prepositional phrase, "out of the earth." Now redundancy was a common rhetorical device that was used for emphasis. The verb in the second clause, "**is** (or: constantly exists being)," is the identical verb used in the main clause of the previous statement about that One being "**above upon all people**," so perhaps our author is grammatically strengthening the contrast between the two. Our present "person," by "being forth from out of the earth," has all of his existence coming from the earth realm – and therefore he "**is habitually speaking forth from out of the earth**." Thus, such a person cannot bring forth unveilings of spiritual matters. He lives in the earth realm and minds fleshly things. We see this same contrast in Rom. 8:6,
"**For the result of the thinking** (mind-set; effect of the way of thinking; disposition; result of understanding and inclination; the minding; the opinion; the thought; the outlook) **of the flesh** (= from the human condition or the System of culture and cultus; or: = Torah keeping) **[is; brings] death, yet the result of the thinking** (mind-set; disposition; thought and way of thinking; outlook) **of the spirit** (or: from the Spirit; which is the Breath-effect) **[is; brings] Life and Peace** (joining)."
We can also observe that the one whose existence is from the earth does not go anywhere. He just keeps on speaking from out of the lower sphere.

The last statement virtually repeats the first statement, but substituting the term, "**the heaven** (or: the atmosphere)" for the term "**back again from above**; again to a higher place." The final clause, "**constantly exists being, above upon** (= has authority and dominion over) **all people** (or: up over upon all things)," brackets these statements about the two spheres of living.

32. "**What He has seen and hears** (or: heard), **to this He continuously bears witness** (or: is repeatedly testifying, attesting and giving evidence), **and yet no one is presently grasping** (or: habitually takes in hand; continues receiving) **His witness** (or: testimony; evidence).

This verse builds upon, and refers to, "**The One continuously coming** (and going) **forth from out of the midst of the heaven** (or: the atmosphere)," of the previous verse. He is living in the Garden, and hears the Voice of God; He is living in the Holy of Holies, communing with the Father. Having "eyes to see and ears to hear," this One (i.e., Christ) lives in the open heavens and bears witness to what the Father is doing. But the person living focused on the earth realm "**is presently not grasping His witness** (or: testimony; evidence)." This was true of many who listened to the immerser, and then of many who heard the witness of Christ, and then of many who heard from His body (*cf* Mat. 13:16-17). Each person has their own time, season or age to be given ears to hear.

33. "**The one receiving** (grasping; taking in hand; accepting; getting hold of) **His witness** (testimony; evidence) **certifies – by setting a seal** (= giving attestation) – **that God is true** (real; genuine; truthful),

If we receive, grasp, take in hand, accept or get hold-of "**His witness** (testimony; evidence)," because this receiving, etc., is a work of the Spirit, within us, it certifies, sets a seal and attests the Truth and Reality of God, and the veracity of His Logos to us. And furthermore, hear Paul, in Eph. 1:13,
> "**Within and in union with Whom you folks also, upon hearing the Word of the Truth** (or: the thought and idea of Reality; the message from the Truth; the Logos which is Reality) – **the good news** (the message of goodness, ease and well-being) **of your** [other MSS: of our] **deliverance** (rescue; return to health and wholeness; salvation) – **within and in union with Whom also, upon trusting and believing, you people are stamped** (or: were sealed; marked for acceptance, or with a signet ring; = personally authorized) **by the set-apart Breath-effect of The Promise** (or: with the holy attitude of assurance; in the sacred essence from the promise; or: for the Holy Spirit which is the Promise)." [*cf* 2 Cor. 5:5]

34. "**for He Whom God sends forth with a mission** (dispatches as an Emissary and Representative) **habitually is speaking the gush-effects from God** (the results of the flows of God; God's declarations or sayings), **for God is habitually** (or: continuously) **giving the Spirit** (Breath; or: Attitude) **[and] not from out of a measure** (= not by a measured portion or limit; = without measure and without limitation).

This pronouncement applies first of all to Jesus, but recall Jesus' words to His followers:
> "**Correspondingly** (or: Accordingly; On the same level; In the same sphere; In line with) **as the Father has sent Me forth with a mission and as an Emissary** (Representative), **I Myself also am progressively** (or: repeatedly; or: one after another) **sending** (dispatching) **you folks**" (Jn. 20:21).

The first clause of vs. 34 could begin, "You see, the person whom God sends forth…" And so, we who hear God sending us forth as emissaries or representatives should be "**habitually is speaking the gush-effects from God**." That is a literal rendering, and so is the second one, "the results of the flows of God," which gives us both another form of God's way of communicating, and another picture of how God is acting and working within His reign – both here on earth, and everywhere. We may more easily relate to the third rendering: "God's declarations or sayings." We can speak these things from God, because we are able to "see and hear" Him (vs. 32, above). And we can see and hear because, "**God is habitually** (or: continuously) **giving the Spirit** (Breath; or: Attitude) **[and] not from out of a measure** (= not by a measured portion or limit; = without measure and without limitation)." And THIS is the Good News.

35. "**The Father continuously loves and fully gives Himself to the Son, and He has given all humanity** (or, as a neuter: all things) **[to Him] so that He has it** (or: them) **as a gift within His hand.**

Now, do not rush over this proclamation. The verb form "**has given**" is in the perfect tense, which means that what was given remains as a gift that Christ continues possessing, or, said otherwise, "**He has it** (or: them) **as a gift within His hand.**" Remember that old song, "He's got the whole world in His hands"? Yeah, it's true.

The form of the word "**all**" is either masculine singular (and thus: **all humanity**), or neuter plural (and thus: all things). Both readings are true. "For thus God loves the aggregate of humanity [and] the world" – vs. 16, above. THIS is also the Good News. In the first clause, I conflated *agapē* as "**loves and fully gives**

Himself." And this is also what the Father expresses and conveys to us. THIS, too, is Good News. Perhaps we should call this the "Good News Chapter." And this includes, the next verse...

36. **"The one habitually trusting into** (or: continuously going on confidently believing with loyalty unto) **the Son is now constantly holding and is presently, progressively possessing** (having) **eonian life**
> (life having the characteristics and qualities of the sphere of the Age; life of and for the ages; eon-lasting life; life whose source is the Age [of Messiah]). **Yet the person now continuing being unpersuaded by the Son** (or: presently being constantly uncompliant, disobedient or disbelieving to the Son; being repeatedly stubborn toward the Son) **will not be catching sight of** (seeing; observing; perceiving) **[this] life. To the contrary** (or: Yet, nevertheless), **God's personal emotion and inherent fervor**
> (or: the teeming passion and **swelling desire, which is God**; the mental bent, natural impulse, propensity and disposition **from God**; or: the ire, anger, wrath or indignation **having the quality and character of God**)

presently continues remaining (keeps on resting, dwelling and abiding) **upon him."**

We discussed the last part of this verse when considering vs. 17, above. But let us now look at 36a. Observe the present tense rendering of the verb, "**is now constantly holding and is presently, progressively possessing** (having)." This comes from "**habitually trusting into** (or: continuously going on confidently believing with loyalty unto) **the Son.**" This is a living, existential relationship. It is not a one-time mental "decision." It comes from "abiding in the Vine," or, "**a person continuously remaining** (dwelling; abiding) **within the midst of [Him] – and [He] within the midst of and in union with him**" (15:5, below). 15:6, below, explains the alternative situation:
> "**If anyone would** (or: may; should) **not continuously remain** (dwell; abide; stay) **within the midst of and in union with Me, he or she is cast** (or: thrown) **outside, in the same way as the tender branch** (or: like that twig or shoot). **And thus, it** (or: he/she) **is caused to dry up and wither, and then they are constantly gathering** (or: leading) **them** [other MSS: it] **together** ["synagogue-ing" them, or it, as in a bundle]. **Later, they are normally throwing** (or: casting) [p66 adds: **them**] **into the fire – and it** (or: he) **is progressively kindled.**"

This seems to be parallel to what Paul said in Gal. 5, in reference to a believer Judaizing (taking up the practices of the Law as a means of union with Christ). So, let us review that passage:
> 2. **See and individually consider! I, Paul, continue saying to you folks, that if you should proceed to being circumcised, Christ will continue benefiting you nothing** (or: an Anointing will continue of use to you [for] not one thing)!
> 3. **Now I continue solemnly asserting** (attesting; affirming; witnessing), **again, to every person** (or: human) **proceeding to be circumcised, that he is, and continues being, a debtor** (one under obligation) **to do** (to perform; to produce) **the whole Law** [= the entire Torah]!
> 4. **You people who in union with** (or: centered in; [remaining] within) **Law continue being "liberated, rightwised and placed in covenant," were at once discharged** (made inactive, idle, useless, unproductive and without effect; or: voided, nullified, exempted) **away from Christ** (or: [the] Anointing) – **you folks fell out from the grace** (or: fall from the midst of the favor)!
> 5. **For you see, in union with [the] Spirit** (or: by [the] Breath-effect; with [the] Spirit; or: in spirit) **– forth from out of faithfulness** (or: [the] trust-faith-loyalty) – **we, ourselves, continuously** (or: progressively) **receive by taking away, as with our hands, from out of [the] expectation which belongs to, comes from and which is [the] rightwising, eschatological deliverance within the Way pointed out** (or: forth from the midst of [the] expected hope, which is the state of being liberated, pointed in the right direction, and included as a participant in the new covenant),
> 6. **for within Christ Jesus** (or: for you see, in union with [the] Anointed Jesus) **neither circumcision continues having strength, for competence or effectiveness, to be availing** (or: be of service for) **anything, nor [does] uncircumcision, but rather, [it is the] faithfulness** (or: trust; faith; loyalty): **of itself continuously working effectively** (operating; being inwardly active and productive) **through Love.**

So we see that it is possible to "**continuing being unpersuaded by the Son**," and for the branch to not remain joined into the Vine, and for the folks in Galatia to turn to the Law and fall out of the Life-stream of Grace. But keep in mind Paul's instruction in Rom. 11:23, concerning the unbelieving branches that were broken out of Israel's olive tree: "**Now they also, if they should not persistently remain in the lack of faith and trust** (or: unbelief), **they will proceed in being grafted in, for God is able** (capable; is constantly powerful) **to graft them back in again!**"

Now consider where this "**faithfulness** (or: trust; faith; loyalty)" comes from:
"**Now the Spirit's fruit** (or: So the fruit from the Spirit; But the fruit which is Breath-effect; Yet the fruit of the Attitude) **is: love** (unrestricted, self-giving acceptance; the drive to overcome existential separation; etc.), **joy, peace** (or: harmonious joining), **length before a stirring of emotion** (slowness of rushing toward something; long-enduring; longsuffering; patience; putting anger far away), **useful kindness, goodness** (virtuousness), **faith** (or: faithfulness; trust; trustworthiness; loyalty; reliance; reliability; allegiance; fidelity), **gentle friendliness** (absence of ego; mildness), **inner strength** (self-control)" (Gal. 5:22-23a).

The Spirit is like the sap of the Vine; it is the source of "**faith** (or: faithfulness; trust; trustworthiness; loyalty; reliance; reliability; allegiance; fidelity)." You see, the Spirit produces Its own fruit, within us.

We should comment on WHAT is "**remaining** (keeps on resting, dwelling and abiding) **upon**" those who are NOT "**continuously remaining** (dwelling; abiding) **within the midst of [Christ]**" (15:6, cited above). It is God's *orgē* that "keeps on resting" upon them. This term has a wide semantic range, and in this phrase it can mean:
God's personal emotion and inherent fervor;
or: the teeming passion and **swelling desire, which is God**;
or: the mental bent, natural impulse, propensity and disposition **from God**;
or: the ire, anger, wrath or indignation **having the quality and character of God**.
Now recall what Jesus said about God, in vs. 16, above. Also, recall what we read in 1 Jn. 4:8 about what God IS (Love)! We suggest that replacing the term "**God**" with the term "**Love**" will give the true meaning of John's words that end vs. 36.

Arthur Eedle has shared instructive insights on the topic of "God's judgment":
"The Bible, replete with picture language, is often found to speak about God's judgments in gross terms, similar to those used by humans, namely, intense fiery anger, slaughter, blazing fire, torture... But the same Bible has many examples of a God who shows amazing compassion towards the waywardness of man. Care is therefore needed for us to be properly instructed about the nature of God and His judgments. Here is an example of what I'm referring to:
'By fire and by His sword the Lord will judge all flesh, and the slain of the Lord shall be many.' (Isaiah 66:16) How shall we understand what God means by His 'fire' and His 'sword'? First of all, fire: *'I will bring the one third through the fire, will refine them as silver is refined, and test them as gold is tested. They will call on my name and I will answer them. I will say, "This is my people," and each one will say, "The Lord is my God."'* (Zechariah 13:9)
Unlocking the picture language is now easy. The process of judgment may be unpleasant, but necessary. The end result is worth all the pain. Now what about the 'sword'?
'The word of God is living and powerful, sharper than any two-edged sword, piercing even to the division of soul and spirit, and of joints and marrow, and is a discerner of the thoughts and intents of the heart.' (Hebrews 4:12)
Now we have the full picture. Just as the Refiner's fires bring us needful cleansing from the 'works of the flesh', so the Sword of the Lord penetrates our minds, discovers and exposes all that is hidden and shameful..."

Chapter 4

1. **Then, as the Lord** (Master; [other MSS: Jesus]) **became personally aware** (or: came to know) **that the Pharisees heard that Jesus is progressively making and immersing** (baptizing) **more disciples than John** – [comment: "Jesus did not reject baptism, but neither did He require it" – Bruce Chilton]
2. **although, to be sure, Jesus Himself had not been immersing, but rather His disciples [were]** –

We are not told how Jesus "**became personally aware**" of what the Pharisees had heard. Someone may have told Him, or, the Spirit/Anointing may have provided this knowledge. Our author is quick to point out that Jesus was not doing this, but rather it was His disciples (perhaps those who had been disciples of John the immerser). Our author seems intent in separating both Jesus' ministry, and thus His status/position in God's reign (cf 1:8, 26-27, above).

3. **He abruptly left** (or: abandoned) **Judea and went** (or: came) **away again into the Galilee [district]**

As with what was described about Him in 2:24-25, above, and discussed there, it seems that He was wanting to avoid notoriety – it was not yet His hour (2:4, above). But, He was also simply doing what He saw His Father doing (5:19, below).

.

4. **Now it was being necessary for Him to be progressively passing through Samaria.**

We suggest that this **necessity** was primarily for what arises at Jacob's Spring, discussed below.

5. **He continues going, therefore, into a city of Samaria, called Sychar** (perhaps: Shechem), **near** (close to) **the small place** (or: the plot of ground [which could be bought, and then become an inheritance, or sold]; the freehold) **which Jacob gave to his son Joseph.**

Observe that Jesus is alone as he comes into the area of Sychar. There may be significance to the fact that the narrative associates this area with Joseph, who had been a savior for ancient Israel, in Egypt. Prior to this, Joseph had been thrown into a dry well, and then sold into slavery. Another Savior now comes into the district called Samaria, where the inhabitants are considered to be like Gentiles, by the Judeans (out from whom comes Deliverance and Salvation – vs. 22, below). Ten tribes of Israel had been deported when overcome by the Assyrians, and now the folks in Samaria were not considered, by the Judeans, to be Israelites. In Mat. 15:24, Jesus makes this statement to His disciples:
> "**I was not commissioned and sent off as an emissary – except into the midst of those sheep having been lost and destroyed, the ones that belong to [the] house of Israel.**"

Was this the necessity for His traveling into Samaria? Were His actions saying that the Samaritans were now included in "the house of Israel"?

6. **Now [the well of] Jacob's Spring** (or: a spring that had belonged to Jacob) **was located there. Jesus, therefore, being wearied from the journey, was sitting upon [the large capstone of]** (or: at) **the Spring. It was about the sixth hour** (= noon, mid-day).
7. **There presently is coming a woman of Samaria to draw** (or: dip up) **water. Jesus now says to her, "Would you give [some] to** (or: for) **me to drink?"**

These verses present the setting of the narrative that follows. It seems to be a very casual encounter, just outside the city. Jesus is tired and thirsty, and so asks this woman for a drink from Jacob's Spring. The fact that this was a well, or spring, that her ancestor Jacob dug anchors, in the history of Israel and the book of Genesis, the following discussion between the two of them. A well, or spring, and water will become important metaphors in this Gospel. Recall how Jesus had the attending servants use water in order to produce wine for the wedding feast, in chapter 2.

But there is another layer to this encounter at the spring: there is an echo to Abraham's servant seeking a wife for Isaac. In Gen. 24:16, Rebecca "went down to the spring, filled her jar and came up again," and then:

> "The servant ran to meet her and said, 'Please, let me sip a little water from your jar.' She replied, 'Drink, my lord'." (vss. 17-18a)

Was Jesus seeking a "bride" in Samaria? Is this also, perhaps, an allusion to Jer. 2? There, in vs. 2, Yahweh calls to Jerusalem to remember, "The love of your bridal days, when you followed after Me in the wilderness, in a land not sown." In vs. 4 Yahweh spoke to the house of Jacob and proceeds to challenge the People. In vs. 8 He says, "The priests, they did not ask, 'Where is Yahweh?' Those who handle the Law, they did not know Me; the shepherds, they transgressed against Me; the prophets, they prophesied by Baal, and went after things that do not benefit." Then vs. 11 asks, "Has any nation changed its elohim (God) – even though they are not God? Yet My people, they have changed My glory..." In. vs. 13b He proclaims, "ME they have forsaken, the Fountain of Living Waters, to hew for themselves cisterns – broken cisterns that cannot contain water." (CLNT)

8. – you see, His disciples had gone away into the city so that they may buy food (nourishing provisions) **in the market place –**
9. The Samaritan woman is then saying to Him, "How is it that you, being a Jew, are requesting to drink from my side – me being a Samaritan woman? You know, Jews are not usually making common use [of vessels, or things] with Samaritans!"

Was it perhaps what Jesus was wearing, or was it His accent, that gave Him away as being a Jew? Recall that at the trial of Jesus, Peter's accent, or way of speaking, betrayed him as being a Galilean, and not a Judean (Mat. 26:73). Whatever the case, this woman was well aware of the dissension between these two people groups. The Jews endeavored to keep themselves apart from the Samaritans. We do not know whether or not the Samaritans felt the same way about Jews. Jesus is obviously ignoring and bridging this cultural/religious barrier (*cf* Eph. 2:11-22). He was walking in the Kingdom of God: a realm where all barriers to union are overcome.

10. Jesus considered and decidedly said to her, "If you had seen, so as to be aware of and now perceive God's gift, and Who is the One presently saying to you, '[Please] give [some] to me, to drink,' you would ask (or: make request of) **Him, and He would give continuously living water to you."** [note: a figure for "flowing water"; metaphorically: water bringing life that continues to live within]

Jesus defines at least one aspect of "**God's gift**" as providing "**continuously living water**" for people. Had she "**seen, so as to be aware of and now perceive**" who He was, she would have asked Him for a drink of water. Jesus, here, seems to presume that this Samaritan woman would equate God's gift with the fact of Him being the Messiah (*cf* vs. 25, below), and that she would expect that the Messiah would provide water for people. Was Jesus alluding to Isa. 12:3?

> "Then you will draw forth water, in joy and with elation, from the wells (or: springs) of salvation."

It is interesting that Jesus tells her that if she knew who He was, she would then ask Him for this water, as though that was all she would need (which is basically what He said, in vs. 14, below). He did not mention anything about her needing to be born back up again, as He did with Nicodemus.

Recall Jer. 2:13, above: there, Yahweh is the "Fountain of Living Water." In this Gospel, Jesus is now the Fountain of Living Water.

11. She [other MSS read: The woman] **says to Him, "Sir** (or: Master; = My lord), **you are not even holding** (or: having) **a bucket or any means of drawing, and the well is deep! From where** (or: From what source), **then, are you holding** (or: having; possessing) **the living water?**

Does the woman's response remind you of the responses of Nicodemus, in chapter 3? The first response from the Adamic nature is always in the realm of the literal. In vss. 19 and 25, below, we will see her beginning to perceive who He is. Jesus, with His opening request of her, is living out a parable for her. He begins on the natural plane in order to get them thinking. First she is surprised at His disregard for the present norms of their cultures. Then He offers her a drink, when He has no physical means of getting physical water for her. Observe how He has drawn her in, so that he can cause a change in her thinking.

12. **"You yourself are not greater than our father Jacob who gave the well to us, are you? Even he himself drank out of it, together with his sons and his nourished and reared ones** (i.e., his livestock).**"**

Now she is focusing on Him, and at the same time affirming her standing in their common ancestry. But still, she is thinking of drinking physical water, and of watering livestock. As with Nicodemus, enlightenment normally takes time, and breaking free from comfortable paradigms is not easy. It takes the work of the Logos, and the Spirit of Life.

13. **Jesus considered and responds to her, and says, "Everyone repeatedly drinking from out of this water will repeatedly become thirsty again.**

So Jesus meets her on her level and sphere of thinking. He states the obvious. She would probably be thinking, "Of course, that is why I repeatedly come here (expressed in vs. 15, below)."

14. **"Yet whoever may** (or: would) **drink from out of the water which I, Myself, will be continuously giving to him will not repeatedly become thirsty, on into the Age, but further, the water which I shall constantly give to** (or: in) **him will progressively come to be** (or: repeatedly become; continuously birth itself) **within him a spring** (or: fountain) **of water, constantly bubbling up** (continuously springing and leaping up) **into a life having the source, character and qualities of the Age** (life of and for the ages; eonian life; = the life of the Messianic age).**"**

But now Jesus springs the trap (to which she positively responds, in the next verse). He takes her into the realm of the kingdom, even though she will not at first understand. This is parallel to how Jesus dealt with Nicodemus. Recall that in 3:5 Jesus spoke of being born of both water and spirit, and how He contrasted the realm of flesh to the realm of spirit (or: Spirit).

The water that Jesus gives will be an ever-present flow within the person that drinks it. It will be constantly bubbling up into the Life of the Age of the Messiah – an eonian fountain that produces water from within the person that drinks from the water that Christ gives to him or her. In effect, the person becomes a living fountain of the water of Life. Jesus spoke again of the Water, below, in chapter 7:

> 37. **Now within the last day – the great one – of the Feast** (or: festival), **Jesus, after having taken a stand, stood and then suddenly cries out, saying, "If ever anyone may continue being thirsty, let him be habitually coming toward** (or: face-to-face with) **Me, and then let the person continuously trusting and progressively believing into Me be constantly** (habitually; repeatedly) **drinking!** [cf Isa. 12:3; 55:1]
> > (or: let him be progressively coming to Me and keep on drinking. The person habitually being faithful unto Me,)
> 38. **"Just as the Scripture says, 'Rivers** (or: Floods; Torrents) **of living water will continuously flow** (or: gush; flood) **from out of the midst of His cavity** (or: his innermost being or part; or: the hollow of his belly; [used of the womb]).'"** [cf Isa. 58:11; Ezk. 47:1; Joel 3:18; Zech. 13:1; 14:8]

Here, in 7:38, the Scriptural quote applied first to Jesus, but could also refer to those who drink from Him. Now in 7:39a, our author explains the metaphor:

"**Now this He said about** (or: with regard to) **the Breath-effect** (or: Spirit; Attitude; [other MSS: Holy, or set-apart Spirit; Sacred Wind]) **of which** (or: of Whom as a source; [other MSS simply read: which]) **they – those trusting and believing into Him – were about to be continuously and progressively receiving**…"

15. **The woman is saying to Him, "Sir** (or: Master; = My lord), **give to me this water, so that I may not constantly become thirsty, nor yet be repeatedly coming over to this place to be constantly drawing** (or: dipping up).**"**

She wants it, so that she, "**may not constantly become thirsty,**" but her thinking is still on the natural plane. Yet she has taken the bait, so she is ready to continue listening. Her ears are developing as the birth back again to a higher place progresses.

16. **He presently says to her, "Be going on your way. At once call out to** (or: summon) **your husband and then come to this place."**

Now He is sending her off to bring others to Christ – first by touching the pain in her life, the situation regarding her husband.

17. **The woman thoughtfully replies, and says to Him, "I am not presently having a husband** (or: I do not continuously hold a man).**" Jesus then says to her, "Beautifully you say that, 'I am not presently having a husband** (or: I do not continuously hold a man),**'**

The Life and Water within His words has brought an honest confession, introducing her present situation. Jesus responds with a Word of Knowledge (1 Cor. 12:8), acknowledging the truth, and thus **beauty**, of her words. Honesty is always beautiful, even in painful situations. But He continues…

18. **"for you had five husbands** (or: at various points held five men), **and whom you now are presently holding** (or: having) **is not your husband. This you have said [is] true** (or: a reality; [other MSS: This you truly and truthfully say]).**"**

He reveals the knowledge of her past. Beyond the literal understanding of her life, up to this moment, and beyond the display (a Sign?) of His knowing her situation apart from any outside source, we wonder if the number of 6 men corresponds to the 6 water jars at the wedding in Cana (chapter 2). Was she living in her figurative "6th day," corresponding to that day of humanity's creation? Was this the day of her "new creation"? Or, was the number "5" an allusion to the 5 Books of Moses (the Samaritan Pentateuch – the only OT books that the Samaritans regarded as Scripture) that she had been under, but now was not living in accord with its Laws? And, as suggested by Dan Kaplan, was she now standing before the One who would soon be her new Husband (following His resurrection)? Keep in mind that signs and symbols are important figures in John's Gospel. The "5 brothers" in the parable of the rich man and Lazarus (Lu.16:28) have been interpreted by some as signifying the 5 Books of the Law.

19. **The woman now says to Him, "Sir** (perhaps, by now: Lord; Master), **in carefully observing, I am perceiving that you, yourself, are a prophet.**

This unveiling of her life by Him, and in her presence, begins an opening of her eyes, to see. She discerns that He is a prophet. This tells us something of what was expected from prophets, in 1st century Palestine. He had light ahead of time (*pro-* "before; ahead of;" *phē-* {a form of *phōs*} "light;" *tēs* "a person having this") – before He learned this from people. Such a person was known to hear from God, and perhaps be a "seer," one who sees visions, etc. But also, in saying this, is she thinking that He might also be "the Prophet" (1:21b, above; Deut. 18:15; Acts 3:22)? Note her conclusion in vs. 29, below.

20. **"Our fathers worshiped** (or: worship) **within this mountain** [i.e., Mt. Gerizim], **and you folks continually say that the place where it continues necessary** (or: is constantly binding) **to be habitually worshiping is within Jerusalem."**

Now some have posited that she is trying to change the subject, away from herself and her marital situation. But with the revelation about the present season, which Jesus builds upon her words, suggests that His Logos and Spirit had lifted her to a realm of thought that was above day-to-day living. She now is no longer speaking about physical water, or human relationships, but rather is seeking a spiritual answer about their current religious life. She knew the history of her own people, and was aware that the Jews maintained that it was "**necessary** (or: is constantly binding) **to be habitually worshiping is within Jerusalem**." She most likely was honestly wondering about this contrast of traditions. Who was right?

21. **Jesus then says to her, "Be constantly trusting in Me** (or: by and with Me; or: Continue believing Me), **O woman** (madam; = dear lady), **because an hour is progressively coming when neither within this mountain nor within Jerusalem will you folks continue giving worship to the Father.**

Jesus uses the imperative, present tense form of the verb, in the first clause. It was first of all an impartation of the Logos, as a creative implanting into her. When speaking to Nicodemus (Jn. 3:16-18), Jesus was referencing God's Son, saying, "**when progressively trusting and successively believing into Him and thus being constantly faithful to Him**," a third-person reference. But here, Jesus is beginning to reveal Himself to her, and in direct address instructs her: "**Be constantly trusting in Me** (or: by and with Me; or: Continue believing Me), **O woman** (madam; = dear lady)." In vs. 26, below, He tells her plainly that He is the Messiah, whom she expects to come.

Next He gives a prophecy that would happen within that generation. The temple in Jerusalem would later be destroyed (in AD 70), and He would be raised up as the Chief Corner-stone of the new, heavenly Temple (the called-out communities). Worship would happen within individuals and among corporate gatherings. There would be a new covenant that would include all races and people-groups; it would be a new arrangement for a joined Jew-and-Gentile as a One New Humanity (Eph. 2:15). There would no longer be the enmity between Jew and Samaritan (or, the rest of the ethnic groups, as well). The old would be passing away. This had already happened by the time Paul wrote 2 Cor. 5:17,

"**Consequently, since someone [is] within Christ** (or: So that if anyone [is] in union with [the] Anointed One; or: And as since a Certain One [was] in Christ), **[there is] a new creation** (or: [it is] a framing and founding of an essentially different kind; [he or she is] an act of creation having a fresh character, a new quality): **the original things** (the beginning [situations]; the archaic and primitive [arrangements]) **passed by** (or: went to the side). **Consider! New, essentially different things have come into existence.**"

22. **"You people are habitually worshiping what you have not seen and thus do not know. We [Jews] are presently worshiping what we have seen and thus know, because the deliverance** (the rescue and being restored; the health and wholeness; the salvation) **continues being** (habitually is; constantly exists being) **from out of the Judeans** (or: from among those of Judah {or: from the Jews}).

Was He saying that they had not seen, or perceived, the Father – and thus did not know Him (cf Jn. 14:6-11)? Or was He referring to the Way, the Truth and the Life? Was He referencing the OT Scriptures? His next statement refers to the deliverance, wholeness and salvation that "**continues being** (habitually is; constantly exists being) **from out of the Judeans**," but He does not end with that...

23. **"Nevertheless an hour is progressively coming – and now exists** (or: is; is being) **– when the true** (real; genuine) **worshipers will proceed to worship** (or: will habitually give worship to) **the Father within spirit and Truth** (or: in breath and reality; centered in the midst of [the] Spirit and a Fact; in union with and centered in Breath-effect, attitude and genuineness of non-concealed actuality), **for the Father**

is also constantly seeking after such folks (habitually searching out such ones as this; continuously looking for and trying to find lost ones to be this kind) – **ones presently by habit worshiping Him!**

Now He alerts her that a new "**hour**" (and this is closer than a "new day" that was coming; it was upon her, and everyone) "**now exists.**" The place where "true, genuine worshipers" would proceed worshiping was the realm of "**spirit and Truth** (or: in breath and reality; centered in the midst of [the] Spirit and a Fact; in union with and centered in Breath-effect, attitude and genuineness of non-concealed actuality)."

We should observe that Jesus did not say, "The Father is seeking folks to worship Me." Jesus always pointed folks to the Father. He was a Pattern for us to follow. Also take note that "**the Father is also constantly seeking after such folks** (habitually searching out such ones as this; continuously looking for and trying to find lost ones to be this kind)." This could mean that the Father did not, at that time, have such people (even in Israel), or, that the Father was constantly looking for more people – enlarging the group that would become "His People." Ponder Rev. 21:3,

> "**Consider! God's tent** (the Tabernacle of God) **[is] with mankind** (the humans), **'and He will continue living in a tent** (dwell in a Tabernacle) **with them, and they will continue being** (will constantly exist being) **His peoples, and God Himself will continue being with them** [some MSS add: their God].'" [Lev. 26:11-12; Isa. 7:14; 8:8, 10; Jer. 31:33; Ezk. 37:27; 2 Chr. 6:18]

24. "**God [is] spirit** (or: [is the] Spirit; [gives] Breath; [becomes] Wind; [is] a Breath-effect and Attitude), **and it is binding** (or: necessary) **for the ones continuously worshiping Him to be constantly worshiping in union with spirit and Truth** (in Breath-effect and Reality; within the midst of [the] Spirit and [the] Fact; centered in [life]-attitude, as well as non-concealed genuineness and open actuality)."

The first clause, "**God [is] Spirit** (or: spirit)," defines what He had just said, in vs. 23, about worshiping "in **Spirit** (spirit) and **Truth** (reality)," for whereas the Law had come to both Samaria and Jerusalem, Christ had brought Grace and Truth (1:17, above). He is moving her to an even higher level of Truth, giving a definition of God, and at the same time explaining the sphere of the new worship: that happens when we are in union with, centered in, and within the midst of God. It means cohabitation between Bridegroom and Bride. It means being One Spirit (1 Cor. 6:17), from being "**joined to the Lord.**" It means "**abiding** (dwelling; remaining) **in the Vine** (15:1ff, below), and producing the "fruit of the Spirit" (Gal. 5:22-23). It means "living in the Spirit and walking in the Spirit" (Gal. 5:25). It produces a birth back up again into a higher place (3:7, above; etc.). It means being filled with the Spirit, Wind and Attitude of God. In fact, it would soon be:

> "**Now there continue being different distributions** (divided-out, assigned apportionments) **of the effects of favor and the results of grace, yet the same Spirit** (Breath-effect; Attitude), **and there are different distributions of attending services** (divided-out apportionments and assignments of dispensings), **and yet the same Lord** (or: Owner; Master; [= Christ or Yahweh])" (1 Cor. 12:4-5).

Jesus is speaking of the realm of the **Second Humanity** that has been resurrected into His Life; about the **Last** (Eschatos) **Adam** (1 Cor. 15:45-47); about:

> "**and likewise, as [is] the Added, Imposed, Heavenly Person** (or: the one made of and having the quality and character of the added-heaven), **of such sort also [are] the added, imposed, heavenly people – those made of and having the quality and character of the added, imposed, heaven** (or: the finished and perfected atmosphere, or the added sky).... **we can and should** [B reads: will continue to] **also bear and wear the image** (likeness; form) **of the Added, Imposed, Heavenly One** (or: belonging to the One having the quality and character of the finished, perfected atmosphere; or: from the fully-heaven [sphere]; of the added-sky person)" (1 Cor. 15:48b, 49b).

This is SO much more than singing hymns, speaking in tongues or dancing in the spirit (but all those can be a part of it). Jesus is speaking of **the new creation** (2 Cor. 5:17). He is speaking of Resurrection

Life. Heb. 12:22-24 expands the description of what Jesus says in these few words of vs. 24. We find it described in Rev. 14:1-5. And so much more…

Recall 1 Jn. 4:8b, "**God continuously exists being Love** (or: for God is Love and Acceptance)." This is the Spirit, and the Truth. "**And so, everyone, who** (or: all humanity, which) **in continuously loving, has been born, and exists being a born-one, from out of the midst of God, and constantly experiences intimate knowledge of God** (or: comes to know by experiences from God; gains knowledge and insight by the experience which is God)" (1 Jn. 4:7b). Loving is worshiping God in Spirit (spirit) and Reality.

25. **The woman then says to Him, "I** [other MSS: we] **have perceived** (or: seen) **and hence know that a Messiah repeatedly comes** (or: an anointed leader periodically comes; Messiah is presently coming) – **the One commonly called** (or: interpreted or translated) **'Christ'** (or: Anointed). **Whenever that one comes, he will bring back a report** (or: fully announce again a message; or: = explain) **to us about all humanity** (or: all things; or: [the] whole [matter])."
26. **Jesus then says to her, "I – the One presently speaking to you – I AM [the One; He]."**

This woman had been taught; she had some basic understanding. She knew and believed that a Messiah (an Anointed One) would come, and would bring Truth and understanding about **all humanity**, and all things (the form of the word "all" functions as either masculine – and thus speaks of "people" – or neuter – and thus would be speaking about "things"). We have addressed the topic of Christ "repeatedly coming; periodically coming" elsewhere (*cf* my rendering of Rev. 1:8b). But possibly, from being in the presence of Jesus, she was perceiving that the Messiah was "presently coming." Jesus makes it clear, in vs. 26. He uses one of the "**I AM**" statements that we will find elsewhere in this Gospel. It is the emphatic personal pronoun combined with the first person, singular and present tense of the verb "to be; to exist." Scholars and theologians debate about just what Jesus meant by phrasing it this way. I have rendered it emphatically, separating the pronoun from the verb by the participial clause that I read as modifying the personal pronoun, "I," and then inserting "**[the One; He]**" as a logical reading of His saying this in answer to her last statement about "**that one.**" Now in writing the narrative of this event, John might have been subtly alluding to the "I AM" statement that Yahweh made to Moses, when Moses inquired about His Name. We will let the Spirit speak to our readers concerning this.

27. **Now upon this [situation], His disciples came, and were** (or: had been and continued) **wondering** (or: amazed; astonished) **that** (or: because) **He had been and continued speaking with a woman. Of course** (or: Indeed, let me tell you), **no one said, "What are You presently seeking or looking for** (= What can we do for You)**?" or "Why are You speaking** (or: What are You now saying) **with her?"**

Our understanding of 1st century Palestinian culture was that men normally did not speak to a woman in public. And since she was a Samaritan, this would be another reason that His disciples would be surprised at His speaking with her, and what He might be wanting from her. But, wisely, they did not challenge Him or make known what they might have been thinking or questioning of His behavior. Their "wonder, amazement, or astonishment" informs us about the issue of custom, in this scene.

28. **Then the woman left behind her water jar** (or: pot) **and went away into the city, and proceeds saying to the people,**
29. **"Come here! See a man who said to me** (or: told me) **everything which I did** (or: all [the] things which [other MSS: as much as] I do)**! Surely this one is not the Christ, is he?** (or: Is this one not the Christ?; Can this one be the Anointed?)"

We have previously cited this verse. We see her illumination by observing what she told the villagers. The second statement can be rendered in the ways on offer – they all represent virtually the same question that she poses to her fellow residents.

30. **They came** (or: at once went) **forth out of the city, and were progressively coming toward Him.**

This statement can be read in two ways: a) literally describing their actions; b) figuratively describing their inner journey to believing in Him.

31. **Now in the meantime** (or: Meanwhile) **the disciples had kept on urging Him, repeatedly saying, "Rabbi, You must eat!"**
32. **Yet He says to them, "I, Myself, continually have** (or: hold) **food to eat which you men have not seen and hence do not know or perceive."**
33. **Thereupon, the disciples were saying to one another, "Did anyone bring Him something to eat?** (or: No one brought Him anything to eat!)**"**
34. **Jesus then says to them, "My food is** (or: exists being) **that I should do** (can perform; would produce; [other MSS: can continuously be doing; or: habitually do]) **the will, intent and purpose of the One sending Me, and that I should and would bring His work to its purposed goal and destiny** (or: can complete His act; may finish and perfect His deed).

The narrative describes the physical discourse between the disciples and their Master. But the explanation that Jesus gives points them to a higher realm of existence, and to a spiritual form of sustenance. It gives them, and us, a parallel picture to His offering water to the woman, and sets everyone up for the stunning things that He will tell folks in 6:27, 33, 35, 45-51, and 53-58, below.

The food for Jesus was to do the will, intent and purpose of the Father, and thus bring **His Father's** work **to its purposed goal.**" His work was His Father's work. The word "**goal**" also means "destiny; a completed act; a finished and perfected deed." His Father's work began in Gen. 1:1. It ends (or begins anew) with a new creation, and as He states in Rev. 21:5,

> "**I am presently making all things new** (or: habitually creating everything [to be] new and fresh; progressively forming [the] whole anew; or, reading *panta* as masculine: I am periodically making **all humanity** new, and progressively, one after another, producing and creating **every person** anew, while constantly constructing all people fresh and new, i.e., continuously renewing **everyone**)!**" [Isa. 43:19; 65:17-25; 2 Cor. 5:17]

35. **"Do you guys not commonly say that, 'It is still** (or: yet) **four months more, and then the process of harvesting progressively comes'? Consider** (or: Look and see)! **I am now saying to you men, 'Lift up your eyes and attentively view** (fix your eyes on, gaze at and consider) **the countryside and fields of cultivated tracts, that they are radiant** (brilliant; or: bleached light to white) **toward a harvest.'**

Keep in mind that they are now in Samaria, not Judea. The harvest includes the Samaritans. The harvest spoke of the end of that current age. The Age of the Messiah was beginning, and the Seed for that was about to be planted, and now the field was not just Palestine (or just Israel), but the world of the aggregate of humanity (Mat. 13:38).

36. **"Already** (or: Even now) **the one habitually reaping** (normally or progressively harvesting) **is constantly receiving** (or: taking in his hand) **a compensation** (a wage; a reward; a payment), **and is constantly** (or: presently; progressively) **gathering** (collecting; bringing together) **fruit into a life having the source, character and qualities of the Age** (eonian life; life of, for and in the ages; eon-lasting life), **so that the one habitually** (or: progressively) **sowing and the one habitually reaping** (or: repeatedly harvesting) **may be continually rejoicing together [in the same place or at the same time],**

This was a period of an overlapping of the ages. One harvest was being reaped while another crop was being planted. Christ was the end of the Law period (Rom. 10:4), and the beginning of the new (Heb. 8:5-13).

37. **"for within this [relation, respect, or, matter] the message** (or: *Logos*; saying; thought; verbal expression; word) **is genuinely true** (dependable; real; [other MSS: the truth]), **'The one is habitually sowing, and another is habitually reaping** (or: One is the sower, and another the harvester).'

38. **"I, Myself, sent you men off as commissioned agents** (or: representatives; emissaries) **to be constantly harvesting** (or: reaping) **[a crop] for which you folks have not labored, so as to be wearied from toil; others, of the same kind, have done the hard labor and are weary** (tired) **from the toil, and you men have entered into their labor** [i.e., into the results and fruit of their work and have thus benefited from it; = entered into the midst, joining with and fulfilling their labor]."

Moses had sown Palestine, the prophets had also labored in that field, and Jesus had recently sent out the twelve (Mk. 6:7-12) to harvest that planting, and gather them into His threshing floor (Mat. 3:12). All agricultural crops take a season, an age, to grow and produce a harvest. Paul described the process this way in 1 Cor. 3:

> 6. **I myself plant** (or: planted), **Apollos irrigated** (or: waters; caused [you] to drink), **but then God was causing [it/you] to progressively grow up and increase** (be augmented).
> 7. **So that neither is the one habitually planting anything [special]** (anyone [of importance]), **nor the one habitually irrigating** (watering; giving drink), **but rather God: the One habitually and progressively causing growth and increase.**

As with agricultural products, in people it is the Life (the Spirit; Christ; God) that causes the growth. When the time is right, God brings the harvest (e.g., *cf* Rev. 14:15).

39. **Now many of the Samaritans from out of that city believed and put their trust into Him through the word** (the message; the communication) **of the woman constantly bearing witness that, "He said to me everything which** [others: as much as] **I did** (or: He tells me all things that I do)!"

She had been brought to a harvest, and now her witness had planted the Seed, and it immediately sprouted.

40. **Therefore, as the Samaritans came toward** (or: to; face to face with) **Him, they began asking, and kept on begging, Him to continue remaining** (or: dwelling) **with them** (or: at their side). **So He stayed** (or: remained; dwells) **there two days.**

The Samaritans were good soil and received the Seed. Like with everyone else, He planted the Life of the Spirit within them, but He did not personally (as Jesus) remain long with them. He was on a journey, and that journey's goal was all humanity and the ages to come. He would not remain with them as He was at that time, but would repeatedly come again to them as the resurrect Christ, via His Spirit (Rom. 8:9b). Let us review what Paul said in Rom. 8:10-11,

> 10. **But since Christ** (or: Yet if [the] Anointing) **[is] within you folks, on the one hand the body is dead** (lifeless) **BECAUSE OF sin** (through failure, deviation and missing the target), **yet on the other hand, the Spirit, Attitude and Breath-effect [is] Life BECAUSE OF an eschatological act of justice that brought a rightwising deliverance into equitable, covenantal relationships within the Way pointed-out** (or: on account of the covenantal Faithfulness of a liberating Turn into the Right Direction of the Living Way/Path).
> 11. **Now since the Breath-effect** (or: Spirit; Attitude) **of the One arousing and raising Jesus forth from out of the midst of dead folks is continuously housing Itself** (making His abode; residing; making His home; by idiom: living together as husband and wife) **within, and in union with, you folks, the One raising Christ Jesus forth from out of dead ones will also continue progressively giving Life to** (or: will even habitually make alive) **the mortal bodies of you folks** (or: your mortal bodies) **through the constant indwelling of His Spirit** (or: the continual in-housing of His Breath-effect; the continuous internal residing of the Attitude, which is Him,) [other MSS: because of His habitually-indwelling Spirit] **within and among you folks.**

[*cf* 2 Cor. 4:14; 5:4-5; Acts 1:8]

41. **And now many more folks believe through** (or: And so many people, in and by much [evidence], placed their trust, because of) **His word** (*Logos*; message; thought; communication; flow of information),

42. **and were saying to the woman, "We are no longer having faith, believing or trusting because of what you said** (your speaking; your speech), **for we ourselves have listened and heard from Him, and have seen to become aware and thus know that this One truly** (really; genuinely; actually) **is the Deliverer** (Rescuer; Savior; Healer and Restorer to health and wholeness) **of the world**
> (of the aggregate of humanity; of the ordered system of culture, religion, economy and government; or: of, or from, the dominating and controlling System; of the cosmos; or: = of all mankind), **the Christ** (the Anointed One; [= the Messiah])."

Here we see the growth from the Seedling (the result of the woman's speaking) into a healthy plant that saw Jesus as who He really was: the Savior of the aggregate of humanity; the Deliverer of the world,
> **"For thus God loves** (or: You see God, in this manner, fully gives Himself to and urges toward reunion with) **the aggregate of humanity** (universe; ordered arrangement; organized System [of life and society]; the world), **so that He gives His..."** (3:16a, above).

Along with Jesus' disciples, this Samaritan village was a part of what John the immerser had proclaimed, in 3:30, above,
> **"It is necessary and binding for That One to be progressively growing and increasing."**

It was His body that was growing, as we read in Acts and the Epistles. He was the Rock that "was cut out of the mountain [Sinai]" (Dan. 2:45) which "became a great Mountain [Zion – Heb. 12:22] that would fill the whole earth" (Dan. 2:35b).

43. **Now, after the two days, He went out from there into the Galilee [area],**

44. **for you see, Jesus, Himself, bore witness** (or: testifies) **that a prophet** (one with light ahead of time) **continues to hold no honor** (or: is not in the habit of having value or worth; is not respected or rightly evaluated) **within his own country** (or: fatherland; native land).

Here, we can recall the words of Isa., as quoted in Mat. 4:
> **"O land of Zebulun and land of Naphtali: a pathway associated with [the] Lake** (or: Sea), **on the other side of the Jordan [River], Galilee-of-the-multitudes** (ethnic groups; nations; non-Israelites; pagans; Gentiles; *Goyim*) –
> **The people continuously sitting within the midst of darkness** (the gloomy dimness of the shadow that lacked the light of the Day) **saw a great Light. And on** (or: to; for; in) **those constantly sitting within [the] province** (or: region) **and shadow of death, Light arises on** (or: rose to and among; dawned for or in) **them."** [Isa. 8:23-9:1; *cf* Jn. 1:4-5]

Like Samaria, the Galilee District had been the land of two of the original tribes of Israel, but now it was considered a non-Israelite territory that was inhabited by Gentiles (etc.). Recall Nathaniel's attitude toward this area, in Jn. 1:46, **"Can anything good be** (or: Is anything virtuous normally able to exist) **from out of Nazareth** [it was in the Galilee District]**?"**

45. **Now then, when He comes into the Galilee [district], the Galileans at once receive and welcome Him, being folks having seen everything: as many things as He did** (performed; produced).

Notice that they receive and welcome Him because of what they had seen Him do. Israel, following Moses in the wilderness, saw all Yahweh's miracles, yet **"they did not have power or ability to enter because of a lack of faith and trust** (or: unfaithfulness; disloyalty; distrust)" (Heb. 3:19).

46. **So Jesus went back again into Cana, of the Galilee [area], where He made the water [to be] wine.**

Now there was a certain royal officer (king's courtier; or: relative of the king; royal one) **whose son was continuing sick** (infirm; without strength in a chronic ailment) **within Capernaum.**

This episode (or, a similar one) is recorded in Mat. 8:5-13, and in Lu. 7:1-10. In those accounts (presuming that they are speaking of the same one as here) the man is a Roman centurion. Our author's term for him is more ambiguous, designating him as simply being in the royal service. He may have been a Roman officer that was attached to the court or household of Herod Antipas. If he was a centurion, then we can assume that he was a Gentile (a non-Jew).

47. **This man, upon hearing that Jesus is presently arriving from out of Judea into the Galilee [district], went off toward Him and began asking and kept on begging Him so that He would walk down** (or: descend) **at once and instantly heal** (or: cure) **his son, for he was progressing in being about to be dying** (or: was at the point of death).

Upon hearing that Jesus was in the area, this man take immediate action. This tells us that he had heard about Jesus, and about the miracles and healings that he had done. He comes straight to the point, and vs. 49, below, shows us that he is not at all put off by Jesus' statement in vs. 48, but rather hold to his mission.

48. **However, Jesus says to him, "Unless you folks see SIGNS and unusual events** (wonders; portents; omens; miracles), **you people can in no way** (or: would under no circumstances) **trust, have confidence, believe or faith-it."**

Recall that the water made to be wine (vs. 46) was the beginning Sign that Jesus produced (2:11, above), and Jesus has returned to the area where He had performed it. Because of the rumor of that event having spread, this **royal officer** came to know about Jesus and the demonstration of His glory (2:11, above). There was also the chance of him having heard about the things he had done in Jerusalem (vs. 45). So when this man heard that Jesus had returned to the area, he "**went off toward Him and began asking and kept on begging Him so that He would walk down** (or: descend) **at once and instantly heal** (or: cure) **his son.**" This would have been a very logical action to take, considering the reputation that was building abound Jesus.

Jesus' response to him (vs. 48) has been taken by some as a rebuke to the people ('**you folks**"), but if we look at the rendering of the verb in the main clause, we see that He may have simply been stating the fact about the human situation. Recall the statement made about His beginning Sign:
   "**Jesus**... set **His glory in clear light** (or: manifested His splendor so as to create a reputation; gave light in a manifestation which calls forth praise and has its source in Him; manifested His assumed appearance), **and His disciples trusted, had faith and believed into Him.**"
The verb in the last clause of vs. 48 is in the subjunctive mood, and this is indicated by the words, "**can;**" or, "**would.**" Just as with the disciples, these folks as well (including the royal officer) could not, or would not, be able to "**trust, have confidence, believe or faith-it.**" But because of the creative Logos (where Jesus instructed the attending servants, in Jn. 2:7), the words (*logos*) of the people who had spread the message about that Sign had reached this man. Verse 49 records this man's insistent, obviously faith-filled request:

49. **The royal officer** (courtier; king's attendant or relative) **continues, saying to Him, "Lord** (or: Sir; Master), **walk down** (or: descend) **at once, before my little boy dies!"**

50. **Jesus then says to him, "Be proceeding on your way** (or: Depart and continue traveling). **Your son continues living." The man trusts by, and believes in, the word** (*Logos*; message; statement; conveyed information) **which Jesus spoke to** (in; for) **him, and so he began proceeding on his way.**

Jesus responds with another Logos, which reinforces the man's trust, and he leaves with confidence.

51. **Now by** (or: during) **the time of his steadily descending, his slaves meet him, and so they report, saying that his boy continues living.**
52. **He then inquired from them the hour within which he began to better hold himself** (or: started to have better health; held a turn to a more trim and improved condition), **and they then said to him, "Yesterday [at the] seventh hour, the fever released from him** (or: let go away from him; divorced and abandoned him; emitted from him; flowed off him; [note: this verb is often translated "forgive"]).**"**

To build his readers' faith, our author provides this beautiful back-story. Jesus spoke the Logos, and the boy was instantly healed. The "**fever released from him** (or: let go away from him; divorced and abandoned him; emitted from him; flowed off him)." As noted in the brackets, about the verb of this clause, this informs our understanding concerning what is commonly rendered "the forgiveness of sins." When that happens, the person is released from sin's hold on them; failures are cause to flow away from them; mistakes are divorced and the effects of missing the target abandon the person. What a beautiful picture.

53. **Then the father knew by this experience that [it was] in that hour within which Jesus said to him, "Your son continues living." And so, he himself believes** (or: experiences trust; or: held conviction; or: was loyal, with faith; or: gives allegiance) **and, later, his whole household.**

Observe how the Samaritan woman, at the well, and "many of the Samaritans of that city believed and put their trust into Him" (vs. 39, above), and here it is one man (likely also an non-Jew) and "**his whole household**" that give their allegiance and trust to Jesus. Like Samaria, Galilee was thought of as being a Gentile territory (Mat. 4:15). Is there significance to the detail given in vs.40b, above, that Jesus stayed two days with the Samaritans? In this chapter there are two groups that come to believe, and our author designates, in the next verse, that this healing of the boy was Jesus' "**second SIGN.**"

54. **Now this, again, [is; was] a second SIGN [which] Jesus makes** (or: did; performed; produces), **upon coming from out of Judea into the Galilee [district].**

First the disciples believe (2:11, above), next the Samaritans (vss. 29, 39-42, above) then others in Jerusalem (vs. 45ff, above), and now this man, and then, through this second Sign, **his whole household** came to believe and trust in Him. Jesus' first two Signs were performed in an area considered by the Judeans to be a Gentile region. We should take note that, as with those of the Samaritan village, it was the work of the Logos, through the Spirit of Jesus' words, that an entire household came to believe in Him. It was due to an encounter with Christ, by the man, and then a witnessing, by the household, of the result of His Logos (the healing of the boy) that progressed unto faith in Christ. No catechism was required; no avowal of church doctrine or verses of Scripture; but rather, a living encounter with Christ, or with the experience of living results that embodied Him. It is the planting of the Seed within the heart, no matter the means or the situation. The Life is in the Seed.

Chapter 5

1. **After these things there was a festival** (or: Feast) **pertaining to the religion and culture of the Jews, and Jesus went up into Jerusalem.**

The opening phrase, "After these things," introduces a new geographical setting: Jerusalem. We will find this same phrase, introducing a different setting, at the beginning of chapter 6 (where Jesus has gone back north, to the Sea of Galilee). Jesus and His disciples had been north of Jerusalem, in Samaria, and then had gone north from there back to Cana in Galilee (the location of the wedding, and Jesus' beginning Sign). John says nothing about His trip down south, from Galilee, but lets us know that this is a

94

new setting, from which the following narrative flows. John does not here indicate what festival (or: Feast) this was. The first episode is a healing of a lame man, and then the central theme of the rest of the chapter is discussions of, and information about, the Father. This theme is woven into the responses that Jesus makes to those who question Him about His activities, and into disclosures regarding the Father and His relationship with Him. John 1:1 opens with the Logos, and Its/His relationship with God and creation. The great theme, begun below, is this same relationship, but now revealed as being between Jesus (the Logos incarnated) and the Father.

2. **Now within Jerusalem, at the sheep gate [which is within the northern city wall], there is a constructed pool [for bathing or swimming] – the one being normally called** (or: named) **in Hebrew "Bethzatha"** (means: House of the Olive; [other MSS: Bethesda, which means: House of Mercy]) – **presently having five covered colonnades** (porticos; porches supported by columns).

> [note: that this structure existed when John wrote this (the verb is present tense) is evidence for this being written prior to A.D. 70 and the destruction of Jerusalem]

Notice that in coming from the north, Jesus would logically first encounter the gate in the northern wall of the City. It is also of note that John points out that the term given for this gate is "**the sheep gate**." The Lamb of God comes to the "sheep gate." John does not miss any opportunity to point us to symbols.

He even gives us the name of the pool, in Hebrew. The alternate MS readings for this term each have symbolic meanings: "House of the Olive" (i.e., the source of olive oil, used for anointing; also, Paul used the olive tree as a symbol for Israel – Rom. 11:17). Or, "House of Mercy" – symbolic of what God, in Christ, was bringing to Israel, and the world. John is the only one to record this incident, and we read the details of his description as being important to his Gospel theme.

Biblical numerologists have assigned the number 5 as a symbol of Grace. So it is further of note that John gives the number of "**covered colonnades**." The act by Jesus, below, is certainly an expression of grace. But more than that, it speaks of Christ's association of Grace with "**the sick** (weak; infirm) **folks, of blind people, of those being lame** (crippled; or: missing a foot), **[and] of withered** (dried up) **folks**," listed in the next verse, who were crowded together, seeking mercy and grace.

3. **Within these and filling them [was] a crowd of the sick** (weak; infirm) **folks, of blind people, of those being lame** (crippled; or: missing a foot), **[and] of withered** (dried up) **folks** [A & later MSS add: periodically receiving (reaching in and taking out) from the moving (or: agitation) of the water].

As with the Samaritan woman at the well, we come, in John's narrative, to another place of water, where Jesus will impart Life.

[4.] [this vs. omitted by WH, Nestle-Aland, Tasker, Panin, following p66 & 75, Aleph, B & other MSS (also absent in Old Syriac, Coptic versions & Latin Vulgate); it is present in A & others: for an agent of {the} Lord used to on occasion (or: corresponding to a season; in accord with a fitting situation) descend (or: step down) within the bathing (or: swimming) pool and it was periodically agitating the water. Then the first one stepping in, after the agitation of the water, became sound and healthy – who was at any time being held down by the effect of a disease (or: sickness).]

5. **Now there was yet a certain man there, having continuously [spent] thirty-eight years within his illness** (weakness; infirmity).
6. **Jesus, having seen this man presently** (or: habitually) **lying [there], and intimately knowing** (or: knowing from personal experience) **that he already continues having [spent] much time [thus], He says to him, "Do you continue purposing to become sound in health?"** (or: "Are you habitually intending or presently wanting to become restored to your original healthy condition?")

As with the Samaritan woman, Jesus initiates a conversation (Jesus, the Logos, is the Beginning of the new situation for people) – this time, also, speaking to the need of this man. Jesus is walking in the open heaven (or, there was something about the man's attire, weathered skin, or something else that was an indicator to Him about the man), so John informs us that He was "**intimately knowing** (or: knowing from personal experience) **that he already continues having [spent] much time [thus].**" Before He addresses the man. John had already told us, in vs. 5, that the man suffered from this illness for 38 years.

Jesus asks the man if becoming sound in health is his purpose and intent (presumably for being at this pool). If that place was also a place for bathing, it would have been possible that someone daily brought him to the pool to socialize and watch the bathers. But Jesus strikes to the center of the man's issue.

7. **The ill** (infirm; weak) **man considered and answers Him, "Sir** (or: Lord; Master), **I do not regularly have a man, to the end that he should cast me into the pool whenever the water may be disturbed** (or: stirred up; or, perhaps: = rippled by a wind). **But within which [time, or, situation] I [by] myself am in progress of coming** (or: going), **another one is always stepping down** (or: descending) **before me!"**

The man's reply may have been the source for vs. 4, above, which has later MS witnesses. There may have been a local belief about "**whenever the water may be disturbed.**" Neither Jesus, nor John (if the critical texts are correct in not including vs. 4), address the issue of the water being "stirred up." But this was the man's belief, and he may have been waiting to be healed in this manner, for decades. We cannot be sure about the reality of what people expected to happen at the pool, but what we observe is years of being at the water – and this calls to mind that the Samaritan woman would have been coming to the well for years, coming for water. In both cases, Jesus answers their thirsts.

8. **Jesus then says to him, "Get on up** (or: Proceed to rise up), **pick up your pallet** (or: mat; cot) **and go to walking about!"**

In Jn. 4:50, Jesus tells the man, "**Be proceeding on your way**…" So once again, the Logos is seen in action, and vs. 9 informs us about the incarnation of this Logos to the ill man. Jesus gives an imperative, and the healing happens instantly…

9. **And immediately the man becomes sound and healthy, and he was raised up** (or: was aroused), **and at once takes up his pallet** (or: mat; cot) **and began walking about.**
– now it was a sabbath on that day –

Observe that it does not say that the man believed on Jesus, or that he even asked for His help. The Logos was uttered: "**immediately the man becomes sound and healthy.**" This "aroused" him, and, we suggest, at the same time "**he was raised up.**" The verb can be rendered either way, so conflating the meanings seemed the right thing to do. Note the passive voice of the verb: termed by theologians "the divine passive," it tells us that it was God that aroused him and raised him up. Being raised up, the man "**at once takes up his pallet** (or: mat; cot) **and began walking about.**" When invaded by the creative Logos, it becomes easy to obey Its instructions. And so it is, with us.

Next, John inserts some information for us: this happened on a sabbath day, and this created a problem for the religious authorities Judeans…

10. **The Judeans** (= religious authorities) **therefore, were saying to the man having been attended and cured** (having received the therapy and healing), **"It is sabbath** (or: It is a sabbath), **and it is not permitted, from [our] existence, for you to lift up or carry the pallet** (mat; cot)."

This Gospel makes reference to "the Judeans" frequently. The common translations often render this term "the Jews," but modern scholarship recognizes that this adjective (used frequently as a substantive, as here) better refers to those who are residents of Judea, and in the Gospels, specifically are members of what has been termed Second Temple Judaism. The term should not be understood as speaking broadly about a race of people, "the Jews," but rather about the local geographic context, time period and interpretation of Israel's religion – within that context. Keep in mind that the disciples and followers of Jesus were mainly "Jews," by race, and also largely Galileans, by geographic context. This understanding will inform our understanding of many texts. Outside of the Palestine context, the terms might well be rendered "the Jews," in contrast to "the Gentiles," but should still be seen through the lens of their religious setting, in Second Temple Judaism.

The statement made by these Judeans presents its basis as being, "**from [our] existence.**" The common versions poorly render this phrase, "it is not lawful." However, we suggest that these folks are drawing on their history, as a people (since the Law {Torah} was given, at Sinai). From their very existence as Israel, work was not to be done on the Sabbath – and to lift up and carry a pallet was thought to be "work." The phrase used here is the third person singular of the verb, "to be," prefixed by the preposition "from": *ex-estin* (from it existing; from it continuously being). It is true that the origin of their being a People was based upon the Law, but a literal rendering of what John actually wrote suggests a more emphatic expression by the speakers. They are outraged! John needs to be read with close attention to detail.

11. **Yet he considered and answers them, "The one making me sound and healthy: that one said to me, 'Pick up your pallet** (mat; cot) **and go to walking about.'"**

The man appeals to a higher authority than their traditional interpretation of the Law. It was the authority of the creative Logos operating within the Healer.

12. **They then asked him, "Who is the person** (or: fellow), **the one saying to you, 'Pick it up and go to walking about'?"**
13. **Now he, being the one being healed, had not perceived so as to know who He is, for Jesus, as a swimmer turning his head to the side, slipped out of the crowd being [there], within the place.**

Jesus was not trying to draw attention to Himself; He was not trying to build a large, physical following. His mission was more focused, and His intent was to begin this earthly mission with a small group of committed disciples (who were specifically and personally called by Him, and who were expected to leave their jobs, homes and families to physically follow His as apprentices of what He was in the process of inaugurating).

Also, specifically being in the presence of Judeans, He did not reveal Himself to the man, as He had to the Samaritans (chapter 4). As He had said to his mother, in Jn. 2, His hour had not yet come – and with God, "timing is everything."

14. **After these things, Jesus is presently finding him within the temple grounds** (or: courts), **and says to him, "Consider** (See; Take note), **you have come to be sound and healthy! No longer continue in error** (or: Do not further make it a habit to stray from the goal), **so that something worse may not happen to you** (or: to the end that something worse should not come to be in you)."

We should note that, in this account, Jesus did not come to Jerusalem with a "triumphal entry" (as given in Mat. 21; Mk. 11; Lu. 19). Remember, John's Gospel is more theme-oriented and is not a sequential record of the events in Jesus' life and ministry. His presence in Jerusalem in this passage may indicate that He came to Jerusalem on a previous occasion, prior to "riding into town" with everyone shouting "Hosanna!" Or, this passage may simply have a theme in mind in which Jesus' mode of entry into the

City did not play a part – for John's purposes. Scholars consider "The Gospels" (Mat., Mk., Lu. and Jn.) as a genre of ancient literature that are unique; they were written to proclaim a message about Christ; they contain history, but were not written to be "histories." Of the four "Gospels," John is unique among them. In our investigations of them, we will endeavor to be alert to recurring themes (such as, e.g., the Signs; the theme of the Logos; the necessity to be born back up again to a higher place; etc.).

So, in vs. 14, Jesus encounters the man from the Pool who is now "**sound and healthy**." Like we will see elsewhere, Jesus gives him a directive, implanting in him a new path of life where he is not "**continuing in error**." The alternate rendering imparts the way that he should live: "Do not further make it a habit to stray from the goal." The Logos (Jesus' words to him) empowers him and creates the ability within him to follow this new way of life. This parallels the experiences of the Samaritan woman and of the royal officer (along with his household, and his son). The Logos, having become flesh, continues creating.

15. **The man then went away and told** [other MSS: informed] **the Judeans** (= religious authorities) **that Jesus is the one making him sound in health,**
16. **so on this account the Judeans** (= religious authorities) **kept in hostile pursuit and were persecuting Jesus** [other MSS add: and were seeking to kill Him], **because He kept on doing these things on a sabbath.**

We can gather, here, that the Judean religious authorities knew who Jesus was and then confronted Him about violating the sabbath, and thus breaking the Law of Moses. This seems to be their main complaint against Him. But John tells us that Jesus answers this charge with the following reason:

17. **But Jesus decidedly answers them, "My Father is continuously working and keeps on being in action until the present moment** (or: up to right now); **I, Myself, also am continually working** (or: and so I, Myself, continue active, regularly performing in [His] trade)." [thus: it was not God's sabbath]

Observe the astounding new worldview that Jesus springs on them: God is not finished with His creation, and, as noted in the bracketed comment in my translation, therefore the seventh day of the Judean week was not God's sabbath (time of resting from His finished work). What a statement: "**My Father is continuously working and keeps on being in action until the present moment** (or: up to right now)." So of course the incarnate Logos is "**also am continually working**." Notice that He did not tell them that healing a person was not actually work. He said that it was. He was a healer, doing a healer's work.

Paul got the message:
"**Consequently, since someone [is]* within Christ** (or: So that if anyone [is] in union with [the] Anointed One; or: And as since a Certain One [was] in Christ), **[there is] a new creation** (or: [it is] a framing and founding of an essentially different kind; [he or she is] an act of creation having a fresh character, a new quality): **the original things** (the beginning [situations]; the archaic and primitive [arrangements]) **passed by** (or: went to the side). **Consider! New, essentially different things have come into existence**" (2 Cor. 5:17).
Well, obviously Jesus was walking and working in the realm of the Christ. He, and the Father within Him (2 Cor. 5:19), were in the process of producing a new creation – and healing was a part of this work. The "archaic and primitive [arrangements] **passed by**." The Law, being an inferior arrangement in comparison to the "better arrangement" (Heb. 8:6ff) went to the side. Now, "**New, essentially different things have come into existence**," and Jesus, together with His Father, was in the process of constructing them. Jesus had moved beyond the Mosaic Law and into the new creation, with its new covenant. The new sabbath lay a little ahead of that time. Heb. 4 spoke of this:
9. **Consequently, a keeping of a sabbath** (a state of rest) **is being left remaining for** (or: to; in; with) **God's people,**
10. **for the person entering into His rest also caused himself to rest from his own works** (actions; deeds), **just as God [did; does; will do] from His own.**

11. **We should at once with diligence hasten, then, to enter into this rest** (or: that ceasing down [from work]; completely stopping), **so that one would not fall in the same example** (or: result of a pattern) **of incompliance** (or: stubbornness; disobedience; lack of conviction; [p46 reads: lack of faith and trust]).

God's rest (Heb. 4:3), in the book of Hebrews, is an allusion to Israel's history with regard to their entering the Promised Land, following their deliverance from Egypt. We read of this in Heb. 3:15-4:11. But figuratively Israel, during the time of Jesus' earthly ministry, was still wandering in the wilderness. Recall the proclamation of John the immerser,

"**A voice! One repeatedly crying out** (shouting; exulting; exclaiming; imploring)**: 'Within the midst of the wilderness** (desert; desolate place; abandoned and uninhabited region) **you folks prepare and make ready the road of [the] LORD** (or: "A sound! One is continuously crying out within the midst of the desert: you folks prepare the road…)" (Mat. 3:3).

Second Temple Judaism was still in the wilderness. It was not yet the Day of the Lord's sabbath.

18. **On this account, therefore, the Jews** (= the religious authorities) **were all the more continuing in seeking to kill Him off, because not only was He habitually loosing and destroying** (or: breaking down; dismantling) **the sabbath, but further, He was also repeatedly saying that God [is] His own Father – making Himself equal to God** (or: casting Himself as the same thing as God; constructing Himself as even, on the same level, in God; formulating Himself as an equal with, or in, the Deity).

Observe that I offer the rendering, "**the Jews** (= the religious authorities)," in the first clause. Not all those in Judea were "**all the more continuing in seeking to kill Him off**," and for this reason I did not render the term, "the Judeans."

According to the reasoning of the Jews, by Jesus healing on a sabbath He was "**habitually loosing and destroying** (or: breaking down; dismantling) **the sabbath.**" But not only that, they reasoned, "**He was also repeatedly saying that God [is] His own Father – making Himself equal to God.**"

Now the bold reading of that last clause is a straight-forward rendering of the Greek text. However, the semantic range rendered "**equal to**" leaves some ambiguity. So the parenthetical options are also worth considering:

     a) casting Himself as the same thing as God;
     b) constructing Himself as even, on the same level, in God;
     c) formulating Himself as an equal with, or in, the Deity.

Each nuance is instructive and worthy of our meditation. In b), the term "even" means "on the same level." Now since the Christ was an Anointed Man who was also the Incarnated Logos, we might ponder how these Jews saw Jesus' words about Himself, and compare the "evenness" to which the risen Christ has brought us:

"**He jointly roused and raised** (or: suddenly awakens and raises) **[us] up, and caused [us] to sit** (or: seats [us]; = enthroned [us]) **together in union with, and among, the heavenly people, and within the things situated upon** [thus, above] **the heavens, within and in union with Christ Jesus**" (Eph. 2:6).

Using a "family metaphor," Paul instruct us:

"**He also marked out beforehand** (determined, defined and designed in advance) **[as] copies** (joint-forms) **of the image** (material likeness; portrait; form) **of His Son** (or: He previously divided, separated and bounded conformed patterns from the image/form of His Son) **into the [situation for] Him to be** (or: to continually exist being) **the Firstborn among, within the center of, and in union with many brothers** (= a vast family from the same womb; Gal. 4:26)!" (Rom. 8:29).

It was not a matter of "making Himself on the same level as God," but rather a matter of God raising Him to that place as the Head of the Second Humanity, the Last Adam (1 Cor. 15:42-49), which is a corporate new creation that also includes us. Ponder that. We see a similar picture in Rev. 3:21,

"**To** (or: In; For) **the person who is habitually conquering** (repeatedly overcoming; normally victorious) **I will continue granting [him or her] to sit** (or: be seated) **with Me within My throne, as I also conquer** (or: conquered; overcome; overcame and was victorious) **and sit** (or: sat down) **with My Father within His throne.**"

19. **Jesus therefore considered and replied, and began saying to them, "It is certainly so** (Amen, amen; It is so, it is so)**! I am now saying to you folks [that] the Son continues unable to do anything from Himself** (or: the Son, from Himself, habitually has no power to be doing anything [independently]) **except He can** (or: unless He should) **continue seeing something the Father is in process of doing** (or: if not something He may presently observe the Father making, producing, constructing, or creating), **for what things That One may likely be progressively doing** (making; constructing; creating; producing), **these things, also, the Son is likewise habitually doing** (or: is in like manner constantly making, producing, creating, constructing). [cf Heb. 4:3, 9; Isa. 11:10]

The Body is always the servant of the Head. Jesus, as the Son, displays for us our own relationship to the Father, and our dependence upon Him. He, the Son, "**continues unable to do anything from Himself** (or: the Son, from Himself, habitually has no power to be doing anything [independently])." This would then, certainly, apply to the sons. They cannot simply decree a thing based upon it coming from themselves, i.e., independently. The Son, and thus, the sons, are able to do only what He "**can continue seeing [that] the Father is in process of doing.**" And so it is with God's sons. Christ's Body has only one Head (1 Cor. 11:3b).

And so we can conclude that the Son was actually SEEING – observing – what the Father was presently "making, producing, constructing, or creating" – which is to say, the new creation. "**The Son is likewise habitually doing** (or: is in like manner constantly making, producing, creating, constructing)" the "**things That One may likely be progressively doing** (making; constructing; creating; producing)." There was only one purpose, one goal: humanity in the image of God, and being inhabited by God (being His temple, or, home). And now, in this new creation, "**let them progressively have primacy of** (or: continuously rule; repeatedly be leaders for) **the fish of the lake and sea, also with regard to the flying creatures of the sky and atmosphere, and of the cattle – even of all the earth – as well as of all of the creeping creatures which move upon the ground!**" (Gen. 1:26b, LXX, JM). We observe this depicted as the Bride, the New Jerusalem, descending out of heaven, from God (Rev. 21:9-27), so that "**the multitudes** (nations; people groups; ethnic groups; or: non-Jews) **will continue walking about** (i.e., living their lives) **by means of her Light** (through light from her)." This was happening in Jesus' day, and continues in our present day.

In the second half of the verse, Jesus repeats what He had said in vs. 17, adding the correlation between the doing by the Father and the doing by the Son. And this is the Pattern for us. He is our Blueprint.

20. "**You see, the Father likes the Son** (or: continuously has affection for and expresses friendship to the Son) **and habitually points out** (constantly shows; progressively exhibits) **to Him** (or: in Him; or: by Him) **everything** (or: all things) **which He is constantly doing, and He will continue exhibiting in Him greater works than these** (or: He will point out to Him greater acts than these), **to the end that you folks may be constantly amazed** (filled with astonishment and wonder).

Jesus continues teaching folks about **the Father**, giving more information about Their relationship and activities. "**The Father likes the Son** (or: continuously has affection for and expresses friendship to the Son)." This seems to reveal more of the Father's personality, and the practical aspects of Their friendship. The Father "**habitually points out** (constantly shows; progressively exhibits) **to Him** (or: in Him; or: by Him) **everything** (or: all things) **which He is constantly doing.**" Now observe the semantic range of the dative case of "Him" (i.e., Christ): "**to Him** (or: in Him; or: by Him)." Because the Father shows everything "to Him," these things are then habitually pointed out "in Him (Christ) and by Him," so that people can see the Father's works and "**may be constantly amazed** (filled with astonishment and wonder)."

"**And He** [i.e., the Father] **will continue exhibiting in Him** [i.e., the Son] **greater works than these** (or: He will point out to Him greater acts than these)." Christ's greatest work lay ahead of Him: the cross and all that came from that (the new creation with its new covenant/arrangement).

21. **"For, just as the Father is habitually** (repeatedly; constantly; presently) **raising up the dead folks, and is repeatedly** (continually; presently) **making [them] alive, thus also, the Son is habitually** (constantly; presently) **making alive which ones He is presently intending** (willing; purposing).

Wait a minute! What did Jesus just say? Really? Well, that's not what we've been taught! Yes, we were not taught this because of translations that do not transmit the force of the Greek present tense: habitual, repeated, constant or presently ONGOING action! Now not only is a resurrection continuously going on (the first clause), the second clause affirms this with a second witness: "**thus also, the Son is habitually** (constantly; presently) **making alive which ones He is presently intending** (willing; purposing)." There seems to be a plan:

"**within the Christ, all humans will keep on being made alive** (or: in union with the Anointed One, everyone will one-after-another be created and produced with Life) [cf Rom. 5:18] **– yet each person within the result of his or her own set position [in line]** (or: effect of ordered placement; appointed class; arranged time and turn, or order of succession; = place in a harvest calendar, thus, due season of maturity)**: Christ a Firstfruit** (a First of the harvest), **next after that, those belonging to the Christ** (or: the ones who have their source and origin in the Anointing; those who are [a part] of the Christ) **within the midst of, and in union with, His presence**" (1 Cor. 15:22b-23).

Jesus is constantly **present**, continuously walking among the called-out communities (Rev. 1:20-2:1). And recall Paul's words, in Acts 17:28,

"**For you see, within the midst of and in union with Him we continuously live** (or, as a subjunctive: could be constantly living), **and are constantly moved about and put into motion, and continue existing** (experiencing Being)."

In chapter 11, below, we read of Jesus physically raising Lazarus from the dead (vss. 43-44) and back to his previous life, with his sisters. But prior to this act, in 11:25-26 Jesus made this remarkable statement to one of those sister, Martha:

"**Jesus said to her, 'I am the Resurrection** (or: the standing back up again; the Arising), **and** (or: that is to say,) **the Life. The one progressively believing and habitually putting trust into Me, even if he may die-off** (or: die-away), **will continue Living** (or: will proceed being alive)! **And further, everyone, who** (or: all mankind, which) **in presently living and progressively trusting-and-believing into** (or: regularly experiencing convinced faith into the midst of; being constantly faithful unto) **Me can by no means** (or: may under no circumstances) **die-off** (or: die-away), **on into the Age [of Messiah].'**"

Was Paul, in Eph. 5:14, speaking in the same way as Jesus did to Martha?

Wherefore He is now (or: it keeps on) **saying,**

"**Let the sleeper** (the person continuously down and being fast asleep) **be waking up, continue rousing, and then stand up** (arise) **from out of the midst of the dead ones, and the Christ will continue shining upon you** (progressively enlightening you)!**"

We understand, in Paul's letter, that he was speaking metaphorically of "the dead ones." How was Jesus speaking, in vs. 21, above? Prior to His death on the cross, and His subsequent resurrection, Jesus told Martha that He WAS the Resurrection. Now in 11:25b, above, Jesus instructs her that, "**even if he may die-off** (or: die-away), **will continue Living** (or: will proceed being alive)!"

When speaking to the Father, Jesus gave a definition of "eonian Life," in 17:3, below,

"**Now THIS is** (or: exists being) **eonian Life** (living existence of and for the ages; life pertaining to the Age [of Messiah])**: namely, that they may progressively come to intimately and experientially know YOU, the only** (or: sole) **true and real** (genuine) **God – and Jesus Christ, Whom You send forth as an Emissary**."

Was this intimate, experiential knowledge of God, and of Jesus, the Life into which "**the Father is habitually** (repeatedly; constantly; presently) **raising up the dead folks**" (vs. 21)? Was this what Paul meant in Eph. 5:14, and what Jesus meant in 11:25-26, below? Keep in mind that we are studying John's Gospel: "**Within It** (or: Him), **life was continuing and progressively existing, And the life was continuing being, and began progressively existing as, the Light of the humans, and the Light is constantly shining in the dim and shadowed places, and keeps on progressively giving light within the gloomy darkness**..." (1:4-5, above). Was this the shining of which Paul spoke in Eph. 5:14? The sleepers there were like Lazarus "sleeping" in Jn. 11:

10. **"Yet, if anyone should habitually walk around within the Night, he constantly stumbles** (strikes against [things]), **because the Light is not** (does not exist) **within him."**
11. **He said these things, and after this He presently says to them, "Our friend Lazarus has been made to sleep** (or: has been lulled to sleep; has been caused to sleep; or, as a middle: has fallen asleep; has found repose), **but even so, I am setting out to proceed in journeying to the end that** (or: so that) **I can awaken him out of [his] sleep."**

Yet Paul was speaking to folks that were physically alive, and Jesus spoke of one who was physically dead. Was this a metaphor with Paul, and an existential reality with Jesus? Or, are we to conclude that on a deeper (or more comprehensive) level, God is viewing both situations as being the same to Him? Regarding Lazarus, Jesus used both "**made to sleep**" (metaphor?) and then He said, "**Lazarus died**" (reality?), in 11:14, below.

22. **"So it follows that, neither is the Father presently** (progressively; constantly) **separating and making a decision about** (evaluating; judging) **anyone, but rather, He has given all sifting and decision-making in the Son** (or: has granted all judging by the Son; has handed over all evaluating of issues to the Son),

The picture that Jesus is describing relates to the incarnation of the Logos (1:14, above), which, in tying this to the language of Father and Son, in this passage, presents the Son of having entered into His own creation (1:3, above) and now assuming jurisdiction over it (as the Last Adam – Gen. 1:28 and 1 Cor. 15:45-50). This could be seen as analogous to a mature son taking over the operation of the family business. This "**sifting and decision-making**" has to do with the orchestrating of the path for humanity, from this point, forward. The Father's business is "the plan for the ages" (Eph. 3:11) and it involves all the people-groups and nations that populate the earth. This is not a reference to some imaginary "final judgment," of which the Scriptures nowhere speak, but to the overseeing of the ongoing lives, which will become lived-out histories, of first our present age, and then "**within the continuously oncoming ages** (the indefinite time periods continually and progressively coming upon and overtaking [us])" (Eph. 2:7).

Jesus said it this way, in Mat. 28:18a,

"**All authority** (or: Every right and privilege from out of Being) **is** (or: was) **given to Me within heaven and upon the earth** (or: in sky and atmosphere, as well as on land)**!**"
This is because Jesus is the Firstborn (Rom. 8:29), and Paul affirms that, "'**You see, we are also a family of the One**" (Acts 28:18b).

23. **"to the end that everyone** (or: all humans) **may and can continuously be honoring the Son** (or: would habitually value, and constantly find worth in, the Son), **correspondingly as they are** (or: may be) **continually honoring the Father. The one not habitually honoring** (valuing; finding worth in) **the Son is not habitually honoring** (valuing; finding worth in) **the Father – the One sending Him.**

What comes to mind is Mat. 25:40,

> "**the King will proceed saying to them, 'I am truly now saying to** (or: It is true, I now tell) **you folks, Upon such an amount** (or: = To the extent) **that you did** (or: do) **and perform(ed) [it] to** (or: for) **one of these belonging to the least of My brothers** (the folks from the same womb as Me; used collectively: = the members of My family; or: = those of My group or brotherhood), **you did and perform [it] to and for Me!'**"

Just as Jesus (as the King, in the parable) shows Himself as being in solidarity and union with people, so here in Jn. 5, it seems, He is showing Himself in solidarity and union with the Father. This appears to be parallel to 1 Tim. 2:5,

> "**God [is] One, and One [is the] Mediator of God and humans** (= mankind), **a Man** (a Human), **Christ Jesus** (or: for [there is] one God, and one medium between God and humans, [the] human, Anointed Jesus [= Messiah Jesus])."

We see Christ "**separating, making a decision about, sifting and evaluating**" in Mat. 25:32-33,

> "**He will continue marking off boundaries and separating them from one another, just as the shepherd is habitually separating** [as in separate pens or groups] **the sheep away from the kids. And so He will continue making the sheep, on the one hand, to stand at [places to] His right, yet on the other hand, the kids** (immature goats) **at [places to His] left**."

So, we see Christ making decisions in regard to His herds' behaviors. And as we see, in the parable, there is a distinction between sheep (a figure of His disciples) and the immature folks (young goats; kids) who did not automatically operate from a heart of love. In the NT, all judging is in reference to behavior (works; acts; deeds; compliance/incompliance) – not about "beliefs."

The reason for the Son making all the decisions (rather than the Father doing this) is "**to the end that everyone** (or: all humans) **may and can continuously be honoring the Son** (or: would habitually value, and constantly find worth in, the Son), **correspondingly as they are** (or: may be) **continually honoring the Father**." In regard to receiving honor from humans, the Father places the Son on the same level as Himself. This is like what Jesus does, for us. But what is the significance of the Son being honored "correspondingly as" the Father? Would it not be because the Father sent the Son as His representative (3:17, above)? And furthermore, because "**for He Whom God sends forth with a mission God is habitually** (or: continuously) **giving the Spirit without measure**" (3:34, above), and because "**the Son is habitually** (constantly; presently) **making alive which ones He is presently intending**' (vs. 21b, above). Having God's Spirit with no limitations and having the power to give Life certainly makes Him worthy of honor that corresponds to God's honor. Often considered equivalent to honor is the idea of being given a name. Paul instructs us that "**God also lifts Him up above and by grace gives to Him the Name – the one over and above every name!**" (Phil. 2:9). The Father wants the same honor that is given to Him to be given to the Son. He does not hold Himself above the Son.

24. "**Most certainly** (Amen, amen), **I continue saying to you folks, that the person habitually listening to, repeatedly hearing and normally paying attention to My Word** (or: My message; the communication of the information, thought and idea from Me; the blueprint and laid out concept {*Logos*}, which is Me), **and continuously trusting by** (or: progressively believing in; habitually being loyal to; faithing-it with) **the One sending Me, presently continues holding** (is progressively possessing; is continuously having) **eonian life** (life having the quality of the Age [of the Messiah]; age-lasting and eon-enduring life; life having its source in the Age), **and is not repeatedly coming into a separating or a deciding** (an evaluating; a judging), **but rather, he has proceeded** (has changed his place of residence; has changed his walk; has stepped over to another place) **forth from out of the midst of 'the Death,' into 'the Life,' and now exists in the midst of 'the Life.'**

There are a number of important points that Jesus makes in this verse:

a) people could at that time "**presently continue holding** (is progressively possessing; continuously have) **eonian Life**"

b) they could possess this by, "**habitually listening to, repeatedly hearing and normally paying attention to [His] Word** (Logos)," and...

c) by "**continuously trusting by** (or: progressively believing in; habitually being loyal to; faithing-it with) **the One** (i.e., the Father) **sending [the Son]**."

This Life that has the quality of the Age of the Messiah (Christ) is the Life of which He spoke in vs. 21b, above; it is the Life into which the Father raises folks from out of the midst of dead ones (vs. 21a, above). Honoring the Son means paying attention to the Blueprint and laid out concept (i.e., the Logos), which He is. Notice in c), above, that "**the One** (the Father)" is in the dative case. First on offer is the instrumental dative, so that a person can be "**continuously trusting by the One**." The Father also enables us to "believe in" Him, "be loyal to" Him, and be "faithing-it with" Him.

A person living in this way (by the power of the Spirit) "**is not repeatedly coming into a separating or a deciding** (an evaluating; a judging)." But rather, he or she:

"**has proceeded** (has changed his place of residence; has changed his walk; has stepped over to another place) **forth from out of the midst of 'the Death,' into 'the Life,' and now exists in the midst of 'the Life.'**"

To step forth from out of the midst of "**the Death**," and "**into 'the Life,'**" is to experience Resurrection. You see, "the Death" is what Paul spoke of in Rom. 5:12,

"**in this way The Death thus also passed through in all directions** (or: came through the midst causing division and duality; went throughout) **into all mankind** (or: into the midst of humanity; or: to all people), **upon which [situation, condition, and with the result that] all people sin**."

Observe that it is because of the Death that people sin (so then, they are still physically alive, although "dead in trespasses and sins" – Eph. 2:1).

Before we move on, we need to grasp that this situation was happening then and there, and we see (due to the perfect tense of the verb: action completed in the past with the result continuing on into the present) that this person, "**now exists in the midst of 'the Life.'**" Such a person "has changed his place of residence; has changed her walk; has stepped over to another place... and now exists centered in the [Christ] Life." This is the being born back up again to a higher place, of which Jesus spoke to Nicodemus, in 3:7, above. This is "eonian Life: age-lasting and eon-enduring life; life having its source in the Age [of the Messiah]."

25. "**Count on it** (Amen, amen), **I am presently continuing to say to you folks that an hour is progressively** (or: presently in process of) **coming, and even NOW exists** (or: = is now here), **when the dead folks WILL be repeatedly hearing the voice of God's Son** (or: the Voice from, and which is, the Son of God; or: the voice of the Son, Who is God), **and the ones hearing WILL proceed to be living!**

Jesus used almost the same phrase when instructing the Samaritan woman, in 4:23, above, "**an hour is progressively coming – and NOW exists** (or: is; is being)." The hour, the Day, and the Age, all came in the Christ! The time was present when Jesus spoke these words. And what was He saying that was existing at that time? The Resurrection (Jn. 11:25) from the Death into the Life:

"**the dead folks WILL be repeatedly hearing the voice of God's Son, and the ones hearing WILL proceed to be living!**"

Paul discusses this Resurrection, in 1 Cor. 15, as the germination and sprouting (or, the birth) of a seed.

The **voice** speaks **the Logos**, and in It (He) was, and continued being, Life (1:4, above).

26. "**You see, just as the Father continuously holds** (or: constantly has) **Life within Himself, thus also, He gives in the Son** (or: to the Son) **to be continuously holding** (or: constantly having; progressively possessing) **Life within Himself,**

The Father was the Original Source of Life, which was in the midst of Himself. He gave birth to the Son, and so the Son now has Life within Himself. Now both the Father and the Son are Sources of Life. In Acts 17:31, Paul speaks of an important aspect concerning the Son possessing "**Life within Himself**,"

> "**In accord with that, He set** (or: established) **a Day within which He continues about to proceed evaluating and deciding about the inhabited area [of the Empire], in fairness and equity of an eschatological deliverance and liberation** (or: in union with rightwised relationships for making things right and in accord with the Way pointed out; or: centered in covenant inclusion; or: within establishment of covenant participation) – **within a Man, Whom He definitely marked out, furnishing faith to all people** (providing trust and confident assurance among, and for, all humans; tendering fidelity, loyalty and faithfulness in all)…"

And thus we have what is described in the next verse:

27. "**And He gives in Him** (or: to Him; for Him) **authority** (or: the right; the privilege; or: out of [His] essence and Being) **to be habitually separating and deciding** (to be constantly sifting and evaluating; to continuously be judging [issues]), **because He is a son humanity** (= because He is human – a member of the human race [= Adam's Son]; or: = because He exists being [the] eschatological Messiah).

We saw this word "**authority** (or: the right; the privilege; or: out of [His] essence and Being)" in 1:12, above, where John spoke of the "right out of Being" to become children of God, and then vs. 13 spoke specifically of being "**born… from out of the midst of God!**" But now, the Son has authority (He comes with the Father's authority, as His Representative) "**to be habitually separating and deciding** (to be constantly sifting and evaluating; to continuously be judging [issues])." And why was the Son given all of this, as described in vss. 26-27? "**Because He is a son humanity**." In Ezekiel, we find this phrase applied to Ezekiel, and the term "son of humanity" meant "a human being; a member of the human race." It could also signify being "Adam's son." But in Second Temple Judaism, primarily from Dan. 7, it had come to mean the "eschatological Messiah" – the One who would establish God's Kingdom. Each of these applications fits vs. 27, above – each one saying something different, as a symbolic term. The Logos became flesh (1:14, above) in order to evaluate "flesh people."

Heb. 2:17 informs us on this last phrase:

> "**Wherefore, He was indebted** (or: obliged) **to be assimilated by** (or: made like or similar to) **the brothers in accord with all things** (or: concerning everything; = in every respect; or: in correlation to all people), **so that He might become a merciful and a faithful** (or: loyal) **Chief Priest** (Leading, Ruling or Beginning Priest) **[in regard to] the things toward God, into the [situation] to be repeatedly and continuously overshadowing the failures** (mistakes; errors; misses of the target; sins) **of the People with a gentle, cleansing shelter and covering.**"

This was the reason for the Incarnation (1:14).

28. "**Don't you folks be constantly amazed at this, because an hour is progressively** (or: presently; or: repeatedly) **coming within which all the people within the memorial tombs** (or: graves) – **will be continuously or repeatedly hearing His voice** (or: the Voice from, and the Sound which is, Him).
29. "**and they will proceed journeying out: the ones doing virtue** (producing, making or constructing good) **into a resurrection which is Life** (or: of, from, and with the quality of, Life); **the ones practicing careless** (base, worthless, cheap, slight, paltry, inefficient, thoughtless, common or mean) **things into a resurrection of separating and evaluation for a deciding** (or: a resurrection which is a judging).

Verses 28 and 29 build upon vss. 26 and 27. In vs. 26 He said that the Father, "**gives in the Son** (or: to the Son) **to be continuously holding** (having; possessing) **Life within Himself**." What the Son does with this Life is to call forth folks from out of their memorial tombs, when they hear His Voice (vss. 28-29a). In 11:43, below, Jesus literally did this, when He called to Lazarus to come from out of his memorial tomb. There, Lazarus was physically resurrected. Now is Jesus speaking of the same thing in vss. 28-29? Perhaps, on a literal level. Time will tell. But recall our discussion on vss. 21-24, above, where we looked at a metaphorical reading of that passage. To aid our perception, here, let us consider the words "**memorial tombs (or: graves)**" where Jesus applied these terms to "people."

In Lu. 11:44, He said,

> "**Tragic will be your fate, you scholars** (theologians; scribes) **and Pharisees – the overly judging and critical folks because you exist being as the unseen** (or: = are unmarked) **memorial tombs** (= graves having the characteristics of Hades), **and so the people** (or: the humans) **habitually walking around on top [of them] have not seen and so do not know** (= without realizing) **[it]!**"

He said, "You exist being as the unseen memorial tombs..." Was this like saying that they were "dead, in trespasses and sins" (Eph. 2:1)? Let us look at Mat. 23:27,

> "**Tragic will be the fate of you Law scholars and Pharisees – you who recite a front of your own opinions and answers** (or: overly-critical folks; [see 6:2, above])! **[It will be] because you continue closely resembling whitewashed** (i.e., smeared or plastered with lime) **tombs** (sepulchers; grave sites), **which indeed, from outside, continue being made to appear in the prime of beauty, for a time – yet inside they contain a full load of bones of dead folks, as well as every uncleanness.**"

Now keeping in mind the metaphorical application of the idea of resurrection discussed a few verses earlier, and in light of His application of "**memorial tombs**" to "people," as just quoted, might the "**memorial tombs**" of vs. 28 be a reference to "people," as well?

We noted the judging and deciding by the King in the parable of the sheep and the kids. In vs. 29a we see a pronouncement (a judgment) similar to Mat. 25:34, 46,

> "'**Come here, you folks having received words of ease and well-being from My Father! At once come into possession of the inheritance of, and enjoy the allotment of,** [the place of, or realm of] **the reign** (or: kingdom; influence and activity of sovereignty).... **into eonian Life.**"

Then, in vs. 29b, we are told about another category of folks:

> "**the ones practicing careless** (base, worthless, cheap, slight, paltry, inefficient, thoughtless, common or mean) **things.**"

These may be compared to the thoughtless and worthless folks described in Mat. 25:42, 43, 46,

> "**I was hungry and you folks did not give to Me [something] to eat; I was thirsty and you folks did not give [something for] Me to drink. I was existing being a foreigner** (or: a stranger), **and you people did not gather Me together [with you]; [I was/am] naked, and you did not clothe Me; [I was/am] sick, weak and in prison, and you folks did not carefully look upon** (or: = visit and look out for or take oversight of) **Me.... these folks will continue going off into an eonian pruning.**"

This second group (the kids, of Mat. 25) can be compared to those journeying out "**into a resurrection of separating and evaluation for a deciding** (or: a resurrection which is a judging)." But let us not forget "**the ones doing virtue**" (vs. 29), as parallel to the sheep (Mat. 25:35-36, 40).

Now the parable of Mat. 25 (sheep and kids) can refer to the judgment that came upon the Judean religious authorities in AD 70 (remember, He said: "**an hour is progressively** (or: presently; or: repeatedly) **coming**"), but also it can be a pattern of the Shepherd continuously pruning His Vine (Jn. 15), or (mixing the metaphors) His immature folks (the kids). Recall that the resurrected Christ had John write to the called-out community in Ephesus,

> "**I am continuously** (repeatedly; habitually) **coming to you** [as a group], **and I will proceed removing** (or: moving) **your lampstand out of its place, if ever you** [as a group] **may not change your way of thinking** (your mind-set, paradigm and state of consciousness)" (Rev. 2:5b).

And to the called-out community in Pergamos,

> "**I am repeatedly** (habitually) **coming swiftly in you** (to you; for you) [again: you, singular], **and I will proceed waging war** (doing battle) **with them within the broadsword of My mouth**" (Rev. 2:16).

Then to Thyatira,

> "**I am presently casting her into a bed**.... **And I will proceed killing her children within death, and all the called-out assemblies shall know that I am the One continuously searching the kidneys and hearts, and I will continue giving to each one of you down from** (in accord to; in the sphere of; to the level of) **your** [plural] **actions** (deeds; works)" (Rev. 2:22a, 23).

Cf Rev. 3:3b, 11, 16 on other warnings of "**separating and evaluation for a deciding,**" as more examples of what we read here, in vs. 29. The Son is with us now: He does not wait until we die to correct our behavior; He does not wait until some phantasy "end of the world" to judge people. When He does make decisions about folks, it is because He has called them from out of their state of metaphorical or "spiritual" death, and as in Mat. 25:45, He will explain to them the areas of their immaturity and need for further child-training. This is an ongoing process, throughout the ages, as people are born, grow and eventually mature.

30. "**I, Myself, am continually unable** (or: As for Me, I habitually have no power or ability) **to be doing anything from Myself: correspondingly as I am continuously hearing, I am habitually sifting, separating, evaluating and deciding** (or: judging), **and My deciding** (separating and evaluating; judging) **is right and just** (continues being in accord with the Way pointed out and is turned in the right direction of fairness, equity, justice and right relationship), **because I am not seeking My own will** (intent; purpose), **but rather the purpose** (intent; will) **of the One sending Me.**

Paul addressed the topic of Christ "judging" people, in 2 Cor. 5:10,

> "**for it continues** (or: is repeatedly) **necessary for us – the all-people** (the whole of humanity) – **to be manifested in front of Christ's elevated place** (a step, platform, stage, or place ascended by steps to speak in public assembly in the center of a city; or: = an official bench of a judge or public official), **to the end that each one may himself take into kindly keeping, for care and provision** (= be responsible for), **the things [done] through** (or: by means of; or: [during our passing] through the midst of) **the Body – [oriented] toward, and facing, what things he practices** (or: she accomplishes), **whether good or bad, whether serviceable or inefficient, whether fair or foul, whether capable or careless.**
>
> > (or: for you see that it continues binding for us all to be set in light so as to be clearly seen in the presence of the judgment seat which is Christ, so that each should keep and provide for the things performed throughout [His] body, with a view to, and face to face with, what things [were practiced], whether virtuous or vile)."

This verse is a continuation of 2 Cor. 5:9, and however we read that verse, in vs. 10, above, there is a continued, or repeated, necessity (the present tense of the verb) "**for us.**" Now Paul qualifies this accusative plural pronoun by the accusative plural adjective, *tous pantas*: **the all-people.** Another way to say this, since the term is masculine (referring to people) is: "the whole of humanity." And just what is this continued necessity? "**To be manifested in front of Christ's elevated place.**" The parenthetical expansion shows that this could be "a step, a platform, a stage, or a place ascended by steps to speak in public assembly in the center of a city." It can also refer to the official bench of a judge or a public official. Since Christ is also the King, this might be an allusion to Mat. 25:31-32ff. It might also be an allusion to Rev. 7:9.

Before we continue, we should take note that Paul uses the same word "**manifested**" about himself and his companions in 2 Cor. 5:11, "**So we HAVE BEEN, and thus remain, manifested** (set in the light so as to be clearly seen) **in God** (by God; for God; to God; with God)," so this is not speaking about some so-called end of time judgment, or even a judgment after this life. It is speaking about a repeated necessity

– in this life. God does not wait until our life is over to make corrective decisions about people, or, to give them awards. Read the OT to observe this, and read Jesus' teachings and parables, as well. We have seen that Jesus' predictions of judgment upon Jerusalem and Second Temple Judaism happened in AD 70 – as set forth in Mat. 24 and Lu. 21.

Now the reason for this manifestation is "**to the end that each one may himself take into kindly keeping, for care and provision** (= be responsible for), **the things [done] through** (or: by means of; or: [during our passing] through the midst of) **the Body.**" In keeping with our corporate reading of this text, I capitalized the term "Body," to suggest that Paul is speaking of the Body of Christ, the called-out communities. A larger reading might be to see this as referring to the Body of Adam – humanity at large, but most likely he has the covenant communities in mind with the term **the Body**, as we saw in 1 Cor. 3:9-17. But what does he mean by "take into kindly keeping for care and provision"? My suggested paraphrase for this is "be responsible for," but these results seem to place a personal effect upon the person, or the group. They must now care for something, or someone. They must now maintain provision for something or someone. This judgment sounds like now having to do something they had failed to do – perhaps such as "care for the sick" or "visit the imprisoned" of "provide clothing for the naked" or "feed the hungry." Yes, this rather reminds us of the kids (immature goats) of Mat. 25:41-46a.

The basis for Christ's decision is: "**[oriented] toward, and facing, what things he practices** (or: she accomplishes), **whether good or bad, whether serviceable or inefficient, whether fair or foul, whether capable or careless.**" This sounds very much like reaping what one has sown. Yes, harvests happen throughout the year, and throughout our lives. This is like Gal. 6:7b-8,

> "'**whatever a person is in the habit of sowing, this also he will reap,' because the person continually sowing into the flesh of himself** (= his estranged inner being), **will progressively reap corruption** (spoil; ruin; decay) **forth from out of the flesh** (= the estranged inner being);
> (or: the one habitually sowing into the flesh [system], of himself will continue to reap decay from out of the flesh [system];)
> **yet the one constantly sowing into the spirit** (or: the Breath) **will be progressively reaping eonian life** (life having the characteristics of the Age [of Messiah]; or: life from the Age that lasts on through the ages) **forth from out of the spirit** (or: the Spirit; the Breath; that attitude)."

Paul made a similar statement in Rom. 14:10, "**For you see, we will all continue** [take note of the durative aspect of the future tense: we stand before Him now: the OT is full of example of people living their lives before God, and of His making decisions regarding them] **standing in attendance alongside on God's elevated place.**" Saul "stood" before Jesus on the road to Damascus and was judged (a decision was made by Christ that changed his life). Jesus was watching what Saul had been doing. We find a promise of Him making decisions about people, in Rev. 22:12,

> "**Consider this! I am continuously** (or: habitually; progressively; repeatedly) **coming quickly** (swiftly), **and My wage** (reward for work; compensation; recompense) **[is] with Me, to give back** (give away; render; pay) **to each one as his work** (accomplishment) **is** (= what he deserves)."

Rev. 20:11-15 does not necessarily speak of some "end of time" or "end of life" situation. This was simply a vision that John saw: it is a picture of God judging folks based upon "**their works.**" He appeared "in His glory" to John in Rev. 1:12-16 – when John was "**within spirit** (or: in union with [the] Spirit; in the midst of a Breath-effect)" (vs. 10). In Rev. 1:8 it was proclaimed to John,

> "**I am continuously the Alpha and the Omega,**" says the Lord God, '**the One continuously being, even the One Who was and continued being, and the One presently and continuously** (or: progressively) **coming and going, the Almighty.**'"

He is constantly active, among us, "**habitually sifting, separating, evaluating and deciding** (or: judging)." He is doing this, "**correspondingly as I am continuously hearing.**" And this is the Pattern for us. We, too, are "**continually unable to be doing anything from [ourselves].**" Our purpose and implanted goal is, "**not seeking [our] own will** (intent; purpose), **but rather the purpose** (intent; will) **of the One sending [us].**"

31. **"If I, Myself, should be giving testimony** (can by habit witness or make claims) **about Myself, is My claim** (or: evidence and testimony) **not valid and true?** (or: My claim is not true or valid [by your standards]).

32. **"There is Another, of the same kind. He is presently** (or: constantly) **bearing witness** (testifying; giving evidence) **about Me, and I have seen, and thus know, that the claim which He is bearing witness about Me is valid and true** (or: credible).

Under the Law of Moses, for something to be accepted as true there was a requirement of two or three witnesses to the fact(s) of the matter. Verse 31 can be read either as a rhetorical question, or as a statement that validates the standards of the Judeans. Jesus goes on to explain to them that He is not a single witness, as set forth in vs. 33 (John, the immerser) and again in vs. 36 (the works that He was doing), and even further, in vs. 37: the Father.

Verse 32 is ambiguous in regard to whom Jesus is referring. My reading of this is that He is referring to the Father, of Whom Jesus says, "**I have seen, and thus know, that the claim which He is bearing witness about Me is valid and true** (or: credible)." Although in vs. 33 He mentions John, in vs. 34 He instructs us that He is "**not by habit taking the witness** (or: receiving testimony or claim) **from a person** (from [the] side of a human)," and for this reason we read Him as referring to the Father (vs. 37) when He speaks of "**Another, of the same kind**," here in vs. 32.

33. **"You folks have dispatched [men] to John, and he has borne witness to the Truth** (or: testified by the Truth; made confirmation in the Truth; attested with reality),

34. **"yet, for Myself, I am not by habit taking the witness** (or: receiving testimony or claim) **from a person** (from [the] side of a human), **but rather, I presently say these things to the end that you folks yourselves may be delivered** (or: could and would be rescued, saved, made healthy and whole, and restored to your original condition).

35. **"That person was continuing being the continuously burning** (ignited; lighted) **and constantly shining lamp, and you folks yourselves, for a short time** (for an hour), **want** (or: purposed) **to exult and rejoice in its light** (or: centered within his light).

Verse 33 refers to 1:19-27, above. Jesus affirms his witness as being "the Truth (or: Reality)." We should not miss the optional readings of the dative case, "by the Truth; in the Truth; with reality." All of these readings, taken together, color-in the situation.

Observe the Jesus was saying these things (and thus: projecting the Logos to them) "**to the end that you folks yourselves may be delivered** (etc.)." He then affirms that John "**was continuing being the continuously burning** (ignited; lighted) **and constantly shining lamp**," but that he would shine only "**for a short time** (for an hour)," and yet He recognized that they had rejoiced in John's ministry, and in what he had said would follow after him (1:28-34, above).

36. **"Yet I, Myself, constantly hold** (or: am continuously having) **the Witness** (or: the evidence) **[that is] greater and more important than [that] from John** (or: the greater testimony compared to the one that John gives), **for the works** (or: actions; deeds) **which the Father has given in Me** (to Me; for Me; by Me) – **to the end that I may bring them to the goal** (finish, mature and perfect them to their destined purpose) – **the works themselves** (or: these same actions) **which I am continuously doing** (performing; producing) **continuously bear witness** (testify; make claim; give evidence) **about Me, that the Father has sent Me forth with a commission** (as a Representative, or Emissary).

So although John was "a burning and shining lamp," the greater witness was "**the works** (or: actions; deeds) **which the Father has given in Me** (to Me; for Me; by Me)." The "**goal** (finished, mature, perfect and destined purpose)" we know to be the cross, along with the resurrection Life that He would bring to humanity. All of His life, on through to His ascension, was to "**continuously bear witness** (testify; make claim; give evidence) **about Me, that the Father has sent Me forth with a commission**." As a Representative, He brought to us the message of Goodness, Ease and Well-being from the Father, which in turn has revealed the Father (and what kind of God He is) to us.

37. "**Also, the One sending Me, that Father, has borne witness** (has testified) **about Me. You folks have neither heard His voice at any time, nor have you seen** (or: perceived) **His external appearance** (shape; figure of what is seen; = what He looks like),
38. "**and further, you people are not holding or possessing His** *Logos* (His Message; His Blueprint; His Thought and Idea; What has been Laid Out from Him; the Word which is Him) **remaining** (or: dwelling) **continuously within you** (or: and you are not having His Word or Information abiding continually among you folks), **because Whom That One sent forth with a commission** (or: as a Representative) **in** (to) **This One you people are not presently trusting, believing or being loyal.**

Verse 37 gives the ultimate witness that a person could have: the Father. In all of their searching of their Scriptures (vs. 39), and in all of the temple cultus of their religion, the religious authorities of the Judeans (vss. 16 and 18, above) "**[had] neither heard His voice at any time, nor [had] seen** (or: perceived) **His external appearance**." That final phrase can also be rendered: shape; figure of what is seen; or = what He looks like." This might seem a strange thing to say to them, if taken on the level of the literal – and on that level, all of this was true, of course. But by the Spirit, they should have been able to hear His voice through what Moses and the Prophets reported of what He had said. The witness of creation and the formation of Israel as His people was "a figure of what could be seen" of Him. The symbols of the Tabernacle (which was to be made according to the pattern shown to Moses on Sinai) would have given a perception of His shape, among them. And the human, itself, should have been seen by them as the image of God. But they were blind, and deaf. They had not seen God, in Jesus (*cf* 14:6-9, below).

Verse 38 is a telling assessment that Jesus made about them. If we read the second half of the verse first, we will see the reason, and condition, for what is said in the first half:

> "**because Whom That One [the Father] sent forth [i.e., the Son] with a commission** (or: as a Representative) **in** (to) **This One [i.e., the Son] you people are not presently trusting, believing or being loyal.**"

Therefore, it was expected of the leaders of the Jews (who had the Scriptures) to trust, believe and be loyal to the Messiah. Because of this, even though they would "**continuously search the Scriptures**" (vs. 39), they were, "**not holding or possessing His** *Logos*." They had the Scriptures, but not "the Word." They were not holding God's "Message, Blueprint, Thought and Idea, what had been Laid Out from Him, or, the Word which is Him." All they had was "the Letter." Paul instructs us that:

> "**the effect of letter habitually kills** (or: Scripture, the result of writing something into a text, repeatedly puts away in death), **yet the Spirit** (or: the spirit; the Breath-effect; the Attitude) **continuously produces Life** (or: repeatedly makes alive; progressively forms life; habitually creates Life)" (2 Cor. 3:6b).

And thus...

39. "**You folks continuously search** (or, as an imperative: Be constantly searching) **the Scriptures, because within them you yourselves are habitually presuming to be presently and continuously holding eonian life**

> (or: because you folks are normally supposing for yourselves to be habitually having – in union with them – life pertaining to, and having the qualities and characteristics of, the Age [perhaps: = the life of the coming age]), **and those [Scriptures] are** (exist being) **the ones continuously testifying about Me** (constantly giving evidence concerning and bearing witness around Me).

The form of the verb in the first clause is either the indicative (a statement) or an imperative (a directive, or a command). The first rendering seems to reflect what the scribes, Pharisees and rabbis actually did. But Jesus may also be instructing them to search more carefully!

Now the second clause is revealing, concerning Second Temple Judaism: they were "**presuming to be presently and continuously holding eonian life.**" What came through Jesus was what they presumed to have already had through Moses and the Prophets. We recall Lu. 18:18,

> "**Then a certain ruler** (or: chief; or: leading person of the ruling class) **put a question to Him, saying, 'Good teacher, by doing what can I be an heir of, and shall I proceed receiving an allotment in, eonian life** (= life in the coming Age when the Messiah reigns; or: life which has the character and qualities of the Age; or: life in the ages and for an indefinite period of time)**?'**"

So, eonian life (etc.) was apparently a life-goal, at least for some, in Second Temple Judaism. Mat. 19:16 is similar. Scholars tell us that during this period of Israel's history, their worldview had two ages: the present one, and the one to come – this latter being the Age of the Messiah. So Judaism of Jesus' time, and Christianity ever since, have viewed the OT as holding prophecies that pointed to the coming Messiah. We could give examples, but the statement by Jesus is ample witness that the OT pointed to Christ, and through this statement He was thus also identifying Himself as the Messiah.

Now as to the final clause, *Cf* Lu. 24: 27, where Jesus opens the OT to the two, on the road to Emmaus, the things found there that applied to Him. And thus do we find Paul identifying the water-giving rock, in the wilderness, as being Christ (1 Cor. 10:4), in reference to the Israelites drinking a "spiritual drink."

40. **"And yet you people continue not willing** (or: presently refuse and habitually do not intend) **to come toward** (or: to; face to face with) **Me, so that you may presently be having Life** (or: would continuously take hold of and possess [this] life).

Here, Jesus implies that they do not have Life, and thus they are dead. If they would come to Him, and be face-to-face (i.e., in relationship with) Him, they could at that very moment "**be having Life**." The same is true today.

41. **"I have no habit of receiving glory from humans** (or: I am not continuing to take a reputation at the side of people, nor do I normally get opinions from [them]),

Jesus seems to be saying that He did not "take a reputation," or an opinion about Himself, from people. He is not dependent upon us "giving Him glory." The Father does that for Him. Then He, in turn gives this glory to us (17:22, below). The best that we can do is:

> "**we all, ourselves – having a face that has been uncovered and remains unveiled** [note: as with Moses, before the Lord, Ex. 34:34] **– being folks who by a mirror are continuously observing, as ourselves, the Lord's glory** (or: being those who progressively reflect – from ourselves as by a mirror – the assumed appearance and repute of, and from, [our] Owner)..." (2 Cor. 3:18).

Our job is simply to continuously observe Him... and then do what we see Him doing. The Glory takes care of itself.

42. **"but rather, I have come to know you folks by personal experience, that you people do not continuously hold** (or: do not presently have) **God's love** (or: the urge toward reunion from, and which is, God; or: love and acceptance from, and pertaining to, God) **within yourselves.**

Not having, or holding (within themselves), **God's love** equates to "**not having Life**" (vs. 40b, above), which they could have had if they would have come to Him. Paul put it this way:

"**And you folks [who were] continuously existing being dead ones in** (or: to; with; or: by) **the results and effects of your stumblings aside** (offenses; wrong steps) **and failures to hit the mark** (or: mistakes; errors; times of falling short; sins; deviations)" (Eph. 2:1).

This is all very simply put, and requires no philosophy or theological formula to explain it. With even a little discernment, we can by personal experience come to know if people are not presently having "the urge toward reunion from, and which is, God," or, "love and acceptance from, and pertaining to, God." We see this by how they live and how they think of, and treat, other people. Eonian Life is very simply "God's love." His Love includes "acceptance of others." To have His love is to give (from within ourselves) His son to others (Jn. 3:16), by our words, actions and mental projections.

43. **"Now I, Myself, have come within my Father's Name, and you folks are not proceeding to receive Me; if another one may come within his own name, you will proceed to receive that one.**

By coming within His Father's Name, He was coming in His Father's authority, as His Father's Representative. He was the King's Son; He was the Son of the Owner of the vineyard (Israel) – Mat. 21:33-39. They could not accept that He WAS the Son of God, that He had been sent by God. They could only accept a person who claimed only to be himself, another human just like they were. They objected to recognizing that He was their Messiah. They may not have liked the message of John the immerser (who had caustic words for them – Mat. 3:7-10), but they did not reject him as a prophet or try to kill him off. What they rejected was that Jesus represented God's reign on earth, which was supplanting their assumed position over the people.

44. **"How are you folks, yourselves, able to trust or believe, when habitually getting a reputation and receiving fame** (or: repeatedly taking opinions and glory) **from one another, and yet you folks are not constantly seeking the glory** (or: the reputation, opinion or manifestation which calls forth praise; or: the assumed appearance) **which comes from the only God** (or: from God alone)**?**

Jesus is saying that if folks are "**habitually getting a reputation and receiving fame** (or: repeatedly taking opinions and glory) **from one another**," and yet are "**not constantly seeking the glory** (or: the reputation, opinion or manifestation which calls forth praise; or: the assumed appearance) **which comes from the only God** (or: from God alone)," then they will not be able "**to trust or believe.**" This should be a sobering revelation to all of us, who can so often put all of our focus on what others think of us. Being content with having only God's opinion of us, or only radiating His glory, is difficult for anyone who is seeking fame from the domination System (the competitive world of culture, religion, politics, etc.).

Another side of the first clause is given by Paul, in 2 Cor. 10:
> 11. **Let such a person take this into account, that the kind of person we are in** *Logos* (word, etc.) **through letters, being absent, such also [are we], being present, in action.**
> 12. **Of course we are not daring to classify ourselves among, nor compare or explain ourselves with, some of those setting themselves together for commendation. But in fact they, themselves, are constantly measuring themselves among** (or: within) **themselves, and are repeatedly comparing themselves with themselves – they continue not comprehending or understanding!**

Their "comparing themselves" was a form of seeking glory and getting fame from other people.

45. **"Stop thinking** (supposing; presuming; having opinions) **that I, Myself, will publicly speak down against** (or: accuse) **you folks to the Father; the one constantly accusing** (publicly speaking down against) **you people is** (or: exists being) **Moses, into whom you folks have put your expectation, and on whom you now rely.**

112

Jesus did not come to be "the accuser of the brothers," but rather He came to cast the "accuser" out of us (Rev. 12:10). They constantly lived with the accuser: Moses. Their expectation, and that upon which they were relying, was that which was "**constantly accusing** (publicly speaking down against)" them!

But now,

"**Nothing, consequently, [is] now a result of condemnation in** (or: a commensurate effect of a decision for; a corresponding result of a negative evaluation which falls in line with a decision or follows the pattern which divides [folks] down, with) **those within Christ Jesus**
(or: In that case, therefore, [there is] now not one thing [that is] really an effect of a downward-judging to, in or with the folks in union with or centered in [the] Anointing of Jesus)!" (Rom. 8:1)

46. **"For if you folks had been trusting by, adhering to, having loyalty for and believing in Moses, you would have been trusting by, adhering to and believing in Me: for that one wrote about Me!**

So the accusation, from their Law (Moses) was that they had NOT "**been trusting by, adhering to, having loyalty for and believing in Moses**." Then He recaps what He has said in vs. 39, above: "**that one** [i.e., Moses] **wrote about Me!**" What a broad, inclusive statement about the Torah. The very foundation of their culture, religion and existence as a nation were writings that pointed to Jesus, as the Messiah, and as the Savior of the world. No wonder John the immerser described Him as:

"**God's Lamb** (or: the Lamb from God; the Lamb having the character and qualities of God; or, in apposition: the Lamb which is God), **the One continuously lifting up and progressively carrying away the Sin of the world, and removing the sin which belongs to and is a part of the System…. the One progressively** (or: habitually) **immersing** (or: baptizing) **within a set-apart spirit** (or: in the midst of [the] Holy Spirit; in union with the Sacred Breath-effect)" (1:29, 33b, above).

John had been trusting, believing and being loyal to Moses, so his eyes were able to recognize who Jesus was.

47. **"Yet if you are not habitually trusting by, adhering to, having loyalty for and believing in that one's writings, how will** [other MSS: do] **you folks continue to trust by, have loyalty for, adhere to and believe in My sayings** (or: My declarations; My gush-effects; the results from flows in Me)?"

This is a foundational statement for all who claim to be a follower, or a believer, in Christ. Now the Pharisees were adhering to, and being loyal to, the literal aspects of Moses (the Law) – they went beyond the Law of Moses, adding many interpretive laws to what was written in the Torah. So obviously Jesus was not speaking about literally adhering to the Law in any religious or cultural way. This was about trusting by and believing in the Spirit of the Logos that was housed in Moses' writings.

Dan Kaplan pointed us to Jer. 11:1-8, and then to Ps. 81:13 (and its context):
"O, if my People were hearkening unto Me; [if] Israel would walk in My ways." *Cf* Jer. 7:22

But without a living, spiritual relationship with God in the old covenant (where they were, at that time), how could they possibly trust or be loyal to His "gush-effects, or the results from the flows in Him" (a literal rendering of *rhēma* – ordinarily only rendered as "sayings" or "declarations")? In the next chapter of John, we will read:

"**The declarations** (gush-effects; spoken words; sayings; results of the Flow) **which I, Myself, have spoken to you folks are** (or: continue to be) **Spirit** (or: spirit; Breath-effect; attitude) **and they are** (or: continue being) **Life**" (6:63, below).

Chapter 6

1. **After these things** (= Sometime later), **Jesus went away to the other side of the Sea** (or: Lake) **of Galilee, the [area] pertaining to Tiberias.**

Our author records another "sign" incident that happened at another time, and another place. The narrative, not the historical sequence, is what is important to this Gospel.

2. **Now a large crowd kept following Him, because they had been attentively viewing the signs which He had been doing** (making; constructing; creating; performing; producing) **upon those who were sick** (without strength; infirm; ill).

Observe that the crowd followed Him "**because they had been attentively viewing the signs**." It was not because of His teachings. But we will see, in vs. 15, that they were beginning to have thoughts about what He could do for them.

3. **So Jesus went back up into the mountain, and was continuing sitting there with His disciples.**

This calls to mind the scene in Mat. 5:1, where Jesus does the same thing: after seeing the multitudes, He went up into a mountain, sits down. But that was the beginning of "the Sermon on the Mount." Here, he says nothing of His teaching (if He did at this time), and instead reports about another "**sign**" which was feeding the multitude. At the wedding He created wine; note here that it is bread and fish.

4. **– Now the Passover, the Feast** (or: festival) **of the Judeans** (from the Jewish culture and religion), **was drawing near –**

Why does he insert this information at this point? Is he preparing his readers for Jesus' teaching about eating His flesh and drinking His blood (vss. 32-58, below) – a reference to the original Passover, when Israel was being delivered from Egypt? John does not record "the last supper" where Jesus refers to the bread as His body and the wine as His blood (Mat. 26:26-28). But what follows, here, is table fellowship for a large crowd (a figure of humanity) – a precursor to the Passover Feast; a parable lived out, but celebrated in the Gentile territory of Galilee. And so we return to Jesus sitting, "**observing that a large crowd was progressively coming toward Him**"...

5. **Then, lifting up His eyes and observing that a large crowd was progressively coming toward Him, Jesus then says to Philip, "From what place may we purchase loaves of bread so that these folks may eat?"**

Jesus sees the need of the people ("I was hungry and you gave Me food..." Mat. 25:35). Jesus' question to Philip was framed around a natural means of supplying their need: "**From what place may we purchase loaves**...?" Now Philip is alerted to the problem that Jesus had foreseen.

6. **– Now he was saying this in process of testing him**
(putting him to the proof; [note: the verb can also mean: to attempt; to try something. Was Jesus perhaps here "teasing" Philip?]), **for He had seen, and thus knew what He was being about to progressively do –**

This gives the readers a clue: In seeing the problem, Jesus also saw the answer to the problem. If we read the verb of the first clause as "testing," Jesus may be wondering if Philip remembers His words to Nathanael, that he would see "greater things" (Jn. 1:50). Or, He may want to see if Philip will remember how Jesus solved the lack of wine at the wedding in Cana. But we also wonder if John is revealing to us the sense of humor that Jesus had – "teasing" Philip about what appeared to be an insurmountable problem, to which Jesus already knew the answer. John's Gospel always shows Jesus in control: He is the Logos incarnated – the Creator is within Him.

7. **Philip considered and answered Him, "Two hundred denarii** [note: a denarius = a day's pay for a laborer, thus = about eight months' wages] **worth of loaves are not continuing adequate** (enough; sufficient) **so that each one might receive** (get; take) **a little** (a short piece).**"**

Philip has done the math. There is no way to feed what John tells us is 5000 men (plus women and children, most likely).

8. **One of His disciples, Andrew, the brother of Simon Peter, then says to Him,**
9. **"There is a young lad** (little boy; young fellow; or: servant; or: lass; young woman) **here who presently has five loaves of barley bread, and two small cooked** (or: dried) **fishes, but what are these unto** (or: for) **so many?"**

Andrew reports the little that they had. Do you notice that neither Jesus nor His disciples brought lunch for this time on the mountain? Only a little boy, or a young lass, had the foresight to bring a lunch for himself/herself, and more to share: 5 loaves! He or she knew that folks would be hungry, but no one else had thought ahead. Of such little ones is the reign of God! (Mat. 19:14). But Andrew came to the same conclusion as Philip – humanly speaking, there was no way to meet the need.

Does this story allude to Israel getting tired of manna, in the wilderness journey, and asking for flesh to eat (Nu. 11:4b)? Moses complained to Yahweh, "Where should I have flesh to give to all the people?" (vs. 13). When Yahweh tells Moses that He will supply flesh for the multitude, Moses was like Philip and Andrew and asks Yahweh, "Shall the flocks and the herds be slain for them to suffice them? Or shall all the fish of the sea be gathered together for them, to suffice them?" (Num. 11:22). Yahweh sent quail to them.

10. **Jesus says, "You guys make the people recline back, as at a meal." – Now there was a lot of grass and plants in the area** (or: the place) **– Therefore the adult men reclined back, about five thousand in number.**

Observe this detail: everyone had a comfortable place to recline for lunch. God considers the details of our needs. Reclining was their normal posture for eating a meal. By having the people "recline back," it was a signal to them that they were going to have a meal. Also, they had entered into His rest.

11. **Then Jesus took the loaves and, expressing gratitude** (while giving thanks; or: in speaking well-being, favor and grace), **He distributes [it] to the disciples, and the disciples to those presently lying back. Likewise, also from out of the small cooked fishes – as much as they wanted.**

What was available was given to Jesus, and He received it. The subordinate participle, "speaking well-being, favor and grace," shows that He was "expressing" this gratitude as He distributes the food (presumably to the disciples, to then give to the people). He was "giving thanks" while He was distributing the food, through the employment of His disciples. This small detail is a pattern for us. Giving thanks while we provide for folks, or expressing gratitude while we do any work, as well as working through those that are with us. He was thanking the Father for what He was seeing the Father doing. And this was not just a snack: they got "**as much as they wanted.**"

12. **Now as they are being filled within and satisfied, He then says to His disciples, "Gather together** (or: Collect) **the excessive abundance of broken pieces** (fragments; or: crumbs), **to the end that nothing may be lost."**

This episode calls to mind the days of Elisha, in 2 Ki. 4, during a period of a famine in the Land. There an incident is recorded where a man brought to Elisha a firstfruits offering of twenty loves of barley bread and new crop grain in a knapsack (note: a loaf of bread in those days were likely small, flat rounds, so twenty loaves could fit into a knapsack).

> "And [Elisha] said, 'Give it to the people that they may eat.' Yet the one ministering to him replied, 'How shall I put this before a hundred men?' He answered, 'Give it to the people that they may eat; for thus said Yahweh: "They are to eat and to have surplus."' So he put it before them and they ate, and they had a surplus according to the word of Yahweh" (2 Ki. 4:42-44; CVOT).

In the story of Ruth, she asked to glean in the field of Boaz, her kinsman. He consents, and even tells her, "If you are thirsty, go and drink from the jars the men have filled" (Ru. 2:9b). Then, in 2:14,

> "When meal-time came round, Boaz said to her, 'Come here and have something to eat, and dip your bread into the sour wine.' So she sat beside the reapers, and he passed her some roasted grain. She ate all she wanted and still had some left over." (NEB)

A detail in this story of the widow Ruth, an ancestor of Jesus, was that she ate "as much as she wanted," and still, there was an "excessive abundance" left over. One wonders if Jesus had these stories in mind when He supplied a surplus of bread. For our author, this detail would point to vs. 35, below, and show that "**the Bread of 'the Life'**" was more than enough for all mankind.

Take note, for His Logos to them is also a SIGN: "**that nothing may be lost**." They were to gather and collect all "**the excessive abundance of broken pieces** [a figure of broken people] (the fragments and crumbs [of society])." But of course, on a natural reading of the text, the next verse affirms that there was not only "as much as the people wanted to eat," but also an excess of supply for them. This Gospel gives us "**signs**" on more than one level of interpretation. God cares about crumbs, the hairs on our heads, and sparrows. Yes, because EVERYTHING came out of Him (Rom. 11:36). He also wants us to consider, and thus learn from, the lilies of the field (Mat. 6:28-29).

13. **Therefore, they gathered** (or: collected) **[them] together and filled twelve wicker baskets of broken pieces** (fragments; or: crumbs) **from out of the five loaves of barley bread which were over-abounded to the folks having eaten.**

Our author's attention to numbers is instructive: 12 baskets of broken pieces (one for each of the 12 disciples; one for each of the 12 tribes of Israel; cf Rev. 21:12b, 14). These were a figure of "the remnant of Israel" that were lost sheep, but this SIGN was also an allusion to the manna for Israel, in the wilderness. In the old covenant, the twelve tribes were represented in the twelve loaves of bread that were kept in the holy place of the Tabernacle. In the new covenant the twelve gates (tribes of Israel) and the twelve foundations (the twelve sent-fort folks/disciples) are integral part of the One New Jerusalem, and as Paul instructs us, we are now "**One Bread** (one loaf of bread), **One Body**," (1 Cor. 10:17).

14. **Then the people, seeing the signs which Jesus did, began to say** (or: kept on saying), **"This One is truly** (or: really) **The Prophet – the One periodically** (or: presently) **coming into the organized system** (or: the world of culture, religion and government; or: the aggregate of humanity)."

The people probably thought of the prophet Elijah, providing meal and oil for the widow (1 Ki. 17:9-16). And **The Prophet** was another designation for the coming Messiah (cf 1:21, above). But as noted above, the main allusion would be to Moses' words, in Deut. 18:15.

The participle "**coming**" is in the present tense, which means it is speaking of repeated action, or these folks may have, because of John the immerser's preaching, thought that (together with all these signs by Jesus) this Prophet was progressively and presently coming. But with the priests and Levites asking the immerser if he was Elijah, perhaps their worldview was that of the spirit of the Prophet periodically coming to Israel to bring correction to the People. Elijah prophesied during a period when Israel had a worthless king (as did the people during the period of Jesus' ministry). Whatever their case was, they interpreted Jesus' signs as God sending the One for whom they had been waiting.

15. **Jesus, therefore – experientially and intimately knowing** (or: coming to perceive) **that they are presently about to be coming and to proceed snatching Him away** (seizing and forcefully taking Him away) **to the end that they may make [Him] king – withdrew Himself, alone, back up** (or: retires; leaves the area and goes back up) **again into the mountain** (or: hill country).

Jesus, again being in control of the situation, perceives what they are up to, and He withdraws back into the hill country, or into the mountain where He had been. His purpose was not to be the kind of king that they wanted to have. His kingdom was not a part of their system of life.

16. **Now as it came to be evening, His disciples walked down** (or: descended) **upon the sea [shore],**
17. **and then, stepping within a boat** (or: boarding a small fishing craft), **they began going and continued coming to the other side of the sea** (or: lake), **unto Capernaum.**
Now it had come to be dim with darkness already (= it had grown dark) **– and Jesus had still not** (or: not yet) **gone toward them –**
18. **and now the sea** (or: lake) **was being progressively roused and stirred up from a great wind continuously** (or: progressively) **blowing.**

The author does not inform us of the details (apparently unimportant to him, with regard to his narrative) of why the disciples left the area without waiting for their Master to come out of the hills. However, Mat. 14 explains the reason:

> 22. **And then, without delay, He compelled His disciples to board** (step into) **the little boat and to be progressively preceding** (going ahead of) **Him unto the other side – while He would be dismissing and dispersing the crowds.**
> 23. **And so, upon dismissing and dispersing the crowds, He went back up into the mountain** (or: hill country) **– in accord with what was His own** (or: corresponding to His own [thoughts and feelings]; or: privately) **– to be praying** (speaking or thinking toward having ease, goodness and well-being). **So then, it coming to be late in the evening, He was there alone.**

Jesus apparently just wanted to be alone, and this would give Him opportunity to display another "sign" to them, revealing to them another aspect of Himself so as to increase their faith and trust in Him...

19. **Then, having been rowing forward about twenty-five or thirty stadia** (= three or four miles), **they noticed and kept on intently watching Jesus continuously walking around upon the sea** (or: lake; or, perhaps: = along the shore) **and progressively coming to be near the boat, and they became afraid** (or: were made to be terrified)!

In vs. 17 we were instructed that, "**it had come to be dim with darkness already** (= it had grown dark)." So their perception of what they were looking-at would not have been clear. Mat. 14:26 tells us that they thought that they might be seeing "**a ghost** (or: a phantom; or: an apparition; or: the effect of something being made visible)." With it being dark, and with a great wind rousing the waves, the combined elements of this situation leave us easily understanding why "**they became afraid**," likely each one of them to varying degrees. Matthew tells us that they even "cried out from fear."

In this storm, they were likely hugging the shore as they rowed on. So at their first sight of Jesus, He may have still been "walking along the shore" (a possible reading of the text). Now Mat. 14:25 informs us that this happened somewhere around 3:00 AM, and amidst this storm we see, here, that "**they noticed and kept on intently watching Jesus continuously walking around upon the sea.**" Not only this, but He was "**progressively coming to be near the boat.**" But they still did not know that it was Him. And so...

20. **Yet He then says to them, "I am!** (or: It is I.) **Stop fearing!** (or: Don't continue being afraid.)"

He revealed His identity to them (possibly on two different levels, as the translation indicates). The Logos has spoken to them; It (He) imparts a directive that changes their response to the situation. If, during the storms of our lives we can call to mind Jesus saying to us, "**I am! Stop fearing!**," what a help this will be to us.

This incident is loaded with practical life-lessons. Storms can bring an experience of the Lord into our lives. These incidents can dispel our fears and give us new understandings about the Lord. We can come to realize that God is within the storm, and that He surmounts the dangerous waves that come against us. The Lord is in control, we need not fear. As David said, long ago,

> "**You see, even if I may** (or: should; would; could) **be caused to journey** (travel; pass from place to place) **within the midst of a shadow of death** (or: death's shadow; a shadow, from death; a shadow which is death), **I will continue not being caused to fear bad [times]** (will not be repeatedly frightened by worthless [situations or people]; will not be habitually afraid of misfortunes, harmful [experiences] or base [schemes]), **because You are, and continue being, with me**…" (Ps. 23:4, LXX, JM)

Christ comes to us with His perfect Love, and, "**Fear does not exist within the Love, and so, perfect love** (mature love; love having reached its goal) **repeatedly** (habitually; progressively) **throws the fear outside**" (1 Jn. 4:18).

21. **Then they began to be willing and proceeded purposing to receive** (or: take) **Him into the boat. And immediately** (or: instantly; all at once) **the boat came to be upon the land** (perhaps: = ran aground) **into which they had been proceeding under way.**

So when you recognize Him, within the storm, welcome Him into your boat.

This Gospel does not mention the incident of Peter walking on the water (Mat. 14:28-31). Also, Mat. 14:32 tells us that when He came into the boat, "**the wind grew weary and died down**." Here in John, we see a different "SIGN": "**And immediately** (or: instantly; all at once) **the boat came to be upon the land** (perhaps: = ran aground) **into which they had been proceeding under way**."

Now of course, these might have been separate incidents, in the two Gospels. Mat. 14:33 records the disciples' acknowledgement that, "**Truly, You are God's Son**," and describes the scene, that they "**paid Him homage by kneeling down and with obeisance kissing toward Him – some reverently kissing His feet**." John sidesteps the disciples' reactions, keeping the focus on the "sign." Also, Matthew's account describes the rest of the boat trip thusly: "**upon cutting right through [the waters] and traversing across [the lake], they came upon land, [entering] into Gennesaret**." Verse 17, above, has their intended destiny as being Capernaum, and this is where John's narrative picks up (vs. 24, below). Again, we must keep in mind that the author's apparent intent is not to give us "history," but report the signs that He performed (referenced in vs. 26, below) as a setting for His lifting their thinking to a higher level (vs. 27) and to present his readers with a revelation of who Jesus was, and of His relationship to the Father, as we will see…

22. **The next day** (or: On the morrow) **the crowd – the one having stood, and still standing, on the other side of the sea** (or: lake) **– saw that there was no other little boat there, except one, and that Jesus did not enter in together with His disciples, but rather His disciples went** (or: came) **away alone.**
23. **And further, boats from out of Tiberias came near the place where they ate the bread, from the Lord giving thanks** (or: upon expressing gratitude, they ate the bread of the Master [or: = Yahweh]).
24. **Therefore, when the crowd saw that Jesus is not there, nor His disciples, they stepped within – into the little boats – and went into Capernaum, progressively seeking Jesus.**

It is important to our author to show how crowds followed after Jesus. In vss. 2-24 he lays out details of how the crowd concluded where He had gone, in order to follow Him. Here we have portrayed two kinds of followers of Jesus. There were His disciples, and then there were the crowds that wanted to track His behavior (vs. 25), and yet, as Jesus explains (vss. 26-27)…

25. **And later, upon finding Him – on the other side of the sea** (or: lake) **– they said to Him, "Rabbi, when** (or: at what time) **have you come to be here** (or: in this place)**?"**
26. **Jesus decidedly answered them, and says, "It is certainly true** (Amen, amen), **I am saying to you folks, you people continue seeking Me not because you saw signs, but rather because you ate from out of the loaves, and you were fed until satisfied.**

Jesus exposed to them their "earth-bound" motives: food! Here "**the loaves**" are a symbol of the daily needs and desires of the natural life. Nothing wrong with that, but this misses the point of Jesus being the incarnation of the Logos. Jesus covered this topic, in Mat. 6:

> 31. **"Therefore, you folks should not fret, be anxious, be full of care or be worrying, constantly saying, 'What can we eat?' or, 'What can we drink?' or, 'What can we put on ourselves to wear?'**
> 32. **"You see, the ethnic multitudes** (the nations; the Gentile people groups) **are habitually in eager pursuit of these things – spending all of their energy in seeking them! After all, your heavenly Father** (or: your Father Who inhabits, and can be compared to, the atmosphere) **has seen and knows that you folks repeatedly have need for all of these things.**
> 33. **"So you people be habitually and constantly seeking God's reign** (or: sovereign activity and influence; kingdom) **and the eschatological deliverance of fairness and equity from Him, as well as His justice and rightwised behavior in the Way, which He has pointed out in covenant participation that has been set right – and all these things will be added to you!**
> 34. **"Therefore, you folks should not fret, be anxious, be full of care or be worrying [with a fixation] into the next day, for the next day will be concerned about itself** (or: will have anxiety of its own). **Sufficient and adequate for** (or: to; in) **the day [is] its own situation as it ought not to be** (bad quality and worthless condition).

Here in John, we have Jesus speaking of "God's reign and eschatological deliverance" in a way more in line with how our author is presenting Jesus' ministry and goals for Israel, and humanity…

27. **"Stop continuously working or doing business for the food which is continuously disintegrating of itself** (loosing itself away; destroying itself), **but rather [for] the Food continuously remaining** (abiding; dwelling) **on into eonian Life**
> (or: unto life originating from, existing in, having the characteristics and qualities of, the Age [of Messiah]; age-enduring and eon-lasting life) **which the Son of the Man** (of Humanity; of the human; of [Adam]; or: = the Human Being; or: = the eschatological messianic figure) **will continue giving to you** (or: in you; for you) **folks, for This One** (or: This Man) **Father God seals**
> (or: for God, the Father, put [His] seal [showing ownership and/or approval and/or authority] upon a person [doing] this; or: you see, this One the Father sealed: God).**"**

The contrast that Jesus presents in this verse, via the metaphor of the two kinds of foods, is also presented by Paul, via two kinds of mindsets and focuses:

> "**For the result of the thinking** (mind-set; effect of the way of thinking; disposition; result of understanding and inclination; the minding; the opinion; the thought; the outlook) **of the flesh** (= from the human condition or the System of culture and cultus; or: = Torah keeping) **[is; brings] death, yet the result of the thinking** (mind-set; disposition; thought and way of thinking; outlook) **of the spirit** (or: from the Spirit; which is the Breath-effect) **[is; brings] Life and Peace** (joining)" (Rom. 8:6).

This is a beautiful promise: "**the Son of the Man will continue giving to you the Food continuously remaining (abiding; dwelling) on into eonian Life**." Jesus will explain this in more detail, later in this chapter.

The final clause has at least the three renderings that are on offer, here:

a) **for This One** (or: This Man) **Father God seals**. This says that the Father, God, seals "**the Son of the Man**."

b) for God, the Father, put [His] seal [showing ownership and/or approval and/or authority] upon a person [doing] this. Here, "this one" refers to and means "a person **working or doing business for the Food continuously remaining**," and so it is this person that God "put [His] seal upon."

c) you see, this One the Father sealed: God. This rendering follows the exact order of the Greek. It seems awkward, but the terms "the Father" and "God" are separated by the verb, "sealed." My reason for presenting this odd rendering is that Jesus seldom uses the phrase "Father God." Is it saying that the Father sealed "the Son of Man," who is "God"? Is this a subtle "I AM" statement? Or, is it simply saying that the Father, i.e., God, is the One who does the sealing? And what is Jesus inferring by using the verb "seals/sealed (the aorist tense)"? The bracketed expansion offers possible inferences: "showing ownership and/or approval and/or authority."

Ponder all of this, and let the Spirit give you a Breath-effect for the possibilities of what Jesus meant by this.

28. **Then they said to Him, "What should we be habitually doing, so that we would be habitually working God's works** (or: actions or labors having the character of, or pertaining to, God; or: the deeds from God; or: = the things God wants us to do)**?"**

The Logos has been effective: they are no longer focused on getting a meal, but have lifted their thoughts to the topic of "**working God's works** (etc.)." This question, by His audience, is virtually asking the same question that we find being asked of Jesus, in Mk. 10:17,

"**Good Teacher! What should I do** (or: perform) **to the end that I can** (or, as a future: will) **inherit** (receive and enjoy an allotment of) **eonian life** (life pertaining to and having the qualities of the Age; life into the unseeable and indefinite future; life of and for the ages)**?**"

Both questions are about "**doing**," instead of about believing into, and remaining faithful unto, the One that God sends with a mission (*cf* next verse). In chapter 15 we will learn about remaining joined unto the Vine – which is a way of living, not something that is done.

29. **Jesus considered and answered, saying to them, "This is God's Work** (the Action which is God; the Deed from God), **so that you folks would continuously trust and progressively believe into** (or: the work of God: that you can remain faithful unto) **Him whom That One sends** (or: sent) **forth with a mission."**

Jesus presents them with a simple explanation. This is parallel to what Jesus would later tell His disciples,

"**I, Myself, AM** (or: exist being) **the true** (genuine; real) **Grapevine, and My Father is** (continues being) **the One who tends the soil.... The person continuously remaining** (dwelling; abiding) **within the midst of Me – and I within the midst of and in union with him – this one is repeatedly bearing** (bringing forth; = producing) **much fruit. [It is the case] that apart from** (or: Because separated from) **Me you folks continue having ability and power to do** (make; construct; create; form; perform; produce) **nothing!**" (15:1, 5, below)

It is the Vine, and its internal sap (the Spirit), that gives the life and ability to "**continuously trust and progressively believe into [Christ]**."

Another picture of this is seen in Ps. 1:

1. **Happy [is] the adult male who does not journey within counsel from profane and irreverent folks who lack awe and respect for God, and does not stand in a road having the character and qualities of folks who miss the target, and further does not sit upon a seat belonging to troublemakers**

> (or: Blessed [is] the man who has not traveled from one place to another in union with [the] deliberated purpose, design or determination of folks who lack a relationship with God, and did not take a stand in union with [the] way pertaining to those in failure or error, nor make [his] place within the midst of a path of people who deviate, as well as did not take a seat on a chair having the character and qualities of folks who are pests).

2. **But to the contrary, his will, intent and purpose is in union with the Law of [the] Lord** (or: resides within the custom belonging to [Yahweh]; is within the midst of the law which is [Yahweh]), **and within His Law** (or: dispensed and established principle) **will he habitually meditate and give careful thought, day and night.**

3. **And thus, he will continue existing, being like the tree [that] has been planted beside the divided-out paths of the waters** (or: outlets of water through [the orchard]; or: rivulets of the waters that pass through), **which will give** (yield; = produce) **its fruit in its season** (or: fitting situation) **and whose leaf will not proceed in falling off. And so, everything that he should continue doing** (or: all things – however much he can make or produce) **will proceed to be thoroughly prospered** (continuously led down an easy path, or along a good road)! (LXX, JM)

"He will be like the Tree [of Life]… or a Vine…" The Creator of the Tree makes the Tree produce fruit. Jesus could only do the works that He saw the Creator doing. Life produces the works of God, and we trust in that Life.

30. **So then they say to Him, "Then what SIGN are you yourself doing** (making; performing; producing), **so that we can see and believe in** (or: trust and have faith by; be loyal to) **you? What are you, yourself, presently accomplishing** (or: actively working; habitually practicing)?
31. **"Our fathers ate manna within the wilderness** (in the desolate place of the desert), **according as it stands written, 'He gave to them bread from out of the atmosphere** (or: the sky; heaven) **to habitually eat.'"** [Ps. 78:24]

Had they not seen the signs that He had done, and it was because of these (especially the multiplication of food) that they were following after Him? They had wanted to be "**working God's works**" (vs. 28), and Jesus told them what God's work is (vs. 29): "**continuously trust and progressively believe into [the Son].**" Now they ask for a sign, "**so that we can see and believe in** (or: trust and have faith by; be loyal to) **[Him].**" To this they add: "**What are you, yourself, presently accomplishing** (or: actively working; habitually practicing)?" They wanted to "see" so that they could duplicate what He was doing. They were not asking to be His disciples, but they wanted His secret (as they assumed that He had), so that they could produce and multiply bread "**from out of the atmosphere.**"

32. **Therefore Jesus says to them, "Count on this** (Amen, amen): **I am now [emphatically] saying to you folks, Moses does NOT give** (or: did not supply) **the bread from out of the atmosphere** (or: the sky; heaven) **to YOU folks! But rather, My Father is presently** (or: continually; progressively) **giving the true, real, genuine Bread from out of the heaven** (or: the atmosphere) **to, for and among YOU people.**

Jesus brings the conversation away from Israel's history, and focuses on THEM, and the present situation. He is reminding them that, first of all God brought the manna to their fathers, but that ended when they entered the Promised Land, with Joshua. The manna was only for Israel's time in the wilderness, and so it did not come to the rest of their ancestors, nor to THOSE folks who were talking with Jesus. However, the Father was then, and thereafter, "**giving the true, real, genuine Bread from out of the heaven** (or: the atmosphere) **to, for and among YOU people.**" THEY now had the opportunity to have the true, real and genuine Bread of heaven, that is, from the atmosphere which they were at that present time breathing.

In Jesus' statement about Moses not giving the bread, the verb is in the aorist (statement of fact, which is indefinite with regard to time) tense, and can be rendered either as a simple present, "**does NOT give**," or a simple past tense, "did not supply." In both renderings, an important point is that God gave, and still gives, "**bread from the atmosphere**," but the rendering, "**Moses does NOT give**," becomes a reference to the Torah and the old covenant, neither of which can be "**giving the true, real, genuine Bread from out of the heaven**." And so He goes on to explain what this Bread is...

33. **"For God's Bread is** (or: You see the bread which is God, and comes from God, exists being) **the One repeatedly descending** (continually or habitually stepping down) **from out of the midst of the atmosphere** (or: heaven) **and constantly** (or: habitually and progressively) **giving Life to the world** (or: in the organized system and secular society; or: for **the aggregate of humanity** and in the universe).**"**

First of all, take note that the verbs "**descending**" and "**giving**" are in the present tense, and so we have on offer the modifying adverbs: repeatedly; continually; habitually; progressively; constantly. It may be easier to receive this information about "**giving Life**," but what about "**descending**"? Is this an allusion to 1:51, above? In Jn. 1 we came to understand that Christ Jesus was the incarnated Logos (1:14, above). In the Greek translation of the OT (the LXX), the Logos is frequently active, and repeatedly comes in messages from, or of, God to the prophets, etc. Was the manna perhaps a manifestation, a kind of embodiment, of the Logos? In 1 Cor. 10:4, Paul interprets the Rock that gave them water as being "Christ." To the disciples Jesus will later say of the bread, "this is My body."

Jesus' words, here, remind us of what He said to Nicodemus, in 3:13, above,
> "**Furthermore, no one has ascended** (or: stepped up) **into the heaven** (or: atmosphere) **except the One descending** (or: stepping down) **from out of the midst of the atmosphere** (or: heaven): **the Son of Mankind** (the Son of the human [= Adam]; Humanity's Son; the Son of man) **– Who is continuously being** (or: constantly existing) **within the midst of the heaven** (or: atmosphere)."

Let us not miss the universal statement that we read in the second clause: "**constantly** (or: habitually and progressively) **giving Life to the world** (or: in the organized system and secular society; or: for **the aggregate of humanity** and in the universe)." The Greek word *kosmos* has a wide semantic range, as is on offer, here. This was the same word that John used in Jn. 3:16. God's intent is for Life to be given to all humanity, as well as to the "organized system" within which humanity lives. Jesus gives Life to the entire universe. What a future he brought to us, almost 2000 years ago. Christ is our "life-support" system, on all levels of existence. He both constantly, and progressively (in both quality and abundance) gives Life **to** us all. But notice that *kosmos* is in the dative case, here. He gives Life "in the organized system and secular society" – and in fact, in the whole "universe." He gives life everywhere – just observe His creation. He is the Source of Life, so He gives Life "for **the aggregate of humanity**." It was worth repeating this!

34. **Therefore they exclaimed to Him, "O Master** (or: Sir; Lord), **always and ever give this bread to us!"**

Does this remind us of the Samaritan woman's response to Jesus, so that she would not have to repeatedly come to that well for physical water? They were still thinking physically, missing the point that this Bread was a Person.

35. **Jesus said to them, "I, Myself, am** (or: exist being) **the Bread of 'the Life'** (or: the bread which is the Life, and which imparts the Life). **The person progressively coming toward** (or: to; or: face to face

with) **Me may by no means at any point hunger** (or: would under no circumstances be hungry), **and the one constantly trusting and believing into** (or being habitually allegiant and loyal unto) **Me will by no means continue thirsting** (under no circumstances be repeatedly thirsty) **at any time.**

So now He speaks plainly to them, identifying Himself as both "**the Bread of 'the Life',**" and at the same time, "**the One repeatedly descending from out of the midst of the atmosphere.**" Take note of the definite article before the word "Life." He is "THE Bread of THE Life." He is speaking of the Christ Life, which is Resurrection Life. Also observe the optional functions of the genitive case: the bread WHICH IS the Life, and which IMPARTS the Life. He is the Source, the Logos.

Just as with the Water of which Jesus said, "**whoever may** (or: would) **drink from out of the water which I, Myself, will be continuously giving to him will not repeatedly become thirsty, on into the Age**" (Jn. 4:14), so with this Bread, "**The person progressively coming toward** (or: to; or: face to face with) **Me may by no means at any point hunger.**" These folks had not been at the well with Jesus, in Samaria, so He adds that this person "**will by no means continue thirsting.**" Now notice the qualifying condition for this to be so: "**the one constantly trusting and believing into** (or being habitually allegiant and loyal unto) **Me.**" He was the necessary ingredient – not some magic formula or religious ritual.

36. "**But further, I say to you that you folks have also seen Me, and yet you continue not trusting or believing** [Concordant Greek Text adds: Me].

Yes, they had seen the "signs," but their hearts and spirits were not joined unto Him.

37. "**All, which** (may = whom [so, D.B. Hart]) **the Father is progressively giving to Me, will progressively move toward** (will one-after-another keep on coming face-to-face with) **Me to finally arrive here, and the person progressively coming toward Me I may under no circumstances** (or: would by no means) **throw forth from out of the midst** (eject; cast out) **[so that he will be] outside,**

If we temporarily remove the subordinate clause from the first main clause, we have:
> "**All will progressively move toward** (will one-after-another keep on coming face-to-face with) **Me to finally arrive here.**"

We can also read this subordinate clause, "**which…,**" in this way:
> "**ALL, whom** (or: which in fact is what) **the Father is, [in fact,] progressively giving to Me…**"

This, rather than limiting the number, or size of the group, is simply stating that the Father is giving everything and everyone to Christ.

This is why Jesus can make the bold statement about All: they "**will progressively move toward Me.**" This is the Plan. Trust the Plan. If Jesus meant "whoever the Father has given to Me," He would have said that. He moves from the general, and inclusive, All to the particular, and individual, "**the person,**" in the second half of the verse. And when they arrive at the judgment seat of Christ, He "**may under no circumstances** (or: would by no means) **throw [them] forth from out of the midst** (eject; cast out) **[so that he will be] outside.**" Paul affirms this in 1 Cor. 15:22-23a,
> "**For just as within Adam all humans keep on** (or: everyone continues) **dying, in the same way, also, within the Christ, all humans will keep on being made alive** (or: in union with the Anointed One, everyone will one-after-another be created and produced with Life) – **yet each person within the result of his or her own set position [in line]…**"

38. "**because I have stepped down to this level, away from the atmosphere** (or: descended, separating off from the heaven), **not to the end that I should continue doing My will** (purpose; intent), **but to the contrary, the will** (intent; purpose) **of the One sending Me.**

This verse gives the reason for what He just said in vs. 37. Now what did He mean, that He had **"stepped down to this level, away from the atmosphere** (or: descended, separating off from the heaven)"? He left the realm of spirit (Jn. 1:1) and became Flesh (Jn. 1:14). He left the realm of being in the midst of God in order to become the Second Human Being – the Last Adam (1 Cor. 15:45-49). Paul gives us a short history of Jesus Christ, in Phil. 2:

> 6. **Who, starting and continuing as inherently existing** (or: beginning under; subsisting) **within God's form** (or: in an outward mold which is God), **He does not consider the [situation] to be equals in and by God a plunder** (or: a pillaging; a robbery; a snatching; or: a thing or situation seized and held),
>> (or: Who, [although] constantly humbly and supportively ruling in union with an external shape and an outward appearance from God, did not give consideration to a seizure: the [situation] to continuously exist being the same things with God, even on the same levels in God, or equal [things; aspects] to God,)
>
> 7. **but to the contrary, He empties Himself** (or: removed the contents of Himself; made Himself empty), **receiving** (or: taking; accepting) **a slave's form** (external shape; outward mold), **coming to be** (or: birthing Himself) **within an effect of humanity's** (mankind's; people's) **likeness.**
>
> 8. **And so, being found in an outward fashion, mode of circumstance, condition, form-appearance** (or: character, role, phase, configuration, manner) **as a human** (a person; a man), **He lowers Himself** (or: humbled Himself; made Himself low; degrades Himself; levels Himself off), **coming to be** (or: birthing Himself) **a submissive, obedient One** (one who gives the ear and listens) **as far as** (or: to the point of; until) **death – but death of a cross** (torture stake)!

As Israel's Messiah, and "federal Head," He was obedient to the Voice of Yahweh (Jer. 7:23), as Israel, and also, as the Last Adam: Paul explains how this works, in Rom. 5:

> 17. **For since** (or: if) **by the effect of the fall to the side** (or: in the result of the stumbling aside; with the effect of the offense) **of the one The Death reigned** (or: reigns; rules as king) **through that one, much more, rather, will the peoples** (= the masses of humanity) **– in continuously receiving and seizing upon** (taking in hand) **the surrounding superabundance** (encircling, extraordinary surplus and excess) **of the Grace and of, from and which is the gratuitous gift of the liberated Rightwisedness** (of the solidarity in fair and equitable treatment; from the placement in right [covenant]-relationship in the Way; of the justification and freedom from guilt while being turned in the right direction and made right) **– continue reigning** (or: ruling as kings) **within and in union with Life through the One, Jesus Christ.**
>
> 18. **Consequently, then, as [it was] through the effect of one fall to the side** (or: the result of one offense) **[coming] into all mankind** ([permeating] into all humanity; = [extending] into the whole race) **[bringing them] into a commensurate effect of a decision** (a corresponding result of a negative evaluation which fell in line with the decision and followed the pattern which divided [us] down), **THUS ALSO and in the same way, through one just-effect and the result of one right act which set [all humanity] right and in accord with the Way pointed out** (through the result of one act of justice, equity and solidarity; through a single decree creating rightwised relationships; through one effect of rightwising which turns [people] in the right direction) **[it comes] into ALL MANKIND** (all humanity; all people; = the whole race) **[bringing them] into a setting right of Life and a liberating rightwising from Life [including them in covenant community]**
>
> 19. **For you see, JUST AS through the unwillingness to listen, or to pay attention, resulting in disobedience** (or: the erroneous hearing leading to disobedience) **of the one person THE MANY** (= the mass of humanity; note: cf Weymouth NT in Modern Speech, 1909 Edition) **were rendered** (established; constituted; placed down and made to be) **sinners** (failures; ones who diverge and miss the target), **THUS – in the same way – ALSO through the submissive listening and paying attention resulting in obedience of the One, THE MANY** (= the mass of humanity) **will continue being rendered "set-right folks"**

(placed down and established [to be] just ones; constituted folks who have been rightwised to be people in the Way pointed out; made righteous ones who are guilt-free, fair, equitable, and rightly-turned in the solidarity of covenant relationships).

What was "**the will** (intent; purpose) **of the One sending [Him]**"? Jn. 3:16 gave us the answer:
> "**that all humanity, which** (or: everyone, who) – **when progressively trusting and successively believing into Him and thus being constantly faithful to Him – would not lose or destroy itself, or cause itself to fall into ruin, but rather can continuously have** (or: would habitually possess and hold) **eonian life.**"

39. "**Now this is the purpose** (intent; will) **of the One sending Me: that all, that** (or: everything, which) **He has given to Me, so that it is now Mine, I will proceed to** (or, as an aorist subjunctive: may; can; should; would) **lose nothing from out of it, but further, I will proceed to** (or: should; would) **raise it up to, in and with This Last Day** (or: by the Last Day; for the final Day).

This verse directly gives the explanation of vs. 38b. The inclusive statements of vss. 37 and 39 simply repeat the message of 3:35, above,
> "**The Father continuously loves and fully gives Himself to the Son, and He has given all humanity** (or, as a neuter: all things) **[to Him] so that He has it** (or: them) **as a gift within His hand.**"

We find this echoed in Mat. 11:27,
> "**All humanity was transferred, given over** (or: All things were delivered and committed) **to Me by, and under, My Father...**"

Eph. 1:22-23 gives another witness:
> "**and then placed and aligned all people in humbleness under His feet** [Ps. 8:6b; LXX]
> (or: and arranges everyone in a supportive position by His feet; or: then by the feet – which are Him – He subjects all things), **and yet gives** (or: gave) **Him, [as] a Head** (or: Source; origin and beginning of a series; or: extreme and top part) **over all humanity and all things, for the called-out community**
> (or: and as a Head over all humanity, gave Him to the summoned and gathered assembly; or: and then by the called-forth congregation He gives Him [to be the] Source over [the situation] of, and for, all humanity),
> **which [community] is His body, the result of the filling from, and which is, the One Who is constantly filling all things within all humanity** (or: humans)."

But here in John we will find yet another inclusive witness, as Jesus addresses the Father:
> "**Correspondingly as You give** (or: gave) **to Him right, privilege and authority from out of Being concerning ALL flesh** (= people) **to the end that ALL, which You have given to Him and that He now possesses, to THEM He will continue** (or: one-after-another be) **giving** [other MSS: would at some point give] **eonian Life** (life having its origin in, and the characteristics and qualities of, the Age [of Messiah]; or: age-enduring life; life of, for and in the ages)" (17:2, below).

That He will "**lose nothing**" echoes what He said about the bread fragments, in vs. 12, above. This reveals the scope and character of His work, and of the Father's purposes. What is temporarily lost, or destroyed, He "**will proceed to raise it up to, in and with This Last Day.**" The form of the verb in this clause functions either as a future tense, or as an aorist subjunctive (on offer in the parenthetical alternative). The bold character of the whole verse leans toward the positive, future reading, but either is possible.

I offer the demonstrative function of the definite article (**This**) modifying "**Last Day**," reading this term as a reference to Himself, and an echo of 5:21, 24-25, 28-29, above. Jesus was that Last Day (just as He was the Last Adam), and He brought the last days of the Mosaic covenant, which ended in AD 70. He uses the same phrase in the next verse, as He gives further explanation of His meaning. But the renderings "the Last Day; final Day" are also parenthetically on offer. The entire phrase is in the dative case, so observe its potential functions: "to; in; with; by; for." Meditate on the differences each preposition offers to our understanding of Jesus' words.

40. **"You see, this is the purpose** (will; intent) **of My Father, to the end and intent that all mankind – which, in continuously watching** (or: the one repeatedly gazing at) **the Son, in contemplative discernment, and then progressively trusting** (believing) **into Him – would possess** (or: can have; may hold) **Life, Whose source is the Age** (or: eonian life; life having the qualities and characteristics of the Age [of Messiah]; an age-enduring and eon-lasting life), **and I will proceed to** (or: can; should; would) **be raising him up to and for this Last Day** (or: in the Last Day; by and with the final day).**"**

The compound, dependent participial clause that is set off in brackets ("**which, in continuously watching** {or: the one repeatedly gazing at} **the Son, in contemplative discernment, and then progressively trusting** {believing} **into Him**") is attributive, modifying "**all mankind**." This compound clause explains how "**all mankind… would possess** (or: can have; may hold) **Life**…" As an analogy, in the natural, a person only has life by continuously breathing. In the realm of the Spirit, or in the sphere of kingdom Life, a person is only alive in this Life by "**continuously watching** (or: repeatedly gazing at) **the Son**," which in turn creates "**progressively trusting** (believing) **into Him**." Compare this to Jesus telling us that we must "abide in the Vine" (Jn. 15:1ff). Furthermore, in the watching and gazing, the Greek term implies that our author meant that this needed to be done "**in contemplative discernment**." Paul put it this way, in 2 Cor. 3:18,

> "**we all, ourselves – having a face that has been uncovered and remains unveiled – being folks who by a mirror are continuously observing, as ourselves, the Lord's glory** (or: being those who progressively reflect – from ourselves as by a mirror – the assumed appearance and repute of, and from, [our] Owner), **are presently being continuously and progressively transformed into the very same image and form, from glory unto glory – in accord with and exactly as – from [the] Lord's Breath-effect**."

The author of Heb. 12:1b-2a gave us this description:

> "**we can and should through persistent remaining-under** (or: relentless patient endurance and giving of support) **keep on running the racecourse** [Gal. 5:7] **continuously lying before us** (or: lying in the forefront within us; or: lying ahead, among us), **turning [our] eyes away from other things and fixing them** (or: looking away) **into Jesus, the Inaugurator** (First Leader; Prime Author) **and Perfecter** (Finisher; the Bringer-to-maturity and fruition; He who purposes and accomplishes the destiny) **of the faith, trust, confidence and loyal allegiance**."

You see, this Life is a life that we actually live, and it involves all of that which these three authors have laid out for us. John gives a further description of the Life that the Father intends for us to possess: it is the "**Life, Whose source is the Age** (or: eonian life; life having the qualities and characteristics of the Age [of Messiah]; an age-enduring and eon-lasting life)." This is more than just physically being alive.

Now this is the first part of what John describes as, "**the purpose** (will; intent) **of My Father**, but it is not the entirety of His "**end and intent**." The second half of the verse tells us what Jesus will DO with this Life: "**I will proceed to** (or: can; should; would) **be raising him up to and for this last Day** (or: in the Last Day; by and with the final day)." This is the same Last Day to which He had just referred, in the previous verse. It is resurrection Life that He gives to us now, while at the same time "**raising [us] up**" together with Him (Eph. 2:6). To get another picture of this, let us visit three verses in Rom. 6:

> 5. **For since** (or: You see, if) **we have been birthed** (have become; have come to be) **folks engrafted and produced together** (or: planted and made to grow together; brought forth together; congenital) **in, by, to and with the result of the likeness of** (or: the effect of the similar manner from) **His death, then certainly we will also continue existing [in and with the effects of the likeness]** of The Resurrection
> > (or: which IS the resurrection; or: from, and with qualities of, the resurrection)….

8. Now since we died together with Christ, we are continuously believing (relying; trusting) **that we will also continue living together in Him** (by Him; for Him; to Him; with Him)....
11. Thus you folks, also, be logically considering (reckoning, accounting and concluding) **yourselves to exist being... ones continuously living by God** (in God; for God; to God; with God), **within Christ Jesus, our Owner** (or: in union with [the] Anointed Jesus, our Lord and Master).

Now, on the idea of "watching/gazing at," see Rev. 14:10, where it speaks of beholding the little Lamb, in His presence. Also read the story of how the Israelites were healed by just "looking at" the serpent on the pole, in Nu. 21:8-9.

41. Therefore the Judeans (= religious authorities of the Jews) **began a buzz of discontented complaining and critical comments, and were progressively murmuring like a swarm of bees concerning Him, because He said, "I, Myself, am** (or: exist being) **the Bread – the One stepping down** (or: descending) **from out of the midst of the heaven** (or: the atmosphere),"

Here, the author is referencing vss. 33 and 35a, above. It could be that their "swarming" discontent about what He had said in those verses made them completely miss what He proceeded to say in vss. 35b-40. They continue on in this way in the next verse. His statement, here, calls to mind 1:51, above.

42. and they kept on saying, "Is this not Jesus, the son of Joseph, whose father and mother we have seen and know? How [other MSS: How then] **is he now presently saying that 'I have stepped down** (or: descended) **from out of the midst of the heaven** (or: the sky)'?"**

There was no spiritual understanding in them. All that they could see was this human being standing before them – and they knew who His parents were, as also Lu. 3:23 records, in Jesus' genealogy:
> "And so this same Jesus, Himself starting to rule (or: progressively beginning), **was about thirty years [old], being a son – as it continued commonly supposed and established by Law, custom, and thus legally – of Joseph.**"

And so Jesus interrupts them...

43. Jesus decidedly answered, and says to them, "Stop the grumbling buzz of murmuring (undertoned mutterings of critical and discontented comments like a swarm of bees) **with one another!**

He first has to silence their buzz of murmuring, and refocus them to what He would now say...

44. "No one is able (or: is presently having power) **to come toward Me unless the Father – the One sending Me – should drag him [as with a net]** (or: draw him [as drawing water in a bucket or a sword from its sheath]), **and I Myself will progressively raise him up** (proceed to resurrect him; continue standing him back up again) **within** (or: in union with) **This Last** (the eschatos) **Day.**

What graphic speech! Consider this picture: "**drag him [as with a net]** (or: draw him [as drawing water in a bucket or a sword from its sheath])!" There can be little doubt from this that Jesus is saying that for a person to "**come toward [Him]**" the Father must do all the action, all the work, and in fact the entire deed of a person "coming to Jesus." There is no "making a decision to accept Jesus as your personal Lord and Savior," which, of course, He is. But there is, in what Jesus just said, no involvement of the human will in a person coming to Christ – any more than there is in a person being born again, from above (i.e., by first the Father/Spirit implanting the Seed of Christ into the person). The Father casts the net, and then drags folks to Christ – while they are yet dead. In the sphere of the Spirit, in the realm of the Life of Christ, and in the kingdom of God, a dead person has no free will – in fact he has no will at all.

And THEN, Christ "**will progressively raise him up** (proceed to resurrect him; continue standing him back up again) **within** (or: in union with) **This Last** (the eschatos) **Day**" – the Day which is Christ Himself. In vs. 65, below, Jesus says this same thing, in a different way. Instead of "dragging," He describes it as "giving; granting":

> "**Because of this I have told you folks that no one is presently able** (or: continues having power) **to come toward** (or: face-to-face with) **Me, unless [the situation] may be existing of it having been granted or given to him from out of the Father** (or: unless he or she should be a person having been given in Him, forth from the Father)."

Life, deliverance, salvation, resurrection – they are all the work and involvement of the Father.

45. **"It exists having been written within the Prophets: 'And all humans** (all people) **will continue existing being God's taught-ones** (or: folks having had instruction from God).' [Isa. 54:13] All humanity – which, in hearing from the Father** (or: the person listening at the Father's side), **and learning** [D and others read: progressively learning] **– is progressively coming toward Me!**

Once again, John uses a dependent participial clause, attributively, to describe the means of people coming to Jesus. And take note that it is through the work and action of the FATHER! Now it is not dragging, or giving, but "**in hearing from the Father**." The Father must speak the LOGOS into them, and as they are listening "**and learning**," then, "**being God's taught-ones**," "**All humanity is progressively coming toward Me**."

This was promised through the prophet Isa., "**All humans** (all people) **will continue existing being God's taught-ones**." Wow! What good news. So how does this happen? In their "**hearing from the Father**." God speaks to them. But Jesus does now explain, or LIMIT, how the Father does this. He leaves it open-ended. It is like His creation: God speaks, and life is created (e.g., in Gen. 1). Now we know that Jesus calls folks to go and do this very thing, but He does not limit the ways or means. Think of Saul, on the road to Damascus…

Observe that Jesus uses the word "ALL" twice in this verse: "All humans," "All humanity." There is no ambiguity here.

46. **"Not that anyone has seen the Father, except the person continuously being at God's side** (or: existing from God) **– this person** (or: One) **has seen the Father.**

Jesus may be speaking generally, "anyone; the person; this person," or, specifically, "this One," referring to Himself, with the final clause, "**this person** (or: One) **has seen the Father**." Jesus was "**continuously being at God's side**," observing what He was doing. From Jn. 14:9, we suggest that the disciples were seeing the Father, but were not aware of it. They were standing at God's side when they stood alongside Jesus and were being "God's taught-ones." In 14:9, below, Jesus' question to Philip seems to indicate surprise when he asked Him to show them the Father. Jesus responded to him:

> "**I continue being (I am) with you folks so much time, and you have not come to intimately and experientially be aware of, know and recognize Me, Philip? The person having discerned and seen Me has seen, and now perceives, the Father!**"

It took time for His disciples to spiritually mature. We read about mature followers of Christ in Heb. 5:14-6:1a,

> "**But solid food belongs to perfected ones** (complete and mature ones; ones who are fully developed and have reached the goal of their destiny) **– those, because of habit, having organs of perception trained as in gymnastic exercise and thus being skilled, because of practice, and disciplined with a view to a discerning both good and evil** (both that which is excellent, ideal, of good quality, profitable and beautiful, as well as that which is of bad quality, worthless, ugly or of bad form), **through which [practice and exercise], in at some point leaving behind** (or: letting flow away) **the word from the beginning, in regard to the Christ**

(or: the message pertaining to the origin of, and Beginning which is, the Christ; or: the primary thought about the Anointed One [= the Messiah]) **[they] can be continuously and progressively brought upon** (or: carried on [to]) **the realization of the end in view** (or: the accomplished goal of maturity; completion of the destined, finished product)…"

Take note of what this says: "**those, because of habit, having organs of perception trained as in gymnastic exercise and thus being skilled, because of practice, and disciplined with a view to a discerning.**" This describes a condition of maturity in which we can discern the Father in people, and see Him continuously working in our world. This is what it means to be "joined to the Lord," and thus, to be "One Spirit (or, spirit)" (1 Cor. 6:17). We are also reminded, here, of Mat. 5:8,

> "**Those who are clean** (clear of admixture; pure; consistent) **in the heart [are] happy and blessed, because they, themselves, will progressively see God!**
>> (or: = The folks that have had the core of their beings made clean [are] happy people, in that they will continue to see the Ground of Being [in everything]!)."

It takes the work of Christ, through His Spirit, within us to make us clean, clear of admixture, pure and consistent.

47. "**It is certainly true** (or: Amen, amen), **I am saying to you folks, the person presently and continuously trusting** (or: constantly believing; progressively faithing-it; continuing loyal) **presently and continuously has and holds eonian Life** (life having its source, qualities and characteristics from the Age [of the Messiah]; age-enduring and eon-lasting life; or: = the life of the coming Age)!

Might we conclude that by saying this, immediately following what He had just said, that Jesus is equating having and holding "**eonian Life (etc.)**" with "**continuously being at God's side**" and "**[seeing] the Father**"? We think so. Now also observe that He did NOT say that you must trust and believe in order to have eonian Life. No, He is instead identifying the person who presently possesses eonian Life: it is the one "**presently and continuously trusting (etc.)**." One must already have and hold eonian Life in order to trust, believe, faith-it and be loyal. Life is the gift of God. Having Life enables everything else that flows from this Life.

48. "**I, Myself, am** (or: continuously exist being) **the 'Bread of the Life'** (or: the bread which is life and which gives and imparts life),

"**The Life**," to which Jesus is referring, is the "**eonian Life**" of which He spoke, in the previous verse. He has not changed the subject, but is expanding it and taking his listeners to a different realm of thinking. He is the Food of this Life, in contrast to what Israel ate in their wilderness wanderings, and in contrast to the bread with which He fed the 5000, in vss.2-13, above.

49. "**– your fathers ate the manna within the wilderness** (desert; desolate place), **and they died.**

Therefore, their fathers did not eat "**the 'Bread of the Life'.**" There is a different "manna" that is promised to the "overcomer," in Rev. 2:17

> "**By and in the one** (or: To the person) **habitually overcoming** (repeatedly conquering), **by and in him** (or: to him; for him) **I will continue giving manna having been hidden…**"

Here the "hidden manna" may be an allusion to the pot of manna which was laid up in the ark, in the holy of holies. We are informed of this in Heb. 9:3-4,

> "**But after the second veil, a tabernacle being called the set-apart of the set-apart ones** (the Holy of Holies; the separated one of the separated ones; = the most set-apart), **having the ark of the arrangement** (or: chest pertaining to the covenant), **having been covered round about by gold, in which [was] a golden pot** (or: urn) **continuously holding** (or: having) **the manna, and Aaron's rod – the one sprouting** (budding) **– and the tablets of the arrangement** (disposition; covenant)."

The concept of "manna from on high" being available "**when the effect of the filling of the time came** (or: that which was filled up by time reached full term)" – Gal. 4:4a – was, among some Jewish groups of this era, understood as an eschatological gift from God at the time of the "consummation." We read in the Syriac Apocalypse of *2 Baruch* 29:3, 6-8 (written in the early 2nd cent. AD) the following:

"And it will happen that when all that which should come to pass in these parts has been accomplished, the Anointed One will begin to be revealed.... And those who are hungry will enjoy themselves... For winds will go out in front of me every morning to bring the fragrance of aromatic fruits and clouds at the end of the day to distill the dew of health. And it will happen at that time that the treasury of manna will come down again from on high, and they will eat of it in those years because these are they who will have arrived at the consummation of time" (translated by A.F.J. Klijn, *The OT Pseudepigrapha*, Vol. 2, ibid pp 630-31).

But Jesus continues in this teaching...

50. "**This is** (or: continuously exists being) **the Bread which is repeatedly** (or: constantly) **stepping down from out of the atmosphere** (or: progressively descending from heaven) **to the end that ANYONE may eat from out of It and not die** (or: he can, or would, not die; [B reads: and he can continue not dying]).

In this verse, and in the next, Jesus again emphasizes where it is that He came from: **the atmosphere,** or, heaven. Was this Jesus' opaque way of saying that He was born from above? He repeats it in vs. 58, below. Whereas the fathers, in Israel's history, had died – even though they ate manna from the atmosphere (vs. 31, above) – **ANYONE may eat from out of [this new Manna], and NOT die.**" This passage, from vs. 32-51, is Jesus teaching the people about the new Exodus, and about Provision that is available in this new arrangement. In this new creation, Jesus is **the 'Bread of the Life.' HE** is "**the Bread which is repeatedly** (or: constantly) **stepping down from out of the atmosphere** (or: progressively descending from heaven)."

No longer is it just Israel who will have access to this new Manna, but ANYONE may eat from out of it (or, Him). Those who do so do not die. The new covenant is not a covenant of death, but a Covenant of Life – the Life of the Age of the Messiah. Recall Jesus' words in 11:25-26, below, where there He said that He is "**the Resurrection and the Life**" and those trusting and believing into Him **will continue Living**.

51. "**I, Myself, am** (or: continuously exist being) **the continuously living Bread – the One stepping down** (or: descending) **from out of the midst of the atmosphere** (or: heaven). **If anyone should eat from out of this Bread, he will continue living on into the Age. Now also, the Bread which I, Myself, will continue giving, over** (or: for the sake of; on behalf of) **the life of the world** (the ordered system; or: = 'the totality of human social existence' – Walter Wink; or: the aggregate of humanity), **is** (or: continuously exists being) **My flesh!**"

From Jesus' statement in vs. 50, His listeners may have still been thinking in terms of "manna" – but perhaps a new kind of manna, where, unlike their ancestors in the wilderness, if they ate from this Bread then they would not physically die – according to what Jesus had just told them. But from this next statement, He removes any such erroneous thinking and tells them plainly that He was referring to Himself as being "**the continuously living Bread,**" and that therefore He, Himself, is "**the One stepping down** (or: descending) **from out of the midst of the atmosphere** (or: heaven)."

Take note of the durative (ongoing) aspect of the verb, "**will continue living on into the Age.**" This is another way of saying that "**ANYONE may eat from out of It and not die**" (vs. 50). The last statement of this verse takes His audience to the logical conclusion: if He is the living Bread, and "**If anyone should eat from out of this Bread,**" then they would have to eat His "**flesh.**" Now the natural mind finds it hard to wrap itself around this saying. But notice the enigmatic qualification which Jesus offers in this last pronouncement: the Bread which He, Himself, is, He "**will continue giving, over** (or: for the sake of; on behalf of) **the life of the world**." Now this is sacrificial language, and His audience would have understood that it was. In effect, He was saying that He was going to be the Passover Lamb, which would give Life to the People on their new exodus journey from out of their existence of slavery. He both repeated and expanded this, in vss. 53-58, below. He was joining an allusion to the original Passover meal to an allusion to God's provision for Israel during their 40 years in the wilderness.

Notice that He did NOT say "over the life of Israel." This was the New Age. Now He was giving Himself as Bread for the sake of "the aggregate of humanity," and this can also be read as, "on behalf of the ordered system" – which could refer to the nation of Israel, or to even the entire Roman Empire, and beyond. His whole BEING was going to feed, and give Life to, EVERYONE!

So, how are we to understand what He meant by, "**My flesh**"? Jesus explained this to His disciples during their private meal before the final Passover:

> "**Now during the progression of their eating [the meal], upon taking the loaf of [unleavened?] bread and saying words of ease and well-being** (or: speaking blessing [to them?]), **Jesus broke [it in pieces]. And then at giving [them] to the disciples, He said, 'You folks take [it]** (or: receive [this]). **Eat [it] at once. This is My body** (or: This is the body which is Me)'" (Mat. 26:26).

Luke's version of this adds, "...**the one presently and continuously being given over you folks** (or: that which is customarily given on your behalf and over your [situation])" (Lu. 22:19b). Paul cited this event, in 1 Cor. 11:

> 24. **and then, with gratitude and expressing the ease of grace, broke it in pieces and said,** "[some MSS add: You folks take {it}; eat {it}.] **This is My body, being now broken over [the situation and condition of] you folks** (or: for you people; on your behalf). **Keep doing this, into the calling up of the memory pertaining to Me** (or: with a view to remembering Me; or: unto a remembering of what is Mine)."

Paul is referencing the tradition that was passed along to him and which he had then passed along to those in Corinth. But let us look at another level of interpretation. Recall 1 Cor. 10:17, "**Because we, The Many, are** (exist being) **One Bread** (one loaf of bread), **One Body**..." As followers and imitators of Christ, THEY should be "**broken**" for those in need among and around them. He gave Himself for others; they (and we) are to do the same! His followers are called to do the works that He did:

> "**It is certainly true, I am saying to you folks, the person habitually trusting and progressively believing into Me, the works** (actions; deeds) **which I Myself am constantly doing** (habitually performing; progressively making, constructing, creating, forming) **that person also will proceed doing**..." (14:12, below).

Dan Kaplan points us to Jesus' definition of "bread" (literally: food) in 4:34, above,

> "**My food is** (or: exists being) **that I should do** (can perform; would produce; [other MSS: can continuously be doing; or: habitually do]) **the will, intent and purpose of the One sending Me, and that I should and would bring His work to its purposed goal and destiny** (or: can complete His act; may finish and perfect His deed)."

He also took us back to the tabernacle/temple setting, where in the holy place (a figure of the called-out community {Rev. 1:20b} and the realm of the ministry of the priests) there was the Table of the "Bread of the Presence" (Ex. 25:30 that was food for the priests. There were twelve loaves put on that Table, daily (their "daily bread" – Mat. 6:11), each loaf representing one of the twelve tribes, a figure of the universal Body of Christ. As Christ's priests, we are to partake of Him (the Bread of Life) daily. While our thoughts are on this setting, let us share more of Dan's insights:

In the holy place, there was also the Lampstand (Ex. 25:31-37), which had 7 branches (alluded to in the 7 communities in Rev. 2-3). Dan sees the center one, as Christ (the Vine; the Head/Source of the Lampstand), and the remaining 6 branches as a figure of the humanity of this Lampstand. He also noted that this Lampstand was the only article of furniture in the holy place that had no measurements given to it (which calls to mind the Spirit being given "without measure" – 3:34, above), and as Dan says, "The Holy Spirit cannot be measured."

The Lampstand burned olive oil (a figure of God's Spirit, the Source of the Anointing, and of Light, within the holy place) – a figure of God consuming Himself (Fire burning the Oil of the Spirit) to give us the Light. Dan posits that the oil was the "blood" of the Lampstand, and was a picture of the blood of Christ giving Life and Light to the communities. Without His Fire, there was no Light in the holy place. Dan pointed out that the Lamp "illuminates our hearts," while the Bread "feeds us." He also posited that the sacrificial Lamb represented Adam, and all the blood had to be drained from it (the life of the old Adam had to be drained out). The soul was in the blood, and in this sacrifice (figure of the cross), the old man of the heart (the soul of the old Adam) was destroyed (Mat. 16:25), in order to "find" the new soul (Mat. 16:25) of the Second Humanity (1 Cor. 15:45-49).

52. **Therefore, the Jews** (= religious authorities of Judea) **began violently arguing** (disputing; warring [with words]) **toward one another, constantly saying, "How is this one presently able to give us his flesh to eat?"**

These particular Judeans were still thinking in terms of the material world, and of the literal flesh of the man in front of them. This is like Nicodemus' response to Jesus telling him that he needed to be born from above. Nic responded in terms of his mother's womb. Jesus' words, here, incited "**violently arguing**." Now observe, they were not arguing directly with Jesus, but "**toward one another**." Does this suggest that some of them might have been perceiving Jesus as having spoken metaphorically? John does not tell us. However, the text does not say that they immediately rejected what He said, but were "disputing" about "**How is this one presently able**" to do this. Keep in mind that this discussion was happening in a synagogue (vs. 59, below). They were familiar with the sacrificial system. The priests ate some of the meat of the burnt offerings and sin-offerings (Lev. 6:25-26). It is possible that Paul was alluding to this passage in John, when in 2 Cor. 5:21 he said:

> "**for you see, He made** (or: formed) **the One not at any point knowing failure** (sin; error; mistake) **by intimate experience [to take the place of; to be] failure over us and our [situation]** (or: He constructed and produced a sin [offering], for our sake, the Person who was not having an experiential knowledge of missing the target or making a mistake)…"

On offer in the parenthetical rendering is the idea of Christ as a sacrifice. You will note that, with the more common rendering of what I first give as "**failure**," we see that God "constructed and produced a **sin** [offering], for our sake…" I have followed the *Concordant Literal NT*, by supplying (here in brackets) the word "offering." Now the rationale and basis for this addition is that the OT reference to a "sin offering" was sometimes indicated by simply using the word "sin." Due to this precedence, I have also offered this potential understanding of Paul's meaning here. We find a similar picture in the vision of Christ as "**a little Lamb standing, as one having been slaughtered**" (Rev. 5:7).

53. **Then Jesus said to them, "Most truly** (Amen, amen) **I am now laying out the arrangement for** (or: saying to) **you people: unless you folks should at some point eat the flesh of the Son of the Human** (the Son of man; = the eschatological messianic figure), **and then would drink His blood** (or: since you would not eat the flesh which is the Human Being, and further, drink His blood), **you are continuing not holding** (or: habitually having or presently possessing) **Life within yourselves!**

This verse, and on through vs. 58, must be taken metaphorically, in the sense that we discussed above (on vs. 51) in reference to Mat. 26:26-29, and Lu. 22:19-20, where Luke's version gives, in vs. 20,

> "**This, The Cup – [being; representing] the new arrangement** (or: the covenant which is new in character and quality) **in union with, centered in, and within the midst of, My blood** (or: the blood which is Me) **– [is] the one presently and continuously being poured out over you folks** (or: that which is customarily being poured out on your behalf)."

In Lev. 17:11, Israel was instructed that "the life (literally: soul) of the flesh [is] in the blood, and I have given it to you upon the altar to make an atonement for your souls..." This was why they were instructed, in Lev. 17:10, that they were not to eat any kind of blood. With Jesus and His audience knowing this, was His meaning that they were to drink in His soul, His inner life and character? Whether bread, flesh, water or wine (used in Jesus' last supper), the idea was to receive the nourishment in order to have Life. Jesus used the Vine metaphor in Jn. 15, where the branches would "suck up" the sap of the Vine in order to produce fruit.

54. **"The person habitually eating** (continuously chewing or masticating) **My flesh and drinking My blood is continuously possessing** (habitually holding; progressively having) **eonian Life** (life derived from and having the qualities of the Age; age-enduring and eon-lasting life), **and I Myself will proceed raising, resurrecting and standing him back up again in this Last Day** (or: for and by the last Day),

Jesus uses the rhetorical teaching device of restatement to drive-home His message. Partaking of Him, by listening, trusting and believing into Him, brought **eonian Life**. You see, He was not speaking of anything physical – He was speaking of Kingdom Life; the Life of the Spirit. And He ends this verse by tying "eonian Life" to resurrection, and the last Day (repeating vss. 39b and 40b) – both of which He was.

55. **"for My flesh is** (or: constantly exists being) **true** (real; genuine) **food, and My blood is** (or: continuously exists being) **true** (real; genuine) **drink.**

Christ is the Messianic Banquet Meal. Christ was the Rock that gave Israel spiritual drink in the wilderness. Paul understood this metaphor, and shared it with the folks in Corinth:
> "**and they all ate the same spiritual food, and they all drank the same spiritual drink, for they kept on drinking from out of a spiritual bedrock** (or: cliff rock; rock mass) – **one continually following along behind** (or: progressively accompanying [them]). **Now the bedrock** (or: cliff rock) **was the Christ** (or: the rock mass was existing being the Anointing)" (1 Cor. 10:3-4).

What Jesus calls "**true food and true drink**," Paul referred to as "**spiritual food and spiritual drink.**"

56. **"The person habitually eating** (constantly chewing [on]) **My flesh and repeatedly drinking My blood is continuously remaining** (abiding; dwelling) **within the midst of, and in union with, Me – and I Myself within the midst of, and in union with, him.**

Where Jesus instructs them about "**is continuously remaining** (abiding; dwelling) **within the midst of, and in union with, Me,**" He explains, in Jn. 15:1ff, about folks being branches that needed to remain (abide; dwell) in the Vine (Jesus), in order to have the Life of the Vine. Here, He is speaking about taking a meal. In Ps. 34:8a we read, "O taste and see, that Yahweh [is] good!" Then in 8b David associates this with "trusting Him."

But notice the locative (location) force of the preposition *en*: **within the midst of, and in union with**. To feed upon Him is to DWELL within the midst of Him. But also, it means that HE also DWELLS within the midst of US! This is amazing! The idea of "union" is also precious, for the metaphor draws upon the concept of copulation, which, as in Jn. 15, signifies being such a "part of" that one can produce Christ's (or, the Spirit's) fruit. I did not include the rendering of *en* as, "centered in" (although that is completely viable), because of its more abstract nature – being both less intimate and less located – but it certainly fits, as well. In an article that he shared with me, Paul Cruice points us to this same concept that expresses the relationship between the Father and the Son, in Jn. 10:38b,
> "**that you may come to experientially know and habitually trust that** (or: because) **the Father [is] within Me, and I [am] within the Father.**" *Cf* Jn. 14:10-11; 1 Jn. 3:24

57. **"Just as** (or: In corresponding accordance as) **the continuously-living Father sent Me off** (or: forth) **as an Emissary** (or: commissions Me as a Representative and sends Me on a mission), **and I Myself am continuously living through** (or: because of) **the Father, likewise the person who is habitually eating** (repeatedly chewing and feeding [on]) **Me, that person will also continue living, through** (or: because of; by means of) **Me.**

Here, Jesus connects **living** with **eating**. How was Jesus "**continuously living through** (or: because of) **the Father**"? It was via the Spirit of God that Anointed Him, and also because of the Logos of God that inhabited Him. It is the same with Jesus and us. We "**continue living, through** (or: because of; by means of) **[Him].**" Below, in vs. 63 we will read a key that will unlock our understanding of all this passage:

> "**The Spirit** (or: Breath-effect; or: spirit; Breath; Attitude) **is** (or: continues being) **the One continuously creating Life** (or: repeatedly making alive; habitually forming life). **The flesh continues being of no help or benefit to anything** (furthers or augments not one thing). **The declarations** (gush-effects; spoken words; sayings; results of the Flow) **which I, Myself, have spoken to you folks are** (or: continue to be) **Spirit** (or: spirit; Breath-effect; attitude) **and they are** (or: continue being) **Life.**"

You see, Jesus was not speaking about His literal flesh.

58. **"This is** (or: continuously exists being) **the Bread: the One stepping down** (or: descending) **from out of the midst of heaven** (or: [the] sky and atmosphere) **– not according as the fathers ate and died. The person habitually eating** (continually chewing and feeding [on]) **this Bread will continue living** [*p*66 & others read middle: will in (or: of) himself continue living; D reads present: is continuously living] **on into the Age."**

Once more, repetition, to drive-home His teaching. We all need to hear things more than once, and the truth of this passage contains multiple witnesses within it. The Bread is a Person: Christ. We must habitually eat Him in order to "**continue living.**" It is not a one-time thing, or even a once-a-week thing. We need to continually chew this Bread. Paul gave us important instruction in 2 Cor. 5:16,

> "**we, from the present moment** (or: from now) **[on], have seen and thus know** (or: perceive; or: are acquainted [with]) **no one on the level of flesh** (= in the sphere of the estranged human nature; = in correspondence to the self that is enslaved to the System; = according to the old covenant), **if even we have intimately, by experience, known Christ** ([the] Anointed One) **on the level of flesh** (or: = in the sphere of estranged humanity; or: = in correspondence to a self that is oriented to the System; = according to the old covenant), **nevertheless we now** (in the present moment) **no longer continue [thus] knowing [Him or anyone].**"

This is why Jesus kept on referring to Himself as the One descending from heaven. We see another one descending from heaven, in Rev. 21:2 – a corporate Bride, New Jerusalem. She has been joined to the Lord, and is one spirit with Him (1 Cor. 6:17).

59. **He said these things, while repeatedly teaching within a synagogue in Capernaum.**
60. **Therefore, many from out of His students** (the learners following His teachings), **upon hearing [this], said, "This word** (message; saying; thought; idea; communicated information) **is hard and rough – who is able to continue hearing from it** (or: listening to its [message])**?"**

Notice that it is not the scribes or Pharisees that say this: it was MANY from among His students that said this. We will see that these folks no longer continued to be His students (vs. 66, below).

61. **Now Jesus, knowing from having seen within Himself that His students** (disciples) **are continuing to buzz in discontented complaint** (murmur; grumble; hold puzzled conversations) **about this** (or: around this [subject]), **says to them, "Is this continuing to trip you folks up** (or: Is this now snaring or trapping you; or: = Is this a problem for you)**?**

134

Jesus confronted them about their discontented complaint and puzzled conversations. Knowing that it was "tripping" and "trapping" them, He gives them something more to contemplate...

62. **"Suppose, then, you could continuously watch** (contemplatively gaze at) **the Son of Mankind** (the Son of the Human; = the Human Being; messianic figure) **progressively stepping back up again** (or: presently ascending) **to where He was being before** (or: continued existing formerly)!

Notice that He speaks in the third person, using the eschatological title "**the Son of Mankind**" of whom Daniel said that He would be "coming with the clouds (i.e., in the atmosphere)" (Dan. 7:13). Jesus was forcing them to really think about the extreme situation that had come to them, and to realize that He was not just another prophet or an ordinary rabbi. He had come from the realm of spirit, and would later step back up to that realm, once again (after His death on the cross). *Cf* 1:51, above.

63. **"The Spirit** (or: Breath-effect; or: spirit; Breath; Attitude) **is** (or: continues being) **the One continuously creating Life** (or: repeatedly making alive; habitually forming life). **The flesh continues being of no help or benefit to anything** (furthers or augments not one thing). **The declarations** (gush-effects; spoken words; sayings; results of the Flow) **which I, Myself, have spoken to you folks are** (or: continue to be) **Spirit** (or: spirit; Breath-effect; attitude) **and they are** (or: continue being) **Life.**

They were still thinking in terms of the physical, material world, and so for those of them whom the Father had given to Him (vs. 65), He gave a more straight-forward explanation. He was speaking about the realm of the Spirit, in contrast to the flesh (i.e., both the physical flesh, and the flesh-level cultus of the old covenant). **Eonian Life** (vs. 54, above) is the **Life** created by **the Spirit**. Material **flesh**, and figurative flesh (the realm of the Mosaic covenant, with its flesh sacrifices and physical purity codes, etc.), "**continues being of no help or benefit to anything.**"

The **declarations**, which Jesus had spoken to them, were **Spirit** and they are **Life**. His "gush-effects" and the "results of the Flow" from Him were the means by which **the Spirit** was "repeatedly making [folks] alive." Think about it: this is the Good News. His gush-effects (a literal rendering of the Greek) brought Grace and Truth (Jn. 1:17). Take note that this was true even before the cross and His resurrection. The Spirit is "the One habitually forming life." The results from His Flow (of Breath and Spirit) were the creations from the Logos. "**Within It** [the Logos] **Life was continuing and progressively existing**" (Jn. 1:4). The Spirit and the Logos are One and the same.

64. **"But in contrast, there continue being some from among you folks who are not continuing faithful or habitually trusting** (or: not presently believing)." **For Jesus had seen, and thus knew from the beginning, which ones are those not habitually trusting or remaining faithful** (or: not presently believing), **and who is the one who will be proceeding to transfer, commend and commit Him** (or: hand Him over).

Jesus **had seen, and thus knew from the beginning which ones** were continuing faithful, and were habitually trusting, and which ones were not so, at that point. John points ahead to the actions of Judah (or, Judas), the one **who will be proceeding to transfer, commend and commit Him** (or: hand Him over). This expanded phrase, in reference to Judah, is the Greek future participle of *paradidōmi*. The common verb *didōmi* has the basic idea of "to give." The preposition that is prefixed to this verb, in our present verse, is *para*, which has the basic meaning of "beside; at the side." So the basic thought in this participle is that of "giving something, or someone, to the side," or, "handing someone over" to another, as given in the parenthetical expansion. But from use in various contexts, the verb has a wide semantic range, and thus also, would its participle. As a religious technical term it can mean "passing along traditions" (e.g., Acts 16:4), as in "transmitting" teachings. It can mean "to commit or entrust," as in Mat. 11:27a,

> "**All humanity was transferred, given over** (or: All things were delivered and committed) **to Me by, and under, My Father**…"

Now the common rendering, here in vs. 64, and elsewhere when it describes the action of Judah (Judas), is the word "betray" – which carries a pejorative, negative connotation that assumes a motivation by Judah of which we cannot be sure. Since it was the practice in old covenant Israel to bring a lamb to a priest in order to sacrifice the lamb, we see that the Israelite "transferred" the lamb, "commending" it as being without spot or blemish, and thus "committing" it into the hands of the priest. We have seen in our present context that Jesus was likely alluding to Himself as being a sacrificial lamb (metaphorically), so it seemed better to not use the word "betray" (which is freighted with negative emotions) and rather use more neutral, and covenant-related, words to describe the actions that Judah would soon take. In Peter's first public message, he uses a cognate of this word, in Acts 2:23a. This was an adjective, *ekdotos*, which is from the verb *didōmi*, prefixed with the preposition *ek-*, instead of *para-*, but it carries the same nuance:

> "**This Man, given forth** (or: lent out; provided out of the Midst [of God]; given out [in marriage]; given from the midst [of one's house]; issued forth [in birth]; or: surrendered; or: **This Fully-given, Emerged and Emptied One**) **in and by the specific, determined, bounded** (limited) **plan** (intended purpose, design and counsel) **and foreknowledge** (intimate knowledge which was experienced beforehand) **of God**…"

The examples of this adjective's use, given in brackets [in marriage; of one's house; in birth], demonstrate the particular nuances of the preposition *ek*, and lend us greater perception of what GOD was doing with Jesus. Within the parenthetic expansion, on offer are three other meanings of the adjective: **Fully-given** (rendering *ek-* as an intensifier); **Emerged**; and **Emptied One**. So this is what God was doing, "**in and by [His] specific, determined, bounded** (limited) **plan** (intended purpose, design and counsel) **and foreknowledge** (intimate knowledge which was experienced beforehand)." Does all of this present us with a different understanding of the action taken by Judah? Details, and the semantic ranges of the words of a text, can make a big difference.

65. **So he went on saying, "Because of this I have told you folks that no one is presently able** (or: continues having power) **to come toward** (or: face-to-face with) **Me, unless [the situation] may be existing of it having been granted or given to him from out of the Father** (or: unless he or she should be a person having been given in Him, forth from the Father)."

Returning to vs. 64, for the moment, notice that there are two categories of which Jesus spoke:
> a) **those not habitually trusting or remaining faithful**
> b) **the one who will be proceeding to transfer Him.**

So we suggest that what He said here, in vs. 65, applied mostly to the "**many**" of vs. 66.

But more than this, grasp the import and depth of this pronouncement: **unless [the situation] may be existing of it having been granted or given to him from out of the Father, no one is presently able** (or: continues having power) **to come toward** (or: face-to-face with) **[Jesus].**

This rather shut out the erroneous idea of people making a "free will" choice to come to Jesus. To be ABLE – to even HAVE POWER – to come toward Jesus is entirely dependent upon the Father granting, or giving, the power and ability to do so. Remember, Eph. 2:1 describes humanity's predicament (when not yet in Christ) as being DEAD, within the midst of trespasses and sins. Without the gift from the Father (called the Promise of, and from the Father, in Acts 1:4), which is His Spirit, there is no hope for humanity.

66. **From out of this [saying, or, circumstance], therefore, many from out of His [group] of students went away into the things back behind** (or: went off to the rear) **and then were no longer continuing to walk about** (or: travel around; = make a way of life) **with Him.**

We do not know whether this was a sudden, mass departure, or if folks just gradually wandered home. His teachings were just too much for them. The requirements for being a disciple (e.g., Mat. 16:24-25), as well as what would amount to a whole new worldview, could only be met by these being granted from out of the Father.

67. **Then Jesus says to the twelve, "You men also are not wanting** (or: intending) **to be going away** (or: to progressively withdraw), **are you?"**
> (or: "Don't you men want to leave, too?")

On offer are two possible forms of the question that Jesus asks the twelve. Apparently most everyone else that had been currently following Him (mostly for free food) went away, at that time. Here, Jesus allows them to count the cost and be sure of their commitments.

68. **Then Simon Peter decidedly gave answer to Him, "O Lord** (Master; Owner), **toward whom shall we proceed to go away? You continue holding** (or: constantly have; habitually hold [out]) **gush-effects of eonian Life** (sayings and declarations of life whose source and origin are the Age [of Messiah]; results of the flows of things spoken pertaining to life of, in and for the ages)!

Gush-effects of eonian Life had become the "ultimate concern" (Paul Tillich's term) for Peter, and history tells us that he spoke for the whole group. They may not have understood it all, yet (and do we, even now?), but they were given, from the Father, to perceive that His teachings were "sayings and declarations of life whose source and origin are the Age [of Messiah]," and they were "results of the flows of things spoken pertaining to life of, in and for the ages." They were receiving revelation, which (again as Paul Tillich maintained) was something that "grasps" a person. Paul pressed on,
> **"I am consistently pursuing** (running swiftly in order to catch), **since I can** (or: if I would) **take down by the hand** (fully seize; forcefully **grasp** and gain possession of) **even [that] upon which I also was** (or: am) **taken down by hand** (fully seized; forcefully **grasped** and taken possession of) **by, and under [the control of], Christ Jesus**" (Phil. 3:12)

This was happening to the twelve, and the power of the Spirit would bring them to the Goal.

69. **– and we ourselves have trusted and are now convinced so as to now be believing, and we by personal, intimate experience have come to know that You, Yourself, ARE** (or: continuously exist being) **God's Holy One** (or: the Sacred One from God; the Set-apart One which is God).**"**

Peter used the perfect tense in both verbs about himself and the others (notice the "we" – he is speaking for the whole group). The action of trusting, believing, becoming convinced and intimately (and experientially) knowing had already happened, and they now existed in the state and results of those past actions that had come upon them.

Notice that he did not say that they knew Him to be the Messiah (or: Christ0, but rather, he was affirming that they knew from whence He had come (from God), and that He was "**God's Holy One**," and (rendering the noun "God" as a genitive of apposition) that He was "the Set-apart One which is God." Even a man in a synagogue who was "**centered in an unclean spirit**," discerned Him and said, "**I have seen to know** (recognize) **you – who you are: God's set-apart one** (or: the Holy One of God; the set-apart one, from God; or, as a genitive of apposition: the Holy One who is God)!" (Mk. 1:24). This is the kind of unveiling that MAKES a person faithful, and fills him or her with faith. If we really KNOW this, we can follow Him.

70. **Jesus considered and gave answer to them, "Do I Myself not select and pick you out – the twelve – for Myself** (or: Did I not choose you twelve Myself)**? And one from among you men is a person who thrusts things through [situations, or, people]** (or: is an adversary; is a devil)!**"**

Later on, Jesus will affirm another witness to His rhetorical question to them:
> "**You yourselves did not choose Me, but to the contrary I, Myself, selected and picked out** (or: chose) **you folks and placed** (or: set) **you…**" (15:16, below).

He chose; the Father granted; they followed.

Verse 71 informs the reader of whom it was He was characterizing as "**a person who thrusts things through [situations, or, people].**" You can observe, by the parenthetical expansion, that THIS is what a or "the" devil actually is. Someone who by word or deed thrusts something painful or deadly through another person, or group of people. The action of Judah caused the whole group to scatter. In a later day, Paul writes to Timothy,
> "**for the people** (the humans; mankind) **will continue being folks that are**…. **devils** (adversarial slanderers; folks who throw or thrust something through people to hurt or cause divisions)" (2 Tim. 3:2, 3).

Writing to Titus, he said,
> "**Old** (or: Aged; Older) **women, similarly** (or: likewise), **[are to be] women in a state and resultant condition proper and fitting for being engaged in the sacred** (suitable in demeanor for serving the temple; or: = living a life appropriate [for] a person [being] a temple), **not folks who thrust-through or hurl [a weapon, or something hurtful] through [someone]** (or: not DEVILS nor slanderous adversaries which bring division and hurt)…" (Tit. 2:3).

71. **Now, He was speaking of Judah** (or: Judas), **[son] of Simon Iscariot, for you see, this person – one from among** [other MSS: being a part of] **the twelve – continued in being about to proceed in transferring, commending, and to keep on committing, Him** (or: to continue in handing Him over).

John makes clear of whom Jesus just spoke, here, and in vs. 64, above. Jesus knew (vs. 64) that – by the Father's lead and direction (and He did only what He saw the Father doing) – He had chosen that one, from this select group, who would transfer Him to the final stage of His ministry among them.

Chapter 7

1. **And after these things, Jesus continued walking about** (moved around) **within the Galilee [area], for He was not intending** (willing; purposing) **to be walking around within Judea, because the Jews** (or: the Judeans; or: = authorities of the second temple Jewish religion/culture of Judea, and its representatives) **had been trying to find Him** (seeking Him; searching for Him), **to kill Him off.**

We should keep in mind that John is not saying that the Jewish people, as a race, were wanting to kill Jesus, it was the religious leaders in Judea that were searching for Him. There were Jews in Galilee, but He felt safe there, for those particular Jews were not trying to kill Him – at least at this time, based upon this text.

2. **Now [the season for] the Jew's Feast of Tabernacles** (*Sukkoth*: the festival of Trumpets, the day of Atonement, and the erecting Booths, or pitching tents, which pertained to the culture and religion of the Jews) **was drawing near.**

This was one of the three major Feasts of Israel to which the Law had required the men within Palestine to attend:
> "Three times in the year all your males shall appear before Yahweh, your God, in the place that He shall choose: at the Festival of Unleavened Bread (= Passover), at the Festival of Weeks (= Pentecost) and at the Festival of Booths (= Tabernacles; also = Ingathering)" (Deut. 16:16).

3. **Therefore His brothers said to Him, "Change your steps from this place, and go away into Judea, so that your disciples will** [other MSS: can; might] **continue watching and thoughtfully observing your work** [= the miracles] **which you are habitually doing,**

It would seem that Jesus' brothers were wanting Him to go more public than He had been. We are not told in what particular year of His ministry that this narrative is set. John's Gospel is not oriented to report the succession of the events that he reports; his focus is on topical, theological and relational issues. This is not a biography or a history, in the modern sense of the word.

4. **"for no one is in the habit of doing anything within a hidden place** (in hiding; under concealment) **and at the same time seeking for himself to be in public openness. If** (or: Since) **you continue doing these things, show yourself in clear light to the world** (cause yourself to be seen by the system [= the religious, cultural and political organizations of the area] and the aggregate of people)."
5. **– you see, not even were His brothers putting their trust into Him, and were still unbelieving –**

So, it was their observation that Jesus was apparently performing signs, miracles and healings only in "**hidden places.**" They presume that He is seeking a public reputation, and so assumed that He was "**seeking for himself to be in public openness.**" We are not told what their motives for suggesting this were, only that they were not yet "**putting their trust into Him, and were still unbelieving.**" Perhaps, like others who were aware of His feeding of the 5000, they wanted to push Him, like our old saying goes, "to either put up or shut up." Their reason was based upon common human practice: "**for no one is in the habit of…**"

6. **Therefore, Jesus is presently saying to them, "My season** (My fitting situation; My *kairos*; My appointed occasion; My fertile moment) **is not yet existing at My side** (is not yet present or here), **yet your season** (the fitting situation belonging to you folks) **is always prepared and ready.**

His response is similar to the one He had first given to His mother, in Jn. 2:4. We may reason that His season was to be at Passover, and not in the fall of the year – at Tabernacles. Or, this may not have been the final year of His earthly ministry. But deeper than these is the "appointed occasion" that had been set by His Father, which would be the "fertile moment" of the planting of the Seed. Perhaps the theme of Jesus being the new Moses, leading humanity on a spiritual exodus from the earthly to the heavenly sphere, meant that His "fitting situation" would be at Passover. This might have been why John mentions that this was the season of Tabernacles.

But what did He mean in saying that their season was always prepared and ready? The next verse gives us a clue…

7. **"The world** (The System; The organization; = the controlling religious, cultural and political society) **is not presently able to be habitually hating you** (to continue radically detaching from and regarding you with ill-will), **yet it is constantly hating and progressively detaching from Me, because I Myself am habitually giving testimony about it** (or: continuously bearing witness and showing evidence concerning it) **that its works are continuously unwholesome** (laborious and such that put others to trouble; apt to shrewd turns; mischievous; wicked; unsound; malignant; gushed with misery).

It would seem that it was always a fertile moment for them because their world (the current system of things and their local society) was "**not presently able to be habitually hating [them].**" They had fair sailing; it was a good time to harvest, and then plant another crop; their lives could continue on uninterrupted because they were not resisting the status quo.

But it was not the season for Jerusalem or the Judean leadership to accept Him. They were "**constantly hating and progressively detaching from [Him].**" He was a thorn in their side, habitually doing the work of the Prophet, which was to critique Israel's leadership when that ruling body was not just or acting in loyalty to Yahweh.

He explains to His brothers that their current domination system (the leaders of Second Temple Judaism) were doing works (deeds; actions) that were "**continuously unwholesome** (laborious and such that put others to trouble; apt to shrewd turns; mischievous; wicked; unsound; malignant; gushed with misery)." Because He was "**habitually giving testimony about it** (or: continuously bearing witness and showing evidence concerning it)," they were trying to find Him so that they could silence Him by killing Him off.

Note the broad semantic range of "unwholesome (etc.)."

8. **"You men walk on up into the Feast** (or: festival). **I, Myself, am not yet walking up into the midst of** (= to be a focal point of) **this feast** (or: festival), **because My season** (or: fitting situation; fertile moment) **has not yet been fulfilled** (made full; filled up)."

The strategy that Jesus displays may be tied to vss. 5 and 6, above. He would not want to enter Jerusalem with them because they might publicly expose Him prior to His "fitting situation." As we see in vs. 10, below, His plan was not to display Himself "**in clear light** (or: as clearly visible)," but instead, "**within a hidden situation**," which may not have been possible were He with his brothers. Timing was important to Jesus: it was the Father's timing, which made it important.

9. **Now, after saying these things to them, He remained within the Galilee [area].**
10. **Yet, after** (seeing as) **His brothers walked up into the Feast** (or: festival), **then later He Himself walked up, not as in clear light** (or: as clearly visible), **but rather, as within a hidden situation.**

John does not tell us how long Jesus waited, but apparently it was long enough for Him to be able to join the Feast in the way that He desired.

11. **Then, the Judeans** (= religious authorities of the Jewish religion, and of Judea) **began persistently looking for Him within the festival, and they kept on saying, "Where is that man?!"**
12. **And there continued being a lot of subdued talk and perplexed buzzing** (murmuring) **about Him within the crowds. Some, on the one hand, kept on saying that "He is a good man** (a virtuous one)." **On the other hand, others were saying "No, to the contrary, he continues misleading** (deceiving; leading astray) **the crowd."**

The Judean authorities were looking for Him, and that, not in His best interests. But He was hidden from them, until He chose to enter the public scene. Like typical, average citizens (even in our own day and country), the folks of the crowds were ignorant of what was really going on behind the scenes, and so (typical of varied personalities) they were divided in their opinions about this potential public leader. Some kept on saying, "**He is a good man** (a virtuous one);" yet others, having a more critical or jaded attitude toward life, were saying, "**No, to the contrary, he continues misleading** (deceiving; leading astray) **the crowd.**" Typical political or religious rhetoric, revealing the hearts. We tend to have strong feelings about things of which we know very little.

13. **Of course no one was in public openness** (or: with the boldness of a citizen) **speaking about Him, because of the fear [which they had] of the Jews** [i.e., the religious/political Judean leaders].

The Judean leadership had apparently let the residents of Jerusalem know that they took a dim view of Jesus. In Jn. 2:23 we are told that "**many believed and put their trust into His Name, constantly gazing upon and critically contemplating His signs.**" But in 9:22, below, we are also informed that,
"**the Judeans** (= Jewish leadership) **had put it together and agreed, so that if anyone should ever confess** (acknowledge; avow) **Him Christ** (or: express the same idea, that He is [the]

Anointed), **he should come to be [put] away from the synagogue** (= be excommunicated; = be cut off from membership in the synagogue, and thus be considered an outcast)."
Cf 12:42 and 19:38, below. Social and religious pressure, and fear of rejection, often restricted "**public openness**" – even though being in a city ruled by the Roman Empire would have given them the right to be bold. Recall in Jn. 3 that Nicodemus visited Him by night, and we will find that, after His death, Joseph of Arimathea went to Pilate **secretly**, "for fear of the Judeans." In later centuries, Christian leaders would burn at the stake those whom they deemed to be heretics, or a danger to their religious system.

14. **Now with it already being in the middle of the Festival** (or: = half way through the feast), **Jesus walked up into the Temple grounds** (or: courts; porches; sanctuary area) **and began teaching.**

He may have been present, although not out in public, for a day or more, depending upon when He had actually entered Jerusalem. A "fertile moment" (or, the Father's directing Him) must have presented itself. So He enters the most prominent place in the city (the Judean headquarters), "**and began teaching.**" Obviously, He had no fear of the Judean authorities and was bold, with "**public openness.**"

15. **The Jews** (or: = religious professionals of the Judeans) **were therefore surprised and kept on being amazed** (or: astonished), **saying, "How has this one seen, and thus known [the] writings, not being one having learned** [i.e., having studied at the schools, to be educated and articulate]**?"**

I chose, first, the rendering "**Jews**" since those listening to Him may have been just ordinary people, but would have expected anyone who knew the Scriptures to have been a scribe or one of the elite of the city. Yet, this rhetorical question could also have been made by the religious professionals of the Judeans. Ordinary folks were not usually among those "**having learned**," and He was apparently being assessed as not being among "the learned," such as those who had studied in the Judean schools, as Saul had, as a student of Gamaliel (Acts 5:34). It is like we have today: "How can you really understand what the Bible means if you have not attended seminary?" Learning from teachers is usually beneficial, but folks often forget what we are instructed in 1 Jn. 2:27,

> "**the effect of the anointing which you folks received** (or: receive) **from Him constantly remains** (abides; dwells; makes its home) **within you folks, and you continually have no use** (or: you are not constantly having a need) **that anyone should keep on teaching you** (or: be repeatedly giving you a course of lessons; coach you; instruct you), **but rather, just as the effect of His anointing is continuously and progressively teaching you about everything** (or: concerning all people), **and is continuously true, and real, and is not a lie, even according as it taught** (or: as He instructs) **you: you are continuously abiding** (remaining; dwelling; being at home) **within and in union with Him.**"

Also, in 16:13, below, Jesus told His disciples,

> "**the Spirit of the Truth**... **will constantly be a Guide and will progressively lead you on the Path** (or: it will continue leading the way for you) **directed toward and proceeding on into all Truth and Reality.**"

Of course, we see that Jesus learned from the One who had sent Him, as He explains in the next verse.

16. **Jesus therefore replied distinctly to them, and says, "My teaching is not My own, but rather belongs to and comes from the One sending Me.**

This means that Jesus' teaching is the Father's teaching. What He says is what the Father is saying. As the Voice told Peter, Jacob and John (on the Mount of Transfiguration), "**This is My beloved Son**... **Listen to, and hear Him!**" (Mat. 17:5).

17. **"Should anyone be habitually wanting or intending to continuously be doing His will** (intent; purpose), **he will progressively come to know by intimate experience concerning the teaching –**

whether it is and continues being from out of the midst of God (or: from that which is God), **or whether I am continuously babbling on, just uttering sounds or randomly talking from Myself.**

The criterion for intimately and experientially knowing "**the teaching**" (whether or not it is from God) is "**habitually wanting or intending to continuously be doing His will** (intent; purpose)." We must stress that this "wanting and intending" comes as Grace; a gift from the Father. Notice, however, that He did NOT say, "You must learn Hebrew, Aramaic, Greek or Latin (etc.), or even be familiar with Israel's history and the culture of Second Temple Judaism" – not that all this is not good and beneficial – but, as we see from Christ's first century disciples, even the unlearned can know the Truth.

Jesus said, "**Should ANYONE be habitually wanting or intending**," and He was speaking to at least some who probably did not even know how to read or write. He was teaching publicly, in the Temple grounds where "anyone" could listen to Him. Even as the Son; even as the Messiah; He did not teach "**from Himself.**" His teaching was "**from out of the midst of God** (or: from that which is God)." We, as teachers, should do no less.

18. **"The one continuously speaking or randomly talking from himself is normally seeking his own reputation** (or: appearance; glory); **yet the One constantly seeking the reputation** (or: glory; appearance) **of the One sending Him, this One is true** (continues being genuine and real), **and dishonesty** (injustice; that which is contrary to fairness, equity and rightwised relationships in the Way pointed out) **does not exist within Him.**

In 5:41, above, Jesus laid out one of His operating principles: "**I have no habit of receiving glory from humans** (or: I am not continuing to take a reputation at the side of people)," and then in 5:44 rhetorically asks,

> "**How are you folks, yourselves, able to trust or believe, when habitually getting a reputation and receiving fame** (or: repeatedly taking opinions and glory) **from one another, and yet you folks are not constantly seeking the glory** (or: the reputation, opinion) **which comes from God alone?**"

Now He once again sets the standard for speaking as a representative of someone else, stating that "**the One constantly seeking the reputation** (or: glory; appearance) **of the One sending Him, this One is true.**" In this, He is setting Himself in contrast to those who would accuse Him, or (cf 7:1, above; vs. 30, below), would be "**seeking to catch hold of and arrest** (or: seize) **Him.**" Attempts at self-glory are **dishonesty**. Seeking to promote oneself is seeking to preserve the life of the enslaved "first Adam" (1 Cor. 15:45). When a person lifts up the heart, in pride, attempting to be great (perhaps because of their beauty, wisdom or brightness), some kind of death awaits them as they are "cast to the ground" (cf Ezk. 28:2-19; Mat. 16:25a, 26).

19. **"Did not Moses give the Law [= Torah] to you folks? And yet not one from among you folks is habitually doing** (or: performing) **the Law! Why are you constantly seeking to kill Me?"**

They were seeking to stop Him, and even kill Him. So Jesus reminds them of the rule of Law that governed their religious lives. What they wanted to do to Him was not just or right, and the Law that Moses gave them was a standard of justice and right living, within their culture. We can better understand His next question to them by reading the disclosure in 1 Jn. 3:15a,

> "**Everyone, who** (or: All humanity, which) **in constantly hating** (or: regarding with ill-will or detaching from) **his brother, constantly exists being a person-slayer** (a murderer)."

What they were in their hearts was being exhibited in their intents. Also consider Jesus' teaching in Mat. 5:21-22,

> "**YOU folks heard that it was said to the original People** (or: for the Beginning Folks; among those of the beginning period [of Israel]),
> > '**You folks will not continue murdering.**' [Ex. 20:13]

Yet whoever may commit murder will continue being held within the decision (= held under the control of the crisis or the judging). **I Myself am now saying to YOU people that everyone, who – from internal swelling or agitated emotions of his natural disposition, or from the fruition of his mental bent – is habitually being randomly impulsive to, or without cause repeatedly intensely angry with, his brother** (= fellow member of this society) **will continue being held within the decision** (= under control of the judging of the local court)."

Jesus' bold revealing what they were up to (via positing it in a straight-forward question to them) took them by surprise and they responded with a wild accusation that did not fit the circumstance...

20. **The crowd considered and replied, "You're demon-possessed** (or: You possess a demon; You constantly hold a demon; You presently have a demon [note: a Hellenistic concept and term: = animistic influence]; = you are out of your mind)! **Who is constantly seeking to kill you?"**

My, this sounds so much like what we hear from Washington D.C., today! If we were to take Jesus' question metaphorically (which we know it was NOT), we could hear a similar response from religious groups, when they reject or excommunicate those who do not agree with them, as they say to those folks, "But you know that we love you." We see, from vs. 25, below, that even the ordinary citizens of Jerusalem were aware that the leadership was seeking to kill Him. Their feigned surprise, with this question to Jesus, would have been quite transparent, even to the crowd.

21. **Jesus decidedly answered, and said to them, "I did one work** (or: I do one act [= miracle]) **and you all continue being amazed** (shocked and stunned with wonder) **because of this.**

Jesus ignores their question, and begins describing the situation.

22. **"Moses has given the circumcision to you – not that its source is from out of Moses, but rather from out of the fathers** (= ancestors) **– and yet, within** (or: on) **a sabbath you folks habitually circumcise a man.**
23. **"If a person** (a human; a man) **is normally receiving circumcision within** (or: on) **a sabbath so that the Law of Moses may not be loosened so as to fall apart** (be untied or undone; be destroyed; = be broken), **are you constantly bitterly angry and progressively enraged** (literally: filled with bile) **with Me because I make** (or: made) **a whole man sound in health within** (or: on) **a sabbath?**

He set a logical parallel before them. He presented a similar argument to healing a man on a sabbath, in Lu. 14:5-6,

> **"Which one of you folks, [if your] son** [other MSS: ass] **or ox will fall into a cistern** (sealed-in well; or: a pit) **on a sabbath day, will [you] not also proceed immediately pulling** (or: dragging) **him, or it, back up again [the same day]?"** And they did not have strength or ability** (were powerless) **to give a decided response in opposition to** (or: to direct back an answer in contradiction toward) **these [reasonings]."**

Arguments from the Law are always trumped by the Logos of the Life.

24. **"Do not be constantly judging** (or: Stop making decisions or evaluations) **according to sight** (= external appearance), **but rather be habitually making just decisions** (or: be judging with fair evaluating which accord with the Way pointed out; form rightwised conclusions)."**

Jesus' **"one work (act)"** brought justice – that which is right and fair. He was acting as "**an Emissary with a mission**" (vs. 29, below). His act was the result from "**making a just decision.**" He had been "judging with fair evaluation which accorded with the Way pointed out, and had formed rightwised conclusions."

Even under the old covenant, they were not supposed to be judging from appearances – from how the situation seemed, by natural sight. He had shown mercy.

"**Thus keep on speaking and thus keep on doing** (performing; producing)**: as those being continuously about to be separated and decided about** (evaluated; judged; made a distinction between; scrutinized) **through means of a Law** (or: custom; principle; [*p*74: a word; a message]) **of Freedom and from unfettered Liberty, and which is Un-restriction. For you see, the separating, evaluating and deciding** (or: scrutinizing and judging) **is merciless in, by and with** (or: to; for) **the one not performing, exercising or producing mercy. Mercy is consistently speaking loudly, boasting and assuming superiority with regard to evaluating, deciding and separating** (or: Mercy is repeatedly bragging from making decisions; or: Mercy keeps on fully boasting in repeatedly triumphing over judging)**!**" (Jas. 2:12-13)

Even in their Scriptures, Habakkuk prayed,

"O Yahweh… within the midst of inherent fervor (or: anger; wrath), remember mercy" (Hab. 3:2). In Neh. 9:32 we are instructed that God keeps covenant AND mercy. In Ps. 25:10, we read that "All the paths of Yahweh [are] mercy." In Ps. 89:14, we learn that "Mercy and Truth will go before [Yahweh's] face." And then Paul informs us that God is "**wealthy and rich in mercy, because of His vast** (much; great in magnitude and quantity; outstretched; long-lasting; repeated) **Love, with which He focused Love on us**" (Eph. 2:4). But religion tends to be legalistic, and to judge by appearances.

25. **Then some of the inhabitants of Jerusalem said, "Is not this one he whom they** (= the group of leaders) **are presently seeking to kill?**
26. **"And look! He continues speaking in public openness** (boldly as though being a citizen) **– and they continue saying nothing to him. The chief rulers** (or: "the authorities"; the ruling class) **have not at some point come to really know personally that this one is the Christ** (the Anointed One; = the Messiah), **have they?**
27. **"On the contrary, we have seen, and thus, we know this one – what place and source he is from. Yet whenever the Christ** (the Anointed One; = the Messiah) **should proceed in coming, no one is getting to know what place or source he is from."**

In vs. 25, we see that the inhabitants of Jerusalem were aware of what was politically/religiously going on. Verse 26a shows us their surprise at the seeming paradox between the "behind the scenes," attempted actions of the ruling class, and the overt action of Jesus. This unexpected boldness that Jesus displayed caused them to wonder if the political/religious atmosphere had changed. Verse 27 displays what is very common in a general populous: reasoning from popular theories that lack real knowledge. We are reminded of Job 38:2, "Who is this who darkens counsel by declarations without knowledge?" This has been the case all through the ages. The chief priests and scribes, knowing the Scriptures, had pointed to Bethlehem (the House of Bread) as the place from which "**will proceed coming forth a Leader and Mentor, which very One will shepherd** (= guide, nourish, care for and protect) **My People, Israel**" (Mat. 2:6; Mic. 5:2). But, especially in that time and place, the general population was uneducated, and in the dark. Sadly, to a great degree, this is still true, today.

28. **Therefore Jesus cries out** (or: spoke in a loud voice), **as He is proceeding with teaching within the Temple grounds** (court yards; porches), **and continuing, says, "You have both seen and know Me, and you have seen and know where I am from** (or: what is my source). **And yet, I have not come from Myself** (= on My own initiative or authority). **On the contrary, the One sending Me is Real** (True; Genuine), **Whom you folks have not seen, neither know.**

Jesus' first statement informs us that He already had a reputation, and folks in Jerusalem had witnessed the signs and miracles that He had performed. Also, they would have at least known that He had recently come from the Galilee District. But now He is getting more specific, if also enigmatic, in referring to "**the One sending [Him]**." He also affirms to them that He has come representing Someone else (He had not come on His own initiative, and was not representing Himself), but that they have neither seen, nor even then knew (the perfect tense of the verb) Who this One is. He is saying that they do not know God.

Notice that He emphasized that this God "**is Real** (True; Genuine)," and not a false god of the pagans.

29. **"I, Myself, have seen and know Him, because I am from His side** (or: I continuously exist being at His side and in His presence) **– and that One sent** (or: that One also sends) **Me forth as an Emissary with a mission** (as a Representative)."

Now He takes them to a higher level of understanding, for those who have been given to perceive with their spirits. He is saying that He has seen, and knows, the Father, for He came from the Father's presence – as the Father's Emissary. The Father sent Him forth "**with a mission**," and to represent Him.

30. **Then they began seeking to catch hold of and arrest** (or: seize) **Him – but still no one laid a hand upon Him, because His hour had not yet come.**

The "they," here, refers to the elite leadership, not the common people. The Judean religious leaders were "**seeking to catch hold of and arrest** (or: seize) **Him**," and yet they apparently could not do so – "**because His hour had not yet come.**" It was the period of His Day, or season, but not the actual time for Him to be taken. Yet, by John using the term "**hour**" we realize that the time was close at hand.

31. **Now many, from out of the crowd, came to believe and so put [their] trust into Him, and so they began and continued saying, "Whenever the Christ may come, He will proceed doing** (performing; making) **no more signs than this Man does** (or: did)!"

They had seen the signs and the miracles, and now "knew" Him (vs. 28), and now through His words to them (the Logos expressed to them), "**many, from out of the crowd, came to believe and so put [their] trust into Him.**" Reason (one of the meanings of the term *Logos*) had arisen in their minds and hearts: "**Whenever the Christ may come, He will proceed doing no more signs than this Man does.**"

32. **So the Pharisees heard the crowd buzzing with these low-toned conversations about Him, and the chief priests and the Pharisees commissioned and dispatched officers** (deputies; those who act under orders; = temple guards) **to the end that they might catch hold of and arrest** (or: seize) **Him.**

This scene reminds us of the "mixed multitude" that came out of Egypt, following Moses. MANY of "the crowd" (the common, unlearned folks) were believing, but the religious professionals wanted to stop Him, and even "**commissioned and dispatched officers** (deputies; those who act under orders; = temple guards) **to the end that they might catch hold of and arrest** (or: seize) **Him.**" They were serious in their intent.

33. **Then Jesus says, "I am still with you folks for a little time, and then I am progressively withdrawing, bringing things, under control, toward** (or: face-to-face with) **the One sending Me.**

Here He predicts His departure from this life and His return to the Father. The Pharisees and the crowd would not have understood this, because they did not understand Who it was that had sent Him.

We want to point to the verb, in the present progressive tense, "**progressively withdrawing, bringing things, under control.**" The Greek word is *hupagō*. The verb *agō*, by itself, means "bring; lead away; guide; conduct; convey; or: take into custody; or: depart; drive off (e.g., as cattle)." Prefixed to this verb is *hupo*, contracted to *hup-* before a vowel, and its basic meaning is "under," often with the idea of motion or action. Thus, the verb can thus have the meaning of "subjection," or "bring things under control."

Because of the preposition which follows, *pros*, the predicate can mean to "**bringing things, under control, toward the One sending [Him]**," or, it can mean for Him to be "**progressively withdrawing**," and vs. 34 indicates that He will no longer be with them, but rather will be in another place – where they cannot find Him. I conflated these two meanings of the verb in order to display the reason that He was withdrawing (to bring things of humanity and the universe under control), and that He was going away from them so as to be "face-to-face with" the Father. It was going to be a productive move, on multiple levels.

34. **"You people will continue seeking to find Me, but you will not be coming across, discovering or finding Me – and where I, Myself, am existing** (or: in what place I Myself continue being), **you folks presently have no power to come** (or: continue unable to go).**"**

Observe the future indicative, in the first clause: "**You people will continue seeking to find Me**." What did He mean by that? Verse 32 said that they were seeking to arrest Him. But they would not continue seeking to find the physical Jesus after they had killed Him (on the cross). Unless, perhaps, He was referring to the empty tomb that He would leave behind. Now if we join this first clause with the last one (which holds a ray of hope for them: not now, but perhaps in the future), we might uncover His subtle prediction: "You people WILL continue seeking to find Me…"

Take note that he uses the present tense "I am existing," or, "I continue being," not the future tense, "I will continue being." He was already in that place, but they could not see that realm (the realm of the Father). They would try to find Him in the natural realm (the only place where they could look), and He was no longer going to continue being in the natural realm (as Jesus, their earthly Messiah). Jesus lived in two realms at the same time: heaven (the atmosphere of the spirit) and earth. His earthly life would soon be over, except when His Spirit would inhabit His corporate body.

Notice that He again uses the present tense, "**you folks presently have no power to come**." But it did not mean that in the future they would not be able to go to Him, by the power of, and in the sphere of, the Spirit.

35. **Therefore, the Jews** (= the authorities) **said to themselves** (= toward each other), **"Where is this fellow about to proceed journeying, that we will not be finding him? He is not about to be traveling into the Dispersion, among the Greeks** (= Greek-speaking Jews; or: = all those having been absorbed into the Greek culture and civilization), **and to continue teaching the Greeks, is he?**

They took His meaning in the realm of natural thinking, that He meant that He was simply going to relocate geographically. The Greek culture surrounded Judea, so they assumed that maybe He meant that He would quit teaching the Judeans, and take His ministry to other ethnic groups.

But is John making a subtle suggestion, through their human reasoning? Via His Spirit, and through His corporate body, He would indeed go into the Dispersion (those Jews living in districts or countries outside of Palestine, among the Greek culture outside of Judea, and there would "**continue teaching the Greeks**."

36. **"What is this word** (discourse; saying; communication; expression) **which he said, 'You people will continue seeking to find me, but you will not proceed to come across, discover or find me – and where I, myself, am** (or: in what place I continue being), **you folks presently have no power to come** (or: continue unable to go)'**?"**

They did not understand that He was speaking of the realm of Spirit, the atmosphere of God's reign, and then, by His Spirit, within the hearts and spirits of people.

37. **Now within the last day – the great one – of the Feast** (or: festival), **Jesus, after having taken a stand, stood and then suddenly cries out, saying, "If ever anyone may continue being thirsty, let him be habitually coming toward** (or: face-to-face with) **Me, and then let the person continuously trusting and progressively believing into Me be constantly** (habitually; repeatedly) **drinking!** [cf Isa. 12:3; 55:1]

> (or: let him be progressively coming to Me and keep on drinking. The person habitually being faithful unto Me,)

This is a reprise of what Jesus said to the Samaritan woman, at the well, in Jn. 4:10-14 He has now taken this message to the whole of Jerusalem. My bold reading has brought the participial clause, which is normally divided off to be the beginning of vs. 38, to serve as the subject of the participle "**be constantly** (habitually; repeatedly) **drinking**." Greek syntax often has the subject follow the predicate. Thus we have a two-stage process being described. The thirsty person first comes to Him, and then in, or by, trusting and believing into Him, this person can be constantly drinking.

The next two verses expand and further explain what He meant. Before going there, note that the syntax of the second half of the verse can end differently, as most translations offer. The parenthetical alternative ends the sentence about "**anyone continuing being thirsty**," with the participle, "keep on drinking," and begins with the common reading of the text as leading into vs. 38. This reading can make what "**the Scripture says**" refer to "The person habitually being faithful unto Me." The Rivers would now flow from out of THIS person. The bold reading of vs. 37 would have vs. 38 referring to Jesus. Either reading makes good sense. The clause, "**let the person continuously trusting and progressively believing into Me**," can be read either before, or after, "**be constantly** (habitually; repeatedly) **drinking**."

38. **"Just as the Scripture says, 'Rivers** (or: Floods; Torrents) **of living water will continuously flow** (or: gush; flood) **from out of the midst of His cavity** (or: his innermost being or part; or: the hollow of his belly; [used of the womb])."** [cf Isa. 58:11; Ezk. 47:1; Joel 3:18; Zech. 13:1; 14:8]

John gives us the meaning of "**living water**" in vs. 39. Notice who is like a source of water, in Isa. 58:11,
> "And Yahweh shall guide you [i.e., God's people] continually, and satisfy your soul in drought, and make your bones fat; and YOU shall be like a watered garden, and like A Spring of water, whose waters do not fail (or: deceive)."

In the vision of the waters, Ezk. 47:1, the waters issued out of the House (i.e., Temple). This would fit both Jesus, and His Temple/body. In Zech. 14:8, "living waters shall go out from Jerusalem."

39. **Now this He said about** (or: with regard to) **the Breath-effect** (or: Spirit; Attitude; [other MSS: Holy, or set-apart Spirit; Sacred Wind]) **of which** (or: of Whom as a source; [other MSS simple read: which]) **they – those trusting and believing into Him – were about to be continuously and progressively receiving. You see, the Holy Spirit** (set-apart Breath-effect; Sacred Wind and Attitude) **was not yet being One having been given** [note: reading with B; with p66c, p75, Aleph, and others: for you see, there was not yet Spirit in existence; D* and three others: for there was not yet a Holy Spirit upon them; *Textus Receptus*: You see, [the] Holy Spirit was not yet being or existing], **because Jesus was not yet glorified** (given repute and an assumed appearance; made into a manifestation which induces praise).

John reports that Jesus had "**said this about** (or: with regard to) **the Breath-effect** (or: Spirit)." Then John goes on to say that "**those trusting and believing into Him were about to be continuously and progressively receiving**" this Breath-effect/Spirit.

The last half of the verse is somewhat of an enigma, and by the diverse MS witnesses, we can see that those who authored those texts may have been confused about what John was saying, and the different scribes came to different conclusions. I chose the reading of B for the bold rendering, but offer the other three readings for contemplation. It seems to us that John was simply indicating that the context of this passage was prior to the Day of Pentecost, in Acts 2.

40. Then from out of the midst of the crowd, [*p*66 and others read: many] **after hearing these words, they began saying, "This one is certainly** (really; truly) **The Prophet!"**
41. Others began saying, "This one is the Christ [= Messiah]**!" Yet they** [other MSS: But others] **continued saying, "Surely the Christ** (the Anointed One) **does not normally come** (or: is not presently coming) **from out of the Galilee [area]!**
42. "Does not the Scripture say that the Christ (the Anointed One; = Messiah) **is proceeding in** (or: normally) **coming from out of the seed of David** [2 Sam. 7:12], **and from Bethlehem** [Micah 5:2], **the village where David was?"**

In vs. 40 we have reasoning from experience, from "**after hearing these words**." Remember Jn. 1:21b, where the crowd ask John the immerser if he was "**The Prophet**." The general population lived in anticipation of "the Prophet" or "the Messiah" (two terms for the same entity), so someone speaking in an unusual manner, as Jesus had just been doing, would naturally have brought this idea to mind. Verse 41a has the same reasoning as vs. 40, just using the other term "Christ [Greek word for the Hebrew word 'Messiah'])." But 41b shows evidence of natural reasoning, based upon the sacred texts, and common traditions: "**Surely the Christ** (the Anointed One) **does not**..." To them He was not fitting the appropriate criterion.

Verse 42 presents other reasoning – perhaps popular; perhaps more learned: the appropriate lineage (**seed of David**) and the appropriate birthplace (**Bethlehem**). Later on, both Mat., chapter 1, and Lu. 3:23-38 settle people's concerns about Christ's lineage, and Lu. 2:1-11 supplies the answer about His birthplace. John's Gospel is not concerned with Jesus' birth situation, but it shows us why it was important for Mat. and Lu. to give this information.

43. Therefore a split-effect (a tearing division) **occurred** (came into being; developed) **within the crowd, because of Him.**

As with most every topic of discussion, or personal viewpoint, people are always divided. Natural reasoning that is not informed by revelation leaves folks confused and torn-apart. As in the past, so also today. He has from the beginning been a source of conflict, for those who live with only natural reasoning. But this is part of the plan. He came to divide the light from the darkness, while bringing about a new creation:
> "**YOU folks should not assume from custom or infer from the Law that I come** (or: go; came) **to throw peace** (a joining) **upon the Land** (or: earth). **I do** (or: did) **not come to throw** (impose) **peace or joining, but to the contrary, a sword** (a curved weapon for close combat)! **You see, I come** (or: came; go) **to disunite** (to make to be two)" (Mat. 10:34-35a).

He came to divide the new covenant from out of the midst of the old; the Light from out of the midst of the Darkness; the Son from out of the midst of the mother.

44. So some of them were wanting (intending; willing) **to catch hold of and arrest Him, but yet no one laid hands on Him.**
45. Therefore the subordinate officials (officers; deputies; those who act under orders) **went to the chief** (or: ranking) **priests and Pharisees, and so those fellows said to them, "Why** (Through what [situation; reason]) **did you not bring him** (or: Wherefore do you not lead him [here])**?"**
46. Then the subordinate officials (= temple guards, or police), **after consideration, replied, "Never** (Not even once) **did a human** (a person; a man) **speak thus** (like this; in this way), **like this man!"**

The "**subordinate officials** (= temple guards, or police)" had better ears to hear than did the ranking priests and Pharisees. His Logos had penetrated their hearts. The subordinate officials responded to the

Logos, rather than to their bosses. Notice their testimony: "**Never** (Not even once) **did a human** (a person; a man) **speak thus** (like this; in this way), **like this man!**" What a proclamation our author has included.

47. The Pharisees then pointedly questioned them, "Have not you men also been led astray (or: been deceived)?

48. "Not anyone from out of the rulers (chiefs; leaders) **or from out of the Pharisees put trust, confidence or belief into him, do they?**

Their question, in vs. 47, shows that they deemed Jesus as someone who was leading the people astray (and away from being under their control – we have repeatedly seen this same response from the leaders in many groups of institutional Christianity). Verse 48 presents their logic: believe what "**the rulers**" tell you; believe what THEY believe. John is unveiling the religious atmosphere and environment of Second Temple Judaism, in Jerusalem.

49. "But this crowd, which is having no habitual, experiential or intimate knowledge of the Law, continues being those under a curse (are those upon whom a curse rests)."

They said this because they viewed the "crowd" as people who did not keep the Law, and so were under the curses of Deut. 28, etc. They also considered them ignorant, and thus easily led astray and deceived.

50. Nicodemus, the one previously going to Him – being one of them (or: = a part of their group), **proceeds saying to them,**

51. "Our Law (or: custom) **is not in the habit of judging** (or: No law of ours is proceeding to decide about) **the person** (man; human) **unless it can** (or: except it should) **first hear from his side and can** (or: should; may; would) **know with intimate experiential knowledge what he is habitually doing** (repeatedly or presently practicing)!"

The Law does not judge from hearsay. It is based upon direct witness and evidence. (It is too bad that many in the U.S. Congress, in our day, are unaware of, or have ignored, this). The leadership of Second Temple Judaism did not keep the Law. It also appears that Nic's visit with Jesus, in Jn. 3, made an impact on him to the extent that he would buck the tide of the leadership.

52. They thoughtfully replied, and say to him, "You are not also from out of the Galilee [area], are you? Search (or: Examine) **and see, that a prophet is not usually awakened** (not normally raised up) **from out of the midst of the Galilee [district]!"**

They first took up an *ad hominem* attack to smear the validity of Nicodemus' argument, and then turn to the history and traditions of Israel to back up their attitudes, which, as Nicodemus chidingly points out, are not in harmony with the Law. Apparently they had forgotten that Jonah had come from Galilee (2 Ki. 14:26; he was from Gath-hepher, a town in Galilee), but they may have been meaning that OT references to "The Prophet" (vs. 40, above) gave no references to Galilee.

53. And they went on their way, each one into his house (= they all went home).

Thus, it seems that John is saying that each one left their gathering still being of the same opinion. No consensus about Jesus seems to have been formally decided – perhaps due to what Nicodemus had said. Recall, from the beginning of this chapter, that this was during the Feast of Tabernacles – not during the time of Passover, which would be the next Feast in their religious calendar.

Chapter 8

1. **Now Jesus went** (or: had gone; or: journeys) **on His way into the Mount of the Olives.**

Many folks tie vs. 1 to 7:53, and this may be correct. However, the previous section that ended ch. 7 was about the Judean leadership, and the final verse, there, may have referred just to them. John does not present a sequential history, but records incidents and teachings that present the Incarnate Logos as the Christ, the Son of God. Here, vs. 1 may have happened many times, indicating that during His visits to Jerusalem, the Mount of Olives was where He often spent the night.

The verb is in the aorist tense, which is the fact, or indefinite, tense as concerning action, and so it can be rendered as a simple past tense, "went," or even as a simple perfect, "had gone" (setting the scene for vs. 2), or as a simple present tense, "journeys on His way." With any of these, we are now picking up Jesus, as well as the scribes and Pharisees (vs. 3), on a different day.

2. **Yet at dawn** (at daybreak; early in the morning) **He came to be alongside, moving into the Temple courts** (porches; grounds; or: cloister), **and all the people began and kept on coming toward Him, and so, after sitting down** (taking a seat; [= teacher's posture]), **He began and continued teaching them.**

Presuming that the context is still during the Feast of Tabernacles, Jesus is once again taking a bold stand to take a public posture of a teacher, as He had in 7:14ff, above, and recall the people's response in 7:25-26. This scene may be the day after 7:37-44. We are probably safe in concluding that this describes His normal activities when visiting Jerusalem, prior to His final Feast of Passover.

3. **Now the scribes** (specialists in the written Scriptures; theologians; scholars) **and the Pharisees are progressively bringing a woman** (or: a wife) – **a woman being one having been taken down** (grasped down with force; overpowered by hand, seized and forced) **upon in an act of adultery – and then, standing** (setting; placing) **her within the midst,**

The religious leaders are attempting to put Jesus in a difficult position. If this woman had committed adultery, they want to see if Jesus would judge her in accord with the Law of Moses (vs. 5, below), and in vs. 6 John explains their motive: to test and entrap Him. They knew that He had a reputation of extending grace to "sinners," and had showed acceptance of them by sharing meals with them.

Careful attention needs to be given to the participle that our author uses to describe this "act of adultery." The NIV renders this as a verb, "caught," i.e., "caught in adultery." This sounds like they just happened to catch her in the act, and then dragged her to Jesus. The KJV is more correct, rendering the verb as "taken," but it still allows for an interpretations as given in the NIV. However, the Greek (a perfect, passive participle of *kata* {down} + *lambanō* {take; grasp; seize}) is more specific and indicates the action of a male upon the woman that likely may have been rape. My bold rendering is that she was a woman (or: a wife) "**being one having been taken down.**" The passive voice indicates that the action is not being ascribed to her, but rather to the male. The alternate translation is, "one having been grasped down with force; overpowered by hand, seized and forced upon." She had been violated. [I was a boy when my father first pointed this out to me, based upon what the Greek text says.] The scribes and the Pharisees knew this, and so the second layer of their duplicity is to see if He is able to discern what had actually happened. Surely the Messiah should have the "wisdom of Solomon."

4. **they proceeded in saying to Him, "Teacher, this woman** (or: this, the wife) **has been taken down, grasped, overpowered by hand and forced, upon the very act: being a woman having repeatedly been adulterated** (or: having the act of adultery habitually performed upon her; gang raped).

Now they tell him straight out what had happened, using the verb form of the same participle that John used in vs. 3. But here they betray themselves by using the phrase, "**upon the very act**," and then also putting the word "adultery" in the form of a present participle: "**having repeatedly been adulterated** (or: having the act of adultery habitually performed upon her; gang raped)."

Of course, if they had "caught" her in "the very act," they would have also caught the man, or men, who had been doing this. Yet, they do not bring him, or them, along with the woman. This was contrary to the Law. *Cf* Lev. 20:10

5. **"Now within the Law, Moses implanted a goal for** (imparted the end in view with; gave an inward directive to) **us to repeatedly stone this sort of woman. Therefore, what are you yourself now saying?"**

Notice that they ask Him to verbally respond to them, to make a pronouncement about the situation. They want Him to judge her.

6. **– Now they were saying this, continuing in putting Him to the proof** (examining so as to test Him; = to trap Him) **to the end that they should continue holding** (or: having) **[something] to be constantly accusing** (or: progressively bringing charges) **pertaining to Him –**
So Jesus, stooping (or: bowing [His] head and bending) **down, began writing down into the dirt** (earth; soil; ground; = dust) **with the finger.**

John reveals their intent. However, Jesus does not give them what they are asking for: He makes no verbal response. Instead, He stoops down and begins writing in the dirt, using His finger. John does not tell us what He wrote, but only describes His action. It is an expression, in writing, of the Logos. The media that He used was the ground upon which everyone habitually walked – a figure for both what people were made of, and for the living of their lives. This was "holy ground," set-apart land, which was the yard around God's House. They were using this area to bring condemnation, and to attempt to gain "grounds" for an accusation against Him. Church history has repeated this same act.

7. **Now as they were persisting, remaining upon [the subject], continuing to question Him, He unbends back up** (or: straightens up) **and says to them, "Let the sinless one** (the one without failure or a miss of the target) **of** (or: among) **you folks [be] first [to] cast** (or: throw) **a stone upon her."**

The religious folks persist in giving an evil report, and are "**continuing to question Him.**" So He straightens up, thus taking a stand in the confrontation. Now we see "the wisdom of Solomon" in action: He gives the judgment of the Law, but the execution of the Law now has a stipulation. For these Israelites to follow-through on what was written in their Law, they must be "**sinless** (without failure or a miss of the target)." Jesus has brought a new Logos that modifies the old arrangement. Recall what He said in Mat. 5:

> 27. **"YOU folks hear** (or: heard) **that it was declared,**
> **'YOU will not continue committing adultery!'** [Ex. 20:13]
> 28. **"Yet I, Myself, am now saying to YOU people that every man who is continuing in, or, repeatedly looking at and observing** (constantly watching or leering at; = fantasizing over) **a [married] woman, with a view toward the [situation, or, condition] to crave her** (to experience strong passion for her, or, to desire to rush in a heat of emotion upon her), **has already committed adultery with her, within his heart!**

With the coming of the Christ, the issues of life must be dealt with at their roots – in the sphere of the heart. We will see in His response to the woman (vs. 11) what the new arrangement looks like. Paul spoke of this in Rom. 8:2,

> "**For the principle and law of, from and which is the spirit and attitude of 'The Life within Christ Jesus'**

(or: For you see, the Law of Life's spirit, joined with [the] Anointing of Jesus; or: For the Spirit's law of life within Christ Jesus; or: the Law [= Torah] from the Breath-effect, which is Life in union with [the] Anointed Jesus)
frees you away from the Law of the Sin and of the Death."

8. **And again, bending** (or: stooping) **down, He was continuing to write into the dirt** (or: earth).

We suggest that Jesus was here acting out the work of The Prophet. Was He possibly writing what had been written in Isa. 1:21?
> "Oh, how the faithful city has become a prostitute! Once her courts were just, and what was right lived there, but now – murderers."

Art White added this insightful observation: It is "a type of Him writing his Logos into, or onto, dust... earth; i.e., the 'earthen vessels' of our hearts." Perhaps this second writing was the first writing of the new covenant, and aimed at the woman standing before Him.

9. **So those hearing [Him] also being progressively convinced, then convicted by the conscience, began going out, one by one, beginning from the elders** (or: the older ones) **until the last ones. Then Jesus was left behind, alone, and also the woman** (or: the wife) **continuing being** [other MSS: standing] **in the midst [of the court, or cloister].**

This new Logos, from Jesus, had hit the mark: their consciences. His new Idea, His creative Blueprint, had progressively convinced them. They made no reply, but one-after-another left the Temple courts, abandoning their original purposes. Some of these were "**the elders**." They would have most likely had a better understanding of Israel's Scriptures, which pointed beyond the Law to mercy, and to the Christ, and to the time of God's principles being written in our hearts (the new arrangement). *Cf* Ezk. 11:19; 36:26; Jer. 31:33; Heb. 8:10-11

Notice that when the men left, the woman stayed with Jesus. Was her conscience clear? Or, was she the only one who was aware that she was in the presence of the Logos-made-flesh? Was she waiting for His judgment upon the matter? Was she simply enthralled with this manifestation of wisdom, grace and mercy? Was she hoping for inner healing from the abuse that she had endured? Was she captivated by God's Love?

10. **Now Jesus, unbending, straightening up and seeing no one but the woman, says to her, "O woman** (or: Madam; = Dear lady), **where are those, your accusers? Does no one condemn you?"**

Observe that once again He takes a stand and confronts the situation, as He had in vs. 6. He now asks her to look around and see the change in her situation, which He had created by His judgment to the men. She is now a new Eve, but with God not asking, "where are you, Adam.... did you disobey Me?" But rather, she is with a Savior, asking where her accusers had gone, and asking if no one condemns her. She was in the presence of the Christ, and:
> "**Nothing, consequently, [is] now a result of condemnation in** (or: a commensurate effect of a decision for; a corresponding result of a negative evaluation which falls in line with a decision or follows the pattern which divides [folks] down, with) **those within Christ Jesus**
> > (or: In that case, therefore, [there is] now not one thing [that is] really an effect of a downward-judging to, in or with the folks in union with or centered in [the] Anointing of Jesus)!" (Rom. 8:1)

11. **Then she says, "No one, sir** (or: O lord; or: Master).**" So Jesus says to her, "Neither am I, Myself, bringing a corresponding decision upon you** (or: proceeding to condemn you according to the pattern). **Be going on your way, and from this moment no longer make it a habit to miss the target** (or: from now on be failing no more; from the present moment no longer practice error or sin).**"

152

This is "the judgment seat of Christ." He asks us, "What happened to your accusers? Does no one condemn you?" And we answer, "No one, O Lord." And He tells us, "**Neither am I, Myself, bringing a corresponding decision upon you**." This story is all of us, when we are in the presence of Christ – and we all are, all the time.

But the Logos is not finished. An empowerment comes next, via an implanted goal: we can "**no longer make it a habit to miss the target**." That imparted Word means that, from now on, we can be "no longer keeping on failing, practicing error, or constantly sinning." My, what freedom! And so much better than being exiled from the Garden!!

12. **Jesus therefore again spoke to them** [i.e., to those whom He had just been teaching, in vs. 2, or at a later time], **saying, "I, Myself, am** (or: continuously exist being) **the Light of this ordered world**
>   (or: of the aggregate of humanity; for the System of domination; of the cultural, political, and religious arrangements; from the cosmos; of 'the theater of history' – Walter Wink).
The one habitually and progressively following Me can by no means walk around (= under no circumstances live his or her life) **within, or in union with, the Darkness [of the old order]**
>   (or: the dim and shaded areas; the gloom and obscurity due to the lack of the Light of the Day; the [realm] of the shadows; [note: = ignorance; = that situation which existed before the Light came; or, could also refer to the dim condition within the holy place of the Temple, or to the darkness of death, blindness or the womb]),
but, to the contrary, he will progressively possess (constantly have and hold) **the Light of 'the Life!'** (or: the light which is life; or: the Light from the Life.)"

His first statement reaches back to the description of the Logos, in 1:4, above, "**Within It** (or: Him), **Life was continuing and progressively existing. And the Life was continuing being, and began progressively existing as, the Light of the humans**." On offer are other potential renderings for "**this ordered world**" which can equally apply. He continually exists being **the Light**:
>   a) of the aggregate of humanity
>   b) for the System of domination (be that religious or governmental)
>   c) of all aspects of the cultural, political and religious arrangements
>   d) of 'the theater of history' – a phrase used by Walter Wink.

Those who "**habitually and progressively follow [Him]**" now walk (i.e., live their lives) in His Light, and no longer live "**within, or in union with, the Darkness [of the old order]**." This is an echo of 1:5, above. Primarily, for Israel, this meant not living in accord with the darkness of the Law, or the old covenant, and therefore living in a new creation (2 Cor. 5:17). A similar change would happen for those of the ethnic multitudes who had not been a part of Israel. They were now joined to Israel (Rom. 11:17; Eph. 2:15). In 1 Jn. 1:6-7, we are instructed:
>   "**If we should up and say that we are continuously having common being** (or: constantly enjoying fellowship, participation and partnership) **with Him and yet may be habitually walking round about** (= living our lives) **within the Darkness and the dim realm of shadows we are constantly lying** (speaking falsely) **and are not in the habit of doing the truth** (or: are not constructing, practicing or producing reality). **Yet if we keep on walking about** (= continue living our life) **within the midst of and in union with the Light, as He exists** (or: is) **within the Light, we constantly have common being and existence** (or: hold common fellowship, participation and enjoy partnership) **with one another, and the blood of, from, and which is Jesus, His Son, keeps continually and repeatedly cleansing us** (or: is progressively rendering us pure) **from every sin** (or: from all error, failure, deviation, mistake, and from every shot that is off target [when it occurs])."
You cannot remain under the Law or the old covenant system and still be in the Light of the new creation.

The "**Light of 'the Life!'**" is the perception and understanding of the Christ-Life, which is a life of union with God, and with all, and with everything – for God is All in all. It is having the single vision that Christ has, seeing and doing only what the Father is doing. It means walking in the new Day of the Lord, and not in the night of a past day.

13. **Therefore the Pharisees said to Him, "You yourself are continuing to bear witness** (or: are now giving testimony) **about yourself! Your witness** (testimony) **is not true** (real; valid)**!"**

Jesus, Himself, said that if He bore witness of Himself, His witness would not be true (5:31, above). Deut. 17:6 or 19:15 may have been what the Pharisees had in mind, with this accusation. The Law required at least two witnesses for a claim to be considered valid and true (vs. 17, below). In the context of 5:32-39, above, Jesus explained to the Judeans that both the works that the Father had given Him to do and the Father, Himself, gave witness to Him. In vs. 18, below, He once again affirms that "**the Father is continuously bearing witness** (constantly testifying and giving evidence) **about Me.**"

There have been many people who have related to others about spiritual experiences that they have had. If we are to believe them, it seems reasonable that either their "works; deeds; actions" or the Father should provide a second witness for them – if we are to accept their story as being true. Otherwise, we are left not necessarily refuting their word, but having questions about the veracity of what they have related. From the giving of the Law, to Israel, on through Rev. 11:3ff, a plural number of witnesses is always stressed. Paul instructed the community in Corinth to have the group discern and judge when someone gave a prophecy (1 Cor. 14:29). So in saying what they said, the Pharisees were not making an unreasonable assertion. The problem that these folks had is explained by Jesus in vs. 15a, below: they were judging the situation and making this decision "**based on the flesh.**" So, in the next six verses, Jesus refutes their public claim. Public accusations, when they are not true, can give opportunity for truth and understanding to be shared with that same public – and then recorded for others, like us.

14. **Jesus considers a reply, and then says to them, "Even if I, Myself, continue bearing witness** (or: am now giving testimony) **about Myself, My witness** (testimony) **is, and continues being, true** (valid; real; genuine) **because I have seen and thus know where** (or: what place) **I came from, as well as under where I progressively lead the way** (or: to where I am going). **Yet you folks, yourselves, have not seen and do not know from where** (or: what place) **I am progressively coming, nor under where I progressively lead the way** (or: to where I am departing and continuing to go).

It may be that with the statement of their accusation, Jesus listened to what the Father would have Him say to them. Or, He might have taken a few moments to consider how best to answer them. Notice that I rendered what the common translations give as "answered," as, "**considers a reply.**" The Greek word is a form of *apokrinō*. This is the verb *krinō* (to separate out the elements of a situation, evaluate and then decide, or make a judgement) prefixed by the preposition *apo-*, which means "from." So, from evaluating what they had said, Jesus "**considers a reply, and then says to them**…" Take note of the complexity of His reply. It was not just an "off-the-cuff rebuttal." It was what we call, "a teaching moment."

Now Jesus adds another dimension to the verification of one person's witness:

> "**My witness** (testimony) **is, and continues being, true** (valid; real; genuine) **because I have seen and thus know where** (or: what place) **I came from, as well as under where I progressively lead the way** (or: to where I am going)."

Ordinary people would be unable to make this claim. Only by the Spirit of God could this be known. Thus, Jesus was implicitly making another claim about Himself: He was the Anointed One; He had the Spirit. The Pharisees were ordinary people, so they had not seen, and thus did not know either where He had come from, nor to where He was "**progressively lead the way** (or: to where I am departing and continuing to go)." This repeats the idea of Jn. 7:33-34, and would leave them questioning again, as we saw in 7:35-36, above. But here, Jesus continues in His explanations.

15. **"You people, yourselves, continue making decisions based on the flesh** (or: constantly separate, evaluate and judge down from, on the level of, and in accord with [the realm and system of] the flesh). **I, Myself, am habitually judging** (sifting, separating, evaluating and deciding about) **no one.**

Paul instructs us concerning "basing things on the flesh," in Rom. 8:

5. **You see, those continuously existing in accord with flesh** (or: = in correspondence to Torah-keeping and cultural boundaries; or: = the human condition) **habitually think about, have an understanding and outlook based upon, are inclined to, set their mind on and are disposed to the things of the flesh** (= the human condition with its cultural traditions, religious cultus and national boundary markers), **yet those in accord with spirit** (or: down from [the] Spirit; on the level of Breath-effect; in line with [His] Attitude) **[think about; have an outlook from] the things and matters of the spirit** (or: the Spirit; Breath-effect; the Attitude).

6. **For the result of the thinking** (mind-set; effect of the way of thinking; disposition; result of understanding and inclination; the minding; the opinion; the thought; the outlook) **of the flesh** (= from the human condition or the System of culture and cultus; or: = Torah keeping) **[is; brings] death, yet the result of the thinking** (mind-set; disposition; thought and way of thinking; outlook) **of the spirit** (or: from the Spirit; which is the Breath-effect) **[is; brings] Life and Peace** (joining).

7. **Because of that, the result of the thinking** (disposition; thought processes; mind-set, outlook) **of the flesh** (= attention to Torah boundary-markers, custom and cultus; or: = from the human condition) **[is; brings] enmity, alienation and discord [streaming] into God** (or: hostility unto, or active hatred with a view to, God), **for it continues not being humbly aligned and supportive** (habitually placed under and submitted; or, as a middle: subjecting, humbly arranging or marshaling itself) **to the principle and law which is God** (or: in God's principle; by the Law from God), **for neither is it able nor does it have power.**

This really sheds light on the situation that Jesus was constantly encountering, with the scribes, the Pharisees and the priests. Because of operating in, and making decisions based on, **the flesh,** they **"continued not being humbly aligned and supportive** (habitually placed under and submitted) **to the principle and law which is God** (or: in God's principle; by the Law from God), **for neither [were they] able nor did [they] have power."** Because of this, Jesus was not **"judging** (sifting, separating, evaluating and deciding about) [them]."

16. **"And yet, if I, Myself, ever proceed in judging** (or: if ever I, Myself, should evaluate or decide), **My deciding** (separating, evaluating and judging) **is, and continues being, true** (valid; real; genuine), **because I am not** (or: I do not exist being) **alone, but to the contrary, [it is] I, Myself, and the One sending Me: the Father.**

Mark well this statement: "**I am not** (or: I do not exist being) **alone.**" Then He goes on to say, "**[it is] I, Myself, and the One sending Me: the Father.**" So we should conclude that either the Father, although unseen to the natural eye, was with Him, or in Him. Paul informs us that:

"**God was existing within Christ** (God was and continued being centered in, and in union with [the] Anointed One) **progressively and completely transforming [the] aggregate of humanity** (or: world) **to be other [than it is]**

(or: progressively bringing [the] ordered System into another level or state; repeatedly changing [the] universe to correspond with other [conditions; perceptions]; progressively altering [the] ordered arrangement of culture, religions, economy and government to be in line with another one; habitually and progressively changing [the] secular realm [of humanity] from enmity to friendship; reconciling [the] world [of mankind]) **in Himself, to Himself, for Himself, by Himself and with Himself, not accounting to them** (not putting to their account; not logically considering for them; not reasoning in them) **the results and effects of their falls to the side** (their trespasses and offenses), **even placing within us the Word** (the *Logos;* the Idea; the Reason; the message; the pattern-forming information) **of the**

corresponding transformation to otherness (or: the full alteration; the change from enmity to friendship; the conciliation)" (2 Cor. 5:19).

Jesus, and His body, were and are "two witnesses" (*cf* Rev. 11:3-11).

During Jesus' earthly ministry, He – as God's Lamb – was not judging or making decisions about other folks. That would come after His exaltation into the realm of the atmospheres, with His body seated with Him (Eph. 2:6; Heb. 12:22-24; Rev. 2:26-27; 3:21). At the "judgment seat of Christ" (2 Cor. 5:10), the "**deciding** (separating, evaluating and judging) **is, and continues being, true** (valid; real; genuine)," for it comes from "**the Way** (or: Path), **the Truth** (the Reality) **and the Life**" (14:6, below).

17. **"Yet even within your own Law it has been written that the witness** (testimony; evidence) **of two people** (humans; men) **is true** (or: exists being valid, genuine and real).

18. **"I, Myself, am the man now bearing witness** (or: habitually testifying; progressively giving evidence) **about Myself, and the Father – the One sending Me – is continuously bearing witness** (constantly testifying and giving evidence) **about Me."**

Verse 17 gives the Scriptural basis for His deciding being true, and vs. 18 is a restatement (rhetorical redundancy) of 16b, above. We will see an expansion of this in 14:9-11, and again, in 17:5, 21-23, below.

19. **Therefore they went on saying to Him, "[So] where is your father?" Jesus decidedly answered, "You folks have neither seen, nor perceived, nor known, nor are you acquainted with Me, nor My Father. If you had seen and knew** (or: were acquainted with) **Me, you would also have seen and know** (or: be acquainted with) **My Father."**

So now His audience challenges His statements about His Father. Observe His first response: "**You folks have neither seen, nor perceived, nor known, nor are you acquainted with Me, nor My Father**." The verb "seen... acquainted with" is based upon an obsolete (at that time) verb that had the core meaning to "to see; to perceive," and being in the perfect tense strictly means "to have seen," but from this now had the extended meanings "perceive," and thus "know" (from having seen/perceived), as well as "to thus be acquainted with" someone or something. Although they had the Law that had given information about God, and His interaction with their ancestors, they really did not know God – and thus, were not acquainted with Who Jesus really was/is. From what has been shared, above, of other statements by Jesus as well as by Paul, we are informed about the union that Jesus had with the Father, and about how the Father was within Him. But these folks did not yet know this. And since they did not know Who He was, they would therefore not know, or be acquainted with, the Father. Sadly, this is still true of many people in our day.

As He had said, in vs. 15, above, they "**continued making decisions based on the flesh**." Since "**God is Spirit**" (Jn. 4:24), they had no ability to see or perceive God, and thus did not know Him. They only knew His rules, under the old covenant, and were aware of some of His actions.

20. **These declarations from the gush** (or: sayings which resulted from the flow) **He spoke within the treasury area, while teaching within the Temple courts** (or: grounds; porches), **and still no one caught hold of or apprehended Him, because His hour had not yet come, so as to be present.**

The Temple rulers, and the religious domination system, did not like what He was saying, but His "hour" was determined by the Father. Here, John is instructing us that although they wanted to catch hold of Him and apprehend Him (arrest Him), they did not have free will to do what was contrary to the Father's plans and program. Modern humanity, in their idolatry of the human "free will" (which is a myth – only God is free) still cannot comprehend the effects of God's reign among us.

21. **Then He** [*p66c* & others: Jesus] **again said to them, "I Myself am progressively leading the way under** (or: I am Myself proceeding to withdraw and go away), **and so you folks will continue looking for Me** (or: seek to find Me) **and you yourselves will progressively** (or: one after another) **die and decay within your errors** (failures; misses of the target; deviations; sins). **Under where I, Myself, progressively lead the way** (or: To where I am Myself proceeding to withdraw and go away) **you folks continue having no power to go** (or: are presently unable to come)."

The bold rendering of the first verb in the first clause, "**progressively leading the way under**," is a literal rendering of the verb "to lead" that is prefixed by the preposition, "under." This is the Path (the Way, of 14:6, below) that Christ was to follow:

> "**And so, being found in an outward fashion, mode of circumstance, condition, form-appearance** (or: character, role, phase, configuration, manner) **as a human** (a person; a man), **He lowers Himself** (or: humbled Himself; made Himself low; degrades Himself; levels Himself off), **coming to be** (or: birthing Himself) **a submissive, obedient One** (one who gives the ear and listens) **as far as** (or: to the point of; until) **death – but death of a cross** (torture stake)!" (Phil. 2:8)

Those who follow Him do the same, and come to, the same place. But the end is resurrection and exaltation. His listeners were unable to come after Him without being joined to the Vine (15:1ff, below). But each, in their own "place in line" would eventually come to where He was going, having in their appointed time been given the power to do so.

22. **The Jews** (= religious authorities of Judea) **were therefore beginning to say, "Surely he will not proceed to be killing himself, will he, seeing that he is saying 'Under where I progressively lead the way** (or: To where I am proceeding to withdraw and go away) **you folks continue having no power to go** (are presently unable to come)'?"

A fascinating response. But, as to where He was going, they were on the right track.

23. **So He went on to say to them, "You folks, yourselves, continuously exist** (presently are) **from out of the things below** (or: You are yourselves presently forth from out of the downward places); **I, Myself, continuously exist** (have My being; am) **from out of the things above** (or: I am Myself forth from the midst of upward places). **You yourselves continuously exist from out of this System** (ordered arrangement; world of culture, economy, religion and politics; this System of control and domination); **I, Myself, do not exist** (do not have My being) **from out of this System** (world; etc.).

They were, as Paul put it, "**the first humans** (persons; humanity), **forth from out of the earth** (Land; ground; soil), **made of moist soil and dust** (or: having the quality and character of moist dirt that can be poured or mounded; soilish)... **of such sort also [are] the people [who are] made of and have the character and quality of moist soil or dust** (soil-ish folks)" (1 Cor. 15:47a, 48). He, on the other hand, "**[is made] out of heaven** (or: [is] from atmosphere and sky... [is] the Added, Imposed, Heavenly Person** (or: the one made of and having the quality and character of the added-heaven)" (1 Cor. 15:47b, 48). This was Paul's way of contrasting "**the one having the qualities and characteristics of a soul** (the soulish; psychical)" with "**the spiritual** (that pertaining to and having the qualities of Breath-effect and Attitude)" (1 Cor. 15:46). This is what Jesus meant by contrasting "**above**" with "**below**," in the first part of vs. 23, above.

A part of being "**from out of the things below** (the downward places)" was "**continuously existing from out of this System** (ordered arrangement; world of culture, economy, religion and politics; this System of control and domination)." That was a reference to living with a focus on earthly things, being shaped by their culture, and the socio-religious System of domination. Remember, Christ came to set folks free from that (e.g., Gal. 4:22-31; 5:1).

24. **"Therefore I said to you that you will progressively die and decay within your errors** (failures; sins; times of falling short or to the side of the target), **for, unless you come to trust and believe that I, Myself, am** (or: that, as for Me, I exist and continue being; or; that I am Myself Existence and Being; or, emphatically: that I AM), **you folks will progressively die and rot within your failures** (sins; etc.)**!"**

What a disheartening thing to hear, if they could not come to trust and believe Who He was, where He came from, and Who was His Father. If they were not inserted into the Vine, or the olive tree; if they did not become born back up, from above (Jn. 3:7), they would not experience the flowing away of their mistakes and failures, and would not become a part of what their Messiah had come to inaugurate: the Messianic Kingdom of God. But still, we later learned that they would at some point be resurrected into a time of cleansing (Mat. 3:12) and purification (Rev. 20:13-15 – the pond of the Fire [i.e., God] and Deity [the transforming divine nature]). They would miss out on participation in the upcoming Messianic Banquet/Wedding Party, of which we read and observe in the tales of the Logos, in the book of Acts.

25. **They then began saying to Him, "YOU! – what** (or: who) **ARE you?" Jesus says to them, "That which I am even habitually telling you: the Beginning, the Origin, the Source and the Chief One** (or: The *Archē*; or, perhaps: Primarily that which I am also constantly telling you). [*Cf* 1:1, above]

The interrogative is normally (and correctly – as I include parenthetically) rendered "who." That would be a logical question to ask Him. Perhaps some thought he was a prophet, like John the immerser. Maybe some thought that He was Elijah, come as prophesied in Mal. 4:5. Some might have thought that He was an Essene, from the Qumran community out in the desert.

But Jesus had said some strange things, in vs. 23, above. And thus did I give my first rendering as "**what ARE you**?" Did they think that he might be a scribe, or one of the priests? Were they wondering about the source of the authority that they perceived Him having? Did they think that He was possibly an agent or messenger that had appeared from the atmosphere? Did they perhaps have the visitation of agents to Abraham, or Joshua, or Gideon in mind? Such things were a part of both their history and worldview. Now, consider His reply to them...

Parenthetically, on offer is a transliteration of the Greek word: *Archē*. This was the word used in 1:1, above, "In *Archē* was the *Logos*." The Greek syntax is a bit ambiguous, but my bold rendering is literal, and I employ a colon to make sense of His answer. He is telling them that He is "**the Beginning, the Origin, the Source**." He is the *Arche*. Another possible rendering is, "the chief One." Now we, having all of the Gospel of John to read, can make sense of this. But what did His listeners think? Well, this is why this verse is often rendered with "*Archē*" not rendered as a noun, but as an adverb, "Primarily..." Now this makes sense to our ears, but it does not really translate the Greek. He had regularly been giving them vague answers, and in John there are a number of "I AM" statements, possibly pointing to the divine. Notice that in the next verse, He again uses the vague "the One sending Me..." They were, apparently, supposed to figure this out. Who was the One who sent Moses to deliver Israel from Egypt? Jesus had come on a parallel mission.

26. **"I continuously hold and habitually have many things to be constantly speaking and deciding** (or: separating, evaluating and judging) **about you folks. However, the One sending Me is truthful** (exists being continuously real and true), **and I, what I hear from His side, these things I constantly speak and utter into the System**
>   (into the world; unto the aggregate of humanity and the ordered arrangement of the culture, religion, economy and government; into the realm of the secular; or: unto the dominating systems of control; or: into the midst of the universe).**"**

This first statement is ambiguous. He had been speaking to those who were obviously NOT His disciples, and they had just put a wide-open question to Him: "Who or what ARE you?" What "many" things did He hold, or have, "**to be constantly speaking**" about them? What were the "many" things that He was to be "**deciding** (or: separating, evaluating and judging) **about**" them?

Whatever these things were, they were **what [He] heard from [the] side [of] the One sending [Him]**," and this One is "**truthful** (exists being continuously real and true)," and so they could depend upon that One, and thus, upon what He, Himself, had been saying to them from the One. In Jn. 14:6, He will tell His listeners that He is "the Way, the **TRUTH**, and the Life." John's Gospel presents a progressive unveiling of the Christ to his readers. This is not just a record of His sayings. The reader (in that day, those listening to this being publicly read to them) was expected to be putting these little pieces together in order to know just Who Jesus was.

Now consider: He was not constantly speaking to the leaders of the Roman Empire. So into what "System" was He constantly speaking? Yes, it was to their "world" of the priests, the scribes and the Pharisees, their Second Temple Judaism culture, as well as to the aggregate of humanity in 1st century Palestine.

27. They did not know or understand that He had been speaking the Father to, and among, them.

At first reading, it may seem that I have omitted a word, just before "**the Father.**" Most translations insert a preposition before this phrase, such as "of" (KJV) or "about" (D.B. Hart). Either of those would be correct if the phrase was in the genitive case, the case of the indirect object. But the noun case is the accusative, the case of the direct object. In vs. 26 we read that He told them, "**what I hear from His side, these things I constantly speak.**" The Logos that He heard from the Father was the Logos that He spoke to them. So He was, literally, "**speaking the Father to, and among, them.**" Through the Words that He spoke, **the Father** was being presented to them, and was coming to them. It is still so, today: In the Word/message of Christ or the Spirit, we are confronted with the Speaker.

Dan Kaplan pointed us to one example for the precedence in the prophets of John's description of Jesus' speeches:

> "Then Zerubbabel, son of Shealtiel, Joshua, son of Jehozakak, the great priest, and all the remnant of the people, hearkened to the Voice of Yahweh their Elohim (God), and to the words of Haggai the prophet when Yahweh their Elohim (God) sent him to them, and the people feared before the face of Yahweh. Then Haggai, the messenger of Yahweh, spoke Yahweh's message to the people, saying, 'I am with you, averring is Yahweh'" (Hag. 1:12-13; *Concordant Version of the OT*).

There, they were confronted with Yahweh, through Haggai, His messenger; here, they were confronted with the same God, identified as Jesus' Father, through His Messenger, the Son.

28. Then Jesus says to them, "Whenever you folks may lift up high (should raise aloft; would elevate; or: can exalt) the Son of man (Humanity's Son; = the Human Being; = the son of Adam; = the eschatological messianic figure), then you will progressively come to know by personal experience that I, Myself, am (or: I Myself continue existing; I Myself am Being and Existence; or, emphatically: I AM), and I from Myself am habitually doing nothing (not one thing), but rather, according (just; correspondingly) as the Father instructs (or: taught) Me, I continue speaking (uttering) these things.

Since the last clause of vs. 28 carries on the thought of vs. 27, we will begin here. It begins with a dependent clause, "**according** (just; correspondingly) **as the Father instructs** (or: taught) **Me.**" The verb is in the aorist tense that just gives the facts of the action. It is the indefinite tense, and can be rendered as a simple present tense (**instructs**) or as a simple past tense (**taught**), and on offer are two meanings of the verb. I first chose the present tense, in light of what He had said in vs. 26, above, "**what I hear from His side,**" which seems to suggest an ongoing process of His hearing the instruction of the Father, and then continuing in "**speaking** (uttering) **these things**." He was a Branch of the Father (Jn. 15:1ff), receiving the Life-Sap which produced the Father's Fruit. He was a Pattern for us, who have become His branches. Just before this He had affirmed to them that He, from Himself, was "**habitually doing nothing** (not one thing)." He received from the Father, and then gave out to others. He, as "**the Son of man**," was dependent upon the Father, Who was His Head (1 Cor. 11:3b).

The opening statement of this verse is a bit obscure. We, knowing that He was speaking of His crucifixion, can understand the dependent clause, "**Whenever you folks may lift up high** the eschatological messianic figure (the Human Being; Adam's son, which corresponds to the Second Humanity, or the Last Adam of 1 Cor. 15:45-47)." But how will they "**progressively come to know by personal experience that I, Myself, am**?" One fulfillment of this was in the Roman centurion, at the cross, in Mk. 15:39, "**Truly** (or: In reality; Certainly) **this man was God's Son** (or: a son of God)." But in 12:32, below, He expanded His meaning in this statement:

> "**And thus I Myself: if** (when) **I should be lifted up from out of the earth** (or: can be exalted from the midst of this Land), **I will progressively** (or: one after another) **drag** [note: drag as with, or in, a net; or: draw, as drawing water with a bucket, or a sword its sheath] **all humans** (or: everyone) **to Myself.**"

When they began to see this happening, in the book of Acts, they might have remembered what He said, here in 8:28, as well as in 12:32.

There is another layer of understanding that can be seen in the three optional renderings in the parenthetical expansion:

> a. I Myself continue existing;
> b. I Myself am Being and Existence;
> c. I AM (*egō eimi*)

This is another of the "I AM" statements by Jesus, in John's Gospel. It echoes the Septuagint (Greek) version of what God said to Moses out of the burning bush, "and so functions as a somewhat veiled but still nearly unmistakable divine name" (David Bentley Hart). Most common translations render this "I am [he]," which would understand Him as saying that He was "the Son of man." Either reading makes sense, but as I have indicated, with the brackets, the pronoun "he" is not in the text. Now if we put "c" with vs. 27, it could read, "**He had been speaking the I AM to, and among, them.**"

29. "**And further, the One sending Me is constantly** (or: continuously exists being) **with Me. He does not leave Me alone** (or: He did not send Me off alone; He does not let Me go away alone; He does not divorce or abandon Me). **For this reason I, Myself, am always constantly doing the things pleasing to Him** (or: making pleasing things by Him; performing and producing the acceptable things in, and with, Him)."

The I AM was with Him. The I AM did not abandon or divorce Him. The Father did not leave Him alone, let Him go away alone, or send Him off alone. Does not this call to mind Ps. 23:4,

> "**For you see, even if I may** (or: should; would; could) **be caused to journey** (travel; pass from place to place) **within the midst of a shadow of death** (or: death's shadow; a shadow, from death; a shadow which is death), **I will continue not being caused to fear bad [times]** (will not be repeatedly frightened by worthless [situations or people]; will not be habitually afraid of misfortunes, harmful [experiences] or base [schemes]), **because You are, and continue being, with me**" (LXX, JM).

This seems to describe Jesus' journey to Jerusalem, and His being "lifted up high," there.

Because the Father stuck with Him, He was "**always constantly doing the things pleasing to Him.**" The verb "doing" has a broad semantic range that can give us more insights to "the work of Christ."

> a) He was making pleasing things BY Him;
> b) He was performing and producing the acceptable things IN, and WITH, Him."

The dative form of "Him" can also show us (a) that the Father was the source and instrument of what Jesus was doing, and (b) the sphere of the work and production of Christ (IN God) as well as that God was a Partner WITH Christ. Christ was the material with which the Father produced Christ's Body. This body, the Last Adam and the corporate Second Humanity, was and is pleasing and acceptable to God, because of what Christ has done with Humans: He cleaned them from the soil that clung to them (e.g., washed their feet); He healed them and gave them Life (10:10, below); He covered over their mistakes (1 Pet. 4:8) with His Love and gave them shelter (1 Cor. 13:7) and protection (Ps. 28:7; Eph. 6:13-17).

30. **During His progressively speaking these things, many at some point believed, and came to put [their] trust and confidence into Him.**

The Word, as a Seed, fell into their earth (their heart and soul) and took root. They were confronted with the Father, and they were given faith and trust so as to have confidence in Jesus.

31. **Therefore, Jesus began laying it out, saying to the Judeans who had trusted and were now believing by Him** (or: in Him), **"If you yourselves would remain** (can dwell; should abide) **within My word** (in union with My *Logos* and information; centered in the thought, idea and message laid out by Me), **you folks are, and continue being, truly** (really; genuinely) **My disciples** (or: learners from Me),

Take note that "Him" which ends the first statement is in the dative case. Therefore, my first rendering is "**by Him**." It was He, Himself, and His presenting the Father to them, which was the instrument of their ability to trust and believe "in Him."

Remaining (dwelling; abiding) within His Logos is stated metaphorically in 15:1ff, below, as branches remaining within the Vine (Christ). This is a presentation of the Gospel. This is an offer to join Him on the Path (the Way, the Road). This is the Life: abiding in union with the information laid out by Him, and dwelling centered in the Thought which is Him; remaining in the midst of His Reason. It is the life and existence of His disciples: being folks who continue to learn from Him. It is really very simple. No theology needed; no philosophical constructs required. No rituals involved: just live in His Logos and follow the Blueprint, which is alive and moving forward.

32. **"and you will progressively come to know the Truth** (or: Reality; that which is unsealed, open and without concealment) **by intimate experience, and the Truth** (Reality) **will progressively liberate and make** (or: set) **you people free!"**

It is the disciple who **progressively come to know the Truth** from **remaining with His Word**. This Reality is known **by intimate experience** – and this implies relationship, not just intellectual information or a "belief system." It is this "Reality which is unsealed, open and without concealment" that **will progressively liberate and make** (or: set) **you people** [that is those who have been enabled to trust Him, and abide in His Logos as His learners] **free**. Now this verse is the conclusion of vs. 31. We cannot take it as an independent aphorism that describes an independent situation that can arise separated from vs. 31. Verse 31 sets down the condition and the requirement for being **liberated** and **set free**. To be free one has to be a part of Him, just as a branch must be a part of the Vine. There is no freedom apart from this union, and being centered within the sphere of His Logos.

33. **The [Jewish leaders] considered and replied to Him, "We are Abraham's seed** (offspring; descendants), **and we have served as slaves to no one at any time. How are you now saying, 'You will progressively come to be free ones'?"**

Ah, now comes the arrangement of the old covenant: being of the right lineage. In 39a, below, they will make the same claim, again, but there they will insist that Abraham is their father. Based upon vs. 37, below, these folks are not the "**many**" of vs. 30, above, who came to believe and trust into Him. These folks who make this reply to Him He confronts, below, as "**seeking to kill**" Him. These folks considered themselves as being **free**. They probably thought that they had "free" wills, too. But Jesus goes to the heart of the matter, in the next verse…

34. **Jesus decidedly answers them, "It is certainly true** (Amen, amen). **I am now saying to you that everyone, who** (or: all humanity, which) **when, or by, habitually doing the failure** (constantly making the mis-shot; repeatedly performing the sin; progressively producing error), **is** (or: exists being) **a slave of the failure** (the error; the sin; the mis-shot; the mistake; the deviation).

This is the real "slavery" that the NT addresses. Paul addresses this issue in Rom. 7:7-25. To correctly understand Jesus' meaning, here, we must take note of the present tense of the participle, "**do**; make; perform; produce." He meant "**habitually**, constantly, repeatedly or progressively" failing, making the mis-shot, performing the sin, producing error. He was describing a way of life, not an occasional making a mistake or failing to hit the target (of reflecting God's image).

The adjective "**everyone**/all" can apply to an individual, or to all humanity (the corporate first Adam). This was the human condition from which Christ came to save us, and make us free from the slavery of "the deviation (etc.)." All had been slaves of "the failure" (Rom. 5:12), because the Death had spread unto all humanity, and because of this, everyone kept on missing the Target.

35. "**Now the slave is not remaining** (dwelling; abiding) **within the House** (= having no perpetual place in the household) **on into the Age** (or: for life). **The son continuously remains** (dwells; abides) **on into the Age [of Messiah]** (or: for life).

Is His reference, here about the slave, reaching back to Abraham, and the story of Hagar and Ishmael (as Paul did in Gal. 4:22-31)? Was the "House" the house of Israel? We see that Abraham was on their minds in vss. 33 and 39, and in vs. 37 Jesus affirms that, at least on one level, they are "Abraham's seed."

But it was Isaac that remained in the house of Abraham, and in him was the promised seed accounted (Heb. 11:18), which Paul affirms to be a reference to Christ (Gal. 3:16-29). Then in Gal. 4:30 Paul echoes Sarah,
> "**Cast out** (or: At once expel) **the servant girl** (the slave-girl; the maid) **and her son, for by no means will the son of the servant girl** (the slave-girl; the maid) **be an heir** (take possession of and enjoy the distributed allotment) **with the son of the freewoman.**" [cf Gen. 21:10]

So, in vs. 35 Jesus is indicating that these folks are not, presently, a part of Abraham's corporate son. It is those who correspond to Isaac ("**the one from out of the freewoman [was] through Promise**" – Gal. 4:23b) that could now correspond to "**the Son.**" And Paul explained,
> "**Now since you folks belong to Christ** (or: have [the] Anointing as your source and origin; or: So since you people have the qualities and character of Christ, and [are] that which is Christ), **you are straightway and consequently Abraham's Seed: heirs** (possessors and enjoyers of the distributed allotment), **down from, corresponding to and in the sphere of Promise!**" (Gal. 3:29)

So is Jesus indicating that these folks, being slaves of deviation (vs. 34b, above), will not be remaining in the House that is classified as Israel (Rom. 9:7-9; 11:17)? Those who are "placed in the Son" remain so "for life." This calls to mind Paul's teaching on "sonship." That term is composed of the Greek word for "son," and the noun form of the verb meaning "to set; to place." We see a precious picture in Rom. 8:
> 22. **You see, we have seen, and thus know and are aware, that all the creation** [note: = Old Covenant Israel] **keeps on sighing, groaning or querulously moaning together, and yet progressively travailing together as in childbirth** (continues suffering common birthing pains), **until now** (to the point of the present moment). [cf 2 Cor. 5:2, 4]

23. **Yet not only [this], but further, even we ourselves – constantly holding** (or: having; possessing) **the firstfruit of, and which is, the Spirit** (or: the Firstfruit from the Breath-effect; or: the first offering, or first portion, which is spirit and breath, and is from the Attitude) **– we ourselves also continually sigh and groan within** (in the center of) **ourselves, continuously accepting and with our hands taking away from out of** (or: fully receiving) **a placing in the condition of a son** (or: [the] deposit of the Son; a setting in place which is the Son; a constituting as a son; a placing in the Son): **the process of the release of our body from slavery**
> (or: [and] the loosing from destruction pertaining to the [corporate, old covenant] body, which is us; or: = the unbinding and release of the body [of Adam; of humanity], which belongs to us).

As to the term, "the age," Dan Kaplan pointed us to the aspect of "age" that speaks of "maturity." Those in the Son remain so unto the age of maturity (Christ is our maturity).

36. **"Therefore, if the Son should** (or: would) **at some point liberate or begin to make** (or: set) **you free, you folks will progressively exist being actually, essentially and ontologically free people.**

Yet, there is hope for them, because, **"the Son would at some point liberate or begin to make** (or: set) **[them] free**." At some point He would graft them back into the olive tree (Rom. 11:23-29), or the Vine (15:1-10, below), and then they would be "**actually, essentially and ontologically free people**." There is freedom only in Christ.

Here, Dan pointed us to Christ as the new Moses. This verse can be seen as an allusion to the Exodus story, where Israel were freed from the slavery to Egypt (a domination System). He was also the new Joshua, leading the people into the land of "the Promise" – which Paul referred to in Gal. 5:1 as "FREEDOM."

37. **"I have seen and know that you people are Abraham's seed** (offspring; descendants), **but now you men continue seeking to kill Me, because My word** (message; thought; idea; discourse; laid-out information; *logos*) **is not continuing to have room and make progress within** (or: among) **you guys.**

You people are Abraham's seed, but...

Folks who are "**not continuing to have room and make progress [for His word] within** (or: among) **them**," usually "**continue seeking to kill [Him]**." Because of this, they have not yet become Abraham's Seed, "**from out of the freewoman [was] through Promise** (or: a promise)" (Gal. 4:23b). Because His "message; thought; idea; discourse; laid-out information; *logos*" did not have room in them, they "**from out of the servant girl** (the maid) **had been born** (generated and birthed) **down from** (in accord with; on the level of; in the sphere of) **flesh**" (Gal. 4:23a). The Greek word, *chōreō*, has the dual meaning of "to make room for or have space for," and also, "to make progress." Having the one usually leads to the other. These Second Temple Jews were full of the traditions of the elders (e.g., Mk. 7:3; Mat. 15:1-20). His Blueprint found no room at the inn.

38. **"I am habitually speaking things which I, Myself, have seen, [being] at the side of** (or: present with) **the [other MSS: My] Father, and you folks are yourselves therefore habitually doing** [*p*75: speaking] **things which you hear** (or: heard) **at the side of your father** [with other MSS: ... and so are you people then by practice doing what you have seen at the side of the Father?]."

The first clause repeats the ideas of vs. 26b and vs. 28b, but those verses speak of what He hears (or, heard) and what He is instructed (or, was taught). Now He brings up another spiritual sense (Heb. 5:14), the sense of sight. He was "**habitually speaking things which [He, Himself], had seen, [being] at the side of** (or: present with) **the [other MSS: My] Father**." Notice that some MSS have "the Father" while others have "My Father." Likewise with the last phrase of the verse, some have "your father" while others have "the Father." In such cases it is best to meditate on both readings, and then listen within, to what the Father says about each reading. There is another ambiguity due to the lack of punctuation in the oldest texts. So I rendered the second clause as a statement of fact, in the bold rendering, and then, with the other MSS, I set this the second clause as a question that He put to them. The statement is a conclusion about, and an assessment of, their normal practices. It also intimates that they have a different father than He does. The question is a challenge for them to think about, which is really asking them if they have spiritual vision, or if they are walking in the realm of the Spirit.

39. **In calculated reply, they said to Him, "OUR father is Abraham!" Jesus then says to them, "If** (or: Since) **you folks are Abraham's children, be continually doing and performing Abraham's deeds** (actions; works).
> [other MSS: If you folks were Abrahams' children, were you ever doing Abraham's works (deeds; acts)?]

Some MSS give the verb "doing/performing" as a present imperative. In other words, "If you say that your father is Abraham, be habitually living like he lived. The other MSS have the verb in the imperfect indicative tense, and with this the syntax suggests that he was putting a question to them: "were you ever doing Abraham's works (etc.)?" These are contrasting textual traditions; only the Breath-effect can lead us to how Jesus answered their assertion.

40. **"So now, proceed in seeking to kill Me!** (or: Yet now you are continually seeking to kill Me; [note: the verb "seeking" is either present imperative or present indicative]) – **a Man** (person; human) **Who has spoken to you the truth which I hear from** (or: heard at) **God's side** (or: in the presence of God). **Abraham does not do this** (or: did not do this).

The ambiguity of the first statement is not a difference in different MSS, but rather that the form (spelling) of the verb serves two different functions, and so can be read in either of the renderings on offer.

Now is He alluding to Abraham going off to sacrifice Isaac? Or, is He setting them up for what He will say to them in 44a, below? Or, with the parenthetical alternative, is He again facing them with the same confrontation that He did in vs. 37, above?

Whatever it was that He spoke to them, and whatever His intent, He now contrasts their potential actions to His own actions, which were, **"habitually speaking things which I, Myself, have seen, [being] at the side of** (or: present with) **the** [other MSS: My] **Father."** Is this any reason to seek opportunity to kill Him? That is not what Abraham did. Abraham did what God instructed him to do. He also "believed God" (Rom. 4:3). We read again of him in Heb. 11:8b-9a, that he:
> "**summarily obeyed to suddenly go out into the place which he was, and continued being, about to take in hand** (or: receive) – **into an inheritance** (an enjoyment of an allotment). **And so he went out, while not presently putting his thoughts on** (or: not acquainted with) **where he was progressively going. In faith, by trust, with confident loyal allegiance, he sojourned** (resided as an alien in a foreign country; lived alongside as a temporary inhabitant) **[settling] into the land of the Promise…"**

41. **"You folks habitually do your father's works** (perform deeds and actions from your father).**" Therefore they said to Him, "We ourselves were not born out of prostitution** (or: fornication). **We have one Father: God!"**

Their reply to Jesus' statement, here, shows that they saw no ambiguity in His words that they habitually "perform deeds and actions from [their] father." They insist that they "**have one Father: God!**" So they took Jesus' description of them as indicating that someone else was their father. In vs. 44, below, He will state clearly that He was alluding to their father being "**the Ancestor who cast [something] through [someone]**." We will discuss this below.

But why would they first of all affirm that they were NOT "**born out of prostitution** (or: fornication)"? Well, they knew their history, and the words of the Prophets, e.g. Isa. 1:21,

"How has she become a prostitute, a town (or: city) that was faithful? Full of right judgment (or: justice) [was] Zion. Righteousness was lodging in her – yet now, **murderers**!"

These folks did not want an identity of being the descendants of THAT Jerusalem. Yet, once again, we find Jerusalem thus characterized, and given a hateful name, Mystery Babylon, in Rev. 17, where she is symbolically seen as sitting upon the Roman Empire (a domination system pictured as a beast). When John saw that vision of her, he was surprised and amazed at who she was (Rev. 17:6b). She was drunk from the blood of the set-apart folks and with the blood of Jesus' witnesses (Rev. 17:6a). In Mat. 23:37, Jesus says:

"**O Jerusalem, Jerusalem! The one repeatedly killing the prophets, and habitually stoning the people sent off with a mission to her**."

In Lu. 13::33, He said:

"**it continues being inadmissible** (not acceptable or allowed; = unthinkable) **for a prophet to be destroyed** (or; be lost; or, middle: ruined himself) **outside of Jerusalem!**"

His sarcasm is hard to miss in this statement. Another prophet, Hosea was instructed to act out the prostitution of Jerusalem by taking a prostitute as a wife. The prostitution of Israel was her idolatry, as Hosea takes pains to bear out. So Jesus touched a sore spot with his audience. They had assimilated pagan teachings from their overlords. They now had beliefs in demons (a word and concept from Greek religions) – a phenomenon found nowhere in the OT Scriptures. Their father (the pagan teachings) had impregnated their more recent ancestors with ideas based upon idol religions, especially Zoroastrianism, from their time under the Persian Empire.

So is it any wonder that Jesus said to them, in vs. 37, above, "**you men continue seeking to kill Me**"?

42. **Jesus said to them, "If God were your Father, you folks would have been, and continued, loving and urging toward union with** (or: progressively giving yourselves fully to) **Me, for you see, I Myself came forth and am arrived here** (or: and here I am) **from out of the midst of God. For neither have I come or gone off from Myself** (= on My own initiative), **but rather that One sent Me away with a mission** (commissions and sends Me forth as an Emissary, [His] Representative).

You know a tree by its fruit (Mat. 7:16). They had not been producing "love," the fruit of the Spirit of the Father (Gal. 5:22-23). Now think about it: love, and the urge toward union with others, indicates whether or not a person has God as the Father of their spirit, attitude, and state of their inner being. These folks had not yet been "born from above" (3:7, above). They were still dead in trespasses and sins (Eph. 2:1). It is the birth of the new human within us that makes God our Father in a new way, so that we can produce the fruit of the Spirit. To better understand this, let us consider how this is expressed in a passage from Eph. 4:

20. **But you folks did not learn the Christ in this way,**
21. **since, in fact, at one point you heard and so listen to Him, and within Him as well as in union with Him and centered in Him you were and are taught – just as Truth and Reality continuously exist within Jesus** (or: in union with the One, Jesus) –
22. **to put off from yourselves** [as clothing or habits] **what accords to the former entangled manner of living** (or: twisted up behavior)**: the old humanity** (or: the past, worn-out person) – **the one continuously in process of being corrupted** (spoiled; ruined) **down from and in accord with the passionate desires** (the full-covering, swelling emotions) **of the deceptions** (or: seductive desires) –

23. **and then to be continuously renewed** (or: from time to time, or, progressively made young again) **by** (or: in; with) **the spirit** (or: attitude; breath-effect) **of your mind** (or: from the mind which is you folks; or: by the Spirit which is your [collective] mind),

24. **and to enter within** (or: clothe yourselves with) **the new humanity** (or: the Person that is different and innovative in kind and quality) – **the one in accord with and corresponding to God** (or: the person at the Divine level) – **being formed** (framed, built, founded and settled from a state of disorder and wildness; created) **within the Way pointed out** (or: in union with fair and equitable dealings with rightwised relationships, justice, righteousness and covenant participation; centered in [His] eschatological deliverance) **and reverent dedication** (or: benign relationship with nature) **pertaining to the Truth** (or: in intrinsic alignment with reality, which is the Truth).

Note the phrases: **the spirit** (or: attitude; breath-effect) **of your mind**... **the new humanity**... **being formed** (framed, built, founded and settled from a state of disorder and wildness; created) **within the Way pointed out**... **pertaining to the Truth**. This sort of transformation makes Jesus "the Firstborn among many brothers and sisters" (Rom. 8:29b). But further, note how this had happened to those in Ephesus: "**at one point you heard and so listen to Him, and within Him as well as in union with Him and centered in Him you were and are taught.**" So put this in our present context of Jn. 8, and especially vs. 43, below.

But let's go deeper, and ponder what Jesus said next: "**I Myself came forth and am arrived here** (or: and here I am) **from out of the midst of God.**" This is a clear affirmation that He is the Son of God, and that God is His Father/Mother. Yet, in His teaching, He is not just dropping a little ontological gem for folks to have a proof-text that Jesus was God. He is speaking as "the Son of the Human Being," who has God as His Father. The expectation for those of Israel was that they (and now we) can have "**God [as] [their & our] Father,**" as He posits the possibility in the first clause of this verse. This was to come to understand that we can say "Our Father" (Mat. 6:9ff) with it having a new meaning based upon an intimate relationship with Him. Jesus taught His audience:

> "**Therefore, you folks will continuously exist being ones that have reached the purposed and destined goal: finished and completed ones; mature and perfected ones – in the same way as your heavenly Father** (or: your Father which has the qualities of, and is characterized by, the atmosphere) **constantly exists being One that is the goal and destiny: finished, complete, mature, perfect!**" (Mat. 5:48).

This is our goal. Union with the Father, through being a part of the Son, is the aim of the Path. Hear the words in Eph. 4:13,

> "**until we – the whole of mankind** (all people) – **can** (or: would) **come down to the goal** (or: attain; arrive at; meet accordingly; meet down face-to-face): **into the state of oneness from, and which is, The Faithfulness** (or: the unity of, that belongs to and which characterizes that which is faith; or: the lack of division which has its source in trust, confidence and reliability, has the character of and is in reference to the loyalty and fidelity), **even which is the full, experiential and intimate knowledge** (or: and from recognition; and of discovery; as well as pertaining to insight) **which is** (or: of; from; in reference to) **the Son of God, [growing] into [the] purposed and destined adult man** (complete, finished, full-grown, perfect, goal-attained, mature manhood) – **into** (or: unto) **[the] measure of [the] stature** (full age; prime of life) **of the entire content which comprises the Anointed One.**"

The last clause of this verse gives perspective to the statement that we just discussed – that He had come from out of the midst of God. It posits: "**that One sent Me away with a mission** (commissions and sends Me forth as an Emissary, [His] Representative)." Now to understand what He is saying in this verse, let us jump ahead to 20:21, below,

> "**Correspondingly** (or: Accordingly; On the same level; In the same sphere; In line with) **as the Father has sent Me forth with a mission and as an Emissary** (Representative), **I Myself also am progressively** (or: repeatedly; or: one after another) **sending** (dispatching) **you folks.**"

And thus, from being in this realm (Eph. 2:6) and when receiving this commission (Mat. 28:19), we can also say, "We, or I, have come forth, and are (am) now arrived here, from out of the midst of God; God is our (or, my) Father." Can you hear that? Well, look at vs. 47, below…

43. **"How** (Through what [situation]) **is it that you folks consistently do not understand** (have personal, experiential knowledge of) **the matter of My discourse or the way I'm speaking** (= Why don't you understand what I'm saying)**? Because you presently have no power and continue unable to keep on hearing My word** (or: to progressively listen to My message, thought or information [*logos*]).

He gave them no chance to answer His rhetorical question, for He knew the answer and so immediately provided it for them. He probably also knew that they had no idea of "through what" this situation had come to be. After all, they had the priests and the scribes to teach them. But they "**consistently [did] not understand** (have personal, experiential knowledge of)" what He was saying. Notice that, in the question, He used a noun that can mean either "**the matter of My discourse,**" or, "**the way I'm speaking.**" We might paraphrase by saying that they did not understand the subject matter of His teaching, or that they had no knowledge of rhetoric or His use of metaphor, or perhaps His way of teaching that was meant to cause them to think, rather than giving them answers. Most of Scripture comes to us as this latter. We are meant to listen to the Breath-effect within us, rather than to learn facts.

Now the reason that He gave them for this state of affairs sounds a bit ambiguous, but He will clarify what He means, in vs. 47, below. It involves their present state of being: slaves, under the old covenant (Gal. 4:25; and, "**the slave has not seen and does not know** {or: is not aware of} **what his owner** {lord; master} **is habitually doing**" – Jn. 15:15); dead, in trespasses and failures (Eph. 2:1); blind and deaf (Mat. 13:13-15; etc.). Therefore, at that time they had "**no power and continued unable to keep on hearing {His} word.**" As the expansion offers, they could not "progressively listen to [His] message, thought, information or the Blueprint (*Logos*)." In that condition, nothing could be expected from them. Paul described their condition this way:

> "**the results of their perceptions, concepts and understanding** (effects of directing the mind and thought processes) **were petrified** (were hardened into a stony concretion and made callous [note: a medical term for being covered with thick skin])…. **until today, whenever Moses should be habitually read** [e.g., in the synagogue], **a head-covering** (veil) **continues lying upon their heart** (= the innermost being of the group)" (2 Cor. 3:14, 15).

This is true, even today, for those who live with an old covenant mentality and worldview. You see,

> "**the folks ordering their behavior/living their lives in accord with flesh** (or: = corresponding to the human condition; or: = on the level of Torah-keeping boundary-markers; with literal interpretations of Scriptures)…. [and with] **the result of the thinking** (mind-set; effect of the way of thinking; disposition; result of understanding and inclination; the minding; the opinion; the thought; the outlook) **of the flesh [are in] death**" (Rom. 8:4, 6a).

44. **"You folks, in particular, are** (continue existing, being) **from out of, and have your source in, the Ancestor who cast [something] through [someone]** (or: the adversary {devil} father; or: the father – the one thrusting [words or issues] through [folks/groups] and dividing them), **and you are habitually wanting** (willing; intending; purposing) **to be constantly doing your father's passionate cravings** (full-rushing over-desires). **That one was existing being a murderer** (a killer of humanity) **from [his; its; a] beginning** (or: from [the] start; from [its] origin; or: from headship, chieftainhood, government or rule), **and he/it has not stood and does not now stand within the Truth** (or: it had not made a stand in union with reality), **because truth is not** (openness and reality does not exist) **within him** (or: it). **Whenever he/it may be speaking the lie, he/it is continuing speaking from out of his own things – because he/it is** (or: continues existing being) **a liar, and its father** [note: either the father of the lie, or of the liar; Could this refer to what Paul called "the first man Adam" – 1 Cor. 15:45?].

So who was that "**Ancestor** (or: father)"? Who would they have assumed that He was talking about? Because of the unfortunate translation "devil," the traditional Christian worldview has taken on a Zoroastrian (Persian) theology of dualism (basically a good God versus a bad god) that was assimilated into Second Temple Judaism, which thereafter has become a central theme of mainline Christian theology. It is assumed that Jesus was speaking of a "spirit entity" or a supposed "fallen angel" in a dualistic spirit-world. We do not find this dualism in the OT Scriptures (e.g., see "the adversary (*satan*)" in Job chapters 1 and 2, and in Nu. 22:22, "a messenger of Jehovah stationed himself in the way for and adversary [Hebrew: *satan*] to him" [Young]). In the NT, we find this word used in:

> 1 Tim. 3:11, "**Women (or: Wives) [of the community], similarly, [should be] serious** (dignified with majestic gravity, inspiring awe), **not devils** (or: adversaries; women who thrust things through folks)."

> 2 Tim. 3:2, 3, "**for the people** (the humans; mankind) **will continue being**.... **without natural affection, unwilling to make a treaty** (implacable; not open to an agreement), **devils** (adversarial slanderers; folks who throw or thrust something through people to hurt or cause divisions)..."

> Tit. 2:3, "**Old women, similarly, [are to be] women in a state and resultant condition proper and fitting for being engaged in the sacred** (suitable in demeanor for serving the temple; or: = living a life appropriate [for] a person [being] a temple), **not folks who thrust-through or hurl [a weapon, or something hurtful] through [someone]** (or: not **devils** nor slanderous adversaries which bring division and hurt)..."

Now I kept the rendering "devil" in these verses so that folks could see how the term was applied to human beings. The Greek word is *dia-bolos*, and literally means "someone casting [something] through [someone, or something]." This basic meaning fits all the contexts of this word's use, throughout the entire NT, where it can be seen as referring to people who act in this way thus described. Paul, when he was still Saul, went about like a roaring lion, seeking what Christians he could devour (as the word was used in 1 Per. 5:8).

Even here, in vs. 44, Jesus is telling these folks that THEY are just like their Ancestor, or father. They were habitually wanting to do what their father did, in his passion. In my translation, I inserted a note, above, with a suggestion that this Ancestor was the 1st Adam, a part of whom we all start out being, until the last Adam is brought to birth within us, and we become God's temple. We suggest that this old humanity, of which we read in Eph. 4:22, above, "**the old humanity – the one continuously in process of being corrupted down from and in accord with the passionate desires** (swelling emotions) **of the deceptions.**" It is in Eph. 4:27 that we are instructed to give no place to this old humanity:

> "**neither be folks constantly supplying nor repeatedly giving a place or position for** (or: to; in) **the person who thrusts things through [folks or situations]** (or: the slanderer; the adversary; the accuser; **the devil**; or: that which casts [harm or division] through the midst of folks)."

Rom. 5:12 explained how the 1st Adam **murdered** everyone, in "his beginning; start; headship,"

> "**through The Sin** (failure; the mistake; the miss of the target; the deviation) **The Death [also], in this way The Death thus also passed through in all directions** (or: came through the midst causing division and duality; went throughout) **into all mankind**..."

We also see that, "**he [Adam] has not stood and does not now stand within the Truth** [what God had told him], **because truth is not** (openness and reality does not exist) **within him.**" And this was humanity's predicament, until the **Truth** (Jn. 14:6) was incarnated in Jesus, and, individually – each in his or her own place in line – incarnated within us. All we had was the serpent's inner lie, within us, and that lie was that humans needed to do something in order to be like God. Then religions expanded and multiplied the lies about who we are, about what God thinks of us, and about our being separated from the Ground of our Being.

The last statement of this verse applies to any who are not joined to the Vine. That lie originated within the Garden which is US! The death that we experience within our Exile from God's intimate presence, and from the inner land (the core of the human) of the Promise (the Promise which is the Father – Acts 1:4b, read in apposition). You see, the Truth is the opposite of the Lie, just as the Light is the opposite of the Darkness. Darkness (lack of Light; the Lie) always comes before the Light (Gen. 1:2-4), and likewise, that which pertains to the soul is first (Gen. 2:7), and afterward that which pertains to the Spirit (the spiritual) – 1 Cor. 15:44-49).

It is within us that the Lie is given birth. Paul described this situation in Rom. 7:

> 5. **You see, when we** [= Adam/Israel] **were existing within the flesh** (or: = in the old alienated Adamic existence, with the flesh sacrifices and markers of the Law), **the effects, impressions, emotions and impulses from the experiences, passions and suffering of the failures** (from the sins and deviations which caused misses of the target) **– the things through means of the Law** [the Torah] **– were continually operating** (working within; energizing and effecting) **within our members into the condition to produce fruit by Death** (in death; to death; for Death)....
> 11. **For the Sin** (failure; error; the miss when shooting at a target; the deviation from the goal), **taking a starting point** (receiving an occasion and base of operation) **through the implanted goal** (impartation of the finished product within; inward directive; commandment [to Adam, then to Israel]), **completely makes me unable to walk the Path** (made me incapable to walk out [customs of the Law]; thoroughly cheats and deludes me, making me lose my Way; deceives me; [comment: reference to Eve in Gen. 3:13]) **and through it kills me off** (or: slaughtered me)....
> 17. **Yet now** (= as the case really stands) **I myself am no longer habitually producing** (continuously working down and effecting) **this, but rather the Sin** (the failure; the personified error of missing the Target; the deviation [from Torah and its boundary markers]) **[which is] continuously housing herself** (or: making its home; inhabiting; dwelling; = living) **within me**....
> 23. **yet I constantly see** (or: observe) **a different principle** (or: law), **within my members, [which is] by the Law** (or: custom; or: [= Torah]) **repeatedly taking the field to wage war against my mind** (or: warring in opposition to, and in the place of, the law of, and which is, my mind), **and repeatedly taking me prisoner and leading me into captivity within the principle** (or: in union with the Law) **of the Sin** (the failure; the error; the miss of the Target; the deviation from [Torah-keeping]) **– the one continuously existing** (or: now being) **within my members.**

There is another layer of understanding that can be traced out from Jesus' pronouncement in this verse: **"That one was existing being a murderer from a beginning."** This could refer to Cain, Adam's firstborn (prefiguring Israel being Yahweh's firstborn – Ex. 4:22b). In Gen. 4, we find his story of how he killed his brother and then was exiled from the land of Yahweh's intimate presence. We can see a connection to Jesus' present situation from His reference to those of His audience (representative here of the Judean leadership, in John's Gospel) who were seeking to kill Him (vs. 37, above). In vs. 59, below, they attempt to stone Him. So they had the same spirit of their father, Cain. Recall our reference to Isa. 1:21, above (under vs. 41, and our discussion, there), how the land had become full of murderers. So Jesus continues this thread of murder. We know that later on they did murder Jesus, via a Roman cross.

The dispute that Cain had fomented with his brother Able was over a religious incident on the subject of what later (under Moses) became the temple cultus. Sacrifices and offerings are threads throughout the story of Jesus, in the Gospels. But there is another aspect of Cain's story that may be observed in the bigger picture of 1st century Second Temple Judaism: God's judgment. As a result of Cain killing his brother,

> "God put (or: set; placed) a SIGN on and in (or: allocated a sign TO) Cain.... Then Cain went away from the presence of God and settled in a house, in a land of wandering (Heb.: Nod), in a place that was in complete opposition to, and was down-against and the opposite of, Eden" (Gen. 4:15, 16; LXX, JM).

Cain lied to Yahweh, when asked where his brother was. He replied to Yahweh, "I do not know..." (vs. 9). In Gen. 4:11, God told him, "And now [there is] a negative prayer upon you (or: you [are] correspondingly cursed) AWAY from the Land" (LXX, JM). Cain was exiled. We suggest that Jesus' words may have been an allusion to Cain, and to his judgment of having to leave God's home (prefiguring Jerusalem and the temple), and thus carried a subtle prophecy of what would soon happen to His present audience, and to the people of Judea (AD 70).

45. "On the other hand – because I, Myself, am continually saying the truth (speaking reality)**! – you folks are not presently trusting Me or believing in Me, nor do you continue loyal to Me.**

Although having the Law, they lived in the Lie. Because they had the spirit and attitude of their adversarial father, they could not at that time be trusting Him, or believing in Him nor continue loyal to Him (the expanded rendering conflates the meanings of the verb, and reflects the connotations of the dative case of "**Me**"). This was their situation, "**because [He was] continually saying the truth** (speaking reality)." We are reminded of 1:5, above, "**the Light is constantly shining**... **yet the darkness does not grasp or receive it on the same level**." Jesus, the Light, was the complete opposite of the Darkness in which they were living. His truth angered them. It is the same, today: the truth often angers those who live in darkness (of religion, or of culture). They love their Law (or: laws; rules), but reject "grace and truth" (1:17, above).

46. "Who of you is presently correcting Me about error
        (or: demonstrating a proof about My being wrong; making a convincing argument which refutes
        Me and exposes Me about having missed the target; arraigning me concerning sin)**? Since** (or:
If) **I am habitually speaking truth** (reality), **how** (through what [situation]) **is it that you folks are not presently trusting Me, believing in Me or pledging allegiance to Me?**

The expanded renderings of "**error** (etc.)" along with the semantic range of the verb (**correcting**; demonstrating a proof about; making a convincing argument which refutes; exposes; having missed the target; arraigning) give us pause amidst the ambiguity.

All those meanings make sense, and perhaps round-out His meaning, in this rhetorical question. It all sets a wide, and potentially complex, contrast to His second question. They could not legitimately bring anything against Him (from any angle), and He was "**habitually speaking truth**" (notice how, in John, this is a central thread), so how was it that they did not trust Him, believe in Him or "**pledge allegiance to [Him]**"? Well, vs. 47 gives further reasons...

47. "The person continuing in being (ontologically existing in essential being) **out of the midst of God is constantly hearing** (repeatedly and habitually listening and paying attention to [implies obeying]) **the effects of the things God says** (results of God's flow of declarations; spoken words from God). **Because of this, YOU folks are not presently in the habit of hearing** (or: listening; paying attention [and obeying])**: because** (seeing that) **you are not presently existing from out of God."**

Now, how many "followers of Christ; believers" within the Christian religion do we suspect of actually believing the first statement in this verse? First of all, do most folks believe that they "**continuing in being** (ontologically existing in essential being) **out of the midst of God**"? Actually, we sense that more and more people are, today, but traditional Christianity does not normally speak much of this. This should be our continuing existential reality (and worldview), else He would not have made the second statement, that they were NOT "**presently existing from out of God**" – and for this reason, THEY were "**not presently in the habit of hearing** (or: listening; paying attention [and obeying])."

We can also conclude that "**presently existing from out of God**" (like, being joined to the Vine, in Jn. 15, and being joined to the Lord, in 1 Cor. 6:17) is a prerequisite for "**constantly hearing** (repeatedly and habitually listening and paying attention to [implies obeying]) **the effects of the things God says** (results of God's flow of declarations; spoken words from God)." This speaks of a life of conscious awareness of His presence, and of continuous communion with His Spirit, and of habitual attentiveness to "listen and pay attention to **the effects of the things God says**." Is not a healthy "body" continuously responsive to the impulses from its "Head"? It is an unhealthy body that is not "**in the habit of hearing** (or: listening; paying attention" to its head. This is what we call "Life." When this is not happening, we call it some form of "death." And, mark well Jesus' use of the present tense in this verse! He was not talking about a "once in a while" occurrence.

48. The Jews (= religious authorities of Judea) **calculated a reply and said to him, "Are WE not expressing it beautifully** (or: finely; ideally; precisely) **when we are saying that you yourself are a Samaritan** [note: a term of loathing and contempt – Barclay] **and constantly have** (or: continuously hold or possess) **a demon** (a Hellenistic concept and term: = an animistic influence)**?"**

Well, they sure put Him in a box, did they not? Notice Barclay's interpretation of calling Him a Samaritan. Not only did they not accept Him as being their Messiah, they dismissed Him as not even being a Jew! The Samaritans were a mixed breed, a result of the Assyrian deportation of most of the ten tribes of Israel, and the planting of Assyrians in their place. The northern tribes had become either assimilated or racially polluted – in the eyes of the Judeans.

Now to say that He had a "demon" (note the explanation of the term, in the text) most likely does not mean what it came to mean in later Christianity. This very likely meant that either He was crazy, or was emotionally sick, or mentally ill, or was deluded, or perhaps that He had an adversarial spirit. We cannot be sure of their exact use of the word. But notice how He responds to this accusation…

49. Jesus decidedly replies, "I, Myself, do not have (or: habitually possess) **a demon, but to the contrary, I continuously honor** (bring value to) **My Father, and yet you yourselves are repeatedly dishonoring** (or: devaluing) **Me.**

He honors and brings value to His Father, while THEY "**are repeatedly dishonoring** (or: devaluing) **[Him]**." He simply took both categories (Samaritan; demon) as terms that they hoped would devalue Him. There was no reference to a paranormal entity in this verbal exchange. He defined exactly what they had said. It was a matter of honor versus shame (a vital contrast within their culture). If the latter, they had a supposed reason for not paying attention to Him.

50. "Now by habit I am not seeking My glory or reputation. There is One constantly seeking [glory; repute] and continuously making decisions (sifting, separating, evaluating and judging).

Again, notice that Jesus categorizes "**honor**" (vs. 49, above) as "**glory or reputation**." This was turning their "honor/shame" society on its head. Everyone else was striving for honor and endeavoring to keep shame at bay. Glory and reputation were high currency in their culture – but He was not seeking these

Next, He simply points them to God, the "**One constantly seeking [glory; repute] and continuously making decisions**." Glory is an important theme throughout all of Scripture. God seeks its presence in us, for we were created to bear His image and reflect His glory. So He is "continuously sifting, separating, evaluating and judging" our progress and development. This was happening during Jesus' encounter with these folks. It happens every day, with everyone. We are created to BE His glory, not to try to gain glory for ourselves.

51. "It is certainly so (or: Amen, amen; Count on it)**! I am now progressively laying it out, and saying to you folks: If anyone should keep watch over, so as to hold in custody, protectively guard, observe and maintain My word** (Blueprint; message; thought; idea; laid-out information; *Logos*),

he or she can under no circumstances (or: may, or would, by no means) **at any point gaze upon death, so as to contemplate it, be a spectator to it or look at it with interest and attention** [note: a Hebrew idiom for 'experiencing' death], **on into** (or: throughout) **the Age [of Messiah]."**

Just what did He mean, in saying, "**keep watch over, so as to hold in custody, protectively guard, observe and maintain**"? This is a conflation of the most common meanings of the verb of the dependent clause. The common use of this word would have been applied to observing the Law and keeping the commandments. So Jesus' is most likely spring boarding from that concept, but taking them into His Logos and the living, interactive relationship that He has with the Father. His teachings, and He Himself, were the new "**the principle and law of, from and which is the spirit and attitude of 'The Life within Christ Jesus'**," as Paul put it in Rom. 8:2.

Here is another version of the Good News: "**keep, observe and maintain My Blueprint**... [and you will never] **gaze upon death** (or, experience it) **on into** (or: throughout) **the Age [of Messiah]**." So His Logos, coming into them via His message and laid-out information, would give them His Life, "**if you yourselves would remain** (can dwell; should abide) **within My word** (in union with My *Logos* and information; centered in the thought, idea and message laid out by Me)" (vs. 31b, above). His emphasis for Life (and for not having one's interest and attention on death) was His Logos. In the Logos was Life, which was the Light of humanity (1:4, above), and thus He was "**the Light of the world**," which gives folks "**the Light of the Life**" (vs. 12, above). It is all about "**holding in custody [His] Word**." He gives us the Blueprint of the Way, the Truth and the Life (14:6, below). But He does not just give us a plan that we now have to follow. We are aware of how all His disciples deserted Him when the Judeans arrested Him (Mat. 25:56). But when the Promise from the Father, the Set-apart Breath-effect, came upon them (Acts 2), they were given the power and ability to hold His Logos in custody and maintain it.

52. **The Jews** (= authorities of Judea) **said to Him, "Now we have come to personally know** (have intimate experiential knowledge) **that you presently have a demon** (= an animistic influence)! **Abraham died** (or: is dead), **also the prophets, and yet here you are now saying, 'If anyone should hold, protect, note and observe my word** (message; idea) **he by no means** (under no circumstances) **may taste of** (= partake of or participate in) **death, on into the Age.**

They repeat their dishonoring accusation, from vs. 48b, and then reason from the realm of the flesh (making a "natural" analogy) as they compare Him to Abraham and the prophets, who all died. Next, they question His assertion about not dying, using the metaphor of "**taste**," as a synonym for "partaking of or participating in" **death**, instead of Jesus' term "**gaze upon**."

53. **"You are yourself not greater than our father Abraham – who died – are you? Even the prophets died! Who are you continually making yourself [to be]?"**

Unhindered, by not understanding what He had said, they press their point and now demand to know just who He is "**continually making [himself] [to be]**."

54. **Jesus decidedly replies, "If I should ever glorify Myself** (build a reputation for Myself), **My glory is** (or: My reputation exists being) **nothing. My Father – of Whom you keep saying, "He is our God"** [with other MSS: that He is your God] **– is actually the One continuously and progressively glorifying Me** (bringing a manifestation of Me which calls forth praise; building My reputation).

His first response needs no comment. But the second statement would have fired their anger toward vs. 59, below. He was plainly saying that God is His Father – in a way that indicated to them that He meant that He was not just a Jew, like them, but that He was divine in His essential Being. He was the Logos that "was God" (1:1b, above), and thus, He was God, the Creator (1:3, above), having been incarnated in Jesus. This is simply unexplainable; it is what has been called "transrational."

He was not glorifying Himself, nor building His own reputation. Rather, God, His Father, was (even through this exchange with these hostile Judeans) "**continuously and progressively glorifying [Him]**." God was progressively bringing a manifestation of Him that was, and would continue, bringing forth the praise to God. His Father was continuously building His reputation.

55. "**Now you have not intimately or experientially known Him, yet as for Myself, I have seen and thus know Him – and if ever** (or: even if) **I should say** (or: = Suppose I say) **that I have not seen nor know Him, I will be a liar, like you folks. But to the contrary, I have seen and know Him** (or: am acquainted with Him), **and I continuously hold in custody, protectively guard, observe and maintain His word** (*Logos*; message; laid-out thought; patterned idea; conveyed information).

Twice He affirms, "**I have seen and know Him** (or: am acquainted with Him)." And then He tells them that He continuously does what He says that others should do (vs. 51, above). He "**continuously holds in custody, protectively guards, observes and maintains [God's] Logos**," and He IS God's Logos.

But His audience, and antagonists, "**have not intimately or experientially known Him**." They had the Law, the rules, but they had no intimacy with God. Furthermore, He posits that they, themselves, are liars. He knew that they were metaphorically blind (Mat. 15:14; Lu. 6:39), so He did not state the fact that they had not seen the Father.

56. "**Abraham, your father, was exceedingly glad** (or: exulted) **to the end that he could see My day, and he saw** (caught sight of; beheld; observed; perceived) **[it] and then was graced** (or: favored; or: rejoiced; was made glad).**"

Now He affirms their literal ancestry, as having Abraham as their "father." Was He, by this, indicating that what He would say next was also literal? But what did He mean by saying that Abraham had seen His day? Apparently He was not just speaking figuratively, as though Abraham had "spiritual vision" and could mentally or spiritually perceive the day of the Messiah and the fulfillment of the promises to him. Verse 58, below, seems to indicate that He was speaking literally, and this is how His audience took it, as vs. 57 indicates.

57. **Therefore the Jews** (= religious authorities of Judea) **said to Him, "You are not yet holding** (or: having) **fifty years – and you have seen Abraham** [*p*75, Aleph, Sin-syr & Coptic read: and Abraham has seen you]?**"

This whole conversation, from vs. 51 to the present (what He was laying-out for them) seems absurd, in both parties of the conversation. Here, vs. 57, seems like a ridiculous assessment, on behalf of the Judeans – who were obviously thinking literally.

58. **Jesus says to them, "It is certainly so** (Amen, amen; Count on it)! **I am telling you, before Abraham comes** (or: was to come) **into being, I, Myself, am** (or: I continuously exist; or: I repeatedly had being; or: I am Being; I am continuous Existence; I AM).**"

Another I AM statement. This can, of course be read metaphorically, as Him speaking as being the Messiah, which was the plan from the beginning. But considering these repeated I AM constructions in John's Gospel, it seems that Hart may be right: He is letting them know that He is a divine Being that somehow (not explained) predated Abraham's birth.

But perhaps there is another explanation: He could have been speaking as Paul characterizes Him, in his first letter to Corinth, i.e., He could have been speaking of being somehow identified with Adam.

Speculation about this only satisfies our imaginary preferences. And yet, these could help us to remain open to fuller, future unveilings – as we are lead deeper into All Truth (Christ).

59. **They therefore lifted up stones so that they could hurl** (throw; cast) **[them] upon Him. But Jesus had been suddenly concealed** (was at once hidden), **and then He went out from the Temple grounds** [Aleph, A & others add: even (or: and) passing through the midst of them as He was proceeding, and He thus was passing by].

This verse takes us back to the incident in vss. 3-11, above. Those Judeans were certainly not adverse to throwing rocks! John does not inform us about how Jesus "**had been suddenly concealed** (was at once hidden)," but perhaps he wanted his readers and listeners to see this as another SIGN. It must have certainly had an effect upon those who were preparing to hurl stones upon Him.

As on offer, some MSS state that He simply left the area, while others give the details of His escape: "even (or: and) passing through the midst of them as He was proceeding, and He thus was passing by." It certainly would have punctuated what He had just said, in vs. 58.

This incident reminds us of the story of Elisha and the Syrian (or: Aramean) army, in 2 Ki. 6:18.
"And Elisha prayed to Yahweh, and said, 'Strike this people, please, with blindness'…"

Chapter 9

1. **Now continuing passing along, He saw a man [who had been] born blind** (blind from out of birth),
2. **and His disciples asked Him, saying, "Rabbi, who failed** (sinned; missed the mark; deviated), **this man or his parents, to the end that he should be born blind?"**

The question that asks about "**this man**" would seem to be based upon a worldview of either pre-existence or reincarnation. It suggests that His disciples may have held one or the other of these concepts as possibly being true. Since Jesus responds with, "**Neither,**" in the next verse, we will pass over this topic, except to note that it was deemed important to include the question with these alternative reasons being offered.

The more plausible idea is seen in the second option offered: "**his parents**." Many have offered the ideas presented in the Heb. text of Ex. 34:7b, but the Greek version can be translated differently:
"and yet He will not continue cleansing or purifying **the person holding [something] within** (or: entertaining a grudge against [someone]; or: held within an entanglement; or: centered in an offense against [someone]) **while repeatedly** (or: continually; progressively) **bringing lawlessness from fathers upon children**, and then upon children's children, upon (or: added to) a third, and even a fourth, generation" (LXX, JM).
This rendering, of the LXX, is saying something different than the common reading of the Heb. text. The present participle, "repeatedly bringing" has as its closest antecedent "the person entertaining a grudge (etc.)," and by doing this, perpetuating lawlessness, from fathers on their children and from generation to generation. Let us now look at the Nu. 14:18b version of this idea:
"by (or: with; in) cleansing He will not be repeatedly cleansing or purifying **the person holding [something] within** (or: entertaining a grudge against [someone]; or: held within an entanglement; or: centered in an offence against [someone]) **while continuing in returning** (repaying) **sins** (mistakes; errors; failures) **from** (or: of) **fathers upon children**, until a third and fourth generation" (LXX, JM).
Deut. 5:9b can read like the Heb. text, or differently – depending upon the rendering of the present participle. Here, God is the antecedent of the participle:
"Because I AM [the] LORD [Heb.: Yahweh] your God, an enthusiastic (or: eager; zealous; jealous) God, **repeatedly restoring failures** (making recompense for errors; or: giving back

deviations; repaying or returning sins) **from** (or: of; pertaining to) **fathers upon children**, upon (or: added to) a third and a fourth generation among (or: to; for; with; by) the folks continuously hating Me (habitually regarding Me with ill will)" (LXX, JM).

I have included these Greek renderings, since the LXX is regarded by many scholars as "the Bible" of the 1st century followers of Christ, and it is the most quoted version in the NT writings. The common translations of the OT (e.g., KJV, NIV, etc.) follow the Masoretic Text (7th to 10th century AD; Heb.) and tend to give a quite different reading than how the Jews of the 3rd century BC apparently read the Heb. texts of that period.

3. **Jesus judged the situation and replied, "Neither this man sinned** (missed the mark; failed) **nor his parents, but rather [it is] so that God's deeds** (the works of God; the acts from God) **could be set in clear light and manifested within him.**

Jesus affirms that the man had not sinned, and thus was not the cause of his own birth defect. He also affirmed that this was not an ancestral issue: his parents had not sinned, so as to cause his blindness. John's inclusion of this question would seem to be so that Jesus could deny the reality of their suppositions. This removed what may have been a cultural assessment of guilt upon people for the tragedies that they seem to endure for no apparent reason. This reminds us of the story of Job. His friends had assumed that he was responsible for the disasters that befell him.

The verb that introduces Jesus' reply to the disciples is most often translated, "answered." This is, in fact, what He did, but in English it obscures the mental/spiritual process that took place before He spoke. The verb is *apokrinomai*, and it is from the common verb *krinō* (to separate in order to evaluate, assess and then reach a decision; to judge) prefixed by the preposition *apo-* (from; off; away). It shows that before Jesus "answered" them, this process took place – which was probably listening to the witness of His Father. So He judged this situation, by His spiritual discernment, and then He replied to them. Perhaps a small point, but an enlightening one and a prime example for us. Hear and discern before speaking.

So in this instance, at least, we have Jesus instructing them that this specific physical situation is neither the individual's fault, nor the fault of his parents, and we see from vs. 1 that the man was born with this birth defect. Yet, Jesus informs us that it is neither "karma," nor the result of what most translations proclaim in Ex. 34:7b, and the other quotes, cited above. But we should refrain from making a general rule from this one situation. Today, we know that addicted mothers often give birth to a child that received the addiction from the mother. We are also aware of genetic disorders that can be handed down. Neither the disciples nor Jesus were addressing such a situation. The disciples were asking a question about the cause of birth defects, and they assumed that it could only be because of one of the two options which they had offered in their question.

However, Jesus offers another option which He will explain in vss. 4-5, and this was also because He knew what He would do. He was in control of the situation, because He always listened to the Father. Because of this, His first reply is that this situation was "**so that God's deeds** (the works of God; the acts from God) **could be set in clear light and manifested within him**." He did not enter into theological debate or ontological reasoning about the general human predicament, and thus did not really answer the disciple's curiosity about such situations. He only spoke what He heard, and addressed this specific situation – since He knew that it would bring glory to God by setting His works in clear light, to be observed by folks. We would be advised not to bring more to this situation than Jesus explains. The disciples' questions have probably been echoed throughout time – and generalized answers have never been given, except by those who have become convinced about the teaching concerning karma, or who read Ex. 34:7b (etc.) as in the common translations.

4. **"It is constantly necessary** (or: binding) **for Me** [other MSS: us] **to be habitually performing the works** (accomplishing the deeds; active in the acts; doing the business) **of the One sending Me** [other

MSS: us] **while it is day; night** (or: a night; = darkness; *cf* Gen. 1:5) **progressively** (repeatedly; habitually) **comes, when no one is able** (or: has power) **to continue performing work** (accomplishing deeds; doing business).

5. **"Whenever I may (can) continue being within the world** (aggregate of humanity and its ordered System; the religious and cultural arrangement), **I am the world's** (system's) **Light**

(or: When I would progressively be within the System's ordered arrangement, I exist being the System's light)."

There is parallelism between the "**day**" of vs. 4 and the "**Light**" of vs. 5, with vs. 5 "shedding light" on vs. 4 and explaining the metaphorical sense of how He was using the term, "**day**." He was "the Day of the Lord." Understanding this will open up many other passages that speak of "day" and "light." With His coming, a new "Day" for humanity had arrived. This reaches all the way back to 1:9, above. He was the Logos,

"**the True and Genuine Light which** (or: Who) **is continuously** (repeatedly; progressively) **enlightening** (giving light to) **every person** (or: all humanity) **continuously** (repeatedly; progressively; constantly; one after another) **coming into the world** (or: the ordered system of culture, religion, economics and government; aggregate of humans; or: the universe)."

He was what made (and still makes) darkness disappear.

So why was it "**constantly necessary** (or: binding) **for [Him]** [other MSS: us] **to be habitually performing the works**"? First of all, because it was still His Day, but also because of what He told folks in 5:17, above "**My Father is continuously working and keeps on being in action until the present moment** (or: up to right now); **I, Myself, also am continually working**."

Another layer of meaning can be seen through the parenthetical alternative of vs. 5, "When I would progressively be within the System's ordered arrangement, I exist being the System's light." We should remember to include His manifestation within any system that we construct. His Light will dispel the darkness of an ordered system, and overcome its domination over people.

Well, then what was the "**night**" of which He spoke, here? We suggest that this was speaking of when the Light would be crucified, when "**about the sixth hour** (= about noon) **darkness was birthed** (or: a dim, gloomy shadowiness came to be) **upon the whole Land – until [the] ninth hour** (mid-afternoon)" (Lu. 23:44), but then continued for three days and three nights, until the Son rose again. With their Messiah in the grave, "**no one was able** (or: had power) **to continue performing work**." During that period, there were also two sabbaths (20:1, below, "**Now on one of the sabbaths** [note: Passover was one sabbath, and the seventh day of the week was another sabbath], **Mary the Magdalene is progressively coming early into the memorial tomb**..."), and folks were not normally allowed to work on the sabbath.

Jesus may also have been alluding to what would come to Jerusalem, such as prophesied in Joel 2:2ff, and which would come to pass in AD 70.

6. **After saying these things, He spits on the ground and makes clay mud from out of the spitted saliva, and then smears** (or: anoints; rubs on; [WH following B read: applies; puts... on]) **His clay mud upon the blind man's eyes,**
7. **then says to him, "Lead on under** (or: Go your way; Depart) **into the swimming-pool of Siloam"** [note: situated south of the Temple, fed by a subterranean tunnel] **– which is normally being translated and interpreted 'Being sent forth on a mission** (or: Commissioned; Being made representative)' **– "[and] wash yourself!"** Therefore, he went off (or: away) **and washed himself and came [back] seeing.**

Jesus healed folks using a variety of methods. Why did John include the details of this healing in his "sign-oriented" Gospel? What are these details meant to convey to us?

The common verb, "**make**," in the first clause of vs. 6, is the same verb used in Gen. 2:4, "the Lord God **made** the sky (heaven) and the dirt (earth; land; ground)" (LXX) – the same dirt from which He formed the human (Gen. 2:7). Are Jesus' actions an allusion to the creation? He used His own body-water (spit) to turn the clay into mud. Was this pointing to the Living Water of Jn. 4:10, 14? The word "**smears**" also means "anoints," and thus speaks to the action and being of the Anointed One (Christ).

His instructions for the man to "**wash**" himself calls to mind the story of Elisha's instructions to the Syrian captain, Naaman, in 2 Ki. 5:1-14, and the cleansing that he received from the skin ailment after washing seven times in the muddy Jordan River. As with that story, here there is a partnership in the healing, between Jesus and the blind man. The only indication of "faith" being involved is the man's obedience, which in turn reminds us of the obedience demonstrated by Abraham.

The giving of the name of the pool, along with the meaning of its name, also seems to tell us something. The man was "sent forth on a mission" to receive healing. Jesus' followers would be "sent forth on a mission" of bringing healing and new creation to others. Jesus characterized the Judean leadership as being "the blind leading the blind" (Mat. 15:14; 23:24), and He came that they might be "**seeing**," as with this man. This incident was another "SIGN" in John's Gospel.

8. **Then the neighbors, and those habitually observing** (being spectators of; carefully noticing) **him formerly – that he was existing being a beggar – began saying, "Is this one not the person normally sitting and constantly begging?"**
9. **Some were saying, "This is he." Others were saying, "No, but he is like him." Yet that man kept saying, "I, myself, am [he; the one]."**

On the level of the literal event, we see that man identifying himself as being the person who had been the blind beggar. However, we wonder if John has subtly slipped in an identification of the source of his healing. The last clause is another "I AM" statement – obviously used as normal speech, yet perhaps worded by John to point to one of his favored meanings, with regard to Jesus. The author's crafting of the narratives was intentional.

10. **Then they began saying to him, "How, then, were your eyes opened up?"**
11. **That man decidedly replied, "The Man called 'Jesus' made clay mud and anointed** (smeared [it] on) **my eyes, and said to me, 'Lead on under into the Siloam, and wash yourself.' And then, upon washing myself, I looked up and saw."**

Now we have a restatement of the whole incident – a second witness for John's listeners/readers. The man recites the essential details to "**the neighbors**" who had "**habitually observed him**" in his former condition. The last clause of vs. 11 uses the verb "to look; to see" with a prefix that here would mean, "up." Was his glance toward the sky? Was he figuratively looking up "to God," in amazement or gratitude? See his explanation in 15b, below.

Here our author shows the natural progression of witnessing – from the incident to the close associates. In vs. 13 we will see the next phase…

12. **And so they said to him, "Where is that one?" He then says, "I have not seen so I don't know."**

The miracle has been observed, and so folks want to now find the miracle-Worker. The SIGN points, and so people want to find. The man's answer is normally simply rendered, "I don't know," but the word that

John used for "know" has the root idea to "to see," and thus, "to know from having seen." This idea of "perception" may also be a subtle suggestion concerning perceiving the Messiah among them.

13. **They are progressively leading him – the once-blind man – to the Pharisees.**

From having been blind all his life, it is logical that he might need to have someone help him find the usual location of the Pharisees that were among them. Also, the Pharisees would have been looked to as being authorities on spiritual matters, so it would be natural for his neighbors to want them to know about what had happened. This was an important event in their community.

14. **Now it was on a sabbath day in which Jesus made the clay mud and opened up his eyes.**

Well, now we see that Jesus had ignored the rules of the culture, and "breaking the rules" was a larger issue than the mercy shown to the blind man. In our day this issue might be compared to "practicing medicine without a license." Rules are rules, you know…

15. **Again, then, the Pharisees also began asking him how he saw again** (= received his sight). **Now he said to them, "He applied clay mud upon my eyes, and I washed myself, and now** (or: the next thing), **I am seeing."**

We now have a third, although abbreviated, recounting of the SIGN. We observe that here the Pharisees use the common verb for "see" or "look" that is prefixed by a preposition that means either "up," or "again." Since he had been born blind, in vs. 11 I rendered this verb "looked up and saw." But here, the Pharisees would not likely have known that he was born blind, so had presumed that at some point he had lost his sight, so they ask how he "**saw again.**" In his explanation to them, he uses the verb without the prefix, and so explains his current situation, "**and now** (or: the next thing), **I am seeing.**"

16. **Some, from out of the Pharisees, therefore began saying, "This man is not on God's side** (or: from God; beside God; in God' presence), **because he is not keeping** (observing; guarding) **the sabbath." Yet others were saying, "How is a person who misses the mark** (a man, a sinner; an erring man; a man who is failing [in regard to the Law]) **able to be constantly doing such signs?" And there was a tearing split-effect** (= a division) **among them.**

We should take note that "the Pharisees" were not a unanimous, single-view group, as they are often referenced as having been. They seem to have been a religious association composed of people who were able to have their own opinions on a matter. Here, the first group appear to hold toward the Law being a determining factor, while the second group appear to give more weight to experience and evidence, and recognized that He had been, "**constantly doing such SIGNS.**" We have the same diversity in traditional Christianity, but that history seems to have been more divisive. The "**split-effect** (= a division)" would seem to be only about the issue before them, not about their continuing as an association that still met together.

17. **Therefore, they continued again saying to the once-blind man, "What are you yourself now saying about him, seeing that he opened up your eyes?" And the man exclaimed, "He is a prophet!"**

Why did they ask the opinion of a beggar about what he thought of Jesus? Were they using him as a one-man polling device to test the waters about the people's opinion of Jesus? The man's answer is one that we could expect from him, as a member of that culture. But the fact of his having been healed did not lead him to say, "He must be the Messiah." But also, he was likely afraid of these folks due to their social and religious power, just as his parents were (vs. 22, below). Among those Pharisees, some thought of Him as a sinner who broke the Law; others concluded that He must be in line with God. But none suggested that He might be their Messiah (*cf* vs. 22, below).

18. **The Judeans** (= religious authorities), **however, did not trust or believe concerning him, that he was blind and saw again** (or: received his sight), **until they summoned the parents of the man being made able to see again,**

19. **and they questioned them, saying, "Is this your son, who you say was born blind? How, then, is he presently seeing now?"**

20. **His parents considered, then replied, saying, "We have seen, and thus know, that this is our son, and that he was born blind.**

21. **"Yet how he now presently continues seeing, we have not seen and do not know, nor who opened his eyes we have not seen and do not know. You men ask him; he is of age** (has maturity; is an adult). **He will speak concerning himself."**

22. **His parents said these things because they had been fearing the Judeans** (= religious authorities; the ruling class), **for the Judeans** (= Jewish leadership) **had put it together and agreed, so that if anyone should ever confess** (acknowledge; avow) **Him Christ** (or: express the same idea, that He is [the] Anointed), **he should come to be [put] away from the synagogue** (= be excommunicated; = be cut off from membership in the synagogue, and thus be considered an outcast).

The **synagogue** (which means "a gathering together") was the social center of the community. To be excommunicated, cut off from membership in the synagogue, would assign a person to the social level of being an outcast. This is why his parents were "**fearing the Judeans.**" The Jewish leadership had "thrown Jesus under the cart," and would not allow anyone to acknowledge Him as being the Messiah. Confessing Him to be the **Christ** would have been the same as the post-resurrection disciples saying that "**Jesus is Lord.**" It was over this issue that Jesus would later be crucified.

23. **Because of this [situation], his parents said, "He's an adult** (He has maturity; He has come of age), **you men inquire upon him."**

24. **Then a second time they summoned the man who had been blind, and said to him, "Give glory** (the credit and reputation) **to God. We have seen and now know that this man is a sinner** (one who misses the goal; or: an outcast).**"**

They were OK with him giving "**glory** (the credit and reputation) **to God.**" That would not affect their religion, culture or place in the Empire. But they could not credit Jesus with this healing, and so went on to smear His reputation. Those Pharisees of vs. 16a must have been the synagogue rulers, or at least the majority opinion, for they won the day over the "**tearing split-effect** (= a division) **among them**" (vs. 16b), for it was their assessment that was given to the man.

25. **So then that man considered and replied, "I have not seen and do not know if he is a sinner** (one who does not comply with the religious rules, thus missing the goal; an outcast). **I have seen and know one thing: that I was existing being a blind man; at present** (or: just now) **I constantly see."**

Notice that he "considered" before he replied. He had not observed Jesus' life to know His character, but he had seen the change that Jesus had brought to him, and thus knew his new "sighted" condition. As the saying goes, "a man with an experience will always win over a person with just a thought or a theory."

26. **So then they said to him** [some MSS add: again], **"What did he do to you? How did he open up your eyes?"**

27. **He decidedly answered them, "I told you already, and you folks did not listen** (or: hear; = pay attention)! **Why are you now wanting to hear [it] again? You are not wanting to become his disciples, also, are you?"**

He saw through their motives and sarcastically confronted them, reckless and perhaps passionate with his words.

28. **So now they hurled abuse at him** (railed and reviled him) **and said, "You are now a disciple of that fellow, but we ourselves are disciples of Moses!**
29. **"We have seen, and know, that God has spoken to** (or: in) **Moses. But this fellow – we have not seen, nor do we know, where he is from."**

Observe that they engage him with arguments – this man who had been a beggar! His words must have stung them. So they accuse him of being a disciple of Jesus, and contrast themselves as being "**disciples of Moses**!" In vss. 28 and 29a they speak emphatically, using the personal pronouns "You" and "we." They have seen from their Scriptures, and know from their traditions, that God spoke to and in Moses. But Jesus is unknown to them. They don't know which school or sect from which He must have arisen – and such would have been unlikely, because He did work on the sabbath!

30. **The man insightfully replied, saying to them, "Accordingly indeed, in this [situation] is the marvelous thing** (the wonder; the astonishing state of affairs)**: that you yourselves have not seen nor know where he is from, and yet he opened up my eyes** (= made me able to see)**!**

His statement devalues them and shames them. In an honor-shame society, they would not be able to receive this, as vs. 34, below, shows us. From this hostile exchange, we get a better picture of why Jesus emphasized where He was from, in vs. 23, above, and Jn. 7:29. We can also get from this a better idea of the importance to them of their genealogies.

31. **"We have seen, and know, that God does not usually listen** (or: normally respond) **to sinners** (to those habitually missing the target; to those continuously being in error)**, but rather if anyone may be one who reveres and stands in awe of God, and may be habitually doing His will** (intent; purpose)**, He continuously listens to** (hears, or, responds to) **this one.**

This once-blind beggar is reciting their own arguments and worldview to them (vs. 16b, above). Although blind, this man knew his OT when he said "**God does not usually listen** (or: normally respond) **to sinners**." Cf e.g., Job 27:9; 35:13; Ps. 18:41; 34:16; 66:18; Isa. 1:15; Ezk. 8:18; Mic. 3:4; Zech. 7:13.

The second half of this verse would have been mainline Pharisee doctrine, as well. He is "preaching to the choir."

32. **"From out of the age [past]** (= from of old; = in known history; = since our world began) **it is not heard that anyone opened up [the] eyes of one having been born blind.**

Now he appeals to the miraculous, unheard-of character of what Jesus had done for him. He points them to their own history: look and see if this has ever happened!

33. **"If this one was not being from God's side** (on God's side; at God's side)**, he would not have been having power** (he would not have been able) **to be doing anything."**

Again he quotes part of the group's own words (vs. 16b) to them. This was their traditional wisdom.

34. **They decisively replied, and said to him, "You yourself were wholly born within sins** [idiom = You bastard!] **– and are YOU now teaching us?" And so they cast him out** (threw him outside).

When all other arguments fail, turn to the *ad hominin* attack: smear his person! Note that they are now devaluing and shaming him. They attack the place from which he arose. He was an unlearned beggar, as well, so how could HE teach them – folks who were Torah students and teachers! So they physically (it appears) cast him out of the synagogue. But this also probably meant that they excommunicated him.

35. **Jesus heard that they threw him outside, and so upon finding him, said to him, "Are you yourself now trusting or believing or putting faith into the Son of man**
> (or: = the son of Adam; = the Human Being; or: = the eschatological messianic figure [A, L and others read: Son of God])**?"**

It was so kind and thoughtful of Jesus to seek him out, having heard of the treatment that he had received. When folks cast you out for standing for the Truth, be of good cheer, the Son of man will seek you out and engage you!! This man had demonstrated and voiced his faith and trust in Jesus to the leaders of the synagogue. Jesus, having heard of the incident, asks him if this was the reason that he, himself, had been thrown out. To paraphrase Jesus question to him: "Did this happen because YOU (emphatic) are actually trusting and believing into Me?" But He used the eschatological title, making it a third-person question.

36. **And in considered response, that one says, "And who is he, sir** (or: my lord; master), **so that I can believe** (or, as a future: to the end that I will believe and progressively put trust) **into him?"**

The man either did not understand what the eschatological phrase meant, or, he did not know who this person was. It is also possible that although the man knew it was Jesus who healed him, after washing his eyes it does not say that he came back to Jesus, but to his neighbors. In vs. 12, when asked where he was, he replied that he had not seen and so did not know. So in the next verse, Jesus makes the connection for him…

37. **Jesus said to him, "You have both seen Him, and the One presently talking** (speaking) **with you, that One is He."**
38. **Then he began affirming, "I am now believing, Lord** (or: Master, I trust, and continue confident)**!"** **And he bowed down to the ground** (did obeisance), **kissing toward Him, and gave worship to Him.**

It is to a person who was blind, but now sees, that Jesus reveals Himself as being "the Son of man (etc., vs. 35, above)." With the revelation of WHO He is, this man immediately confesses his belief, calls Him Lord, and does obeisance to Him. This has been a story of a person's journey from blindness, to healing, to a confrontation with the religious domination system, and then to allegiance to Christ.

39. **Then Jesus says to him, "I came into this world** (or: ordered System of control and subjection) **into a result of sifting and deciding** (an effect of separation; a judgment)**: to the end that the folks NOT habitually seeing and observing can** (or: may; would) **be constantly seeing and observing, and the ones habitually seeing and observing should** (or: would; may) **become blind ones."**

Jesus' opening clause, "**I came into this world** (etc.)," can be read as an ontological statement, perhaps alluding to the Logos incarnating (becoming flesh). It can also be read as referring to entering the public scene after having been anointed for His ministry to the "ordered System of control and subjection."

The next phrase is commonly translated, "for judgment." But in the text, the preposition here is the same preposition rendered "into" in the phrase "**into this world**." The rendering "for judgment" implies an understanding of "for" as meaning "purpose." Translating it literally, "into," explains that by coming "into this world" He came "into a judgment." That judgment was made in the Garden of Eden and its result was the expelling of the humans out of the Garden and into a world of control and subjection, elsewhere rendered, "a domination system."

The Greek word commonly rendered "judgment" is *krima*, a form of the noun with a –*ma* ending which thus indicates that it means "**a result**" or "an effect" of "**sifting** (thus separating out the issues), and **deciding**" what should be done. The result of the sifting, separating and deciding was the human situation (theologically called "the fall") and predicament. Mankind was separated from the Garden, which was a symbol of a place of intimate fellowship with God – as that story displays. You might say that Jesus entered the prison house of darkness, blindness and slavery.

Following these two phrases is a conjunction that indicates that what follows it will explain the purpose for His coming. That purpose was: "**to the end that the folks NOT habitually seeing and observing can** (or: may; would) **be constantly seeing and observing**." This nicely fits the subject of the story that we have just read. The SIGN (which was the healing) points to a larger purpose, beyond the individual, for all of humanity. The terms "seeing and observing" become metaphors for enlightenment.

So what about the reversal in the second half of the couplet: **the ones habitually seeing and observing should** (or: would; may) **become blind ones**? This must be understood as irony (the use of words to express something other than and especially the opposite of the literal meaning). The Pharisees who opposed Jesus would likely have considered themselves as being the ones who had light from the Torah, and could see all the fine details about keeping the Law. But Jesus had elsewhere affirmed that they were blind to the Truth and were thus unaware of the presence of God's reign and sovereign activities. It was for this purpose, as well, that Jesus had come into the effect of God's decision, and as Paul put it:

> "**a petrifying, from a part** (a stone-like hardening in some measure; a callousness [extending over] a part), **has been birthed and come into existence in Israel** (or: has happened to Israel) **until which [time]** (or: to the point of which [situation]) **the effect of the full measure** (or: the result of the entire contents; or: = the full impact and full compliment of forces) **from the nations** (or: of the ethnic multitudes; or: – which are the Gentiles –) **may enter in**" (Rom. 11L25b).

In Mat. 13:13-15 Jesus cites Isa. 6:9-10, where we read,

> "… they squint their eyes! At some point should they not see with [their] eyes, and continue listening so as to hear with [their] ears, and thus understand in the heart? And then they can turn around, and I will continue healing them!" (vs. 15b).

So there is hope for them, too.

40. And so those from out of the Pharisees – being with Him – heard these things, and said to Him, "We ourselves are not also blind ones, are we?"

They got the message with its implication. They had been "sifted" and now realized that He had decided that they were among the blind.

41. Jesus says to them, "If you men had been and were continuing being blind ones, you were not holding and would not be having sin (error; a miss of the goal; failure). **Yet now you continue saying that, 'We are continuously seeing and habitually observing.' Your error** (sin; failure; miss of the target; deviation) **continues remaining** (is habitually dwelling; constantly abides).

There is no sin in not seeing, when one is blind. But when one IS blind, and yet professes to see, that profession is error (a sin) and that person is mistaken. Because they thought that they could see, and would not admit to their blindness, their error remained with them. It was a two-sided error: that of actually being metaphorically blind, and that of continuing to say that they were "**continuously seeing and habitually observing**."

They were the Torah experts, yet they did not see who He was. Recall 5:39, above,

> "**You folks continuously search** (or, as an imperative: Be constantly searching) **the Scriptures… and yet those [Scriptures] are** (exist being) **the ones continuously testifying about Me**."

In Lu. 24 we read an insightful incident:

> 27. **And so, beginning from Moses, and then from all the prophets, He continued to fully interpret and explain to** (or: for) **them the things pertaining to** (or: the references about) **Himself within all the Scriptures**....
>
> 31. **At that their eyes were at once fully opened wide, and they experienced full recognition of Him**..."

One only sees when his blindness has been healed and his eyes have been opened.

Jesus made a similar affirmation in 15:22, below,

> "**If I did not come and speak to** (or: among) **them, they had not been holding failure** (or: were having no sin or error; continued possessing no deviation). **But now** (at this time) **they continue holding nothing which like a specious and deceptive cloak appears in front around their sin**
>
> > (or: they are not continuing to hold that which is put forward to hide the situation concerning their failure; they are not habitually having an excuse or pretense about their deviation, error and miss of the target)."

When beginning His ministry, we read in Lu. 4:18 where He quoted Isa. 61:4 (apparently from a version of the LXX) that said, "**to** (for; among) **blind folks a seeing again** (a recovery of sight)." This was the mission of the Light which was the Logos. This chapter portrayed an example of its fulfillment.

Chapter 10

In the last verse of chapter 9, Jesus was speaking, and Pharisees were in His audience and had asked Him if they were also blind (vs. 40). In vs. 41 He gave them a response, and the chapter ends. Since our present chapter begins with Jesus speaking, we assume that the setting is the same, and thus chapter 10 is a continuation of chapter 9. It was probably divided off to keep chapter 9 from being too long. So, to begin, Jesus continues...

1. **"I tell you folks it is certainly true** (amen, amen; count on it): **the person not habitually entering in through the door** (or: gate; opening for entrance/exit) **into the sheepfold** (the walled-in pen for the sheep), **but rather repeatedly climbing up elsewhere** (or: stepping back over [the wall] from another place), **that one exists being a thief and a plunderer** (one who seizes by violence; or: an insurrectionist; a brigand).

With the prior comments in mind, we may be safe in concluding that Jesus is aiming this characterization at the Pharisees. In vs. 7, below (since vs. 6 informs us that they were not tracking with what He was saying), Jesus clearly identifies Himself as the Door for the sheep (the "narrow gate," as it were, through which the sheep can enter into safety from wolves and thieves).

Now the **sheepfold** would correspond to the "house" in other metaphors, such as "the house of Israel" (Mat. 15:24), the city of Jerusalem, or the temple (Mat. 23:38), or the place symbolizing the marriage feast of the Messiah (Mat. 25:10-13). In that last reference, they were just termed "foolish virgins" who ran out of oil (their lamps – i.e., their light – ran out of fuel), and missed out on the celebration of the arrival of the "Son of man." In Lu. 12:39, the metaphors of house and thief were combined in a setting similar to the sheepfold of vs. 1, here. There, we read:

> "**Now you normally know this by personal experience** (or, as an imperative: But be coming to experientially know this), **that if the householder had seen, or by foresight had perceived so as to be aware, at what hour the thief is proceeding in coming, he would stay awake and be watchful – and thus not allow his house [wall] to be dug through**..."

The word "thief" is used again, in vss. 8 and 10, below:

> "**All – as many as go before, or ahead of, Me** (or: precede, in front of Me; or: came or went before Me) **– are thieves and plunderers** (continue being those who seize by violence, are brigands, or are insurrectionists), **but yet the sheep do** (or: did) **not listen to** (or: hear, pay attention or [obey]) **them**"....
>
> "**The thief does not constantly come, except to the end that he may steal, slaughter** (slay for food – as for a feast – or, for a sacrifice) **and destroy** (utterly loose away). **I, Myself, come so that they can progressively possess** (would continuously have; could habitually hold)..."

The thief comes to steal; Christ came that we might possess and continuously have. We will discuss these verses in more detail, below. But this gives us some idea of where He is headed with all these metaphors and symbols. But before moving on, let us ponder Jesus' use of the term "thief," in Mat. 6:

> 19. **"Stop accumulating and storing up treasures for yourselves upon the earth** (or: on the Land) **– where moth and corrosion progressively causes [things] to disappear, and where thieves constantly dig through** (i.e., as to break in through a wall) **and then proceed in stealing.**
> 20. **"So you folks be continuously accumulating and storing up for yourselves treasures within heaven** (or: [your] atmosphere) **– where neither moth nor corrosion causes [things] to disappear, and where thieves do not constantly dig through** (or: penetrate) **nor are they repeatedly stealing.**
> 21. **"You see, where your treasure is, there also will be your heart** (= the core of your being)."

Notice, above, that the term "**plunderer**" can also refer to "an insurrectionist; a brigand." Palestine in 1st century AD had all of these, in the natural realm. But we need to keep in mind that Jesus is using all of these verbal pictures as analogies to be compared to or contrasted with – as the case may be – Himself, His followers, and the reign of God. Furthermore, we must hold in our thoughts the topic of "**the door.**"

2. **"But the person habitually entering through the door is the sheep's own shepherd** [note: root meaning of 'shepherd' is 'to protect'].

Observe that His topic is only secondarily "**the sheep**;" the central theme of His teaching is Himself, as the Door and the Shepherd of these sheep. From the root meaning of "shepherd," we are instructed about "safety" and "salvation." The sheep are kept safe from present danger, within this life. He is not speaking of "the afterlife" in this passage. Take note of 9b, below, speaking of the sheep:

> "**he will be habitually going in** (entering) **and going out** (exiting), **and he will continue finding pasture** (something to feed on)."

That is the life of a sheep that is living on this earth. But we will look at this more closely, below.

3. **"The doorkeeper** (the one who takes care of the gate and has charge of the sheep in the fold at night) **is regularly opening up to** (or: for) **him, and the sheep are constantly hearing and listening to his voice, and he habitually summons** (or: calls out to) **his sheep, [each] by its own name, and is constantly leading them forth** (or: out).

The figure of the doorkeeper does not come up again, in this passage, so we will pass over this as merely a stage prop for the play that He is setting forth. We can note, that whoever tends the door when the shepherd and the sheep are away from the fold (out getting a bite to eat) is a fixture of the fold itself, and he knows who the shepherd is, and facilitates the return of the flock. Might this be a veiled reference to the tribes of Israel, whose names were on the gates of the New Jerusalem (Rev. 21:12)? There, each gate also had an agent (a gatekeeper?). If we combine the picture here to the picture in Rev. we see that the redeemed Israel opens their gates to welcome the True Shepherd, and His sheep.

The second half of this verse dives directly into the meat of the message:

"**the sheep are constantly hearing and listening to his voice**" (reminds us of the relationship of Jesus to the Father);"

"**he habitually summons** (or: calls out to) **his sheep, [each] by its own name**" (he calls them; he has an intimate relationship with each one);

"he **is constantly leading them forth** (or: out)."

And, like His disciples, the sheep follow the Shepherd – in fact, He is the Way that they trod. This does not describe a static life. It describes the life of Peter, Paul, Silas, Timothy, etc., as they are led from city to city, from group to group. His SHEEP are His apprentices who will carry on His work after He leaves this realm. But they also live in the same realm (Eph. 2:6; Heb. 12:22-24; Rev. 3:21). He is the Path through this realm of the atmospheres – the realm of His reign – where "heaven" touches "earth."

4. "**And whenever he may drive out** (eject; herd forth) **all his own sheep, he is habitually passing on in front of them, and the sheep progressively follow him, because they have been acquainted with and recognize his voice.**

Yes, He often has to "drive" us "out." He ejects us from our comfort zones and herds us into the pastures. We progressively follow Him, because "**He is habitually passing on in front of [us]**" – AND, we "**have been acquainted with and recognize his voice.**" If we do not yet know His voice, we are not yet His sheep (disciples). It takes time and experience to, once born, learn to **recognize His voice.**

5. "**Yet to that [voice] belonging to another person they simply will not continue following; on the contrary, they will progressively take to flight** (flee) **from it** (or: him), **because they have not been acquainted with nor recognize the voice belonging to the other ones** (or: strangers)."

My how this has applied to His sheep, down through the ages. Many "shepherds" do not speak with the Shepherd's voice – and so, we do not follow them. Rather, we "**will progressively take to flight** (flee) **from it** (or: him)." There are many voices in the domination systems of the world; if they do not speak Life, they are not the Shepherd.

In vs. 1, Jesus introduced the negative character whom the sheep might encounter: "**a thief and a plunderer.**" This might also be a reference to, "**another person [whom] they simply will not continue following,**" here, in vs. 5. He refers to "**thieves and plunderers**" in vs. 8, and then describes the intent of the thief, in vs. 10: "**that he may steal, slaughter and destroy.**" We will look at these again, in vs. 8, but His reference there, to those who "came or went before Him," as well as to these same folks from vs. 1 on to our present verse, may be an allusion to the days of Ezekiel. In Ezk. 34, The Logos of Yahweh came to him and told him to prophesy against "the shepherds of Israel." We will highlight some of the complaints against those shepherds when we discuss the hireling, in vs. 13, below.

6. **Jesus told them this proverb** (common saying), **yet those did not intimately experience nor come to know or understand what things they were which He has been speaking to them.**

He was not, at that time, their shepherd. They currently belonged to another fold. They were lost sheep, but in time He would search them out and BRING (or: drag) them back to the fold, for as vs. 16b, below, instructs us: "**and they** [other MSS: it; there] **will progressively become One Flock, One Shepherd.**"

7. **Therefore, again, Jesus said to them, "I tell you, and it is certainly true** (amen, amen), **I Myself AM the Door for the sheep** (or: the sheep's Gate and Entrance).

Here, and through vs. 14, we have four "I AM," or "identity" statements. He affirms twice that He is the Door, and then twice that He is "the Ideal Shepherd." Things that are repeated are being emphasized. Furthermore, these emphatic affirmations are paradoxes. How can He be the Entrance, and at the same time be the One who Enters? Well, He is saying that He is all that these sheep need. Each metaphor gives His audience a picture of what He IS to them, and what He DOES for them. We find another metaphor in Jn. 14:6, part of which gives the same message as does the Door, here:

> "**Jesus then says to him, "I, Myself, AM** (exist being) **the Way** (or: Path), **the Truth** (the Reality) **and the Life. No one is presently going to, or progressively coming toward, the Father, except through Me** (through means of Me, or, through the midst of Me)."

They enter into the place of safety through Him. He keeps them safe from the wolves and thieves and plunderers. But not everyone had performed this way for the sheep. In fact...

8. **"All – as many as go before, or ahead of, Me** (or: precede, in front of Me; or: came or went before Me) **– are thieves and plunderers** (continue being those who seize by violence, are brigands, or are insurrectionists), **but yet the sheep do** (or: did) **not listen to** (or: hear, pay attention or [obey]) **them.**

The common way of rendering the first, dependent clause, "All who came before Me," has been a consternation to commentators. The question that arose was, "To whom was He referring?" The verb means either to come, or, to "**go.**" The verb is in the aorist tense, the indefinite (timeless) tense that can be rendered either as a simple English past tense (came; went), or as a simple English present tense (go). It seems to me that rendering as a present indefinite removes the difficulties. Notice, too, that the copulative that follows (**are**; continue being) is in the Greek present tense. The verb "**listen**; hear; pay attention," is also in the Greek indefinite (fact, point in time, snapshot tense), and so "**do not listen**" corresponds to the indefinite "**go.**"

Observe that this verse is bracketed by the two statements that He is "**the Door**," so this gives us the context for vs. 8. My wife, Lynda, mentioned that He is the only way in, and so anyone going ahead of Him would have to enter by another way. In vs. 1, above, He explained that anyone "**repeatedly climbing up elsewhere exists being a thief and a plunderer.**" This explains His terming those who go in front of Him as being in this category. "**The sheep do** (or: did) **not listen to them**" for the same reason as He explained in vs. 5, above: "**because they have not been acquainted with nor recognize the voice belonging to the other ones.**"

We suggest that He is referencing His current situation (and His contemporaries), and this comment is aimed at the Pharisees in His audience: those who were preceding Him into God's sheepfold by another way (religion and/or tradition that is not Christ, i.e., not Anointed, not grace, but instead is the way of Law). He was the Forerunner, and we have this promise, as we read in Heb. 6:

> 16. **For you see, men are swearing by** (or: according to) **the greater, and to** (or: for; with; among) **them the oath [is] an end** (limit; boundary; termination) **of all contradiction and dispute** (or: from talking-back in face-to-face opposition), **unto an established confirmation.**
> 17. **In [line with] which God – intending** (or: willing; purposing) **more abundantly to fully demonstrate to the heirs** (or: possessors) **of the promise the unchangeableness of His intent** (will; purpose) **– interposed with an oath,**
> 18. **so that by two unchangeable transactions in which [it is] impossible [for] God to deceive** (to lie or be false), **we – those fleeing to refuge – may be constantly having strong consolation** (services of the Paraclete) **to be strong to get into one's power the prescribed and settled expectation continuously lying before [us],**
> 19. **which we continuously have as an anchor of and pertaining to the soul, both secure from falling and established, even habitually entering into the interior** (or: then progressively going fully into the inner part) **with reference to the veil** (= entering into the interior [behind] the curtain [of the Holy of Holies; of the Temple])
> 20. **where a Forerunner, Jesus, entered over us** (or: on our behalf; over our [situation]), **down from** (or: in accord with; in the line of [succession of]) **the station** (order; placement) **of Melchizedek, being born** (or: coming to be) **a Chief** (or: Ranking) **Priest on into the midst of the Age** (or: [proceeding] unto the Age [of Messiah]).

Any attempt to enter prior to His entry, would be considered an action of brigands or insurrectionists against the reign of God. They would be acting like thieves trying to steal the goods of the inheritance. It would be an attempt to steal God's glory. The Door was for the Shepherd, and for the sheep. Verse 3, above, mentioned the door/gatekeeper who guarded the sheepfold at night. This was to ward off thieves who would open the gate/door and steal sheep. A parallel situation is described in regard to a house, in Mat. 24:43,

> "if the householder had seen and known in what sort of watch (= which of the watches) [of the night] the thief is normally coming, he would have kept awake, remained alert and kept watchful, and then he would not let (permit) his house to be dug (or: tunneled) through."

In Acts 20:29-30, Paul warned a local congregation:

> "Now I myself have seen and am aware that, after my spreading forth as dust and ashes (= going away, so as to be out of reach), heavy (burdensome and oppressive; fierce; vicious) wolves will enter into the midst of you folks – folks by habit not sparing the little flock, and men from among you yourselves will of themselves proceed standing up, repeatedly speaking things having been thoroughly turned and twisted (things that are distorted and not straight), to progressively drag (or: draw; [D & p41 read: turn]) away the disciples behind themselves."

This describes one example of plunderers, who Jesus also describes as wolves, in vs. 12, below. Notice that Paul spoke of them "speaking things having been thoroughly turned and twisted." This shows us that they would have a false *logos* that is contrary to the Logos of Christ. They would have a false blueprint, a false idea about God and His reign, a false message about His grace and the purpose of His decisions (judgments), and a false image of the character of the Father. They would be false shepherds.

Winslow Parker has added this insight, that this verse could "be a reference to Christ being the head, the firstborn from the dead, etc. In this, the 'going before would be one who intends to supplant, supersede, take the place of Jesus Himself.'"

John Gavazzoni offers this perception: "My innermost man equating to a sheep who follows the Shepherd, AS He knows that sheep, is always following Him, and will not listen to the voice of another, even as my outer man, the man of the flesh, goes its own way very attracted to the voice or voices of the false shepherds."

9. "I Myself AM the Door (or: Gate; Entrance); if anyone should enter in through Me he will be constantly kept safe and protected (made whole and returned to his original condition; rescued; delivered; saved), and he will be habitually going in (entering) and going out (exiting), and he will continue finding pasture (something to feed on).

Entry into the sheepfold (a metaphor for the kingdom, later expressed as the called-out community) had to be done through the Door, i.e., through Christ. The being "constantly kept safe and protected" offered by the sheepfold, and the Door, is a picture of the "salvation" spoken of elsewhere in the NT – in fact it is the verb form of that noun, as can be seen in the parenthetical expansion. The "habitually going in (entering) and going out (exiting)" is a picture of walking the Path, following Christ (living the cruciform Life, in Him). The pasture represents the nourishment gained by "eating His flesh and drinking His blood" (6:56, above).

10. "The thief does not constantly come, except to the end that he may steal, slaughter (slay for food – as for a feast – or, for a sacrifice) and destroy (utterly loose away). I, Myself, come so that they can progressively possess (would continuously have; could habitually hold) Life, and may continue possessing [it] in superabundance (or: and may have a surplus surrounding them in excessive amounts).

Remember, the thief is the person that tries to climb into the fold by another way. Here, Jude 4 lends insight for us:

> **"You see, some people came in unobserved, from the side – those having been previously written of old into this judgment** (or: people having from long ago been written into the effects and result of this decision)**: [to exist being] impious ones, people continuously changing the grace and favor of God into licentiousness, as well as repeatedly contradicting, saying, "No," to or about, disclaiming, denying and disowning our only Sovereign and Lord** (or: Supreme Ruler and Owner)**, Jesus Christ** [= Messiah]**."**

Now in that context, Jude 5 gives us an illustration of what he was speaking about:

> **"Yet I am repeatedly purposing and intending to remind you** [p78 adds: brothers] **– you folks having once seen** (or: perceived) **and thus being aware of all [these] things – that the Lord** [= Yahweh; other MSS: Jesus (= Joshua); some MSS: God] **after delivering** (rescuing; saving) **a people out of Egypt's land, [in] the second [phase] brought to ruin and loss those folks not trusting, believing or being loyal."**

He was speaking about Israel, during their wilderness journey. Judah (Jude) compared them to those in the 1st century that came into their communities "**unobserved, from the side,**" i.e., not through **the Door.** So this shows us who the "**thief**" is, to whom Jesus was speaking, here in vs. 10. We can generalize and just refer to this one as the 1st Adam. Isa. 14 spoke of this one:

> "Nevertheless, to the unseen shall you be brought down; to the remote parts of the crypt! Those who see you shall peer at you; they shall examine you closely: 'Is this the man who was disturbing the earth, making kingdoms quake?' He made the habitance like a wilderness and demolished its cities; he would not open a homeward way for his prisoners" (vss. 15-17, CVOT; *cf* also Ezk. 28).

Jesus may have been alluding to Jer. 23:1,

> "Woe to the shepherds (pastors) who destroy and scatter the flock of My pasture, averring [is] Yahweh" (CVOT; *cf* the rest of this chapter).

11. **"I, Myself, AM the Ideal Shepherd** (the Beautiful Protector of, and Provider for, the sheep). **The Ideal** (Fine; Beautiful) **Shepherd continually places His soul over the sheep** (or: habitually sets [p45 & others: gives] His inner life and consciousness for, and on behalf of the situation of, the sheep).

There may be here, in this I AM statement, an allusion to the blessing that Jacob gave to Joseph, in Gen. 49:24,

> "But taut was his bow, his arms ever-moving, through the hands of the Champion of Jacob, through the name of the Shepherd, and Israel's Rock" (trans. by Robert Alter).

The CVOT reads the last phrase, "Because there [is] the Shepherd of the Israel-Stone." Also, *cf* Ps. 23, below.

The adjective describing Christ as a Shepherd is commonly rendered "good," which is not wrong, but fails to give the essential ideas of this adjective. *Agathos* is the normal word for "good," and signifies the opposite of *kakos*, "bad." But here, John uses the word *kalos* which has the core ideas of "ideal; fine; beautiful" the opposite of "ugly, deformed, defective or unfit." The LXX used *kalos* to describe the trees in the Garden, in Gen. 2:9, in describing them as "ideal, or fine, for food." The word was also in that same verse to describe:

> **"the tree of the [situation] to know of beauty and of worthlessness by intimate experience**
> (or: to experience insight concerning what is fine and ideal, as well as what is harmful, unprofitable, painful and freighted with sorrow, bad conditions and wearisome labor)**."**

Considering the description of the contrasting negative fruit of this tree gives us greater insight into the idea of what Jesus meant here, in using the word "ideal, fine, beautiful" to describe Himself. Let us meditate on Ps. 23 as a classic description of "**the Ideal Shepherd.**" On offer is my rendering of the LXX version, but keep in mind, as parenthetically indicated, that the word LORD is Yahweh in the Heb. version – and that vs. 11, here, is another "I AM" affirmation:

1. **[The] LORD (= Yahweh) continually shepherds** (habitually cares for and tends, repeatedly leads to pasture and constantly protects) **me [as a part of the flock], and He will continue causing me to lack nothing** (or: so, by habit, in not even one thing will He fail me, or come too late [for; to] me; or: and thus will He keep on causing me not to be in need of even one thing).
2. **Into a place of [the] tender shoot** (or: Into the midst of a verdant place), **there** (in that place) **He encamped me** (or: causes me to settle down in a tent); **upon water of rest** (or: at restful water; on a water of ceasing) **He nourishes and rears me.**
3. **He turned my soul around** (or: He turns upon my whole being; He restored my self-life; He turned-about my inner being)**: He leads and guides me upon the well-worn Path of the Way pointed out, in righted covenant-participation, because of and for the sake of His Name.**
4. **For you see, even if I may** (or: should; would; could) **be caused to journey** (travel; pass from place to place) **within the midst of a shadow of death** (or: death's shadow; a shadow, from death; a shadow which is death), **I will continue not being caused to fear bad [times]** (will not be repeatedly frightened by worthless [situations or people]; will not be habitually afraid of misfortunes, harmful [experiences] or base [schemes]), **because You are, and continue being, with me: Your rod and your staff – these, from a call to be at my side, give me aid and impart relief, encouragement and comfort** (these are paracletes to help me).
5. **You prepare a table** (= spread a meal) **before me right opposite the folks habitually afflicting me** (or: You make ready my table, in my sight, from within the midst of the people constantly bringing pressure against me and rubbing me the wrong way); **You anoint** (or: fatten) **my head in** (or: with) **olive oil, and Your cup is progressively** (or: continuously; repeatedly) **intoxicating – as the best** (as the most excellent, or strongest, [wine]).
6. **And thus, Your mercy and compassion will in itself continue eagerly pursuing in order to track me down – all the days of my life, and [this is for] the [situation; occasion] for me to continuously settle down and dwell within** (or: to be habitually residing centered in) **[the] LORD'S [= Yahweh's] house on into a long duration of days.**

The clause "**continually places His soul over the sheep**" gives us not only a picture of protection, but also of "covering," the central idea of the word normally rendered "atonement," and reminds us of 1 Pet. 4:8b,

> "**Love** (the urge toward union; self-giving) **is constantly covering** (habitually throwing a veil over; progressively concealing; [and with other MSS: will continue covering]) **a multitude of failures** (mistakes; errors; misses of the target; sins).**"** [cf Prov. 10:12]

Lev. 17:11 instructed Israel that "the soul [LXX: psuchē] of the flesh is in the blood." If we connect this with 1 Jn. 7b, "**the blood of, from, and which is Jesus, His Son, keeps continually and repeatedly cleansing us from every sin,**" we get a more complete picture of Him placing His soul (which is in His blood) over the sheep.

12. "**The hireling** (hired hand working for wages) **– not even being a shepherd [and] the sheep are not his own – continues attentively watching the wolf progressively coming, and proceeds to abandon the sheep and to take flight – and so the wolf continues ravenously snatching them away and progressively scattering and dispersing them –**
13. "**but the hired hand flees, because he is a hireling, and it is not a concern to him** (or: a care for him) **about the sheep.**

The obvious take-away from this is that an owner will have greater concern for the safety of his sheep than someone who is hired to do the job – and especially in the face of danger. But who is "the hireling" in this analogy? Well, first of all we realize that God is the true Owner (Lord) of the sheep, which, of course, are human beings. As we saw in Ps. 23, above, Yahweh was the true Shepherd of Israel. But, just as we have today, people served as shepherds that represented the Owner. Let us look at the time of Ezekiel, and at a situation and time when the shepherds in Israel acted like hirelings:

"The word of Yahweh came to me, saying, 'Son of humanity, prophesy against the shepherds of Israel: prophesy, and you will say to them, to the shepherds, Thus says my Lord Yahweh: Woe to the shepherds of Israel who have been grazing themselves! Should the shepherds not graze the flock? The curds you eat, and with the wool you clothe [yourselves]; the plump you slaughter, but the flock you do not graze. The ailing you do not make steadfast, and the ill you do not heal, and the broken you do not bind up; the outcast you do no bring back, and the lost you do not seek, but with brunt [force] you [hold] sway [over] them, and with rigor..." (Ezk. 34:1-4, CVOT; *cf* the rest of the chapter).

Jesus had more explicit things to say about the scribes and Pharisees, in Mat. 23:

2. **"The scribes** (scholars; theologians; experts in the Law [Torah]) **and the Pharisees sit upon Moses' seat.**

3. **"Therefore, you people be constantly doing and keeping** (observing; maintaining) **everything – as many things as they should tell you. But do not continue doing or performing according to their works or actions, for you see, they are habitually 'saying,' and yet they are not doing or performing** (= they are 'all talk and no action').

4. **"So they habitually tie up and bind heavy loads** (or: burdensome cargos), **and then constantly place [these] as an addition upon the shoulders of the People** (or: belonging to persons) **– yet they, themselves, are not willing to budge or put them in motion with their finger** (or: = to 'lift a finger' to help carry them)!....

13. **"And so, tragic will be the fate for you, scribes** (scholars; theologians; Law experts) **and Pharisees – [you] overly critical and perverse folks who make decisions from a low point of view! – because you consistently shut and lock up the reign of the heavens in front of the People** (humans)

> (or: the sovereign rule of the atmospheres, which is in the presence of people; or: the activity and influence of the realm of the sky and heaven which is resident within, and moves toward, the humans; or: the kingdom moving from within the midst and face to face with people). **For you, yourselves habitually do not enter, nor yet are you by practice allowing** (or: letting flow on) **those repeatedly coming into [your realm of influence] to continue to go in."**

14. **"I, Myself, AM the Ideal** (the Beautiful; the Fine) **Shepherd, and I intimately know those [that are] Mine by experience, and those [that are] Mine are now intimately coming to know** (or: progressively are intimately knowing) **Me by experience –**

15. **"just as the Father has continuous, intimate knowledge of Me, and I Myself have continuous, intimate knowledge of the Father – and so I am constantly placing My soul-life over the sheep.**

Intimate knowing that comes from personal experience are the key notes of these two verses. This describes the fundamental and central component of kingdom living. This knowledge comes first of all from **constantly hearing and listening to His voice** (vs. 3, above), and through that, His Logos. He expresses this idea in 8:31b-32, above,

> "**If you yourselves would remain** (can dwell; should abide) **within My word** (in union with My *Logos* and information; centered in the thought, idea and message laid out by Me), **you folks are, and continue being, truly** (really; genuinely) **My disciples and you will progressively come to know the Truth** (or: Reality; that which is unsealed, open and without concealment) **by intimate experience, and the Truth** (Reality)..."

Notice that the same relationship that He has with the Father (vs. 15) He has with those that are His (vs. 14). And what He stated as one of His functions as an Ideal Shepherd in vs. 11b, above, He affirms again here, in 15b, "**and so I am constantly placing My soul-life over the sheep.**" We want to point out that this rendering, here and in 11b, give a more accurate rendering of the Greek terms. The KJV renderings, "gives his life for" (11b) and "I lay down my life for" (15b), are slanted toward sacrificial language that interprets His death on the cross. But notice the present tense (signifying continual or constant action) of the verb in these two verses, and then the intimate, relational context of vss. 14-15.

Furthermore, the "**continuous, intimate knowledge of the Father**" is the reason for WHY He is "**constantly placing [His] soul-life over the sheep**." This is the Heart of the Father! This is "**God... existing within Christ** (God being centered in, and in union with [the] Anointed One) **progressively and completely transforming [the] aggregate of humanity** (or: world) **to be other [than it is]**" (2 Cor. 5:19). When He lays Himself upon you, His Son is inserted into you, and you become pregnant with Christ (Gal. 4:19).

John Gavazzoni observes: "[It is] my inner sheep who the Lord "knows." The contrarian outer sheep, God has no fellowship with...does not '*gnosis*' it."

Dan Kaplan has shared these insights in regard to that with which Covers us:
    a) The **soul** speaks to all that a person is, the whole of the person, including the personality, the desires and passions, the will, the mindset and worldview – even the occasional "wrath." God's wrath (*orgē*) means: "**God's personal emotion and inherent fervor**
        (or: the teeming passion and **swelling desire, which is God**; the mental bent, natural impulse, propensity and disposition **from God**; or: the ire, anger, wrath or indignation **having the quality and character of God**)" (Jn. 3:36b).
    b) Jesus instructs us that we:
        "**will continue loving** (fully giving yourself to; urging toward reunion with) **[the] LORD** [= Yahweh], **your God, in union with your whole heart – and within the midst of the core of your being, and in union with your whole soul – and within the midst of your entire soul-life** (consciousness)..." (Mat. 22:37)
    And this is what Christ does, as He places God's soul over us (*cf* Jn. 3:116-17).
    c) This covering, like a warm blanket, allows us to have rest – His rest, as we are informed of in Heb. 4:9-11a. Furthermore, Jesus instructed His disciples, in Mat.11:
    29. "**You folks at once lift up My crossbeam** (or: the yoke which is Me; the balance beam that comes from and pertains to Me) **upon you, and instantly LEARN from Me, because I am** (or: I continuously exist being) **mild-tempered** (gentle; kind; considerate) **and humble** (low) **in the heart, and 'you folks will continue finding refreshment and discovering rest in and for your SOULS** (= consciousness and whole inner person; the mind, emotions and responses).' [Jer. 6:16]
    30. "**You see, My crossbeam** (or: the yoke which is Me; the balance beam that comes from and pertains to Me) **is useful, well-fitting and kindly obliging, and My load** (the burden that is Me and which pertains to Me) **continues being light** (not heavy)."

16. "**And I constantly have** (hold; possess) **other sheep which do not exist** (or: are not) **from out of this fold** (or: sheep pen), **and it is binding** (or: necessary) **for Me to progressively lead those also, and they will continue listening to** (will habitually hear and pay attention to [implying: obey]) **My voice, and they** [other MSS: it; there] **will progressively become One Flock, One Shepherd.**

Most likely, the "**other sheep**" of a different fold would be a hint of the ethnic multitudes, commonly called the Gentiles. In Jn. 4 we observed that He had sheep in Samaria, and that area was considered to be non-Israel, by Second Temple Judaism, and thus in another fold. We, of course, see in the book of Acts, and after that, that the call to follow Christ went throughout the whole world of that time (i.e., into all the Roman Empire, and beyond – Mat. 28:19).

In Acts 10 we read of Peter with the household of Cornelius. Then in Rom. 11:17ff we see that the ethnic multitudes were grafted into Israel's olive tree, and in Eph. 2:11-22 that the economy of God was changed to no longer recognize the distinctions of "circumcision" and "uncircumcision," "**making** (forming; constructing; creating; producing) **The Both [to be] one**... **within His flesh**.... **to the end that He may frame** (create; found and settle from a state of wildness and disorder) **The Two into One qualitatively New and Different** [*p*46 & others: common] **Humanity centered within the midst of, and in union with, Himself, continuously making** (progressively creating) **Peace and Harmony** (a joining)" (vss. 14-15b).

And that was just the beginning…

17. **"On this account the Father continuously loves** (or: fully gives Himself to) **Me, because I Myself am constantly placing** (or: repeatedly setting) **My soul-life** (or: progressively laying My inner self, being and consciousness [over them]), **so that I may take it in My hand** (or: would receive it) **again.**

Here again, as in vss. 11 and 15, He uses the same verb, "**constantly placing** (or: repeatedly setting)," in reference to His soul/**soul-life,** or, "progressively laying [His] inner self, being and consciousness" over them. Jesus makes good use of the rhetoric of repetition.

Now the final, dependent clause has traditionally been associated with His resurrection (the "placing" or "setting" of His soul/soul-life being taken as a veiled reference to His crucifixion). However, His death and resurrection was a "once for all" situation (Heb. 9:26; a reference to the Day of Atonement). But in this passage He repeatedly used the present tense, not the aorist or the future. He gives further explanation in the next verse, and there we continue seeing Him use the present tense (continuous, repeated, habitual or progressive action).

His words create a picture of His having control of His Soul-Life/Consciousness. He sets it upon someone or some situation, and then takes it in hand again. This could be seen as a process of imprinting – or of forming a clay pot into His image. His Soul/Spirit – expressed in His Logos – keeps on creating folks as containers of His glory.

18. **"No one at any point lifts it** [with other MSS: Not one person is presently lifting it] **up and carries it away** (or: proceeds to remove it) **from Me; on the contrary, I Myself continue putting** (keep on placing; am repeatedly setting; am progressively laying) **it away from** (or: off) **Myself. I constantly hold authority** (continuously have the right and hold the 'position'; or: continue possessing privilege from out of the midst of Being) **to place it** (put it; lay it), **and I constantly hold authority from out of being** (continuously possess the right, forth from [My] existence; = am in the authoritative position) **to take it** (or: receive it; resume it) **again. This implanted goal** (purposed impartation of the finished product within; inward directive and destiny) **I received from** (or: at) **My Father's side."**

Notice vs. 21, below. This is the same extended teaching and conversation that the Pharisees started with Him in ch. 9: they refer to His opening up blind eyes, and here we have another "**tearing split-effect**" among them (vs. 19). So is this an example of that to which He was referring? Was His spitting to make clay, and then applying (anointing) it upon the blind man's eyes actually "**placing His soul and consciousness**" upon Him? In vs. 10b, above, He explained His current mission:

> "**I, Myself, come so that they can progressively possess** (would continuously have; could habitually hold) **Life, and may continue possessing [it] in superabundance** (or: and may have a surplus surrounding them in excessive amounts)."

He gave Life to the eyes of the blind man.

Now when He said, "**No one at any point lifts it** [with other MSS: Not one person is presently lifting it] **up and carries it away** (or: proceeds to remove it) **from Me**," the "**it**" refers to His soul, self, consciousness and soul-life" to which He referred in vs. 17. We must read "crucifixion" into these words to make them say that. Was He making a veiled allusion to His upcoming death? Perhaps. But this can also be read that no one controls Him. This was all gift and grace – it could not be demanded or "**lifted up and carried away from Him**. There was no demand from the Law that He should do ANYTHING that He did.

Recall our discussion, in chapter 9, of how His actions demonstrated allusions to the creation. Light was shining into the darkness of that man's eyes (1:5, above). He had "privilege from out of the midst of Being," and "the right and held the 'position'" of "the Messiah," "the Son of humanity." He "**constantly held authority** (continuously had the right to hold the 'position'; or: continued possessing privilege from out of the midst of Being) **to place it** (put it; lay it), **and [He] constantly held authority from out of being** (continuously possess the right, forth from [His] existence; = [was] in the authoritative position) **to take it** (or: receive it; resume it) **again**. This all referred to **His soul**, and we might say, His "Christ consciousness and awareness." In vs. 24, below, their questions are about Him being the Christ. His response had to do with "**The works** (The deeds; The actions) **which [He Himself was] continually doing** (or: progressively performing; regularly producing)."

Consider the context of this chapter: the Door of the sheepfold; the Shepherd; the sheep. In vs. 9 He functions as the Door: that function is for protection of the sheep, for in vs. 10 He brings up the danger of the thief who might come to steal the sheep. In vs. 11 He is the ideal Shepherd: again, for protection, as explained in vs. 12 where the hireling will not protect the sheep. Verse 14 affirms again that He is the ideal Shepherd, then vs. 15 gives us a key to vss. 17-18, stating that He is "**constantly placing [His] soul-life over the sheep**." But then He takes it off of them, giving them the needed freedom to go out to find pasture. This is like opening "the Door" for them. His soul is not a prison, but is protection. The ideas of sacrifice or of crucifixion just do not fit the context.

What we suggest is that He was repeatedly (and still continues) placing His SOUL upon people, and then repeatedly taking IT up again so as to place IT and US into the Vine (ch. 15), thus JOINING us to Himself. Dan reminds us that, "**He empties Himself** (or: removed the contents of Himself; made Himself empty)" (Phil. 2:7a), and lived the cruciform life, placing His soul upon others in order to raise them up. Verse 28, below, adds another aspect to the action of setting His soul over them, which is that He gives **Life** to them, and then He adds, "**no one will be snatching them** (or: taking them by force) **from out of My hand**" (once, again: protection – the function of a Shepherd).

During a discussion with Dan, the picture of the vision in Isa. 6 came to mind as being parallel to what Jesus said, here in vs. 18. In Isa. 6:2 Isaiah saw the Burning Ones (Heb. *seraphim*). In vs. 6 one of the Burning Ones (a symbol of Christ, the Anointed One, but now functioning as the Purifier – cf Mal. 3:2-3) comes to Isaiah with a "live coal" from the altar, then in vs. 7 He laid the coal upon his mouth, and thus withdrew his perversity (or: iniquity; LXX: lawlessness) and sheltered his mistake (covered his failure and error; his sin was atoned; LXX: purified his deviations). The "live; glowing" coal had the "soul" of the Burning One. Our God is a consuming Fire that purifies and transforms. This is the character of the Soul of Christ. When placing of His burning Soul (Person; Fiery Presence and Character) upon His sheep (vs. 15, above), He knows when to "**take or receive it again**" – as Dan said: "He knows just how much we can take at one time."

In 15:13, below, Jesus uses the same phrase that we can see applies to Him, but also to us, as well:
"**No one continues holding** (or: having) **greater Love** (full self-giving; urge toward reunion) **than this: that someone should place** (set; lay; put) **his soul** (or: inner being; self; person; consciousness which is him) **over [the situation or circumstances of; = cover]** (or: on behalf of) **his friends**."
This is something He did during His years of ministry, as well as for all humanity, on the cross. It is a Pattern for us, during our lifetime.

19. **Then a tearing split-effect** (= a division) **occurred again among the Judeans** (= religious authorities; ruling class in Judea) **through these words** (or: on account of these ideas {*logoi*}; because of these blueprints).

Verses 17-18 apparently had a huge emotional effect upon the crowd: some liking it, but the usual critics strongly objecting to the implications of the blueprints that He was laying out.

20. **Now many of them began saying, "He continues having a demon** (a Hellenistic concept and term: = animistic influence) **and is insane** (mad; manic; crazy; deranged). **Why do you continue listening to** (or: hearing; = paying attention to) **him?"**

Their first statement seems to be one of their default critiques (Jn. 8:48, 52). And as to this Hellenistic term, *demon*, notice that they connect this word with a person being **insane** (deranged; etc.). So these folks are asking other people, "Why continue listening to a crazy person?"

21. **Others were saying, "These are not the gush-effects of** (or: result of a flow from; spoken words of; declarations from) **a demoniac** (of one being constantly affected or afflicted by a demon). **A demon** (= an animistic influence) **is not able and has no power to open up blind people's eyes!"**

This was approximately the same reasoning that they gave in Jn. 9:16b, but there using the word "sinner," and here, "demoniac." These folks did see clearly on this matter that no animistic influence, or adversarial spirit, is able to open blind eyes.

22. **At that time [the feast** (or: festival) **of] the Dedications** (or: celebration of renewals or rededication; Feast of Lights; Hanukkah) **occurred within Jerusalem – it was winter** (the rainy and stormy season).
23. **Jesus had been walking around in the Temple grounds, within Solomon's Colonnade** (Portico; covered porch attached to the Temple buildings).
24. **Then the Judeans** (= religious authorities) **surrounded** (or: encircled) **Him, and began to say to Him, "Until when are you continuing to lift up our soul** (= How long are you going to constantly keep us in suspense, or with high expectations)**? If YOU** (or: you yourself) **are the Christ** (the Anointed One; = the Messiah), **openly** (outspokenly; boldly and publicly, with freedom of speech, as a citizen) **tell us!"**

He was presenting Himself publicly in an area that today might be called city hall, or the state capital buildings. It was their civic and religious center, in Jerusalem. Whether this time immediately followed the confrontation above, or not, cannot be ascertained with certainty from the text, nor from the non-sequential character of John's Gospel. But since the religious leaders "**surrounded Him**," it was likely soon after His previous engagement with them. They were wanting to silence Him.

Now with the discussion regarding the term "soul," in vs. 18, above, take note of how these Judeans are using this term: "**Until when are you continuing to lift up our soul?**" The parenthetical expansion offers a potential paraphrase of their idiomatic use of the term. Their second question demonstrates their meaning: they want a straight-forward answer, spoken to them openly and publicly. Is He the Christ?

25. **Jesus directly answered them, "I did tell you folks, and you continue not trusting or believing with conviction. The works** (The deeds; The actions) **which I Myself am continually doing** (or: progressively performing; regularly producing) **within My Father's Name, these are continuously bearing witness** (giving testimony; showing evidence) **about Me.**

In considering Christ's works, we are reminded of Paul, in Gal. 4:19, "**O my little children** (born ones), **with whom I am progressing, again, in childbirth labor** (travail; labor pains) **until Christ may be suddenly formed within you folks.**" This is what Jesus was doing, as we saw with the healing of the blind man, and then revealing Himself to him (Jn. 9:35-39). Here, He repeats the affirmation that His works bore witness about Him, and showed evidence concerning Him. We saw this same response by Him in Jn. 5:36; His life and actions were a testimony to them. It should be the same with us. Once again, He side-steps their question, yet indicates that the works that He was continuingly doing should have given them the answer to their question. They should be able to come to a conclusion from the testimony and evidence that His deeds and actions proclaimed of themselves. He also affirms that He had done them "**within [His] Father's Name**," and they had taken this to mean that God was His Father (8:38, 42, 49 and 54, above).

26. **"But you folks yourselves are not in the habit of trusting or believing, because you are not from among My sheep** (or: because you presently exist being no sheep of Mine), **just as I told you,**
27. **"because My sheep are constantly hearing and listening to** [implying: obeying] **My voice, and I Myself am progressively** (or: continuously) **knowing them by intimate experience, and they are progressively** (or: habitually) **following Me,**
28. **"and I Myself am continuously giving eonian life** (age-enduring life; life having the qualities and characteristics of the Age [of Messiah]; a life from, of and for the ages) **to and in them and so by no means** (or: under no circumstances) **can they at any point be lost or destroyed, or even cause themselves to perish; and further, no one will be snatching them** (or: taking them by force) **from out of My hand.**

Next, in vss. 26-28, He turns the conversation to the subject of His **sheep**, affirming that these Judeans that are questioning Him "**are not from among [His] sheep.**" Verse 27 repeats vs. 3, "**My sheep are constantly hearing and listening to** [implying: obeying] **My voice,**" and then He repeats vs. 14 to them, "**I Myself am progressively** (or: continuously) **knowing them by intimate experience,**" but here adding "**and they are progressively** (or: habitually) **following Me.**" He affirms again that He is the Shepherd of the sheep, and He is leading them out for food, and then leading them back for protection and rest.

Then vs. 28 explains what **placing His soul on them** imparts: "**and I Myself am continuously giving eonian life** (age-enduring life; life having the qualities and characteristics of the Age [of Messiah]; a life from, of and for the ages) **to and in them.**" He is telling these Judeans that His **sheep** have entered **God's reign**, and have the new Life that corresponds to the Messiah's presence among them.

We observe an allusion to Jn. 3:16 with the announcement, "**and so by no means** (or: under no circumstances) **can they at any point be lost or destroyed, or even cause themselves to perish.**" The last clause, "**no one will be snatching them** (or: taking them by force) **from out of My hand**" is echoed by Paul in Rom. 8:35, 38, 39,

> "**Who or what will be separating, dividing or parting us away from the Love of and from Christ?**…. **neither death, nor life** (or: living existence), **nor agents** (or: messengers), **nor sovereignties** (rulers; those in prime position; or: beginnings), **nor things being now here** (being placed within, at present), **nor things about to be** (impending, or about to consecutively come), **nor powers** (or: capabilities), **nor height** (effect of being high), **nor depth** (or: deep places), **nor any other or different created thing** (or: founded thing; institution; = the Law; = old covenant; = adversaries) **will be having power or be able to separate, divide or part us from God's Love** (or: from the acceptance from God; from the urge toward reunion, which is God; God's full giving of Himself to us) **which is within Christ Jesus, our Owner.**"

29. **"My Father, Who has given [them] to Me, is greater than all** (or: everything; all things or people; [other MSS read: What My Father has given to Me is greater than all]), **and no one** (not even one person) **has power or is able to proceed to snatch from out of the Father's hand.**

By stating that His Father "**is greater than all,**" He is in effect saying that God is His Father. The last clause repeats their security in Him that he proclaimed in 28b, but now THEIR SOURCE (His **Father**, who gave them to Him, and thus who had POSSESSED them in order to give them; recall: Ezk. 18:4, "all souls are Mine") also has them in His hand – indicating that Jesus' **hand** and "**the Father's hand**" are either the same **hand**, or else Jesus' hand is within the Father's hand. We see this same picture of a concentric sphere in an assertion from Paul"

"your life has been hidden so that it is now concealed together with the Christ, within the midst of God" (Col. 3:3).

30. **"I, Myself, and the Father are** (continuously exist being) **ONE** (or: I and Father: We are one thing [= essence, nature or being]; or: = unity; union)."

Now this can either be a statement of "unity, or union," or, it was/is an ontological bombshell: "I and Father: We are one essence, nature and Being." Traditional Christianity has been, and remains, on both sides of this issue. This one-liner previews more enigmatic affirmation, such as, vs. 38b, below, and 14:9, below, **"The person having discerned and seen Me has seen, and now perceives, the Father."** Then 14:10, proclaims, **"it is continuously** (it constantly exists being) **I, Myself, within the midst of the Father, and the Father within the midst of Me;"** and added to that are the verses in chapter 17. All of what is rendered for this verse is probably true, and Jesus wanted us to ponder the ambiguity of what He said.

31. **Then the Judeans** (= leaders of the Jewish religion) **again picked up stones and brought them so that they could stone Him** (pelt Him with stones; or: kill Him with stones).

Another audience did the same thing, in 8:59, above. This is typical of fanatical groups – be they religious, political or cultural. Offend their idols and they will stone you, burn you at the stake (in the old days) or burn your building, or verbally trash you one way or another (shadow ban you, etc.), or make a pontifical pronouncement, like, "Goodbye, Rob Bell." We saw this in Adam and Eve's first son, who, for a religious reason killed his brother. The "unplugged soul" always wants to destroy the opposition.

32. **Jesus discerningly replies to them, "I exhibited** (pointed out, showed, displayed) **to** (or: among; for) **you folks many beautiful works** (ideal acts; fine and noble deeds) **issuing from out of the midst of the** [other MSS: My] **Father. Because of what kind** (sort; character) **of work, of them, are you men proceeding to stone Me?"**

He knows that His works are not the reason, He just wants them to say it. When He related Himself to Abraham and said, **"before Abraham comes** (or: was to come) **into being, I, Myself, am"** (8:58, above), and the group reached for the rocks, it was over an ontological, and thus religious, statement that Jesus had made. Verse 30, above, fits into this category. But furthermore, He is bringing to this public forum a proclamation that He has been doing **"many beautiful works** (ideal acts; fine and noble deeds),"** and that these have **"[issued] from out of the midst of the Father."** His ending question drips with sarcasm.

33. **The Judeans** (= religious authorities) **considered and answered Him, "We are not proceeding to stone you about beautiful works, but rather, about blasphemy** (villainous, impious slander; defaming communication and misrepresentation [of God]) **– even because YOU** (or: you yourself), **being a human** (a man), **continue making yourself God** (or: frame yourself [to be] a god)."

Well now, we can surmise, from the stated reason that they gave for their attempted execution, that they took Jesus' statement, in vs. 30, as an ontological statement. They deduced that by Him saying that He and the Father were One (One and the same thing?), that He was **"making [himself] God,"** when to their view He was only a human being. So how do we take His statement? Just listen to the Breath-effect, within…

34. **Jesus judiciously replies to them, "Is it not standing written within your Law** [other MSS: the Law; = the Torah] **that 'I say, you people are** (or: exist being) **gods'?** [Ps. 82:6]

Well, Jesus just gets right down to it. So how do we suppose His listeners normally interpreted that Psalm? Paul made an instructive quote of a Greek poet, and then adds his own comment about who we really are:

> "'**You see, we are also a family of the One** (or: we even continuously exist being a race whose source is the One; or: we also are His species and offspring; we are even a family which is composed of the One and which is the One).' [a quote of Aratos, and of Keleanthes]
>
> **Therefore, continuously and inherently subsisting from under a beginning, being God's family** (a species of God; a race whose source is God; [the] kind of being having the qualities and characteristics of God; [the] offspring birthed from God)..." (Acts 17:28b, 29a).

Paul further defines the relationship of Jesus to us, in Rom. 8:29,

> "**He also marked out beforehand** (determined, defined and designed in advance) **[as] copies** (joint-forms) **of the image** (material likeness; portrait; form) **of His Son** (or: He previously divided, separated and bounded conformed patterns from the image/form of His Son) **into the [situation for] Him to be** (or: to continually exist being) **the Firstborn among, within the center of, and in union with many brothers** (= a vast family from the same womb; Gal. 4:26)!"

In Mat. 6:8, Jesus used the phrase, "**God, your Father.**" Then in vs. 9 He taught His followers to begin their address to their Father with: "'**O our Father – the One within and in union with the heavens!** (or: in the midst of the atmosphere and firmament!)..." We all came from the same place (womb?) that Jesus did, as Paul indicates in Rom. 11:36,

> "**forth from out of the midst of Him, then through the midst of Him** (or: through means of Him), **and [finally] into the midst of Him, [is; will be] the whole** (everything; [are] all things; or: = Because He is the source, means and goal/destiny of all things)."

The word for "gods" in the Heb. text of Ps. 82:6 is *elohim*, and the LXX renders this in the Greek as the plural of *theos*, as is used here in 10:34, 35. In the LXX of Ps. 82:1, we read: "**The God** [= Elohim] **stood** (or: takes a stand) **within a synagogue** (gathering together; assembly) **of gods; and so within the midst, He continuously makes decisions throughout gods** (or, as a future tense: will keep on or progressively thoroughly discern and evaluate gods)." The LXX of Ps. 82:6 reads:

> "**I Myself said, 'You folks are** (exist being) **gods, and all people [are] sons of the Most High! But yet you folks continue** (or: are one-after-another; are progressively) **dying-off as** (or: like) **human beings, and even as** (like) **one of the beginning ones** (or: rulers; original people) **you continually** (or: one-after-another; repeatedly; progressively) **fall** (or: collapse)'" (LXX, JM).

But more importantly, how did Jesus interpret Ps. 82:6? Let's just move ahead to His explanation...

35. "**Since He said 'gods'** [= *elohim*] **to whom God's** *Logos* (the Word which was laid out from God) **came to be** (or: toward whom the Idea and Blueprint, which is God, was birthed; toward whom God's message proceeded and was directed into existence) – **and it is not possible** (or: there is no power) **for the Scripture** [= the Tanakh] **to be loosened, to be undone so as to nullify, or to be destroyed** –

The dependent clause, "**to whom God's** *Logos* **came to be,**" bears investigation. As we have offered elsewhere, the forms of the nouns present us with choices, the meaning of *Logos* offers more choices, and then the verb can be variously rendered. So let us begin, being aware that the combinations can be switched, between noun functions and their semantic range:

a) **God's** *Logos* – this rendering expresses the possessive function of the genitive case; the *Logos* belongs to God; it pertains to God; it's what God said; *Logos* is a transliteration of the Greek word, and I use it here so that the reader is helped to trace this significant word from 1:1, above, on through the entire text of John's Gospel.

b) the first parenthetical rendering, "the Word which was laid out from God," gives the common rendering and meaning, "word," but also conflates a central idea of *logos*: "that which is laid out,"

197

like a thought that has been presented; the word God is rendered as an ablative (the same spelling as a genitive), indicating that it expresses a source: "FROM God."

c) the second parenthetical rendering picks up the whole phrase, offering another rendering of the preposition: toward whom (instead of to whom), which indicates direction and aim (the target being the people to, or toward, whom the Logos "**came to be**"); *Logos* is here conflated "Idea and Blueprint," and "God" is rendered as a genitive of apposition (definition): "which is God." The verb is now rendered in the basic meaning of a family of words: "was birthed," indicating how it came to be.

d) with only slight further explanation, the last offering is "toward whom God's message proceeded and was directed into existence" – another meaning of *logos*, the preposition demonstrating the sense of directed movement ("proceeded and was directed"), and another core meaning of the verb: "into existence."

The interjected clause, set off by dashes, may have a bit of "tongue-in-cheek" humor to it (striking a chord among the Pharisees, as it were, saying, "Yes, I agree with you," or, "Yes, I know that this is important to you," or, it may be a bare statement of fact – or, all three. But for His argument, it is essential, for He is basing what He had previously said in vs. 30 upon a line of Scripture. Loosing, undoing, nullifying or destroying any part of the Torah was unthinkable.

But His main point is that God's Logos had said that the people of Israel were "**gods**." Many have tried to explain this away by affirming that the Hebrew *elohim* had a semantic range of meaning, in the OT. But the LXX (translated in the 3rd century BC) renders *elohim* by the Greek plural of the word, *theos* – the word for "god" or "God," in Greek. Furthermore, we can see from our present context, that this was the way Jesus was using the word. He meant "**gods**." So open your mind to the possibilities. He chose this verse to make His point.

36. **"are you yourselves now saying to the One Whom the Father set apart** (consecrated as holy) **and sent forth as an Emissary** (on a mission; as a Representative) **into the organized domination-System** (into the world; into the cosmos; unto the religious, political and cultural complex; into the midst of the aggregate of humanity) **– that 'You are blaspheming** (speaking impious villainy and giving a false image [of God])**,' because I said, 'I am God's Son** (I exist being the Son of, and from, God)**'?**

If Israel was addressed by God as being "gods," would that not make them "sons of God"? Paul, in Rom. 8:14, declares plainly, "**For it follows that as many as are being continuously led by God's Spirit, these folks are God's sons**" – a clear reference to Israel wandering in the wilderness, of whom God said (corporately), "Israel is My son – My firstborn" (Ex. 4:22). He could have ended His argument to the Pharisees with the rhetorical question that this verse offered them, but He continued…

37. **"If I am not habitually** (continually; progressively) **doing My Father's works** (deeds; actions), **do not make it a habit to put trust in Me** (or: Don't proceed to believe Me or give allegiance to Me).

In vs. 36 He posited that He was "**set apart** (consecrated as holy) **[by the Father] and sent forth as an Emissary** (on a mission; as a Representative) **into the organized domination-System**." So now He follows with the logical suggestion that if He was not engaged in His Father's works and deeds, then they should not trust Him or give allegiance to Him. However…

38. **"Yet since I am constantly performing** (habitually doing; repeatedly making; progressively producing), **even if you folks cannot now be trusting and believing in Me or continue loyal to Me, continue to** [other MSS: at some point] **trust, believe and put faith in and by the results** (acts; works; deeds) **so that you may come to experientially know and habitually trust** (or: believe [other MSS: continue knowing]) **that** (or: because) **the Father [is] within Me, and I [am] within the Father!"**

The Pharisees had propaganda; Jesus had the facts. He WAS "**constantly performing** (habitually doing; repeatedly making; progressively producing)" on behalf of His Father. So even if they can't believe what He says, "**trust, believe and put faith in and by the results** (acts; works; deeds)." If they would even do THIS, they could "**come to experientially know and habitually trust** (or: believe [other MSS: continue knowing]) **that** (or: because) **the Father [is] within Me, and I [am] within the Father**." His works were SIGNS; if they believed these signs they would be pointed to Him, and personally come to trust in the relationship between, as well as the "interpenetration" of and intertwining of the Father and the Son.

39. **Therefore they kept on seeking [opportunity], again, to lay hold of and arrest** (or: seize; grasp) **Him at some point, but He went** (or: slipped) **forth out of their hands** (or: from their clutches).

But all of His words were at that time of no avail. It made them all the more desire to arrest Him. But again, as in 8:59, above, He "slipped from their clutches."

40. **So He went off** (or: away), **again, to the other side of the Jordan [River], into the place where John had been habitually immersing [folks] the first time** (or: formerly), **and continued remaining** (abiding; dwelling) **there.**

His Father saw that He needed a break, and led Him out into nature, away from the maddening crowds.

41. **Then many came to Him, and they began saying, "John, indeed, did not perform a single** (or: one) **sign, yet all – whatever John said about this one – was true."**

We are not told how long of a break and a rest that He had before folks learned that He was in their area. When the Son of God is manifested, you can't keep folks away. They had heard of, or perhaps at one point seen, His SIGNS and knew that they were TRUE.

42. **And so many believed and put convinced trust into Him** (or: were loyal unto Him) **there.**

Notice that these, probably common, folks DID exactly what Jesus advised the Pharisees to do, in vs. 38, above. They believed and trusted that His **results** were reliable, and this led them to "**put convinced trust into Him**," and to be loyal unto Him.

Chapter 11

1. **Now there was a certain man being constantly ill** (habitually weak; progressively infirm; repeatedly sick) **– Lazarus, from Bethany, from out of the village of Mary and her sister Martha.**
2. **In fact, it was the Mary who at one time rubbed and anointed the Lord** (the Master) **with perfumed oil** (ointment) **and then wiped off His feet with her hair, whose brother, Lazarus, had been continuing ill** (weak; sick).
3. **So the sisters dispatched a message to Jesus, which was saying, "O Lord** (Master), **take note, he whom You habitually regard as a friend** (constantly treat with fondness and affection; continuously cherish and love as a congenial associate) **continues being weak and sick."**
4. **Now Jesus, hearing [this], said, "This weakness** (sickness; infirmity) **is not directed or leading toward death, but to the contrary [is] over [the issue of] God's glory** (or: reputation; appearance; manifestation; recognition), **to the end that through it God's [other MSS: His; the] Son would be glorified** (may receive recognition, a good reputation and a manifestation which calls forth praise)."

Jesus' initial response calls to mind how He answered His disciples about the cause of blindness in the man that was born blind (Jn. 9:3b). We might expect, then, that this incident will involve another SIGN, along with His added teaching. Here, He adds that "**this weakness** (illness)" has a purpose (note: "**to** the end that through it"), and this purpose is that "**God's Son would be glorified** (etc.)." Is His message to us, in this, that we should see all difficulties and negative situations as opportunities for God and Christ to receive glory from the manifestations of Himself that He will bring praise to them? The word **glory** is used 19 times in this Gospel; it is an important theme in Jesus' messages, and John's narratives. God's reputation would naturally be an important feature in an honor/shame culture, which was the environment of the life and times of Jesus and His followers. Glory and honor were the highest social values, while shame and disgrace were at the bottom. Jn. 17:24 reports Jesus expressing to the Father His desire that His disciples, "**can** (or: may; could; would) **constantly look upon and keep on contemplatively watching My own glory** (assumed appearance; manifested Presence which incites praise)."

5. **Now Jesus was loving and continued in loyal appreciation of Martha, her sister, and Lazarus.**
6. **Even so, when He heard that he continues being sick and weak, He then, indeed, remained two days within [the] place in which He was [staying].**

His actions are a Pattern for us: He did not operate out of His emotions, but listened to the Father's instructions of when He should go to Lazarus. All through His life, timing was everything (Jn. 2:4). The Father's plan was for Him to arrive when it was too late for a healing, and the situation called for a miracle – and a teaching moment.

7. **Thereupon – after this – He is saying to His disciples, "We should proceed going into Judea again."**
8. **The disciples are then saying to Him, "Rabbi, at the present time the Judeans** (= leaders of the Jewish religion) **have been seeking to stone You – and You are proceeding to go there again?"**

The disciples had a good point, and they were probably referring to the incidents in the previous chapters. However, they were thinking in human terms, and apparently did not remember how He had said that He only did the things that He saw the Father doing (5:19; 8:28, above). Still, it is commendable that they were staying with Him through those times of attempted physical rejection. Consider Thomas' almost dire remarks, in vs. 16, below.

9. **Jesus decidedly replied, "Are there not twelve hours [in] the day** (= of daylight)**? If anyone may habitually walk around** (= live his life) **within the Day, he does not constantly stumble** (cut toward or strike against [something])**, because he continually sees** (looks at; observes) **the Light of this world, or from the aggregate of humanity**
> (or: of this cosmos; this System's light; or: = because he progressively perceives the light and understanding that guides this System and secular society).
10. **"Yet, if anyone should habitually walk around within the Night, he constantly stumbles** (strikes against [things])**, because the Light is not** (does not exist) **within him."**

This statement of apparent "common wisdom" seems out of place considering the context of their discussion. But recall His words associated with healing the blind man, in 9:4, above,
> "**It is constantly necessary** (or: binding) **for Me** [other MSS: us] **to be habitually performing the works… while it is day; night progressively comes, when no one is able to continue performing work**."

We suggest that in these two verses, the "**anyone**" that may "**habitually walk around**" has reference to His disciples. When they were with Him (**the Light**) they would "**not constantly stumble.**" But when He left them, during the upcoming Night between the two ages (the close of the Mosaic age blending into the dawn of the New Age of the new creation/covenant), they would "**constantly stumble,**" as they fled the Judean and Roman authorities. The same would hold true for anyone, during the following centuries, who would walk away from the Light and turn back into the darkness (e.g., Gal. 3:1-4; 5:3-4).

"All (everyone)" is followed by a relative pronoun, "**who**," that is the subject of two present participles, "**in presently living and progressively trusting-and-believing**," that describe the situation described in the predicate of the main clause: "**can by no means** (or: may under no circumstances) **die-off** (or: die-away), **on into the Age**." This corresponds to the necessity of abiding in the Vine (15:1ff, below). By the branch continuing to dwell in the Vine it continues living. Here, "**in presently living and progressively trusting-and-believing into** (or: when regularly experiencing convinced faith into the midst of and being constantly faithful unto) **Me**," is a subordinate clause that gives another description of being His sheep, or His branches. With this dependent, subordinate clause we have a description of what it means to participate in the Life and be a branch of the Vine, or to be included in Kingdom Life. It is not giving a requirement that must be met in order to be a sheep or a branch, it is a description of the Life of both of those metaphors: a life of trust (etc.).

Not dying-off means "**will continue Living**" (vs. 25, above). But take note of what Jesus also said, in vs. 25, "**even if he may die-off** (or: die-away)." This is not a contradiction, but a revealing of the two realms of life/Life to which He repeatedly refers. In 3:7, above, He told Nicodemus that the Judeans needed to be born back up again. He was not speaking of physical birth, just like in our present verse He is not speaking of a physical "continue living." The contrast was between dying physically, like Lazarus, in this passage, and the Life in Christ, which is continuous and has no end – unless someone ceases to remain in the Vine by ceasing in "trusting-and-believing." What happens to a person that does not abide in the Vine and ceases "regularly experiencing convinced faith (etc.)"? Cf 15:6, below! An example is turning back to living in the dead covenant of Law. Paul gave a warning about turning back to physical symbols (citing circumcision as an example of a yoke of bondage to the Law of the bondwoman – Gal. 4:21-5:1) and in Gal. 5, gives this strong warning:

1. **For the [aforementioned] freedom, Christ immediately set us free** (or: [The] Anointed One at once frees us in, to, for and with freedom)! **Keep on standing firm, therefore, and do not again be habitually held within a yoke of slavery** (or: a cross-lever [of a pair of scales] whose sphere is bondage)

    (or: Continuously stand firm, then, in the freedom [to which the] Anointing sets us free, and let not yourselves be progressively confined again by a yoke pertaining to servitude)!

2. **See and individually consider! I, Paul, continue saying to you folks, that if you should proceed to being circumcised, Christ will continue benefiting you NOTHING** (or: an Anointing will continue of use to you [for] not one thing)!

3. **Now I continue solemnly asserting** (attesting; affirming; witnessing), **again, to every person** (or: human) **proceeding to be circumcised, that he is, and continues being, a debtor** (one under obligation) **to do** (to perform; to produce) **the whole Law** [= the entire Torah]!

4. **You people who in union with** (or: centered in; [remaining] within) **Law continue being "liberated, rightwised and placed in covenant," were at once discharged** (made inactive, idle, useless, unproductive and without effect; or: voided, nullified, exempted) **away from Christ** (or: [the] Anointing) – **you folks FELL OUT from the Grace** (or: fall from the midst of the favor)!

Now this is not speaking about possibly going to an afterlife of torment; it is speaking of the present life, of returning to Law, or legalistic religion, that is outside of the Life of the Age of the Messiah – living outside the City (New Jerusalem – Rev. 21:24, 27; 22:11, 15). Nonetheless, there is still opportunity for them, for consider Jesus' message to them in Rev. 22:17,

> "**And now the Spirit and the Bride are continuously saying, 'Be repeatedly coming!' Then let the one continuing to listen and hear say, 'Be continuously coming!' And so let the person constantly thirsting continuously come; let the one habitually willing at once receive Water of Life freely.**"

You see, "**Jesus Christ [is] the same yesterday and today and on into the ages**" (Heb. 13:8) – note the plurality of "ages" in this verse. And we can keep in mind Paul's insight in Eph. 3:10-11,

> "**to the end that now** (at this present time), **in union with the heavenly people, God's greatly diversified wisdom could be made known – through the called-out community – to the governments** (or: rulers; sovereignties; chief ones) **as well as to the authorities and folks with**

privilege among those situated upon elevated positions in accord with (or: down from; corresponding to) **a purpose of the ages** (a fore-designed aim, plan and object [which He is bent on achieving] of the unspecified time-periods) **which He formed** (forms; made; constructs; creates; produced) **within the Christ by our Lord and Owner, Jesus** (or: in union with Jesus the Anointed One)."

It follows that, His sheep have a job to do – and we see that begun in the book of Acts. We now have the privilege of reading of this history, and of now experiencing God's reign in action. But Jesus did not explain all this to Martha. He only asked her if she was "**presently believing this, trusting this and having convinced faith of, or in, this** [thumb-nail sketch]" that He had stated to her.

27. **She says to Him, "Yes, Lord** (Sure, Master). **I have trusted, and now believe, that You, Yourself, are the Christ** (Anointed One; = Messiah), **God's Son – the One habitually** (repeatedly; or: presently) **coming into the world** (into the ordered System; or: unto the aggregate of humanity).**"

For her time and situation, this was all that she needed to believe, and to trust: that He, Himself, was the Christ, and that their Messiah was God's Son. This statement affirms and expands upon what she saw and recognized (vs. 22, above).

John does not step in and explain her final Christological statement: "**the One habitually** (repeatedly; or: presently) **coming into the world** (into the ordered System; or: unto the aggregate of humanity)," but we may surmise, at least, that she associated it with "the Last Day" (vs. 24, above). But we should take note that John records her as using the present tense (repetition?, or possibly just "presently") with the participle "**coming**."

28. **And upon saying this she went off** (or: came away) **and summoned** (or: called) **Mary** (or: Miriam), **her sister, secretly** (covertly) **saying, "The Teacher is present** (= is now here), **and He is calling for** (or: summoning) **you."**

Apparently Jesus sent her on the mission (short-term emissary) to announce to Mary that Jesus was calling for her.

29. **So that one, as she heard, was quickly roused and was proceeding to go toward Him.**

She wasted no time in answering the call. The contemplative will be responsive to the Master's summons. Apparently Jesus planned to raise Lazarus before going to the house, where Mary had remained. She was "called-out" to Him. Burial was outside of the village, just as Jesus' would also be outside of Jerusalem. This SIGN, as well as Jesus' resurrection, would be outside of Jerusalem.

30. **Now Jesus had not yet come into the village, but rather was yet** (still) **being within the place where Martha met Him.**
31. **Then the Judeans – those constantly being with her within the house, and repeatedly giving words of comfort, consolation and encouragement – seeing Mary, that she quickly stood up and went out, follow her, supposing** [other MSS: one after another saying] **that she is on her way** (progressively going) **unto the memorial tomb so that she could cry** (or: weep; mourn) **there.**

Here, we not only get a picture of the Judean society, with their solidarity with folks who are grieving a loss, but also that with their attentiveness to Mary they would by this be witnesses of what Jesus would do, in regard to Lazarus.

32. **Then Mary – as she came where Jesus was – on seeing Him, falls at His feet, saying to Him, "O Lord** (Master), **if You had been here my brother would not [have] died away."**

33. **Jesus, therefore, as He saw her continuously weeping** (crying) **– and the Judeans coming with her [also] crying** (mourning; audibly weeping or wailing) **– inwardly snorted** (as with violent displeasure) **and groaned, being deeply moved in spirit** (or: by [the] Spirit; with Breath-effect; to an attitude and mood), **and then stirred Himself up** (shook Himself; or: disturbed and troubled Himself),
34. **and says, "Where have you folks laid** (put; placed) **him?" They proceed saying to Him, "Lord** (Master), **come and see."**
35. **Jesus sheds tears** (let tears flow; gave way to tears; or: bursts into tears).

We can only guess at the reason for why Jesus "**inwardly snorted** (as with violent displeasure) **and groaned, being deeply moved in spirit**." Knowing what we know from having read the text, below, and what Jesus had said to Martha, above, we might surmise that His deep emotions were due to the lack of trust that He perceived in them. They obviously kept crying because they considered Lazarus to be beyond hope of restoration – until the "last Day." He also may have just had a human reaction because of His solidarity with them, responding to their deep grief. We should also not miss the other potential readings, that He was deeply moved "by [the] Spirit," or "WITH Breath-effect" – the Spirit moved within Him. And then, this groaning may have moved Him "to an attitude and mood" which enabled Him to "stir Himself up, shake Himself (from their grief and/or unbelief), or even "trouble Himself." By repeated meditation upon these verses, we may receive multiple pictures of what was going on within Him.

And so, having "stirred Himself UP (however we are to understand that), He asks direction to the tomb and then they lead Him there. Whether vs. 35 comes immediately after their short exchange (which seems likely), or whether it happened at the gravesite, we cannot be sure. John does not inform us of just what brought Him to tears. The comments by the Judeans, in vss. 36-37, seem to have affected Him in the same way as seeing the crying of the Judeans, in vs. 33, as we observe in vs. 38.

36. **The Judeans therefore began saying, "Consider** (Look; See) **how he was feeling affection for** (how fond he was of; what affection he used to have for) **him."**
37. **Yet some of them said, "Was this one – the one opening up the eyes of the blind one – not able** (or: powerless) **to make also this one so that he would not die off?"**
38. **Jesus therefore, again continuing inwardly snorting, groaning and being deeply moved within Himself, is progressively going into the memorial tomb [area]. Now, it was a cave, and a stone was lying upon** (= against) **it.**

Again, the reason for His "**continuing inwardly snorting, groaning and being deeply moved**" is not explained, but it was happening while He was "**progressively going into the memorial tomb [area]**."

39. **Jesus is then saying, "Lift up** (Remove; Take away) **the stone."**
Martha, the sister of the one having come to his end (or: of the one having reached the goal; = of the deceased), **then says to Him, "O Lord** (Master), **he is already progressively giving off a smell** (or: there is already an offensive odor increasing), **for it is [the] fourth [day]."**

Notice that here, and again with the resurrection of Jesus, it is recorded that the stone that covered the entrance, or opening, of the cave (or carved out chamber) was removed. Obviously, in this situation with Lazarus, it would be so that he could bodily exit the cave. Was this the same reason, in the case with Jesus' resurrection? Of course, with Jesus, the women expected to enter the cave and wondered how they would be able to remove the stone.

Martha, ever practical, warns Jesus that to remove the stone from the grave of one that has been dead for four days will bring an unpleasant experience. Remember that Jesus had purposely waited before coming to do the Father's work. There is always purpose in God's "waiting," even when we deem that His act will now bring unpleasantness, due to His delay. With this being the fourth day for Lazarus, it would mean that he has been in the grave for three days and three nights. Do you believe in coincidences?

Jesus said that He would be in the grave for three days and three nights (Mat. 12:40). Resurrection comes on the fourth day.

40. **Jesus proceeds saying to her, "Did I not say to you that if you would trust and believe** (faith-it) **you will be habitually seeing God's glory and appearance**
> (God's manifestation which calls forth praise; or: a notion which is God; God's recognition and reputation; the vision and fancy of God; God's expectation; the imagination from God)**?"**

Because of the significance and timing of Jesus' statement, on offer is a wide semantic range of the word commonly translated **glory**:
> a) God's appearance – i.e., God showing up on the scene, as He did with Israel, at the Red Sea;
> b) God's manifestation which calls forth praise – a SIGN; a miracle;
> c) a notion which is God – that is, an example of what God is thinking about this situation;
> d) God's recognition and reputation – a realization that what has happened is God in action;
> e) the vision and fancy of God – what God has in view; what He wants and likes;
> f) God's expectation – what God expects to happen; the results of what He intends;
> g) the imagination from God – a depiction, and embodiment of what, God pictured was to be.

Trusting and believing (or, as it has been coined: faithing-it) will habitually open our eyes to see His glory. We will, via this sphere of trust and confidence, see the appearance of God at work in a situation.

41. **Then they lifted up the stone and took it away. Yet Jesus lifted His eyes upward, and said, "O Father, I continually thank You that You hear and respond to Me,**
42. **"and I, Myself, have seen and thus know that You habitually listen and constantly hear Me at all times** (always), **but nevertheless, because of the crowd standing around, I spoke – to the end that they could trust, believe and have faith that You commissioned and sent Me forth as an Emissary** (Representative).**"**

They "**lifted up the stone**" (can we see a figure of the removal of the Law from the realm of death, to let the prisoners go free?), while Jesus "**lifted His eyes upward**" – literally, looking toward the sky, but, as a symbol (for His life acted out parables):
> "**Be constantly minding** (thinking about; setting your disposition and sentiments toward; paying regard to) **the upward things** (or: the things above), **not the things upon the earth**" (Col. 3:2).

And then, they hear Him speaking to the Father, expressing gratitude, as was His habit, for the fact that the Father hears and responds to Him. What a witness to what the Christ Life looks like. But He goes on to underscore the fact that the Father "**habitually listens and constantly hears [Him] at all times.**" That witness is hammered home for us – our Father habitually does the same for us.

Next, He tells the Father the reason for His outward vocalization of this private conversation with the Father. Jesus spoke this "prayer" aloud, only so that the crowd could hear His words. There is no need to speak aloud to the One who dwells within, Whose mind has been joined to ours, by His Spirit. Jesus is rehearsing a drama "**to the end that they could trust, believe and have faith.**" Have faith in God? Have faith in Jesus as their Savior? No, it was so that they could trust "**that [the Father] commissioned and sent [Him] forth as an Emissary** (Representative)." He wanted people to believe that God had sent Him as His Representative. We will see another SIGN, this time from their atmosphere (or, the sky), in the form of a Voice that answers Jesus' request to the Father, and that also happened for the sake of the crowd (12:28-30, below). That folks would know where He came from and what was His authority seemed to be important things that He wanted them to understand (*cf* 8:14, 23, 28, 29, 42; 10:36, above).

43. **Upon saying these things, He suddenly shouted with a loud** (or: in a great) **voice, "Lazarus! Here! Outside!"**

Contrary to the common translations that have Jesus using a verb, in the imperative (like a command), the Greek has no verb. Jesus shouts his name, then informs him about the location: here; outside. We assume that He meant for Lazarus to come outside, which appears to be a correct assumption, for the next verse narrates that he, in fact, came out of the tomb. Lazarus was in another place – and we again assume that he was within the tomb, perhaps still within his body. But John does not explain all that we would like to know about the "state" and "realm" of the dead. Those around Jesus probably had no such questions. The dead Lazarus was simply where he had been put, after his body had been prepared in accord with their burial customs. So, I wanted our readers to know what Jesus actually said, which can sound like a parent alerting a wandering or lost child of their whereabouts. Inquiring minds may want to know: if Jesus had not said, "Outside," might Lazarus have instead looked for Him within the realm of the dead? Just wondering...

44. **And out comes the man having been dead, still being bound, having been wrapped in grave-clothes** (with swaths, bands, or bandages of cloth, such as linen) – **even binding the feet and the hands – and his face having been wrapped around with a face-cloth** (or: sweat-cloth; handkerchief; napkin). **Jesus says to them, "You folks loose** (unwrap; unbind) **him and release him** (let him go off) **to proceed leading the way** (or: to be departing).**"**

When we think of "resurrection," we normally picture people loosed and free – and perhaps flying upward, if that fits with our eschatology, or pictures that artists have painted of "the resurrection." This is the only place, in Scripture, where it speaks of a resurrected person still being bound and in need of others to unbind him so that he can go off, departing.

Now we can reason that he appeared, coming out of the tomb as he had been put there, so that folks would realize that this was the same person, and that he had actually died, etc. But in this book of SIGNS, we wonder if there is another layer to be seen underneath those grave-clothes. For one thing, he was alive, but he still needed to be released from his clothes of their traditions around the topic of death, or the dead. John even gives us the details about the face-cloth. 20:7 also gives this detail. We are reminded of the words of Paul, in 2 Cor. 4:6,

> "**because the God suddenly saying** (or: the God Who once was saying), **"Light will shine forth** (give light as from a torch; gleam) **from out of the midst of darkness** (dimness and shadiness; gloom and the absence of daylight),**" [is] the One who shines forth within the midst of our hearts, with a view to illumination of the intimate and experiential knowledge of God's glory – in a face of Christ**."

Here we have an enigmatic statement that includes Light, out of darkness, God' glory, and a face – a face of Jesus Christ. Paul was speaking in a figurative allusion to the creation, in Gen. 1:3-5, and John's Gospel both begins, and from time to time continues, with references to the creation.

Was this story about Lazarus set to be a SIGN with allusions to Ezk. 37:1-14, where God characterized Israel as a "valley of dry bones," saying that He would open their graves and cause them to come out? Was this what Jesus was about to accomplish, on a spiritual level, when He was raised, and we with Him (Rom. 6:4-11; Eph. 2:5-6)?

45. **Therefore, many from out of the Judeans – those coming to Mary and being ones attentively watching what He did – put faith and trust into** (or: believed and were loyal unto) **Him.**

Jesus' purpose, expressed in vs. 42b, above, was fulfilled in **many** of these folks, but vs. 46 informs us that, as usual, "**some of them**" did not believe, and instead returned to their religion.

46. **Yet some of them went off to the Pharisees and told them what** [other MSS: how much; how many] **things Jesus did.**

207

47. **Consequently, the chief** (or: ranking) **priests and the Pharisees gathered [the] Sanhedrin** (= convoked a council of the leaders of the Jewish religious and political culture), **and they began to say, "What are we presently doing, seeing that this man is repeatedly doing many SIGNS?**

Jesus presented a problem for the institutional religion of His people. They did not know what to do about Him. The Sanhedrin was the cultural and religious ruling body of Judea, at that time. Before He could be recognized as their Messiah, they wanted to impeach Him – well, actually kill him, which corresponds to the political arena of our day: to politically do away with Him. Which they eventually did, in the way of the Roman Empire.

But notice that they affirmed that He was actually "**repeatedly doing many SIGNS.**" Although spiritually blind, they did this with their eyes open.

48. **"If we let him go on in this way** (or: If we disregard him in this manner; or: Suppose we thus abandon, neglect or leave him alone), **all** (everyone) **will one-by-one put trust into him** (or: will continue believing, being allegiant unto him)**, the Romans will proceed to come, and they will progressively take away both our place and our nation** (= political station, culture and corporate ethnic identity).**"**

This was their main fear, and the central reason for wanting to be rid of Jesus. As vs. 51, below, suggests, their chief priest could envision what would happen if Jesus was left unchecked. Their "place" was on the back of the seven-headed beast (Rev. 17:3) of the Roman Empire. Their "nation" was their political station via the temple, in Jerusalem, as well as their "culture and corporate ethnic identity." All of this would change, after AD 70, and there would only be the Diaspora (the dispersion of them, among the ethnic multitudes). Much of Second Temple Judaism was already in this condition, although maintaining their culture, religion and ethnic identity. But as a nation, this had been tied to the Land. Those in Judea would soon experience another phase of the Exile.

49. **Yet one of them, Caiaphas, being chief priest of that year, said to them, "You people have not seen, nor perceived, nor know anything,**
50. **"neither are you logically reasoning or taking into account the fact that he is progressively bringing it together for you** (or: it is advantageously bringing things together among you), **so that one man can die over** (or: to the end that one person should and would die away for the sake of [in the sense of "instead of"]) **the People, and not [that] the whole nation should destroy itself!"**

Caiaphas understood that his fellows had no political insight, and so did not realize that, in his view, "**the whole nation would destroy itself**" if they did not do something about Jesus. He viewed the entire Sanhedrin was not "**logically reasoning or taking into account the facts.**" What they did not see can be rendered with the next clause having its subject as either "**he** (meaning Jesus)," or "it (referring to the general situation)." This clause can therefore read, "**he is progressively bringing it together for you,**" or, "it is advantageously bringing things together among you."

But what he perceived was that it was good for the People that, "**that one man can die over** (or: to the end that one person should and would die away for the sake of [in the sense of "instead of"]) **the People.**"

51. **Now, he did not say this from himself, but to the contrary, being chief priest of that year, he prophesied that Jesus was being about to be dying away over [the situation of]** (or: for the sake of) **the Nation** (or: ethnic group),

Here, our author seems to affirm that the high priest prophesied this, about Jesus, and that he could do this because of having the position of being the chief priest. Perhaps he meant that the intentions of Caiaphas turned out to be what really happened. At that time, and for one generation (about 40 years) this was a literal reality. Jesus did die-away, and their nation remained intact, for a while. But the author might also be suggesting that this was a self-fulfilling prophecy that Caiaphas himself would instigate.

Many have also seen in this statement an understanding of the function of Jesus' death as being the Nation's fulfillment of both their Passover tradition combined with Him fulfilling the Day of Atonement (the first and the last of Israel's three major feasts, as described in the Law).

52. **and not over [the condition of] the Nation** (or: on behalf of the ethnic group) **only, but further, to the end that He could gather God's children together – those having been thoroughly scattered – into one** (or: so that He would lead together into unity God's divided, dissipated and disintegrated born-ones that have been dispersed throughout). [cf Gen. 11:8; Eph. 2:11-17]

From this verse, along the references suggested, in Gen. and Eph., we can see an application of John's statement to the Diaspora, and to all the peoples of the earth – who all compose "**God's children**," and who all will be "**gathered together**," as this passage in Eph. 2 describes.

53. **Therefore, from that day they deliberated and consulted together to the end that they should** (or: would) **kill Him.**

So their plot was solidified, and we will see that in time they carried it out.

54. **Jesus, therefore, was no longer walking about publicly** (openly; with outspoken boldness as a citizen) **among the Judeans** (or: = religious authorities), **but rather, He went away from there into the country** (or: region; territory) **near the wilderness** (desert; desolate area), **into a city called Ephraim, and there He remained** (or: dwelled; [other MSS: was passing time]) **with His disciples.**

Here we can discern that Jesus discerned their plans, and since it was not yet "His season," he ended public ministry in Judea, and went to Ephraim.

55. **Now the Passover of the Jews** (of the Jewish culture and religion) **was coming to be near, and many went up into Jerusalem from out of the region** (country; territory), **before the Passover, so that they could purify** (or: perform ritual cleansing for and of) **themselves.**
56. **Consequently, they began trying to find** (or: were looking out for or continued seeking) **Jesus and would periodically converse with one another, as they had been standing within the Temple courts, saying, "What do you think or suppose** (or: What is your opinion)**?" "Surely he is not likely to come into the festival** (or: Feast)**!"**
57. **As it was, the chief** (or: ranking) **priests and the Pharisees** (= the Sanhedrin) **had given goal-oriented directions, with imparted authority, so that if anyone may come to know where He is, he should disclose** (or: report) **it, so that they might lay hold of and seize Him.**

So for a while, He left them guessing, with the Sanhedrin trying to find Him. But they would not have long to wait…

Chapter 12

1. **Accordingly then, six days before the Passover feast, Jesus came into Bethany where Lazarus – the one having died – was, whom Jesus raised up out from the midst of dead folks.**
2. **So they made dinner** (the evening meal) **for Him there, and Martha was serving [them]. Now Lazarus was one of those still reclining** (lying back) **[at the meal] with Him.**

The narrative seems to pick up Jesus' activities from where it left off tracking His location, in 11:54, in "**a city called Ephraim**." Jesus has returned to the Jerusalem area, being hosted by Lazarus and his sisters. In 11:55 we saw that many Jews had come early on, before the Passover, in order to make themselves ritually pure so that they could participate in the Passover. This corresponds to the time period of Jesus drawing near to Jerusalem.

3. **Then Mary, taking a pound** (Roman pound = about 12 oz.; about a pint) **of very costly** (of much value; precious) **genuine** (= pure) **perfumed ointment** (or: oil; aromatic juice distilled from plants) **extracted from the spike-nard plant, anoints and rubs** (as in preparing the body with oil for gymnastics) **the feet of Jesus, and then wipes His feet off with her hair, and so the house was filled full with** (or: from) **the fragrance** (aroma; odor) **of the perfumed ointment.**

It is interesting that our author referenced this act, by Mary, in 11:2, above. Lu. 7:37-38 records another time where Jesus' **feet** were anointed with ointment. That incident happened in Galilee (possibly in or near the town of Nain – Lu. 7:11) at the house of Simon, a Pharisee, and it was performed by an unidentified woman (described only as a "sinner," the reputation of whom was known, by Simon) who first washed His feet with her tears and kissed them. Jesus said of her:
> **"Pertaining to this gift, and from its grace, I am now saying to you, her many failures** (mistakes; miss-shots; deviations; sins) **had been caused to flow away, and continue sent-off, divorced, forgiven – because she loved much** (or: so that she urges much for reunion)!" (Lu. 7:47a)

We find Jesus being anointed by another unidentified woman, in Bethany, but this time it is at the house of Simon the leper (Mat. 26:6-7; Mk. 14:3) and it was His head that was anointed, not His feet. Mark's version, of the anointing of His head, gives Jesus' response to this act as:
> **"She undertakes, beforehand** (in anticipation), **to anoint My body with aromatic ointment, with a view to the preparation of [My] corpse for burial"** (Mk. 14:8).

Notice that in Mark's account of the head anointing, Jesus gave the same characterization for what Mary had done here (vs. 7, below) when anointing His **feet.** Here, in vs. 3, there is no mention of His feet needing to be washed, since it was probably done (as was the custom) when He entered their home. In pointing out that the act of anointing can also be rendered "rubbing," Mary's motive may simply have been to ease tired feet, as well as to honor their guest using expensive "**perfumed ointment,**" and not the usual olive oil. The fact that she "**wipes His feet off with her hair,**" means that she, too, became "anointed," and her moving about the house would be another reason that "**the house was filled full with** (or: from) **the fragrance** (aroma; odor)." This description brings a picture of the House of God (the Temple) with the priest burning incense that would have filled the holy place. Her action was a lived-out prayer (*cf* Rev. 8:4). Call to mind what Paul said concerning a woman's long hair (and Mary's would have needed to be long in order to use it as a towel):
> **"if a woman should have plumes or long, luxuriant hair it is a glory to her"** (1 Cor. 11:15).

She took the function of a servant, and applied her personal glory to His feet. Perhaps Mary was thinking of Isa. 52:7,
> "How beautiful upon the mountains are the feet of the heralds who bring and announce peace, who bring and announce salvation, saying to Zion, 'Your God reigns!'"

The picture described in vss. 2-3 calls to mind this Psalm:
> Psalm 133 (132, LXX)
> An Ode of the Stairs (the Steps Back Up Again; the Acts of Ascending; the Means of Ascent)
> [other MSS add: pertaining to David]
> 1. **Look at this** (or: Consider now): **What [is] beautiful** (fine; ideal), **or what [is] pleasant and delightful, more than** (or: surely rather than; except for) **the [situation of] folks from the same womb** (kindred; brothers) **to continue settled down** (to remain housed-down and keep on dwelling) **together** (on the same [level; sphere]).
> 2. **[It is] like perfumed ointment upon [the] head, which continues running down on [the] beard – the beard of Aaron – which keeps on running down upon the border** (or: fringe) **of his clothing** (= robe).

3. **[It is] like dew of Hermon, which is continuously running down on the mountains of Zion, because there [the]** LORD **implanted the goal** (imparted the destiny and end in view; gave the inner directives), **the Blueprint of Goodness** (the Thought, Idea and Message of Ease; the *Logos* of well-being; the Good Word; the blessing): **LIFE, unto the Age** [of Messiah]. (LXX, JM)

4. **Now** [other MSS: Then] **Judah** (or: Judas) **of Simon Iscariot, one of His disciples – the one continuing about to proceed commending, and thus transferring and committing, Him** (or: giving Him over; presenting Him at the side; turning Him in; entrusting Him along) **– proceeds in saying,**

Attention should be paid to the expanded (and conflated) renderings of the infinitive in the dependent clause that is set off by dashes. On offer are other meanings of the compound verb *para-* (beside; along) plus *didomi* (to give; grant; offer; surrender; yield; entrust; present). The common rendering, "betray," carries negative baggage that is not necessarily in view. I thus render it: "**commending, and thus transferring and committing, Him** (or: giving Him over; presenting Him at the side; turning Him in; entrusting Him along)." Judas played a role in bringing the temple guards to Jesus so that He could be arrested at night and outside of public view. Had it been part of the Plan (Acts 2:23; 3:18 – trust the Plan), He could have been arrested when He taught in the temple courts. But to complete the type of a lamb being offered at the brazen altar, at Passover or on the Day of Atonement, an Israelite man had to bring the lamb to the priests to be slaughtered. Judas transferred and committed Jesus to drink the cup that the Father had given Him to drink. He "commended Him" and "entrusted Him along" as

"**God's Lamb** (or: the Lamb from God; the Lamb having the character and qualities of God; or, in apposition: the Lamb which is God), **the One continuously lifting up and progressively carrying away the Sin of the world, and removing the sin which belongs to and is a part of the System**" (1:29, above).

5. "**Why** (Through what [reason; situation]) **was this perfumed ointment not sold for three hundred denarii** (= a year's wages) **and given to** (or: for) **destitute** (poor) **people?"**

We find a similar statement made about a different woman, and a different anointing (this time on His head), in Mat. 26:

8. **Now on seeing [this], the DISCIPLES became annoyed** (or: resentful; indignant; angry), **[various ones] saying, in turn, "Why** (or: Unto what [purpose is]) **this waste** (or: loss; destruction; ruin)**?**

9. "**For this was able to be sold for a lot [of money] and then given to the destitute folks and beggars!"**

Notice that in that situation it was not just Judah that complained about the "wasted ointment," but apparently, the whole group of disciples felt the same way.

6. **He said this, though, not because it was normally a care** (or: of interest) **to him about the destitute** (the poor people), **but rather, because he had been existing as a thief, and, normally holding** (or: having; [other MSS: used to be in possession of]) **the money box** (or: case; originally a receptacle for the "tongues" {i.e., mouth-pieces} of musical instruments), **had been regularly carrying** (or: bearing; supporting; providing for) **the things being repeatedly** (or: habitually) **deposited.**

The verb of being (**had been existing**), in the second clause, is the imperfect tense, and can refer to past practice; thus, John is not necessarily saying that Judah was currently a thief, but he is pointing out his disposition toward money. The verb for **carrying** (bearing), in the last clause, can also be used in the sense of "bearing away," "removing," or "pilfering;" or, it can be used to signify "supporting; providing for" – this latter giving a different slant to John's words. Recall that Mark says that "some" had indignation, and Matthew says "the disciples" did, so Judas expressed a consensus. Also, in Mat. 26:6, they were in the same town, but at a different place – the house of Simon the leper – and an anonymous woman enters while they are eating, and this time pours the costly ointment on His head. It behooves us not to jump to conclusions when there is ambiguity in the language of the text. In the Mat. 26 passage, Jesus gives a response similar to what we have here, below.

7. **Then Jesus says, "Let her flow on** (or: Allow her; or: Pardon, forgive and release her; or: = Leave her alone) **so that she can keep it in view** (watch over, observe, take note of and guard it) **on into the day of the preparation for My burial,**

The verb, **Let her flow on** (etc.), is imperative, singular, so He is addressing Judah, and his comment in vs. 5, above. This verb has a wide semantic range and is used in many contexts. One of the root ideas is the motion of flowing away, in the sense of "keep going on" with what someone is doing. An associated meaning is, "allow." It can be used to mean "pardon" or "forgive," but here in a social sense of politeness – like, "forgive her for her indiscretion." The extended meaning may be paraphrased, "Leave her alone (i.e., don't bother her)." I included the meaning of "release" (literally, "Let her flow away"), for this context, to mean, "Release her from your judgment of her action."

The dependent clause adds a purpose to His instruction to Judah, "**so that she can keep it in view** (watch over, observe, take note of and guard it)…" Now does the "it" refer to the ointment (assuming that she did not use all of it, at this time), or to the act of anointing/rubbing and wiping His feet with her hair? The verb leaves us with some ambiguity about what He meant. The translations vary, due to the broad semantic range. We suggest that He did not want her interrupted, so that she could keep in her view, that is, in her thoughts and perceptions, the fact of what she had done for Him: she had anointed Him. On the day of **the preparation** for His burial, she would remember this act, and realize that it had been a SIGN that the Path that He had walked was that of High Priest and Messiah. She would be able to "take note of" the significance of what she had been led to do. She could guard this truth in her heart.

Another central idea in this verb is to "watch over and observe." She was to be one of His witnesses of the Christ Event. In Lu. 10:39, she:
> "**after sitting alongside near to and facing the Lord's** [other MSS: Jesus'] **feet, began listening and kept on hearing His word** (or: the thought, idea and message from Him)."

She had sat at His feet (the position of a disciple) and received the Blueprint (the *Logos*), and may well have had more insight, than did the rest of the disciples, into why He had returned to Jerusalem at this time. She may have understood that her act was a prophecy of His burial.

8. **"for you see, the destitute ones** (the poor people) **you folks are always having with yourselves. Yet, you are not always holding** (or: having) **Me."**

He was not just saying that He was worth this apparent extravagance, but was alerting them to His upcoming exodus (Lu. 9:31). He would still be with them, but they would no longer know Him "**on the level of flesh** (or: = in the sphere of the first humanity; or: = in correspondence to a self that is oriented to the System; and: = according to the old covenant)" (2 Cor. 5:16b). He was also right that humanity has continued having **the destitute ones** (the poor people). What Mary had done was integral to His journey to the cross. At different times and occasions, two women (two witnesses) had anointed the One who was to be a Priest, after the order of Melchisedec (Heb. 5:5-6).

9. **Then many of the common folks** (or: the vast crowd) **from out of the Jews** (or Judeans) **became aware** (or: got to know) **that He is there, and they come** (or: came) **– not only because of Jesus, but also so that they might see and become acquainted with Lazarus, whom He raised up from out of the midst of dead ones.**

It was the "common folks" of the Jews who were drawn to Him and to His works, but not so most of the "elites" of their society…

10. **So the chief priests** [note: representing the Sadducees] **deliberated and resolved** (or: purposed and made a plan) **to the end that they should also kill off Lazarus,**
11. **because many of the Jews** (or: Judeans) **had been repeatedly going, on account of him, and then were progressively believing and continuing to put their trust and loyalty into Jesus** (or: = believing what Jesus was saying; or: = being convinced that Jesus was the Messiah; = being followers).

So they thought to destroy the evidence of His work (the resurrected Lazarus) in order to discredit Him. His SIGNS were causing the common folks of Judea to continue putting their trust and loyalty into Jesus. Recall Jn. 11, which recounts the death and resurrection of Lazarus: many Jews had come to mourn with Martha and Mary. These had seen the miracle, and must have spread the word in Jerusalem. They seemed to have no problem in believing in the miracle of someone being raised from the dead.

12. **The next day** (or: On the morrow), **the vast crowd going unto the Feast** (or: i.e., the one coming into the festival) – **upon hearing that Jesus is on His way into Jerusalem** –
13. **took the branches** (or: fronds) **of the palm trees** (date palms) **and went out into a meeting with Him, and they began and kept on shouting, "Ho-san'na** [Heb. word meaning: Save now; Send your salvation]! **O One having been blessed, now coming** (or: repeatedly coming) **in [the] Lord's Name** (= in [the] Name which is Yahweh): **even the King of Israel!"** [Ps. 118:25, 26]

News traveled fast among the crowds coming for the Feast of Passover. The "common people" had in their minds that it was a time for the fulfillment of prophecy (quoted in vs. 15, below), and prepared to give Jesus a proper welcome to the capital city as "**the King of Israel,**" who would, according to the Psalm quoted, be "**now coming in [the] Lord's Name.**" He was being seen as Yahweh's Representative who would bring salvation to Israel, and was being hailed as Israel's King. Mat. 21:8 records some of them as spreading their garments on the path.

Lu. 19:38b adds another testimony of what others of the crowd were saying:
"**Peace and shalom from the Joining within the midst of heaven** (or: A joining in [the] atmosphere), **and a manifestation which calls forth praise** (glory; a good reputation; an assumed appearance) **in union with the highest places, and in [the authority of the] highest Ones!**'"
Mark 11:10a records some saying: "**Blessed and praised in having received the good word and message of ease and wellness [is] the progressively coming kingdom of our father David!**" They were expecting something far different than what would happen.

14. **Now Jesus, finding a donkey colt** (or: a small donkey, or, ass), **sits down upon it – according as it stands, having been written,**
15. **"Do not continue fearing** (or: Stop fearing), **O daughter of Zion! Look and consider, your King is progressively coming – presently sitting upon a donkey's colt."** [Zech. 9:9]
16. **Now His disciples did not notice, become personally aware of, or understand these things, at the first, but when Jesus was glorified, recognized, made to appear, and became renowned** (or: was given an assumed appearance) **they were then reminded that these things were written upon Him** (= had been written about Him), **and that they did these things for Him** (or: to Him; with Him).

It would seem, from vs. 16, that the crowd was more aware of the significance of His manner of entering Jerusalem than were His disciples. The crowd seemed to have a greater expectation of Jesus than did His intimate followers.

17. **Accordingly, the crowd of common folks – the one constantly being with Him when He summoned Lazarus forth from out of the memorial tomb and raised him out of the midst of dead ones – kept on bearing witness and giving testimony.**

18. **[It was] on account of this, [that] the [other] crowd also came to meet with Him, because they heard [that] He had performed** (done; made; produced) **this SIGN.**

So our author explains both their actions, and their high expectations. It was because of the SIGN of having raised Lazarus from the dead, and they were spreading the news. They had high hopes.

19. **So the Pharisees said among themselves** (to one another), **"You are observing** (noticing; or, as an imperative: Be watching and considering) **that your efforts are futile** (that you men are benefiting nothing; = that you are getting nowhere). **Look and consider! The whole world** (or: The entire mass of society; or: The whole system of our culture; or: The entire inhabitants of our organized society; or: This whole aggregate of humans) **went off after** (or: goes away behind) **him!"**

Lu. 19 reports what other Pharisees said to Jesus:
> 39. **Then some of the Pharisees from the crowd said to Him, "Teacher, at once give [your] valued advice to your disciples [to restrain and silence them]!"**
> 40. **And yet, giving discerning and decided response, He said, "I am now saying to you folks, If these people will proceed to be silent and continue keeping quiet, the stones will proceed crying out, screaming and continue in exclaiming** (or: breaking into cheers)**!"**

The actions of God, within His creation, seems to always bring mixed perceptions and varied reactions. Those Pharisees quoted in this verse were having a negative reaction, realizing that their previous efforts to stop Him were futile, and so were fearful of what might follow.

20. **Now there were certain** (or: some) **Greeks** (or: Hellenists; those of the Greek culture; or: Jews who had acculturated to Hellenistic philosophy or culture) **out of** (or: among) **those progressively coming up so that they could worship in the Feast** (or: pay homage at the festival).

These folks were probably from the Diaspora, living outside of Galilee and Judea, and so this is probably the first time that they had heard of Jesus. Since they were coming to observe the Feast, they were probably either Jews, or converts to Judaism, but were either raised in, or had adopted, the Hellenistic lifestyle or philosophy that had been spread by the conquests of Alexander the Great. These may have been among the folks of whom we read, in Acts. 2:5-6.

21. **These, then, approached Philip** [note: this is a Greek name] – **the one from Bethsaida of the Galilee [area]** – **and began inquiring with a request of him, saying, "Sir** (or: My lord), **we desire** (or: wish) **to see and become acquainted with** (or: = have an interview with) **Jesus."**

They would have likely heard the witnessing and testimonies of the Judeans, about Jesus (vs. 17b, above), and so were seeking to learn more about this One who had raised a man from the dead, and who was now being anticipated, by the Judean citizens, as being Israel's Messiah.

22. **Philip proceeds to go and he tells Andrew** [note: also a Greek name]. **Andrew and Philip then continue on to Jesus, and proceed telling Him.**

This encounter may have been a seed of the Gentile missions that would soon follow.

23. **Yet Jesus is deliberating a reply for them, [and] proceeds saying, "The hour has come and is here so that the Son of Mankind** (Humanity's Son; = the Son of Adam; or: = the Human Being; or: = the eschatological Messianic figure) **can be glorified** (or: may be recognized with a reputation of renown; should be made a manifestation which incites praise; would be given an assumed appearance).

Jesus seizes this request as a teaching moment, and informs Philip and Andrew that His "**hour has come and is here**," and then (in the next verse) gives them a metaphor that pointed to this hour, and to the Son of Mankind being glorified. Observe the parenthetical expansion of what that last word can mean, or imply. In 13:31-32, below, He made a similar statement, once again referring (in a third-person construction) to Himself as the eschatological figure of Dan. 7, and to Himself and God being "**glorified**." *Cf* 17:1, below.

24. "**Most assuredly** (It is certainly true; Yes, indeed; Count on it; Amen, amen), **I am saying to you folks [that] unless the grain of wheat** (or: kernel of corn; = seed of an agricultural crop), **upon falling into the earth** (the ground; the field), **should die, it by itself continues remaining alone. Yet if it should die, it proceeds to bear much fruit** (= it produces a harvest of many grains, or, seeds).

This is a metaphor of both the Gospel and of God's kingdom (sovereign influence, activities and reign). In 15:8a, below, He explains,

> "**In this is My Father glorified** (caused to appear and be recognized; given a good reputation and a manifestation which calls forth praise): **that you men can continuously bear** (or: would keep on bringing forth) **much fruit**..."

That passage uses the metaphor of a grapevine, which involves habitual pruning. Here it involves a kind of death, which He goes on to explain in vs. 25. In speaking on the topic of resurrection (which Jesus is – Jn. 11:25), Paul uses the same metaphor as did Jesus (vs. 24, here) in 1 Cor. 15:36,

> "**What you are habitually sowing is not being progressively brought to life unless it should die off.**"

We see Jesus' fruit described in Heb. 2:

> 10. **You see, it was fitting for Him – on account of Whom [is] the collective whole** ([are] all things that exist) **and through Whom [is] the collective whole** ([are] all things that exist) **– in, when and by leading many sons** [note: a figure for all humanity] **into glory** (a good reputation), **to finish and perfect the Leader who first walked the Path of their deliverance**
> > (to bring to a complete state the Originator and Chief Agent of their rescue; to script the final scene for the Chief Conveyor of their restoration; to bring the Pioneering Bringer of their salvation to the destined goal) **through the effects of sufferings and results of experiences** [note, *paschō* means: to be affected by something - either good or bad; to feel, have sense experiences; thus, also: to suffer or undergo passion].

Paul gave us another picture of what Jesus' metaphor looks like, in Rom. 8:

> 28. **Now [look], we have seen, and thus know and are aware, that to those habitually or progressively loving and giving themselves to God – to the folks being called and invited according to [the] purpose**
> > (or: for, in and with the people progressively experiencing participating acceptance in, unambiguous love for, and the urge toward union with, God – in, with, by and for the people being invited down from an advanced placing, congruent with a design and corresponding to a before-placing and a prior setting forth)
> **– He is constantly working all things together into good and is progressively working all humanity together into that which is advantageous, worthy of admiration, noble and of excellent qualities,**
> > [with other MSS: Yet we know that God is continuously joining everything together (or: working together with everything) into goodness by those continuously loving God...]
> 29. **because those whom He foreknew** (whom He knows from previous intimate experience), **He also marked out beforehand** (determined, defined and designed in advance) **[as] copies** (joint-forms) **of the image** (material likeness; portrait; form) **of His Son** (or: He previously divided, separated and bounded conformed patterns from the image/form of His Son) **into the [situation**

for] Him to be (or: to continually exist being) **the Firstborn among, within the center of, and in union with many brothers** (= a vast family from the same womb; Gal. 4:26)!

Jesus was the First Seed to fall into the ground and die, and the letters to the Hebrews and to Rome present us with His "**much fruit**." But let us proceed to His explanation of His metaphor...

25. **"The person being constantly fond of** (maintaining an emotional attachment to; continuing in devoted affection for) **his soul** (or: soul-life; interior self; perceived image) **progressively destroys it, and yet in contrast, the one continuing to radically detach from and regard with less affection** (or: habitually hates with distaste) **his soul** (or: inner life; conscious self) **[that is] centered in this System** (world; ordered arrangement of cultural, political and religious society) **will safeguard** (keep in watchful custody and preserve) **it, into the midst of eonian life** (life of and for the ages; life having the qualities and characteristics of the Age; life for, pertaining to, and having its source in, the Age [of Messiah]).

He said this in a similar, but expanded, fashion, in Mat. 16:

> 24. **At that point Jesus said to His disciples, "If anyone continues intending** (purposing; willing; wanting) **to come on behind Me, let him at once completely say, 'No,' to, deny and disown himself, and then in one move lift up his execution stake** (pole for suspending a corpse; cross), **and after that proceed to be by habit continuously following after** (with) **Me!**
> 25. **"You see, whoever may intend** (or: should purpose; might set his will; happens to want) **to keep his soul-life safe** (rescue himself; preserve the conscious life that he is living) **will continue loosing-it-away and destroying it. Yet whoever can loose-away and even destroy his soul-life** (the consciousness of self) **on My account, he will continue finding it!** [*cf* Mat. 26:38]
> 26. **"For what will a person** (or: mankind) **proceed being benefited, or in what will he** (or: it) **continue helped or augmented, if he** (it) **can or would advantageously procure and gain the whole ordered system of society: government, economy, culture, religion – even the whole universe, yet would be undergoing the loss of, receive damage to, or be made to forfeit, his soul-life** (the consciousness which he is; or: its interior self [in its reality])**? Or what will a person** (or: mankind) **proceed giving as a result of a change-instead** (or: in exchange) **pertaining to his** (or: its) **soul** (or: as an effect corresponding to transformation of the consciousness of, or which is, himself/itself which makes him/it other than he/it is)**?**
> 27. **"You see, the Son of the Man** (or: mankind's son; or: = the Son of Adam; or: [the eschatological Messianic figure]; or: the Human Being) **is presently about to continue progressively coming** (or: repeatedly passing from place to place) **within the glory** (the manifestation which calls forth praise; the assumed appearance) **of His Father, with His agents** (messengers; folks with the message). **And at that time, He will proceed giving back** (or: repaying; recompensing) **to each one in corresponding accord with his practice, behavior and operation of business.**
> 28. **"It is so** (or: In fact; Amen), **I am now telling** (laying it out for) **you men, that there are some** (or: certain ones) **of the folks presently standing here who under no circumstances can** (or: may) **taste** (= partake of, or, experience) **death, until they can** (or: should) **perceive and see the Son of the Man** (mankind's son; = the eschatological Messianic figure; = Adam's Son) **progressively coming** (or: continuously coming and going; repeatedly passing from place to place) **in His reign** (or: within His kingdom; joined to His sovereign activities).**

He answers Mat. 16:25 here, in vs. 25-26,

> "**the one continuing to radically detach from and regard with less affection** (or: habitually hates with distaste) **his soul** (or: inner life; conscious self) **[that is] centered in this System** (world; ordered arrangement of cultural, political and religious society) **will safeguard** (keep in watchful custody and preserve) **it, into the midst of eonian life**."

26. **"If anyone would habitually give attending service** (raise dust throughout in hastening to provide for material needs) **with, by, in and for** (or: to) **Me, let him habitually and progressively follow with, by and in Me, and then where I Myself AM, there My attending servant will also be** (exist; have his or her being). **If anyone would habitually give attending service with, by and in Me or provide for or to Me, the Father will value and honor him.**

Notice how He describes a disciple, here: "**habitually give attending service** (raise dust throughout in hastening to provide for material needs)," and that this is to be done in conjunction with Him:

    a) **with Me** – a joint-effort and partnership;
    b) **by Me** – by the power and ability of His Spirit; He is the instrument and essence of our service;
    c) **for Me** – we are His representatives, just as He did the work for the Father;
    d) **in Me** – by abiding in the Vine, Jn. 15:1ff;
    e) **to Me** – this is explained in Mat. 25:40,

    "**And then, giving a decided reply, the King will proceed saying to them, 'I am truly now saying to** (or: It is true, I now tell) **you folks, Upon such an amount** (or: = To the extent) **that you did** (or: do) **and perform(ed) [it] to** (or: for) **one of these belonging to the least of My brothers** (the folks from the same womb as Me; used collectively: = the members of My family; or: = those of My group or brotherhood), **you did and perform [it] to and for Me!'**"

These optional readings express the potential functions of the dative form of the personal pronoun **Me**. We are reminded of the term *koinōnia*, found in 1 Cor. 1:9,

    "**God [is] full of faith, trustworthy, loyal and faithful – through Whom you folks were called** (summoned) **into a common being of and existence from** (or: partnership, participation, fellowship, sharing and communion with) **His Son, Jesus Christ, our Lord** (Owner; Master)."

This verse contains another I AM statement. If we are with Him and in Him, it follows that we are "**where [He Himself IS]**." This calls to mind Eph. 2:6.

27. **"At the present time, My soul** (the consciousness which is Me; My inner self, feelings, emotion and will; My inner being) **has been stirred up** (shaken; disturbed; troubled), **and what can** (or: should) **I say? O Father, deliver** (rescue; save) **Me from out of the midst of this hour!** (or: ?) **But to the contrary, on account of this I come into the midst of** (or: came unto) **this hour.**

Verse 22, above, leaves us thinking that Philip and Andrew may have been speaking privately to Jesus about the folks that wanted to see Him. As is often the case, Jesus does not apparently reply to what they had just told Him, but seems to give a teaching, from vss. 23-26. Now, in vs. 27-28a, what He says seems more personal (27a), and is possibly spoken primarily to His disciples. After the rhetorical question, "**what can** (or: should) **I say**," what follows may be a request spoken directly to the Father, or it might be another rhetorical question. With either reading, "**But to the contrary, on account of this I come into the midst of** (or: came unto) **this hour**" could be seen as saying, "No, cancel that request, Father," or (if spoken to the disciples) He just continues sharing His inner reasonings concerning the stirrings of His soul (27a) and affirms to them His determination to do the Father's will. Verse 28a is definitely directed to the Father...

28. **"O Father, glorify Your Name** (bring glory, recognition and a renowned reputation to Your Name in a manifestation which calls forth praise)**!" Then a Voice** (or: sound) **came from out of the midst of the heaven** (or: the sky; the atmosphere)**: "I both bring glory** (or: brought recognition and a reputation) **to [it], and I will continue glorifying** (bringing a manifestation that calls forth praise to) **[it] again!"**

He does not say, "Father, I will glorify Your Name." Although being the Anointed One, and having been acknowledged by the Father as being His Son (Mat. 3:17; 17:5; Lu. 3:22), He still asks the Father to bring glory to the Father's Name. He asks the Father to "bring glory, recognition and a renowned reputation to [the Father's] Name in a manifestation which calls forth praise." Jesus does nothing from Himself, nor apart from the Father. His aim and goal is to be an image-bearer of His Father in a way that will glorify the Father. The inner shaking and disturbance in His soul has brought Him to a place similar to what He would later face in Gethsemane (Lu. 22:42; etc.). By virtually saying, "Do it, Father," He is answering the questions of His soul in vs. 27, above, with the conclusion that He stated at the last of that verse.

The immediate response from the Father, as the "**Voice**" from out of their immediate atmosphere (note vs. 29, below, that others heard a "sound"), calls to mind His immersion by John, in the Jordan River, and the Mount of Transfiguration, in Mat. 17:5, which Peter, Jacob and John heard (and then fell on their faces). 2 Pet. 1:17 recalls the experience that they had on that mountain.

What the Father's Voice said is somewhat ambiguous, unless the Father was referring to His immersion, and then His transfiguration, in the past, and the "**again**" aspect was what He was presently doing, via the voice. Other speculations are possible, but the Father left the statement open-ended.

29. **Hence the crowd of common folks, the [crowd] standing around and hearing [it], began to say that it had thundered. Others were saying, "A messenger** (or: An agent) **has spoken to him."**

Some thought that the Voice was natural thunder, and others assumed that an agent from the atmosphere (e.g., like with Moses; Ex. 3:2-4) had spoken to Him. Such occurrences were not unknown to them.

30. **Jesus decidedly replied, and said, "This Voice** (or: sound) **has occurred** (happened; come to be) **not because of Me, but rather because of you folks** (= for your benefit).

Recall Jn. 11:41-42, where Jesus was speaking out loud to the Father, for the sake of those standing by. Here, Jesus explains that this Voice came as a witness to all those who heard it – it brought "glory," i.e., an affirming testimony to the validity of Jesus being God's Son. It gave "weight" (the literal meaning of the Heb. word for glory) to what He had been saying, and would now say…

31. **"At the present time** (or: Now) **is an evaluation OF and a decision PERTAINING TO** (or: a sifting of and separation for; or: a judging **FROM**) **this System** (or: this ordered arrangement; this world; this polity, culture and religion; or: this system of control and subjugation; or: this aggregate of humanity). **Now the Ruler** (the one invested with power; the **Leader**; the chief; the ruler; or: the Original One; **The Beginning One**; the **Prince**) **of this System** (or: cosmos) **will progressively be ejected outside**
> (or: At this time the Chief of this world of culture, religion and government, the Originator and Controlling Principle of this cosmos and ordered arrangement of the universe, will proceed in being thrown out, [to the] outside [of it]).

This verse is normally interpreted from a dualistic world view, where the term "**the Ruler** (etc.)" is deemed as being a negative, or evil, spirit-being – often called satan, or the devil. A studied consideration of how I have rendered the terms in this verse will reveal that the normal interpretation is not necessarily, and as we read it, is definitely not, correct. We maintain that, "**the Ruler** (the one invested with power; the **Leader**; the chief; the ruler; or: the Original One; **The Beginning One**; the **Prince**) **of this System** (or: cosmos)" was standing before them, speaking these words to them. He had discerned that the priesthood and the Pharisees had come to **an evaluation OF** Him, and **a decision PERTAINING TO** Him, and that it was a judging **FROM this System** of their religion and cultus, that He **will progressively be ejected outside** (or: will proceed in being thrown out, [to the] outside [of it]). Recall their reasonings in vss. 10 and 19, above.

Jesus was, and is, "**the Ruler** (the one invested with power; the **Leader**; or: the Original One; **The Beginning One**; the **Prince**, the Chief, the Originator, the Controlling Principle) **of this System** (or: cosmos)." He had come into their "world of culture, religion and government" as their King and Messiah.

He was the Incarnate Logos that had originated and was the Controlling Principle of their Law. He was **The Beginning One**, the eschatos Adam, the **Leader** and **Prince** of **the Second Humanity**, made "**out of heaven**.... **the Added, Imposed, Heavenly Person** (1 Cor. 15:45-48). The next verse (32, below) describes how they will throw Him out and kill Him (to be "lifted up" was a common phrase that signified killing someone – *cf* vs. 33, below).

32. **"And thus I Myself: if** (when) **I should be lifted up from out of the earth** (or: can be exalted from the midst of this Land), **I will progressively** (or: one after another) **drag** [note: drag as with, or in, a net; or: draw, as drawing water with a bucket, or a sword its sheath] **all humans** (or: everyone) **to Myself."**

The first clause echoes 3:14-15, above,
> "**And so, just as** (or: correspondingly as) **Moses lifted up** (elevated) **the serpent, within the wilderness** [Num. 21:7ff], **thus it is necessary and binding for the Son of Mankind to be lifted up with the result and end that all – this progressively believing and successively** (one-after-another) **trusting humanity – in union with Him** (or: in order that all humanity, who being constantly loyal, centered in and within the midst of Him), **would continuously have eonian Life**."

This short, simple verse is a summary of the Christ Event and the whole "**purpose of the ages** (a fore-designed aim, plan and object [which He is bent on achieving] of the unspecified time-periods) **which He formed** (forms; made; constructs; creates; produced) **within the Christ by our Lord and Owner, Jesus**" (Eph. 3:11). The utter inclusiveness of this verse is beyond doubt or objection.

Take note of what He says that HE will do: "**drag** [note: drag as with, or in, a net; or: draw, as drawing water with a bucket, or a sword its sheath] **all humans** (or: everyone) **to Myself**." As the inserted note makes clear, this is a forceful action that will be made upon EVERYONE. Saul of Tarsus (who became Paul, a representative of Christ) is a classic example, when he was on the road to Damascus (Acts 9).

What He has said, this He WILL do.

33. **Now He was saying this continuing to indicate, by a SIGN, by** (or: with; in) **what sort of death He was progressively being about to be proceeding to die.**

This statement, by Jesus, was another SIGN, pointing them to the Goal which He had just explained to them. Consider the statement that He made in Mat. 12:39b-41a,
> "... **the SIGN of Jonah the prophet: You see, just as Jonah was within the midst of the belly of the huge fish** (or: sea monster) **[for] three days and three nights** [Jonah 1:17], **thus in this way will the Son of the Man** (humanity's son; = Adam's son) **continue being within the heart of the earth [for] three days and three nights.** [comment: then the message went to the Gentiles, vs. 41] **Adult males – Ninevites – will stand back up again with this generation, in the separating and deciding** (the judging)…"

That verse gives an allegorical interpretation of the story of the prophet Jonah, and forecasts His resurrection, and then points ahead to the mission to the Gentiles.

The sort of death (being literally lifted up from the earth) was indicating death by crucifixion – the Empire's mode of suppressing opposition to its rule. But Jesus foretells, in 32b above, how this would be transformed (via the death of God, for God was within Christ – 2 Cor. 5:19) into a Tree of Life.

34. **Therefore the crowd considered and replied to Him, "We, ourselves, hear** (or: heard) **from out of the Law that the Christ continuously remains** (abides; dwells) **on into the Age; so how are you, yourself, now saying that it continues necessary and binding for the Son of Mankind** (= the Human

Being; = the eschatological Messianic figure) **to be lifted up? Who is THIS Son of Mankind** (or: = son of Adam)**?"**

John recalls the unenlightened crowd's question and reference to the Law as a dark backdrop for the Light that would be shared by Jesus' response, in vs. 35. They did not have the view of "**the Son of Mankind** (= the eschatological Messianic figure, in Dan. 7)" being killed. He was to be the savior of Israel, from their enemies (in this case, the Romans), in their view. So who is this new sort of deliverer, who would not seem to be someone that would rescue Judea from the Romans? Furthermore, they did not associate Jesus with being this longed-for Messiah. So they ask, Who are you talking about?

35. **Jesus then says to them, "The Light continues being** (or: is) **among you folks, yet a little time** (= for a little while). **Continue walking around** (= living your lives; = order your behavior) **while you folks continue having the Light, so that Darkness** (the dim shadow-land of obscurity; = the ignorance of the system of shadows) **can** (or: could; would) **not grasp you with force and take you folks down. And the one constantly walking around within the Darkness has not seen nor does he know under what place he progressively leads [his path]** (or: where he is humbly going; where he is constantly withdrawing).

As usual, He does not give them a direct answer, but instead gives them an admonition for their present time. Remember 1:4-5, above?

> 4. **Within It [the *Logos*]** (or: Him), **life was continuing and progressively existing**
>   (or: In It was life [as a source]; [Aleph, D and other witnesses read present tense: In union with it there continues being life; Life progressively exists within the midst of It]).
> **And the life was continuing being, and began progressively existing as, the Light of the humans** (or: Furthermore, the Light progressively came to be the life known as {or: which was} the humans, and was for the human beings; or: Then later the life was existing being the light from the humans).
> 5. **And the Light is constantly shining in the dim and shadowed places, and keeps on progressively giving light within the gloomy darkness where there is no light** (or: within the midst of the obscurity of The Darkness where there is no light of The Day; or: = in the ignorant condition or system).
> **And yet the darkness does not grasp or receive it on the same level**
>   (or: Furthermore, the Darkness did not take it down, so as to overcome it or put it out; or: = the ignorant condition or system would have none of it, nor receive it down into itself [in order to perceive it]; But that darkness does not correspondingly accept It nor commensurately take It in and so as to follow the pattern or be in line with Its bidding).

His words (the expressions and manifestations of the Logos) had been shining the Light to them, but in their realm of **darkness** (the old covenant, as an expression of the realm of the first Adam) **does not grasp or receive it on the same level**.

Still, there was still time, the Day was still with them. Recall His admonition in Jn. 9:

> 4. **"It is constantly necessary for Me to be habitually performing the works of the One sending Me while it is day; night** (or: a night; = darkness; *cf* Gen. 1:5) **progressively comes, when no one is able** (or: has power) **to continue performing work.**
> 5. **"Whenever I may continue being within the world** (the religious and cultural arrangement), **I am the world's Light.**

The Darkness of domination systems (especially religious ones) can "**grasp [us] with force and take [us] folks down**" – as it would soon do to Jesus, and later, to His followers. Those "**constantly walking around within the Darkness [do] not [see] nor [do they] know under what place [they] progressively go.**" But, nonetheless, Jesus will say of them:

"**O Father, let it flow away in them** (or: send it away for them; forgive them), **for they have not seen, so they do not know or perceive, what they are now doing**" (Lu. 23:34a).

36. "**While you continue having the Light, progressively trust and believe into the Light, to the end that you folks can yourselves come to be** (or: would yourselves be birthed) **sons of Light** (= folks having the quality and characteristics of light; folks whose source is Light; [note: this could be considered a Hebrew idiom for 'enlightened people'])."

Now He speaks more specifically: "**progressively trust and believe into the Light… to be sons of Light**." Notice the parenthetical expansion: "would yourselves be birthed." This explains His words to Nicodemus, in 3:7, above, about being born back up, again. Just as He kept on speaking of Himself rather abstractly, as "the Son of Humanity," here He speaks of Himself as the Light, as He did in 8:12, above. He is telling them to put their trust in Him, and believe into what He has been sharing. These words of His were full of faith, and were true – they could be trusted (Rev. 21:5b).

Jesus spoke these things, and then after going off, He was hidden (or, as a passive with a reflexive idea: kept Himself concealed) **from them.**

John does not explain just how He was hidden, or how He kept Himself concealed, but we can assume that it was not His time to do or say more – He was following the direction of His Father.

37. **Yet, [even with] His having performed** (done; made; produced) **so many signs in front of them, they were not proceeding to believe or place their trust into** (or: not continuing loyal unto) **Him,**
38. **to the end that the word of** (or: message laid out from) **Isaiah the prophet could** (may; should; would) **be made full** (or: fulfilled), **which he said:**
    "**O Lord** [= Yahweh], **who trusts or believes in our report** (tidings; the thing heard from us)? **And to whom was the Lord's** [= Yahweh's] **arm unveiled** (revealed; uncovered)?" [Isa. 53:1]
39. **On account of this they were unable** (or: they had no power) **to progress in trusting or believing** (or: to continue loyal), **because again** (= elsewhere) **Isaiah says,**
40. "**He has blinded their eyes with the present result that they are still blind, and He hardened** (or: petrified) **their heart, to the end that they could** (or: should; would) **not see with [their] eyes nor could they direct [their] mind so as to perceive and get the thought in** (or: with) **the heart and be turned, so I, Myself, will proceed to heal** (or: will progressively cure) **them.**" [Isa. 6:10]

The author first instructs us that "**they were not proceeding to believe or place their trust into** (or: not continuing loyal unto) **Him**" (vs. 37b), then he continues, informing us that their unbelief had a purpose: "**to the end that the word of Isaiah the prophet could** (would) **be fulfilled**" (vs. 38a). This may seem strange, to us, but we need to read this through John's understanding that the prophecies of Israel's past were expected to be fulfilled, and not read this through the lens of our own unbelief about such things. John perceived that Isa. 53:1 was the reason that they did not **place their trust into Him**. This is in line with the words of Jesus, in Mat. 13:
    14. "**And so the prophecy of Isaiah is progressively being filled up in** (or: for; by) **them – the one continuing in saying,**
        '**In listening you folks will keep on hearing, and yet you can by no means have things flow together so as to get the picture or see the relationships** (or: comprehend or understand), **and while constantly looking, you will continue observing, and yet you can by no means see so as to perceive.**
    15. '**For the heart of this People was made thick and fat, and thus has become impervious, dull and insensitive, and with the ears they hear heavily, and are thus hard of hearing, and they shut** (or: closed) **their eyes** (or: they squint their eyes), **lest at some time they might see with [their] eyes and should then be listening and**

221

hearing with [their] ears, and with the heart they could make things flow together so as to comprehend – and they might turn about! And so, I will progressively cure and heal them!' [Isa. 6:9-10]

In that passage, Jesus ends vs. 15 with an expectation for Israel: He will heal them.

To drive his point home, John gives the same passage (vs. 40) that Jesus had cited (Mat. 13, above) and we read in vs. 39 that "**they were UNABLE** (or: they had NO POWER) **to progress in trusting or believing** (or: to continue loyal) **BECAUSE**" of what Isaiah had said, in the second quote (Isa. 6:9-10). But all this was, "**On account of**" Isa. 53:1 (vs. 38b). So there are at least two things that we can take away from this:

a) prophecies in the OT had a fulfillment in the circumstances of the coming of Israel's Messiah;
b) Our author assigns no guilt upon these Judeans for their unbelief or their lack of loyalty to Jesus.

A theological point that we might conclude from this is that John did not view these Judeans as having a "free will." All people are subject to the plans and purposes of God – the only existence of "FREE" will. In vs. 40 it is affirmed that God "**has blinded their eyes with the present result that they are still blind.**" Not only that, "**He hardened their heart, to the end that they could not see with [their] eyes nor could they direct [their] mind so as to perceive and get the thought in the heart.**" Paul put it this way:

"**And you folks [who were] continuously existing being dead ones in** (or: to; with; or: by) **the results and effects of your stumblings aside** (offenses; wrong steps) **and failures to hit the mark** (or: mistakes; errors; times of falling short; sins; deviations)" (Eph. 2:1).

Jesus used an analogy to say virtually the same thing about the Law scholars and Pharisees:

"**you continue closely resembling whitewashed tombs** (grave sites), **which indeed, from outside, continue being made to appear in the prime of beauty, for a time – yet inside they contain a full load of bones of dead folks**" (Mat. 23:27).

Now we do not blame a dead person for his or her lack of faith or unbelief, and we see, above, that Jesus and John considered this to be God's fault.

41. **Isaiah said these things because he saw His glory** (or: appearance; splendor; manifestation) **and knew His recognized reputation, and so spoke about Him.**

This may be due to the vision that was given to Isaiah, in Isa. 6:1ff. There he saw the Burning One (*seraph*) that was a manifestation of Christ's **glory**. The verb used here for "**saw**" also has the meaning to "**know** or **recognize**" (from having seen). Thus, I conflated the rendering, adding, "**and knew His recognized reputation.**" Isaiah was a person to whom the Logos of Yahweh periodically came and shared a message or laid out prophecies. Isaiah was one of those who,

"**died off, not taking hold of the promises, but still, after SEEING them forward at a distance, and drawing them to themselves and clinging to them**..." (Heb. 11:13).

42. **Just the same, however, many of the rulers also** (or: many, even from among the chiefs and ruling class) **believed and placed their trust into Him, but still, because of the Pharisees, they did not begin confessing** (= openly avowing their faith) **or keep on speaking in agreement – so that they would not become ones cut off from** (separated away from) **the synagogue,**

This reminds us of the parents of the blind man (who Jesus healed). They, too, were afraid of the Pharisees and of being excommunicated from the synagogue, by them (9:22, above). Now despite their lack of courage, if these rulers "**believed and placed their trust into Him,**" it means that God had opened their eyes and their hearts (vss. 37-40, above). Once again, it is not our place to blame or make decisions about them.

43. **for you see, they loved, held precious and accepted the opinion, esteem and reputation** (or: the recognition; the glory; the appearance; the manifestation which calls forth praise) **of the humans** (or: from the people) **rather than even the opinion, esteem and reputation** (or: the recognition; the glory; the appearance; the manifestation which calls forth the praise) **of, from, and which is, God.**

John points out their failure to hit the target, but this does not necessarily place guilt upon them – as we have often been prone to do, while thinking better of ourselves. Remember the great social pressure that they would have experienced in an honor/shame-base culture. Being an "outcast" was then, and is now, a hard thing to endure. The Seed from the Logos had been planted in their hearts, so they believed that He was the Messiah, and placed their trust into Him. It's just that the Seed had not yet sprouted in their outward lives – the baby Christ had not yet come to birth in them.

44. **Now later, Jesus suddenly gives out a loud exclamation** (or: cries out) **and says, "The person progressively believing and continuing to put trust into** (or: constantly being loyal unto) **Me is not continuously believing and placing loyal trust into Me, but rather, into the One sending Me;**
45. **"and further, the person continuing in attentively gazing at and contemplatively watching Me continues looking at** (contemplatively viewing; watching, discerning and seeing) **the One sending Me.**

This would have applied to those rulers mentioned in vs. 42, above. They were now informed that by placing loyal trust into Him they were really placing trust into God. Verse 44 calls to mind Mk. 9:37b,
> "Further, whoever may (or: should; would) continue welcoming and receiving Me in this way is not [simply] giving Me a hospitable welcome and an embraced reception, but further, [he does this to] the One sending Me off with a commission (as an Emissary)."

Now consider the verb that Jesus uses here, in vs. 45: **continuing in attentively gazing at and contemplatively watching… continues looking at** (contemplatively viewing; watching, discerning and seeing). This does not necessarily mean to have "spiritual insight" of Him, or to perceive "by the Spirit," or see in a "visionary" way. It can mean to simply be a spectator, to look at. But it often means attentive gazing or contemplatively watching. This calls to mind Nu. 21:6-9, where the folks who were bitten by the *seraphim* (fiery serpents) only had to look at the bronze serpent that Moses put on the pole, and they lived. Jesus identified Himself with that bronze serpent. *Cf* vs. 32, with discussion, above.

More on this "**continuing in attentively gazing at and contemplatively watching [Him]**," compare the result of beholding Him, as Paul explains in 2 Cor. 3:18,
> "But we all, ourselves – having a face that has been uncovered and remains unveiled [note: as with Moses, before the Lord, Ex. 34:34] – being folks who by a mirror are continuously observing the Lord's glory are presently being continuously and progressively transformed into the very same image and form, from glory unto glory – in accord with and exactly as – from [the] Lord's Breath- effect (or: from [the] Spirit and Attitude of, and which is, [the] Lord)."

Verse 45 states what Jesus says to Philip, in 14:9, below. Jesus was an image-bearer of the Father. But more than this, there was identity and solidarity involved. Consider the imagery in Rev. 3:12, one of the promises to the overcomer:
> "I will proceed to write upon him My God's Name, and the name of the City of My God: 'The New and different Jerusalem' – the one habitually descending from out of the atmosphere (or: heaven), from God – and My Name, the one new in character and quality."

46. **"I, Myself a Light, have come into, and am now within, the world** (the organized domination System of religion, culture and government; the ordered and adorned arrangement; or: secular society; or: the cosmos or universe; the aggregate of humanity), **to the end that everyone, who** (or: that all humanity, which) **in habitually trusting and progressively believing into Me, cannot** (should not; may not; would not) **remain** (abide; dwell) **within the midst of the Darkness, or in union with the dim shadiness, or centered in the obscurity.** [*Cf* 1:4-5, above]

> [note: darkness is perhaps a figure for their religious system, or for the world that does not know what God is really like, or for the Night, that period before the coming of the Day]

This is a brief description of His life and His purpose; it is His "mission statement" (one of a number of them). He has returned to the topic on which He spoke in vss. 35-36, above: **Light** entering into the realm of **the Darkness**. He came into, and is still within, our world – amidst the aggregate of humanity. This may be an allusion back to Gen. 1:2-4. There, the Deep (= the sea of humanity) was covered by the Darkness, but during that creation there came Light, and in turn that Light was separated from the Darkness. This may also be an allusion to the new creation (2 Cor. 5:16) that He was in the process of forming.

"**In habitually trusting and progressively believing into [Him],**" the Way out of this Darkness is seen, and it is seen because of the Light having come. We saw, in vs. 42 that many among the rulers trusted and believed into Him. Then, in vs. 44, He informs us that those that believe into Him also believe into the Father, and in vs. 45 He implies that His audience, by watching Him, is watching the Father. They are able to continue looking at the Father because He has brought Himself, the Light, into their darkness. And so now, in their trusting and believing, they **cannot** (should not; may not; would not) **remain** (abide; dwell) **within the midst of the Darkness, or in union with the dim shadiness, or centered in the obscurity.**"

The construction "**everyone, who** (or: that all humanity, which)," which is the subject of the dependent participial clause that follows, can be read either as speaking of an individual, or as corporate singular (all humanity). Habitually trusting and progressively believing (and being loyal) are the way of life that leads folks out of the Darkness (the ignorance inherent in a Law-based system; the blindness of death).

47. "**And yet, if anyone can listen to and would hear** [implying: obey] **results of the flow of My sayings and declarations** (the gush-effects said by Me) **and yet cannot** (may not; should not) **keep** (guard; maintain; watch-over and protect) **them, I Myself have no habit of separating him so as to make a distinction with him, or to evaluate, decide and then be judging him. For you see, I did not come to the end that I should** (could; would) **constantly separate, make distinctions, evaluate, then decide about and be judging the world** (the domination System; secular society; the arranged religious structure; aggregate of humans), **but to the contrary, to the end that I could, and will** [note: the verb form is both an aorist subjunctive and a future indicative], **progressively save the world**

> (restore the universe to its original state and condition; or: make the ordered System healthy and whole; rescue and deliver the ordered and adorned arrangement of religion, culture and secular society; or: heal the aggregate of mankind). [*cf* 3:16, above]

In this context, the first people to which Jesus' first statement (in this verse) refers would be those rulers that John mentioned in vs. 42, above. Even though they "**believed and placed their trust into Him,**" they apparently could not "**keep** (guard; maintain; watch-over and protect)... **results of the flow of My sayings and declarations.**" But even though this was the case concerning them, He, Himself, "**[had] no habit of separating [them] so as to make a distinction with [them], or to evaluate, decide and then be judging [them].**"

Evaluating or deciding about the situations of those who could not keep or maintain "the gush-effects said by [Him]" was not why He had come. Rather, "**to the contrary, [it was] to the end that [He] could, and will** [note: the verb form is both an aorist subjunctive and a future indicative, so I have rendered it both ways], **progressively save the world** (the aggregate of mankind)." On offer, at the end of this verse, is a parenthetical expansion of alternate renderings of the final clause.

48. "The person habitually displacing, disregarding, rejecting or setting-aside Me, and not progressively taking in hand and receiving or getting the effects of what I have gushed in speech (the results of My sayings and declarations which flowed), **is constantly having that which is** (or: the One) **continuously evaluating, progressively deciding and repeatedly judging him: the Word** (the message, laid out *Logos*) **which I spoke** (or: speak)**! THAT will continue to sift, separate, evaluate and make a decision about** (or: be judging) **him – within** (or: in union with) **this** (or: the) **Last Day –**

What He left with them and with all of us, through the centuries, are "**the effects of what I have gushed in speech** (the results of My sayings and declarations which flowed)" which are a part, a beginning, of the Blueprint (*Logos*) which founded the new creation and the attending new arrangements (covenant). The roots of this new Vine/Olive Tree are grounded in the old creation, with the age(s) that corresponded to it. As Paul said,

> "**you also came to be** (are birthed; are become) **a joint-participant** (a partner taking in common together with; a co-partaker) **of the Root and of the Fatness** (= sap) **of The Olive Tree** (or: of the oil of the olive). **Stop boasting against** (or: Do not be constantly vaunting or exulting over) **the branches! Now since you are habitually boasting and exulting** (priding yourself), **you yourself are not bearing** (supporting; sustaining; carrying) **The Root, but rather, The Root you!**" (Rom. 11:17b-18).

The Anointed Root was composed of the Logos; that, together with the Logos which He spoke, is that which "**will continue to sift, separate, evaluate and make a decision about** (or: be judging) **him – within** (or: in union with) **this** (or: the) **Last Day.**"

We maintain that the Christ Event, and the judgment upon Jerusalem which followed within THAT generation, comprised "THAT **Last Day.**" HE was that Day. The phrase "**this** (or: the) **Last Day**" offers two functions of the definite article: a) the demonstrative, used as a "pointer" (its original use), **this;**" and b) the simple, definite article, "the." The sifting was happening immediately upon the expression of the Logos from Him. This was especially happening with His disciples (sifting begins first with God's house – 1 Pet. 4:17). Also,

> "**You see, the Word of God** (or: God's thought, idea and message; or: the expressed *Logos* and Blueprint from God; or: the Word which is God) **[is] living** (or: alive), **and active** (working; operative; energetic; at work; productive) **and more cutting above every two-mouthed sword, even passing through** (penetrating) **as far as a dividing** (or: parting; partitioning) **of soul and spirit** (or: of inner self-life/consciousness and breath-effect), **both of joints and marrows, even able to discern** (separate; judge; decide) **concerning thoughts** (ponderings; reflections; in-rushings; passions) **and intentions** (notions; purposes) **of a heart** (= core of the being)" (Heb. 4:12).

In Rev. 19, John saw an apocalyptic, symbolic vision that we read as applying first to the judgment of Jerusalem, in AD 70, but which can also be seen as a figure for the Overcomer and His body functioning in kingdom activities, as directed by the Father, down through the centuries:

> 11. **Then I saw the atmosphere** (or: sky; heaven), **having been opened back up again – and consider! A bright, white horse. And the One continually sitting upon it being constantly called "Faithful** (Full of Faith; To Be Trusted; Trustworthy; Loyal) **and True** (or: Real)**," and He is continuously judging** (making decisions and evaluations) **and battling** (making war) **in eschatological deliverance** (within equitable dealings; in justice, fairness and righted relations which accord with the covenantal Way pointed out).
> 12. **And His eyes [are]** [other MSS add: as] **a flame of fire; and upon His head [are] many diadems** (kingly bands), **having a name having been written** [other MSS: having names written, and a name] **which no one knows except Himself,**
> 13. **and having been clothed** (or: cast around) **with a garment having been dipped in** (immersed; [other MSS: sprinkled with]) **blood** (or: dyed with blood), **and His Name is being**

called "**The Word of God** (God's Logos; The Message from God; The Idea which is God; The Expression about God)."

14. **And the armies in the atmosphere** (or: heaven) – **ones having been clothed with** (invested with; entered within) **clean** (or: pure) **bright, white fine cotton – continued following Him upon bright, white horses.**

15. **Also, a sharp two-edged broadsword repeatedly goes out** (issues forth; proceeds) **from His MOUTH, to the end that in it He would bring a blow to** (or: could touch; should strike) **the multitudes** (nations; ethnic groups). **And then He will continue SHEPHERDING them with an iron staff. Furthermore He is continually treading, [as on a path],** (or: trampling) **the tub** (the wine vat) **of the wine of the strong passion of the internal swelling fervor** (natural impulse; mental bent; personal emotion; or: indignation; wrath) **of the All-Strong** (Almighty) **God.**

16. **And upon His garment and upon [His] thigh He has a Name having been written: "King of kings and Lord of lords."** [*cf The End of the Old and the Beginning of the New, Comments on Revelation*, Harper Brown Pub., 2017, Jonathan Mitchell]

Now common eschatology has put this passage of Rev. 19 in the "someday" of our future. But let us consider Jesus' words in Mat. 10 that spoke of His time among them THEN, in the 1st century:

> "**YOU folks should not assume from custom or infer from the Law that I come** (or: came) **to throw peace** (a joining) **upon the Land** (or: earth). **I do** (or: did) **not come to throw** (impose) **peace or joining, but to the contrary, a sword! You see, I come** (or: came) **to disunite** (to make to be two)…" (vss. 34-35a).

Jesus' words in Mat. 10, and the prophetic vision given to John in Rev. 19 (given probably around AD 68, as suggested by John. A.T. Robinson, *Redating the New Testament*) can be seen in application to the sphere of the flesh, and the history of 1st century Judea. But we suggest that both of these contexts have their primary meaning understood by interpreting Jesus' words as metaphor (in the sense described in Heb. 4:12, cited above) and John's vision as symbol. Notice that Rev. 19:13 names (i.e., identifies) this figure on the white horse (figure of a pure action of the King) as being "**The Word of God** (God's Logos)." Furthermore, observe that the "sword" of 19:15 comes out of "**His MOUTH**" (a figure of the Logos as described in Heb. 4:12). The divisions that we find listed in Mat. 10:35bff, speak to the "**separation**" aspect of the judging, of which we read in vs. 48, above. This is what Paul referred to in Gal. 1:15 – an allusion to his conversion experience:

> "**Yet when God – the One marking off boundaries to separate and sever me from out of my mother's womb** (or: cavity; [comment: a figure of the religion of the Jews]), **and calling [me] through His grace and favor…**"

The divisions, such as here in Gal. 1 and those listed in Mat. 10:35b--38, speak to the calling-out of the *ekklēsia* (the called-out covenant communities) that were being SHEPHERDED (Rev. 19:15) by the Logos, through Paul and other sent-forth representatives of Christ.

49. "**because I Myself do not speak from out of the midst of Myself, but to the contrary, the One sending Me – [the] Father, Himself – has given an implanted goal** (an impartation of the finished, purposed product within; an inward directive of destiny) **to Me: what I could** (or: should; would; may) **say, and what I will proceed to** (or, as an aorist subjunctive: could, should, would or may) **speak.**

He repeats to this audience the same thing that He said in Jn. 8:38. He basically functioned as the Father's Mouthpiece: He was The Prophet (1:21, above). So the Logos, the Vehicle of Creation (1:3) did, and does, "**not speak from out of the midst of [Himself]**." What Jesus said and taught was "**an implanted goal** (an impartation of the finished, purposed product within; an inward directive of destiny)" given to Him by the Father. That "inward directive of destiny" was "**what I could** (or: should; would; may) **say, and what I will proceed to** (or, as an aorist subjunctive: could, should, would or may) **speak**." He spoke "an impartation of the finished, purposed product within" into the hearts of His audience. He implanted the Seed from His Father into other humans, to make them incarnate words of God.

50. **"And I have seen and know that His implanted goal** (purposed impartation of the finished product within; inward directive of destiny) **is, and continuously exists being, eonian Life** (life of and for the ages; Life having the qualities and characteristics of the Messianic Age; an eon-lasting life which pertains to, and comes from, the Age). **Therefore, the things which I Myself am habitually** (or: continuously; periodically) **speaking, just and according as the Father has told Me** (or: declared to Me), **thus I am habitually and continually speaking** (= When I speak, I repeat what the Father has told Me)."

Now He defined just what that **implanted goal** was, and is. What He SPOKE "**continuously exists being, eonian Life** (etc.)." He was continuously hearing from the Father, and then habitually speaking those same things to those who came to Him. This would continue being His pattern, all through the rest of His journey. This is our Pattern, too. We, His sheep, need to be continuously listening to what He is habitually speaking within us. In this chapter, alone, recall vss. 24-26, 32, 35-36, then 44-50. The words in those verses express the depths of the Message of Goodness, Ease and Well-being: the Gospel.

Chapter 13

1. **Now before the festival** (or: Feast) **of the Passover, Jesus, having seen and thus knowing that His hour comes** (or: came) – **to the end that He could** (or: should; may; would) **change His steps and move** (walk differently; transfer; pass over to another place) **from out of the midst of this world** (ordered System; secular society; **human aggregate**; cosmos) **toward the Father – in loving** (accepting and driving toward union with) **His own** [people? humans? friends? disciples? created ones?], **[i.e.,] those within the world** (the System; culture; ordered universe; aggregate of mankind), **He loves and fully gives Himself to them unto the end** (or: the goal and attained destiny; the finished, purposed product; the accomplished and completed work; the consummation; or: = to the uttermost extent).

Jesus knew that His hour comes, because He constantly listened to the Father. Also, He probably discerned the climate of the Jerusalem environment: how the Judean leadership desired to be rid of Him. But how beautiful a picture comes to us in the way that John describes this. **His hour** has a personal purpose for Him: **to the end that He could change His steps and move from out of the midst of this world toward the Father.** His hour meant that He would be walking differently: not as a free person, a wandering rabbi, but as a prisoner that had been beaten, carrying an execution timber to a painful death. Still, this would be His "transfer;" He would "pass over to another place," a journey which He termed as being "**toward the Father.**" Those of us who have been joined to Christ can have the same vision of the destination of our final journey from this life, but, by His grace, without the pain or shame that accompanied His journey. He so often mercies many of us, although many do have similar pain. Each of us has our own "valley of the shadow of death" (Ps. 23).

The next part of the verse begins with a participle, "**in loving** (accepting and driving toward union with)," and then uses a finite form of the same verb, followed by a descriptive predicate, to form a rather poetic construction to explain Jesus' inner emotions that are coupled with outer conduct, as we will observe in this chapter. Following the participle (in loving) John gives us an object of that love (**His own**) without defining what or who they were. We are reminded of John's Prologue, where 1:11 tells us (likewise ambiguously), "**It** (i.e., the Logos; or: He) **came into Its** (or: His) **own things** (possessions, realms, or people), **and yet Its own** (or: His own) **people did not grasp, receive or accept It** (or: Him) **or take It** (or: Him) **to their side**." In 1:11 the first "own" is neuter, plural, while the second one is masculine, plural – thus the differences in renderings. Because even though we know that He is speaking of people, here in vs. 1, I inserted some potential meanings of the phrase, since, in reality He owned everything. Of course He loved His disciples and friends, but we are sure that He also had the Father's love within Him (3:16, above) – and that included **the aggregate of humanity** and the cosmos ("the world").

The next phrase, "**those within the world** (the System; culture; ordered universe; aggregate of mankind)," shows the potential inclusiveness of His love, but does not help us in understanding specifically what John meant here. Was he, perhaps, contrasting the humans still living on earth with those now living in the realm of spirit (e.g., the Patriarchs, or those who had passed from this earthly life)? Did he mean that Jesus was loving His own people (Israel, to whom He was sent – Mat. 15:24) who were still under the culture and cultus of the old covenant – or under the domination of the Empire? Since we cannot be sure, let us keep as inclusive a paradigm as possible.

The final clause, "**He loves and fully gives Himself to them unto the end**," is also somewhat ambiguous, and this is why I offered a variety of possibilities, especially for the term "**end** (*telos*)":
         a) the goal and attained destiny – the salvation of humanity; the new creation; etc.;
         b) the finished, purposed product – the completion of His major opus, the Second Humanity;
         c) the accomplished and completed work – eschatological deliverance; atonement; restoration;
         d) the consummation – the end of the Mosaic Age; the end of the old arrangement;
         e) = to the uttermost extent – taking the phrase as an adverb, modifying the extent of His Love.

2. **So, while the evening meal was progressively going on** [other MSS: with, or after, the occurring of the evening meal] – **the adversary** (the one who thrusts something through the midst of situations, or of people; traditionally: the *devil*) **having already thrust** (cast; hurled; thrown; = put) **[the idea or conviction] into the heart of Judah** (or: Judas), **[son] of Simon Iscariot, that he should transfer, commend and commit Him** (or: hand Him over; or: = turn Him in) –

People can be adversaries. In 6:70, above, Jesus says to His disciples, "**And one from among you men is a person who thrusts things through [situations, or, people]** (or: is an adversary; is a *devil*)." There, he was speaking of Judah (Judas). In our comments on 6:70 and on 8:44, we have gone into more detailed explanations about the term "adversary (*diabolos*)" and point to 1 Tim. 3:11 and Tit. 2:3 where Paul admonishes **people** not to be "**adversaries** (those who thrust something through the midst of situations, or of people; or, traditionally: *devils*)." So how is John using the word, here? Was he speaking of a mindset or of an adversarial idea to Jesus' plans? Recall what Jesus said to Peter, in Mat. 16:23,

> "**Now, being turned, He said to Peter, "Proceed leading the way** (or: bringing things under control) **behind Me, O adversary. You are My bait-stick, ensnaring and leading Me into a trap, because you are not in the habit of setting your mind on or having the attitude pertaining to the things of God, but instead, [you continually have opinions which align with] the things of the People** (or: humans)."

There, Peter just did not want Jesus, "**to experience and suffer many things from the elders and chief** (or: ranking) **priests, as well as the scribes** (scholars and theologians of the Law), **and then to be killed off**" (Mat. 16:21). So what does John mean, when Judah is going to "**transfer, commend and commit Him** (or: hand Him over; or: = turn Him in)" to the folks of whom Jesus spoke in Mat. 16:21, where Jesus said to His disciples, "**that it is necessary [for] Him – even continues being binding [on] Him – to go away into Jerusalem, and to experience and suffer**..." by these very people?

An adversary to God's plans can simply be a plan of our own which is contrary to God's plans. Perhaps our answer can be found in the words of Paul, in Rom. 8:7,

> "**Because of that, the result of the thinking** (disposition; thought processes; mind-set, outlook) **of the flesh [is; brings] enmity, alienation and discord [streaming] into God** (or: hostility unto, or active hatred with a view to, God), **for it continues not being humbly aligned and supportive** (habitually placed under and submitted; or, as a middle: subjecting, humbly arranging or marshaling itself) **to the principle and law which is God** (or: in God's principle; by the Law from God), **for neither is it able nor does it have power**."

And Paul had just said,

> "**You see, those continuously existing in accord with flesh** (or: = in correspondence to Torah-keeping and cultural boundaries; or: = the human condition) **habitually think about, have an understanding and outlook based upon, are inclined to, set their mind on and are**

disposed to the things of the flesh (= the human condition with its cultural traditions and religious cultus)" (Rom. 8:5a).

So perhaps the result of the thinking of Judah's flesh had thrust itself into his conscious focus, as an idea or a conviction, concerning the path that he thought Jesus should take. Here, we can only speculate. But below we find that Jesus washed Judah's feet, and then instructed him to quickly do what he was intending (vs. 27, below, where we find it stated that "**the adversary** (opponent; "*satan*") **enters into [him]**").

3. **Jesus, having seen and now knowing** (or: being aware) **that the Father has given** [other MSS, aorist: gives/gave] **all humanity and all things to Him – into [His] hands – and that He came out from God – forth from the midst [of Him] – and now is continuously leading and bringing [all] under [His] control to God** (or: is progressively humbly withdrawing and continues underway, going back [to be] face to face with God), [*Cf* Jn. 1:1]

We are reminded of His statement in Mat. 28:18,
> "**All authority** (or: Every right and privilege from out of Being) **is** (or: was) **given to Me within heaven and upon the earth** (or: in sky and atmosphere, as well as on land)!"

That is, we suspect, what John meant by "all" being "**given into [His] hands**." But here, John specifies that this meant that "**all humanity and all things [have been] given to Him**." The reason for the conflation of "things" and "humanity" is that the form of the word "**all**" functions both as neuter and masculine, thus implying both realms of meaning. And more than this, it means that He is functioning as God, in all realms of existence. Or, as He says, "I and My Father are One" (10:30, above).

But further, Jesus is aware of from whence He came (**out from God – forth from the midst [of Him]**}, and that He has seen (from what the Father is doing) that the Father "**now is continuously leading and bringing [all] under [His] control to God** (or: is progressively humbly withdrawing and continues underway, going back [to be] face to face with God)." The last phrase "**to God**" also means "[to be] face to face with God." It is the same phrase used in both 1:1 and 1:2, above. The Logos is at work, forming the new creation, and the goal (*telos*, vs. 1, above) is for all humanity to be with, and face-to-face with, God. This was always the Plan, from the Beginning to the End, from the Alpha to the Omega. From out of the midst of God to ultimately end in God (Rom. 11:36).

With this knowledge, He now acts...

4. **He presently proceeds to get up** (or: arise) **from the meal** (dinner, or, supper), **continues to lay aside [His] outer garments, and then taking a linen cloth** (a servant's towel; [note: symbol of a priest's clothing?]) **He ties it around Himself** (around His waist; or: He girds Himself).

This physical act, and what follows, was a SIGN acted out by Him of what the Christ Event would accomplish for all humanity. It calls to mind the words of Paul, in Phil. 2: 7-8,
> "**He empties Himself** (or: removed the contents of Himself; made Himself empty), **receiving** (or: taking; accepting) **a slave's form** (external shape; outward mold), **coming to be within an effect of humanity's likeness. And so, being found in an outward fashion, mode of circumstance, condition, form-appearance** (or: character, **role**, phase, manner) **as a human** (a person; a man), **He lowers Himself** (or: humbled Himself; made Himself low; degrades Himself), **coming to be a submissive, obedient One...**"

In Lu. 22:27b, Jesus told His disciples,
> "**I Myself am in your midst as the person constantly giving attending service.**"

5. **Next, He proceeds to cast** (= pour) **water into the washbasin and was beginning to successively wash the feet of the disciples, and to continue to wipe [them] dry with the linen cloth** (or: towel) **with which He had girded Himself.**

6. So then He continues coming toward Simon Peter, and that one then exclaims to Him, "O Lord, You, Yourself – are you preparing to wash my feet?!"
7. Jesus decidedly replies, and says to him, "What I Myself am presently doing, you yourself have not seen and do not understand at present (or: just now), **yet after these things you will progressively gain insight and then intimately learn and realize through experience."**

So much was yet to happen: the arrest, the trial, the cross, the resurrection, the sending of the Promise from the Father, in the form of the Holy Spirit. Until the resurrection, they would experience their hopes and expectations being dashed to pieces. And then, things would be so much different. Then Paul would be shown so much more. So, yes, how could they in that moment understand what He was presently doing? We would be advised to learn a pattern from this: most of what comes to us, in our lives, we do not understand at the moment in which they occur.

8. Peter then says to Him, "Under no circumstances can (or: should) **You wash my feet ... unto the Age** (in this lifetime)!" **From discerning, Jesus replied and said to him, "Unless I can** (or: If I should not) **wash you, you do not continue to hold** (or: have) **a part** (portion) **with Me."**

Peter could not understand this reversal of function, and thus social position: their Master washing the feet of His disciples. They had been with Him for over three years (as is commonly calculated); He had called them. Why did He need to wash their feet in order to "**continue to hold** (or: have) **a part** (portion) **with [Him]**"? And what did He mean by "**a part** (portion) **with Me**"?

In Lu. 7:38 we have the incident of the woman washing His feet with her tears. Then, in Lu. 7:44, He says to Simon the Pharisee, "You gave me no water [to wash] My feet..." So first of all, we need to look at the first level of interpretation: people walked on dirt roads and paths – their feet (a figure of the "walk" of living their lives) would get dirty; usually a servant would wash the feet of someone entering the house. Cf Gen. 18:4; 19:2; 24:32; 43:24.

Next, there may be an allusion to the preparations of animals for sacrifice (Lev. 1:9, 13). Another allusion may be to Moses washing Aaron and his sons (Lev. 8:6) in their being installed as priests. Then, in Lev. 15 there were given situations where purification by washing was required for people, in general, (such as sexual intercourse, vss. 16-18). This act of washing the disciples' feet, along with the communal meal, were all symbolic, and may have pointed to a number of things, as we have noted. His disciples were now becoming a reign of priests (Rev. 1:6a). They would also need habitual spiritual cleansing, as they lived their lives (1 Jn. 1L7b; 1 Tim. 5:10). Eph. 5:25b-26 speaks of Christ love for the called-out folks:

> "**Christ also loved** (or: to the degree that, and commensurately as, the Anointed One loves and unambiguously accepts) **the called-out community, and gave Himself up** (or: commits and transfers Himself over) **in behalf of** (for the sake of; **over** [the situation of]) **her, to the end that He may set her apart** (**separate** her; consecrate and make her holy), **cleansing** (purging) **[her] by the bath of the Water [that is] within a result of a flow** (or: in union with a gush-effect; or: in the midst of a spoken word, a declaration, or an utterance)."

Take note of how Paul saw Christ giving Himself up, committing and transferring HIMSELF over – he sees beyond the instrument of Judah (Judas, vs. 21ff, below) to the One who really orchestrated the Event.

Then, we read in Tit. 3:5,

> "**not from out of works [which arise from] within religious performance which we ourselves do** [= observances associated with the temple cultus, or codes of the old covenant]
>> (or: not forth from actions in union with an act of righteousness which we, ourselves, did; not in a relationship based upon our own performance; not deeds in a system of justice, equity and fairness which we, ourselves, constructed), **but to the contrary, down from and corresponding to His mercy, He delivered us** (or: He saves, rescues and restores us to

the wholeness and health of our original condition) **through a bath of and from a birth-back-again** (or: [the] bathing of a regeneration; a washing which is a return-birth) **and a making back-up-new** (of a different kind and quality)-**again from a set-apart Breath-effect**."
The symbolism in Jesus' act seems to be multivalent.

9. **Simon Peter then says to Him, "O Lord ... not my feet only, but also [my] hands and [my] head."**
10. **Jesus in turn says to him, "The person being one having bathed himself or herself** (or, as a passive: being one having been washed and cleansed) **does not continue having a need to wash himself or herself – except the feet – but rather she or he continues to exist being wholly clean. And so you men continue being clean folks – however, not all [of you folks]."**

This is an important insight that is shared with us by Jesus. We suggest that the "**bathing**" of oneself would refer to the PERSON being immersed into Christ, there being, "**ONE effect of SUBMERSION and envelopment which brings absorption and permeation to the point of saturation** (or: baptism)" (Eph. 4:5b). That event involves what Paul referred to in Eph. 4:21-24,

> "**at one point you heard and so listen to Him, and within Him as well as in union with Him and centered in Him you were and are taught – just as Truth and Reality continuously exist within Jesus** (or: are in union with the One, Jesus) – **to put off from yourselves** [as clothing or habits] **what accords to the former entangled manner of living** (or: twisted up behavior): **the old humanity** (or: the past, worn-out person) – **the one continuously in process of being corrupted** (spoiled; ruined) **down from and in accord with the passionate desires** (the full-covering, swelling emotions) **of the deceptions** (or: seductive desires) – **and then to be continuously renewed** (or: from time to time, or, progressively made young again) **by** (or: in; with) **the spirit** (or: attitude; breath-effect) **of your mind** (or: from the mind which is you folks; or: by the Spirit which is your [collective] mind), **and to enter within** (or: clothe yourselves with) **the new humanity** (or: the Person that is different and innovative in kind and quality) – **the one in accord with and corresponding to God** (or: the person at the Divine level) – **being formed** (framed, built, founded and settled from a state of disorder and wildness; created) **within the Way pointed out** (or: in union with fair and equitable dealings with rightwised relationships, justice, righteousness and covenant participation; centered in [His] eschatological deliverance) **and reverent dedication** (or: benign relationship with nature) **pertaining to the Truth** (or: in intrinsic alignment with reality, which is the Truth)."

Here in Eph. 4, the idea of "**to enter within** (or: clothe yourselves with)" corresponds to Immersion (aka: baptism) which in turn corresponds to "washing oneself" in our present text of Jn. 13. Jesus put it this way, in 15:3, below,

> "**You folks, yourselves, are already clean** (cleansed), **cleared and pruned ones through and because of the word** (*Logos*; laid-out message; thought; idea; pattern-conveying information) **which I have spoken to you** (in you; for you; among you) **folks.**"

There, the term "clean" was used in an agricultural metaphor, in that case, a Vine, and so it referred to being "**cleared and pruned**."

The exception, to our new existential state of being "in Christ" and thus having no need for a full bath, is in the phrase, "**except the feet**," which refers to our daily "walk" in life. Once again, Eph. 4 sheds light on this, where in vs. 1 Paul admonishes them:

> "**repeatedly calling you folks, as it were, alongside: exhorting, admonishing, imploring and entreating you to WALK [your path]** (= behave; = live your life) **worthily pertaining to** (or: in a manner suitable to the value of) **the calling and invitation in regard to which you folks are called** (or: from which you were summoned)."

His concluding explanation to Peter (and all) regarding "**bathing**," affirms that: "**she or he continues to exist being wholly clean. And so you men continue being clean folks.**"

11. For He had seen and knew about the person in process of transferring and committing Him (or: handing Him over). **On account of this He said, "Not all you people exist being clean ones."**

John was impressed to repeat the final exception to His disciples being "clean folks." We suggest that He meant that Judah (Judas) had been in contact with a dead body, which would have rendered him to be ceremonially unclean. Recall that Jesus had characterized the scribes and Pharisees as being like "**whitewashed tombs, full load of bones of dead folks, as well as every uncleanness**" (Mat. 23:27). So contact or dealing with them made Him unclean. Recall Isa. 28:15,

> "For you say: We have contracted a covenant with death, and with the unseen we have made a public treaty…"

In Mat. 26, we observe:

> **14. At about that time, one of the twelve – the person normally called Judah** (or: Judas) **of Iscariot – was going on his way to the chief** (or: ranking) **priests.**
> **15. He said, "What are you presently willing to give to me? – and I, myself, will proceed in transferring and committing Him by turning Him over** (or: delivering Him) **to you men!"**
> **16. And so, from that point on, he kept on seeking a good opportunity for the purpose of committing and transferring Him** (or: a suitable situation so that he could hand Him over).

As we see, this had happened before the supper recorded here in Jn. 13, and in Mat. 26:20ff. Here, we can look to Paul's advice in 2 Cor.6:15-17,

> 15. **And what joining of voice** (concord, agreement and harmony of sound) **has Christ [when faced] toward** *belial* [Hebrew word for "worthlessness;" not a proper name]? **Or what part for one full of faith and trust** (or: portion in a loyal believer) **[corresponds] with one who lacks faith** (an unbeliever; one who is not trustworthy or loyal)?
> 16. **Now what mutual deposit** (or: concurrence or agreement arrived by group decision) **[does] God's Temple [have] with idols** (or: external forms or appearances; or: phantoms of the mind; unsubstantial images or forms)? **For you see, we ourselves** [other MSS: you folks] **continuously exist being** (indeed we/you are) **a temple of [the] living God, just as God said,**
> > **"I will proceed to make My home and will continue walking about within and among them** (or: I will habitually reside {dwell}, as in a house, and live My life within and among them), **and I will continue existing being their God, and they will continue existing being My people."** [Lev. 26:12; Rev. 21:3]
> 17. **On which account [the] Lord** [= Yahweh] **says,**
> > **"Instantly go forth from out of their midst and be instantly marked off by boundaries so as to be defined and restricted – and do not continue** (or: stop) **touching what is unclean** (= ceremonially defiled), [Isa. 52:11] **and then I, Myself, will constantly admit you folks and receive you into [Myself; My family],** [Ezk. 20:41]

Also consider what Paul quotes in 1 Cor. 15:33,

> "**Worthless associations, conversations or interminglings in a crowd** (or: Companionships of corrupt quality [note: this can refer to sexual encounters]; Bad company or communication) **habitually and progressively corrupt, decay, spoil and ruin useful habits, kind customs and profitable characters.**"

This may explain Jesus' words about Judah. Call to mind what was needed for the "sons of Levi" (from whom came the priesthood):

> "For He is like a refiner's fire, and like the soap of launderers. And He will sit like a refiner and a cleanser of silver. And He will cleanse the sons of Levi, and refine them like gold and like silver" (Mal. 3:2b-3a).

Another insight may be seen in 1 Cor. 6:

> 15. **Have you folks not seen so as to know that your** [other MSS: our] **bodies are** (exist being) **members** (body parts) **of Christ? Upon lifting up and carrying off** (or: bearing away) **the members** (body parts) **of the Christ, will I proceed then in making** (or: could or should I at any point yield) **[them] members** (body parts) **of a prostitute? May it not come to be or happen** (= Heaven forbid; = No way)!

16. **Or, have you folks not seen so as to know that the man continually joining himself** (or: being habitually glued in intimate union) **to** (or: in) **a prostitute exists being one body [with her]? For, He says,**

   "The two will continue existing, being [joined] into one flesh." [Gen. 2:24]

We find that Prostitute pictured in Rev. 17:1-18, which, we submit, is 1st century Jerusalem that rides on the back of (was in collusion with) the Roman Empire. Judah (Judas) had joined forces with the Jerusalem leadership, and became one flesh with her. It was a flesh relationship between him and the flesh system of the old covenant. In Lu. 22:42, Jesus was about to drink the cup. What cup? The woman of Rev. 17:4 had **a cup** in her hand. Rev. 17:4 explains that this cup was **full of the blood** of the set-apart folks and the witnesses of Jesus. Mat. 23:24 gives further identification of this woman: "**O Jerusalem, Jerusalem! The one repeatedly killing the prophets, and habitually stoning the people sent off with a mission to her**..." We know that Jesus drank of (= experienced) her cup.

12. **After He had washed their feet, He took His outer garments** (= He put them back on) **and reclined back again, [and] says to them, "Are you men coming to know and personally understand what I have done for you** (to you; in you; with and among you folks)**?**

In vs. 4, above, He stripped off His outer garments before performing the symbolic act of cleansing their walk. Was that a SIGN pointing to the Romans stripping Him before His crucifixion? Was the fact that "**He took His outer garments**," after completing the task, pointing to His resurrection? We see this whole episode as something more than just a "foot-washing service" (as beautiful as those are). Did they "**[come] to know and personally understand what [He had] done for [them]**," at that time? We doubt it. But they would, later on.

13. **"You men are repeatedly addressing** (calling) **Me, 'Teacher** (= Rabbi)**' and 'Lord** (Master),**' and you keep on speaking** (or: saying [it]) **beautifully** (ideally; finely), **for I am.**

Now He sets up a comparison between His role and theirs.

14. **"If** (or: Since) **I Myself, then, the Lord and the Teacher, wash your feet, you men also are constantly indebted** (obliged; continuously owe it) **to be habitually washing one another's feet,**
15. **"for I give** (or: gave) **an underlying example** (or: result of something pointed out as a specimen or illustration shown under your eyes) **to, and for, you folks, so that just** (accordingly; correspondingly) **as I, Myself, do** (or: did) **for** (to; in; among) **you, you men should also be repeatedly doing.**

You see, they would become teachers, and masters of students, and they were not to be shepherds that operated in a forced manner with the sheep,

   "**Nor yet as ones constantly exercising down-oriented lordship** (acting as owners or masters, bearing down with demands) **of the members of the inheritance** (of those who are the allotments of the heritage; or: of those considered to be small objects to be used in assigning positions or portions), **but to the contrary, progressively becoming beaten models** (types made by the strike of a hammer; examples) **for the little flock**" (1 Pet. 5:3).

We suggest that He was not speaking about literally "**habitually washing one another's feet**," but rather about doing that of what the ceremony was emblematic: taking the role of a servant, and cleaning from one another the dust (manifestations or behaviors from their flesh realms) from one another's walk (daily living) as His followers.

16. **"Most assuredly** (It is certainly true; Amen, amen)**, I am saying to you, a slave is not greater than** (superior to) **his lord** (owner; master), **nor [is] one sent with a mission** (an emissary; a representative) **greater than** (superior to) **the one sending him.**

These were practical admonitions, presented as wisdom sayings, that they would need to keep in mind, since He would soon be physically leaving them, and they would carry on doing the works that he had been doing. The implications were that they should deem themselves as slaves of the Lord (as did Paul; Rom. 1:1). He (via His Spirit) would now be the One sending them, and they should remember their "place" in that relationship. Jesus had modeled this for them: He did and said ONLY what He heard from the Father.

17. **"Since** (or: If) **you have seen and know these things, you are happy** (continue being blessed and fortunate) **ones – if you can** (or: would; should) **be habitually doing** (performing; producing) **them.**

"**you are happy** (continue being blessed and fortunate)" – IF… "**habitually doing** (performing; producing) **them**." Vision and knowledge are not enough: we must live these things. It's not about doctrines, it's about a way of Life: the Path, the Reality and the Life (14:6, below).

18. **"I am not now speaking about all of you men. I Myself have seen and thus know which ones** (or: whom) **I select and pick out for Myself, but to the end that the Scripture may be fulfilled** (made full; filled up): **'The one habitually eating** (crunching; chewing) **My bread** [other MSS: the bread with Me] **lifts** (or: lifted) **up his heel on** (= walked away from; or, = turned against) **Me.'** [Ps. 41:9]

He was not speaking about the entire group, but about a certain person among them. Notice that Jesus uses the Scriptures as being the reason for this person "walking away" from Him. All of the disciples would have known this Psalm, and would have realized that it began, "My own familiar friend, in whom I trusted…"

One verse from an OT passage would bring to mind the entire passage, in that day and in the Jewish culture. This was a Psalm of David, and it is the ending psalm (#41) in Book One of the psalms. It begins with:
> 1. Blessed [is] the person that considers the poor (or: the weak or sick): Yahweh will deliver him (or: provide his escape) in the day of evil.

This was the focus of Jesus' teaching (e.g., Mat. 5:3; Lu. 6:20), and many of His actions. It continues:
> 2. Yahweh, He shall guard him and preserve his life… and He shall certainly not give him over to the soul of his enemies.

These words must have been on Jesus' mind, when He cited vs. 9, above. How ironic – both for David, and for Jesus. But he also would have remembered the first half of vs. 10,
> "Yet You, O Yahweh, be gracious to me and raise me up…"

And then, in vs. 12, "You uphold me…" Jesus saw beyond the immediate, heartbreaking situation to the end, as vs. 12 continues, "And You station me before You for the Age."

Just as Jesus was still seeing the Father within the midst of His upcoming ordeal, the Blueprint (*Logos*) still lies before us to continue beholding the Father, and know that our end is secure.

19. **"From now** (or: this moment) **on, I am saying [it] to** (or: telling) **you folks before the [situation for it] is to come to be** (is to be birthed; is to occur; = before it happens), **so that when it may come to be** (happen; occur) **you can** (or: would) **continue trusting and believing that I am** [what I say I am; He] (or: I AM; because I Myself am Being; for I am continuous Existence; or: that I continue existing).

The purpose of prophecy – of being told "**before the [situation for it] is to come to be** (is to be birthed; is to occur; = before it happens)" – is to enable us to "**continue trusting and believing that I AM**." The emphatic personal pronoun coupled with the verb of being (with no predicate following it) would have pointed them to the "I AM" of Ps. 41 that He quoted: Yahweh. Since the verb is in the present tense, He could have also been reminding them that the Father was speaking to them through Him, saying, "I am continuous Existence... I Myself am Being." Again, a really multivalent statement (more than His just being the Door, the ideal Shepherd, etc.).

20. **"Most assuredly** (It is certainly true; Amen, amen), **I am saying to you, the person habitually receiving** (taking with the hand, embracing and accepting) **whomever I will send** (or: may send) **is continually receiving Me** (welcoming, embracing and accepting Me). **Now the one habitually receiving Me is continually receiving** (welcoming, embracing and accepting) **the One sending Me."**

The solidarity and connectedness, and dare we say "implied identity," of the objects of the verbs in both statements are profound, and point us to "**the Depths of God**" (1 Cor. 2:10b). Recall Jn. 12:44-45, where the verbs were "**trusting and believing**." Compare these to what He said in Lu. 10:16,

"**The person continuing to listen to and hear you folks is habitually listening to and hearing Me. And the person habitually setting you aside and disregarding you continues to set Me aside and disregard Me. Yet the person setting Me aside continues to set aside and disregard the One sending Me off with a mission and as a representative** (emissary)."

These all remind us of what He said in Mat. 25:40, "you did it to them, and in that you thus did it to Me." Whether it be receiving, hastening/hearing, or doing, there is existential oneness involved between us and Him (cf 17:21, below).

21. **[On] saying these things, Jesus was shaken by the Spirit** (or: troubled in mood or disturbed in the spirit; or: **stirred with** the Breath-effect and Attitude), **then gave witness** (testified) **and said, "Most assuredly** (It is certainly true; Amen, amen), **I tell you** (I am saying to you) **that one from among you men will proceed in transferring, commending and committing Me** (or: handing Me over)."

The first clause recalls 12:27, above, where John tells us that it was His "soul" that was shaken and troubled. Here the dative form of the phrase "**the Spirit**," etc., injects ambiguity, or it reveals different aspects of what was happening to Him. Let us lay these out:

   a) **the Spirit** was shaking Him, or, His spirit was shaking Him;
   b) He was troubled in mood;
   c) He was disturbed in His spirit;
   d) He was **stirred with** the Breath-effect and Attitude.

The verb is in the passive voice, so the objects of the prepositions (Spirit; spirit; Breath-effect; Attitude; mood) were acting upon Him. Maybe He was experiencing all of these at the same time. The **witness** (or: testimony) that He then expressed would certainly reveal to us the reason for His being shaken, troubled, disturbed and/or stirred.

What He had hinted at, by quoting Ps. 41:9 in vs. 18, He now clearly states. What Jesus says in the last half of this verse was spoken of in Jn. 6:64, 71; 12:4; 13:2, 11, and now stated here. The same verb is used, in regard to this act, five times in ch. 18, twice in ch. 19, and once in ch. 21. It is revealing that John used it of Jesus in Jn. 19:30b, "**and so, bowing [His] head, He transferred the Spirit** (or: committed [His] spirit and life-force; or: gave over and surrendered to the side the Breath-effect)."

If we connect the dots, we see that Judah was an instrument that began a sequence of events which ended in Jesus transferring the Spirit... ultimately to us.

Paul used this same verb, multiple times. Let us review a few of them that may speak to Jesus' situation, in this verse:

   In Eph. 5:

   1. **Keep on becoming** (or: Progressively come to be), **then, imitators** (those made exactly alike so as to portray, express and represent by means of imitation) **of God, as beloved** (or: like loveable) **children,**

2. **and so, keep on walking** (walking around; = progressively living and maintaining your life) **within, and in union with, Love** (self-giving acceptance and the urge for union), **according as the Christ also loves** (or: to the same level and commensurately as the Anointed One loved, accepted and achieved reunion with) **you folks, and also gives** (or: gave) **Himself over in our behalf** (or: then commits and transfers Himself over us and our [situation]; [other MSS: you]): **a bearing toward and a bringing to be face to face, even an offering by** (or: in; with; or: to; for) **God [turning] into a fragrant odor** (or: and unto a sweet-smelling incense-sacrifice amid God)....

25. **O husbands, be constantly loving, and urging to unity with, [your] wives** (or: Men, continue giving yourselves for and accepting the women), **accordingly and correspondingly as the Christ also loved** (or: to the degree that, and commensurately as, the Anointed One loves and unambiguously accepts) **the called-out community, and gave Himself up** (or: commits and transfers Himself over) **in behalf of** (for the sake of; over [the situation of]) **her.**

Notice that Paul admonishes us to imitate God, and then Christ, who **gave** THEMSELVES **in Love**; he does not say that they were "betrayed." Our love for others is to be a committing and a transferring of ourselves (like "placing our souls" – 15:13, below) over the situations of other people.

In 1 Cor. 5:

5. **[you are] to commit** (surrender; hand-over) **such a man, with the adversarial [spirit]** (or: in the adversary; by the opponent; or: to *satan*), **into a loss of the flesh** (or: an undoing and destruction of this [distorted human nature]; a loss of [his "dominated existence" – Walter Wink]) – **to the end that the spirit may be saved** (rescued; delivered; restored to health, wholeness)...

As with the case of Jesus, this "commitment" had salvation and deliverance in view.

In 2 Cor. 4:

11. **For we, ourselves – the continuously living ones – are ever being repeatedly handed over and committed into death** (or: = continuously delivered into life-threatening experiences) – **because of Jesus – to the end that the Life, also, of Jesus** (or: so that also the life which comes from and is Jesus; or: so that Jesus' life) **can** (may; could; would) **be set in clear light and manifested – within our mortal flesh!**

Take note of the "divine passive" voice of the verb "handed over/committed" – Paul meant that God was the Actor in this verb.

In 1 Tim. 1:

20. **of whom are Hymenaeus and Alexander, whom I gave over** (or: commit; commend; transfer; handed along; deliver) **to the adversary** (or: entrust and render as a yield to be matured in and with the opponent; or: pass along to and deliver by this satan) **to the end that they would be child-trained, educated and disciplined with a view toward maturity, [so as] not to constantly blaspheme.**

With these examples in mind, then to describe the action of Judah (Judas) as "betrayal," with this word's pejorative baggage, would limit our understanding of the role that he played in the Passion narrative.

When sharing these thoughts with Dan Kaplan, he took us back to Genesis, and the story of Joseph. There, it was ten of the twelve that sold their brother into slavery, and yet it all ended with him telling his brothers,

"God sent me here before you, with a view to life.... Now therefore it is not you who have sent me here, but rather God, and He made me a father to Pharaoh and lord (master) of all his house and ruler of all the land of Egypt" (Gen. 45:5b, 8, LXX).

Take note that Joseph had no condemnation for his brothers, but rather saw God behind it all. In the upcoming Passion of Jesus, we can see Judah, as the representative of the twelve tribes of Israel, who passed along Jesus (the One who would be King of kings and Lord of lord, over all the earth) to His adversary, the Judean leadership – but it was actually God who sent Him to them, to be the Savior of the world (*cf* Acts 2:22-36). Here, Dan calls to mind 1 Cor. 2:8,

"**For if [the rulers] had known, THEY would not likely have crucified the Owner of, and Who is, the Glory [of Israel, and of all].**"

Then Dan pointed us to the story of Job, and how God instigated his trials, using the adversaries of Sabean raiders, lightning, the Chaldeans, a great wind, and then sore boils on his body, from head to foot (Job 1 and 2), as a test of his faithfulness. His story ended in restoration, but it had no condemnation for the role of "*satan*," in the form of those various adversaries, in that story. They were all "part of the plan," and a part of the story.

22. **Therefore the disciples began to glance and continued looking into one another, being perplexed** (at a loss; confused) **about whom He is speaking.**

We find it interesting, that they had no idea of whom He was speaking. Apparently no one had any suspicions of Judah. They had been together for three years. Apparently nothing in his personality, his disposition, his mannerisms, his family, his friends, his side conversations, ever gave any hint of what he was up to. The disciples were "**perplexed** (at a loss; confused) **about whom He is speaking**." Fascinating.

23. **Now one from among His disciples, whom Jesus had been loving** (progressively urging for accepting union, as being on common ground; giving Himself to), **was by habit lying back** (reclining at the table) **at the chest** (or: on garment fold; = close at the right, the place of honor/intimacy) **of Jesus.**

The designation of this disciple, along with the fact that John does not name him either here, or later, has led tradition to conclude that this disciple was the author of this Gospel. But this is merely an assumption. Some have suggested that he was not named for the sake of this person's safety. It remains a curious aspect of the narrative. We wonder if, as some have suggested, since there are so many symbols and signs in this book, whether he might be a representative "place-holder" for all the disciples, and all of us, who would in turn have this closeness to the Lord, and be loved by Him, in return.

Dan Kaplan has raised a startling candidate for this mysterious disciple who is so close to Jesus. We will share this conjecture, so that our readers can wonder about it, too…

24. **Therefore Simon Peter repeatedly nodded to this one, and then says to him, "Tell who it is** [other MSS: Ask which one it might be], **about whom He is now saying [this]."**

Here our author refers to him as simply "**this one**," and Simon Peter wants "this one" to inform the group of whom Jesus is speaking! Why did not Peter ask Jesus directly? Were they all in shock? Well, "**that one**" complies with Peter's request…

25. **Therefore that one, thus leaning back upon the chest of Jesus, says to Him, "Lord** (Master), **who is it?"**

Does "**that one's**" question, here, correspond with the account in Mat. 26:25?
> "**So Judah** (or: Judas) – **the one in process of transferring, committing and turning Him in** (delivering and handing Him over) – **making a discerning response, said, "I, myself, am not the one who You mean, am I, Rabbi?** (or: No way is it I, myself, Teacher!)"
> **Jesus then says to him** (or: continues laying it out for him), **"You, yourself, are saying [it]**."

26. **Jesus considers and then replies, "It is that one for whom I, Myself, will dip the morsel** (bit of bread) **and will give [it] to him." Then, after dipping the morsel in, He continues taking it in His hand and proceeds to give [it] to Judah** (Judas), **[son] of Simon Iscariot**

Now we have seen all along that our author has known who "this one" was, as noted in 6:71, above. And consider that in 6:70 Jesus describes Judah thusly: "**one from among you men is a person who**

237

thrusts things through [situations, or, people] (or: is an adversary; is a *devil*)." Yet Judah was one of the "**twelve**" that Jesus "**selected and picked out** (chose) **for [Himself]**."

So, back to Dan's suggestion: What if "**this one**" was the person "**whom Jesus had been loving** (progressively urging for accepting union, as being on common ground; giving Himself to)"? What if Jesus had taken this person to His side, and had made him sit right next to Him? Remember: their manner of taking a meal was "reclining" (**leaning back**), one next to another. So if Jesus was going to hand **the morsel** to the person that He was designating as being "the one," that person would most likely have been within arm's length of Jesus. Was Jesus answering the one who asked Him the question, by handing the morsel to this one who had just asked the question? The special designation for "**this one**" is used again in 19:26; 20:2 and 21:7, below, and these contexts, as well as how they inform us, need to be considered as we ponder the identity of "**this one**." But as a preview, Jn. 21:2 tells us that the sons of Zebedee (those would be James and John – Mat. 4:21) were among the seven disciples that went fishing. Two of the seven are not named. It was "**this one**" (21:7) who first recognized Jesus, on the shore. So why was Peter asking about "**this one**," in 21:20-21, and why does our author point out that this is the same one who asked Jesus the question about who it was that was transferring Him? Enquiring minds want to know :) Then Jesus responds enigmatically to Peter, "**If I am intending** (willing; purposing) **him to continue remaining until I am progressively coming, what [is it] to you?**" Jn. 21:24 is commonly taken to mean that "**this one**" is the author of this Gospel:

> "**This is the disciple: even the one constantly witnessing and testifying about these things, even the one writing these things – and we have seen and know that his witness** (testimony) **is true** (genuine; real)."

But this need not be the case. It can mean that "**this disciple**" was constantly witnessing, and was also the written source for the incident described, above. Or, the tradition may be true (assuming that "**This is the disciple**" is referring to our author, yet there is no conclusive evidence, either way. Note that our author ended this Gospel:

> "**not even the organized System** (world; society at large; arranged order; cosmos) **itself will [be able] to contain the scrolls being constantly written**."

Of course, tradition has Judah (Judas) already dead by this time. But was he? Could the author of the Gospel of John (no MS has this title) actually been Judah (Judas)?
Consider Acts 1:

> 16. "**Men! Brothers** (= Fellow believers)! **It was continuing necessary and binding for the Scripture to be fulfilled in which the Holy Spirit** (or: the Set-apart Breath-effect and Sacred Attitude) **foretold** (or: spoke in advance) **through the mouth of David, concerning** (or: about) **Judah** (or: Judas) **– the one coming to be a guide for** (or: to) **the folks seizing and arresting Jesus –**
> 17. "**because he was one having been actually numbered** (or: counted down; = enrolled and assigned) **among us** (or: within our [group]) **and thus he obtained by lot the allotted portion** (or: share) **of this attending service.**"
> 18. **– This man** (or: "**This one**"), **indeed therefore, acquired a small parcel of ground** (a farm; an estate; a freehold: a place not subject to allotment which could be bought or sold) **from out of wages of injustice** (that which is contrary to solidarity and the Way pointed out; inequity; unfairness), **and so, having come to be flat on his face** (prostrate), **[his] heart** (the core of his being in the midst of him) **broke and his deep feeling and affections were poured forth**.

The last clause of vs. 18 is reading the Greek metaphorically, since a literal reading makes no sense.
Now let us consider Mat. 27:

> 3. **At that time, upon seeing that He was correspondingly judged against** (or: condemned), **Judah** (or: Judas) **– the person transferring and committing Him – after changing his judgment and concern on the matter so as to be regretting and caring differently, returned the thirty silver [coins]** (or: pieces of silver) **to the chief** (ranking) **priests and elders,**
> 4. **while saying, "I made a grave mistake** (erred; failed to hit the target; sinned; fail to attain the goal) **in transferring, committing and giving-over just and innocent** (rightwised) **blood.**"

But those men said, "What [does this mean] to us? You, yourself, will proceed seeing!"
5. **And so, upon hurling the silver [coins; pieces] into the inner Temple** (shrine; = the holy place), **he withdrew, and then going off, he at one point hugged, embraced and, as it were, compressed himself away [as in grief]** (or: suddenly squeezed or choked himself off; or, perhaps: strangled or hanged himself [note: only here in NT; only once in OT]).

Both of these passages about the response of Judah to the condemnation of Jesus, by the chief priests and elders, can be read as expressions of deep grief, not necessarily as indications that (in Mat.) Judah killed himself. Notice that in Mat. 27:3 we see Judah had a change of heart: "**after changing his judgment and concern on the matter so as to be regretting and caring differently, returned the thirty silver [coins]** (or: pieces of silver) **to the chief** (ranking) **priests and elders**."

Let us read on…

27. **– and with** (accompanying) **the morsel, at that time, the adversary** (opponent; "*satan*") **enters into that one. Therefore Jesus proceeds to say to him, "What you are in process of doing** (or: proceeding to do), **do more quickly** (or: promptly)."

We know the story, so often we can miss details. Observe that Jesus does not openly name Judah as the one, but subtly, with a SIGN that points him out to Peter, and the others: "**It is that one for whom I, Myself, will dip the morsel** (bit of bread) **and will give [it] to him**." Neither does He condemn him, or ask him, "How can you do this?" Rather, Jesus tells him to hurry, and get on with it!

Now with all that we have considered re: "**the adversary** (opponent)," what did the author mean, here, that it "**enters into that one**" (i.e., Judah)? And notice: it happened "**at that time**" – i.e., when he receives the dipped bit of bread from Jesus! It was when taking "communion" that the adversary enters into him! How ironic!

We suggest that "**the adversary**" was the thinking of Jesus' "opponent," the Judean leadership. This mindset, or the minding of the functioning that he was chosen to do that would facilitate a nighttime capturing of Jesus by the temple authorities, came to his mind. Perhaps Jesus had pre-arranged this as a signal, which Jesus may have previously given to him. Or, perhaps "**the morsel**" reminded him that Jesus had said that people must "eat His flesh," and that memory entered his mind, and then he remembered what he was supposed to do. Jesus may have realized the inner working of Judah's mind – perhaps a questioning of whether or not transferring Jesus was really God's will, or even, whether the will of the priests was correct – and so He affirms what Judah is supposed to do, and that NOW was the time.

Before leaving this conjecture about Judah, let us recall the incident where Jesus had just informed His disciples that it continued binding on Him that He must go to Jerusalem and suffer many things from the elders and chief priests (Mat. 16:21). Peter remonstrated that this should not happen to Him, and so Jesus replied to him:
> "**Proceed leading the way behind Me, O adversary. You are My bait-stick, ensnaring and leading Me into a trap, because you are not in the habit of setting your mind on or having the attitude pertaining to the things of God, but instead, [you continually have opinions which align with] the things of the People** (or: humans)" (Mat. 16:23).

The thinking (expressed in Peter's remonstration) and an attitude, which were **adversarial** to what Jesus had just said, had entered Peter, at that time – and thus came Jesus' strong response.

28. **Now none of those presently reclining knew** (at any point had personal knowledge) **toward what end He said this to him.**

Recall that in Matthew's version of this incident, when Jesus made the announcement, "**one from among you will proceed transferring and committing Me**," we find ALL the disciples questioning themselves:

> "continuing being tremendously pained, caused to be distressed and filled with sorrow, each one commenced to be saying to Him, in turn [or, with p45, D, the Magdalen fragments, and others: each of them, joining in and speaking at once, were saying], "I, myself, am not the one who You mean, am I, Master (Lord)?" (Mat. 26:21, 22).

Did they all realize their own weaknesses and vulnerabilities? Now Luke records another surprising incident, afterwards,

> "they themselves began to seek, each one in face to face discussion among themselves, who really it could be from their [group] that is progressively about to be committing this thing" (Lu. 22:23).

The very next verse (vs. 24) records:

> "Now this also birthed a readiness to quarrel resulting in a dispute (or: a fondness for contention with a love for victory which spawned "mimetic rivalry" [– Walter Wink]) among them about who of them is now seeming to be greater [than the rest] (or: who is normally presuming to be the most important)."

No wonder that they were clueless: they were still just thinking about their sitting on thrones, ruling with Christ – as is often the case with us. And so…

29. **Some in fact thought** (supposed; imagined), **since Judah** (Judas) **had been holding** (in possession of) **the money box, that Jesus is saying to him, "Buy at the marketplace things of which we presently have need, with a view to the feast [days]," or, "for the destitute folks," so that He could give something.**

The rest of the disciples were blind as to what was going on. They did not suspect that Judah was part of a plot, and certainly did not imagine that God might be the author of the plot.

30. **Then, upon accepting** (or: receiving) **the morsel, that one went out set for goodness, ease and well-being** (or: a straight, direct, upright and true one; or, as adverb: immediately). **Now – it was night.**

The phrase, "**set for goodness, ease and well-being**," is *euthus*, and can function as an adjective, a noun or an adverb. The common adverbial rendering is "immediately" or "straightway" or "at once." However, it also means "straight; direct; upright; true." This latter I gave as the first parenthetical rendering, where it functions as a noun that has those characteristics. But the bold, and first, rendering is an expanded rendering of *eu-* (goodness, ease and well-being) + *thus* (from the verb that means to set or place). This expanded phrase functions as an adverb that modifies the verb "**went out**" suggesting the goal, purpose and/or mindset/mood in which he left the group. This suggests that what Jesus had just "commissioned" him to do was taken by him to mean that his actions would end in goodness, ease and well-being – which ultimately they did!

This reading shines a different light on the character of Judah, on his immediate paradigm and worldview, and perhaps on the mood he was in, or even perhaps on the perception of the goal that he had in mind. We suggest that there was more to Judah than what normally meets the eye, due to the traditional renderings and interpretations. It is interesting that Mark does not mention Jesus designating who it was of which He spoke. There (Mk. 14:20) He simply said, ""[It is] one of the twelve – the person repeatedly (or: normally) dipping [a morsel] into the common bowl with Me." That is similar to His quote of Ps. 41:9, in vs. 18, above.

31. **Then, when he went out, Jesus proceeds to say, "Now is** (or: At this moment was) **the Son of Mankind glorified** (or: given an appearance, a recognized reputation and caused to receive opinions), **and God is** (or: was) **glorified** (or: made to appear; recognized; receives opinions and a reputation; given a manifestation which will call forth praise) **within Him** (or: centered in union with Him).

Think of it! With Judah going off on his mission, Jesus announces that "**NOW is** (or: At this moment was) **the Son of Mankind glorified** (or: given an appearance, a recognized reputation and caused to receive opinions)." Take note! This is in conjunction with the action of Judah (Judas), which was to transfer Him to the next phase of His ministry and purpose as the Messiah. Judah has a role in God being glorified, within Christ – or, with God being centered in union with Christ. In 9:3, above, Jesus said that the healing of the blind man was so that the works of God could be manifested. Jesus will now be committed to the Judean leadership so that all of Israel, and the whole aggregate of humanity, would be healed.

In the Christ Event, "God was made to appear, be recognized, receive opinions and a reputation, and was given a manifestation which has called forth praise!"

32. **"Since God is glorified in union with Him, God will also progressively glorify Him within** (in union with) **Himself, that is, He will continue giving Him an assumed appearance set for goodness, ease and well-being** (or: and He will keep on manifesting Him as a straight, direct, upright and true One which calls forth praise).

First of all, take note that Jesus states that God will continue giving Him "**an assumed appearance** (glory) **set for goodness, ease and well-being**," and He uses the same term that our author used for Judah, in vs. 30, above. All of this is Jesus' response to what Judah (Judas) had gone out to do.

In considering what would have become of Judah, Marge White raised the question of what Jesus said regarding him, in Jn. 17:12,

> "**I Myself was continually watching over, caring for, observing, keeping, guarding and maintaining them in union with** (or: centered in) **Your Name – which You have given to Me, and I now have – and I protected [them], and NOT ONE from among them lost himself** (or: destroyed himself), **except** (or: since not) **the son of "the loss"** (the son of the dissolution, or, from the destruction; the person having the characteristics of loss, dissolution or destruction), **so that the Scripture could and would be fulfilled.**"

Judah had become "the son of the loss." We will look at this more fully when we observe Jn. 17, but for now let us just recognize that Judah had become a lost sheep. He had recognized his Shepherd's voice, in vs. 27, above, and had rightly responded. But his path involved his becoming lost – for a time. We read of what the Ideal Shepherd does in regard to a lost sheep, in Lu. 15:4-7, where we read about the Owner of the sheep:

> "**What person… upon losing one of them, is not normally leaving the ninety-nine down within the wilderness** (desolate and uninhabited place) **and then continuing on his way upon [the track of] the lost one – until he can find it? Later, after finding [it], he proceeds to place it on his shoulders, amidst rejoicing! And so, upon coming into the house, he proceeds calling together [his] friends and neighbors, saying to them in turn, 'Celebrate** (or: Be glad and caused to rejoice) **together with me, because I have found my lost sheep.**"

In this verse, observe the rhetorical repetition (beginning in vs. 31b) of the verb "**glorified… glorify… giving Him an assumed appearance** (manifesting… which calls forth praise)." His emphasis could hardly be stronger. But notice the intermingling and inter-penetration going on here. The glory – the assumed appearance – is one of mutual co-habitation. There is also the evidence of past, present and future which speaks to a divine continuity of all that has been said. Observe the alternate rendering of *ethus* in the parenthetical expansion: "and He will keep on manifesting Him **as a straight, direct, upright and true One** which calls forth praise."

33. **"Little children, I am with you yet a little while** (or: longer). **You folks will continue seeking, and trying to find Me, and just as I said to the Jews** (= Judean leaders), '**To the place that I Myself progressively lead under** (or: am going away), **you yourselves are continuing unable** (still have no power) **to go** (or: come),**' I am also now saying to and for you right now** (at present).

In all of this, Jesus had been speaking obscurely, as was often His manner of communicating. He was not shocking them with words about His upcoming death (as He had in Mat. 16:21, referenced above). But to what time was He referring? When would they try to find Him? From the Gospel accounts we do not see them physically seeking Him – unless He was referring to what Mary Magdalene and the other women would do when going to see Him in His tomb, and later Peter (Lu. 24:1-12). The account in 20:1-10, below, records Mary coming alone, finding the tomb empty then running to Peter, and "**the** (or: that) **other disciple for whom Jesus was continuing feeling friendly affection and showing devotion**," then it reports the three of them going to the tomb but finding it empty. Next, the two men left the scene, "**But Mary had taken a stand outside, facing the memorial tomb, and still stood there**..." (20:11).

34. **"I am giving to you folks a new implanted goal** (an inward purposed directive different from that which had been formerly; an impartation of a finished product and destiny that is new in kind and character)**: that you folks are to be continuously and progressively loving** (or: should constantly accept, and give yourselves to,) **one another, just as** (correspondingly as; to the same level as; in the sphere as) **I love, accept, and fully give Myself to, you folks so that you also may constantly** (or: would habitually) **love, accept, fully give yourselves to, and drive toward union with, one another.**

In the previous verse, Jesus addressed the remaining disciples as "**Little children**." This should be a clue to us about their mental/emotional/spiritual growth, at that time. What, near the end of His physical presence and time of instruction, He had evidently not given to them before, He now imparts to them. Before getting into what He gave them, let us examine the term that He used to describe the gift: *entolē*. This word is composed of a cognate of the word *telos* that is prefixed by the proposition, *en*. It is from the root idea of the preposition that I suggested "implanted; inward; impartation." The *Concordant Greek-English Concordance* gives the meaning of the Greek elements as: "in-finish."

The common rendering, "commandment," seems strange to the ears, when what follows is "**to love**." But even in a military setting, when a commander gives a command to his troops, his words are implanting into the minds of his troops the goal that he has in mind. He imparts his intent into their consciousness. And thus, on offer here are as follows:

a) **implanted goal** – which is continuous and progressive love to others;
b) inward, purposed directive – the Master speaking a "heart-matter" to His disciples;
c) impartation of a finished produce and destiny – He planted the Seed that would produce His fruit.

This was also actually true of the Law and the Sinai covenant. It was to be lived out, but come from the heart. Jer. 31:33 proclaimed, "I will put My law within them, and I shall write it on their heart." Isa. 59:21 explains His covenant as, "My Spirit which is on you and My words which I place in your mouth shall not be removed from your mouth..." Ezk. 11:19a promises, "Then I will give them another heart, and a new spirit shall I bestow within them..." Jer. 31 is represented in Heb. 8:10,

"'**progressively giving My Laws into their thought** (into that which goes through their mind; into their perception and comprehension), **and I shall progressively imprint them** (write or inscribe marks) **upon their hearts, and I shall continue being in and among them**."

Heb. 10:16 gives a second witness to Jer. 31. These simply give a different picture than what normally comes to mind when we read, or hear, the word "commandment." What Jesus says, here, is both relational and ontological; it speaks to the new creation and the new humanity.

The adjective "**new**," signifies "different from that which had been formerly" and "new in kind and character." It refers to the New Age of the Messiah, with life on a higher plain than before. This also calls to mind the literal meaning of *katallassō*, in 2 Cor. 5:19, "**progressively and completely transforming [the] aggregate of humanity to be other [than it is]**

(or: progressively bringing [the] ordered System into another level or state; repeatedly changing [the] universe to correspond with other [conditions; perceptions]; progressively altering [the] ordered arrangement of culture, religions, economy and government to be in line with another one)."

And now, to the **implanted goal**: "**to be continuously and progressively loving** (or: should constantly accept, and give yourselves to,) **one another**." However, He adds a qualifier: "**just as** (correspondingly as; to the same level as; in the sphere as) **I love, accept, and fully give Myself to, you folks**." Let us break down this qualifier:

a) **just as I love you folks** – so it behooves us to contemplate just HOW He loved/loves us;
b) correspondingly as He **accepts** them/us;
c) to the same level as He "**fully give Myself to**" them/us (as in Jn. 15:13, "soul-placing");
d) in the sphere as He **drove toward union with** them/us – in Spirit, in Truth and with Grace.

35. "**Within this, all people will come to know by personal experience and insight that you are** (or: continue being) **My disciples** (students; learners; apprentices) – **if you should constantly hold love centered in, and in union with, one another** (or: have acceptance which overcomes separation and drives toward union among yourselves)."

They will come to know it because they will both observe and experience the disciples' love in their actions, their attitudes, and by the spirit of Love which existentially emanates from them. As they intimately experience this through relationships with them, they will gain the "**insight that you are** (or: continue being) **My disciples** (students; learners; apprentices)." Notice another qualifier:

a) **if you should constantly hold love centered in, and in union with, one another**, or,
b) have acceptance which overcomes separation and drives toward union among yourselves.

Here 1 Cor. 13 comes to mind. The "qualifier," as I call it, simply means that this Love must be lived out.

36. **Simon Peter then says to Him, "Lord** (Master), **to what place are you proceeding to lead under** (or: where are you going)?" **Jesus decidedly answered, "To what place I proceed leading under** (or; departing) **you continue unable** (still have no power) **to follow Me now, but you will keep on following afterwards** (will subsequently proceed following).

Peter seems to ignore what Jesus had just said, and goes back to His announcement in vs. 33. Apparently Jesus' presence with them, and them being with Him, was more on his mind than the "**new implanted goal**" that He had just given to them. It is the same with us.

Jesus does not answer Peter's question, but rather restates what He had said before, in vs. 33b, above.

37. **Peter now says to Him, "Lord** (Master), **why** (through what situation or circumstance) **am I not presently able to keep on following you right now? I will continue placing my soul over You** (or: I will proceed to be laying [down] my soul-life, inner being, and conscious self for Your sake)."

Peter affirms his commitment to Jesus, and an intent to have the greater Love of which Jesus will speak in 15:13, below.

38. **Jesus continues in discerning reply, "You will continue to place your soul over Me** (or: lay you soul-life and self [down] for My sake)? **Most assuredly** (It is certainly true; Amen, amen; Count on it), **I now say to you, a cock** (or: rooster) **will** [other MSS: can] **under no circumstances crow until you will proceed to disown** (renounce; deny) **Me three times. Don't let the heart of the group be continually shaken or concerned** (unsettled; agitated; troubled; disturbed; distressed)."

The response that Jesus gave to Peter reveals WHY he was "**not presently able to keep on following [Him]**" at that time. The next admonition is normally placed at the beginning of the next chapter, but due to the subject matter of vss. 36-38 – the inability of the disciples to follow Jesus through His iminent ordeal, and rather the disowning, renouncing and denying, and then with all eventually forsaking Him, it seemed more appropriate to connect it to this verse. The construction of this imperative statement is odd, but He seems to still be talking to Peter. The verb is 3rd person, singular (which corresponds to the singular form of the direct object, "**heart**"), passive, in the imperative voice. But the personal pronoun is plural – referring to the whole group. Thus, I rendered it, "**the heart of the group**." Peter would lead the denial and abandonment of Jesus; he would also lead the group not to let their hearts (or their corporate heart) to be "**continually shaken or concerned** (unsettled; agitated; troubled; disturbed; distressed)." The next chapter begins with His teaching about trusting God, and also trusting Him. Lu. 22 reports a similar statement, by Jesus:

> 31. **"Simon, O Simon! Look, and consider. The adversary** (or: opponent; *satan*; = Jewish leaders?) **makes** (or: made) **a request** [to God; cf Job 1:9-11; 2:4-5] **concerning you men: to winnow [you folks] as grain!**
> 32. **"But I Myself urgently asked [God] concerning you, [Simon], to the end that your trust, allegiance and faithfulness would not leave from out of [you]** (or: default; = give out). **And so at some point, you yourself, upon turning around, make your brothers immovable** (or: stabilize and establish your fellow members [of God's Family])."

Chapter 14

1. **"You folks are constantly trusting and believing into and then continue faithful unto God; you are also progressively trusting and believing on into Me**
> (or, as an imperative: Keep on believing and putting faith into the midst of God, and also keep on putting your trust, confidence and loyalty into Me). [cf 2 Cor. 5:1-2, 4, 6, 8]

Having just spoken a word of peace and ease to Peter, for the entire group (13:38b, above), Jesus now affirms their allegiance to God, as well as their constant life of trust of, and belief in, God. And then He goes on to affirm their progressive trusting and believing into Him. This reading comes from the form of the verbs in these statements functioning as a present tense, indicative. However, these same forms can also function as a present tense, imperative. This latter reading is given in the parenthetical expansion. As imperatives, He is giving them parallel directives in regard to their trust (etc.): Just as their faith is to be put into the mist of God (and here, the picture is of shooting their arrows of trust, with God being the imagined Target that they want to penetrate), so also they must "keep on putting your trust, confidence and loyalty into [Jesus]."

The preposition "**unto; into; into the midst of**" is *eis*. In some Greek grammar books, it is symbolically graphed as an arrow, coming from outside of a circle, and entering into the midst of the circle. Likewise, the preposition *en* (in; within the midst of; in union with; etc.) is graphed as a dot within the midst of the circle. The NT frequently uses both of these prepositions: they are both locational and relational – as well as other functions, dependent upon the contexts. *Eis*, used in this verse, primarily implies direction (i.e. destination of the "arrow") and movement, as well as final destination. To give the reader a mental picture is the reason for the renderings "into the midst of God" and "into Me." The idea of "penetration" is both relational and locational in the implied intent of the verb, when this preposition is used. Notice, then, the progression of the conflation of verb meanings and preposition functions in: "**are constantly trusting and believing into and then continue faithful unto**." The idea of movement (this is an active Life that we are called to live) can be seen in the less-conflated second statement that ends in "**progressively trusting and believing ON into**…" Our Life in the Kingdom of God describes movement ON INTO deeper and deeper experiences of God in Christ.

Dan Kaplan picked up the arrow metaphor (from my grammar explanation) and applied it to 8:56-58, above, and the "faith of Abraham" that was like an arrow shot from his spirit into the future, resulting in his being able to "see Christ's Day." This reminded us of a tapestry thread that began on one end of the picture, in the Beginning (the Alpha; the first Adam) and wove all the way through to the end of the picture/story, ending dead-center in the Target: the Last Adam (the Goal; the Omega; the End). Faith, trust and loyal obedience were a constant goal toward which Israel's story plodded through history, from its first creation (on Sinai) on into the new creation (Mt. Zion – Heb. 12:22-24) and the New Jerusalem (Rev. 21-22). When you see the whole tapestry, the Story becomes clear.

2. **"Within My Father's house** (or: household) **are many abodes** (staying places; dwelling places; homes; rooms). **Now if not, I would at once tell you folks, because I am progressively passing** (or: traveling) **along to prepare and make ready a place in you** (or: for you; with and among you folks).

His **Father's house** is the Temple (2:16-19, above). The "**many abodes** (staying places; dwelling places; homes; rooms)" are we, His body (1 Cor. 6:15-19; 2 Cor. 6:16). He was "**progressively passing** (or: traveling) **along to prepare and make ready a place in [them; us].**" Reading it this way, the many abodes were the many people who would be "places" for Him to live. The personal pronoun "you" is in the dative case, so on offer are other potential readings: "for you; with and among you folks." Now on the last two, "with/among," we have the witness of Rev. 21:3,

"**Consider! God's tent** (the Tabernacle of God) **[is] with mankind** (the humans), **'and He will continue living in a tent** (dwell in a Tabernacle) **with them, and they will continue being** (will constantly exist being) **His peoples, and God Himself will continue being with them.'**" [Lev. 26:11-12; Isa. 7:14; 8:8, 10; Jer. 31:33; Ezk. 37:27; 2 Chr. 6:18]

Paul seems to be referring to this topic, in 2 Cor. 5:1,

"**You see, we have seen, perceived and know that if our House – from the Tabernacle which was pitched on the Land – would at some point be dismantled** (or: that whenever our house, which is this tent upon the earth, should be loosed down), **we constantly have** (continuously hold; presently possess) **a dwelling structure or place** (a building for an abode; or: **a household**; = a family or a possession) **forth from out of the midst of God: an eonian act of building a roofed house** (or: a covered building for dwelling having qualities and character which pertain to the Age [of the Messiah]; a structure of edification for, and pertaining to, the ages) **– not made by hands** [cf Heb. 9:1-8, 11; Dan. 2:34, 45; Eph. 2:11; Col. 2:11] **– resident within the atmospheres** (or: in union with the heavens)." [cf 6:16, below; 1 Tim. 3:15; Heb. 9:24]

"**Preparing and making ready a place for [us]**" is also a beautiful picture. Having our own place, in Him, in His Father's House (or: household – another layer of meaning), satisfies the longing in our hearts to be rescued from exile, and returned to the Garden, in the new Eden. We see this place pictured as the New Jerusalem, with the names of people in its gates (Rev. 21:12) and on its foundations (Rev. 21:14).

The metaphor is both a "house," that has places, such as "dwelling places, or rooms," and it is also a "household," and in that sense, the word "**place**" can also signify "a position" in the household, or, an "opportunity." So these latter meanings can refer to functions, such as are described in Eph. 4:11-13, or grace-effects, such as are listed in 1 Cor. 12:8-10.

3. **"Even if I should journey on and prepare** (make suitable, fit and appropriate) **a place** (or: a spot; a position; a role) **in you folks** (or: with, among and for you), **I am now presently** (or: progressively; repeatedly; habitually) **going and coming again, and then, I will progressively take you folks in My arms and receive you to Myself, directing you toward Myself so as to be face to face with Me, to the end that where I, Myself, am** (or: exist) **you folks also can continue being** (or: would ongoingly exist).

First of all, He spoke these words to folks that were with Him at that time. He was not speaking about some "end-time second coming" off in the distant future (for which, sadly, many folks are still waiting, not enjoying His real presence, right now). Next, notice that the words "**going and coming**" (conflating the two meanings of *erchomai*) is in the present, indicative. He was saying that He was "**presently** (or: progressively; repeatedly; habitually) **going and coming**." I listed four potential functions of the present tense, including "presently," since the context implies imminent departure (Jn. 13:33), but also a coming **again** to "**take you folks in My arms and receive you to Myself**." He was saying that to them, not to someone else. But the idea of "habitual or repeated" going and returning can also include us into His pattern of activity. When He returned to them, He would be in an altered state of existence from having been resurrected. But the point that He was making was the end of His present, upcoming **journey**: His return to THEM!

The future progressive describes a beautiful, intimate scene: "**I will progressively take you folks in My arms and receive you to Myself, directing you toward Myself so as to be face to face with Me**." This clause conflates the meanings of the verb: **take in [one's] arms; receive**." Along with this is the conflation of the preposition: **to; direction toward; face-to-face; with**. When these are joined together, we see the touching picture of His personal, even emotional, return to them. What a promise, considering what they would soon experience.

So what about the purpose clause that ends this verse? His coming again was, "**to the end that where I, Myself, am** (or: exist) **you folks also can continue being** (or: would ongoingly exist)." What did He mean by that? As is our practice, we will answer that by insight from the NT authors, as they seem to apply. As usual, there are layers to the answer of this question. Notice that He did not say "where I, Myself, WILL be," but rather "**where I, Myself, am** (or: exist)." Now in vs. 10, below, He said,

"**it is continuously** (it constantly exists being) **I, Myself, within the midst of the Father**."
Since He would have known that they probably didn't get this, in vs. 11 He said,

"**[it is] I within the midst of the Father**."
In verse 20 He gives an expanded explanation:

"**you yourselves will personally be coming to progressively realize and then be knowing that I Myself [am; exist] within the midst of My Father, and you folks within the midst of and in union with Me, and I Myself within the midst of and in union with you people**."
So He was speaking, first of all, of a new sphere of existence: within Him, and within the Father. That was the Target to which the "arrow" of vs. 1 was aiming. He will give a metaphorical explanation in the next chapter, where He speaks of Himself being the Vine, and they are His branches – if they "**remain** (dwell; abide; stay) **within and in union with [Him]**" (15:4a, below), that is, take up residence in His Father's House (which He, and they, are).

Paul informed those in the Province of Galatia that they lived in a new existence. In Gal. 3, he wrote:

26. **For you folks are all** [i.e., Jew and non-Jew; male and female; slave and freeman] **God's sons, through the faithfulness located and resident within Christ Jesus** (or: by means of the trust in union with an Anointing from Jesus; [*p*46: through Jesus Christ's faithfulness])!

(or: You see, all you folks [who are] **located and centered in Christ Jesus** exist being sons of God, by means of that Faithful One!)

27. **For you see** (or: It follows that) **as many of you folks as were immersed into Christ, at once clothed yourselves with Christ** (or: were plunged into so as to be enveloped by, then saturated and permeated with, Anointing – or, the Anointed One – instantly entered within and put on [the/an] Anointing)!

We read in Rom. 6:3-4 he spoke of being "**immersed** (or: were at one point soaked or baptized) **into Christ Jesus**.... **thus also we can walk around** (or: we also should likewise conduct ourselves and order our behavior) **within newness of life**." And then, in Rom. 6:18, we find that,

"**Now since we died together with Christ, we are continuously believing** (relying; trusting) **that we will also continue living together in Him**."
Rom. 8:1 refers to "**those within Christ Jesus**." And he used apocalyptic language and a seat/throne metaphor in Eph. 2:6 to picture this same new situation:

"He jointly roused and raised (or: suddenly awakens and raises) **[us] up, and caused [us] to sit** (or: seats [us]; = enthroned [us]) **together in union with, and among, the heavenly people, and within the things situated upon** [thus, above] **the heavens."**

Paul was speaking of a new existence that he and the called-out communities were at that time experiencing.

Now after His resurrection, He came to them many times, and in Acts 1:9, "**a cloud from underneath [Him] took and received Him.**" Now Heb. 12:1 speaks of their "**continuously having such a big cloud-mass** (figure for a dense throng) **of witnesses** (spectators; folks bearing testimony; people with evidence) **environing us** (lying around for us and [they] themselves surrounding and encompassing us)." And then Heb. 12:22-24 describes their (and our) present location:

22. **But to the contrary, you folks have approached so that you are now at Mount Zion – even in a city of a continuously living God; in "Jerusalem upon heaven"** [Heb. 11:16]
(or: in a Jerusalem pertaining to and having the character and qualities of a superior, or added, heaven and atmosphere; or: in Jerusalem [situated] upon, and comparable to, the atmosphere; centered in a heavenly-imposed Jerusalem) – **also among ten-thousands** (or: myriads) **of agents and messengers** (people with a/the message)**:**
23. **[that is] in** (or: to) **an assembly of an entire people** (or: an assembly of all; a universal convocation) **and in** (or: to) **a summoning forth** (or: a called-out and gathered community) **of firstborn folks having been copied** (from-written, as from a pattern; or: enrolled; registered) **within [the; or: various] atmospheres** (or: heavens), **and in** (or: to; with) **God, a Judge** (an Evaluator and Decider) **of all mankind, even among** (or: to; with) **spirits of just folks** (or: breath-effects from those who are fair and equitable and in right relationship within the Way pointed out) **having been brought to the destined goal** (perfected; finished; matured; made complete), [cf Rev. 3:12; 21:1-2; Eph. 2:6; Phil. 3:20; Rev. 14:1-5; Ex. 4:22; Gal. 3:19]
24. **and in** (or: to) **Jesus, a Medium** (or: an agency; an intervening substance; a middle state; one in a middle position; a go-between; an Umpire; a Mediator) **of a new and fresh** (young; recently-born) **arrangement** (covenant; settlement; a deposit which moves throughout in every direction; a placing through the midst; a will and testament), **and to and in blood of sprinkling, and to One continuously speaking something superior to** (or: stronger and better than) **Abel.**
[cf Mat. 17:1-5; Gal. 4:22-26; Rev. 21:1-2; 9b-22:5; Jn. 4:21; Ps. 46:4; 132:13; Isa. 28:16; 33:5]

In Rev. 21:10b, John was shown the New Jerusalem descending out of the atmosphere, from God. This is where we "**can continue being** (or: should ongoingly exist).

4. **"And to the place under, where I Myself am progressively leading the way** (or: where I am submissively going), **you have seen and know the Way** (or: path; road)."

They had seen the Way and knew the Path, because this is what He was, and is, as He explained in vs. 6, below. Another understanding of **the Way** was suggested by Jesus' words in vs. 3, above: "**directing you toward Myself so as to be face to face with Me.**" This in turn calls to Paul's picture in 2 Cor. 3:18,
"**But we all, ourselves – having a face that has been uncovered and remains unveiled – being folks who by a mirror are continuously observing, as ourselves, the Lord's glory, are presently being continuously and progressively transformed into the very same image and form, from glory unto glory – in accord with and exactly as – from [the] Lord's Breath-effect.**"

It is the Way of Transformation. It is the Way of the Life of Christ, where His Light illumines our darkness. It is the Way of placing our soul upon another to give shelter, healing and life (15:13, below). It is the Journey back into the midst of God (Rom. 11:36), and as vs. 6, below reveals, the Way is Him. He is both the Path into, and the destiny which is, the New Creation.

5. **Thomas then says to Him, "O Lord** (Master), **we have not seen nor do we know under what place You are leading the way** (or: where You are humbly going), **so how are we able to have seen and** [other MSS: how do we] **know the way?"**

They have not yet seen because they are still blind. They are still the moist soil that has been formed to be a human, but the Breath-effect from God has not yet given them Life.

6. **Jesus then says to him, "I, Myself, AM** (exist being) **the Way** (or: Path), **the Truth** (the Reality) **and the Life** (or: = I am the way to really live). **No one is presently going to, or progressively coming toward, the Father, except through Me** (through means of Me, or, through the midst of Me).

Rather than seeing this statement as a simplistic religious formula, or making it the basis of the Christian religion, let us pause and consider the context, the import of the second statement, and the verse that follows. First of all, observe that this is another I AM statement. He is the Logos that was made flesh. His is the Door of the sheepfold. He is the Ideal Shepherd. He is the source of Living Water. He is the Resurrection and the Life. He is the Reality of all these metaphors.

As **the Way**, He enables us to journey on into the midst of the Father. The Father is the goal, our destiny. As the Door, we pass **through** Him – and All that He is – to **come toward the Father**. But also, through means of Him (through means of the Christ Event) we are "**presently going to the Father**." As **the Way**, He is "**the True and Genuine Light which** (or: Who) **is continuously** (repeatedly; progressively) **enlightening** (giving light to) **every person** (or: all humanity) **continuously** (repeatedly; progressively; constantly; one after another) **coming into the world**" (1:9, above).

As **the Truth**, He is that to which the shadow (Heb. 10:1; Col. 2:17) of the old covenant pointed. The word Truth also means "the Reality."

And just as He is the Resurrection (11:25, above) and the Life of the Age of the Messiah. He embodies that of which the vision of the valley of dry bones prophesied (Ezk. 37:1-14), and thus – with all of this – He is Israel (Ex. 4:22), and the Seed of the woman (Gen. 3:15); He is the Son of David, and the eschatological Deliverer – the Son of the Human (Dan. 7), the Last Adam (1 Cor. 15). In the next chapter we will find that He is the Vine, out of whom grow the branches of humanity. He is all of the Messianic metaphors, but He embodies and represents the Pathway to the Father. The Father is the emphasis of what He is saying here – even Philip got that (vs. 8, below)! And He devotes the next verse to the Reality of personally, intimately, experientially and progressively knowing and recognizing **the Father**.

7. **"Since you men have personally and experientially known Me** (or: If you folks had insight of Me or were acquainted with Me), **you also will continue personally and experientially knowing and perceiving My Father** [other MSS: you would likely have seen and now know (or: perceive) My Father, as well]. **And so from right now** (this moment) **you are intimately, experientially and progressively knowing and recognizing Him** (or: you folks continue gaining insight of Him), **and have seen Him."**

You see, Jesus was, and is, **the Way** to **see the Father**. Look (2 Cor. 3:18) at Jesus, the Son, the Glory, and **see** the Father. Also, know Jesus and you know the Father. He came to open the "spiritual" eyes of the blind. Jesus was also **the Life of the Father** (Jn. 5:26). And speaking of **Life**, Paul instructs us that, "**the Spirit and Breath-effect [is] Life, BECAUSE OF an eschatological act of justice**" (Rom. 8:10), where,

> "**God was existing within Christ** (God was and continued being centered in, and in union with [the] Anointed One) **progressively and completely transforming [the] aggregate of humanity** (or: world) **to be other [than it is], in Himself, not accounting to them the results and effects of their falls to the side** (their trespasses and offenses)" (2 Cor. 5:19).

We can all know Him and see Him because,

"**He drags us out of danger** (or: rescued us) **forth from out of the midst of the authority of the Darkness and changes [our] position** (or: transported [us], thus, giving [us] a change of standing, and transferred [us]) **into the midst of the kingdom and reign of the Son of His love**" (Col. 1:13).

Notice Who did/does the dragging here: Col. 1:12 instructs us that it is, "**the Father: the One calling you**… **within the Light**," Who then does the dragging and transporting. You see, the Light shines on everyone (each in his or her own time – 1 Cor. 15:23), and from the mist of that Light calls us (e.g., Acts 9:3-4). All the divine metaphors in this Gospel express the "I AM." The Father and the Son are One (Jn. 10:30), which equates to *the Shema* (Deut. 6:4).

8. **Philip then says to Him, "O Lord** (Master), **show us the Father** (point the Father out to us), **and it is continuing to be sufficient** (adequate; enough) **for us."**

Clearly, Philip was still blind. He might as well have said, "Show us the Light."

9. **Jesus is then saying to him, "I continue being** (I am) **with you folks so much time, and you have not come to intimately and experientially be aware of, know and recognize Me, Philip? The person having discerned and seen Me has seen, and now perceives, the Father! How are you now saying, 'Show us the Father'?**

These are amazing questions, framing an astounding statement that, "**The person having discerned and seen ME has seen, and now perceives, the Father!**" But also, in His first question to Philip, He did not say, "have you not recognized the Father," but rather "**have you not come to intimately and experientially be aware of, know and recognize ME**"? That is like saying, "Don't you know who I AM?"

10. **"Are you not continuing to trust and presently believe that it is continuously** (it constantly exists being) **I, Myself, within the midst of the Father, and the Father within the midst of Me** (or: I Myself centered in union with the Father, and the Father centered in union with Me)**? The gush-effects** (results of the flow; or: utterances, declarations, words spoken) **which I, Myself, am constantly saying to you men, I am not constantly saying from Myself. But the Father, continuously dwelling and remaining** (abiding; staying) **within the midst of Me, is habitually** (constantly) **doing** (making; constructing; creating; forming; performing; producing) **His works** (actions; deeds).

The question that Jesus asks Philip, in the first part of this verse, is repeated as an affirmation within the imperative that opens vs. 11, below. When a statement concerning Reality and Truth is repeated, its importance is underlined for us. What He said is obviously mystical, and was probably hard for Philip, and others who may have heard it, to either believe or understand. But He expected both of these responses from them, so how are we to perceive His meaning? Since He had become human on our behalf (due to God's love for us – Jn. 3:16), and He expected us to follow Him, it seems reasonable to expect for us to have to do what He did in order to enjoy this kind of relationship with the Father, and be His sons. So, what did He do? Paul tells us, in Phil. 2:7,

"**He empties Himself** (or: removed the contents of Himself; made Himself empty), **receiving** (or: taking; accepting) **a slave's form** (external shape; outward mold), **coming to be** (or: birthing Himself) **within an effect of humanity's** (mankind's; people's) **likeness.**"

Did He do this so that He could, as a human, be filled with the Father? We expect that this is part of the reason. But this was also the path to His becoming the Resurrection, and the Life (11:25, above). This act of self-emptying is also the probable reason for the terms of discipleship, as given in Mat. 16:24-25,

"**If anyone continues intending** (purposing; wanting) **to come on behind Me, let him at once completely say, 'No,' to, deny and disown himself, and then in one move lift up his execution stake, and after that proceed to be by habit continuously following after** (with) **Me! You see, whoever may intend to keep his soul-life safe** (rescue himself; preserve the conscious life that he is living) **will continue loosing-it-away and destroying it. Yet whoever**

can loose-away and even destroy his soul-life (the consciousness of self) **on My account, he will continue finding it**."

This implies that Jesus was already carrying His execution stake, and that those who would follow Him already had their execution stakes (He did NOT say, "Come here; I have an execution stake for you"). Loosing-away the old Adam consciousness allows us to be filled with the new Adam consciousness (which is the awareness of the Father being in us, etc.). The cruciform life is the Way of self-emptying.

But now let us focus on "**I, Myself, within the midst of the Father, and the Father within the midst of Me**" – for this is how "**it is**" with Him, and in that same way, it is to be with us. This condition and existential reality is a kind of "mutual habitation." It corresponds to how both Jesus and Paul described our new existence as both us in Christ (like the branch in the Vine – Jn. 15) and Christ is us (e.g., Col. 1:27). But Paul also used the analogy of a man being joined to a woman as a picture of us being joined to Christ, with the result being that,

> "**the person continually joining himself** (or: being habitually glued in intimate union; in himself being continuously welded) **to** (or: in; with) **the Lord exists being one spirit** (or: one Breath-effect; one Attitude; one Spirit)" (1 Cor. 6:17).

This new relationship will now allow us to ask of others the same question that Jesus asked of Philip. And also, we will be able to say what Jesus said to Philip, in vs. 9, above: "The person having discerned and seen me has seen, and now perceives, the Father." But in order to be able to say this, we must be living in constant union with Christ. And that requires making a place for Him, and remaining conscious of His being present with us, His Temple.

Notice that in the last statement He instructs them that "**the Father, continuously dwelling and remaining** (abiding; staying) **within the midst of Me, is habitually** (constantly) **doing** (making; constructing; creating; forming; performing; producing) **His works** (actions; deeds)." And then, in vs. 12, below, He informs them (and us) that they, and we, will proceed doing the works that He was/is doing. It follows that for this to happen the Father must continue dwelling within us (and that is the point of Paul referring to us as being God's Temple, i.e., His Home).

When He said, "**The gush-effects** (results of the flow; or: utterances, declarations, words spoken) **which I, Myself, am constantly saying to you men, I am not constantly saying from Myself**," He was indicating that the Father was the Source of the Flow which was being expressed by the Incarnate Logos. Recalling what was said of the Logos, in Jn. 1:1-3, we may conclude that these "**gush-effects** (results of the flow; or: utterances, declarations, words spoken)" were the Beginning (Jn. 1:1) of the New Creation (2 Cor. 5:17; Gal. 6:15; Eph. 2:10-22; 4:17-24; Col. 1:15-23; 3:1-17; Rev. 21:5). So let us move on...

11. "**Keep on trusting and progressively believe Me** (or: by Me and in Me,) **that [it is] I within the midst of the Father, and the Father within the midst of Me** (or: that I [am] in union with the Father, and the Father [is] in union with Me). **Otherwise** (or: But if not), **keep trusting and constantly believe Me** (or: in Me) **because of the works** (actions; deeds) **themselves.**

So what is our part? "**Keep on trusting and progressively believe [Him]**." And what is the content of this trust and progressive belief? "**that [it is] I within the midst of the Father, and the Father within the midst of Me** (or: that I [am] in union with the Father, and the Father [is] in union with Me)."

Now this is a little different than the usual evangelistic fare that is served to "the lost." Yet Jesus seems to make this a central part of "trusting and believing." Remember, He said it twice (vs. 14 was only stated once). You see, vs. 12, below, has other things in mind than "going to heaven, or escaping the alternative: their pagan doctrine of 'hell.'"

But Jesus is not a demanding Master. He offers them an alternative: "**keep trusting and constantly believe Me** (or: in Me) **because of the works** (actions; deeds) **themselves**." The first imperative involves a higher level of spiritual perception; the second one involves natural reasoning (such as Nicodemus offered, in 3:2, above). But recall that Jesus told Nicodemus that something more than the natural reasoning of the Pharisees was required for entrance into God's reign, and participation in His sovereign activities (cf 3:5, above). So this second offer is for those not yet "born back up, again, from above" (3:7, above).

12. **"It is certainly true** (Most assuredly; Amen, amen), **I am saying to you folks, the person habitually trusting and progressively believing into Me, the works** (actions; deeds) **which I Myself am constantly doing** (habitually performing; progressively making, constructing, creating, forming) **that person also will proceed doing** (performing; making; creating; producing), **and he will progressively be doing and producing greater than these, because I Myself am progressively journeying** (constantly going from one place to another) **toward** (or: facing; face-to-face with) **the Father.** [Cf 1:1]

Now this is that to which He had called these folks to be disciples. They (and we, if we have been awakened to this call) were called to continue His (and thus, the Father's) **works** (actions; deeds). It was not a call to go off to heaven, but to be the Body of Christ in the earth.

Now many have wondered, "How could anyone be doing greater works than Christ did?" That is a reasonable question. Jesus did not explain what He meant by this, so we are once again faced with some ambiguity. But we suggest that He actually gave the answer to this question in Jn. 12:24,
> "**unless the grain of wheat** (or: kernel of corn; = seed of an agricultural crop), **upon falling into the earth** (the ground; the field), **should die, it by itself continues remaining alone. Yet if it should die, it proceeds to bear much fruit** (= it produces a harvest of many grains, or, seeds)."

We posit that His 1st century followers were the first crop of "many grains (seeds)" that resulted from His teaching, and then further, from His death, burial and resurrection – followed by His Spirit anointing them on the Day of Pentecost. These would all follow Him, being impregnated by His Logos, and would then carry His offspring to be planted in the fertile soil of others, just as He was implanting His Logos in them. This multiplication will not come to an end, but will likely eventually spread throughout the universe (as it possibly is now doing, via those who have passed from this life – who knows; why should we limit out thinking to centuries-old doctrines that had only suppositions for the activities in the next existence?).

This would all happen, "**because I Myself am progressively journeying** (constantly going from one place to another) **toward** (or: facing; face-to-face with) **the Father.**" He was completing His circuit: He came from out of the midst of God, passed on through the midst of God, and was now returning back into the midst of God (Rom. 11:36). And because He functioned as the Eschatos (Last) Adam, within Him were all those of the first Adam (1 Cor. 15:44-49), in Seed/Ovum form. You see, Paul informed us of a secret, in Col. 1:15-17, 19-20.
> 15. **It is [this Son] Who is the Image** (portrait; the Exact Formed Likeness; the Figure and Representation; visible likeness and manifestation) **of the not-seen God** (or: the unable to be seen God; the invisible God), **the Firstborn of all creation**
>> (or: of every creature; or: of every framing and founding; of every act of settling from a state of disorder and wildness; or: pertaining to the whole creation; or: = the Inheritor of all creation Who will also assume authority over and responsibility for every creature [note: this is the duty of the firstborn]),
> 16. **because within Him was created the whole** (or: in union with Him everything is founded and settled, is built and planted, is brought into being, is produced and established; or: within the midst of Him all things were brought from chaos into order) – **the things within the skies and atmospheres, and the things upon the earth** (or: those [situations, conditions and/or people] in the heavens and on the land); **the visible things, and the unseen** (or: unable to be seen; invisible) **things: whether thrones** (seats of power) **or lordships** (ownership systems) **or governments** (rulers; leadership systems; sovereignties) **or authorities – the whole has been**

created and all things continue founded, put in order and stand framed through means of Him, and [proceeds, or were placed] into Him (or: = He is the agent and goal of all creation). 17. **And He is before** (prior to; or: maintains precedence of) **all things and all people, and the whole has** (or: all things have) **been placed together and now continues to jointly-stand** (stands cohesively; is made to have a co-standing) **within the midst of and in union with Him**….

19. **because WITHIN Him all – the entire contents** (the result of that which fills everything; all the effect of the full measure [of things]) **– delights to settle down and dwell as in a house** (or: because He approved all the fullness [of all existence] to permanently reside within Him) [*cf* 2:9] 20. **and THROUGH Him at once to transfer the all** (the whole; = all of existential creation), **away from a certain state to the level of another which is quite different**
> (or: to change all things, bringing movement away from being down; to reconcile all things; to change everything from estrangement and alienation to friendship and harmony and move all), **INTO Him – making** (constructing; forming; creating) **peace** (harmonious joining) **through the blood of His cross** (execution stake/pole)**: through Him, whether the things upon the earth** (or: land) **or the things within the atmospheres and heavens!**

Now THAT is the Gospel!

13. **"And because** [reading *hoti an*] **you would have sought in petition within My Name** (or [reading *ho ti an*]: Also whatever you could seek in petition in union with My Name), **I will proceed doing it: to the end that the Father can** (could; would) **be glorified** (recognized; be given a good reputation, a good opinion and a manifestation which incites praise; have an assumed appearance) **within the Son.**

In the oldest MSS, there was no separation between words in the texts. The two (or, three) words that follow the conjunction, "**And**/Also," are an example of occasional ambiguity that faces the translator. The next thing to consider, is how this verse has grown out of the previous verse of "**the works** (actions; deeds) **which I Myself am constantly doing** (habitually performing; progressively making, constructing, creating, forming) **that person also will proceed doing** (performing; making; creating; producing)." It is from this context – and because He has left them and returned to be face-to-face with the Father – that He spoke of them "**seeking [for something] in petition**."

Furthermore is the stipulation that they would make the request "**within My Name** (or: in union with My Name)." In that time and region of the world, a person's name represented who he or she was, their place in that particular society, and in the case of someone representing that person, it could mean that the representative had the authority of that person (like having the person's signet ring). So the Name of the Lord implied His character, His mission and His authority. Dan Kaplan also instructs us that "His WILL is wrapped up in His Name." This verse does not speak to access for personal advantage. It does not speak to just saying His Name. It involves relationship. Jesus said this to His disciples, and these petitions would be expected to relate to their mission as carrying on His work in this world.

This is an important topic, for He speaks of it in the next verse, as well as in chapters 15:6, 16; 16:23-26, and we also find it in Mat. 21:22. Also, recall what He stipulated in 5:19, above,
> "**the Son continues unable to do anything from Himself** (or: the Son, from Himself, habitually has no power to be doing anything [independently]) **except He can** (or: unless He should) **continue seeing something the Father is in process of doing** (or: if not something He may presently observe the Father making, producing, constructing, or creating), **for what things That One may likely be progressively doing** (making; constructing; creating; producing), **these things, also, the Son is likewise habitually doing** (or: is in like manner constantly making, producing, creating, constructing)."

This would create parameters for what things that the disciples should petition Him, or the Father. In 1 Jn. 5:14 we read another insight on this topic:

"**if we ourselves should keep on asking or persistently request anything in line with** (or: down from; in the sphere of; that accords with) **His will** [A reads: Name], **He is continuously hearing us.**"

A negative view of human petitions is explained in Jas. 4:3,

"**You continue asking** (requesting), **and yet you continue not receiving** (taking [it] in hand; grasping [it]) **because you are asking inappropriately** (worthlessly requesting; or: = asking for a wrong purpose) **to the intent that you may spend** (= waste) **it in** (or: on) **your pleasures.**"

Kaplan has also pointed us to Mat. 6:33,

"**So you people be habitually and constantly seeking God's reign** (or: sovereign activity and influence; kingdom) **and the eschatological deliverance of fairness and equity from Him, as well as His justice and rightwised behavior in the Way, which He has pointed out in covenant participation that has been set right – and all these things will be added to you!**"

Jesus gave this implanted goal to His audience after addressing the topics of concern for having food, drink and apparel. In vs. 32 He reminded them that, "**the ethnic multitudes** (the nations; the Gentile people groups) **are habitually in eager pursuit of these things – spending all of their energy in seeking them.**" – as they still are, today. These "things" are not the objects of the **petitions** to which He refers, here in vs. 13.

The final qualifying characteristic for our petitions must be: "**to the end that the Father can** (could; would) **be glorified** (recognized; be given a good reputation, a good opinion and a manifestation which incites praise; have an assumed appearance) **within the Son.**"

He "**will proceed doing it**" presuming that it brings glory within the Son, but also, because it is done within His Name, this very realm (i.e., in the Name) of activity brings glory to the Father.

14. "**If you folks should petition Me for something** (or: anything) **within, in union with, and centered in, My Name, I Myself will proceed performing** (doing; making; creating; forming) **this.**

Once again, we see emphasis by means of repetition: He wants them to really understand this. Also, recall His words to the multitudes, in Mat. 7:7,

"**Be habitually requesting** (or: Keep on asking), **and it** (or: He) **will proceed being given to** (or: for; in) **you people. Be habitually seeking** (or: Keep on searching and trying to find), **and you folks will repeatedly find. Be repeatedly** (or: Keep on) **knocking, and it** (or: He) **will habitually be opened up to** (or: for; in) **you.**"

But notice the continued personal involvement that He affirms here: "**I Myself will proceed performing** (doing; making; creating; forming) **this.**" Now to more fully understand this verse, we must perceive what He is saying in the next three verses...

15. "**If you folks are habitually loving and accepting Me** (or, as a subjunctive: would continue urging toward union with, and fully giving yourselves to, Me), **you folks WILL continue observing** [other MSS, subjunctive: you folks can or should observe (or: note and keep watch over; guard and preserve; keep in view; hold in custody); other MSS, the imperative: Keep in view and take note of] **My implanted goals** (impartations of the finished product within; inward directives; interior purposes and destiny),

Paul Tillich's definition for love (*agapē*), here, "urging toward union," spoke to Dan Kaplan of the purpose of marriage, as seen in Gen. 2:24, "Therefore a man… clings to his wife, and they become one flesh." Paul cites this vs. in Eph. 5:31, when speaking of Christ and the called-out folks. Eph. 5:25 gave an admonition based upon this Christ/called-out relationship, as a practical analogy:

"**O husbands, be constantly loving, and urging to unity with, [your] wives** (or: **Men**, continue giving yourselves for and **accepting the women**), **accordingly and correspondingly as the Christ also loved** (or: to the degree that, and commensurately as, the Anointed One loves and

unambiguously accepts) **the called-out community, and gave Himself up** (or: commits and transfers Himself over) **in behalf of** (for the sake of; **over** [the situation of]) **her**."
We are all called to live-out the Reality of the Good News.

In regard to His "**implanted goals**," Dan referred to God's original goal for humanity, as given in Gen. 1:26-30. In our discussion, what also came to mind was the end that God had in view, in Rev. 21-22, the new atmosphere (or: heaven) and the new people (Eph. 2:14-18; the new land/earth), the New Jerusalem (Christ's Bride), and the new creation of 2 Cor. 5:17, and:

> "**Consider this! I am presently making all things new** (or: habitually creating everything [to be] new and fresh; progressively forming [the] whole anew; or, reading *panta* as masculine: I am periodically making **all humanity** new, and progressively, one after another, producing and creating **every person** anew, while constantly constructing all people fresh and new, i.e., continuously renewing **everyone**)!" (Rev. 21:5).

All this He has **imparted** into our hearts as we live in His kingdom of "**eschatological deliverance of fair and equitable dealing which brings justice and right relationship in the Way pointed out** (being turned in the right direction; rightwisedness; also = covenant inclusion and participation), **peace and harmony from the joining and joy within set-apart Breath-effect**" (Rom. 14:17).

Meeting the requirement of the first clause leads to the fulfillment of the second clause. The form of the verb serves as a present indicative (**are HABITUALLY loving and accepting**) or as a present subjunctive, where additional meanings of the verb are on offer: "would continue urging toward union with, and fully giving yourselves." In either reading, in order to "**CONTINUE observing My implanted goals**" there needs to be Love operating within His followers. Loving – accepting others despite their demonic state of being; urging toward union with others by fully giving oneself to another – IS the implanted goal, the impartation of the finished product, within us, and the inward directive that drives us toward our purpose and destiny. Here, Dan pointed to another "inner directive" for us:

> "**Within the midst of everything, be continuously giving thanks** (or: In union with all people, be habitually expressing the goodness of grace and the well-being from favor), **for this is God's intent** (will, purpose) **unto you in Christ Jesus** (or: [proceeding] into the midst of you folks, in union with [the] Anointed Jesus)" (1 Thes. 5:18).

All this is the sphere of being "**in His Name**" which He referenced in vss. 13b-14.

We should note that the object of the verb, in the first clause, is Jesus. You see, if you love Him, you are loving the One that sent Him. Did it take God incarnating Himself in order for Israel to be able to do what was promised in Deut. 6:4?

> "**You will be constantly loving** (fully giving yourself to; urging toward reunion with) **[the] Lord** [= Yahweh] **your God from out of your whole** (= entire) **heart, and in union with your whole soul** (or: consciousness, self and soul-life), **and in union with and in the midst of your whole** (= entire) **strength, and in union with and within your whole** (= entire) **mind** (intellect; comprehension; understanding)." (Lu. 10:27; [also: Lev. 19:18])

Here, Jesus did not say, "Love God," or "Love Yahweh," but rather, be "**habitually loving and accepting Me**." As Moses functioned as a god to Pharaoh (Ex. 7:1), so Jesus was the "one medium and mediator between God and humans, a human, Anointed Jesus" (1 Tim. 2:5). Jesus gave God a face and a personality, and through Him we have come to love the Father.

As can be seen, the verb of the second clause has different MS traditions: some as a future tense (**you folks WILL continue observing**), others an aorist subjunctive (you folks can or should observe), and others an aorist imperative (Keep in view and take note of). Through these various renderings, on offer is the semantic range of the verb for your consideration. But there is more, for He continues...

16. **"and I Myself will continue asking** (making a request of) **the Father, and He will proceed to be giving another Helper** (One called alongside to give assistance, relief, comfort and encouragement;

Paraclete), **of like kind, to you folks – to the end that He** (or: It) **can continue being** [other MSS: would be constantly remaining and dwelling] **with you folks on into the midst of this** (or: the) **Age –**

In order to do what He promised in vss. 13b and 14, and with explanation of the sphere of "within His Name," in vs. 15, He now instructs them how He "**will proceed doing it**." He "**will continue asking** (making a request of) **the Father**," and then the Father "**will proceed to be giving another Helper of like kind to [them]**." The Paraclete will be the means and sphere of "**performing** (doing; making; creating; forming)" in response to their petition (vs. 14). Up to this point, Jesus had been their Helper (Paraclete), but the Father would send them another Helper, which/who is the Spirit of what Jesus declares Himself to be: the Truth (vs. 6, above; vs. 17, below). Can you see why it was a "**Helper of like kind**"?

Now this Paraclete would "**continue being** [other MSS: would be constantly remaining and dwelling] **with you folks on into the midst of this** (or: the) **Age**." After His resurrection, and His returning to be face-to-face with the Father, Jesus Himself sent this Paraclete to them:

> "**I Myself am now progressively sending forth the Promise from out of the midst of, and from, My Father** (or: am out from within repeatedly sending forth My Father's promise, as an Emissary; [with other MSS: From where I now am, I now continuously send off the Promise, **which is My Father**]) **upon you people**" (Lu. 24:49a).

Having done this, on the Day of Pentecost, they were able to "**clothe [themselves] with** (or: enter within the midst of) **power and ability from out of the midst of exaltation**" (Lu. 24:49b; *cf* Eph. 2:6).

17. "**the Spirit of the Truth** (or: the spirit and breath of reality; the Breath-effect and Attitude which is this Reality), **whom** (or: which) **the System** (world; ordered arrangement of religion, politics and culture; the system of domination) **has no power** (is not able) **to receive, because it is not habitually gazing upon It** (or: Him) **with contemplation** (continually viewing and watching it with attentive interest), **nor is it coming to intimately and experientially know It** (or: Him). **Yet YOU folks are progressively knowing It** (or: Him) **by intimate experience, because It** (or: He) **is continuously dwelling** (remaining; abiding) **alongside you folks – in your presence – and It** (or: He) **continuously exists** (or: is; [other MSS: will continue being]) **within, in union with, and among you people.** [*Cf* 2 Cor. 5:5]

Before diving into this verse, let us just ponder the three renderings of the first clause, which are on offer:

a) **the Spirit of the Truth** (this would be the Spirit of Jesus, or the Spirit of Christ – Rom. 8:9);
b) the spirit and breath of reality (this would be the spirit of God's reign and the Life of Christ);
c) the Breath-effect and Attitude which is this Reality (i.e., God in His Reality of the new creation).

The domination System of government, culture, religion, etc., cannot receive this Spirit – just like they could not receive Jesus, the embodiment of the Truth. These realms have "**no power** (are not able)." Why? Well,

a) "**because it is not habitually gazing upon It** (or: Him) **with contemplation** (continually viewing and watching it with attentive interest);" *Cf* 2 Cor. 3:18
b) "**nor is it coming to intimately and experientially know It** (or: Him)."

You see, the Breath-effect of the Truth IS, the Way the Truth and the Life.

But Jesus had good news for them: They were "**progressively knowing It** (or: Him) **by intimate experience, because It** (or: He) **is continuously dwelling** (remaining; abiding) **alongside [them] – in [their] presence**." Now recall the immersion of Jesus, by John the immerser:

> "**[the time and situation] had come to be [for] the heaven to be opened back up again, and [for] the Set-apart Breath-effect** (or: the Holy Spirit) **to descend – in bodily perceptual appearance as a dove – upon Him...**" (Lu. 3: 21,-22a; *cf* Mat. 3:16b; Jn. 1:32)

The Paraclete was remaining and dwelling upon Jesus. You see, it was the Spirit of the Truth that had Anointed Jesus, making Him the Messiah (the Anointed One). Without realizing it, It (He) had been

255

continuously dwelling with them, in their presence – within and upon Jesus. Not only that, "**It** (or: He) **continuously exists** (or: is; [other MSS: will continue being]) **within, in union with, and among you people.**" Notice the two MS traditions: I accept the first, and affirm the second. There is no need for any doctrinal or theological arguments concerning this. This is simply Good News.

18. **"I will not be leaving you abandoned or be sending you off as orphaned ones** (or: folks without family). **I am repeatedly** (or: habitually) **and now progressively coming to** (or: face to face with; toward) **you people.**

The first statement is a beautiful promise. The second statement would have filled them with a glorious expectation. And since Jesus is still the same, today (Heb. 13:8), it behooves us to have this same, ongoing, expectation – daily! The common translations do not bring out what is implicit in the present tense of the verb: constant, repeated, habitual and progressive **coming to [us].**" Now observe the preposition of the final phrase, and the first parenthetical expansion, "face to face with." First of all, this is how we can behold Him (2 Cor. 3:18). Second of all, we saw this term in the relationship between the Logos and God, in 1:1, above,
> "**the Logos was, and continued being, face to face with God.**"
The relationship, experience and presence that the Logos/Christ has with the Father is the same relationship, experience and presence that we have with God, the Father.

But when He is "**coming to** (or: face to face with; toward)" us, He does not come alone. Speaking of Himself, and the Father, vs. 23b, below, instructs us that:
> "**We will continue coming to him and will be progressively making** (constructing; forming; creating; producing) **a home** (an abode; a dwelling place; a place to stay) **with [anyone loving, accepting, fully giving himself to, and urging toward union with, Him].**"

19. **"Yet a little [while; longer] and the domination System** (world; ordered arrangement of religion and culture) **no longer continues viewing** (attentively watching) **Me, but YOU people are constantly watching** (attentively and contemplatively viewing) **Me. Because I, Myself, am continuously living, you folks will also continue living** [other MSS: will also from, or in, yourselves keep on living].

Recall 5:19, quoted in the discussion of vs. 13, above, where Jesus said of Himself that "**He can continue seeing something the Father is in process of doing**…" Now Jesus tells His disciples that they are able to be "**constantly watching** (attentively and contemplatively viewing) **Me,**" even when the domination System no longer continues viewing Him. In vs. 9 He told Philip that they should be able to see the Father within Him, even though He is journeying on to the Father (vs. 12). But also, He would be repeatedly coming to them (vs. 18).

The last clause gives a wonderful promise: **Because I, Myself, am continuously living, you folks will also continue living.** This reprises His words to Martha,
> "**The one progressively believing and habitually putting trust into Me, even if he may die-off** (or: die-away), **will continue Living**" (11:25b, above).
Later, it would be revealed to Paul that:
> "**Now since we died together with Christ, we are continuously believing** (relying; trusting) **that we will also continue living together in Him** (by Him; for Him; to Him; with Him), **having seen and thus knowing and perceiving that Christ, being aroused and raised forth from out of the midst of dead folks, is no longer dying**" (Rom. 6:8-9a).
We are blessed to be able to live with this realization. This is the Good News.

Here, Dan Kaplan points us to another level of dying and living (the spiritual/metaphorical):
> "**You see** (or: For it follows that) **I, myself, through [the]** (or: through means of; by) **Law died by [the] Law** (or: to Law; in [the] Law; with [the] Law), **to the end that I could and would live by**

God, in God, for God, to God and with God! [*cf* Rom. 7:13-23] **I was crucified together with Christ** [= the Messiah], **and thus it remains... yet I continue living! [It is] no longer I, but it is Christ continuously living and alive within me!**" (Gal. 2:19-20a).

20. **"Within That Day you yourselves will personally be coming to progressively realize and then will continue intimately and experientially knowing that I Myself [am; exist] within the midst of My Father, and you folks within the midst of and in union with Me, and I Myself within the midst of and in union with you people.**

What He refers to as being "**That Day**" had a historical inauguration, and we might determine that to be "the third Day," or, "the Day of the Lord," or, "the Day of Jesus Christ." *Cf* 1 Cor. 1:8; 5:5; 2 Cor. 1:4; Phil. 1:6; 2:16. In Phil. 1:10 we read the phrase:

> "**a Day of, and which is, Christ** [*p*46: the Day from Christ (or: an anointing)]."

When we live in **That Day**, we "**progressively realize and then continue intimately and experientially knowing that [He] [Himself] [is; exists] within the midst of [His] Father.**" The Father was, and is, His realm of His existence. But He did not stop there:

> "**and you folks within the midst of and in union with Me, and I Myself within the midst of and in union with you people.**"

OK, now how many of us really, day-by-day, believe that this is our present reality? Really? Well, this is where walking in faith and trust comes in, but in time we progressively realize and then we continue intimately and experientially knowing the truth of this statement. When we live in this reality, we are changed by it, and life is not the same as it once was. This is because He has transferred us away from the authority of the Darkness (of ignorance; of religion; of the first Adam) into the reign of His Son (Col. 1:13).

21. "**The person continuously holding** (or: constantly possessing and having) **My implanted goals** (impartations of the finished product within; inward directives; interior purposes and destiny) **and habitually observing** (watching over to keep, protect and maintain) **them – that one is** (exists being) **the person continuously loving, and fully giving himself to, Me. Now the one continuously loving and accepting Me will continue being loved, accepted and urged toward union** [*p*75 reads: watched over and cared for] **by** (or: under) **the Father, and I Myself will continue loving that person and I will progressively** (or: habitually) **cause Myself to be seen in clear light in him or her**
> (or: will continue inwardly manifesting Myself by her/him; will continuously inwardly make Myself visible to her/him; will progressively show Myself within for him/her; or: = will continue showing to, in, or by him/her what I am really like)."

The first statement of this verse is a repeating of what He said in vs. 15, above, but reversing the order of the two clauses. Again, repetition is a sign of importance. The reversal can also imply equivalence – each part can be substituted for the other part. Here, Jesus identifies "**the person continuously loving, and fully giving himself to, [Him]**, and that is the,

> "**person continuously holding** (or: constantly possessing and having) **My implanted goals** (impartations of the finished product within; inward directives; interior purposes and destiny) **and habitually observing** (watching over to keep, protect and maintain) **them.**"

This is not a statement about what one must do in order to be loved by God, but rather, it gives a description of the person who is loving Jesus. He is speaking of a reciprocal relationship. The last half of the verse begins by describing the benefits, or fruit, of this interpersonal relationship:

> "**the one continuously loving and accepting Me will continue being loved, accepted and urged toward union** [*p*75 reads: watched over and cared for] **by** (or: under) **the Father.**"

We read in 3:16, above, that God already loves the whole aggregated of humanity (the world). By loving and accepting Jesus we get intimately plugged into the Love (it is like being joined to the Vine, and abiding in the Vine, as we will read in chapter 15), and as we read in vs. 15, above, the person "**habitually loving and accepting**" Jesus "**WILL continue observing [His] implanted goals.**" The abiding union with the Lord keeps the flow of this dynamic continually going. This verse is a promise, not a statement of a prerequisite that must be met in order for God to love us. And the relationship with Jesus includes an interpersonal relationship with the Father. Verse 23, below, is simply a restatement of this progressive dynamic:

> "**If anyone continues loving, accepting, fully giving himself to, and urging toward union with, Me, he WILL continue constantly watching over so as to observe, guard, preserve keep and maintain My word** (*logos*: thought, idea; blueprint; message; laid-out, patterned information), **and My Father will continue loving, fully giving Himself to, and urging toward union with, him**…"

Jesus is describing the life in Christ – not setting conditions that must be met. In loving Jesus we are empowered to observe and maintain the "thought, idea, blueprint, message, and laid-out, patterned information" that a relationship with Jesus implants within us. This is the Way (the Path that we walk), the Truth (the reality of being a part of the Vine) and the Christ-Life (vs. 6, above). The verbs "**will continue being loved**" and "**will continue loving**" are in the future tense, which (like the imperfect tense and the present tense) is a durative tense that signifies continuing action (or: repeated or progressive action). God's love does not start or stop, for He IS Love. When we read that God loves (in 3:16 it is the aorist tense, the "fact" tense) the world, we must realize that this does not change.

The second statement begins with the last part of the first statement, signaling an expansion of the same topic, but now moving on to the Other Side of this reciprocal relationship: "**being loved, accepted and urged toward union** [*p*75 reads: watched over and cared for] **by** (or: under) **the Father**." The core idea of the preposition in the last phrase, "**under**," really creates a dynamic picture of being overshadowed, covered, sheltered, and intimately loved by the Father being in union with His Wife.

But more than this – as majestic and overwhelming as it is presented to us – we see Jesus saying:

> a) **and I Myself will continue loving that person** – and all that this word "love" implies;
> b) **and I will progressively** (or: habitually) **cause Myself to be seen in clear light in him or her**.

We must have our eyes unveiled by Him, for us to be able to see this; and so it is: "**But we all, ourselves – having a face that has been uncovered and remains unveiled**" – 2 Cor. 3:18a. This may be what John was referring to in 1 Jn. 3:2,

> "**it has not yet been made visible** (or: it is not yet apparent or manifested) **what we will proceed in being. We have perceived, and thus know** (or: are aware) **that if it** (or: He) **should be** (or: whenever it {or: He} may be) **made visible, apparent and manifested, [then] folks like to Him** (like-ones to Him; ones like Him; people resembling Him) **we will be existing, because we will continue seeing and will be progressively perceiving Him just as** (according and exactly as; in the manner that) **He constantly exists** (or: He is)."

This may be an allusion to Ps. 17:15, "As for me, in righteousness [eschatological deliverance – LXX] I shall perceive Your face; I shall indeed be satisfied – when I awake to Your semblance" (CVOT). This in turn calls to mind 1 Cor. 1:30,

> "**Now you folks are, and continuously exist being, forth from out of the midst of Him – within and in union with Christ Jesus, Who came to be Wisdom in and among us** (or: to us; for us), **from God: both a rightwising, eschatological deliverance into righted, covenantal existence in fair relationships of equity in the Way pointed out** (or: likewise a just covenantal Act from God) **and a being set-apart to be different** (a being made sacred), **even a redemptive liberation** (an emancipation; a loosing-away from [a condition of bondage])."

Also, there is the beautiful promise in Col. 3:4,

> "**Whenever the Christ, our life, can be brought to light** (or: may be manifested), **you folks also will proceed being brought to light, together with Him, within the midst of glory** (or: in union with a manifestation which calls forth praise; or: in a good reputation; or: = in His manifest presence)."

258

More insights are on offer in the parenthetical expansion of the last clause:

    a) will continue inwardly manifesting Myself by her/him;
    b) will continuously inwardly make Myself visible to her/him;
    c) will progressively show Myself within for him/her;
    d) a potential paraphrase: will continue showing to, in, or by him/her what I am really like.

22. **Judah** (Judas) – **not Iscariot – is then saying to Him, "Lord** (Master), **what has come to be** (or: has happened) **that you are now about to progressively and continually show Yourself plainly** (make Yourself to be inwardly seen in clear light) **to us** (or: in us) **and not to** (or: in) **the world** (or: domination System; ordered arrangement of the religious and political culture; aggregate of humanity)**?"**

This Judah was not fully tracking with Jesus, but he at least realized that something was happening that would be different from how things had been, with Jesus and thus with the group. Jesus does not tell him that anything has happened, but rather, He returns to the same topic of which He had been speaking...

23. **Jesus conclusively replies, and says to him, "If anyone continues** (or: may be habitually) **loving, accepting, fully giving himself to, and urging toward union with, Me, he WILL continue constantly watching over so as to observe, guard, preserve keep and maintain My word** (*logos*: thought, idea; blueprint; message; laid-out, patterned information), **and My Father will continue loving, fully giving Himself to, and urging toward union with, him, AND, facing toward him, We will continue coming to him and will be progressively making** (constructing; forming; creating; producing) **a home** (abode; dwelling place; place to stay) **with him** (or: at his side and in his presence).

Here, repeating the same thing about "**loving** Him," He makes it clear that this inner urge of the Spirit (for only the Spirit of God can cause us to love, in the way that Jesus means by using this word, *agapē*) is the Way and the means of "**watching over so as to observe, guard, preserve keep and maintain [His] word** (etc.)."

Notice the key, "**loving**," that enables the "constant watching over (etc.), and these are accompanied by:

    a) **My Father continuing in loving, fully giving Himself to, and urging toward union with, him;**

    b) **AND, facing toward him, We will continue coming to him and will be progressively making** (constructing; forming; creating; producing) **a home** (abode; dwelling place; place to stay) **with him** (or: at his side and in his presence).

Just as an aside: He did NOT say that He would come to take us off to heaven. No, they come here, to be with us (Rev. 21:3).

These two promises can only be perceived by illumination from the Spirit, with us. They are far above our natural reasoning. The FATHER "fully giving Himself to us"? The FATHER "urging toward union with us"? The Father and the Son "creating a home with us" – "making a place to stay with us"? No wonder Paul advised us to"

    "**Be constantly minding** (thinking about; setting your disposition and sentiments toward; paying regard to) **the upward things** (or: the things above), **not the things upon the earth**" (Col. 3:2).

Jesus gives further insight of this through His prayer, in 17:21, below,

    "**to the end that all humans would** (or: all people can and should) **continuously exist being one, correspondingly as You, O Father, [are] within the midst of Me, and I [am] within the midst of You – so that they, themselves, may and would also continuously exist being within the midst of Us**..."

Also, 17:22b-23a,

    "**to the end that they can continuously exist being one correspondingly as** (just as; according as; to the same level as; in the same sphere as) **We are one: I within the midst of**

and in union with them and You within the midst of and in union with Me, to the end that they would continuously exist being folks having been perfected (brought to the destined goal; finished; completed; matured and purposed) **into one...**"

The end result is that we are made to participate in the "mutual indwelling" of the Father and the Son. We are reminded of the concentric spheres described by Paul, in Col. 3:3, "**for you folks died, and your life has been hidden so that it is now concealed together within the Christ, within the midst of God** (or: in union with God)." Take note: your life, within the Christ, who is within the midst of God.

24. "**The one not habitually loving or fully giving himself to Me is not habitually observing, watching over or keeping My words** (laid-out thoughts, ideas and messages), **and the word** (that which has been laid out; *Logos*; thought; idea; message) **which you folks are continually hearing is not Mine, but rather belongs to, is from and pertains to the Father [Who is] sending Me.**

Without loving and fully giving ourselves to Christ, we are unable to be "**observing, watching over or keeping [His] words** (laid-out thoughts, ideas and messages)." Notice the connection between the two. Also take note that Jesus was not just speaking His own message (*Logos*), but rather **the Father's Logos**. He was speaking the Father's Blueprint – not some "gospel" that was inferior to Paul's message! His words were the Foundation of the Building upon which Paul taught the covenant communities to build.

> "**for you see, no one can** (or: continues able to; is having power to) **lay another foundation** (or: to place or set another foundation [Stone] of the same kind) **beside** (or: in addition to and distinct from) **the One lying** (or: continuing being laid): **which is** (continues being) **Jesus Christ**" (1 Cor. 3:11).

25. "**I have spoken these things to you folks while constantly remaining** (dwelling; abiding) **with you** (in your presence; at your side or at your house).
26. "**Now the Helper** (the One called alongside to aid, comfort, encourage and bring relief; the Paraclete), **the set-apart Spirit** (or: the Sacred Breath; the holy Breath-effect; the holy attitude), **which the Father will proceed sending within, and in union with, My Name, that One will be progressively teaching you all things** (everything) **and will continue reminding you of** (calling to your mind and causing you to think about) **everything** (all things) **which I, Myself, said to you.**

Here He identifies **the Helper**, "**the set-apart Spirit** (or: the Sacred Breath; the holy Breath-effect)." It was **the Father** that would proceed sending the Spirit, and observe: The Breath-effect will be "**within, and in union with, My Name**." OK, recall our discussion on His Name, in vs. 13, above. This presents us with another clue as to what He meant by making a request in union with His Name. Those requests would need to be in union with the Spirit that INHABITED the Name.

The Breath-effect will be another Teacher, and will instruct them concerning making requests. But what is more:
> a) **that One will be progressively teaching you all things** (everything);
> b) **and will continue reminding you of** (calling to your mind and causing you to think about) **everything** (all things) **which I, Myself, said to you.**

So how have so many Christians, who claim to have the Holy Spirit, disregard that which the Spirit is continuing to remind them: **everything** (all things) **which I, Myself, said to you**? Yes, He taught Paul and the other representatives more, but what He had taught His first twelve (and the others) were instructions that all followers would need to remember, and apply as directed by the Father (who would be residing within them).

27. "**I am continuously sending off** (releasing away; hurling off) **peace** (joining) **to** (or: for; by; in; with) **you people. My peace** (joining) **I am constantly giving to you** (or: in, by, for you folks). **I, Myself, am not giving [it] to you the way** (or: according as) **the System** (the world of religion, politics and culture)

continually gives [it]. Do not let the heart of the group be constantly shaken, disturbed or agitated, neither let it be habitually timid (shrinking; responding cowardly). [Deut. 31:8; Josh. 1:9]

OK, was this just "inner peace," or "an absence of war," or the prosperity of *shalom*? No, it was His **peace**. In the first statement, notice the parenthetical expansion of the word "peace" – "**joining**." You see, it is the "joining" which we discussed in vs. 10, above, when speaking of "mutual habitation," and the "joining" of a man with a woman which results in union. On the natural level, when kingdoms or governments "join" in some aspect, there is "peace" in that area of joining.

There was also, via the work of Christ, a joining, and then peace, in what we find described concerning the union (in Christ) of the circumcision and the uncircumcision (Eph. 2:10-22). Let us focus on three verses from that passage:

> 14. **You see, He Himself is our PEACE** (or: continuously exists being our JOINING and harmony) – **the One making** (forming; constructing; creating; producing) **The Both [to be] one, and within His flesh** (= physical being; or: = system-caused crucifixion) **is instantly destroying** (unbinding; unfastening; loosing; causing to collapse) **the middle wall of the fenced enclosure** (or: the partition or barrier wall)**: the enmity** (cause of hate, alienation, discord and hostility; characteristics of an enemy),
> 15. **rendering useless** (nullifying; rendering down in accord with inactivity and unemployment) **the Law** (or: the custom; = the Torah) **of the implanted goals** (or: concerning impartations of the finished product within; from commandments; which was inward directives) **consisting in decrees** (or: prescribed ordinances), **to the end that He may frame** (create; found and settle from a state of wildness and disorder) **The Two into One qualitatively New and Different** [*p*46 & others: common] **Humanity centered within the midst of, and in union with, Himself, continuously making** (progressively creating) **Peace and Harmony** (a JOINING);
> 16. **and then should fully transfer, from a certain state to another which is quite different, The Both – centered in, and within the midst of, One Body in God** (or: make completely other, while moving away from what had existed, and fully reconcile The Both, in one Body, **by, to,** with and for **God), through the cross** (execution stake) – **while in the midst of Himself killing the enmity and discordant hatred** (or: killing-off the characteristics of enemies within it).

Very simply, the word peace comes from the verb that means "to join."

But in our current context, He was meaning the **joining** of them to Himself (as branches are joined to the Vine – Jn. 15), and of our thus being **joined** to the Father (e.g., 1 Cor. 6:17).

The systems of culture, religion and government (especially, Empire) brought peace by the physical sword. Domination was the method – even in religion: cross them and you are out! Christ does not create peace or joining by a sword, or a joining by domination. He creates it by placing His soul over us.

We can, of course, see allusions to the OT in His words. Isa. 9:7a, "Of the increase of His dominion, and of *shalom* (peace; well-being; prosperity) there shall be no end…" Isa. 26:12a, "O Yahweh, You will ensure *shalom* for us…" From the LXX, Isa. 32:17,

> "And so the works (acts; deeds) of the eschatological deliverance and from the rightwising, and which is the turning in the right direction of the Way pointed out, belonging to covenant inclusion, will continue being **peace** (or: will progressively be a **joining**)…" (JM)

And those are just a beginning. Paul unveils more of this in Phil. 4:7,

> "**and God's peace** (or: peace from God; or: the harmonious **joining, which is God), which is continuously having a hold over** (habitually having sway over; or: constantly being superior and excelling over) **all mind and inner sense** (or: every intellect; all power of comprehension; or: all process of thinking), **will continue garrisoning** (guarding; keeping watch over; protecting) **your hearts and the results from directing your minds** (or: effects of your perceptions,

concepts, thoughts, reasonings and understandings; or: dispositions; designs; purposes; [*p*16 adds: and bodies]), **centered within, and in union with, Christ Jesus.**"

Then, of course, there is the famous admonition from Paul in Col. 3:15,

"**Furthermore, let the peace and the joining of the Christ** (belonging to and originating in the [Messiah]; the harmony which is the Anointing [other MSS: God]) **continuously umpire** (act as a judge in the games) **within your hearts** (= in union with the core of your being) **– into which [peace] you folks are called** (were called; were invited), **within one body. And progressively come to be thankful people** (or: continue becoming folks expressing gratitude for the goodness, ease and well-being that comes in grace; be habitually graceful folks)."

The second statement in this verse ends with the plural personal pronoun in the dative case, so this can also read: "**My peace** (or: joining) **I am constantly giving by you folks.**" You see, He gives it to us, and we are to pass it on to others. This peace was also to be within them, among them and for them. Because of this, He repeated the last line of 13:38 (or, commonly: the first line of this chapter): **Do not let the heart of the group be constantly shaken, disturbed or agitated.** They were **joined** to Him and to one another… and to all humanity. When we can see this, we are not easily shaken or disturbed, "**neither [should we] be habitually timid** (shrinking; responding cowardly)." *Cf* Deut. 31:8; Josh. 1:9

The JOINING was to bring us into His Oneness. Paul was given this picture, in Eph. 4:

1. **I myself – the prisoner within, in union with, and centered in [the] Lord – am therefore repeatedly calling you folks, as it were, alongside: exhorting, admonishing, imploring and entreating you to walk [your path] worthily pertaining to** (or: in a manner suitable to the value of) **the calling and invitation in regard to which you folks are called,**
2. **with all lowliness of attitude** (or: humility in frame of mind) **and gentle kindness and friendliness, with longsuffering** (even-tempered, forbearing patience; a long wait before rushing in passion; putting anger far away; passionate perseverance unto the goal), **continuously holding one another up** (or: bearing with each other with tolerance) **within the sphere of, and in union with, love** (unqualified acceptance and the urge toward union),
3. **repeatedly hurrying to make every effort to constantly keep** (watch over to guard and protect; maintain) **the Spirit's ONENESS** (or: the unity from the Breath-effect, and of spirit; the oneness which is the Spirit; = agreement of [your] attitude) **within the Bond** (the link, tie and connection that joins two things; the binding conjunction which results in union) **of the Peace** (or: which is from **THE JOINING**),
4. **[making] ONE BODY and ONE SPIRIT** (attitude and effect of the Breath), **according as you folks were also called within the midst of ONE expectation** (or: in union with one expectant hope) **of your calling,**
5. **[with] ONE LORD, ONE FAITH** (or: faithfulness, fidelity, loyalty, reliability, confidence, conviction, assurance, and trust), **ONE effect of SUBMERSION and envelopment which brings absorption and permeation to the point of saturation,**
6. **ONE God and Father of all humans – the One upon all people and [moving] through all people, and within the midst of all humanity and in union with all people and all things.**

28. "**You heard that I, Myself, said to you, 'I am progressively leading away under** (or: humbly departing, but bringing things under control), **and yet I am presently progressively** (or: repeatedly; habitually) **coming toward** (face-to-face-with) **you folks.' If you had been loving and giving yourself to Me, you should have at some point been caused to rejoice, because I am progressively journeying toward the Father, because the Father is greater** (or: = more important) **than I.**

And thus should we not rejoice when a friend or loved one journeys on to the Father? Do they not, also, habitually come to be face-to-face with us? Well, that is speculation, on our part, but does not the logic follow – since we are all joined to Him? What did Judah mean, in Jude 14b?

"**Behold, the Lord came** (or: comes and goes) **within His set-apart myriads** (or: in union with innumerable holy multitudes, which are Him)."

But we digress. Even though He was "**progressively leading away under** (or: humbly departing, but bringing things under control)," He was also, "**presently progressively** (or: repeatedly; habitually) **coming toward** (face-to-face-with) **you folks** [or, us]." Remember when He came to Saul, on the road to Damascus (Acts 9)? Recall how He came to John on the Isle of Patmos (Rev. 1). The verb (**coming**) in this last statement is in the present indicative: it speaks of repeated, continual, habitual or progressive action. In Rev. 1:8 we have the present participle of this verb, where the Lord identified Himself to John as, "**the One continuously being, even the One Who was and continued being, and the One presently and continuously** (or: progressively) **coming and going, the Almighty**." All through the OT, we observe God coming and going, and then coming again...

Recall that He had emptied Himself and took the form of a servant (Phil. 2:7), when He was incarnated within this life and realm. Now He was in the process of "**progressively journeying toward the Father**," completing His circuit (Rom. 11:36). But why did He say that He was going to be face-to-face with the Father, "**because the Father is greater than I**"? Was this because He was still in the form, and role, of a servant? Forget what some theologians have read into this text, creating a false picture of a hierarchy. A hierarchy in God was not found in the OT Scriptures. His disciples still were seeing Him as human. Also, He had told them, "**I, Myself, am continually unable** (or: As for Me, I habitually have no power or ability) **to be doing anything from Myself...**" (Jn. 5:30). Also, in 5:19, above,

> "**the Son continues unable to do anything from Himself** (or: the Son, from Himself, habitually has no power to be doing anything [independently]) **except He can** (or: unless He should) **continue seeing something the Father is in process of doing...**"

Jesus was modeling the role of a son for them. You see, those who are continually LED by the Spirit (Breath-effect) are God's sons (Rom. 8:14). Jesus would later say to the Father, "Not my will but yours be done."

29. "**And now** (at the present time) **I have told you** (declared [it] to you) **before it comes to be** (is birthed; occurs), **so that whenever it would come to be** (or: should occur) **you people would trust, can believe, should be loyal and may faith-it.**

When folks see a prophecy fulfilled, it does build faith in the one who spoke it. But we think that there is more to what He says, here, for in 13:34, 14:15 and 14:21, above, He had spoken of the implanted goals that He had imparted to them. He will speak of them again, in 15:10, and then in 15:12, below He gives a particular definition:

> "**This is My implanted goal** (impartation of the finished product within; inward directive; interior purpose and destiny)**: that you keep on loving, urging toward union, and accepting one another – correspondingly as** (to the same degree as; in the same sphere as) **I love and accept you folks.**"

Now put this with vs. 23a, above, "**If anyone continues loving, accepting, fully giving himself to, and urging toward union with, Me, he WILL continue constantly watching over so as to observe, guard, preserve keep and maintain My word** (*Logos*: thought, idea; blueprint; message; laid-out, patterned information)." His *Logos* included EVERYTHING that He had told them – not just His going and coming. It included the peace and joining, of which He spoke in vs. 27, above. It included His reference to loving Him and giving themselves to Him, of which He spoke in vs. 28. It is the entire LOGOS, when IT comes to fruition, that enables folks to **trust**, **believe**, **be loyal** and "**faith-it**." When we observe the Spirit's Fruit in our lives, this builds trust in the Spirit, produces belief in His Logos, and causes us to be loyal to the imparted goals.

30. **"I will no longer converse** (be speaking) **with you folks [about] many things, for the ruler** (the one in first place; the chief) **of the System** (or: of this ordered arrangement of the political, economic, religious and cultural world) **is progressively coming, and yet he is holding nothing within Me**
>   (or: it [i.e., the domination system] continues to have and possess nothing in Me and has no hold on Me; or: = he [note: this could refer either to the chief priest, or to Pilate] has nothing to do with Me, and there is nothing in Me that is to his advantage),

Of whom was He speaking, when He said "**the ruler** (the one in first place; the chief) **of the System**"? Who was it that would send out the temple guards to apprehend Him? Recall Peter's first sermon, on the Day of Pentecost:
>   "**Men! Israelites!**.... **you folks – through the hand** (= agency) **of people not bound by the Law** (= folks without knowledge of and not living in accordance to the Torah) **– took up and assassinated by fastening [Him] to [an execution stake** (or: a cross)**]**" (Acts 2:22, 23b).

Later, Paul would explain,
>   "**not one of the rulers** (leaders; chief people) **of this age know** (or: came to know) **by intimate experience or insight. For if they knew, THEY would not likely have crucified** (hung or suspended on a pole) **the Owner of, and Who is, the glory**
>>   (or: For if they know, they would not stake-execute the Lord of the Manifestation which calls forth praise, and Who is the Appearance with a good reputation)" (1 Cor. 2:8).

Our author spoke of a particular "**ruler**" of the System of Second-Temple Judaism, in 3:1, above,
>   "**a man from out of the Pharisees, Nicodemus by name, a ruler** (leader; chief; head man) **of the Judeans**..."

In Jn. 7, during the Feast of Tabernacles, Jesus was openly teaching in the temple courts and the crowd was surprised at this because they knew that the Judean leadership was wanting to kill Him. In 7:26b they asked one another, "**The chief rulers** (or: "the authorities"; the ruling class) **have not at some point come to really know personally that this one is the Christ, have they?**" Then, in 7:32, "**the Pharisees commissioned and dispatched officers**" to arrest Him. When they returned without Him, the Pharisees said to them, "**Not anyone from out of the rulers** (chiefs; leaders) **or from out of the Pharisees put trust, confidence or belief into him, do they?**" (7:48, above).

We have rehearsed all this to support our conclusion that "**the ruler** (the one in first place; the chief) **of the System**," to which Jesus referred, here in vs. 30, was the Chief Priest, to whom Jesus would first be taken. This title could then extend to Pilate, the representative of the Roman Empire (the greater System, at that time). His arrest, and then crucifixion, was the reason that He would, "**no longer converse** (be speaking) **with you folks [about] many things**."

31. **"but rather, even correspondingly as the Father gave an implanted goal and destiny in Me** (imparted the finished purpose within and gave an inward directive to Me), **thus and in this manner I continue habitually performing** (constantly doing and producing), **to the end that the System** (the ordered arrangement of the world; the system of control; religious and secular society) **can come to know by experience that I am continuously loving, and fully giving Myself to, the Father.**

Here we see that He had been given "**an implanted goal and destiny**" imbedded within Him, by the Father. Now Jesus had done the same thing to, for and within, His disciples.

Next, observe the context in which He purposed to "**continue habitually performing** (constantly doing and producing)": it was within the midst of this very same "**System** (the ordered arrangement of the world; the system of control; religious and secular society)." And what was His reason for doing this? It was, "**to the end that the System can come to know by experience that I am continuously loving, and fully giving Myself to, the Father**." After this, He said to His disciples...

Be progressively caused to rise up, and be habitually awake and excited (or, as a middle: Now rise up). **We can** (or: should) **now progressively lead the way from this place** (or: = Let's get out of here)."

Chapter 15

1. **"I, Myself, AM** (or: exist being) **the true** (genuine; real) **Grapevine, and My Father is** (continues being) **the One who tends the soil** (the Farmer; the One who tills and works the Land; the Cultivator, Gardener, Husbandman).

In 14:6, the pictures were "the Way, the Truth and the Life." In 11:25, He is the Resurrection. Now, as we will see, the metaphor associated with this "I AM" statement is corporate, and it is organic. It is a production of the soil, and of the land (Gen. 1:11), and it speaks of a vineyard that is tended by the Creator, the Son's Father. He is here "Creation" (a Plant; a Vineyard) that is cultivated by the Creator. The Father has complete control of Him, as well as responsibility for Him – as does Yahweh, with regard to Israel. The Son, like Israel, like Creation, is owned by God. All souls are His (Ezk. 18:4). This is another picture of the Son emptying Himself, and becoming a kind of vegetation – in the metaphorical sense that Christ was the Rock that followed Israel in the wilderness (1 Cor. 10:4), and the Consuming Fire that inhabited a bush, which Moses observed as burning, but not consumed.

Jesus takes up a figure, for Himself, which was an OT figure for Israel. He is the whole plant, here, so He is corporate Israel, Yahweh's Firstborn (Ex. 4:22b). We find an allusion to Joseph, in Gen. 49:22, he was "a fruitful bough by a well (or: spring), whose branches (or: daughters) climbed up straight, and run over the wall [of Israel, and beyond Palestine]." The first cultivation by Noah, in the new creation, was a vine (and then a vineyard). In Isa. 5:7, we read:
"You see, the vineyard of Yahweh of hosts [is the] house of Israel, and each man of Judah His plant delectable" (CVOT).
Ps. 80:8, "You brought a Vine out of Egypt..." And so, we see that Jesus drew upon a long tradition of this metaphor, in Israel's history.

Paul picked up this metaphor in 1 Cor. 3:9,
"**For we are God's fellow-workers** (or: we are co-workers of, and from, God, and are people who work together with God; we exist being workings-together who belong to God, synergies of God; attending deeds which are God). **You folks are God's farm** (or: field under cultivation; husbandry)..."
Then Jacob selected this same metaphor in Jas. 5:7,
"**Be patient** (long-tempered; long-passioned; slow to rush; or: Have long-term feelings and emotions, with anger pushed far away), **then, brothers, during the continuance of the Lord's presence and His being alongside. Consider! The worker of the land repeatedly receives** (takes out into his hands from within) **the precious fruit of the land** (or: ground; soil), **being patient** (slow to rush and with long-term feelings; with anger far from him) **upon it, during the continuance where it can receive "an early as well as a latter** (or: late) **rain."** [cf Deut. 11:14]

2. **"Every tender branch** (shoot or twig which can easily be broken) **within Me not habitually bearing** (bringing forth; = producing) **fruit He regularly lifts up and takes it away. And every one consistently bearing the fruit He periodically clears and cleans** (or: seasonally cleanses) **by pruning, to the end that it can continue bearing more** (a greater amount of) **fruit.** [cf Mat. 25:46]

What Jesus is describing is the normal "vine dressing," and cultivation, of a vineyard – that happens every year, in order to keep the vines productive. He is faithful to take away from our lives that which is not productive. We see similar care of a field in Heb. 6:8, where fire is used to burn off unwanted growth and weeds, in preparation for sowing a new crop. Another picture is seen in the seasonal "cleansing" His threshing floor, following the harvest (Mat. 3:12).

The word for "**prune**" also means "**clear, clean and cleanse**." The vine is cleared from dead branches (as Dan Kaplan suggests: dead works; that which has no life and provides no nourishment), and the area is "cleaned up." He is still speaking in terms of the vineyard. In the next verse He will turn the metaphor on His disciples…

3. **"You folks, yourselves, are already clean** (cleansed), **cleared and pruned ones through and because of the word** (*Logos*; laid-out message; thought; idea; pattern-conveying information; blueprint) **which I have spoken to you** (in you; for you; among you) **folks.**

Now He has indicated that they are a part of the Vine, and that He has been doing the Father's work on them (remember, the Father is the Farmer, Vine Dresser – vss. 1-2, above). It is the *Logos* that is the instrument for pruning and cleaning in preparation for the new growth season – the new creation (Jn. 1:3; 2 Cor. 5:17). The Blueprint (Christ) is used in building the New Temple (1 Cor. 3:9-17).

He spoke the Logos "to" them, but also His implanted goals were spoken "in" them, and were, of course, "for" them. We suspect that it was through words – whether spoken or live out – that the called-out communities, such as Corinth, were building one another up – constructing God's Temple (1 Cor. 3). They were cleansing one another, perhaps "washing their feet," in their daily living together.

4. **"You folks remain** (dwell; abide; stay) **within and in union with Me – and I, Myself, [will remain] within and in union with you. Correspondingly as the tender branch is not being consistently able** (having continuing power) **to repeatedly bear fruit from itself unless it should continually remain** (stay; dwell) **within** (in union with; on) **the grapevine, in the same way, neither [can] you folks, unless you may constantly remain** (stay; dwell) **within** (in union with; centered in) **Me.**

They were already "**within and in union with**" Him, that is why He used the word "**remain**," or "stay." Having been set free (8:36, above), they now had the ability to remain, or to depart, to withdraw. The person that is dead in trespasses and failure (Eph. 2:1) has no such ability. Neither does a slave. In organic reciprocity, Jesus promises that He will remain "**within and in union with**" them. That would hold true, even when He momentarily departed from them, physically.

Now He returns to the grapevine metaphor: the tender branch must remain connected to the Vine in order to produce fruit. And this is the reason for having the Vine: fruit – in this case, fruit of the Spirit (Gal. 5:22ff). Next, He plainly explains the analogy as it relates to them, and returns to the point with which He opened this verse: mutual indwelling; organic union – the spiritual marriage of Yahweh/Christ with Israel; Israel as God's vineyard.

5. **"I, Myself, AM the Grapevine; you folks [are] the tender branches** (shoots or twigs that can be easily broken). **The person continuously remaining** (dwelling; abiding) **within the midst of Me – and I within the midst of and in union with him – this one is repeatedly bearing** (bringing forth; = producing) **much fruit. [It is the case] that apart from** (or: Because separated from) **Me you folks continue having ability and power to do** (make; construct; create; form; perform; produce) **nothing!**

In His typical rhetorical redundancy, He repeats vs. 1 to them, now affirming plainly that they were His "**tender branches**." This corresponds to them being what Paul would later refer to as "the body of Christ" (1 Cor. 12:27). This meant that they were actually the ones who would produce His (i.e., the Spirit's) fruit. They would existentially be a part of, and an extension of, Him. Just as when a vineyard is in full growth and is bearing fruit, what is observed is mostly branches, leaves and fruit – while the trunk is more obscured from view and the matured source of the new branches of the Vine is hidden – so would He be mostly hidden and mostly observed in the new branches, the leaves and the fruit.

Next, He emphasizes the person "**continuously remaining** (dwelling; abiding) **within the midst of [Him]**" and likewise, He "**within the midst of and in union with him,**" i.e., within the person, and then He makes the conclusion that those who do this will be "**repeatedly bearing** (bringing forth; = producing) **much fruit.**"

Just as He apart from the Father would be able to do nothing (5:19, 30, above), likewise they (and we) apart from Him "**continue having ability and power to do** (make; construct; create; form; perform; produce) **nothing.**" This means that if folks endeavor to build God's house while being separated from union with Christ, they can only build with wood, hay and stubble (that which will not endure the Fire – 1 Cor. 3). This is why He would later advise the called out community of Laodicea:

"**I continue advising you** [singular] **to buy from Me gold having been refined** (set ablaze) **forth from out of fire**..." (Rev. 3:18; *cf* Mal. 3:2-3).

6. "**If anyone would** (or: may; should) **not continuously remain** (dwell; abide; stay) **within the midst of and in union with Me, he or she is cast** (or: thrown) **outside, in the same way as the tender branch** (or: like that twig or shoot). **And thus, it** (or: he/she) **is caused to dry up and wither, and then they are constantly gathering** (or: leading) **them** [other MSS: it] **together** ["synagogue-ing" them, or it, as in a bundle]. **Later, they are normally throwing** (or: casting) [*p*66 adds: **them**] **into the fire – and it** (or: he) **is progressively kindled** (repeatedly ignited; or: habitually lit and progressively burned).

So, what does he mean by "**he or she is cast** (or: thrown) **outside**'? Of course the rest of the verse adds to the description of what someone does with unproductive branches that have been pruned, but before looking at that, let us look to other places where Jesus used the term, "**outside.**"

In Mat. 8:12, Jesus speaks about some in Israel (figures as "the sons of the kingdom) of whom Paul spoke, in Rom. 11, about "**their casting away**" (vs. 15) and then in vs. 17 said of them:

"**Now since some** (or: if certain ones) **of the branches are broken off** (or: were at one point broken out of [the tree])..."

But in our Matthew text, Jesus prophesied of these same folks:

"**Yet the 'sons of the kingdom** (or: reign; = those who were in line to inherit the kingdom; or: = those who were supposed to manifest its reign and dominion)' **will be progressively thrown out into the external darkness** (external obscurity of the shadows). **There** [= outside the banqueting building] **it will continue being 'the weeping and the grinding of teeth'** (or: The crying and the gnashing of teeth will continue being in that [outdoor] place, or situation)" (Mat. 8:12; [note: grinding/gnashing of teeth = either regret, or anger])

In Mat. 22, in the parable of the wedding feast (a figure of participation in the reign of the coming Messiah) Jesus used a similar metaphor about a person not properly attired for the celebration:

"**At that point, the king said to the servants, 'Upon binding his feet and hands, you men throw him out into the darkness** (dim obscurity) **which is farther outside. In that place there will continue being the weeping** (or: lamenting) **and the grinding of the teeth.'**"

[comment: compare the "binding of feet" in Hos. 11:1-4, LXX:

1. Because Israel [is] a young child, I Myself also love him, and I once called his children together from out of Egypt.

2. The more I called them [to Me], the more they distanced themselves and kept away from My face (or: immediate presence). They sacrificed to the Baals, and then burned incense to the carved and chiseled images (= idols).

3. And so I, Myself tied the feet of Ephraim together (i.e., restrained him; = hobbled him to keep him from wandering) [then] I took him up upon My arm – and yet they did not realize (or: know) that I had healed them.

4. In the thorough ruin and destruction of humans I stretch out to them and lay [My hand] on them in binding ties (or: bonds) of My love. And so I will be to them as a person slapping (or:

striking) [someone] on his cheek, then I will look upon him (= either: keep an eye on him; or: give respect to him). I will prevail with him and then give ability and power to him. (JM)]

In a parable about a "worthless slave," Jesus ends the story in this way:

"**and so he will proceed to be cutting him in two** [hyperbole for: severely punish; or, metaphor: cut him off from employment] **and then he will proceed putting** (placing; setting) **his part with the perverse, opinionated scholars who have all the answers and are hyper-critical and overly judgmental. The weeping, moaning and the grinding of the teeth will continue being in that place and situation**" (Mat. 24:51).

Then, in Mat. 25:30, we read the ending of another story about a worthless slave:

"'**And now, you men at once throw the useless slave out into the darkness** (dim obscurity and gloominess) **which is farther outside. In that place there will continue being the weeping** (or: lamenting) **and the grinding of the teeth.**"

We suggest that the subject of these parables in Matthew are the same topic of which Paul wrote, in Rom. 11, cited above, as well as of those "**cast** (or: thrown) **outside**," in vs. 6a, above. As the Vine, Jesus spoke of Himself as Israel's Messiah (and thus as the Representative of Israel), and His branches (the disciples) represented those who would function as leaders within His reign. Jesus signified this in a prophetic picture spoken to His disciples in Mat. 19:28,

"**I am now laying it out and saying to you men – in the Rebirth** (Birth-back-again; Return-birth) **when the Son of the Man** (or: = the eschatological messianic figure) **would sit upon the throne of His glory** (or: which is His assumed Appearance), **you yourselves – the folks following Me – you also will be habitually sitting down upon twelve thrones** (or: seats) **repeatedly separating-out [issues], evaluating and making decisions for, or administering justice to, the twelve tribes of Israel.**"

Not to remain within the Vine means not to continue in the sovereign activities of His reign, and not to continue in the Life of the Messiah – it would be to return to the Darkness that is outside of the Lighted banquet hall.

Returning to Jesus' description of what happens next:

"**And thus, it** (or: he/she) **is caused to dry up and wither, and then they are constantly gathering** (or: leading) **them** [other MSS: it] **together ["synagogue-ing" them, or it, as in a bundle].**"

Again, since this Gospel is filled with SIGNS (figures that point to something), I have on offer a transliteration of the verb phrase, "**gathering them together**," which is: "**synagogue-ing them.**" Those who did not stay with Jesus would have returned to their synagogues. Just as with Mal. 3:2-3, God still has plans for them: Fire (a figure of a purifying, cleansing activity, by God, as in Heb. 6:8, where a field is burned off in order to get rid of the weeds and brambles that have overtaken it – preparation for a new planting). Mat. 25:46 described this Fire (God, Himself being applied to a person) as an unspecified period of pruning – for the young goats who were not bearing the fruit of caring-for-others (love).

Jesus went on to explain that, "**Later, they are normally throwing** (or: casting) [p66 adds: **them**] **into the fire – and it** (or: he) **is progressively kindled** (repeatedly ignited; or: habitually lit and progressively burned)." The metaphor is about what the Father would put them through – His serious dealing with them – not about the end of their personal existence. Recall what Paul said about the branches that were broken out of Israel's olive tree (which, of course would also have dried up, as the Vine branches in our present text):

"**Now they also, if they should not persistently remain in the lack of faith and trust** (or: unbelief), **they will proceed in being grafted in, for God is able** (capable; is constantly powerful) **to graft them back in again!**" (Rom. 11:23).

Since Second-Temple Judaism has been a central topic during the earthly ministry of Christ, we suspect that the last part of vs. 6 may have been a veiled prophecy about the destruction of Jerusalem, in AD 70.

7. **"If you people can** (or: would; should) **remain** (abide; dwell; stay) **within the midst of and in union with Me – and My gush-effects** (results of spoken words) **can** (should; would) **remain** [with *p*66 and others: and the flow of My declarations continues abiding] **within the midst of and in union with you – seek in petition** [other MSS: you will continue asking] **whatever you folks may habitually purpose** (constantly intend; repeatedly will; continuously want or desire), **and it will proceed coming to be within and among you folks** (or: will progressively occur for you people; will continue being birthed by you folks; will habitually happen to you folks).

While vs. 6 discussed what would come by NOT remaining joined to Him, now He again expresses the double, or mutual, indwelling: they remaining "**within the midst of and in union with**" Him, and He, in the form and presence of His "**gush-effects** (results of spoken words)," remaining "**within the midst of and in union with**" them. This union and co-indwelling gives them both power and ability to "**seek in petition whatever you folks may habitually purpose**," the result being that "**it will proceed coming to be within and among you folks**." This suggest that the answer to their requests would happen within them (in their souls or spirits or bodies), or, if appropriate, among the group. Now take note of the plural personal pronoun, used twice in this compound clause: "**you folks**." This seems to be mainly speaking of petitions made by the group, and not just requests by individuals. All along, He has been addressing a corporate Vine, or vineyard. When abiding within the Vine, they are one corporate "being." This does not disallow personal request being made to the Lord, but this teaching was focusing on "**If you people can**," in the first clause. They were "the twelve," a SIGN, in themselves, of the "born-from-above" twelve tribes of Israel (*cf* Jas. 1:1; Rev. 7:5ff; also, the twelve gates and foundation stones of the New Jerusalem – Rev. 21:12-21) that was being resurrected from the dead (Ezk. 37), as the beginning of the New Creation.

The form of the final "you folks" is dative, without an expressed preposition in the text, so the potential ambiguity of function allows for the other readings in the parenthetical expansion:
  a) will progressively occur for you people;
  b) will continue being birthed BY you folks;
  c) will habitually happen to you folks.
All of these readings can apply, according to the multitude of situations that they (and we) would have.

8. **"In this is** (or: was) **My Father glorified** (caused to appear and be recognized; given a good reputation and a manifestation which calls forth praise)**: that you men can continuously bear** (or: would keep on bringing forth) **much fruit, and thus can** (or: would) **come to be** [with other MSS: will continue becoming] **disciples** (learners; students; apprentices) **by Me** (or: in Me; to Me; for Me; with Me; [other MSS: My disciples]).

This verse builds upon the premise of the stipulation of 7a, above: the mutual indwelling of them within Him and His **gush-effects** remaining within them so as to "**continuously bear** (or: keep on bringing forth) **much fruit**." HE is the source of the fruit that He desires to see in them! It is His Life, His Spirit and His Logos – all of which comprise His implanted goals which produce the Fruit (from the result of the flow of His Breath streaming into them). Since He is the Light of the aggregate of humanity (8:12, above), and He now indwells them, they (and we) are now able to do what He said to do in Mat. 5:16,
  "**Let the Light, which you folks possess** (or: which has a source in you folks; or: which you people are), **shine in front of the People** (before the humans), **so that people can see your fine works** (or: the beautiful works that you are; the ideal acts which come from you folks) **and they can give glory to** (or: and [these deeds; or: these works of beauty] will bring a good reputation to, and a manifestation which incites praise for) **your Father – the One in union with the atmospheres [that surround you folks]** (or: within the midst of the heavens)!"
Light is the "fruit" of the Light. Paul's prayer for those in Philippi gave us another picture of what Jesus says, here in vs. 8.
  "**being people having been filled full with [the] Fruit of fair and equitable dealings which bring right relationship within the Way pointed out** (or: from covenant inclusion)**: the one

269

[that is] through Jesus Christ [that is] leading into God's glory (good reputation and manifestation of that which calls forth admiration) **and praise** (approval and commendation) (or: being those filled full of fruit of the eschatological deliverance of a rightwised nature through Jesus Christ, which proceeds into glory and praise that belongs to and pertains to God; or: ... through Jesus Christ, with a view to inhabiting the qualities and characteristics of God's reputation and praise)" (Phil. 1:11).

So it is through the union of mutual indwelling, which in turn enables the production of His Fruit, that is now presented as the basis in which, "**thus [they] can** (or: would) **come to be** [with other MSS: will continue becoming] **disciples** (learners; students; apprentices)." But as we saw, there is more. They (and we) can, or will, come to be disciples "**by [Him].**" This happens when He "places His soul over us (His sheep)" (10:11, above). It happens when He implants Himself (via His Logos, His Spirit) into us.

As is other cases, the personal pronoun, "**Me**" is in the dative case, so this final phrase can also read:
   a) learners in Me – this emphasizes our dwelling within Him;
   b) students and apprentices to, for or with Me – these speak of our relationship with Him, and of our participation with Him.
We are reminded of His words in Mat. 11:29, where He gave an invitation to the yoke of discipleship:
   "**You folks at once lift up My crossbeam** (or: the yoke which is Me; the balance beam that comes from and pertains to Me) **upon you, and instantly learn from Me, because I am** (or: I continuously exist being) **mild-tempered** (gentle; kind; considerate) **and humble** (low) **in the heart, and 'you folks will continue finding refreshment and discovering rest in and for your souls** (the consciousness and whole inner person; the mind, emotions and responses)'" [cf Jer. 6:16]

9. "**Correspondingly as** (or: In the same sphere as; To the same degree as) **the Father loves and accepts Me – and I, Myself, also love and accept you folks – at once begin to remain** (abide; dwell; stay) **within the midst of** (and: in union with; centered in) **My own Love** (acceptance; drive toward reunion)!

The doing of this implanted goal would be impossible for them (and us), unless they (or we) were a part of the mutual indwelling, discussed above. Only by being joined to the Vine can folks "**correspondingly as** (or: in the same sphere as; to the same degree as) **the Father**" accomplish what He says. Only God can do what God does. Only He can "correspondingly love as He loves." But now we can also do this,
   "**because God's love** (the urge toward reunion and the unambiguous, uniting acceptance from God; God's giving of Himself to [us]) **has been poured out in a gush and shed forth so that it now floods within our hearts, permeating the core of our being, through the Set-apart Breath-effect** (or: Holy Spirit; Sacred Attitude) **being given to us** (in us; for us)" (Rom. 5:5).
And because it is God, Himself, it is "in the same sphere as, and to the same degree as," They love and accept us.

First of all, it is because He loves and accepts us that we are able to Love (1 Jn. 4:19). But to "**remain** (abide; dwell; stay) **within the midst of** (and: in union with; centered in) **[His] own Love** (acceptance; drive toward reunion)" is also a work of His Spirit, within us, and the presence of His "**gush-effects** (results of spoken words)" also remaining in us (vs. 7, above). His Love is the Vine in which we are to remain – vss. 4-5, above – and He is the Love – vs. 10, below. We can only do what the Father and the Son, within us, do. It is the Life of the Vine that produces the Fruit of the Vine.

10. "**Whenever** (or: If) **you would** (can) **observe, watch over, guard, keep in view and maintain My implanted goals** (impartations of the finished product within; inward directives; interior purposes and destinies), **[by this] you will continue remaining** (abiding; dwelling) **within the midst of, in union with, and centered in the Love which is Me** (My love; the acceptance and urge toward union, from Me),

correspondingly as (or: to the same level as) **I, Myself, have watched over, observed, guarded, keep and now maintain My Father's implanted goals** (impartations of the finished product within; inward directives; interior purposes and destinies) **and continuously remain** (or: dwell) **within the midst of the Love, acceptance, Self-giving and urge toward union, from, and which is, Him.**

He returns, again, to His "**implanted goals** (impartations of the finished product within; inward directives; interior purposes and destinies)." These are the seeds, or sources, of the inner "finished products" and the "interior purposes and destinies" which He purposes to produce within us and then to spread to others, through us. And now He further explains how this works: "**Whenever [they] would observe, watch over, guard, keep in view and maintain**" what He has planted within them (recall 1 Cor. 3:6-9, we are God's farm; also Gen. 2:15, the human was to till and keep the Garden), then they (and we) "**will continue remaining** (abiding; dwelling) **within the midst of, in union with, and centered in the Love which is [Him].**"

Jesus then goes on to remind them that He had done the same thing, in regard to the goals that the Father had implanted within Him, and so He also "**continuously remains** (or: dwells) **within the midst of the Love, acceptance, Self-giving and urge toward union, from, and which is, Him.**" He walked the Path (Way) before us, and now explains that we can walk the same Path (Way) by following Him and doing what He has done – by "observing (etc.)" the goals that He implants within us.

11. "**I have spoken these things to you to the end that My joy would** (or: can; should) **remain and continuously exist within the midst of you people, and that your joy may be filled full** (or: fulfilled).

And so we see that one of the implanted goals is "**His joy.**" And His intent is that this JOY **would remain and continuously exist within** us, and would apparently increase to the end that OUR joy **may be filled full** (or: fulfilled). In Gal. 5:22, Paul described one aspect, and quality, of the Fruit of the Spirit as being "**joy.**" In Rom. 14:17, we note that "**joy**" is one ingredient of God's reign. Now **His joy** was so great, or of such quality, that the writer of Hebrews instructs us that it was:

> "**instead of and in place of the joy** (or: in the position on the opposite side from the happiness) **continuously lying before Him** (or: lying in the forefront within Him; lying ahead for Him), **[that He] remained under a cross – despising shame** (or: thinking nothing of [the] disgrace) – **and has sat down and now continues seated, remaining at the right [hand] of God's throne**" (Heb. 12:2).

Before that, in Heb. 10:7, it is explained:

> "'**Consider! I am arriving to do** (make; form; create; produce; perform) **Your will** (purpose; intent; resolve), **O God!' – in a little head of a scroll** (a summary of a little scroll), **it has been written concerning Me.**'" [Ps. 40:6-8]

The will of the Father is the Path to Joy.

Now How it is to be fulfilled in them, He does not explain, but in 17:13b, below, He prays:

> "**that they can continuously hold** (or: would habitually have) **My own joy** (the joy that is Mine) **existing having been filled full** (made full and continuing full) **within the midst of themselves.**"

In Lu. 2:10, the agent from the Lord brought good news of great Joy to the shepherds. In Lu. 15:10, Jesus informed us that,

> "**joy is habitually birthed** (or: constantly happens) **in the sight and presence of God's agents** (or: the messengers from God; the folks with the message of God) **upon** (or: on the occasion of) **a progressive changing of the mind** (or: a continued change in thinking and state of consciousness) **by one outcast** (habitual failure; person who constantly makes mistakes; sinner)."

Cf Jn. 16:25; 17:13; 1 Jn. 1:4

12. **"This is My implanted goal** (impartation of the finished product within; inward directive; interior purpose and destiny)**: that you keep on loving, urging toward union, and accepting one another – correspondingly as** (to the same degree as; in the same sphere as) **I love and accept you folks.**

This is the overarching umbrella that is the ultimate destiny for all humanity. It began with Jesus, the First Seed that was planted, sprouted (resurrected) and grew into His first crop, in the 1st century AD, and there have been seasons and crops ever since – some 30-, some 60- and some 100-fold. Of the INCREASE of His government and rule, there will be no end. Jesus implanted the goal – the plan of the ages (Eph. 3:11) – in His first apprentices, and then they continued planting into successive generations, *ad infinitum*. Just as, **"thus God loves** (or: You see God, in this manner, fully gives Himself to and urges toward reunion with) **the aggregate of humanity** (universe; ordered arrangement; organized System [of life and society]; the world)…," now with His Love shed abroad in our hearts, we likewise **"keep on loving, urging toward union, and accepting [the aggregate of humanity] – correspondingly as** (to the same degree as; in the same sphere as) **[He]"** does.

1 Jn. 3:10b-11 affirms:
> **"the one not continuously loving** (unconditionally accepting and seeking union with) **his brother – is not existing out of God** (= is not living with God being his source of life and direction), **because this is the message** [other MSS: promise; or: complete announcement] **which you heard from [the] beginning, so that we are habitually** (or: to the end that we would or could progressively be) **loving** (accepting and participating in) **one another."**

We also have the witness from Paul, in 1 Thes. 4:9,
> **"But now concerning loving one like a brother** (or: brotherly love; = fondness for fellow sharers of the community), **we have no need to continually write to you, for you yourselves are folks continuously taught by God** (God-taught ones) **to continuously love** (accept; urge toward reunion with; totally give yourselves to) **each other."**

13. **"No one continues holding** (or: having) **greater Love** (full self-giving; urge toward reunion) **than this: that someone should place** (set; lay; put) **his soul** (or: inner being; self; person; consciousness which is him) **over [the situation or circumstances of; = cover]** (or: on behalf of) **his friends.**

We are instructed, in 1 Pet. 4:8, that:
> **"Love** (the urge toward union; self-giving) **is constantly covering*** (habitually throwing a veil over; progressively concealing; [and with other MSS: will continue covering]) **a multitude of failures** (mistakes; errors; misses of the target; sins).**"** [*cf* Prov. 10:12]

Paul wrote an essay on *agapē* in 1 Cor. 13. There, in vss. 7-8a, we read an enlightening perception of God's Love:
> **"[Love] continuously covers all mankind; it is habitually loyal to all humanity; it constantly has an expectation for all mankind; it is continuously remaining under and giving support to all people.**
>> (or, since "all" can also be neuter: It [i.e., unambiguous acceptance] progressively puts a protecting roof over all things; it is habitually trusting in, and believing for, all things; it is continually hoping in or for all things; it keeps on patiently enduring all things.).
>
> **The Love** (or: This unrestricted, self-giving drive toward reunion) **never – not even once – fails** (collapses or falls into decay; = becomes ineffectual; [other MSS: falls out or lapses])."

When we place ourselves over the needs of others, and for their supply and protection, we, as God's representatives, become their shield and their fortress of safety, our Life flows into them. A river of Life flows from within us to quench their thirst, and we (as One Loaf – 1 Cor. 10:17) feed and nourish them. We have other admonitions from Paul, in Eph. 5:
> 1. **Keep on becoming** (or: Progressively come to be), **then, imitators** (those made exactly alike so as to portray, express and represent by means of imitation) **of God, as beloved** (or: like loveable) **children,**

2. **and so, keep on walking** (walking around; = progressively living and maintaining your life) **within, and in union with, Love** (self-giving acceptance and the urge for union), **according as the Christ also loves** (or: to the same level and commensurately as the Anointed One loved, accepted and achieved reunion with) **you folks, and also gives** (or: gave) **Himself over in our behalf** (or: then commits and **transfers Himself over us and our [situation]**; [other MSS: you]): **a bearing toward and a bringing to be face to face, even an offering by** (or: in; with; or: to; for) **God [turning] into a fragrant odor** (or: and unto a sweet-smelling incense-sacrifice amid God).

14. **"You folks are** (exist continuously being) **My friends! So if you can – or would – [simply] keep on doing** (or: be habitually producing) **whatever I, Myself, am constantly imparting as the goal in you** (or: repeatedly giving as inner direction to you; progressively implanting as the goal and end for you; now implanting as the interior aim, purpose and destiny by you)! ...

They were like Abraham:
> "**Now Abraham believed** (or: put trust and confidence) **in God** (or: became persuaded by God; adhered to God), **and he was counted into the Way pointed out by Him, and later, he was called 'God's friend'**" (Jas. 2:23; [Isa. 41:8]).

His instructions were to "**keep on doing** (or: be habitually producing) **whatever [He is] constantly imparting**." This was the **goal**, the inward *telos*, which He would be habitually implanting IN them. Otherwise said, we are to habitually bring to fruition what He is repeatedly giving as inner directions to us. These will be His aims, purposes and destinies that He places in the reign that is within us, and that He intends to be accomplished by us – as we abide in Him. Remember: we are His branches!

15. **"I am no longer calling** (or: terming) **you people slaves, because the slave has not seen and does not know** (or: is not aware of) **what his owner** (lord; master) **is habitually doing. Yet now I have declared you folks friends, because I make intimately and experientially known to you everything** (or: all things) **which I heard and hear at My Father's side and in His presence.**

They have completed the first phase of their apprenticeship with Him, and now He has adjusted their status, in relationship to Him. With this increased intimacy, they will now "**intimately and experientially known**" what He had heard, and what He now hears, "**at [His] Father's side and in His presence**." He, too, had now finished His course, and was being caused to ascend back into the atmosphere from which He had descended. He had become the Foundation Stone upon which they, and others, would proceed in building. This is a multi-generational affair. He was now going to be ascending the ladder, but He (along with other agents – Jn. 1:51) would repeatedly descend it to them, as the Ladder (also known as, "the Way"), constantly calling them to a higher place (Rev. 4:1) within the Path that Paul called "**God's invitation to an above place** (or: the prize from, and which is, **the upward calling** from, and which is, the God) **within the midst of and in union with Christ Jesus**" (Phil. 3:14).

The final, dependent clause of this verse reminds us of what Paul said, in Acts 20:27,
> "**I did not draw back from recounting to, for, and among you folks all the purpose, will and counsel of God** (or: from the [situation] to at some point announce again all God's design and determination for you people)."

We live in a time of disclosure. Things are being no longer hidden from us. We live in a day of deliverance.

16. **"You yourselves did not choose Me, but to the contrary I, Myself, selected and picked out** (or: chose) **you folks and placed** (or: set) **you, to the end that you would** (or: can; may) **progressively lead and bring [situations] under control** (or: humbly go your way) **and would** (or: can; should) **be

constantly bearing (bringing forth) **fruit, and your fruit may continuously remain** (stay; abide), **so that whatever you people may seek in petition from the Father – in** (or: centered in) **My Name – He at a certain point would** (or: may suddenly; [other MSS: will proceed to]) **give [it] to** (or: supply for) **you folks.**

We find these ideas put in another way, in 1 Jn. 4:10,

> "**Within this exists** (or: is) **the Love, not that we ourselves have loved** [other MSS: not that we ourselves love or accept] **God, but in contrast, that He Himself loves us and sends** (or: urged toward reunion with us and sent) **His Son as a Representative** (Emissary)**: a cleansing, sheltering covering around our sins** (failures to hit the target, errors, mistakes, deviations)."

The first clause, where Jesus affirms His being the one that did the choosing, in regard to their becoming His apprentices, leads us to recall that it was Yahweh who initiated the personal relationship with Abram, in Gen. 12:1. Later, Jacob was met by God's agents (Gen. 32:1) and then Gen. 32:24-29 we read the story of "a man" wrestling with Jacob all night, and then giving him the name, Israel. With the story of Joseph, his dreams were fulfilled, and he told his brothers that it was God who had sent him to Egypt. And then Moses was chosen (at the burning bush encounter) to lead Israel's Exodus. We have the stories of God choosing Saul to be Israel's first king, and then His choosing of David. God chooses those who will serve a specific function within His developing plan of the ages. Jesus said that He had chosen the twelve, in 6:70, and repeats their choosing in 13:18, above. Even the Judeans expected the Messiah to be God's "**Chosen One**" (Lu. 23:35b). Later, 1 Pet. 2:6 would describe Christ as, "**a chosen** (picked-out), **precious** (held in honor and value) **cornerstone**" (quoting Isa. 28:16).

We also see that the Lord said of Saul,

> "**this one is** (exists being) **a vessel of choice to Me** (or: a picked-out and chosen instrument by and for Me) **to lift up and carry My Name before** (in the sight and presence of) **the ethnic multitudes** (or: nations; Gentiles; non-Israelites) **– as well as [before] kings and [the] sons** (= people) **of Israel**" (Acts 9:15).

So why were the twelve chosen? Here, in vs. 16, He told them that it was "**to the end that you would** (or: can; may) **progressively lead and bring [situations] under control** (or: humbly go your way) **and would** (or: can; should) **be constantly bearing** (bringing forth) **fruit, and your fruit may continuously remain** (stay; abide)." Now the first verb in this compound purpose-clause is commonly just rendered "go," but the primary meaning is "lead," or, "bring under control." Considering the fact that He has made numerous references to giving them "implanted goals" and "inner directives," it seems appropriate to hold to the strict meaning of the verb. They were to **progressively lead** the Way. And we see this in the book of Acts, as well as in the NT letters. The thought of "**bring [situations] under control**" would be necessary in the Jerusalem called-out community, as well as in all the other covenant communities. Since "go" is so frequently used to render this verb, I parenthetically offer, "humbly go your way," since this verb is constructed with the prefix that means "under." It is like Jesus telling His followers to "take the low position" (Lu. 14:10). Doing this will promote the "**fruit**" of "**length before a stirring of emotion** (slowness of rushing toward something; long-enduring; longsuffering; patience; putting anger far away)" and "**gentle friendliness** (absence of ego; mildness)" (Gal. 5:22, 23). Paul was one who certainly "led the way," and also wrote about fruit being produced, and then increasing, in Col. 1:6,

> "**This [Word; message] is being continuously present alongside [and proceeding] into you folks, just as it is also continuously existing within all the ordered System** (within the every world of culture, society, religion, economics and government; centered in the entire aggregate of humanity, the whole universe and all the Roman Empire), **repeatedly bearing fruit of itself and constantly being grown and caused to be increasing, just as also within you folks, from [the] day in which you heard and at once fully experienced – in intimate knowing and accurate realization – the grace of God, within Truth** (or: God's favor resident within [the] truth; God's grace in the midst of reality; or: the favor which, in reality, is God).

The idea of fruit remaining is that, first of all, it has the time needed to mature, and then, so that it will be accessible for folks to partake of it. Following the purpose-clause that we have just discussed is a conjunction, "**so that**," which signals that another purpose-clause is following:

> "**whatever you people may seek in petition from the Father – in** (or: centered in) **My Name – He at a certain point would** (or: may suddenly; [other MSS: will proceed to]) **give [it] to** (or: supply for) **you folks**."

Once again we see that the idea of "petitioning the Father" is tied to:

> a) **in** (or: centered in) **My Name** – discussed under vs. 7, above;
> b) **constantly bearing** (bringing forth) **fruit**.

17. "**I repeatedly give you these goal-oriented, inner directions** (or: I am progressively imparting these purposed aims leading to the union-centered end-and-destiny, by, for and among you folks) **so that you can and would habitually be Loving** (accepting; seeking union with) **one another.**

Observe the repeated and/or progressive action in the first clause:

> a) **I repeatedly give you these goal-oriented, inner directions**;
> b) I am progressively imparting these purposed aims leading to the union-centered end-and-destiny, by, for and among you folks.

As you see, the parenthetical expansion in "b)" also offers the multiple functions (by, for and among) of the dative form of "**you**." He gave it first TO them, and next He will be giving it BY them to other folks.

This verse is virtually a restatement of vs. 12, above. This was a typical mode of Jewish teaching, and a common rhetorical device throughout the Hellenistic world, in that day. The inner, implanted direction about "**habitually Loving** (accepting; seeking union with) **one another**" was a primary ingredient of the Good News. It is what God does with the aggregate of humanity (Jn. 3:16). The Second Epistle of Jn. re-affirms this:

> 5. **And so now I am asking you, Lady, not as writing a strange or newly different implanted goal** (impartation of the finished product within; inward directive of destiny) **to you, but one which we have had from [the] beginning** (or: one which we originally had), **to the intent that we may continuously be loving** (urging toward accepting union with) **each other.**
> 6. **And this is Love: that we may be continuously walking about** (= go on living our lives and ordering our behavior) **according to** (or: down from; in line with; on the level of; in the sphere of; commensurate with) **His implanted goals** (impartations of the finished destiny within; inward directives). **This is the imparted and implanted goal, even as you heard from [the] beginning** (or: even which you originally heard)**: that you would** (or: could) **be continuously walking about within it** (= go on living your lives in union with it)**!**

Also consider 1 Jn. 3:14,

> "**We ourselves have seen, and thus know** (or: are aware), **that we have walked together** (or: proceeded to change, passing from) **out of the Death into the Life, because we are habitually loving the brothers. The person not habitually loving continues remaining** (dwelling; abiding; staying) **within the Death**."

Dan Kaplan observed: "If you are eating from the tree of the knowledge of good and evil (the Law), then you are not loving, because you are dwelling in death."

18. "**Since** (or: If) **the System** (world; controlling ordered arrangement of the political and religious culture) **is constantly regarding you folks with ill-will** (or: hating or radically detaching you), **you continue knowing by experience** (or, as an imperative: be now knowing) **that it has socially detached Me, hated Me and still regards Me with ill-will first – before you people.**

A similar thought is echoed in 1 Jn. 3:1,

'**You people at once consider** (or: look and perceive) **what kind of** (what sort of; what unusual, foreign or exotic) **love** (or: acceptance) **the Father has given to** (or: in; for) **us** [other MSS: you], **which we now have as a gift, to the end that we can** (may; should; would) **be called** (or: named) **God's children** (born-ones; bairns)! **And we are! Because of this** (On account of this; Therefore) **the System** (the world; the realm of the secular and religious; the ordered arrangement of culture, religion, economy and government) **is not habitually having experiential or intimate knowledge of us** (does not know or have insight into us [other MSS: you]), **because it did not know** (or: it does not have an intimate, experiential knowledge of) **Him**."

19. "**If you had been and yet had your being from out of the domination System** (or: world of culture, religion and government) **as a source, the System** (world of control by religion and economy) **would have been being friendly toward and fond of its own production and possession. Yet now, because you do not exist from out of the System** (cosmos) **as a source – but to the contrary I have selected** (or: chosen) **and picked you out from the midst of the System** (world's organization: culture, religion and politics) **– on account of this, the System** (world; institutional religion; society; government) **continues treating you with ill-will** (or: habitually hates you and socially detaches you).

The domination Systems normally just love and accept their own – what they produce and possess. Jesus' apprentices had been called out of those systems (out of the authority of the Darkness, and into the reign of His dear Son – Col. 1:13) and so were no longer their possession, and they also no longer were representatives of what those domination systems were producing. So now, "**because [they] do not exist from out of the System**… **the System** (world; institutional religion; society; government) **continues treating [them] with ill-will** (or: habitually hates [them] and socially detaches [them])." They would be cast out of the synagogues (16:2, below).

20. "**Continually bear in mind** (or: Keep on remembering) **the *Logos*** (Word; thought; message and information that was laid out) **which I, Myself, said to you. A slave is not greater than** (does not exist being superior to) **his owner** (lord; master). **Since they pursue and persecute Me, they will also continue pursuing and persecuting you folks. If they keep** (or: observed and cared for) **My *Logos*** (Word; laid-out message), **they will also proceed to be keeping** (observing and caring for) **yours.**

They are instructed to "**Continually bear in mind** (or: Keep on remembering) **the *Logos***" which He had delivered to them. This was more than wisdom literature, like the book of Proverbs, which spoke of how to have a successful life. It was the Seed that had been planted in them which would grow to produce the Christ in them. It was the Sap that flowed from the main stem of the Vine, and gave Life to His branches.

However, the fact was that those of the domination System would "**continue pursuing and persecuting**" them as they had, and still were, doing the same to Him. Furthermore, His disciples should not expect those of the System to "keep, observe or care for" their *Logos*. To the contrary…

21. "**But to the contrary, they will proceed doing** (accomplishing; making; performing; producing) **all these things unto you and bringing them forth into the midst of you folks, on account of My Name, because they have not seen nor do they know the One sending Me.**

Those who are united to the domination System (vs. 18) do not know God. That of course referred to those who made up, and had the worldview and way of thinking as, the Empire. But it also included Second-Temple Judaism. It was from this second group that the front line of persecution (vs. 20) would enter into their midst, because His followers would bear His Name.

22. **"If I did not come and speak to** (or: among) **them, they had not been holding failure** (or: were having no sin or error; continued possessing no deviation). **But now** (at this time) **they continue holding nothing which like a specious and deceptive cloak appears in front around their sin**
> (or: they are not continuing to hold that which is put forward to hide the situation concerning their failure; they are not habitually having an excuse or pretense about their deviation, error and miss of the target).

The "**they**" of vs. 20b, vs. 21, here in vs. 22, as well as in vss. 24-25, below, all refer to the same group: the Judean leadership of the religious system which scholars now refer to as Second-Temple Judaism. These were the ones that would execute Jesus and foment the persecution of the Christ-followers, of which we read in the book of Acts. Later, the beast upon which Jerusalem rode would continue the persecution which was begun in Jerusalem (Mat. 23:37), and then would continue throughout the Diaspora within the Empire.

But the execution of the Innocent One would remove the "**specious and deceptive cloak**" from those who instigated the act, and the persecutions that would follow. They would now be disclosed as being Babylon the Great, the mother of the prostitutes (Rev. 17:3-6). But Jesus had seen through their disguise, and had proclaimed:
> "**[You] snakes! [You] offspring** (brood) **of vipers** (poisonous serpents)! **How can you flee and escape from the judging which has the qualities, character and significance of the valley of Hinnom** (= the sentence to the city dump [Greek: Gehenna; = the Valley of Hinnom]; the deciding which pertains to the waste depository of the city)**?** [*cf* Jer. 19:1-15] **Because of this – look and consider! – I, Myself, am continuing in commissioning and sending off to you people prophets, wise people and scholars** (scribes; theologians of the Law). **Of them, [some] you folks will proceed to be killing, and [some] you will proceed to crucify** (hang and put to death on stakes). **Further, of them [some] you people will continue severely whipping** (scourge; lash) **within your synagogues, and then you, yourselves, will continue pursuing and persecuting [them] from city to city** (or: town to town), **with the result that upon you, yourselves, can** (or: would; should) **come all [the] just** (equitable; rightwised) **blood being continuously poured out** (or: spilled) **upon the** (or: this) **Land – from the blood of rightwised** (just; fair; in-right-relationship; upright) **Abel, until the blood of Zechariah, the son of Barachiah** (or: Baruch), **whom you people murdered between the Temple and the altar. Assuredly** (Amen; Count on it), **I am now saying to you people, it will progressively move toward this point, and then arrive – all these things! – upon THIS generation!**" (Mat. 23:33-36).

23. **"The one who by habit hates Me, detaches from Me or treats Me with ill-will also continues hating My Father, habitually treats Him with ill-will and keeps on radically detaching from Him.**

Although this can apply to anyone, we suspect that he was referring to those who were wanting to kill Him – the Judean leadership. In their rejection of Jesus, they were rejecting the God of their ancestors. Let us consider what we have in 1 Jn. 2:22-23a,
> "**Which one is** (exists continuously being) **the liar, if not the person habitually denying** (repeatedly disowning; constantly contradicting), **[saying] that Jesus is not the Christ** (the Anointed One [= Messiah])**? This person is** (exists being) **the anti-anointing** (or: anti-anointed person; the one taking the place of and being in the opposite position of the anointing and of Christ)**: the one habitually denying** (contradicting; saying, "No," about) **the Father and the Son. Everyone, who** (or: All mankind, which) **in continuously contradicting or denying the Son, does not even have** (or: not even is he possessing; neither holds) **the Father...**"

24. **"If I did not do** (perform; produce; create) **the works** (actions; deeds) **among them or within them – which no one else** (or: no other one) **did** (performed; produced) **– they were having no sin or error**

(they had not been holding a failure or a miss of the target). **But now** (at this time) **they have both seen and hated with radical detachment from both Me and My Father.**

His first statement repeats the same idea as vs. 22, above, so He is employing restatement to underline His point. In vs. 22, it was His words; here it expands to His works. These verses echo 9:41, above,
> **"If you men had been and were continuing being blind ones, you were not holding and would not be having sin** (error; a miss of the goal; failure). **Yet now you continue saying that, 'We are continuously seeing and habitually observing.' Your error** (sin; failure; miss of the target; deviation) **continues remaining.**"

Here, in vs. 24, He affirms that they **have seen** His works, but still they "**hated with radical detachment from both [Him] and [His] Father.**"

25. **"But then, [this is] so that the *Logos*** (Word; message; pronouncement; blueprint) **having been written in their Law would** (could; should; may) **be fulfilled: 'They hated, treated badly and radically detached from Me for no cause** (for no reason at all; gratuitously).**'** [Ps. 35:19; 69:4]

Jesus viewed this situation (pertaining to the Judean leadership) as a part of Israel's story, and thus part of the Plan. This is a remarkable statement: their hate and rejection of Him was a fulfillment of their Law; it was that to which their Torah would lead. Paul would refer to this in Rom. 10:4a,
> "**you see, Christ [is] an end of Law** (or: for Christ [is] Law's goal and destiny; for Christ [was the] final act of [the] Law) **[leading] into the Way pointed out...**"

26. **"Whenever the One called alongside to aid, comfort, encourage and bring relief** (the Helper; the Paraclete) **can** (or: may; should would) **come – the Spirit of the Truth** (or: the Breath-effect of, and which is, Reality; the attitude which is genuineness) **Which** (or: Who) **is constantly** (habitually; progressively) **proceeding and traveling out from beside the Father** (= emanating from the Father's presence; or: from a presence which is the Father), **[and] Which** (or: Whom) **I, Myself, will continue sending to you from the Father's side** (or: from the presence which is the Father) **– THAT** (or: that One) **will continue bearing witness** (giving testimony; showing evidence) **about Me.**

He now takes them back to the topic of 14:16 and 26, above, where He first mentions the Paraclete, giving Its same identity (**the Spirit of the Truth**) in 14:17. There, He affirmed that, "**the System** (world; ordered arrangement of religion, politics and culture; the system of domination) **has no power** (is not able) **to receive**" the **Spirit of the Truth.** That was because they were "**continuously existing being dead ones in** (or: to; with; or: by) **the results and effects of your stumblings aside** (offenses; wrong steps) **and failures to hit the mark** (or: mistakes; errors; times of falling short; sins; deviations)" (Eph. 2:1). *Cf* 1 Jn. 3:14, above. Those who are dead have no power to do anything.

Take note of the present tense of the verb in the dependent clause, "**Which** (or: Who) **is constantly** (habitually; progressively) **proceeding and traveling out from beside the Father** (= emanating from the Father's presence; or: from a presence which is the Father)." God is a dynamic God, and this clause gives us a picture of His Reality. From this, we have the durative future tense where Jesus says, "**Which** (or: Whom) **I, Myself, will continue sending to you from the Father's side** (or: from the presence which is the Father)." He will continue sending from the constant proceeding of this Spirit of Truth.

When "the Breath-effect of, and which is, Reality" comes to us, "**THAT** (or: that One) **will continue bearing witness** (giving testimony; showing evidence) **about Me,**" because Jesus IS the Truth and Reality. This Breath-effect (this Spirit of the Truth) IS, in fact Jesus, the Christ, Who will continuously breathe His Life and Reality into us who are the Second Humanity (the Last Adam – 1 Cor. 15:45-47).

Testimony was given about Him, in 1 Jn. 5:6,

"**This is the One at one point coming through water and blood and breath** (or: spirit; Breath-effect), **Jesus Christ. Not within the water alone** (or: not in only water), **but rather within the water and within the blood** (or: in union with water and in union with blood; [other MSS add: and within spirit; note: figure of a human birth, or natural lineage]), **and then there is the breath – that which is continuing to give evidence** (or: and the Spirit {Breath-effect} continuously exists being the One repeatedly testifying), **because the breath is** (or: Spirit or Breath-effect exists being) **the Truth and Reality!**
> (or: and the spirit is the One {or: one} continuously witnessing that the Spirit is The Truth! or: the breath is that which constantly gives testimony that the Breath-effect is reality...)."

27. **"Now you folks, also, continue giving witness** (are habitually testifying; are progressively being evidence), **because – from [the] beginning** (= the start or the outset) **– you are with Me** (or: because you constantly exist, being with Me from [the] origin).**"**

Just as the Spirit of the Truth/Reality continues bearing witness about Him, so too, they "**continue giving witness** (are habitually testifying; are progressively being evidence)." Their mission is the same as the mission of the Spirit of this Reality. Because they abide in this new Reality (the Vine), their very existence gives evidence of this new reality. And, "**since someone [is]* within Christ, [there is] a new creation.**"

Is this an allusion to Jn. 1:1, "Within a Beginning was the Logos..."? Is He speaking of the "**beginning**" of this new creation, that started with the incarnation of the Logos, or when Jesus began His ministry and they were with Him from the start? The potential ambiguity may be speaking of the first level reading – that of Jesus' earthly ministry in the 1st century AD. Or, is could be referring to the concept of Rom. 11:36, that just as He came from out of God, so did they... and all things. The same could be said of the other Witness (vs. 26), the Spirit/Breath-effect of the Truth/Reality.

We have another witness to this verse, in 1 Jn. 1:
1. **The One who was continuously existing from a beginning** (or: He Who was progressively being parted away from [the] Source, Headship and Rule). **The One whom we have listened to, and still hear; the One whom we have discerningly seen, and now yet perceive with our eyes** (or: in our eyes); **the One whom we contemplatively gazed upon as a public spectacle** (as an exhibit in a theater) **and our hands handled in investigation** (felt about for and touched) **– groping around the Word of the Life** [cf Lu. 24:39]
> (or: the Logos, which is the Life; the thought which pertains to life; the Information and Idea from the Life; the message with the character and qualities of the Life; the Reason which belongs to the Life; [note: I have treated *ho* as the definite article in the first four phrases here and in vs. 3; many treat it as a neuter relative and render it: That which]),
2. **and the Life was manifested** (or: is brought into the clear light and made visible)! **And so we have discerningly seen, and still perceptively observe, and are repeatedly testifying** (bearing witness; giving evidence) **and in a message are constantly reporting to you folks the Life which has the character and qualities of the Age** (or: the life of, for and pertaining to the age [of the Messiah]; eonian life) **which Certain [Life] was continuously existing [oriented and proceeding] toward** (or: was face to face with) **the Father, and was manifested** (or: is made visible; appeared) **to us, in us, by us, among us and for us.** [cf Jn. 14:26]
3. **The One whom we have seen, and still now see, and we have heard, and now continue listening to and hearing, we are also constantly reporting to you, to the end that you, too, may be continuously having common being and existence** (or: would be progressively holding partnership and participation) **with us. And yet, our common being and existence** (or: participation; fellowship; partnership; sharing) **[is] with the Father, even with His Son** (or: as well as with the Son from Him; or, in apposition: and with the Son which is Him), **Jesus Christ.** Cf Acts 1:8; 2:32; 4:33; 1 Pet. 5:1; 2 Pet. 1:16

Chapter 16

1. **"I have spoken these things to, for and among you folks so that you would** (could; may; should) **not at any point be caught in a snare** (or: trap) **by surprise, or be made to stumble or falter.**

A snare is usually a trap that is not recognized as such, so the one caught in it is taken by surprise. Things were about to suddenly and drastically change for the disciples – their Master and Teacher, their Leader, would be taken from them and it would seem that they were vulnerable and like scattered sheep, without their Shepherd. He goes on to explain…

2. **"They will continue making you gathering-outcasts** (synagogue-exiles) **– ones turned away from the synagogues** (= they will continue cutting you off from the rights and privileges of the Jewish society). **But further, an hour is progressively coming with the result that everyone in the process of killing you folks off may imagine** (suppose; hold the opinion of; think) **[himself] to be proceeding in presenting** (bearing forward) **an offering of sacred service to, and for, God,**

Not only did it seem like Israel was still in exile (with even those within "their own" Land being ruled by a foreign power), but the followers of Jesus would be like exiles within their own communities – cut off from their own culture and from the centers of their religious and social life: the synagogues.

Saul, in the book of Acts would come to be an infamous example of Jesus' second statement (Acts 8:1; 9:1; 26:9). This has continued to be the case all through history wherever religious, radical extremists have had power – in both literal and metaphorical (or, social) application of their power and authority. When this happens within religions, those who are "**in the process of killing folks off**" demonstrate that they are walking in the Darkness.
> "**The person who keeps on speaking [thus, as though] to be within the Light, and yet is constantly hating** (or: regarding with ill-will or detaching from) **his brother** (or: = fellow believer; or: fellow member of his society), **is a liar and continues being within the Darkness** (the obscure dimness of the realm of the shadows and lack of the light of the Day; = the prior night) **until the present moment…. that Darkness blinds** (or: blinded) **his eyes**" (1 Jn. 2:9, 11b).

3. **"and they will continue doing** (or: performing) **these things because they neither personally know** (or: intimately or experientially recognize; have insight into) **the Father, nor Me.**

This statement applied to Second-Temple Judaism, and then to institutional Christianity, ever since, as history (and our present day) gives witness. Paul references this fact, in Rom. 10:2,
> "**For you see, I can repeatedly bear witness to and for them that they constantly hold God's zeal and they continuously have a boiling jealously and hot aspiration concerning God, but however, NOT down from** (or: on the level of and in accordance with) **full and accurate experiential, personal knowledge, recognition or insight.**" *Cf* 1 Cor. 2:8

4. **"Nevertheless, I have spoken these things to you so that whenever their hour may** (or: should; would) **come, you folks can call them to mind** (or: would remember them), **that I, Myself, told you. Now I did not tell you these things originally** (from out of [the] beginning; from [the] start; = at first), **because I was being with you.**

If we knew, as children, the things that we would have to endure later in life, we would be burdened with that knowledge for years, before it came to pass. The disciples had been with Him for around three years (according to the calculations of some) and had seen so much of the works that He had done, had been implanted with the goals that He had in view for them, and had produced some of the same works when He had sent them out on a mission. Furthermore, in that time they had been producing Fruit, from being joined to the Vine. Also, what he was referring to was about to happen, so they would really have no time to worry about it. The strength gained by seeing that what He had said had come to pass would add to their trust and help them through the dark hours that were just about upon them.

Jesus reprises 14:28-29, above, where He had told them that when this came to pass they could trust and believe.

5. **"Yet now** (at this time) **I am progressively leading [the way] under** (or: humbly going away) **toward the One sending Me, and no one from among you folks is presently asking** (or, as a subjunctive: should keep on inquiring of) **Me, 'To what place are you progressively leading [the way] under** (or: submissively departing)**?'**

Observe that He framed the upcoming event, which we now know would be His physical death, as "**leading [the way] under** (or: humbly going away) **toward the One sending [Him]**." The Life that He led was the Way to the Father. The fact that He was humbly "**leading**" meant that others would follow Him. In Eph. 4:8 we find Paul reaching back to Ps. 68:18 to explain Christ's journey back to the One sending Him:

"**Going up** (or: Stepping up; Ascending) **into a height** (unto [the] summit) **He led** (or: leads) **captive a captive multitude** (or: He led 'captivity' captive). **He gave** (or: gives) **gifts to mankind** (or: for, in and among the humans; to humanity)."

As "'**to what place [He was] progressively leading [the way]**," Heb. 6:19b-20a informs us that it was: "**the interior** (or: then progressively going fully into the inner part) **with reference to the veil** (= entering into the interior [behind] the curtain, which was the Holy of holies, in the Temple) **where a Forerunner, Jesus, entered over us** (or: on our behalf; over our [situation])."

That "**place**" was with our spirits (keep in mind that we are the Temple), within the midst of the core of our beings. Also, recall 14:2, above, "**I am progressively passing** (or: traveling) **along to prepare and make ready a place in you**." And then, in 14:3 He told them:

"**Even if I should journey on and prepare** (make suitable, fit and appropriate) **a place** (or: a spot; a position; a role) **in you folks** (or: with, among and for you), **I am now presently** (or: progressively; repeatedly; habitually) **going and coming again, and then, I will progressively take you folks in My arms and receive you to Myself**..."

6. **"But now because I have spoken these things to you people, grief, sorrow and sadness has filled the heart of you folks** (or: = the core emotion of the group; or: = your hearts).

They were probably unable to fully take it all in, but they perceived enough to be filled with grief and sorrow. This is a normal, human reaction. Even when we understand the reasons, and perceive those reasons to be good ones, it is still a time of grief when a loved-one departs from us. Also, they were probably unaware of how soon, and in what manner, He would return to them.

7. **"Nevertheless, I, Myself, am continuously telling you folks the Truth** (or: repeatedly laying-out Reality to, for and among you folks; habitually *Logos-ing* within you a revealed reality that is based upon an appearance, and which is neither hidden nor deceitfully false). **It progressively bears together for you people** (It continues being advantageous and expedient in you; It is now for your benefit) **that I should go away. For if I should not go away, the One called alongside to aid, comfort, encourage and bring relief** (the Helper; the Paraclete) **will not come** [other MSS: may by no means come] **to you and be face to face with you folks. Yet if I should journey on** (or: would travel on to another place) **I will be repeatedly sending Him to you folks.**

Let us take time to contemplate these four statements. In Jn. 14:6 He told them that He WAS the Truth, the Reality. Now He affirms that He is saying "**the Truth**" to, for, among and within them. Jesus used a different verb, "have spoken," in vs. 6, above. But now He uses the verb *legō*, which is the source of the noun *logos*, which is what He was. His words were "repeatedly laying-out Reality to, for and among" them, but considering the verb that He chose to use, I have offered a unique rendering of it. He was "habitually *Logos-ing* within you a revealed reality that is based upon an appearance, and which is neither hidden nor deceitfully false." Obviously, in this last rendering, I have also given an expanded definition of the word more normally rendered "truth" of "reality." What was considered to be "true" was that which could be seen to be what it is, shown in adequate light to be clearly seen. It was thus the opposite of that which is hidden or deceitfully false. He was creating Truth/Reality within them by the *Logos* of the implanted goals, and the imparted end that He had in view for them. But, recalling 14:6, He was also planting Himself within them.

The second sentence gives us a clear reason for why Christ had to die: "**It progressively bears together for you people** (It continues being advantageous and expedient in you; It is now for your benefit) **that I should go away**." He was leaving for their benefit. He was dying so that the Paraclete would come to them and thus be available to be "**called alongside to aid, comfort, encourage and bring relief**" to them. The coming of the Paraclete was dependent upon His departure. Now this may sound strange to us, until we realize that this would be the form in which He, Himself, would come to them. Recall that He has said to them, "**I am presently progressively** (or: repeatedly; habitually) **coming toward** (face-to-face-with) **you folks**," in 14:28, above. He termed the Paraclete as "**the Spirit of the Truth**," in 15:26. Can we discern the connection? He leaves, and then He, the Truth, comes; He leaves and then He sends the Spirit of the Truth. Rather than try to "figure this out" or fit into a philosophical formula, we may be better off to simply accept the seeming paradox. We suggest that it is the same thing as Philip seeing Jesus, and thus seeing the Father. His words describe a reality that we can observe, not a "logical conclusion" that our flesh-oriented mind can comprehend.

He restates the reality of His second sentence in His fourth sentence: "**Yet if I should journey on** (or: would travel on to another place) **I will be repeatedly sending Him to you folks**." Notice the habitual aspect of the verb: **repeatedly sending**. This is because He describes Himself, in Rev. 1:8, as "**the One continuously being, even the One Who was and continued being, and the One presently and continuously** (or: progressively) **coming and going** (or: habitually being on the go and repeatedly moving about)."

Again, let us stress this: Jesus did NOT say that He needed to depart so that they (or: we) could be saved or forgiven of their sins. He did not have to leave in order to do either of those things. He had to leave so that He (and the Father, and the Breath-effect) could return in a different form in which His Presence could dwell within our hearts and spirits – and be in their/our midst whenever two or three are gathered together in His Name (Mat. 18:20).

8. "**And upon coming, that One will be progressively testing and putting the domination System** (or: the aggregate of humanity; or: the world of culture, society, religion, economy and politics) **to the proof** (or: exposing and presenting convincing arguments about the aggregate of humanity) **concerning error** (failure; deviation; missing the target; sin) **and about fairness and equity in rightwised relationships which comprise the Way pointed out** (or: concerning eschatological deliverance that produces covenant inclusion) – **and about dividing and separating** (sifting) **for evaluating and deciding** (or: concerning judging).

Now He speaks in third-person ("that One") in the same manner as He spoke of "the Son of Man." We must remain aware of His style of speaking, and not focus on the arithmetic or philosophy of later theologians. Here, His point is about what the Paraclete would do:

a) **be progressively testing and putting the domination System** (etc.) **to the proof concerning error** (etc.) – these are part of the refining process;

b) **about fairness and equity in rightwised relationships which comprise the Way pointed out** (etc.) – this has to do with how we "walk the path" and live as a covenant community;

c) **about dividing and separating** (sifting) **for evaluating and deciding** (etc.) – this can be about the condition of His "threshing floor" (Mat. 3:12), or about the material that was used to build His Temple (1 Cor. 3:12-17).

Functionally, the Paraclete replaces the Law. It "exposes and presents convincing arguments [to us] about the aggregate of humanity;" It speaks to us and teaches us about "failure, deviation, missing the target and sin;" It instructs us "concerning eschatological deliverance that produces covenant inclusion;" It informs us "concerning judging." This is how Paul received his unveilings (revelations), and how he shepherded the called-out communities.

9. **"About error** (failure; missing the mark; sin; deviation), **on the one hand, because they are not constantly trusting, continuing faithful, or progressively believing into Me.**

This now defines sin and failure to hit the Target (Christ). It defines failure and deviation as a lack of "**constantly trusting, continuing faithful, or progressively believing into [Him]**." Notice the preposition: **into**. In the previous chapter He had been speaking to them of His being the Vine, and them as being His branches. Branches are joined "**into**" the Vine – they participate in the Life of the Vine.

Let us consider Paul's understanding in Gal. 3:21b-22,

"**For if a law** (or: [the] Law) **were given which continued having power or being able at any point to make alive** (to construct or create living folks; to engender living ones; to impart life), **really, the eschatological deliverance of fairness and equity resulting in righted relationships** (the liberating and rightwising qualities of justice, freedom from guilt, and life as it ought to be within the Way pointed out; or: = new covenant inclusion) **was likely being from out of the midst of [the] Law** [= Torah; other MSS: residing within law]. **But to the contrary, the Scripture encircles and encloses [as fish in a net] all things, shuts them up together and locks the whole** (the totality of everything) **under** (or: by) **failure** (error; deviation; the missing of the target; sin), **to the end that, from out of Jesus Christ's faithfulness** (or: forth from the midst of the faith from Jesus Christ; from the midst of the trust and conviction which is Jesus, [the] Anointed One), **the Promise would suddenly** (or: could at some point) **be given to** (or: in; for; by) **the folks habitually experiencing trust** (or: progressively believing with faith's conviction)." [cf Rom. 11:32]

Observe the role of Jesus' faithfulness, the faith that comes "from" Him, and the conviction which IS Jesus (rendering the phrase first a possessive, next as an ablative, then lastly as apposition).

We also have Paul's insight from Rom. 14:23b,

"**everything which [is] not forth from out of faith** (or: [does] not arise from trust and conviction) **is a failure to hit the target** (exists being an error; is a deviation from the goal; continues being sin and a mistake)."

10. **"About justice, fairness and equity in rightwised relationships of the Way pointed out** (or: concerning eschatological deliverance that produces covenant participation), **on the other hand, because I am progressively leading [everything] under control by withdrawing toward** (or: to; [to be] face-to-face with) **the Father, and so you folks are no longer continually gazing upon and contemplatively watching Me.**

It may be easier to understand His explanation if we begin with the second half of the verse. It is because He was leaving them (in His current form) that they would need the Paraclete to be the One who would test folks and put their actions to the proof, in regard to "**justice, fairness and equity in rightwised relationships of the Way pointed out**." As He would lead them into all Truth (vs. 13, below), He would progressively teach them "concerning eschatological deliverance that produces covenant participation."

Now the work of the Paraclete was not just for the called-out, covenant communities. It is for everyone, for as vs. 8 declares, His work is for all of "**the domination System** (or: the aggregate of humanity; or: the world of culture, society, religion, economy and politics)."

11. "**And about dividing and separating** (sifting) **for evaluation and decision, because the ruler** (one in first place; chief) **of this System** (world of culture, economics, religion or politics; domination system) **has been sifted, separated, evaluated and decided about, and now stands judged**
> (or: Yet concerning judging, because the Prince and Leader of this universe and the aggregate of humanity has had a decision made about Him, and He now stands judged [by the System]).

Observe the beautiful ambiguity: this verse can be speaking of two different subjects. We suggest that both readings are correct, each applying in its own way, to its own subject.

The first reading can be speaking of the chief priest, or even the Sanhedrin (speaking of the corporate group of elders), or of the decision that has been made (by God) about the ruler of the Empire, as prophesied in Dan. 2:21-45.

The parenthetical reading understands Jesus to be speaking of Himself, as "the Prince and Leader of this universe and the aggregate of humanity." The Judean leadership had made "a decision made about Him, and He now stands judged [by the Judean religious System]." This reading would then be a parallel to Jn. 12:31,
> "**At the present time** (or: Now) **is an evaluation OF and a decision PERTAINING TO** (or: a sifting of and separation for; or: a judging FROM) **this System** (or: this ordered arrangement; this world; this polity, culture and religion; or: this system of control and subjugation; or: this aggregate of humanity). **Now the Ruler** (the one invested with power; the **Leader**; the chief; the ruler; or: the Original One; **The Beginning One**; the **Prince**) **of this System** (or: cosmos) **will progressively be ejected outside**
>> (or: At this time the Chief of this world of culture, religion and government, the Originator and Controlling Principle of this cosmos and ordered arrangement of the universe, will proceed in being thrown out, [to the] outside [of it])."

12. "**I still have** (or: hold) **many things to be progressively telling** (laying out for; informing) **you folks, but yet, you continue not yet being able** (or: having no power) **to habitually or progressively pick it up and carry** (or: bear) **it right now** (at present).

We find this statement echoes in Paul, in 1 Cor. 3:
> 1. **And yet I myself, brothers, was not able to speak to you folks as to spiritual people** (= having the effect of the Breath; led by the Spirit/Attitude), **but to the contrary as to fleshly folks** (= people of flesh, being focused thereon; = as "natural" people, unaffected by the Breath/Spirit) – **as to infants in Christ** (or: babies/adolescents in Anointing).
> 2. **I gave you folks milk to drink, not solid food, for you were continuing not as yet being able or having power. But then, neither are you yet now** (at present) **able** (or: having power), **for you are still fleshly ones** (= people of flesh, focused on ordinary life, with natural thinking).

We hear another echo in Heb. 5:
> 11. **concerning Whom the Word** (*Logos*; Blueprint) **[has] much to say to us – and [it is] difficult to be explained** (or: about whom the message [is] great and [is] hard to be understood [or] for us to say; or: concerning Whom, for us [there is] much to say – and [it is] hard to be understood), **since you have become sluggish** (dull) **for hearing.**
> 12. **For also, being indebted** (or: obligated) **to be teachers, because of the time [gone by], you again have a need of someone to be teaching you folks the elementary things** (or: fundamental principles; rudiments and rules) **of the beginning of the brief spoken words** (or:

which are the principle of the short thoughts; concerning the Beginning, from the little messages) **of and from God, and so you have become folks having need of milk, and not solid food.**
13. **For everyone partaking** (sharing in) **milk [is] untried** (inexperienced) **pertaining to [the] Word of the Way pointed out** (from the message of fair and equitable dealing or an idea about rightwised relationships; also: = in regard to the idea of, and the reason derived from, covenant membership), **for he is a babe** (a non-speaking infant, or one who is still childish and unfit to bear weapons).
14. **But solid food belongs to perfected ones** (complete and mature ones; ones who are fully developed and have reached the goal of their destiny) – **those, because of habit, having organs of perception trained as in gymnastic exercise and thus being skilled, because of practice, and disciplined with a view to a discerning** (or: when facing the act of separating, making a distinction and then a decision about) **both good and evil** (both that which is excellent, ideal, of good quality, profitable and beautiful, as well as that which is of bad quality, worthless, ugly or of bad form; or: = between right and wrong),

It would first of all take the coming of the Paraclete (Acts 2), and then it would take a period of growth and maturing (Eph. 4:13-16).

13. **"Yet, whenever THAT** (or: that One) – **the Spirit of the Truth** (or: the Breath-effect from Reality; the Spirit which is the Truth; the attitude which is genuineness) – **would come** (or: Nonetheless, at the time when that spirit which is truth and reality should come), **It** (or: He) **will constantly be a Guide and will progressively lead you folks on the Path** (or: it will continue leading the way for you) **directed toward and proceeding on into the midst of all the Truth and Reality** [other MSS: in union with all this truth and reality] – **for It** (He; it) **will not habitually speak from Itself** (or: Himself), **but rather, as many things as It** (He; it) **continuously hears, It** (He; it) **will proceed speaking, and will continue reporting back to** (or: in; among) **you folks the things presently and progressively coming, as well as those that are habitually coming and going.**

In 14:26, above, we read that, "**the Helper, the set-apart Spirit**… **will be progressively teaching you all things**…" It was later reported that,

"**you folks continue having the effects** (or: constantly hold and progressively possess the results) **of an anointing from the set-apart One** (or: the Holy One), **and so you all have seen and are aware** (or: know; perceive; [other MSS: and you know all {those} folks]).… **and the effect of the anointing which you folks received from Him constantly remains** (abides; dwells; makes its home) **within you folks, and you continually have no use** (or: you are not constantly having a need) **that anyone should keep on teaching you, but rather, just as the effect of His anointing is continuously and progressively teaching you about everything** (or: concerning all people), **and is continuously true, and real, and is not a lie, even according as it taught** (or: as He instructs) **you: you are continuously abiding** (remaining; dwelling; being at home) **within and in union with Him**" (1 Jn. 2:20, 27).

The Way, or the Path, is clearly laid out as progressing from one's current place, on to another. Truth's Spirit "**will constantly be a Guide and will progressively lead you folks on the Path** (or: it will continue leading the way for you)." The goal of this journey is being in "**the midst of all the Truth and Reality.**" The "Breath-effect from Reality" directs us toward, and causes us to be, "**proceeding on into the midst**" of this new Reality. Like we read in Rom. 11:36, it is "from Him (who IS the Reality)," and then back "into Him."

When Jesus was on earth, with them, He spoke to them what He heard from the Father (Jn. 7:18; 12:49-50). So now "**the Spirit** which is **the Truth**" (reading the phrase as apposition) is doing the same thing: "**It** (He; it) **will not habitually speak from Itself** (or: Himself), **but rather, as many things as It** (He; it) **continuously hears, It** (He; it) **will proceed speaking, and will continue reporting back to** (or: in;

among) **you folks.**" And now what is reported to us are, "**the things presently and progressively coming, as well as those that are habitually coming and going.**" This is a vital, ongoing Life of being connected to the Vine, receiving what Truth is telling us – being informed by the new Reality of this new creation.

We see this interaction expressed, when Paul told Timothy,
> "**Now the Spirit** (or: Breath-effect) **is explicitly saying that within subsequent seasons** (in fitting situations and on appropriate occasions which will be afterwards)..." (1 Tim. 4:1a).

Hearing from the Spirit is the normal Christian Life. In Acts 11:12, Peter told his audience, "**So the Breath-effect** (or: Spirit) **told me to at once go with them...**" Of course this sort of thing was nothing new. Yahweh spoke to Cain, in Gen. 4, and to Noah in Gen. 6, to Abram in Gen. 12, etc., all through the OT. What is new is the constant abiding in the Vine, in intimate relationship via the Spirit, as well as our now BEING God's home.

14. "**That One will progressively glorify Me** (will keep on giving Me an assumed appearance, recognition, and a good reputation, with a manifestation of Me which calls forth praise), **because It** (He; it) **will constantly take from out of what is Mine** (or: receive from the one from, and which is, Me) **and will repeatedly report back to you folks** (or: will continue announcing to and informing you).

The Spirit of the Truth (and: Reality) will **glorify Jesus.** Let us lay out the optional renderings of the verb, and the object of the verb, Jesus:
> a) The Spirit of the Truth (and: Reality) will **glorify [Jesus]** – and if it does not, it is another spirit; it will give glory TO Jesus, or present Him as "the glory of God," the Shekinah;
> b) The Spirit will keep on giving [Jesus] an assumed appearance – in other words, it will make Jesus discernible, recognizable, or able to be perceived within the vessel/instrument (i.e., person; group; action; event) within whom, or which, He is present;
> c) It (or: He) will give Jesus a good reputation;
> d) It will create some manifestation of Jesus' presence which will call forth praise to Him.

What did He mean by, "**It** (He; it) **will constantly take from out of what is Mine**"? We suggest that one aspect of what He meant was that which was revealed through the Spirit to Peter, Paul and the others, and was, in fact, His message – His *Logos,* His Blueprint, His Idea, etc. (*cf* 1:1, above). The parenthetical optional reading, "receive from the one from, and which is, Me," means that the Spirit, the Paraclete, may function as a communication link, bringing programmed information from one member of the body and reporting it to other members of the body – as did the prophets – and the message would be Christ, Himself, that is being announced.

The Spirit of the Truth will present Jesus to the called out communities, and to others, as Christ's sovereign activities, and the Logos, expand, grow and spread-out into all of humanity.

15. "**All things – as many and as much as the Father continuously possesses** (or: whatever the Father has and constantly holds) **– progressively, then continuously, exists being Mine. On this account I said that from out of what is Mine It** (or: from the one from, and which is, Me, He) **is continuously receiving** (habitually taking) **and will continue reporting back** (announcing) **to, for, and among, you folks.**

The scope of His first sentence leaves nothing out. So, of course the Spirit of the Truth "**is continuously receiving** (habitually taking) **from out of what is [His].**" So what It continues reporting back to us (as well as for us and among us) is the real deal. The Spirit of the Truth passes on the Truth, the new Reality. It also passes on information concerning the Way, and the Life. And since Jesus IS the resurrection, It passes on the Resurrection to us. In 17:10, below, He affirms, "**all My possessions are**

Yours, and Your possessions are Mine, and I have been – and remain – glorified (made to be a recognized appearance and a manifestation which calls forth praise) **in and among them**."

The Spirit of the Truth brought something more, as a further affirmation on this topic, to Paul, as we read in Col. 1:19; 2:9,

"**All humanity was transferred, given over** (or: All things were delivered and committed) **to Me by, and under, My Father, and yet no one is by habit completely or accurately knowing the Son in an intimate and personal way – except the Father – nor does anyone continue having an intimate experiential full-knowledge of the Father – except the Son, as well as to, or in, whomever the Son would continue desiring** (or: determining) **to unveil or reveal [Him]**…. **because within Him all the effect of the fullness of the Deity** (the result of the filling from the Godship and feminine aspect of the Divine Nature) **is repeatedly corporeally** (or: bodily, as a whole; embodied; as a body) **settling down and progressively taking up permanent residence** (or: is continuously dwelling in person)."

We are informed in Mat. 11:27 that He said it this way:

"**All humanity was transferred, given over** (or: All things were delivered and committed) **to Me by, and under, My Father, and yet no one is by habit completely or accurately knowing the Son in an intimate and personal way – except the Father – nor does anyone continue having an intimate experiential full-knowledge of the Father – except the Son, as well as to, or in, whomever the Son would continue desiring** (or: determining) **to unveil or reveal [Him]**."

As a side note, the verb in the first clause of Matthew's text is that same verb used of Judah's (Judas') action in regard to Jesus, in 13:21, above.

16. "**A little [while; time], and then no longer do you folks continue attentively watching** (gazing at) **Me, and yet then again a little [while; space of time], and you will continue seeing** (or: perceiving) **Me**." [other MSS add: because I, Myself, continue leading the way under, toward the Father.]

In the common translations, the verbs in both clauses are rendered the same: "see." However, in the Greek text, each clause uses a different verb, as my renderings offers: "**attentively watching** (gazing at)," in the first clause, and, "**seeing** (or: perceiving)," in the second clause. The first one has the sense of a person being a spectator, such as in watching a play. The second one carries the sense of perceiving, i.e., seeing with understanding. They would be watching and gazing at Him until His crucifixion, and then for a short time after His resurrection. But then they (and now we) would be able to continuously see and perceive Him – by His Spirit, and in ours. A good example is 2 Cor. 3:18.

The older, and considered "better," MS witnesses do not include the bracketed addition, and most modern translations omit it. This may have been added in, by later MSS, to give the reason for vs. 17b, below.

17. **Therefore some of His disciples said to one another, "What is this which He is presently saying to us, 'A little [while], and then you do not continue attentively watching Me, and yet then again a little [while] and you will continue seeing Me'? And, 'Because I am progressively bringing [everything] under control and departing toward the Father'?"**
18. **Hence, they went on saying, "What is this** (= What does this mean) **which He is saying, 'In a little [while]'? We have not seen nor do we know what He is speaking** (= what He is talking about)."

The disciples had been watching Him, and gazing at Him, but they still did not really "see" Him, nor perceive Him. Verse 18 repeats the first question of vs. 17: our author wants to emphasize the fact the His disciples did not understand what He was meaning, in vs. 16. Whenever Jesus would speak enigmatically, He would usually have to then go on to explain Himself, as we see below…

19. **Jesus knew** [with other MSS: then came to know] **that they were wanting and intending to be questioning** (or: asking) **Him, so He said to them, "Are you folks continuing to seek with one another** (among yourselves) **about this, because I said, 'A little [while] and you do not continue attentively watching Me, and yet then again a little [while], and you will continue seeing Me'?**

The rendering "**knew**" is a simple past tense rendering of the aorist verb. Other MSS add "then," and with these MSS I have rendered the verb as an ingressive aorist, "then came to know." The first can seem to imply that His knowing was like "a word of knowledge," or simply that He knew that He has spoken enigmatically, and that they would want to ask Him what He had meant. The second reading can be a simple human perception, such as observing the expressions on their faces as they looked at each other, or their body language, etc. Perhaps He observed them whispering to one another, such as Peter had done to "the disciple that Jesus loved," at the dinner, earlier. And so, He openly askes them...

20. **"Most assuredly** (It is certainly true; Amen, amen), **I now say to you folks that you yourselves will continue to weep** (shed tears and lament) **and will be from time to time shrieking out** (wailing in mournful funeral songs), **yet the world** (controlling System of culture, religion and politics; or: religious and secular society) **will continue rejoicing. You yourselves will periodically be made sad and distressed with grief, but yet your sadness, grief and distress will repeatedly birth itself into joy.**

And as was His habit, He begins an explanation by speaking obscurely, speaking of the situation that would follow what He has said, in vs. 16. His style of teaching was that of a wisdom teacher: He wanted them to think, not just take in information. He is wanting them to connect the dots of what He has been saying, such as about the sending of the Paraclete, in 14:26, and the fact of His going to the Father, in 14:25, and again of the Paraclete being sent, in 15:26, and then what He said in vs. 5, above, "**I am progressively leading [the way] under** (or: humbly going away) **toward the One sending Me**."

So now He turns to how they will react, and what they will experience: weeping, shrieking, sadness, distress and grief. But then He encourages them: all these negative experiences will give birth to **joy**." This, too, is a SIGN to them (and to us) regarding the characteristics of the Path, as they (and we) follow Him.

21. **"The woman, whenever she may be progressing in giving birth, is progressively having pain and distress** (sorrow and grief), **because her hour comes** (or: came). **Yet, whenever she may give birth to the little child** (infant), **she continues no longer calling to mind** (remembering; bearing in mind) **the pressure** (the squeezing, anguish and tribulation) **because of the joy that a human being** (a person) **is born** (or: was given birth) **into the world** (the system of culture; or: the universe).

And now He gives them an analogy: a pregnant woman, and the process of giving birth to the child. We need not comment on the analogy, but this illustration may also be a SIGN. Consider the vision given to John, in Rev. 12:

> 1. **Next a great sign was seen within the atmosphere** (or: sky; or: heaven)**: a Woman having been clothed** (cast around) **with the sun, and the moon down under her feet, and a wreath of twelve stars upon her head.**
> 2. **And being pregnant** (continuously having or holding within the womb), **she is constantly crying** (or: repeatedly uttering a cry), **travailing with birth-pangs, and being progressively tested and tried in the labor pains** (or: experiencing the touchstone) **to bring forth** (= to bear a child).

We will not comment on that passage in this study, but we suspect that there is a connection to what He has said here. In regard to what Jesus would soon experience, and endure (that to which He is alluding in this passage), Dan Kaplan pointed us to Heb. 2:8-18. We will quote six verses from that passage:

9. **But yet, we are continuously seeing Jesus – having been made inferior for a brief time beside agents – having been encompassed with glory** (or: crowned by a good reputation) **and with honor** (or: in value) **on account of** (or: through) **the effect of the experience of death**
>   (or: Now in this certain short bit of time, we keep on observing Jesus – having been made less because of the result of the suffering from, and which was, death – now having been encircled with the Victor's wreath in a manifestation which calls forth praise and with esteemed respect, at the side of the folks with the message), **so that by the grace of and from God** (or: for God's grace; in the favor which is God; [note: MSS 0243 & 1739, plus a Vulgate MS and in the works of Origen, Ambrose and Jerome and quoted by various writers down to the 11th century, the reading is: apart from God]) **He might taste of** (or: eat from) **death over [the situation and condition of] all mankind** (or: for and on behalf of everyone).

10. **You see, it was fitting for Him – on account of Whom [is] the collective whole** ([are] all things that exist) **and through Whom [is] the collective whole** ([are] all things that exist) **– in, when and by leading many sons** [note: a figure for all humanity] **into glory** (a good reputation), **to finish and perfect the Leader who first walked the Path of their deliverance**
>   (to bring to a complete state the Originator and Chief Agent of their rescue; to script the final scene for the Chief Conveyor of their restoration; to bring the Pioneering Bringer of their salvation to the destined goal) **through the effects of sufferings and results of experiences** [note, *paschō* means: to be affected by something - either good or bad; to feel, have sense experiences; thus, also: to suffer or undergo passion]….

14. **Since, then, the young children have participated in and commonly shared existence of blood and flesh** (= humanity), **He, nearly alongside as neighbor or lover, also partnered, took hold with, participated in, and shared theirs in common** (partook of the [ingredients] which comprise them), **in order that through means of death He might render useless** (or: deactivate; idle-down; discard) **the one normally having the strength** (or: the person presently holding the force) **of death** (or: which is death; or: whose source is death), **that is, the adversary**
>   (or: that which throws folks into dualism with divided thinking and perceptions; or: the one that throws something through the midst and casts division; the one who thrusts things through folks; the slanderer who accuses and deceives; or, commonly called: the "devil"),

15. **and would set them free** (or: could fully change and transform these; or: should move them away to another [situation; existence]): **as many as were through all of life held within slavery by fear of death** (or: in fear, from death: or: with fear, which is death)….

17. **Wherefore, He was indebted** (or: obliged) **to be assimilated by** (or: made like or similar to) **the brothers in accord with all things** (or: concerning everything; = in every respect; or: in correlation to all people), **so that He might become a merciful and a faithful** (or: loyal) **Chief Priest** (Leading, Ruling or Beginning Priest) **[in regard to] the things toward God, into the [situation] to be repeatedly and continuously overshadowing the failures** (mistakes; errors; misses of the target; sins) **of the People with a gentle, cleansing shelter and covering.**

18. **For you see, in what He has experienced Himself, having been tried in ordeals, He is able to run to the aid of those who cry for help – those being tried** (put through ordeals). [*cf* Heb. 13:5b-6; 1 Cor. 10:13; 1 Pet. 2:21-25; 3:19; 4:1; 5:10; 2 Pet. 2:9]

Here, the writer of Hebrews gave a reason for Jesus' incarnation and death, and then explained how He would function as our Paraclete (figured in 2:17 as a merciful and faithful Chief Priest). This sheds light on what Jesus was saying, here in Jn. 16.

22. **"And you yourselves, therefore, are now progressively having** [other MSS: will continue having] **sadness, distress and grief. Yet I will repeatedly see you folks again, and your heart will repeatedly rejoice, and no one will continue lifting up and carrying** [other MSS: now takes] **your joy away from you folks.**

Just as the pain and distress of a woman giving birth produces a child for the world, so will their sadness, distress and grief be productive. It will give birth to the Fruit of the Spirit: **JOY**. Recall what He told them in 14:27, above – the peace and joining that He was giving them. It will be the repeated joy of repeatedly seeing Him again. No one can ever take away the things that we experience – even if, at the time, we do not completely, or even partially, understand the experience. But consider the experience of seeing a Person that had been crucified and dead, now alive again. Consider that kind of joy, for not only will it also grant relief and wonder, but expectation for a future. It was to be an Event that would change everything. *Cf* Lu. 24:41. Peter spoke of the new, joyous condition, and of all that attended it, in 1 Pet. 1:

3. **Well-spoken of** (or: Eulogized; Blessed; or: Well-gathered, laid-out with ease, and worthy of praise) **[is] the God and Father of our Lord, Jesus Christ** (or: Who is our Owner, Jesus Christ), **the One bringing us to birth again** (regenerating us; begetting us back up again; causing us to be born again) **down from, in line with and in correspondence to His abundant mercy** (or: the much-existing sympathizing and active compassion which is Him) – **through Jesus Christ's resurrection forth from out of the midst of dead folks. [We are born again]:**

> into a progressively living expectation (or: into the midst of continuously living hope);

4. **into the midst of an incorruptible** (unspoilable; imperishable; unruinable; undecayable), **unstained** (undefiled), **and unfading** (or: unwithering) **inheritance** (or: enjoyment of and participation in an allotted portion as a possession) –

> > **one having been kept in view, watched-over, guarded, and which continues being maintained and kept intact within the midst of [the, or our] atmospheres** (or: in union with heavens; = in realms of spirit)

– [which things were and are being birthed and entering] into the midst of you folks,

5. **the ones being continuously garrisoned within** (or: kept, maintained and guarded in the center of) **God's power, in union with an ability which is God, through [His] faithfulness,**

> **into a deliverance** (a rescue which brings health, wholeness and a return to your original state and condition; salvation; a [period of] rescue) **[which is now] ready to be unveiled** (revealed; disclosed) **within the midst of and in union with [this] last season** (or: resident within a final fitting situation; in a final fertile moment; on [this] last occasion),

6. **within which [season and deliverance] you folks are presently feeling constant JOY and happiness and are continuing to rejoice exceedingly – though for a little while, at present, since** (or: if) **it continues being binding and necessary, being pained** (distressed; grieved; sorrowed) **within various tests** (or: different trials and ordeals) **to put you to the proof.** [*cf* 2 Thes. 1:4-8]

7. **[This is] to the end that the examined and tested approval of your faith** (of the trust and faithfulness of you folks) **– [being] of much greater value and worth, and more precious, than of gold that constantly loses itself away** (perishes of itself) **despite being progressively tested and examined through fire – might be found [progressing] into praise** (approval; commendation) **and glory** (or: a good reputation) **and honor** (value; worth) **within an unveiling of Jesus Christ** (or: in union with a revelation whose source is, which has the character of, and which is, Jesus, [the] Anointed One; in the midst of a disclosure from [Messiah] Jesus),

8. **Whom not seeing** (or: perceiving), **you folks are continuously loving and accepting** (or: experiencing the urge for reunion); **into Whom at the present moment you folks are not constantly looking, yet are habitually believing** (or: continuously placing [your] trust and loyalty). **You folks are repeatedly REJOICING and being very happy in indescribable** (or: incapable of being spoken out) **JOY which also exists having been made glorious**

> > (or: by unspeakable and glorified joy; in joy [that is] inexpressible and has made a notable reputation; with joy that is glorious beyond words, and which is filled with imagination and good opinion),

9. **being ones constantly bringing to, or conveying in, yourselves – as provision, attentive care and kindly keeping – the promised goal** (the finished product; the aim and result; the purpose and destiny) **of the** [other MSS: your] **faith and trust: deliverance of souls** (or: [the] restoration to wholeness and health of the consciousness of people; a rescue from [our distorted] selves; a healing of [folks'] inner beings; a salvation of people)!

In a practical situation, after having been rejected, we find that:

> "**the disciples continued being repeatedly, or progressively, filled with JOY and a consecrated attitude** (a set-apart Breath-effect; or: [the] Holy Spirit)" (Acts 13:52).

23. **"And within that Day you will continue asking Me nothing** (or: will not repeatedly request even one thing [from] Me). **Most assuredly** (It is certainly true; Amen, amen), **I am now saying to you, if you folks should petition the Father for anything** (or: whatever you people may corporately request of the Father), **He will proceed giving [it] to you corporately, within** (or: in union with) **My Name.**

Why? Well, recall that Jesus had said, in 14:20, above,

> "**Within That Day you yourselves will personally be coming to progressively realize and then will continue intimately and experientially knowing that I Myself [am; exist] within the midst of My Father, and you folks within the midst of and in union with Me, and I Myself within the midst of and in union with you people.**"

It is because of the new relationship that we have with Jesus and the Father, "**within that Day,**" and within the sphere of existence into which He has resurrected us – so that we are within the midst of Him, and He within the midst of us. Also, see our discussion about petitioning "**within** (or: in union with) **[His] Name,**" in Jn. 15:16. Observe, also, that the plural personal pronouns imply that He is speaking primarily about corporate requests, concerning the called-out communities, and that "**He will proceed giving [it] to you corporately.**" As stated before, the individual is included, but His message was about Israel, and about Adam. The twelve (to whom He was presently speaking) were called to be a SIGN that pointed to Israel and to the promise made concerning Abraham's Seed (Christ, corporately) that was to be a blessing to all families of the earth. These promises were made to those who would begin the leadership roles (as His representatives: His body upon the earth) within the new humanity that was about to be brought to birth in His resurrection.

24. **"Until the present time** (right now) **you folks petitioned nothing within** (or: in union with) **My Name. Be habitually making petitions, and you folks will habitually receive, to the end that your JOY may constantly exist being having been filled full and continuing filled up** (or: complete).

His second statement is in the imperative voice. He is instructing them to do this. We find this expanded in Mat. 7:

> 7. **"Be habitually requesting** (or: Keep on asking), **and it** (or: He) **will proceed being given to** (or: for; in) **you people. Be habitually seeking** (or: Keep on searching and trying to find), **and you folks will repeatedly find. Be repeatedly** (or: Keep on) **knocking, and it** (or: He) **will habitually be opened up to** (or: for; in) **you.**
> 8. **"You see, everyone habitually requesting is repeatedly receiving. He who keeps on seeking and searching is constantly finding. And to** (in; for) **the person repeatedly knocking it will be opened up.**"

He wants them to have JOY. The Greek word for "joy" is *chara*; the word for "grace" is *charis*, which is literally "joyous favor." This is a key to His reign. We have quoted this before:

> "**God's kingdom** (or: reign) **is**... **eschatological deliverance into fair and equitable dealing which brings justice and right relationship in the Way pointed out, peace and a joining, and JOY within set-apart Breath-effect**" (Rom. 14:17).

25. **"I have spoken these things to you within comparative illustrations** (in figures of speech, proverbial sayings, similes, and veiled language placed alongside the course of the way). **An hour is progressively coming when I will no longer continue speaking to you in comparative illustrations, but rather, I will proceed in outspoken freedom of speech, as a citizen, reporting back to you folks about** (or: concerning) **the Father.**

His style, or mode, of communicating with them was soon to change. In fact, He does in the next two verses, and in vs. 29 we will read that His disciples notice the difference. The comparative illustration mode of teaching was characteristic of a wisdom teacher who most of all wanted his students to think, rather than just receive information. But His relationship with them was about to change. Recall that in 15:15, above, He told them, "**I am no longer calling** (or: terming) **you people slaves**... **now I have declared you folks friends, because I make intimately and experientially known to you everything** (or: all things) **which I heard and hear at My Father's side and in His presence**." He would now be treating them as branches that were joined to Him. The end in view for them, their goals, had been implanted, and now they were coming to have a new role within His reign. He would no longer be physically with them, and as Paul would learn,

"**if even we have intimately, by experience, known Christ** ([the] Anointed One) **on the level of flesh** (or: = in the sphere of estranged humanity; = according to the old covenant), **nevertheless we now** (in the present moment) **no longer continue [thus] knowing [Him]**" (2 Cor. 5:16b).

26. "**Within that Day you will continue making petition within My Name – and I am not saying to you that I, Myself, will continue asking** (or: requesting of) **the Father about you folks,**

He repeats the phrase that He used in vs. 23, above, "**Within that Day**." He was "that Day," and they were a part of it, too. It would later be revealed to Paul that Christ's followers,

"**all are** (or: exist being) **sons of** (from; associated with and having the qualities of; or: which are) **Light and sons of** (from; associated with and having qualities of; or: which are [the; this]) **Day! We are** (exist) **not of night, nor of darkness**" (1 Thes. 5:5).

The coming of the Messiah (Christ) was the coming of the Day of the Lord. The darkness was the situation into which the Light had come (Second-Temple Judaism), as our author states in Jn. 1:5. It was the time of the dawning of the New Day, and the Age of the Messiah. Because of this, the old (including Jesus' then present mode of speaking to them, and His relationship to them, at that time) was passing away (2 Cor. 5:17). So He would no longer be an intermediary between them and the Father. He had brought them to the Father, in Himself, and now they had direct access to the Father because of being branches that were joined to Him (Jn. 15:5). The "Sap" of the Spirit (Vine) would flow directly into them.

Now you might ask, "Well, what about 1 Tim. 2:5?" Well, that is a different context and it is speaking about those who are not yet joined to the Vine. Let us look at that verse, and its context:

3. **This [is] beautiful** (fine; ideal) **and welcomingly received from the presence of, and in the sight of, God, our Deliverer** (our Savior; the One Who heals us and makes us whole, restoring us to our original state and condition, and keeps us safe),

4. **Who is constantly willing** (continuously intending and purposing) **all humans** (all humanity; all mankind) **to be saved** (delivered; rescued; made healthy and whole), **and** (or: even) **to come into a full, accurate, experiential and intimate knowledge and insight of Truth** (or: that is, to go or come into a complete realization of Reality),

5. **for God [is] One, and One [is the] Mediator of God and humans** (= mankind), **a Man** (a Human), **Christ Jesus,**

6. **the One giving Himself a correspondent ransom** (a ransom in the place of and directed toward the situation) **over [the situation of and] on behalf of** (or: for) **all** (everyone; all humanity and all things) **– the witness** [note: "the witness" is omitted by A; other MSS: the evidence of which] **[will come] in its own fitting situations** (or: the Witness for their own seasons; the Testimony to and for His own particular occasions; the evidence [appears] in its own fertile moments).

Jesus remains as the "**one Mediator between God and humans**," or, in a different metaphor, "the Ladder between earth and the atmosphere (or; heaven)" – Jn. 1:51. But once they are joined to the Lord (1 Cor.6:17), they are joined to the Father (17:21, 23, below). You see, those that are still in the System have not yet known the Father (Jn. 17:25a). And so, for them (and in other ways for us), it is still: "**Jesus Christ, the same yesterday and today and on into the ages**" (Heb. 13:8).

27. **"for the Father, Himself, continuously likes, has fond affection for, and is constantly friendly to you people, because you have liked and been friendly to, and even have shown fond affection for Me, and further, you folks have trusted and still believe that I came out from God's side** (or: came forth from beside God; [other MSS: the Father]).

In 3:16, above, we read that God (the Father) loved (*agapē* love) the aggregate of humanity, the cosmos and the organized System. But here we have a different verb (which Peter, and then Jesus also, will use in Jn. 21. It is the verb *phileō*, the meanings of which I have offered, as a conflation: "**continuously likes, has fond affection for, and is constantly friendly to.**" This shows a more personal and relational feeling and interaction between the Father and the disciples, in the same way that the disciples have been personal and relational with Jesus. It is in the realm of what we would term "brotherly love." This reveals a great deal about the heart and personality of the Father. God likes us. It is sad that the KJV rendered the verb "love" (as is used in Jn. 3:16), because it obscures this beautiful reality. God was friendly to the disciples. Isn't this just like a human father? "You like my kids; I like you!" "Aint it good to know… you've got a Friend"? [These clauses: courtesy of Carol King]

But there is more: the Father knows that they "**have trusted and still believe that I came out from God's side.**" Remember, He is the Logos that was focused toward, and with, God (Jn. 1:1). Only the Father could reveal that Truth to them (Mat. 16:17). And it would take Christ's faith to make them believe it. From His repetition of this fact, we just have to realize how important a fact it is. He IS the Truth of the Father. This is more than His just being "the Prophet" (Jn. 1:21) – that phrase meant to be one like Moses (Deut. 18:15).

28. **"I came from out of the midst of** [other MSS: I went forth from beside] **the Father and I have come back** (or: again [*palin*]) **into the ordered arrangement** (the world; the System of culture, religion, economics and politics; or: the aggregate of humanity).
       (or: reading *palin* modifying *aphiēmi*: **Furthermore** {or: Again}) **I am continuing in forgiving the world and aggregate of humanity** (or: releasing [*aphiēmi*] the system of culture and religion; or: leaving this ordered arrangement; or: divorcing the arranged system), **and then I am progressively journeying on** (traveling to another place), **directed to and facing toward the Father."** [note: *palin* can modify either "come" or "forgive"]

Now He really lays it out for them – but wait, at least for us, there is some ambiguity. As noted, *palin* can modify either the verb "come" (**come back** {or: again}), or the verb, "**forgiving; releasing; leaving.**" It can mean "**back; Furthermore; again.**" And then, which meaning we choose for *aphiēmi* affects how we understand what He was saying. May we suggest that before we proceed in our comments, just pause, read this verse again, and again, and consider the optional meanings of the words, which way the adverb *palin* is pointing (back, to "come," or forward, to "forgiving/releasing/leaving/divorcing"), ponder the optional renderings of *aphiēmi*, and then listen for the *Logos* within you…

This verse is composed of four clauses. We will examine each one, beginning with the first: "**I came from out of the midst of the Father.**" This establishes His origin in a manner that seems to be ontological. Now He can simply be saying by this that God is His existential Father. He can be saying that He came from the presence, and realm, of God, and then the final clause explains that He is journeying on, back to that same place – the place that the Logos had (Jn. 1:1) – "**directed to and facing toward the Father.**" This phrase is the same as in the second clause of 1:1, except there the object is "God," while here the term "Father" is used.

The alternate MS reading, "I went forth from beside the Father," would speak of location or authoritative "position," rather than of origin, in the sense of birth or existence, as we have in the first MS reading. Verse 30b argues for the first reading, rather than this alternate MS tradition.

The second clause (in my first rendering) would be controversial, but we should consider it, nonetheless: "**I have come back** (or: again [*palin*]) **into the ordered arrangement**." The rendering reads the adverb with this clause, rather than with the third clause that immediately follows it. The idea in "have come back, or have come again," would mean that He had been in the ordered arrangement before. Now if we chose to look for a proof-text, we could call up 1 Cor. 10:4, "**they kept on drinking from out of a spiritual bedrock – one continually following along behind. Now the bedrock was the Christ.**" Our thoughts could go in a number of directions and visit a number of OT passages where students have concluded that Christ did come into Israel's history, on occasion. But we will let our readers trace out these trails, on their own. The rendering is simply here for your consideration.

The first reading of the third clause gives us the most excitement: "**Furthermore** {or: Again}) **I am continuing in forgiving the world and aggregate of humanity**." Now is this not what He said on the cross (Lu. 23:34)? He used this same verb in that verse, while on the cross. This is the main verb that is rendered "forgive," in the NT. However, it does have other applications, and thus this clause can read, "I am continuing in releasing the system of culture and religion." That fits well, too. As to the third rendering on offer, "leaving this ordered arrangement," this also fits what He has said elsewhere, about leaving them, but with this rendering of *kosmos* as "ordered arrangement," what comes to mind is that He might have been saying that He was leaving the old covenant order and the age of the Law. Like God had done before, He might have been speaking of "leaving their house desolate" (Lu. 13:35; Mat. 23:38), and we can see in this an allusion to 1 Sam. 4:21, "Ichabod... The glory is departed."

The last parenthetical offering of the third clause presents the previous idea of "leaving" in a more specific, and covenantal, context: "divorcing the arranged system." Yahweh had been symbolically married to Israel, but she had been unfaithful (*cf* the story in Ezk. 16), and we find in Jer. 3:8 Him saying regarding her, "I had put her away, and given her a bill of divorce..." Hos. 2:1-23 tells a similar story, addressed, in vs. 1, to His people (Ammi), saying in vs. 2, 5, 10, 12,

> "Contend with your mother, contend – for she [is] not My wife, and I [am] not her husband.... For their mother committed prostitutions.... And now I will expose her decadence.... And I will desolate her vine and her fig tree..."

However, Jesus now taught against divorce in the new arrangement of the realm of God's reign (Mat. 19:9). And so Paul explains what Christ had to do, in Rom. 7:

> 2. **For instance, the married woman** (the woman under subjection to a husband or to an adult male) **has been bound and remains tied up by Law and custom to the living husband** (or: has been wrapped up and stands tied to law [= Torah; or: custom] by the living man). **Yet if the husband may die, she has been released from employment and stands idle** (or: has been brought down to living without labor and rendered inactive; she is discharged and brought down to unproductivity, being idled down) **away from the husband's law** (or: from pertaining to the Law [= Torah] and custom of the adult man).
> 3. **Consequently** (or: Accordingly), **then, [with the] continued living of the husband, she will be dealing as an adulteress** (or: bear the title "adulteress") **if she should become [attached] to, or [a lover] for, or [involved] with a different man** (or: husband); **but if the husband may die, she is free** (she exists in a state of freedom) **from the Law** [= Torah], **not to be an adulteress, pertaining to her becoming [a wife] for** (or: to) **a different man** (or: husband).
> 4. **So that, my brothers** (folks from the same womb), **you folks also were made dead to the Law** (or: were put to death by the Law [=Torah] and with the Law), **through the body of the Christ, [proceeding] into the situation to become [the wife] for** (or: to; in; with) **a different One – in** (to; for) **the One being roused and raised forth from out of the midst of dead folks – to the end that we may bear fruit by God** (or: produce a harvest in, for, to and with God).

This was how Yahweh was divorcing Israel, under the old covenant, by His metaphorically dying with Christ (2 Cor. 5:19 – "God was within Christ") so that she could be married to Christ in a new covenant. Israel was "made dead to the Law (her marriage covenant, instituted at Sinai) through the body of the

Christ," now to be married to the risen Christ with a new covenant, symbolized by a new mountain (Zion) and a New Jerusalem (Heb. 12:22-24; Gal. 4:22-31; Rev. 21). So this could be what Jesus was meaning, in this reading of this third clause.

Ken Nichols comments: "Best explanation of Romans 7 I've read. It's so often read as a literal instruction on "proper divorce" or how to follow the Law in divorce, when the whole thing is simply giving an example of how our obligation to something/someone DIES when that person/thing dies. Jesus EMBODIED the Law (or the CURSE of the Law) while on the cross, and it DIED with Him, releasing Israel from the law (and anyone else from any OTHER law-following paradigm). It was bringing humanity up to a higher ORDER of thinking that didn't involve rules, obedience and punishment." (from a personal email)

Now the final clause, "**then I am progressively journeying on** (traveling to another place)," obviously refers to His leaving them and traveling the Path to the Father. This is the Way (Road) that we, also, are called to travel. We can see Paul's sketch of the circular (or, spiral) journey in Rom. 11:36, "from out of... through the midst of... [back] into Him." The normal renderings, "came from... have come into... again am leaving... going to" (NRSV), trace the same circuit, but the redundancy of "am leaving... going to" seems less attractive to us than "am forgiving/releasing... and then traveling on..." Our preferred readings offer so much more, and still describe the completed circuit of the Path. As you are led to choose, all of these ways are a blessing. *Cf* 13:3b, above.

29. **His disciples are then saying to Him, "Look! (See!) You are now speaking in [the] outspoken boldness of speech of a citizen, and are saying not even one comparative illustration.**

Yes, He did not speak in a parable or use metaphors. He told them where He had come from, what He had come into, what He was doing at that time, and to where He was progressively traveling on.

30. **"Now we have seen and continue to know that You have seen and know all things** (or: everything) **and have no need that anyone should continue questioning You. Within this we constantly trust and progressively believe that You came forth from out of God."**

Apparently the Spirit had opened their eyes, through the Logos that He had just spoken to them. They were coming to realize something of who He was – shall we just say, "More than the average wisdom teacher"? Yes, notice how they phrased the second statement: "**Within this**..." That can refer either to what He had just disclosed to them, or to the fact of their "knowing" from having "seen" – in their spirits (1 Cor. 2:11). Whichever – probably both – they came to "**constantly trust and progressively believe that [He] came forth from out of God**." This statement gives evidence for the first MS reading of the first clause in vs. 28, above. We find this same affirmation, "**You have seen and know all things**," in Peter's mouth, in 21:17, below. They now "**saw**" that there was **no need** for anyone to question Who He was, or from where He had come, or Who had sent Him.

31. **Jesus discerningly replied to them, "At present** (or: Right now) **you continue trusting and believing with loyal allegiance** (or: Just now you are believing!?).

The ambiguity, suggested in these two readings, is whether He was making an affirmation, or, almost in surprised disbelief at their statement, whether He was asking a rhetorical question. Jesus affirms the fact that they do, in Jn. 17:8b, below.

32. **"Look and consider. An hour is progressively coming – and it has come and is here – to the end that you folks should be scattered and dispersed [as sown seed], each one into his own [places; life; home; paths; destiny; things], and Me you folks can let go off alone** (or: should at once release, leave and send off alone). **And yet I am not alone, because the Father is constantly being with Me.**

He had given them one reason for His going away, in vs. 7, above: so that the Paraclete would come to them. Now He gives another reason: "**to the end that you folks should be scattered and dispersed**." He was breaking up the band of the twelve (even though they attempted to keep it together – Acts 1:15-26). Now this can be read as a momentary scattering – on the night of His arrest – but we see a larger picture in His words. Traditions tells us that some went to other countries, carrying the Good News.

They would let Him go off alone, or "should at once release, leave and send [Him] off alone" (*cf* Mat. 26:56b), but He wanted them to be assured that He was "**not alone, because the Father is constantly being with [Him]**." They could, and should, do this (the subjunctive aorist tense) because this was His Path, His journey. They needed to release Him so that He could go off to release the aggregate of mankind.

33. **"I have spoken these things to you so that you may continuously have** (hold; possess) **peace and a joining centered in, within the midst of, and in union with, Me. Within the System** (dominating and controlling world of culture, religion, economy and government; or: among and in union with the aggregate of humanity) **you normally have pressure and stress** (or: continually have squeezing; repeatedly have tribulation and oppression), **but nonetheless, be confident and take courage! I, Myself, have overcome and conquered the System** (dominating world; organized arrangement of religion and society; aggregate of humanity) **so that it stands a completed victory!"**

We will look at the last statement first. The verb "**overcome and conquered**" is in the perfect tense, which means that the action was completed in the past with the results of the completed action continuing on – into the present, and on into the future. Paul later explained how we can "**be confident and take courage**," since Christ gained the victory for us, and now, "**within all these things we are habitually over-conquering** (we are remaining completely victorious; we continue more than overcoming) **through the One loving, urging toward reunion with, and giving Himself to, us**" (Rom. 8:37). In that passage, Paul goes on to explain that nothing can separate us from God's Love (vss. 38-39). 1 Jn. 5 gives us a corroborating witness:

> 1. **Everyone, who** (All mankind, which) **in continuously believing, constantly being convinced and progressively trusting that Jesus is** (or: exists being) **the Christ has been brought to birth and is now a born-one** (= is a child) **from out of God. And everyone, who** (or: all mankind, which) **in continuously loving** (urging toward reunion with) **the One bearing and giving birth** (the Parent), **should and would also love** (accept in unity) **the person having been born** (the child) **out of Him.**
>
> 2. **Whenever we are habitually loving God, and then may be habitually doing or producing His implanted goals** (impartations of the finished product within; inward, purposed directives), **in this [condition and situation] we progressively come to know by insight and intimate experiences that we are [also] normally loving God's children.**
>
> 3. **You see, that we would continuously observe His imparted and implanted goals is itself the Love of God** (or: the love which pertains to God; the Love which is God)
>
>> (or: For this exists being love from God so that we can progressively watch over, keep, maintain and guard His interior finished product) **– and His implanted goals**
>
> (impartations of the finished product within; inward directives) **are not heavy** (weighty, thus, burdensome) –
>
> 4. **because everything having been born from out of the midst of God continuously overcomes** (habitually conquers and is progressively victorious over) **the controlling System** (ordered world of religion, secular culture, economy and government). **And this is the victory** (or: conquest) **at once overcoming** (conquering; victorious over) **the controlling System** (ordered world of religion, culture, economy and government): **our trust, confidence, faith and loyalty!**

5. **Now who is the person continuously overcoming** (or: progressively conquering) **the ordered System** (world; secular realm; religious arrangement) **if not the one continuously believing, progressively trusting and being constantly loyal to [the fact] that Jesus is** (continuously exists being) **the Son of God!**

Here we also have a reprise of Jn. 14:27. Then, in 1 Cor. 15:27a, Paul affirms,

"**For you see,**

'**He completely arranges, humbly aligns and then appends and puts under shelter all humanity** (or: subjoins, supportively arranges in subordination, and brings under full control, all things) **under His feet** (= as supporting forces in His kingdom).'" [Ps. 8:6]

More encouraging words are found in Gal. 6:14-15,

"**Now may it not happen to me** (or: in me) **to take up the practice of boasting, except within the cross of our Lord, Jesus Christ, through Whom** (or: through which [i.e., the cross]) **the organized System** (or: the world of culture, economy, government and religion) **has been, and continues being, crucified in me** (or: to me; for me; by me; or: through Whom the aggregate of humanity has been, and is now, crucified with me), **and I by** (to; in; with; for) **the domination System. For you see** [some MSS add: within Christ Jesus], **neither circumcision nor uncircumcision continues being anything, but rather: a new and different creation** (a founding and settling [as a village] with a new character and quality, in a place that was wild and without order; an innovative, new act of framing and building)."

THIS is why they, and we, should be confident and take courage. Yes, "**Within the System** (dominating and controlling world of culture, religion, economy and government; or: among and in union with the aggregate of humanity) **[they would] normally have pressure and stress** (or: continually have squeezing; repeatedly have tribulation and oppression)," but nonetheless, He had spoken all these things to them (and now to us), "**so that [they, and we] may continuously have** (hold; possess) **peace and a joining centered in, within the midst of, and in union with [Him].**" And you see, this is because we continue "abiding in the Vine." His provision of peace is an allusion to Isa. 9:6-7a,

"**Because a child was born for us** (among us; to us; with us), **and a Son was given to us** (for us; among us), **whose beginning** (primacy; rule; sovereignty) **was born** (made to be) **upon His shoulder, and His Name is normally called Messenger** (or: Agent) **of Great Purposed-Design** (or: Will; Disposition; Determined-Counsel), **Wonderful Counselor, Strong God, Person of Authority and Privilege from out of Being, Ruler of Joining and Peace, Father of the Impending Age. For you see, I will progressively bring a joining and peace upon the rulers** (chiefs; beginning positions; original situations), **and Health with Him** (or: health by Him, in Him, for Him and to Him). **His Beginning** (or: origin; rule; sovereignty) **is** (exists being) **great, and of the peace from His joining there is no boundary and will be no end...**" (LXX, JM).

Included in these thoughts are the results that Paul describes in Eph. 2:14,

"**You see, He Himself is our Peace** (or: continuously exists being our joining) – **the One making** (forming; constructing; creating; producing) **The Both [to be] one, and within His flesh is instantly destroying** (unbinding; unfastening; loosing; causing to collapse) **the middle wall of the fenced enclosure** (or: the partition or barrier wall)**: the enmity** (cause of hate, alienation, discord and hostility; characteristics of an enemy)..."

And we cannot leave out Col. 1:

19. **because WITHIN Him all – the entire contents** (the result of that which fills everything; all the effect of the full measure [of things]) – **delights to settle down and dwell as in a house** (or: because He approved all the fullness [of all existence] to permanently reside within Him)

20. **and THROUGH Him at once to transfer the all** (the whole; = all of existential creation), **away from a certain state to the level of another which is quite different**

(or: to change all things, bringing movement away from being down; to reconcile all things; to change everything from estrangement and alienation to friendship and harmony and move all), **INTO Him – making** (constructing; forming; creating) **peace** (harmonious joining) **through the blood of His cross: through Him, whether the things upon the earth** (or: land) **or the things within the atmospheres and heavens!**

Of course, the middle part of our verse is still there: "**Within the System** (dominating and controlling world of culture, religion, economy and government; or: among and in union with the aggregate of humanity) **you normally have pressure and stress** (or: continually have squeezing; repeatedly have tribulation and oppression)." That is just a description of life, here on earth. We have a second witness in Acts 14:22b, "**It continues binding and necessary for us to enter into the reign of God** (or: God's kingdom; the sovereign activities which are God) **through the midst of many pressures, squeezings, tribulations, afflictions and oppressions**." This reminder calls to mind the process of a human birth! And in 2 Tim. 2:11b-12a, we have these encouraging words,

> "**You see, since we died together with [Him] we will also continue living together** (or: proceed in jointly living; constantly co-live); **since we are continuously remaining under for support** (or: if we continue patiently enduring), **we will also continue reigning** (performing royal activities and influence) **together with [Him]…**"

And then 2 Tim. 3:12 affirms Jesus' words, above:

> "**And indeed, all those habitually resolving** (intending; willing) **to be continuously living in a reverent, devout and pious manner with virtuous conduct from ease and goodness within Christ Jesus will be repeatedly pursued, persecuted and harassed.**"

Chapter 17

1. **Jesus speaks** (or: spoke) **these things and then, lifting up His eyes into the sky** (or: the atmosphere; the heaven), **says, "O Father, the hour has come and is now here: bring glory** (give a good reputation; bring an assumed appearance and a manifestation which calls forth praise) **to Your Son, to the end that the Son can bring glory** (or: may give a recognized appearance and a good reputation; would bring a manifestation which calls forth praise) **to and for You.**

Consider the setting: His disciples are still there with Him, and hear Him speaking intimately to His Father. What a privilege they had. In Lu. 11:1, one of His disciples asked Him to teach them to pray, and then vss. 2-4 record Luke's version of the "Our Father…" But here, Jesus is taking them deeper, and higher. This entire chapter teaches them what intimacy with the Father looks like; what the goal and intent of a son should be: to **bring glory to, and for [the Father]**. Remember: He had called them to follow Him on the same Path (Way). He had implanted this goal into them, through His *Logos*, which would give birth to Himself within them so that they would bear the Father's image (Gen. 1:26) and have His Name in their foreheads (Rev. 3:12; 14:1).

Now Jesus, as a Son who can do nothing of Himself, asks the Father to "bring [Him] an assumed appearance and a manifestation which calls forth praise to [His Father]." This is a prayer that we, too, can pray. When the Father does this for us, then people will see "a recognized appearance and a good reputation, which would bring a manifestation which calls forth praise to [our Father]."

2. "**Correspondingly as You give** (or: gave) **to Him right, privilege and authority from out of Being concerning ALL flesh** (= people; = critters; Gen. 1:26-28) **to the end that ALL, which You have given to Him and that He now possesses, to THEM He will continue** (or: one-after-another be) **giving** [other MSS: would at some point give] **eonian Life** (life having its origin in, and the characteristics and qualities of, the Age [of Messiah]; or: age-enduring life; life of, for and in the ages).

We see in the first clause an allusion to Gen. 1:26-28. Notice the third person construction, "**to Him.**" He is referring to the third person construction of vs. 1, "**Your Son… the Son.**" Do you think that rather than saying "Me," He used the relational term, "Son," so that His disciples could better relate to this communication? Is He alluding to Adam? to Israel (Ex. 4:22)? to His disciples, as His "branches" (whom Paul would later refer to as being "His body")?

Because of Who He is – and this is "**from out of [the] Being**" of God – as the incarnate Logos, He was **given right, privilege and authority concerning ALL flesh**. That leaves no flesh out. Observe my parenthetical interpretations: people and critters! And now comes another "purpose" phrase, "**to the end that**." What follows this is the "purpose" for which He was given such right and **authority**: it is so that "**He will continue** (or: one-after-another be) **giving eonian Life to THEM**." And so who are the THEM? Well, He identified them as being that which the Father "**[had] given to Him and that He now possesses**." OK, but what had the Son been given? Privilege and authority "**concerning ALL flesh**." Well, we suggest that the "ALL" in both clauses speaks of the same group: the WHOLE (people and critters). The second "**ALL**" is neuter (or, neutral), and thus is all-inclusive of EVERYTHING. Paul later echoes this worldview, in Col. 1:17, 19, 20,

> "**And He is before** (prior to; or: maintains precedence of) **all things and all people, and the whole has** (or: all things have) **been placed together and now continues to jointly-stand** (stands cohesively; is made to have a co-standing) **within the midst of and in union with Him**.... **because WITHIN Him all – the entire contents** (the result of that which fills everything; all the effect of the full measure [of things]) – **delights to settle down and dwell as in a house** (or: because He approved all the fullness [of all existence] to permanently reside within Him) **and THROUGH Him at once to transfer the all** (the whole; = all of existential creation), **away from a certain state to the level of another which is quite different**
>
> > (or: to change all things, bringing movement away from being down; to reconcile all things; to change everything from estrangement and alienation to friendship and harmony and move all), **INTO Him – making** (constructing; forming; creating) **peace** (harmonious joining) **through the blood of His cross** (execution stake/pole)**: through Him, whether the things upon the earth** (or: land) **or the things within the atmospheres and heavens!**"

By way of translation, "**eonian Life** is life having its origin in, and the characteristics and qualities of, the Age [of Messiah], or, age-enduring life, that is, life of, for and in the ages." Well, those are linguistic representations of the semantic range of the term "age" – which originally held the concept of the lifetime of a person, but was expanded to refer to indefinite periods of time, of one sort, or another. Scholars inform us that Second Temple Judaism had a world view of two ages: the current age in which they were living, and the coming age which the Messiah would inaugurate. This would have been the understanding of this phrase which His listeners, and first century readers, would have held. But in the next verse, Jesus gives a clear and specific definition of this specialized phrase...

3. "**Now THIS is** (or: exists being) **eonian Life** (living existence of and for the ages; life pertaining to the Age [of Messiah])**: namely, that they may progressively come to intimately and experientially know You, the only** (or: sole) **true and real** (genuine) **God – and Jesus Christ, Whom You send forth as an Emissary** (or: as well as Jesus [as the] Anointed One, whom You sent off as a Representative).

Really, this is pretty clear. No theological or philosophical terms need to be used to confound what He just said, and further comment may just muddy the Water of Life that we have just been given.

4. "**I Myself glorify You** (or: brought a recognized appearance for You; present a good reputation with a manifestation which called forth praise to You) **upon the earth** (or: the Land), **finishing and perfecting** (bringing to its goal, purpose, destiny and fruition) **the Work** (the Deed; the Act) **which You have given to** (or: in; for) **Me, to the end that I could do** (or: would perform; may produce) **[it]**.

For those who have been given eyes to see, He had "brought a recognized appearance for [the Father], had presented a good reputation [for Him] with a manifestation which called forth praise [to God]." That had been His work "**upon the earth** (or: the Land [of Israel])." He, Himself, had brought glory to the

Father by "**finishing and perfecting** (bringing to its goal, purpose, destiny and fruition) **the Work** (the Deed; the Act) **which You have given to** (or: in; for) **Me, to the end that I could do** (or: would perform; may produce) **[it]**." Now consider that He said this before He had been crucified. The work that was left to be done would be done by others: the Judean leadership and the Romans. The Seed had been finished and perfected: it was now for others to plant It.

5. **"So now You Yourself, O Father, glorify** (bring a good reputation and a manifestation which calls forth praise to) **Me alongside Yourself** (or: with the presence of Yourself) **in, by and with the glory** (recognition; good reputation; manifestation which calls forth praise) **which I was having** (or: used to hold) **and continued holding at Your side and in Your presence, before the universe** (or: system; world of culture, religion and government) **is continuing to have being** (or: which I was constantly possessing, alongside Yourself, before the aggregate of humanity continued to exist with You).

As can be seen in the history and writings of OT Israel, the glory of God is really just His presence (called the Shekinah, in the old covenant). God IS His own glory. Jesus (or, the Son, if you will) was "**at [the Father's] side and in [His] presence, before the universe** (or: system; world of culture, religion and government) **is continuing to have being**." We do not wish to dilute this statement by endeavoring to explain it. May the Spirit that indwells you speak to you whatever level of Truth concerning this that you can receive, at this time. We all likely have different perceptions about the situation of which He spoke. And we are all still learning. The final parenthetical rendering is pregnant with possibilities, and the next verse (6b) expands upon this…

6. **"I brought Your Name to clear light and manifest it to the humans** (people) **whom You gave to, and for, Me from out of the midst of the System** (or: aggregate of humanity; organized culture and religion; world of a dominated society). **They were existing in You** (or: with You; by You; for You; [living] to You) **and to Me** (for Me; in Me) **you give** (or: gave) **them, and they have kept, observed, taken care of and watched over Your** *Logos* (Word; thought; laid-out idea; message; blueprint).

The first clause is very revealing, concerning what this culture and time meant by "**Name**." Nowhere did He mention the "name" Yahweh. What He set in "**clear light and manifested**" was what we would call a title, or an ontological, biological and relational term: **Father**. But a "name," in that setting, referred to a person's character and reputation, and it stood for the person. It was a person's identity, but not as a spelled-out or pronounced word. One's name was really one's "glory" (or lack thereof). THIS is what He had manifested to them.

Therefore, only those who had been with Him really knew God's Name. These disciples had been chosen to bring His Name to the rest of their world. They had been picked, by the Father, "**from out of the midst of the System** (or: aggregate of humanity; organized culture and religion; world of a dominated society)."

He does not explain what, or how, He meant the next clause: "**They were existing in You** (or: with You; by You; for You; [living] to You)." Once again, we will not attempt to explain this for you, but we will lay out the options for the personal pronoun, **You**, that is in the dative case:
   a) **They were existing in You** – this is either an ontological statement, an origin statement (as with Rom. 11:36), or a metaphorical picture similar to our being "in Christ";
   b) with You – like the Logos was "with God"? or, does this mean that their "hearts" were on God's side in matters of human relationships and deeds?
   c) by You – God was their Father, or creator (as a pot formed by the Potter)?
   d) for You – vessels for God's service? on His team?
   e) [living] to You – living with a focus toward, and a commitment to, God?

Again, "your" choice – as the Spirit impresses you. We suggest that all of these apply, and describe the variegated, multi-colored relationship that God has with all of His souls – for they all belong to Him (Ezk. 18:4).

The Father gave them to Jesus, and He now affirms that, "**they have kept, observed, taken care of and watched over Your** *Logos* (Word; thought; laid-out idea; message; blueprint)." Can any greater praise or recommendation be given to a human? He is saying that first of all, "they possessed the Father's blueprint." They had observed and taken care of His incarnated *Logos*, and had kept and watched over the Father's message (or, laid-out idea).

7. "**Now** (or: At this moment) **they have intimately and experientially known that all things – as many** (or: much) **as You have given to Me, so that I now possess – continuously exist from You and are at Your side, in Your presence,**

Generally speaking, this would have been their worldview, as members of the Second Temple Judaism society within which they had grown up. There is one Creator, and all things exist from Him who is their Father. God had been actively involved with Israel, all through their history, and from the creation of humanity, as well. He had Israel build a tent so that He could live beside them, within their midst.

But He seems to be indicating that these disciples had a greater understanding of this, from having spent time with Him, and they also apparently perceive that Jesus now possesses **all things**, as was revealed to Paul (Col. 1, above). He was the heir of all things, as we read in Heb. 1:2, being:

"**a Son whom He placed** (or: sets) **[as; to be] Heir of all** (or: One who receives **all humanity** as an allotment; or: One who received everything as His allotted inheritance) **through Whom He also made the ages**."

8. "**because I have given to them the gush-effects** (results of the flow; spoken words; sayings; declarations) **which You gave to Me, and give in and by Me, and they themselves took and received** (accepted) **[them], and they intimately and experientially know truly** (or: with reality) **that I came out from beside You** (or: went forth from Your presence), **and they trust and believe that** (or: they are faithful because) **You, Yourself, sent Me forth as an Emissary** (a Representative).

Now the Father did not need Jesus to give this information to Him, but rather, this is for the disciples to hear. What an affirmation Jesus is giving to them. Now they can realize that both Jesus and the Father know that "**they themselves [had taken] and received** (accepted)" the "**gush-effects** (results of the flow; spoken words; sayings; declarations)" which He had received from the Father and had passed on to them. Also, He affirmed that they had personally, and intimately, come to know that He had come from the Father, and that it was the Father, Himself, that had sent Him on this mission. What foundational and earth-shaking information had come to them. Jesus was so much more than a prophet, a rabbi or a wisdom teacher. He was the Father's Son. He was the embodiment of the Patterned Information (the *Logos*) through which all things had come to be. And He had just given them a fantastic job reference. But He continues...

9. "**I, Myself, am now requesting about** (or: concerning) **them. I am not presently requesting about the System** (religious, political and cultural world; or: society; the aggregate of humanity; system of domination), **but rather, about** (or: concerning) **those whom You have given to Me, and I possess,**

His focus was on His first crop of grapes (from His branches). Once they were ripe for harvest, and then pruned for another crop, the focus would turn to the rest of the System, through them. They would now be the Vines in the earth (or, the branches of the olive tree – Rom. 11:17), each one producing more branches as His Vineyard spreads throughout the aggregate of humanity. And of the increase, from His Beginning, there will be no boundary, nor end (Isa. 9:6). At that time, however, "**the whole ordered System** (or: the entire realm of the religious and the secular) **is continuously lying outstretched** (lying as asleep, idle or dead; reclining) **within the gush of misery** (within the disadvantageous, laborious and worthless situation; within the sorry plight; in union with wickedness and evil; in the midst of the misery-gushed [attitude and existence])" (1 Jn. 5:19).

10. **"because they continuously exist** (or: are) **in You** (or: by You; for You; with You). **Thus, all My possessions are Yours, and Your possessions are Mine, and I have been – and remain – glorified** (made to be a recognized appearance and a manifestation which calls forth praise) **within, in union with, and among, them.**

This first clause is a continuation of the last clause of vs. 9. These folks, of whom He was speaking to the Father, were now existing **in the Father, by the Father, for the Father and with the Father**. How would this information hit the ears of His disciples? Would their ears be ringing? I would imagine so. They had been brought to the place and position of which He had described concerning Himself. They were His possessions, and the Father's possessions – and Jesus affirms a mutual ownership by Him and the Father.

Similar to what He had said about Himself in vs. 1, above, He now says about them: **He had been, and now remained, glorified within, in union with, and among, them**. In, and among, them He had been "made to be a recognized appearance and a manifestation which calls forth praise." Because of their union with Him, and His union with them, they shared in His glory, and He was glorified within them. Paul would later inform us that,

> "**Now further, those whom He rightwised** (or: liberates and turns in the right direction; or: = included in covenant), **these He also instantly glorified**
>> (or: makes of reputation which calls forth praise; gives a splendid appearance; gives honorable thoughts and imaginations; clothes with splendor)" (Rom. 8:30b).

11. **"Also, I am no longer within the System** (or: And yet I no longer exist being in union with, or centered in, the world of culture and religion, or the domination arrangement), **and yet they themselves are continuing to be within the System** (world; ordered arrangement of the current society) **– and I, Myself, am progressively going toward You** (or: constantly coming face to face with You). **O Father, O Set-apart and Holy One, watch over and care for them** (observe, keep and guard them) **within, and in union with, Your Name – which You have given to Me, and I now have – to the end that they can** (or: would) **continuously exist being one, correspondingly as** (just as; in the same sphere as; to the same degree as; on the same level as) **We Ourselves [are].** [Cf vs. 22, below]

What Jesus later says to Pilate will help us to understand what He means in the first clause here. There He says, "**My kingdom** (My sovereignty; the realm and activity of My reign and influence; My kingship) **is not** (does not exist being) **from out of this System**…" (18:36a, below). When Jesus was immersed by John, and then Anointed by the Spirit, He left the domination System. We suggest that this means that He was no longer in union with Second Temple Judaism: the old covenant, the Law of Moses, the Pharisees, etc. He was born under the Sinai Law (Gal. 4:4b), but He was the new Law, as Paul said it,

> "**the principle and law of, from and which is the spirit and attitude of 'The Life within Christ Jesus'**
>> (or: For you see, the Law of Life's spirit, joined with [the] Anointing of Jesus; or: For the Spirit's law of life within Christ Jesus; or: the Law [= Torah] from the Breath-effect, which is Life in union with [the] Anointed Jesus)
> **frees [us] away from the Law of the Sin and of the Death**" (Rom. 8:2).

He exited that System in order to bring us into His freedom, and as Paul informs us in Gal. 5:1, "**For the freedom, Christ immediately set us free**."

He was the Forerunner into this new Freedom in Christ, and yet at the time of this prayer, "**they themselves [were] continuing to be within the System** (world; ordered arrangement of the current society) **– and [He, Himself, was] progressively going toward [the Father]**." But once there, with the Father, He would,

> "**jointly rouse and raise [them] up, and caused [them] to sit** (or: = enthrone [them]) **together in union with, and among, the heavenly people, and within the things situated upon** [thus, above] **the heavens**" (Eph. 2:6).

But for the time being, since they were not yet where He would be, He continued praying: "**O Father, O Set-apart and Holy One, watch over and care for them** (observe, keep and guard them) **within, and in union with, Your Name…**" So, as He is leaving them, He is passing on custody of them to His, and their, Father. The Father would guard them while He was going through His ordeal, and until He would be resurrected. Being cared for in the Father's Name means belonging to the Father's Family, and being kept safe, as God's children. Yes, they belong to Jesus (the Father had **given to the Son**), but the Father will be their "baby sitter" while He is on His journey of the cross.

In vss. 14 and 16, below, He will twice affirm of them, "**They do not exist** (are not being) **from out of the System** (world of society, religion or politics) **just as I, Myself, am not from the System**." Remember, this prayer to the Father (Who is within Him) is for the disciples to hear. In 15:19b, above, He had told them,

> "**I have selected** (or: chosen) **and picked you OUT FROM THE MIDST of the System** (world's organization: culture, religion and politics)."

Even though they were in, and would remain physically living within, the System, that System was no longer their source or realm of existence. Their source and realm of existence was Christ. This is why Paul would instruct those at Rome:

> "**And stop constantly conforming yourselves in fashion** (or: external show or appearance; guise; scheme) **to** (or, as passive: So then, quit being repeatedly molded by, fashioned for or patterned together with) **this age** [with other MSS: and not to be continuously configured to this age, or not to constantly remodel yourself for this time-period], **but on the contrary, be progressively transformed** (transfigured; changed in form and semblance) **by the renewing** (or: in the renewal; for the making-back-up-new again) **of your mind**" (Rom. 12:2).

Now the role of Guardian, within which Jesus asks the Father to serve, was for more than safety. Its main function was: "**to the end that they can** (or: would) **continuously exist being ONE, correspondingly as We Ourselves [are]**." We should pause, and then consider the other meanings of the compound conjunction:

> a) just as,
> b) in the same sphere as,
> c) to the same degree as,
> d) on the same level as,

THEY, Themselves, are **One**! Recall 10:30, above, "**I, Myself, and the Father are** (continuously exist being) **ONE**." No wonder Paul said what he did in Eph. 2:6 (quoted, above). This kind of "oneness" was entirely new for them, and for humanity. It is the "oneness" of the new arrangement (covenant) within the new creation. Peter would later speak of the Father guarding them. They would be:

> "**the ones being continuously garrisoned within** (or: kept, maintained and guarded in the center of) **God's power, in union with an ability which is God, through [His] faithfulness, into a deliverance** (a rescue which brings health, wholeness, salvation; and a [period of] rescue) **[which is now] ready to be unveiled** (revealed; disclosed) **within the midst of and in union with [this] last season** (or: resident within a final fitting situation; in a final fertile moment; on [this] last occasion), **within which [season and deliverance] you folks are presently feeling constant joy and happiness and are continuing to rejoice exceedingly…**" (1 Pet. 1:5-6a).

All of what Peter spoke is the source of the "oneness" of which He will speak more, below (vs. 21ff)…

12. **"When I was being with them** [other MSS add: within the System], **I Myself was continually watching over, caring for, observing, keeping, guarding and maintaining them in union with** (or: centered in) **Your Name – which You have given to Me, and I now have – and I protected [them], and NOT ONE from among them lost himself** (or: destroyed himself), **except** (or: since not) **the son of "the loss"** (the son of the dissolution, or, from the destruction; the person having the characteristics of loss, dissolution or destruction), **so that the Scripture could and would be fulfilled.**

In the first clause, He is speaking as though He was already gone away from them. Yet they are there, listening to Him. We suggest that His words, His Logos, is taking them into their immediate future, within their minds and imaginations. They are observing Him as already being gone, and with the Father, making His report to the Father. We discussed "the Name" in the previous verse. Here, they are hearing that He has His Father's Name (should we say, "the Family Name"?), and this is a restatement of the assertion which He made in vs. 11 – He is being emphatic.

Let us consider: "**NOT ONE from among them lost himself** (or: destroyed himself)." The verb "lost/destroy" is in the middle voice. It means the subject does the action upon itself, but here it is a negation – not one of them did this to himself. EXCEPT: "**the son of 'the loss'**." This is usually understood as a reference to Judah (Judas). But what does this phrase mean? Of what "loss" or "destruction" is He speaking? The phrase may have the idiomatic significance of meaning "the person having the characteristics of loss, dissolution or destruction," but of what loss or which destruction? Is this an allusion to Adam (Gen. 3; Rom. 5:12)? Was this what Paul meant in 1 Cor. 15:22a,
> "**within Adam all humans keep on** (or: everyone continues) **dying**"?
Perhaps Jesus had in mind what He had said, as recorded in Mat. 15:24,
> "**I was not commissioned and sent off as an emissary – except into the midst of those sheep having been destroyed, the ones that belong to [the] house of Israel**."
If this is applicable to vs. 12, here, then this "son of the loss" was one that He was sent for, and would search, until He found him (Lu. 15:4b). Even though this one was momentarily experiencing loss, we have Jesus declaring, in Jn. 18:9, "**I lose** (or: destroyed) **not one from out of them whom You have given to Me as a possession**." We should keep in mind that this Gospel has a focus on SIGNS. If He was referring to Judah, and his assignment to facilitate Jesus being transferred to the Judean authorities, was Judah a representative of Israel rejecting their Messiah? Did this "son from the destruction" represent either Adam, in his state of metaphorical deadness, or Israel, as she was observed in Ezk. 37, being a figure of their continued condition of being in exile? Or, was this "son of the dissolution" a SIGN pointing to the dissolution of Jesus' physical ministry where, for a time, the sheep would be scattered?

This sheep lost himself "**so that the Scripture could and would be fulfilled**." He had a vital role in the Christ Event.

13. **"Yet now** (at this moment) **I am progressively coming toward You, and I am repeatedly speaking these things aloud, within the System** (world of culture, politics and religion; aggregate of humanity), **so that they can continuously hold** (or: would habitually have) **My own joy** (the joy that is Mine) **existing having been filled full** (made full and continuing full) **within the midst of themselves.**

He was speaking "within the System" because they were still within the System, and as we noted, above, He was saying this prayer for them to hear, "**so that they can continuously hold** (or: would habitually have) **[His] own joy**." The "they," here, are His disciples. But they would take these things to the "world of culture, politics and religion, i.e., the aggregate of humanity." As they would hold this joy "**within the midst of themselves**," it would be "**existing having been filled full** (made full and continuing full)," because this is the goal that He had in view. They would be joined to His joy, and then would reproduce and increase that joy as they continued imparting it to others. Joy, in the set-apart Breath-effect, is a main ingredient in God's reign (Rom. 14:17). Paul imparted a wonderful blessing involving joy to those in Rome:

"**Now may the God of Expectation** (or: the God Who is the Expectant Hope) **make you full of all JOY and peace of the joining, within the midst of constant trust and in union with continual operation of faith and believing, [leading] into the midst of continually surrounding you with abundance within The Expectation** (or: in union with expectant hope) – **within [the] power of a set-apart spirit** (or: within [the] Holy Spirit's ability; or: in union with a power which is, and whose source is, set-apart Breath-effect and sacred attitude)" (Rom. 15:13).

Peter wrote of this joy, in 1 Pet. 1:8b,
> "**You folks are repeatedly rejoicing and being very happy in indescribable** (or: incapable of being spoken out) **joy which also exists having been made glorious**
>> (or: by unspeakable and glorified joy; in joy [that is] inexpressible and has made a notable reputation; with joy that is glorious beyond words, and which is filled with imagination and good opinion)."

But Jacob had a different admonition regarding joy, which would frequently attend them, as we read in Jas. 1:
> 2. **O my brothers** (= fellow Israelites, or, fellow believers; or: = My family), **lead every rejoicing** (or: lead the path of all JOY) **whenever you may fall into – so as to be encompassed by – various trials** (or: multi-faceted ordeals; [a tapestry of] tests and provings; or: experiments and attempts of varying hues),
> 3. **while habitually knowing, from intimate experience and insight, that the thing by means of which your faith, trust and confidence is tested and proved** (or: the testing and proof of your faithfulness and loyalty) **keeps on producing** (or: is progressively working down-in the results and accomplishing) **persistent patient endurance**
>> (a steadfast remaining and dwelling under some ordeal or situation; or: a holding up under sustained attacks; or: a relentless giving of sustaining support).
> 4. **But patient endurance** (remaining under and/or sustained support) **must habitually be having a work brought to completion** (a complete action; a perfect work; a mature production which reaches its goal) **to the intent that you may be** (or: can exist as) **perfect ones** (complete, matured and finished folks who have attained the goal), **even ones having an entire allotment** (or: whole folks having every part), **being left behind in nothing** (or: lacking not one thing).

This sounds very much like something Jesus would have said. *Cf* Jn. 16:20-24

14. **"I, Myself, have given Your *Logos*** (Your Word; the thought and idea from You; the laid-out message and blueprint, which is You) **to them, and the domination System** (world of government and religion) **hates them** (treats and regards them with ill will; detaches from them), **because they do not exist from out of the dominating System as their source** (= are not being a product of that world), **correspondingly as I, Myself, am not from out of the dominating System, as My origin** (or: just as, in Myself, I do not exist [springing up] from the midst of the world of religious or governmental dominance).

The first clause is like saying that He had given Himself to them, for Jesus was the Father's *Logos*. But as we revisit the semantic range of that last word, consider all that He had said to them during the previous three years of teaching them. What He shared with them was "the thought and idea from [the Father]." It was the Father's Plan, His "the laid-out message," and "the blueprint which is [the Father]."

Saul would later be an example of the domination System hating them. Peter would personally experience this after Jesus was taken to the home of the chief priest, when different ones would accuse him of being part of Jesus' followers. The book of Acts gives multiple examples of how the leaders of Second Temple Judaism "treats and regards them with ill will." Even in our day, we have experienced folks "detaching" themselves from us. Why? Because just as the His disciples "**do not exist from out of the dominating System as their source** (= are not being a product of that world)" – that system being the Judaism of the 1st century, which was in collusion with the Roman Empire – so too, we are not a product of the religions of today, or of the "mountains" of our current empire of government, economy, politics or cabals. We have come out of them, and have moved from their mindsets (*cf* Rev. 18:4), in order to stand with the little Lamb, on Mt. Zion (Rev. 14:1; Heb. 12:22-24). We read an echo of Jesus, in 1 Jn. 3:13,

> "**Stop marveling** (Cease wondering; Quit being astonished), **brothers, if** (or: since) **the ordered System** (world of culture and religion; or: the estranged secular system of governmental control) **is constantly hating and detaching from you** (habitually regarding you with ill-will)."

His apprentices had been birthed into the kingdom just like He said of Himself: "**correspondingly as I, Myself, am not from out of the dominating System, as My origin** (or: just as, in Myself, I do not exist [springing up] from the midst of the world of religious or governmental dominance)." And so the call would continue to be:

> "**Now then, we can keep on coming out** (or: should be progressively going out) **toward Him – outside of the Camp – habitually bearing His reproach** (= the censure and disgrace which He bore; or: the insult which pertains to Him)" (Heb. 13:13). [*cf* Heb. 11:26; 1 Pet. 4:12-14, 17] [comment: this was a call to participate in His sacrifice, and also to leave Judaism (or: religion), and thus to bear the same reproach and insults that He bore; it is also a call to bear away from them the mistakes and failures of others – Jn. 20:23]

And so Paul would affirm:

> "**For, take a comprehensive look at** (or: as an indicative: To be sure, you folks are progressively seeing and observing) **your calling** (or: summoning; vocation; social role) **brothers, that [there are] not many wise folks – according to flesh [= the world's wisdom]**
>> (or: corresponding to a flesh [system of philosophy or religion]; on the level of [the estranged human situation]; with a consciousness oriented toward a domination System),
> **not many powerful ones** (those with [political or financial] ability), **not many well-born ones** (ones born to social ease and profit; those of noble birth; folks with distinguished genealogy), **but to the contrary, God collects His thoughts and speaks forth** (or: selects and picks out; chose) **the stupid things** (or: the foolish ones) **of the organized System** (from the world of religion, culture and its secular society)" (1 Cor. 1:26-27a).

15. **"I am not now making a request to the end that You should pick them up and carry** (or: remove; take) **them out of the System** (world; ordered arrangement of culture, religion, economy and government; human aggregate), **but rather that You should observe, guard, protect, maintain, care for and keep them out of the worthless or bad situation, the sorry plight, the effect of the knavish and good-for-nothing person, the oppressive toil and the base or evil influence.**

Jesus did not want His first disciples, nor us, to be "whisked off to heaven" – or even to create their own separated communities, as did the folks at Qumran (the community that created the Dead Sea Scrolls). He wants us to be within the ordered arrangement, but not be "of" it. We are to be the "yeast" that permeates the entire batch of dough (Mat. 13:33). And it is for this reason that He requested that the Father would "**observe, guard, protect, maintain, care for and keep them**" – they would be right in the middle of the mix. Let us consider what He wanted the Father to keep them "**out of** (*ek*)":

> a) **the worthless or bad situation**;
> b) **the sorry plight**;
> c) **the effect of the knavish and good-for-nothing person**;
> d) **the oppressive toil** – an allusion to Israel enslaved in Egypt?
> e) **the base or evil influence**.

Now the common translations often render this last phrase, of which on offer is its semantic range, as "the evil one" – which is OK, so long as we don't read "*satan*" or "*the devil*" into this text. Jesus is speaking about a whole range of negative situations into which His followers will be thrust, as they spread the Good News of Christ's reign. We need not look at this verse through a "spooky" lens, or through the eyes of "Jewish myths" (Titus 1:14), that were so prevalent during the period of Second Temple Judaism. Persian and Hellenistic religious inventions and superstitions had infiltrated the Jewish worldview of that day. The followers of Jesus would have to combat pagan ideas within both Judaism and the paganism of the Empire. Institutional Christianity would become extremely infected with these imaginations following the rule of Constantine who made "Christianity" the official religion of the Empire: it would become Babylon riding the beast, once more.

Paul gives a witness that the Lord has done this:
> "**Jesus Christ, the One at one point giving Himself, over [the situation of]** (or: on behalf of; for the sake of; [p46, Aleph*, A, D & other MSS read: concerning]) **our failures** (situations and occasions of falling short or to the side of the target; deviations; mistakes; errors; sins) **so that He could carry us out from the midst of the present misery-gushing and worthless age**
>> (or: bear us forth from the indefinite period of time – characterized by toil, grievous plights and bad situations – having taken a stand in [our] midst; or: extricate us from the space of time having been inserted and now standing in union with base qualities),
> **corresponding to** (or: down from; in accord with; in line with; in the sphere and to the level of) **the effect of the will** (or: intent; purpose; design) **of our God and Father**" (Gal. 1:4).

He said this again, in 2 Thes. 3:3,
> "**But the Lord** [= Yahweh or Christ] **is** (or: exists) **continuously faithful** (loyal; full of faith), **who will progressively establish** (set you to stand fast and stable) **and keep** (guard; protect; maintain) **you folks away from the malicious person** (or: the unsound and unprofitable; the painful labor; the malignant situation)."

16. **"They do not exist** (are not being) **from out of the System** (world of society, religion or politics) **as a source or origin, just as I, Myself, am not from the System** (world) **as a source or origin.**

Again, a rhetorical restatement for emphasis to His listeners.

17. **"Set them apart** (or: Make them different from the norm) **within the midst of the Truth** (or: in union with, and centered in, reality). **Your *Logos*** (Word; blueprint; patterned idea) **exists being Truth**
> (or: Your thought, patterned information and expressed message of divine rational meaning and purpose is Reality; Your laid-out, communicated reason continues with Being [as] Reality).

Truth – the new Reality – was a realm of spiritual existence, and a worldview/mindset, into which He wanted the Father to set them. Once again, Paul echoes the result of this request, in Eph. 2:6. Note the functions of the preposition: within the midst of; in union with; centered in. In other words, "immerse them" into this new creation. And now He further explains this, for His listeners:
> a) **Your *Logos*** (Word; blueprint; patterned idea) **exists being Truth**;
> b) Your thought, patterned information and expressed message of divine rational meaning and purpose is Reality;
> c) Your laid-out, communicated reason continues with Being [as] Reality.

The domination System was neither truth nor reality, and it certainly was not Life. It was death; it was exile. It was the fruit of the "tree of the knowledge and experience of good-and-evil from which He asked the Father to guard them (vs. 15). But, as Dan Kaplan has reminded us,
> "**Now the ax already continues lying [positioned with its aim] toward** (face to face with)) **the root of the trees. So then, every tree not seasonally producing beautiful** (fine; ideal; choice) **fruit is customarily being cut out [of the orchard or garden] and is regularly being tossed into a fire [to heat or to cook]**" (Lu. 3:9).

So the work of the Spirit is to cut down the tree of the knowledge of good and evil (the Law) that grows within "the Garden" of every person. We do not find this tree in Rev. 22:2; in the New Jerusalem there is only the Tree of the Life.

The Truth – "the Tree of the Life" – was the Blueprint that provided the Plan of the Ages, and that Logos contains the Power to bring about all His will and intent. Rev. 21 and 22 contain pictures of this Truth, in apocalyptic symbols. And, of course, joining Jn. 1:1 to Jn. 14:6, we see that Jesus embodies this new Reality.

18. **"Correspondingly** (or: Just; In the sphere; On the level) **as You sent Me into the System** (world of religious and political dominance; human aggregate) **as an Emissary, I Myself also send them forth as emissaries** (representatives) **into the prevailing, organized system of the human aggregate,**

Take note of the opening compound conjunction: "**Correspondingly** (or: Just; In the sphere; On the level) **as**." Jesus is now sending His apprentices into the "world" in the same way, in the same sphere, on the same level, and correspondingly as the Father sent Jesus into the System (etc.). This begs the question: just how did the Father send Him? In what sphere did He send Him? On what level did He send Him?

To answer these questions we must look at Jesus' origin – the place from where He was sent. On what level did Jesus operate, in His ministry? In 3:34, above, we read:

> "**for He Whom God sends forth with a mission** (dispatches as an Emissary and Representative) **habitually is speaking the gush-effects from God** (the results of the flows of God; God's declarations or sayings), **for God is habitually** (or: continuously) **giving the Spirit** (Breath; or: Attitude) **[and] not from out of a measure** (= not by a measured portion or limit; = without measure and without limitation)."

The apprentices would be sent forth in this same way. Just as the Spirit came upon Jesus, when John immersed Him, in this same way and to the same degree will this same Spirit come upon, and anoint, His apprentices. They will operate in the sphere of God's reign, just as Jesus did. We are informed later on, in 1 Jn. 2:20, that:

> "**you folks continue having the effects** (or: constantly hold and progressively possess the results) **of an anointing from the set-apart One** (or: the Holy One), **and so you all have seen and are aware** (or: know; perceive)."

19. **"and I, Myself, am continuously setting Myself apart over them** (progressively making Myself different from the norm, in their behalf) **to the end that they themselves, also, can** (may; would) **continuously exist being ones having been set-apart within the midst of reality** (centered in Truth).

The first clause, "**setting Myself apart over them**," is a further explanation of 10:11, 15, above,

> "**The Ideal** (Fine; Beautiful) **Shepherd continually places His soul over the sheep**…. **I am constantly placing My soul-life over the sheep**…"

Then, He goes on to explain the purpose for "setting [Himself] apart": "**to the end that they themselves, also, can** (may; would) **continuously exist being ones having been set-apart within the midst of reality** (centered in Truth)." This last phrase, concerning the sphere and center of Reality and Truth, points to the reason for "making [Himself] different from the norm." Jesus was in the process of progressively moving into the higher sphere of the atmospheres/heaven – the realm of spirit and the Breath-effect. He is journeying on into the Holy of holies, the fullness of the new creation. He was metaphorically becoming a Chief Priest, after the order of Melchizedek (read the book of Hebrews, especially chapters 5-10, for this topic).

Paul lends further insight to Christ's work, here, in 1 Cor. 1:30,

> "**Now you folks are, and continuously exist being, forth from out of the midst of Him – within and in union with Christ Jesus, Who came to be** (or: is birthed) **wisdom in and among us** (or: to us; for us), **from God: both a rightwising, eschatological deliverance into righted, covenantal existence in fair relationships of equity in the Way pointed out** (or: likewise a just covenantal Act from God) **and a being set-apart to be different** (a being made sacred), **even a redemptive liberation** (an emancipation; a loosing-away from [a condition of bondage])."

Then Heb. 10:10 informs us that, "**we are folks having been made set-apart ones** (sanctified folks; sacred and holy people) **through the offering of the body of Jesus Christ once for all.**" *Cf* 1 Thes. 4:7

20. "**I am not now making a request about these only, but further about those habitually trusting and progressively believing into Me through their word** (or: *logos*; message; what they lay out),

Here He is letting His listeners know that they will be fruitful branches – that they will carry on His mission, being sent in the same way and with the same power (the Holy Spirit) as He was sent, and was empowered. He is looking to their future, and "**making a request about... those habitually trusting... through their word** (or: *logos*; message; what they lay out)." He saw their future, and spoke into it. He was, indeed, "The Prophet."

21. "**to the end that all humans would** (or: all people can and should) **continuously exist being one, correspondingly as You, O Father** [other MSS: Father], **[are] within the midst of Me, and I [am] within the midst of You – so that they, themselves, may and would also continuously exist being within the midst of Us, to the end that the aggregate of humanity** (the System: world of culture, religion and government; or: secular society) **can** (may; could) **continuously trust and progressively believe that** (would continue faithful because) **YOU sent Me forth as an Emissary with a mission,**

This verse begins with a purpose clause which is a continuation of the previous verse. The word "**all**" is in the nominative case and stands as the subject of the sentence. Most of the normal translations add the pronoun "they" as the subject of the verb, prompting the rendering, "that they all," but this pronoun is not needed. David Bentley Hart's recent translation reads, "that all may be one," rendering "all" as the subject of the verb, as I have it here. James A. Kleist's translation (in Kleist & Lilly) offers, "All are to be one... The world must come to believe..." Here, again, we have the word "all" in masculine form, thus my rendering, "**all humans**." In verse 20, Jesus projects to the future, speaking of the results of sending out His apprentices, generation after generation. The end, or goal, that He has in mind is the peace and the joining that comes in God's reign. This joining (as Paul describes in Eph. 2:13-19, in reference to the two groups: the circumcision and the uncircumcision, which means, the JEWS and the GENTILES) will make "**all humans exist being one.**" Eph. 2:14-16 are most revealing:
> "**You see, He Himself is our Peace** (or: continuously exists being our Joining) – **the One making** (forming; constructing; creating; producing) **The Both [to be] ONE, and within His flesh is instantly destroying the middle wall of the fenced enclosure** (or: the partition or barrier wall)**: the enmity** (cause of hate, alienation, discord and hostility; characteristics of an enemy), **rendering useless** (nullifying; rendering down in accord with inactivity) **the Law of the implanted goals** (or: concerning impartations of the finished product within; from commandments; which was inward directives) **consisting in decrees** (or: prescribed ordinances), **to the end that He may frame** (create; found) **The Two** [i.e., the Jews and the Gentiles] **into ONE qualitatively New and Different** [*p*46 & others: common] **HUMANITY centered within the midst of, and in union with, Himself, continuously making** (progressively creating) **Peace and Harmony** (a Joining); **and then should fully transfer, from a certain state to another which is quite different, The Both – centered in, and within the midst of, One Body in God** (or: make completely other, while moving away from what had existed, and fully reconcile The Both, in one Body, **by, to,** with and for **God**), **through the cross – while in the midst of Himself killing the enmity and discordant hatred.**"

Verse 21 also sheds light on Eph. 3:14-15,
> "**On account of this I continually bend my knees** (= in loyalty, respect and reverence) **to** (toward; or: face-to-face with) **the Father** [other MSS add: of our Lord Jesus Christ], **forth from Where** (or: out of the midst of Whom) **every family** (lineage; kindred; descent; paternal group) **within heaven and upon earth** (or: in [the] sky or atmosphere, and on [the] land) **is one after another being named** (or: spoken of, or to, by name; or: designated)."

In Eph. 3:18 he speaks of "the breadth and length and depth and height," and then in vs. 20 he rather explodes into that which goes beyond our imaginations:

> "**the One being continuously able and powerful to do** (make; form; create; produce) **above and beyond all things – surpassingly above, over and beyond things which we are repeatedly asking for ourselves or are normally grasping with the mind** (apprehending; imagining; considering; conceiving) **– in accord with** (or: down from; corresponding to; in the sphere of and along the line of) **the power and ability [which is] continuously operating** (making itself effective; energizing itself; working and developing) **within US, and in union with US**."

Now mark well the degree, sphere and level of unity – of all humans being one – to which He compares the destiny of mankind: "**correspondingly as You, O Father, [are] within the midst of Me, and I [am] within the midst of You**." THIS is His point of comparison! None of us can imagine such a thing. It only happens within the realm of the atmospheres – in the kingdom of the atmospheres. No wonder Rev. 21 and 22 are described with such opulence and beauty. THIS is the result of the work of Christ. It only happens via Resurrection Life.

But He continues on – and notice the scope and inclusiveness of the end that He has in view: "**so that they, themselves, may and would also continuously exist being WITHIN the MIDST of US, to the end that the aggregate of humanity** (the System: world of culture, religion and government; or: secular society) **can** (may; could) **continuously trust and progressively believe**." This is the plan of the Ages (Eph. 3:11). In time, each one in his or her own order (1 Cor. 15:23) will come to believe that,

> "**the Father has sent forth** (dispatched as a Representative) **the Son – [the] Savior of the world** (or: a Deliverer from the ordered and controlling System of religion and society; Restorer of the cosmos; or: a Rescuer and Healer of **the aggregate of humanity**)" (1 Jn. 4:14).

22. **"and I, Myself, have given to them** (or: in them), **and they now possess, the glory** (the notion; the opinion; the imagination; the manifestation which calls forth praise) **which You have given to Me, and which I now possess, to the end that they can continuously exist being one correspondingly as** (just as; according as; to the same level as; in the same sphere as) **We are one:**

This verse is a continuation of vs. 21, and continues the same focus of His words that were begun in vs. 20. The closest antecedent of "**them**," in the first clause, is "**the aggregate of humanity**" in the last clause of vs. 21. That inclusive group is the end that He has in view with this far-reaching prayer. Paul makes this clear in Col. 1:

> 26. **the Secret** (or: sacred mystery) **having been hidden away and remaining concealed away from the ages** (or: from [past] eons), **as well as away from the [past] generations, yet now** (at the present time) **is set in clear light in His set-apart folks** (or: was manifested to His holy ones; is caused to be seen by His saints; is shown for what it is, for His sacred people),
> 27. **to whom God wills** (or: at one point purposed; or: intends) **to make known by intimate experience, what [are] the riches of the glory of this Secret** (or: the wealth which has its source in this sacred mystery's manifestation which calls forth praise) **within the multitudes** (among the nations; in the Gentiles; IN UNION WITH the swarms of ethnic groups), **which is** (or: exists being) **Christ within you folks, the expectation of and from the glory**
>> (or: which is [the] Anointed in union with you people: the [realized] hope of the manifestation which called forth praise; or: which is [the] Anointing [and the Messiah] within the midst of you folks – the expectation which is the glory),

You see, we were informed in 3:16, above, that, "**For thus God loves** (or: You see God, in this manner, fully gives Himself to and urges toward reunion with) **the aggregate of humanity so that He gives His only-born Son**..." (Jn. 3:16a). His followers were (and we also are) "**a specific** (or: a certain; some) **firstfruit** (first portion) **of, and from among, His created beings**" (Jas. 1:18), but He has the whole harvest in mind. We are a means of bringing in this harvest, over time.

Let us also revisit 1:9, above, where we are informed concerning the Logos:

> "**It was** (or: He was, and continued being) **the True and Genuine Light which** (or: Who) **is continuously** (repeatedly; progressively) **enlightening** (giving light to) **every person** (or: all humanity) **continuously** (repeatedly; progressively; constantly; one after another) **coming into the world** (or: the ordered system and **aggregate of humans**)."

That Light infuses the Glory. Or, as Paul describes it:

> "**But we all, ourselves… being folks who by a mirror are continuously observing, as ourselves, the Lord's glory, are presently being continuously and progressively transformed into the very same image and form, from glory unto glory**" (2 Cor. 3:18).

The vision of God is not just about the firstfruit that He called from out of the harvest, but rather, it is for all of the crop: all humanity:

> "**Now when the whole** (or: all things) **would be completely supportively-aligned in Him** (or: attached and appended to Him; subordinately sheltered and arranged by and for Him), **then… God can be all things within the midst of and in union with all humans** (or: may be everything in all things; or: should exist being All in all; or: would exist being everything, within the midst of everyone)" (1 Cor. 15:28).

The end in view is: **that they can continuously exist being one correspondingly as** (just as; according as; to the same level as; in the same sphere as) **We are one.**" We get a more in-depth picture of this in 1 Jn. 1:3,

> "**The One whom we have seen, and still now see, and we have heard, and now continue listening to and hearing, we are also constantly reporting to you, to the end that you, too, may be continuously having common being and existence** (or: would be progressively holding partnership and participation) **with us. And yet, our common being and existence** (or: participation; partnership) **[is] with the Father, even with His Son, Jesus Christ.**"

23. "**I within the midst of and in union with them and You within the midst of and in union with Me, to the end that they would** (or: could; should; may; can) **continuously exist being folks having been perfected** (brought to the destined goal; finished; completed; matured and purposed) **into one – so that the human aggregate** (or: the domination System) **can** (or: could; would) **progressively come to experientially know that** (or: experience insight [gnosis], because) **YOU commissioned and sent Me forth, and You love, accept, and urge toward reunion with, them correspondingly as** (or: just as; in the same sphere and to the same level as) **You love, accept, and give Yourself fully to, Me.**

When this union and mutual indwelling becomes the human experience, it means to "**continuously exist being folks having been perfected** (brought to the destined goal; finished; completed; matured and purposed) **into ONE.**" This is a picture of the entire harvest, and it is "**so that the human aggregate can** (or: could; would) **progressively come to experientially know…**" To "experience insight [have *gnosis*]" of the Father and the Son is one definition of eonian Life (vs. 3, above). Once again, Jesus' prayer and the Father's plan of the ages are all-encompassing. His vision has all humanity (Adam) in view. It is a plan for the whole world, not just one people-group, or one religion. It is to end religions and all the divisions between people. Universal oneness is the goal, as all are dragged back into union with God, and thus, with each other. It is a message of Peace, which is a Joining, which brings Oneness.

Knowing that the Father "**commissioned and sent [Him] forth**" is now tied to the Father's "**love, accept, and urge toward reunion with, them**" (i.e., with the **aggregate of humanity**), and this, in turn, takes us back to Jn. 3:16 – God so loves the world, i.e., the aggregate of humanity.

24. "**Father, I continue purposing and intending** (or: willing; wanting) **that those also, whom You have given to Me and that I now possess, would continuously exist being with Me where I, Myself, AM** (or: where I AM, and continuously exist Being), **so that they can** (or: may; could; would) **constantly**

look upon and keep on contemplatively watching My own glory (assumed appearance; manifested Presence which incites praise), **which You have given to Me as a possession because You loved** (accepted; fully gave Yourself to) **Me before [the; a] casting-down of [the; a] universe**

> (or: tossing down of a world; or: [the] founding of an organized system; a sowing [as seed] or [impregnating] of [the] aggregate of humanity; founding of [the] system of culture and society; or: a casting corresponding to and in agreement with an ordered disposition of [the] Dominating System).

Here He seems to move back to focus on His current group of apprentices, although this could also be read as His having in mind the full harvest, being the Visionary that He was. We should listen to His heart in these words, and also hear the heart of His Father. The desire is to have Family with Him, and Paul will later reveal that He took them, and us, with Him:

> "**as many as are immersed into Christ Jesus are immersed into His death. We, then, were buried together in Him** (or: by Him; with Him), **through the immersion into the death, to the end that just as Christ was roused and raised forth from out of the midst of dead folks THROUGH THE GLORY of, from, and which is, The Father, thus also we can walk around within newness of life. For since we have been birthed** (have become) **folks engrafted and produced together** (or: planted and made to grow together; brought forth together; congenital) **in, by, to and with the result of the likeness of His death, then certainly we will also continue existing [in and with the effects of the likeness] of The Resurrection**" (Rom. 6:3-5).

Now THAT is "**being with [Him]**." Here, it is not only "**contemplatively watching [His] own glory**," but being resurrected by that Glory. Being in this resurrected realm is the means of which we can observe His assumed appearance (as we have noted, by citing 2 Cor. 3:18).

Just how we interpret a "**casting-down of [the; a] universe** (etc.)" depends upon which lens of the semantic range of *kosmos* we choose to view this event, as well as the lens for the word *katabolē* (casting-down; founding; etc.). Did this refer to Adam's expulsion from the Garden, or to the founding of creation? Might it refer to the "founding of the organized system for Israel, at Sinai"? This second word is used of Sarah "conceiving seed" in Heb. 11:11, so on offer for this phrase is, "a sowing [as seed] or [impregnating] of [the] aggregate of humanity." By rendering *kosmos* as "Dominating System," we could have:

> "a casting corresponding to and in agreement with an ordered disposition of [the] Dominating System."

Although this last rendering may seem out of line with the context, He could be referring to the glory that He has had, with the Father being within Him, prior to the casting of the decision made about Him, by the Judean authorities, that corresponded to an agreement, which led to a disposition, concerning Him. We can tend to think "cosmically" when He might have been referring to the present "world" of Second Temple Judaism. We offer these possibilities, just for your consideration.

Whichever rendering resonates with us, the Father loved Him before it all happened, or was about to happen. The casting-down could also refer to the upcoming destruction of Jerusalem, and of the old covenant "ordered arrangement (customs and Law)."

25. **"O fair and equitable Father** (O Father, who are the paradigm of justice, uprightness, honesty and rightwised relationship – the source of what is right; O deliverance-bringing Father who puts things right), **though the aggregate of humanity** (System; world of culture, religion, economy and government) **does not have intimate, experiential knowledge of You, yet I Myself experientially and intimately know You** (or: the world, also, did not know you by experience, yet I personally knew You), **and these people personally know that** (recognize because) **YOU sent Me forth as a commissioned Emissary,**

Here His words pertain to the then-present contrast between "**the aggregate of humanity**" and "**these people**." Those who were presently His apprentices/learners at least "**personally know that** (recognize

312

because) **YOU sent Me forth as a commissioned Emissary**." This was the beginning revelation upon which their future would be based. The world at large did not yet have this knowledge: correcting this situation was, and is, the mission of His disciples. But see how important it is for them to know, and recognize that the Father is the One that sent Him off on this mission, as the Father's Emissary. He was there representing the Father. All His work was the Father's work. His Name meant "Yah is the Savior."

26. **"and I made Your Name intimately known to, for, in and among them – and I will continue making It experientially known, to the end that the Love** (acceptance; urge toward union with, and Self-giving to, [all]) **[in; with] which You love** (accept; give Yourself to) **Me can** (would; may; could) **continuously be** (or: progressively exist) **within the midst of and among them – and I Myself within the midst of, among, in union with, and centered in them."**

In this chapter, He manifested the Father's Name to them (vs. 6), asked the Father to watch over and keep them in His Name (vs. 11), saying that He had observed and kept them in the Father's Name (vs. 12), and now proclaims that He had "**I made Your Name intimately known to, for, in and among them**," and would continue to do so. All of this was "**to the end that the Love** (acceptance; urge toward union with, and Self-giving to, [all]) **[in; with] which You love** (accept; give Yourself to) **Me can** (would; may; could) **continuously be** (or: progressively exist) **within the midst of and among them**." Recall Paul's essay on Love (1 Cor. 13), and the fact that we are informed that God IS Love (1 Jn. 4:8, 16). So He is saying that the goal is God, Himself, "**continuously being** (or: progressively existing) **within the midst of and among them**." Here, the ground is prepared for the revelations that would be given to Paul (e.g., we are God's Home/Temple, etc.).

Then He ends this long prayer with announcing that, although He was presently journeying on, "**[He] [Himself] would continuously be within the midst of, among, in union with, and centered in them**." The place to where He was journeying on was going to be "within them." This is the Good News, the expectation of Glory.

Chapter 18

We suggest that the rest of Jesus' life as a servant (Phil. 2:7-8) is described, below, as a lived-out apocalyptic parable that embodies the first Adam's and Israel's eschatological story: part 1 being the cross and the resurrection of Jesus, followed by the sending of the Promise of the Father (Acts 2); part 2 coming in the destruction of Jerusalem in AD 70, which ended old-covenant-Israel's story and the continued beginning of the Last Adam – begun with Jesus; progressively fulfilled in the One New Humanity (Eph. 2:14-15). We will begin this chapter with our eyes open to see symbolic details and SIGNS, as this Gospel approaches its conclusion.

1. **[After] saying these things, Jesus, together with His disciples, went out to the other side across the winter flow of the Kedron** (the "brook, torrent or wadi of the Cedars"; or: the Kidron Valley) **to where there was a garden** (a place planted with trees and herbs), **into which He Himself – and His disciples – entered.**

Jesus is taking Adam back to the scene of the crime. It is the prelude to the Eschatos (Last) Adam's death, as He prepares to take the first Adam to the grave – and all humanity with Him, for you see:
"**One Person** (or: Man) **died over [the situation of] all people** (or: for the sake of all humans); **consequently all people died** (or: accordingly, then, all humans died)" (2 Cor. 5:14b).

With having His disciples with them (the figurative 12, representing Israel, which in turn represented the world of humanity) the rest of humanity (as the corporate Seed) is pictured as being participants in this divine play. The group will figuratively die, through deserting Him (Mat. 26:56b). Our author mentions "the winter flow" of "the Cedars." The cedars may allude to the other trees in the original Garden. Winter is the season that symbolizes death, but the flow points to the resurrection season (the return of life, in the spring). Our author is still giving SIGNS.

Significantly, the brook Kedron (or: Kidron) was mentioned in 2 Sam. 15:23, when "all the country wept" at the time when David was fleeing from Jerusalem to "stay in a place that was far off," due to the rebellion of Absalom. At that time David had the priests take "the ark of the covenant" back into Jerusalem, but now it was the priests that were rebelling against the true Ark – of the new covenant.

2. **Now Judah** (or: Judas) – **the one presently transferring, commending and progressively committing Him** (or: handing Him over) – **also had seen and knew the place, because Jesus had many times** (or: frequently; often) **been gathered there with His disciples.**
3. **Therefore Judah** (Judas), **getting and taking the detachment** (or: squad [of Roman soldiers]) **and subordinates** (those who act under orders; deputies; Temple guards or Sanhedrin officers) **from the chief** (ranking) **priests and from the Pharisees, is proceeding to come there with lanterns, torches and weapons** (or: arms).

Judah had to come, to complete the 12 being back in the Garden. There are no cherubim guarding the entrance to this Garden, so the Temple guards and Sanhedrin officers enter with the purpose of cutting down the Tree of Life – and the others trees, as well, but Jesus intervenes (vs. 8, below). The ranking priests prefer the tree of the knowledge of good and evil (darkness: 1:5, 11; 3:19, above) rather than the Tree of Life. They come in the night, because they are of the night and the darkness (1 Thes. 5:5, 7). They come with weapons set for fighting flesh and blood (2 Cor. 10:4-5).

4. **Then Jesus, having seen and being aware of** (or: knowing) **all the things progressively coming upon Him, went out and proceeds saying to them, "Whom are you folks presently seeking** (looking for; or: What things are you men now trying to find)**?"**

This edition of the story presents Jesus as the Logos, the Anointed Messiah: He is in charge of the situation, even though He will submit to them in order to play out His part, in the rest of the story.

5. **They decidedly replied, "Jesus, the Nazarene." He then says to them, "I AM** (or: I, Myself, am; or: I am Being)**"** [B reads: "I am Jesus."]. **Now Judah** (Judas) – **the one transferring, commending, committing and handing Him over – had also been standing with them,**
6. **then, as He said to them, "I, Myself, am** (or: I AM; I am continuous Existence),**"** he [other MSS: they] **went off into the rear** (into the [area] back behind) **and they suddenly fell to the ground.**

Here He proclaims another "I AM" statement – which our author records twice (two witnesses) – and there is a demonstration of the power of the Logos, their God. This may be an allusion to Lev. 9:23-24, where the glory of Yahweh appeared unto all the People (Israel), and a Fire from before Yahweh consumed the offering upon the altar, and "all the people… fell on their faces." Judah, **standing with them,** would also have fallen to the ground. Why did Judah go off "**into the rear** (into the [area] back behind)**"**? Was their falling due to the force and power of His words, or was this done in reverence, as at the time in Lev. 9:24?

7. **Then He again inquired of them, "Whom are you presently seeking** (looking for; or: What things are you men now trying to find)**?" Now those men say, "Jesus, the Nazarene."**

Why did Jesus a second time ask them whom they were seeking? Was He simply bringing them back to their senses – returning them to the issue at hand? Why did they say, "**Jesus, the Nazarene**"? Is our author drawing us back to the beginning of His story, where Philip identifies Him as a Nazarene (i.e., a person from Nazareth; Jn. 1:45-6)? That is the only place in this Gospel that gives this designation (other than the title that Pilate put on His cross – 19:19, below). But we do find the mention of Nazareth, in Mat. 2:23, and Acts 24:5 refers to "the sect of the Nazarenes." So it is possible that His being the Jesus from

Nazareth was more well-known (e.g., Mat. 26:71) than is shown in the records that we now possess. Of course, the name Jesus was a common name, at that time. Perhaps it was because Judah had thus designated who it was that this crowd wanted. The name Nazareth is Aramaic, and was imported into the Greek text by transliteration. Aramaic was a later development of Hebrew during and after the Captivity of the Jews, in Babylon. The root of this name is the Hebrew, *nazar*, and has the basic meaning, "separated." We know this term for its use to describe a person who was under a vow to live a life that was characterized by certain restrictions that "separated" him or her from the rest of the culture. Such a person was called a "Nazarite" (*cf* Nu. 6:2, 13, 18-21).

I handed off the baton to Dan Kaplan on this question, and he first takes us to the story from the history of Israel; the story of another Deliverer for Israel, the story of a "strong man" who reminds us of Jesus' enigmatic statements in Lu. 11:

> 21. **"Whenever the strong person – being one that has fully armed and completely equipped himself – may habitually watch over, guard and protect his own courtyard, his possessions and the things that sustain him continue being in peace** (joined [to him]).
> 22. **"Yet as soon as** (or: if ever) **a person stronger than him, after coming upon [him], can conquer** (or: may overcome) **him, he progressively lifts up and carries off his full armament** (all the armor and weaponry) **upon which he had trusted and placed his confidence – and now progressively distributes his spoils** (booty).
> 23. **"The person not continuing in being with Me is down on Me** (or: The one not existing accompanied by Me exists being out of line and out of step with Me, and is thus against what is Mine) **– and the person not habitually gathering or presently leading [folks] together with Me is constantly scattering and dispersing.**

The person not being with Him, personified as "the strong person" in this sage saying, was the chief priest, the head of the Judean leadership, which was riding the 1st century beast system that corresponded to the Philistine empire in Israel's past. During the time of the Judges, Yahweh raised up "a strong man" to spoil Israel's arch enemy, in that era. We find the story in Jud. 13. We will share some parallel points that Dan has highlighted. Let us sketch out the context, and then the birth and life of Samson. He was born during a period when "Israel did (or: committed) [what was considered to be] evil, in the eyes of Yahweh; so Yahweh delivered them into the hand of the Philistines, for forty years" (Jud. 13:1). [This was a significant, and symbolic number, within Israel's story – and it will be approximately 40 years from the time of Christ until the destruction of Jerusalem, in AD 70] This sets the context for the parallels that we will see between Samson's story, and Jesus' story.

Samson's story begins with a barren woman who had born no child, and "A messenger of Yahweh appeared to the woman and said to her: 'Behold, you are barren... but you will become pregnant and you will bear a son" (vss. 2-3). Next, the messenger instructs her to restrict her diet, because her son would be a Nazarite to God, from the womb, on, and he shall start off with saving Israel from the hand of the Philistines" (vs. 5). Compare the annunciation by Gabriel to Mary, in Lu. 1:26-35. At that time, Mary was living in Nazareth.

Jud. 13 continues with the woman telling of the event to her husband, Manoah (whose name means "rest"), and she described the messenger as "a man" who had the appearance of a messenger. He then seeks Yahweh about the message, and asks Yahweh, "O! my Lord, the man of God, whom You sent, let him, I pray, come again to us so that he may direct us." Yahweh complies, and the messenger came again to the woman, who ran to get her husband (notice that the interaction, up to this point, has been with the woman, a foreshadowing of the annunciation to Mary), and Manoah asks the messenger if he was the same one that had come before, and he answered, "I [am]." So Manoah responds, "Now let your words come to pass" (vs. 11; *cf* Lu. 1:38).

There comes an exchange between them, then Manoah offers to feed the messenger a meal of a young goat that he had prepared, but the messenger refused to eat, instructing him to make any burnt offering to

Yahweh. Then the author explains that Manoah did not know that this "man" was a messenger from Yahweh (vs. 16). But when the flame ascended from the altar, the messenger of Yahweh ascended in the flame, "and Manoah and his wife fell on their faces to the ground" (vs. 20; *cf* Judah/Judas and the detachment, in vs. 6, above). Samson was born, and grew, "and Yahweh blessed him and the Spirit of Yahweh began to move him at times..." (vss. 24-25). His parallels to Jesus' birth and ministry can be easily discerned, though of course his life characterized the failure of Israel – collusion with their enemy, via the prostitute, Delilah. Of note is the manner of his death, where he destroyed the temple of Dagon (Jud. 16; *cf* the mirrored counterpart in Jn. 2:19, "Destroy this Temple..."), and in 16:30b, we are informed that, "the dead which he put to death at his death were more than those whom he had put to death in his life." As we saw in our discussion of Jn. 17, when Jesus (the One) died, all died (2 Cor. 5:14), but that was so that He could resurrect all, having mercy upon all (Rom. 11:32).

In taking this thread, from "the Nazarene" back to Samson, we must view this old story in the same way that Paul viewed the story of Sarah and Hagar (Gal. 4). We must look with the eyes of the Spirit to see shadows of Christ in Israel's story (as did Jesus, in Lu. 24:27). Those old stories were a back-story, roots, which would over the centuries come to produce the Promised Seed.

Dan also pointed us to Zech. 6:12-13,
> "Behold the Man, whose name is The Branch; He will grow up out of His place and He shall build the Temple (LXX: House) of Yahweh... and He will bear (carry) the Glory (LXX: will receive excellence, distinction and virtue), and will sit and rule upon His throne and will be a Priest upon His throne. And the counsel of Peace (or, LXX: a joining resolve and peaceful purpose) will be between them both."

The Branch calls to mind the metaphor of the Vine, in Jn. 15, and the "glory" takes us back to Jn. 17. The building of the Temple/House echoes Mat. 16:18,
> "**And you see, [it is] upon this, this rock-mass** (or: the bedrock), **[that] I will progressively be constructing and building up My House – the called-out, covenant community**."

Just one term, or phrase, can be a code word for those that knew Israel's story, and her Scriptures. We find this all through the NT. The NT writers were scribes who were instructed in the Kingdom of the heavens, and they brought forth from their treasures "things new, and old" (Mat. 13:52; *cf* Song of Sol. 7:13).

8. **Jesus decidedly replies, "I told you that I, Myself, am** (or: I AM). **Since** (or: If), **then, you men are presently seeking Me, allow these men to proceed departing,"**

So we have a third time that Jesus says "I AM." And as noted, He keeps His disciples safe.

9. **so that the word** (or: saying; that which was laid out) **may be fulfilled which He said: "I lose** (or: destroyed) **not one from out of them whom You have given to Me as a possession."**

We assume that here He was referring to Jn. 17:12, and our author reminds his readers about this. We are also reminded of the short-term losses of the sheep, the coin and the son, in Lu. 15:4-32.

Observe that the disciples are characterized as Jesus' "**possession**." Recall that in Rom. 1:1 Paul terms himself as "a slave of Jesus Christ." As to Christ's ability to keep and protect us, Paul rhetorically asks:
> "**Who or what will be separating, dividing or parting us away from the Love of and from Christ?**" (Rom. 8:35)

Then he lists all the things that in this life might be able to do so, but ending in the affirmation that in fact nothing "**will be having power or be able to separate, divide or part us from God's Love which is within Christ Jesus, our Owner**" (Rom. 8:39).

10. Then Simon Peter, holding (or: having) **a small sword, suddenly draws** (or: unsheathed) **it and hits** (struck) **the chief priest's slave, and cuts off his right ear. Now the name of the slave was Malchus.**

Was Peter remembering that Jesus had said that he would deny Him (Mat. 26:34), and so defend his assertion that he would "**never** (not even once) **proceed being ensnared or cause to stumble**" (vs. 33)? In Lu. 22:33 Peter pledges to go with Jesus both to prison, and to death. It is a kind touch that our author mentions the name of the slave. He now lives on throughout history. It is interesting that our author knew his name. It has been suggested that "it could be that only the author of this Gospel knew that the servant's name was Malchus because only this author was formerly of that crowd" (a comment at: https://hermeneutics.stackexchange.com/questions/4974/in-john-1810-why-does-john-note-the-name-of-the-servant-whose-ear-was-cut-off). A relative of Malchus was also present (vs. 26, below), and later confronts Peter about having been there. In the excitement of the moment, he apparently did not see that it was Peter who cut off this relative's ear. Perhaps all were amazed that Jesus performs His final act of healing, there in the Garden. Is it significant that an ear was healed in this Garden? Apparently Eve did not have "an ear to hear" the instructions from Yahweh that were passed on to her – as her carnal and Law-oriented reasoning got the better of her.

All three of the Synoptic Gospels mention this incident, but none of them give this man's name, and only Lu. 22:51 informs us that Jesus touches his ear, and healed him. Why did the other Gospels mention this? As Dan Kaplan observed, Jesus was doing good to His enemies.

The name Malchus means "king or kingdom." If Malchus happened to be one of the priests, was Peter's strike later seen by our author as a symbolic strike against the head of the Judean kingdom? Or was this just Peter not understanding that Jesus' Kingdom was not of that domination System? Here, we see, in the next verse that Jesus rebukes Peter...

11. Therefore Jesus says to Peter, "Thrust the small sword into the sheath (scabbard). **The cup which the Father has given to Me and which I now have – should I not by all means drink it?"**

The cup, and the drinking of it, referred to the experience that lay immediately before Him: extreme pain and death on the cross. We suggest that this is the same cup that was in the hand of the woman on the beast, in Rev. 17:4 (Mystery Babylon). She had been drinking from that cup, and was "drunk with the blood of the set-apart folks, and with the blood of the witnesses of Jesus" (vs. 6). Jesus had told His apprentices that they would indeed drink of the cup of which He was about to drink (Mk. 10:38-39). Nonetheless, Jesus saw the upcoming suffering as the cup "**which the Father has given to [Him].**"

Even Job had realized this, and answered his wife: "Shall we receive good at the hand of God, and shall we not receive evil?" (Job 2:9). And the prophet Amos rhetorically asked, "Shall there be evil in a city, and Yahweh has not done it?" (Amos 3:6b).

12. Then the detachment (or: squad [of Roman soldiers]) **and the military commander** (tribune; commander of a thousand soldiers) **and the subordinates** (deputies) **of the Judeans** (= religious authorities) **together seized** (apprehended; arrested) **Jesus and bound Him** (tied Him up),
13. and then they led Him first to Annas (or: Hannas), **for he was father-in-law of Caiaphas, who was [the] chief priest of that year.**

The Lamb of God is being led away to the slaughter.

14. Now Caiaphas was the one joining in counsel with and advising the Judeans (= religious authorities) **that it is progressively bearing together as an expedient advantage for one man to be dying over [the situation of]** (or: on behalf of) **the People.**

This statement was made by Caiaphas in 11:50, above. Our author is emphasizing the point. We should give attention to it. Recall what Paul said – if One man dies, then all die (2 Cor. 5:14). In 11:51, our author informed us that the chief priest had prophesied "**that Jesus was being about to be dying away over [the situation of]** (or: for the sake of) **the Nation.**" And not only that, but that "**to the end that He could gather God's children together – those having been thoroughly scattered – into one**" (vs. 52; but also see Jn. 17:20-23). Now some may interpret this as applying to the Jews of the Diaspora, but we suggest that it applied to all who through the disobedience of Adam (*cf* Rom. 5:12ff) were living in exile from the Garden (Gen. 3).

15. **So Simon Peter and another disciple kept on following Jesus. Now that [other] disciple was personally known by** (or: intimate with; or: = a close friend of) **the chief priest, and he went in together with Jesus into the courtyard of the chief priest's house.**

Now if this anonymous disciple was known by the chief priest, and was confident enough to accompany Jesus into the chief priest's house, why did they need Judah (Judas) to identify Jesus to the detachment of soldiers? Why does our author not name this disciple? Is it because the author is referring to himself? Is this disciple Judah, himself?

16. **Yet Peter had been, and remained, standing outside, facing toward the gate** (or: door). **Therefore the other disciple – the one well-known to the chief priest – went out and spoke to the girl who kept** (or: guarded) **the gate** (portress; doorkeeper) **and then leads Peter into the midst.**

This disciple seems to be known by the gate keeper, and he exhibits almost familiarity with the household. It is emphasized that this other disciple was "**well-known to the chief priest.**" Was this the reason that our author wants to keep him anonymous? Is this our author, who is giving this detail that others would not have known, who for this reason does not want to draw attention to himself? In chapter 21 we find "that disciple whom Jesus loved" anonymously mentioned in vs. 7, and then again in vs. 20, with Peter asking Jesus about him, while not mentioning his name (vs. 21). This is a curious aspect of this Gospel. It tells what happened, but leaves us wondering who this disciple was who stayed with Jesus during His inquisition, below, apparently with no fear of the priests. When this disciple brought Peter into the courtyard, it would have seemed logical and natural for this other brave man (Peter), who had just charged the crowd with his sword, to have stayed with this disciple who went on to be with Jesus.

17. **Then the young woman** (or: young female servant) **– the gate keeper** (portress) **– says to Peter, "Are you not also one of this man's disciples?" That one then says, "I am not!** (or: No, I'm not.)"

Why did this young woman NOT say the same thing to "**the one well-known to the chief priest**"? That one seemed to have no fear, but we see that Peter did. It would seem like this "unknown" disciple displayed courage and a certain amount of heroism during this incident.

18. **Now the slaves and the subordinates** (deputies; those under orders), **having made a charcoal fire and keeping the embers going because it was cold, had been standing and kept on warming themselves, and so Peter, also, was standing with them and continued warming himself.**

So Peter is now in the same courtyard, with Jesus and the anonymous disciple – but he is not standing with Jesus or this other disciple. He is standing with those of the chief priest's household, as though he were one of them, or a curious bystander who had been allowed to come in. In Jn. 19:25-26, below, we find the women by the cross of Jesus, and "the disciple standing by, who He loved" next to Jesus' mother. Once more he is not named, but He is there, with Jesus. He was the only "disciple," so designated, that followed Jesus to the cross, and stayed with Him until He died. Is he perhaps unnamed so that he can stand for all those who follow Christ unto the end, having no fear? That disciple will now have Jesus' mother as his own mother (19:27, below).

19. **Then the chief priest questioned Jesus about His disciples and about His teaching.**
20. **Jesus considered and replied to him, "I, Myself, have publicly** (outspokenly with boldness and freedom of speech which is the right of a citizen) **spoken in the System** (or: to the world of religion, culture, economics and government; for the cosmos). **I at all times taught in a synagogue, and within the Temple courts, where all the Jews are habitually coming together, and I have spoken nothing within a hidden place.**
21. **"Why are you men now proceeding in questioning Me? Question those being ones having heard what I spoke to them. See and consider** (or: Look [to them]), **these people have seen and know** (are aware of) **what things I, Myself, said."**

Our author does not record that Jesus gave any answer concerning His disciples. He also does not give the chief priest any information about His teaching, but deflects the question to those who had heard Him teach. Was it that His teaching was not for the Judean leadership? He made no attempt to win over the chief priest or to reveal Himself to that assembly of men.

22. **Now [upon] His saying these things, one of the subordinates** (deputies, or Temple guards) **[who] had been standing at the side gave a striking blow to Jesus, with some instrument [such as a rod or a whip], saying, "Are you answering thus** (or: in this way) **to the chief priest?"**

This subordinate may have also noted the tone with which Jesus spoke and the posture that He assumed before them. He obviously did not cower in their presence. Our author portrays Him as being the One in control of the situation.

23. **Jesus considered and replied to him, "If I spoke inappropriately** (in an ugly way; badly; meanly; basely; worthlessly; abusively), **testify** (give evidence) **concerning the inappropriateness** (bear witness about the abuse, the base words, the mean and ugly attitude, the bad thing). **Yet if ideally** (beautifully; appropriately; excellently), **why are you now lashing Me** (flaying Me so as to remove My skin; beating Me)**?"**

The subordinate was already treating Him as a felon or riff-raff. To what must have been a painful blow, Jesus seems to have responded calmly, with reason (the *Logos*). We find a parallel situation involving Paul, in Acts 23, but his first response to the chief priest was with a little more vehemence:
> 1. **So Paul, looking intently** (riveting his gaze) **at the Sanhedrin** (Jewish High Council) **said, "Men! Brothers! I myself have lived and behaved as a citizen in all good conscience to and for God up to this day!"**
> 2. **But Ananias, the chief priest** [note: nominated as high priest by Herod, King of Chalcis in A.D. 48], **placed a directive upon those standing beside him to proceed in striking his mouth.**
> 3. **At that point Paul said to him, "God is now about to be striking you, you whitewashed wall! And so you yourself are now sitting, continuing in judging me according to the Law, and at the same time [you are] transgressing the Law** (acting illegally) **[by] proceeding in ordering me to be repeatedly struck!"**
> 4. **So those standing by say, "Are you now reproaching and reviling God's chief priest?"**
> 5. **At this Paul affirmed, "Brothers, I had not seen so I was not aware that he is a chief priest, for it has been written,**
> > **'You will not continue speaking badly [of] a ruler of your people.'"** [Ex. 22:28]

24. **At that, Annas** (or: Hannas) **sent Him off** (or: away) **– having been bound** (tied up) **– on their mission to Caiaphas, the chief priest.**

25. **Now Simon Peter was yet standing and warming himself. Then they said to him, "Are not you yourself, also, from out of His disciples?" That one says, "No," contradicts and denies** (or: disowns), **and says, "I am not."**

In Mat. 26:69 we read: **"And one servant girl came toward him, then is saying, "You, too, were with Jesus the Galilean."**

26. **One from out of the slaves of the chief priest – being a relative of the one whose ear Peter cut off – is then saying, "Did I not see you within the GARDEN with him?"**

Peter is probably in more danger, here, than he would have been if he had stayed with "the other disciple" and Jesus. But consider that he had been watching his Master standing bound before the Judean authorities. Jesus is led away, and so those gathered turn to this stranger that seems vaguely familiar. In Mat. 26:71 we find that "**another girl saw him and then proceeds saying to the folks in that place, 'This fellow was with Jesus the Nazarene'.**" *Cf* Mk. 14:69; Lu. 22:58.

27. **Then again, Peter contradicted** (denied; disowned) **– and immediately a cock** (rooster) **crowed.**

Peter, here, represents all the disciples. This incident confirms Jesus as being a Prophet. He had "Light (= knowledge; insight) ahead of time." We are not told whether or not "the other disciple" had gone with Jesus to Caiaphas, but he must have still been there to see, and now record, this incident.

28. **They then are progressively leading Jesus from Caiaphas into the Roman governor's headquarters** (the Praetorium). **Now it was early in the morning** (between 3 and 6 A.M.), **and they did not enter into the governor's headquarters so that they would not be polluted** (defiled; made ceremonially impure), **but rather could still eat the Passover meal.**

There was a rebellion by some of the leaders in Israel (among them some of the sons of Levi, from whom came the priests) against the anointed ones of that time, Moses and Aaron. The story is found in Nu. 16:1-50. First the families of Korah, Dathan and Abiram (the leaders in the rebellion) were swallowed up by the earth, and then Fire from Yahweh consumed 250 more, who had offered incense, and finally Yahweh sent a plague that killed 14,700, beside those who had died over the matter of Korah. What would happen to those who committed Jesus to Pilate, to be killed? AD 70 would bring an answer to this rebellion against the Lord's Anointed.

Our author skips over the details of Jesus before Caiaphas, and moves the story directly to Pilate. The setting of being just before the Passover connects Jesus to being the Passover Lamb. Israel was instructed in Deut. 16:2,
> "So you will sacrifice a Passover to Yahweh your God, from a flock and a herd, in the place where Yahweh your God shall choose to tabernacle His Name."

Being ignorant of what they were doing (Lu. 23:34), these Judeans were fulfilling the type that was set forth in the Law.

29. **Therefore, Pilate went forth outside to them and began his interrogation: "What accusation** (formal charge) **are you presently bringing with regard to** (or: which pertains to; [other MSS add: against]) **this man?"**
30. **So they decided a reply and said to him, "If this one were not continually doing an inappropriate thing** (habitually doing bad or wrong), **we would not commit or give him over to you."**

Here we may have an allusion to the vision in Zech. 3:1
> "**And the LORD showed me Jesus, the Great Priest, standing before an agent of** (or: messenger from) **[the] LORD, and also the one who thrusts something through another** (or:

the *devil*; [Heb. text: the adversary; *satan*]) **having taken a stand at His right to oppose, resist and be an adversary to Him**" (LXX, JM).

Here, in vs. 30, it is Caiaphas and the other priests who stand as Jesus' opponent/adversary. It is worthwhile to read all of Zech. 3 and 4 where "shadow" prophesies can be seen to apply to Jesus. In Zech. 3:3-5 can be observed Jesus first in His servant role, and then in His resurrected status.

In Mark's version of the exchange of words between Pilate and the priests, it is stated that "the chief priests accused Him of many things, but He answered nothing" (Mk. 15:3). Then Pilate asked Him why He remained silent at these accusations, "But Jesus yet answered nothing" (vs. 5). The lack of response to the charges made against Him has called to mind Isa. 53:7,

> "**Yet He did not open His mouth because of** (or through) **the [occasion] to have been ill-treated in an ugly situation: just as a sheep is led upon a slaughtering** (or: like a sheep, He was led onto [the] slaughter), **and as** (or: like) **a lamb [that is] set in position against the person shearing it [is] without a voice** (mute; voiceless; = silent), **in like manner He continues not to open up His mouth**" (LXX, JM).

31. **Then Pilate said to them, "You men, yourselves, take him and decide about** (or: judge) **him corresponding to** (or: in accord with) **your Law." The Jews** (= religious Judean authorities) **said to him, "It is not allowed, or permitted from [our] existing, for us to kill anyone,"**

Pilate points them to their Law; in this telling of the story. They had broken the Law and rushed to a judgment: they would have killed Him, were they "allowed to" by the rule of the Romans. In the picture given in Zech. 3:2, Yahweh rebukes Jesus' adversary. We can also see Ps. 2:2 acted out in this scene, but the rest of Ps. 2 projects the rest of the story, which will follow Jesus' resurrection.

32. **so that the word of** (laid-out message and information from) **Jesus could be fulfilled which He said, repeatedly indicating by SIGNS** (showing by symbols, omens, signals and tokens) **by what kind of death He was being about to be progressively dying away** (or: off).

It would be death at the hands of the Romans: crucifixion (alluding to Jesus' words, in Jn. 12:32, and the explanation in Jn. 12:33; *cf* Mat. 20:18-19).

33. **So Pilate entered again into the governor's headquarters** (the Praetorium) **and summoned Jesus and then said to Him, "You are yourself the king of the Judeans?** (or: So YOU are the king of the Judeans.)"**

As offered, Pilate's words can be rendered as a question, or as a statement, with emphasis (he uses the personal pronoun, which signifies emphasis). Taken as a statement (even if said in irony) we have a Roman ruler pronouncing Him as the King of the Judeans. If taken as a question, it might present Pilate as seriously considering the matter about Jesus, which we see in the dialogue which follows.

34. **Jesus considered and replied, "Are you yourself now saying this from yourself, or did others tell you about Me?"**
35. **Pilate considered and replied, "Surely I myself am not a Jew** (or: Judean)! **Your nation** (ethnic group) **and the chief priests committed and gave you over to me. What did you do?"**

Notice that Pilate identifies the **nation**, and its leaders (**the chief priests**) as being the ones who committed and gave Jesus over to the Romans. Pilate was not aware of Him as being a rebel leader or an insurrectionist. He apparently had never heard of Him, but now learns that rumor has it that Jesus was being considered to be "**the king of the Judeans.**" Our author does not say where he got this information, but Jesus' reply, in vs. 34, implies that probably someone had told him. In 19:15, below, the chief priest will avow that they (speaking for the Judeans) have no king but Caesar.

36. **Jesus decidedly replied, "My kingdom** (My sovereignty; the realm and activity of My reign and influence; My kingship) **is not** (does not exist being) **from out of this System** (world of organized government, culture, economics or religion; or: universe) **as its source or origin. If My kingdom** (or: reign, realm and sovereign influence) **were from out of this System** (or: world of government, culture, religion and economy; secular society), **as a source or origin, My subordinates** (deputies; officers; those under My orders) **would have been progressively contending, struggling and fighting, to the end that I could** (or: would) **not be commended, committed or given over to the Jews** (= religious Judean authorities). **But now** (= As a matter of fact, and as it is) **My kingdom and reign is not** (sovereign influence does not exist being) **from that source** (from within this place; thence or hence)."

First of all, can we assume that "the disciple that Jesus loved" was still with Jesus, to hear His reply to Pilate? We are not told, but someone heard it and this instructive conversation was recorded for us. Let us lay out His statements, and observe:

   a) **My kingdom** (My sovereignty; the realm and activity of My reign and influence; My kingship) **is not** (does not exist being) **from out of this System** (etc.)

   b) **If My kingdom were from out of this world of government, culture, religion and economy; secular society, as a source or origin, My subordinates would have been progressively contending, struggling and fighting, to the end that I could** (or: would) **not be commended, committed or given over to the Judeans**

   c) **But now** (= As a matter of fact, and as it is) **My kingdom and reign is not** (sovereign influence does not exist being) **from that source** (from within this place; thence or hence).

This is a structured rhetorical response, with c) repeating a), while b) sets forth what the situation would be if a) and c) were not the case. This alludes to what Jesus told Peter, in the Garden, about using a sword to defend Him (vs. 11, above). It also explains an aspect of His prayer to the Father, in 17:14-24, above. But what do a) and c) mean for us? First of all that we should not fight for Jesus. We have His words in Mat. 26:52b, "**You see, all those taking [up] a knife** (or: a sword) **will proceed in destroying themselves in union with a knife** (or: continue losing themselves [being] centered in a sword)." It is too bad that the Zealots of the Jewish Rebellion of AD 66-70 could not hear His admonition, and so many of them would end up in Gehenna, outside Jerusalem.

But the instruction about the kingdom in Matthew is most enlightening. He uses the phrase "**the sovereign reign, dominion and activity of exercising the sovereignty of the heavens** (or: kingdom from the skies and the atmospheres)" (Mat. 4:17, *et al*). God's reign, or Christ's kingdom and sovereign influence, is in the realm of our atmospheres, or, the sphere of the heaven, or, the dimension of spirit. In fact, Jesus plainly stated,

   "**God's reign** (the kingdom and royal rule, which is God; the sovereign influence and activity from God) **continually exists inside you folks** (or: is on the inside of you people; or: is within the midst of you folks, in your community; exists centered in you people)" (Lu. 17:21).

And this is why Paul would write: "**Christ within you folks, the expectation of and from the glory**" (Col. 1:27). But at the same time, we are to understand that the heavens (the sky; our atmosphere) reach all the way to the earth, where we are. And so God's sovereign activity is right here on earth – as Jesus repeatedly said, "**God's kingdom** (the reigning and ruling of God as King; God's activity of exercising sovereignty) **has approached and is now near at hand and is close enough to touch** (= has arrived and is now accessible)!" (Mk. 1:15a). And because of this, His message was:

   "**You folks be progressively and continuously changing your thinking – change your perceptions, frame of mind, mode of thought, state of consciousness, your direction, and thus turn back [toward God] – and be progressively loyal and believing, while constantly placing your trust in the good news** (the message of goodness, ease and well-being)!" (Mk. 1:15b; [*cf* Rom. 12:2]).

His "Kingdom" is primarily about our "thinking." Also, it involves being turned in the right direction, having peace and experiencing being joined to everyone else, and lots of joy within the midst of a set-apart Breath effect (Rom. 14:17). Need we say more?

37. **Therefore Pilate said to Him, "Are you yourself not, then, a king?** (or: So then... you are yourself a king!)" **Jesus discerningly replied, "You yourself continue saying that I am a king. Into this [position, or purpose] I, Myself, have been born, and I have come into this System** (world and culture; social arrangement; cosmos) **and continue being present: to the end that I could and would bear witness to this Reality** (or: give testimony to and evidence of the Truth). **Everyone being** (or: who is existing) **from out of this Reality** (or: the Truth) **is habitually hearing, progressively listening to [and thus: continually obeys] My voice."**

Pilate's questions call to mind the questions and statements by His inner adversary (the 1st-Adam nature) during His wilderness testing (Lu. 4:1-13), following His heaven being opened back up again (Lu. 3:21b). In His discerning reply to Pilate, Jesus reaches back to His personal origin, His birth, affirms His entrance into this System and His continuance there until that present moment, and then presents the purpose of His life's journey: "**to the end that I could and would bear witness to Reality** (or: give testimony to and evidence of the Truth)." Our author records this purpose statement for the benefit of his readers to know this, as well. As the next verse will attest, this likely meant next to nothing to Pilate, but it apparently got him to thinking.

The next statement is a synopsis of Kingdom Life, the new Reality that Christ's incarnation brought into being. His disciples were hearing His voice, so it follows that they were "**existing from out of this Reality**." Only those who have been born back up again (from above), and were thus His sheep, would be "**habitually hearing, progressively listening to [and thus: continually obeys] [His] voice.**" In Jn. 8:47a, it speaks of hearing "God's voice." Peter gives a more detailed picture of this in 1 Pet. 1:

22. **Having purified your souls** (= inner selves) **within the hearing obedience** (the humble, attentive listening and submissive hearing) **of the Truth and from Reality [which directs and leads] into unhypocritical** (non-hypercritical; non-hyper-separating so as to over-evaluate; not determined from below; non-nit-picky; or: unpretended; unfeigned; thus: genuine) **brotherly affection** (= fondness for the fellow believers), **love one another with acceptance in a stretched-out and extended way, from out of a clean** [other MSS: true; genuine] **heart,**
23. **being folks having been born again** (been regenerated; been given birth back up again), **not from out of a corruptible** (or: perishable) **seed that was sown, but rather from an incorruptible** (imperishable; undecayable) **one: through God's continually living and permanently remaining** *Logos*

> (or: through a message or expressed thought of [the] continuously living and constantly abiding God; or: through means of a living and dwelling Thought, Idea and Logically laid out Expression, Communication and Word, which is God).

This relationship between Voice and existing from out of God will be birthed into Jesus' disciples, as we read in 1 Jn. 4:6,

> "**We, however, continuously exist** (or: are) **from out of the midst of God. The person habitually and progressively coming to know God by intimate experience is continually hearing US** (or: listening and paying attention to what comes from, or pertains to, us). **He who does not exist from out of God is not hearing** (or: listening to) **US. From out of this we constantly know by intimate experiences the Spirit** (or: spirit; Breath-effect; influence; Attitude) **of the Truth** (or: of Reality), **and the spirit** (influence; breath-effect; attitude) **of wandering** (deception; error; straying).

This next-generation situation existed because He was dwelling within them, and their voice was His Voice.

38. Pilate then says to Him, "What is Reality (or: Truth)?"
And upon saying this, he again goes out to the Jews (= religious Judean authorities), **and then says
to them, "I, myself, continue finding not one cause for accusation** (or: fault, responsibility, or reason
for a case) **within him.**

Jesus had been specific in speaking of "this Reality" (that being "the Reign/Kingdom of God/the heavens,"
or "the new creation"), or "The Truth." Pilate's quip to Him was a generality (no definite article in front of
Reality/Truth), and so it bypassed Jesus' affirmation, and he walks out to the Judeans. Of course, from
14:6, above, we know that Jesus IS this Truth/Reality.

Pilate was functioning as a priest, having examined the Lamb in preparation for the Jewish sacrifice (he
gives as second, and double, witness to this Lamb's purity, in Jn. 19:4b, 6b). Here, the lived-out parable
is entering the transition stage before He returns to the Garden, in 19:41; 20:1-17, below. We are seeing
another phase of the Passover events. The false priesthood was blind and had failed to see the purity of
the Truth that this Lamb embodied. But, of course, they were not, at that time, His sheep. They were
kids (young goats), at best (Mat. 25:41-46).

**39. "Now for you people there is a joint custom of intimate friendship and intercourse, for our
mutual use, to the end that I should release one man to you within** (at; during) **the Passover. Are
you men therefore continuing deliberately intended and purposed to the end that I should release
to you the king of the Judeans?"**

Once again, the representative of the Roman Empire terms Jesus **"the king of the Judeans."** We need
not wonder about what Pilate actually thought of Him. The point of this parable is that He has been
proclaimed King – regardless of what the Judean leadership (Christ's real adversary) thought of Him.

We are reminded of the story in 2 Ki. 11, where, in vs. 1, Athaliah destroyed all the royal seed, so she
thought. In vss. 2-16 we see another story that finds an echo in the life of both Moses and Jesus. There,
one of the king's sons was hidden, as a baby, and raised in the house of Yahweh for six years (a
significant number – the number of the day that God created the human). In the seventh year the plot of
the faithful came to fruition and young Joash was brought to light, crowned, and the guard of soldiers
anointed him as the rightful king, clapped their hands and cried, "God save the king." Here, it's Jesus'
story, He is brought to light (and soldiers will crown Him with thorns), and a soldier proclaims Him as the
King.

40. Then they all yelled again, saying, "Not this fellow, but rather, Bar-Abba [meaning: a father's
son, or: the son of the father]!" **Now Bar-Abba had been a robber** (one who appropriates what is not
his by violence, and openly; = a Zealot; = an insurrectionist; cf Mk. 15:7; Lu. 23:19).

So the people, as representative of Jerusalem and Judea, reject their Messiah. They reject the Tree of
Life and hold to the tree of the knowledge of good and evil, and thus seal the fate of the city and of Judea.
Peter will bring up to them this response that they gave to Pilate, in Acts 3:14. In Matthew's version, the
chief priests and elders answered Pilate saying,
> **"His blood [is] upon us** (or: [be splattered] on us; = the responsibility for his death falls on us),
> **and upon our children!"** (Mat. 27:25).
This is the real reason why the potter's field would be called the **"Field of Blood"** (Mat. 27:7-8).

Both Jesus and Bar-Abba are sons of a father. Both of them are Adam: the first, here, is the Last
(eschatos) Adam, the latter is the first Adam. Humanity, in its state of exile from the fellowship in the
Garden, will always choose the man after the flesh, rather than the Man after the Spirit. And the parable
continues...

Chapter 19

1. **Thereupon** (or: At that time), **therefore, Pilate took Jesus and scourged** (with a whip [having pieces of metal embedded, so as to rip off flesh] severely flogged) **[Him].**

This is the real, physical beginning of Jesus' immersion, of which He spoke, in Lu. 12:50,

> **"Now I continue having an immersion** (or: a baptism) **[in which] to be immersed and saturated** (plunged and baptized) **– and how am I continuing being held together, until it can be brought to its purposed goal and destiny?"**

He spoke of this same experience, but used a different metaphor, along with the metaphor of immersion, in Mk. 10:28, in a response to Jacob (James) and John:

> **"Do you now have power and do you continue able to drink the cup which I Myself am now progressively drinking, or to be immersed in** (or: baptized with) **the immersion** (baptism) **which I Myself am now progressively being immersed** (baptized)**?"**

Also, recall His words to Peter when they were in the Garden (Jn. 18:11), **"The cup which the Father has given to Me and which I now have – should I not by all means drink it?"** Both the metaphor of immersion and the metaphor of drinking from a cup each refer to experiencing something. Jesus' "scourging," by the order of Pilate, begins the steps to His death on the cross. This points to the killing of the Passover Lamb, which in turn calls to Israel's present time that was being initiated by Jesus: a new exodus into freedom from slavery, and the beginning of a journey (a new Path, or Way) into a new place. Instead of being "baptized unto Moses, in the cloud and in the sea" (1 Cor. 10:2), Israel, that is now about to be joined to the Gentiles into being one New Humanity (Eph. 2:15), the Second Humanity (1 Cor. 15:47), is now to be immersed (baptized) with Him, into His death (Rom. 6:3-11), and then into His Life.

What has also been found, here, is an echo of Isa. 50:6,

> **"My back I have given unto whips, and my jaws** (or cheeks) **unto effects of slaps and blows, and I turned not away my face from the shame of** (or: from) **spittings"** (LXX, JM).

This lived-parable shows the Path that His apprentices will follow, whether literally or metaphorically.

2. **And then the soldiers, upon weaving** (intertwining; braiding) **a victor's wreath from [branches] out of a thorn-bush** (or: prickly weeds; thistles), **placed [it] upon His head, and threw a purple cloak** (outer garment; robe; [note: Matt. 27:28 reads: scarlet robe – the color robe worn by Roman officers of rank]) **around Him,**
3. **and they kept coming toward Him and were repeatedly saying, "Be rejoicing** (= Hail; Greetings), **O King of the Judeans** (or: Jews)**!" And they kept on giving Him slaps in the face with the open hand** (or: strikes with a whip, rod or club).

Mocking and abuse give evidence to the human that is not bearing the image of God, and that is not a part of God's Vineyard (does not produce the fruit of the Spirit – Gal. 5:22-24; *cf* Jn. 15:1ff). We see a description of humanity before it became distorted and thorn-infested, and then the result of this latter, in Heb. 6:

> 4. **For you see, those once being enlightened, besides tasting** (= experiencing) **the imposed-heavenly gift** (or: the granted bounty from the One [holding sway] upon the atmosphere; the gift which has the character of the added-atmosphere) **and after being born** (or: coming to be) **common-holders** (partners; sharing possessors; joint-participants; associates; partaking members) **of set-apart spirit** (or: of a holy Breath-effect; or: of [the] Holy Spirit),
> 5. **and then tasting** (= experiencing) **a beautiful gush-effect of God** (or: an ideal result of the flow from God; or: God's fine speech; an excellent declaration pertaining to God; a profitable thing spoken, which is God) **– besides abilities and powers of an impending age,**
> 6. **and yet then falling by the side along the way, [are] powerless and unable to be repeatedly renewing again into a change of mind and state of consciousness: [they are]**

continuously suspending back up on a pole (or: crucifying) **again in, with, to, for and by themselves the Son of God, and [are] constantly exposing [Him] to public shame/disgrace.** Heb. 6:4-5, above, describes the condition of how Adam (humanity) was in the Garden of Eden, before the exile from that environment – before the weeds were sown into his field (Mat. 13:25; *cf* Gen. 3:1-8). The results of those false seeds/words being sown into what was "very good" soil (Heb. 6:7; *cf* Gen. 1:31) are next described in vs. 6, and we see that they "**fall by the side along the way, [and are] powerless**." Now these three verses (Heb. 6:4-6) speak of people, and then these same sorts of people are portrayed metaphorically as a field, in Heb. 6:7-8,

7. **For you see, a piece of land** (or: ground; soil; = a field; or: a territory) **which is drinking** (= soaking in) **the rain often coming upon it, and producing vegetation** (pasture; produce) **fit for and useful to them through whom it is habitually being cultivated, [is] also continuously sharing in and partaking of a blessing from God;**
8. **but when repeatedly and progressively bearing forth thorns and thistles [it is] disqualified** (worthless; unable to stand the test [for planting a new crop]) **and [is] close to** (or: near) **[the] curse** (or: a down-prayer and a corresponding wish against [the situation] is at hand), **the end** (the resultant situation) **of which [the thorns, briars, thistles and the field is] into [a time of] burning** (or: = the field ends up being burned off).

> [comment: this is a time-honored agricultural practice for preparing a field for planting a crop – the competition has been removed and the ground has been enriched by the ash]

The Land was a well-known metaphor for Israel, in the OT. Just as the farmer does not throw away a good productive field, even when it gets overgrown with weeds, but may burn it off (e.g., as in 1 Cor. 3:13-15), so these soldiers will have their time in God's Fire, for purification. Dan Kaplan has reminded us of the penalty that humans would undergo due to Adam listening to his wife (a figure of the soulish part of us) and then eating from that tree in the Garden:

> "Cursed is the soil (earth; land) for your sake.... Thorn and thistle shall it sprout for you...." (Gen. 3:17b-18a).

Paul, in Gal. 3:13, noted that Jesus had become a curse for us. This would referred specifically to Deut. 21:23, but He also represented Adam (Rom. 5:12-21), and Israel (the Land/soil) and so this wreath of thorns and thistles shows that He was bearing the curse that had come upon the soil (of which Adam was formed), the Land (Israel) and the earth. But the action of these soldiers, in "crowning Him" with a "**victor's wreath**," symbolically proclaimed (even if, unintentionally) that He was the Victor over that curse, in Gen. 3:18. This humiliating act was another SIGN in this lived-out parable. Kaplan also pointed us to another insight regarding this symbol of having dominated (become the Victor): it represented dominion over our thorny thoughts of hate and darkness inherent in our estranged/disconnected flesh; it was victory over the disease of carnal thinking and fear. It also spoke to dominion over our spiritually-dead self, and thus over abuse, doubt and bearing false witness, etc.

Humanity had come to have, and reflect, what John Gavazzoni has called a "disfigurement" of the image of God. Isa. 52:14 has been applied to what Jesus went through, in His humiliation:

> "So marred (ruined; disfigured) was His appearance, beyond human semblance, and His form beyond that of the sons of Adam."

This Gospel does not record a description that corresponds to that prophecy, but it might represent the condition of the humanity that He had taken on. Those Roman soldiers reflected from themselves a dishonoring, inhuman image, which they then symbolically placed upon Him. In Isa. 53:6b-7a, 8b, we read,

> **"Yet Yahweh Himself causes the depravity of us all to come upon Him. Hard pressed is He, and He Himself is humbled, yet He is not opening his mouth.... Because of the transgressions of My people, He is led unto death."**

The abusive actions of these soldiers have their roots portrayed in apocalyptic language in Ezk. 28:2b-10. This is a figurative passage that on the first level of interpretation was aimed at the prince of Tyrus, but on a symbolic level depicts the human predicament. This "prince" wanted to see himself as a god, which was the temptation in the Garden of Eden (Gen. 3:1-8) where the tree of law could make one wise (Gen. 3:6). Now in Ezk. 28:3-4, we find this person described as having great wisdom, yet we read on to see his (and our) fall. Next. Ezk. 28:12-19 describes the king of Tyrus in a similar fashion. In vs. 12b we find him "full of wisdom and perfect in beauty." And look at vs. 13 – "You have been in Eden, the garden of God..." Notice his beauty! In fact, vs. 14 tell us, "You [were] the anointed cherub that covered [the mercy seat]... on the holy mountain of God... you walked amidst stones of Fire." Folks, this is temple language, and the Garden of Eden was the proto-temple. In vs. 15 we see that this "man" was "perfect in his ways from the day that he was created, until perversity (or: iniquity) was found in [him]." By the way, the word for man, in "yet you [are] a man" (28:2), is the Heb. adam. In vs. 16 we find that a "multitude of merchandise" caused him to be filled with "violence." His judgment was being cast to the ground (a typical judgment for empires, in the OT). Man's wisdom and beauty corrupted him, and he defiled his sanctuaries and was brought to ashes (or: dust), upon the ground. Both Jerusalem, and later Rome, would see this same judgment.

Recall Phil. 2:7-8 where we find that Jesus,

> "**empties Himself, receiving** (or: taking; accepting) **a slave's form, coming to be within an effect of humanity's** (mankind's; people's) **likeness. And so, being found in an outward fashion, mode of circumstance, condition, form-appearance** (or: role) **as a human** (a person; a man), **He lowers Himself** (or: humbled Himself; made Himself low), **coming to be a submissive, obedient One as far as** (or: to the point of; until) **death – but death of a cross.**"

The picture in these verses, and what follows, are that to which Paul was referring. He entered into the judgment that both the prince and the king of Tyrus (figures of humanity) had entered, and endured the shame and violence that the "field" of humanity was producing. As Heb. 2:17-18 puts it,

> "**Wherefore, He was indebted** (or: obliged) **to be assimilated by** (or: made like or similar to) **the brothers in accord with all things** (or: concerning everything; = in every respect; or: in correlation to all people), **so that He might become a merciful and a faithful** (or: loyal) **Chief Priest** (Leading, Ruling or Beginning Priest) **[in regard to] the things toward God, into the [situation] to be repeatedly and continuously overshadowing the failures** (mistakes; errors; misses of the target; sins) **of the People with a gentle, cleansing shelter and covering. For you see, in what He has experienced Himself, having been tried in ordeals, He is able to run to the aid of those who cry for help – those being tried** (put through ordeals)." [cf Heb. 13:5b-6; 1 Cor. 10:13; 2 Pet. 2:9]

He became us – just as those Judean priests and Roman soldiers are us in this lived-out parable. The irony is that they both crowned Him with their own thorns, and clothed Him in royal color – the parable proclaiming Him to be humanity's King, even though they were blind to the fact, and could only produce worthless fruit with a parody. Enemy soldiers were the first to proclaim Him "king of the Judeans," and the Roman governor would do the same – even though the leaders of His own people rejected this.

4. **So Pilate goes outside again and says to them, "Look and consider! I am leading him outside to you, so that you folks can come to know by experience that I am still finding no cause for accusation** (no fault, responsibility or reason for a case) **within him."**

The Lamb is declared to be faultless; He is appropriate and qualified to serve as their Passover. Later, Paul would attest to this, in 2 Cor. 5:21,

> '**for you see, He made** (or: formed) **the One not at any point knowing failure** (sin; error; mistake) **by intimate experience [to take the place of; to be] failure over us and our [situation]** (or: He constructed and produced a sin [offering], for our sake, the Person who was not having an experiential knowledge of missing the target or making a mistake), **to the end that we may be birthed God's just and rightwising act of eschatological deliverance**
> > or: would come to exist in righted, liberated relationships of equitable fairness; would become God's justice, the Way pointed out; could become participants in the new

covenant from God: expressions of well-ordered living of the way it should be, which is God), **within Him and in union with Him**." *Cf* 18:38, above.

5. **Then Jesus came forth, outside, still wearing the thorny victor's wreath and the purple garment** (cloak; robe). **And he** [i.e., Pilate] **says to them, "Look at the man!"** (or: "See and consider this person.")

He was, in fact, saying: "Look at Humanity (Adam)." But there is a deeper message in his words: "See and CONSIDER this Person!" Think about Him! Perceive Who He is! The thorny victor's wreath was proclaiming Him as the Overcomer. He will later tell the called-out community in Laodicea,

> "**To** (or: In; For) **the person who is habitually conquering** (repeatedly overcoming; normally victorious) **I will continue granting [him or her] to sit** (or: be seated) **with Me within My throne, IN THE SAME WAY AS I also conquer** (or: conquered; overcome; OVERCAME and was VICTORIOUS) **and sit** (or: sat down) **with My Father within His throne**" (Rev. 3:21).

6. **When, then, the chief priests and the subordinates** (deputies; Temple guards) **saw Him, they yelled and shouted, repeatedly saying, "Crucify [him]** (or: Suspend [him] from a pole; Impale [him] at once; affix [him] to the stake)!" **"Crucify** (Suspend; Hang) **[him] on a pole!"**

Behold the enmity! They were drunk on the blood of the set-apart folks (Rev. 17:6 *cf* Mat. 23:31-38). But this was some of the kind of enmity that He would kill:

> "**and then should fully transfer, from a certain state to another which is quite different, The Both – centered in, and within the midst of, One Body in God** (or: make completely other, while moving away from what had existed, and fully reconcile The Both, in one Body, **by**, **to**, with and for **God**), **through the cross** (execution stake) **– while in the midst of Himself killing the enmity and discordant hatred** (or: killing-off the characteristics of enemies within it)" (Eph. 2:16).

This enmity was later seen in Saul (Acts 9:1-2, 4b). This enmity and hatred was the fruit of their Law (see vs. 7, below).

Pilate then says to them, "You, yourselves, take him and you crucify (hang) **[him] on a pole, for I, myself, am still finding no cause for accusation** (no fault, responsibility or reason for a case) **in him."**

As noted, above, the Roman governor pronounced the Lamb as spotless.

7. **The Jews** (= religious Judean authorities) **decidedly replied to him, "We, ourselves, are continuously holding** (or: having) **a Law, and corresponding** (or: according) **to the Law, he continues bound** (indebted; obliged) **to be dying away, because he makes** (constructed; creates) **himself God's son** (or: [the] Son of God)!"

Notice their Law: "**corresponding** (or: according) **to the Law, he continues bound** (indebted; obliged) **to be dying away**." Now where do you suppose that Law was written? In Israel's origin story, Yahweh told Moses to say to Pharaoh, "Israel is My firstborn son" (Ex. 4:22). Another example of their traditions making God's Word of no effect. Of course, in Pilate's worldview, this title belonged to Caesar. We see in the next verse that this made Pilate "more afraid." Certainly he would not equate Jesus as having the same authority or power that Caesar had, so why the fear? Did he, perhaps entertain a Hellenistic world view, or religion, where "the gods" sometimes cohabited with human women and produced demigods? The Judeans wanted to kill Jesus for making Himself to be "God's son," or so they said. So might Pilate have joined their expression to his own mythological worldview?

8. **Then, when Pilate heard this statement** (word; what was laid out), **he was made more afraid,**

9. **so he enters again into the headquarters** (the Praetorium), **and asks Jesus, "As for you, from what place are you?** (or: From whom were you, yourself, born and what is your origin?)**" Yet Jesus gives him no reply.**

Does Pilate think that Jesus might be some kind of "divine being"? Of course Christian Trinitarians will rush right over Pilate's obvious inner turmoil, and say, "Well of course He is!" Well, OK, but was our author just trying to point to Pilate's primitive or pagan thinking, or is he pointing to something more than what is obvious? Just asking… Why did he want to know where Jesus came from? Recall, in Jn. 18:38, Pilate's rhetorical question to Jesus: "What is truth/reality?" Pilate may have been a deeper thinker than his reputation as a cruel and violent man might first suggest. Recall more recent history and the complex personality of General Patton. Or, is our author, on behalf of his audience, making an allusion to "the sons of God" joining with "the daughters of humans," in Gen. 6? Jesus' silence (other than being as a Lamb before His shearers) seems to mitigate against whatever He perceived Pilate to be thinking. And His silence is a position of strength, as we will see, below.

Another possibility is that Pilate may have been insecure in his position as governor – we learn from history that it was not long after Jesus death that he lost that position. Was he paranoid that this man before him might be an adopted son of Caesar, here to displace him? Was he satisfying his assessment that Jesus was not the leader of some heretofore unperceived rebellion? Perhaps my speculation is too far astray, but the next verse shows that his question in this verse was apparently important to him.

10. **Hence Pilate continues saying to Him, "You are not speaking to me? Have you not seen to know that I continually hold authority** (the right) **to release you? I also constantly have authority** (the right) **to crucify you** (impale you; attach you to, or suspend you from, a stake)**!"**

Notice that he is emphasizing his position and stressing his authority – in contrast to this "supposed" king of the Judeans. Is this (apparent) outburst an unveiling of his insecurity? Or, is it merely exasperation? Is it surprised wonder, considering that Jesus came to him bound? Jesus was silent because He was drinking the cup that His Father had given Him to drink, so He made no defense for Himself; this was part of the Blueprint, the Plan.

11. **Jesus decidedly replied to him, "You were** [other MSS: continue] **holding no authority at all** (or: in even one thing) **down on** (or: against; with regard to; in the sphere of) **Me, except that it is existing having been given to you from above** (or: from [One; someone] above [you]). **Because of this, the person commending, committing and giving** (transferring) **Me over to you continues holding a greater mistake** (or: having a greater failure, error, sin or miss of the target)**."**

The implied "giver/Giver" of authority may refer to Caesar, or to God. Each case would be true; both were "**above**" Pilate. Yet another interpretation might refer to the Judean authorities who "gave" Jesus over to Pilate. But most likely, Jesus was referring to one or both of the first two situations. However, Jesus' final statement about who holds the "**greater mistake** (or: is having a greater failure, error, sin or miss of the target)" points us to the Judean authorities, in this reply to Pilate. Now this does not necessarily suggest that Jesus was referring to them in His first statement. So, in our narrative, could Jesus have been alluding to Gen. 1:26? "Let us make humankind (Heb.: *adam*)… and let THEM have dominion…" Dominion and sway over others came from God, in the first creation. Lisa Sharon Harper (*The Very Good Gospel; How Everything Wrong Can Be Made Right*, Waterbrook, 2016 p 30) has shared insights on this Genesis creation passage, and how the concept of ordinary humans being bearers of God's image was revolutionary in this time of history: only kings and queens had been seen as bearing God's image. But there is more: in Gen. 1:27b we read that "male and female He created them." Harper observes:

"Imagine how this would have been received by the original hearers. The writers challenge the culturally entrenched Hebrew worldview that defines women as property. In their song, the writers declare that both men and women are made in the image of God. Both men and women are born with inherent dignity and worth. Women bear the image of God equally, with no distinction in the way that image is manifest. They share equally in the call to exercise dominion."

12. From out of this, Pilate was continuing to seek to release Him, but the Jews (= religious Judean authorities) **yelled and shouted, repeatedly saying, "If you should release this fellow, you are not Caesar's friend! Every man progressively making himself the king is progressively speaking in opposition to** (or: continues to declare himself against and in the place of) **the Caesar!"**

Jesus obviously impressed Pilate. Perhaps Pilate even liked Him. But the Judean leaders pulled the political card. They make Jesus a political adversary to the Roman Empire. Notice that first their complaint was that He had made Himself to be God's son. Does this altered accusation ("**making himself the king**") shed light on what they meant in vs. 7b? Are they equating the two titles as, say, with the situation of King David, of Israel's history? Are they really just rejecting Jesus as their Messiah, and they want Pilate to get rid of Him for them? *Cf* Acts 17:7

13. Pilate, therefore, hearing of these words, led Jesus outside and sat down upon [the] elevated place – a platform, or stage, which is ascended by steps and from which men spoke to public assemblies, or judges and public officials performed their duties – into a place normally being called "The Stone Pavement," yet in Hebrew, "Gabbatha."

He now moved to the position that symbolized his authority: he "**sat down upon [the] elevated place**." This is the place from where rulers and judges render a decision about a matter. The Judeans have maneuvered him into the proverbial corner. But he will try another angle…

14. Now it was [the] preparation (= the Preparation Day) **of the Passover** [Feast; Festival], **being about the sixth hour** (= noon time), **and he proceeds saying to the Jews** (or: Judeans), **"Look at and consider your king!"**

He repeats what he had said, in vs. 5, above, but instead of saying "the/this man," here he says, "**Look at and consider your king!**" In Jn. 18:33 he had asked Jesus if He was the King of the Judeans, and in 18:39 – when speaking to the Judean leaders – he referred to Him as "the King of the Judeans." For whatever reason, Pilate was not letting this title go (see vs. 19, below). In vs. 22, Pilate is firm about what he had written for the placard that he had attached to Jesus' cross. Was he rubbing this in their faces (since they were against him saying and writing this – vs. 21, below)? Or did he have a deeper motive, either political or spiritual?

15. Therefore those men yelled and shouted, "Lift [him] up at once and carry [him] away!" "Lift [him] up and carry [him] away!" "Crucify (Suspend; Hang) **him** (Put him to death on the stake)!" **Pilate says, "Shall I proceed to crucify** (suspend and put to death on the stake) **your king?" The chief** (ranking) **priests decidedly answered, "We are not having a king** (or: we continue holding no king) **except Caesar!"**

Note, again, he refers to Jesus as their "**king.**" Observe how many times our author has the Roman official designate Jesus as the King of the Judeans. Our author presses the point by the Judeans' political renunciation of Jesus, through voicing their exclusive allegiance to Caesar. This emphatic message was not just to Pilate, but it was also for Caesar to at some point hear, thus assuring their position as being the leaders of/among the Judeans (recall Jn. 11:48). They were not remembering the proclamation of Gen. 49:10, "The scepter shall not depart from Judah…" They were afraid of the very thing that would later happen, in AD 70. They lost their place, and their nation.

16. At that time, therefore, he [Pilate] committed Him, and gave Him over to them, to the end that He would be crucified (hung on a pole; suspended and put to death on a stake).

They then took (or: received) **Jesus alongside and led Him away.**

This scene has traditionally taken interpreters back to Isa. 53:7,

> "**Yet He did not open His mouth because of** (or through) **the [occasion] to have been ill-treated in an ugly situation: just as a sheep is led upon a slaughtering** (or: like a sheep, He was led onto [the] slaughter), **and as** (or: like) **a lamb [that is] set in position against the person shearing it [is] without a voice** (mute; voiceless; = silent), **in like manner He continues not to open up His mouth**" (LXX, JM).

In Jn. 10:11ff, He had the role of being the Good Shepherd of his sheep. Now He enters the role of being one of the sheep. As such, He is following the Father's Voice (Jn. 10:3-5; I owe this insight to Dan Kaplan).

Philip would explain this verse to the Ethiopian eunuch (Acts 8:30ff), and then Peter would later write about humanity being "**unbound and released by a ransom**" that was accomplished by the event to which He was "**led away**" on this day, coupled with the resurrection that would happen three days later. Peter said that we were,

> "**unbound and released by a ransom.... by Christ's precious blood – as of a flawless** (unblemished) **and spotless Lamb: being One having been foreknown** (previously known by intimate experience), **indeed, before [the] casting down** (as of debts: a paying down by installments) **of, or pertaining to [the; or: an] ordered System** (a particular order or arrangement of things; or: the aggregate of humanity), **yet One being set in clear light and manifested upon [the] last part of the times** (or: of the [or: these] successive chronological time periods) **because of [us]**" (1 Pet. 1:18-20).

This one scene, lived-out by Jesus, would be unveiled as an integral part of the Christ Event which had its roots in the Prophets of Israel. But also *cf* Ex. 12:3 and Jn. 1:36.

17. **So, carrying, supporting and progressively bearing away the cross** (torture pole; execution stake) **by Himself, He went out into the commonly-called "Skull's Place"** (or: the place of a skull), **which is normally called "Golgotha," in Hebrew,**

Our author was informing his readers of the geographical, and historical, location of the crucifixion. A skull is a term for the "head" of a skeleton (this is an allusion to Ezk. 37:1-14, the vision of the valley of dry bones, which represented "the whole house of Israel," vs. 11; here, Jesus is the Head of the skeleton, representing Israel of the old covenant). It signified a place of death. It was another SIGN. This event brings us to the scene that is the turning point of His lived-out parable. It answers to Mt. Sinai, the place that began Israel's Law, which the Judeans were using as their reason for having Him killed. Paul described their condition, in Rom. 7:5,

> "**You see, when we** [= Adam/Israel] **were existing within the flesh** (or: = in the old alienated Adamic existence, with the flesh sacrifices and markers of the Law), **the effects, impressions, emotions and impulses from the experiences, passions and suffering of the failures** (from the sins and deviations which caused misses of the target) – **the things through means of the Law** [the Torah] – **were continually operating** (working within; energizing and effecting) **within our members into the condition to produce fruit by Death** (in death; to death; for Death)."

Murder (in this case, the Judeans killing Jesus) is listed by Paul as one of the "works of the flesh," specifically for those under the Law (Gal. 5:18b-21). Just as in vs. 21 of that passage Paul informed folks that those who do those things will not inherit God's reign, recall that Jesus told the chief priests and elders that the reign (kingdom) would be taken from them and would be given to a people-group (the new creation humanity – Eph. 2:14-15) that would bring forth fruit from God's reign (Mat. 21:43; *cf* Gal. 5:22-23). Kaplan has reminded us that the will of mankind is to kill, while the will of God is for Life. It started with the desire for fruit that would cause death, and from that seed grew to Cain killing his brother. In Jesus' lament over Jerusalem, He referred to the blood of Abel, and tied it to Jerusalem killing the prophets and stoning those that were sent to her (Mat. 23:35-37). Soon, her house would be left desolate (Mat. 23:38), which happened in AD 70.

Instead of the Heb., Golgotha, Lu. 23:33 gives the Greek term, Calvary, which has the same meaning. Heb. 13:12 instructs us that He, "**suffered** (and/or: had experiences of His bodily senses and emotions) **outside of the gate**" (cf vs.18, below), which corresponds to "outside of the Garden" of Gen. 3:24. This "place of the skull" was the place where "the Seed of the Woman" would "boot and crush" the head of the serpent (Gen. 3:15). Now recall what Jesus had said to the scholars of the Law and the Pharisees:

> "**[You] snakes! [You] offspring** (brood) **of vipers** (poisonous serpents)**! How can you flee and escape from the judging which has the qualities, character and significance of the valley of Hinnom** (= the sentence to the city dump [Greek: Gehenna; = the Valley of Hinnom]; the deciding which pertains to the waste depository of the city)**?** [cf Jer. 19:1-15]

The Judean leadership had become "the serpent." It would be the Romans who would be His instrument to finally crush them and many of their bodies would fill Gehenna, but the work on the cross did this for all humanity. Christ has defeated the serpent within us – we simply have to be resurrected from the Edenic death (Eph. 2:1) in order to come alive to the finished work of Christ.

18. **where they crucified Him** (hung or suspended Him; attached Him to a pole; impaled Him), **and with Him two others – [one] on each side** (or: hence and hence) **– yet Jesus in the middle.**

The fact that He "**went out**" of the city, to be crucified, is recalled by the author of Heb. 13, where that author includes us within this lived-out parable:

> 11. **For you see, the bodies of those animals, whose blood is still repeatedly being brought** [some MSS add: concerning sin] **into the set-apart** (or: holy) **places by means of the chief priest, are habitually being burned down outside of the Camp.** [Lev. 16:27]
> 12. **Wherefore Jesus also suffered** (and/or: had experiences of His bodily senses and emotions) **outside of the gate** [p46 and others: the Camp], **so that He may set-apart** (or: would make holy and sacred) **the People through His own blood**.
>> [comment: this was a fulfillment of the Day of Atonement]
> 13. **Now then, we can keep on coming out** (or: should be progressively going out) **toward Him – outside of the Camp – habitually bearing His reproach** (= the censure and disgrace which He bore; or: the insult which pertains to Him). [Heb. 11:26, above; 1 Pet. 4:12-14,17]
>> [comment: this was a call to participate in His sacrifice, and also to leave Judaism (or: religion), and thus to bear the same reproach and insults that He bore; it is also a call to bear away from them the mistakes and failures of others – Jn. 20:23]

Isa. 53:11b-12 has also been seen as pointing to what was happening through His crucifixion:

> "**And so He himself will continue taking and bearing-up their failures** (deviations; errors; mistakes; sins) **[in order] to bring eschatological deliverance and turn folks in the right direction** (or: to institute the Way pointed out; to demonstrate fairness and equity; to establish righted relationships) **in and by [the] Just One who is pointed in the right direction – the One continuously slaving well for and among [the] Many** (or: within many people). **Because of this, He himself will continue inheriting [the] Many and will keep on causing [the] Many to inherit, and thus will progressively divide the spoils of the strong folks, because His soul was transmitted into** (or: delivered unto and committed to; surrendered and entrusted into the midst of) **death and He was considered and viewed among the lawless folks. So He, Himself, took up and carried the failures** (deviations; errors sins; etc.) **of [the] Many, and through these acts of lawlessness He was transmitted, entrusted, committed, delivered, surrendered, handed over and given to [our] side**" (LXX, JM).

You see, this divine drama was written long before it was played-out upon the stage of history. Paul instructs us, in Gal. 3:

> 13. **Christ bought us [back] out** (or: redeems and reclaims us out [of slavery] and liberates us) **from the midst of the curse** (or: adversarial prayer; imprecation) **of and from the Law, while**

becoming (or: birthing Himself to be) **a curse** (or: an accursed One; an [embodied] adversarial prayer) **for our sakes** (or: over our [situation]) – **for it has been and now stands written:**
> **"A curse** (an adversarial prayer) **[is settled] upon all** (or: [is] added to everyone) **continuing hanging upon a tree** (or: wood; a stake or pole)**"** [Deut. 21:23, omitting the phrase "by God," after the word "curse"] –

14. **to the end that the Good Word** (the Blessing; Good *Logos*, Word of goodness, ease and well-being) **pertaining to Abraham** (belonging to and possessed by Abraham; from, and whose intermediary source is, Abraham) **could within Jesus Christ suddenly birth Itself** (or: may from Itself, within Anointed Jesus, at once come into being [and be dispersed]) **into the multitudes** (the nations; the ethnic groups; the Gentiles), **so that we** [note: "we" = the new "one" mankind; *cf* Eph. 2:11-16] **could receive the Spirit's promise through the Faithfulness [of Christ]**
> (or: to the end that we [all] may take in hand the Promise from the Breath-effect, through faith and trust; or: in order that we [Jew and Gentile] can lay hold of and receive the Promise – which is the Spirit – through that loyalty; [*cf* Isa. 44:3]).

In Phil. 2:8 Paul reminded folks that Jesus,
> **"being found in an outward fashion, mode of circumstance, condition, form-appearance** (or: character; role) **as a human, He lowers Himself** (or: humbled Himself; made Himself low; degrades Himself; levels Himself off), **coming to be a submissive, obedient One** (one who gives the ear and listens) **as far as** (or: to the point of) **death – but death of a cross!"**

The cross (pole from a tree) was an allusion to Adam experiencing the result of eating from the tree of the knowledge of good and evil, in the Garden. They nailed His hands (a figure for the ability to do work) so that He could not keep on doing the works that He had been doing; they nailed His feet (a figure for the ability to walk) so that He could no longer walk the Path that He had been taking. They did not realize that this was the destination of His Path (1 Cor. 2:8).

Kaplan has pointed out that He was "suspended on a pole," above the earth, in the first heaven, our atmosphere. In Jn. 12:32, He had told His apprentices that if this happened to Him, He would draw all humanity up to Himself (in the atmosphere/heaven), and Paul affirms that He did, in Eph. 2:6. This was so that where He is, we could be with Him (Jn. 17:24a).

19. **Now Pilate also wrote a notice** (or: title) **and posted it upon the cross** (stake; execution pole). **And that which stood written was:**
> **"Jesus the Nazarene, the King of the Judeans."**

This is one of the most obvious SIGNS of this Gospel. Pilate may have had multiple motivations for doing this. We could even consider this the first public proclamation of the Good News. It announced that the time of Israel's long-awaited Messiah had actually arrived – even though it was not what the Judeans, or the Jews of the Diaspora, were expecting.

It is possible that Paul was alluding to this in Gal. 3:1,
> **"O senseless, unreflecting and foolish Galatians! Who suddenly harmed you with malicious words, or bewitched you folks with the evil eye – before whose eyes Jesus Christ was graphically placarded** (= as though portrayed in writing before your own eyes) **one having been crucified on a stake** (suspended on an execution pole)**?"**

Now just before this, Paul was speaking of Jesus' crucifixion, and God's grace that came through that, in juxtaposition to the way that was pointed out by the Law, in Gal. 2:
> 20. **I was crucified together with Christ and thus it remains... yet I continue living! [It is] no longer I, but it is Christ continuously living and alive within me! Now that which I, at the present moment, continue living within flesh I am constantly living within [His] faithfulness – in and by that [faithfulness] which is the Son of God, the One loving me and giving Himself over to another for the sake of me** (or: even transmitting Himself, over my

[situation and condition]; or: also passing Himself along for me; committing and transferring Himself over me).

21. **I make it no habit to displace** (shove aside; upset; thus: reject; thwart; repudiate; nullify) **God's grace and favor! For if rightwising deliverance into justice, equity and freedom from guilt with right relationships within the Way pointed out** (= transforming-inclusion into the new covenant) **[is] through Law** (= by legalistic behavior or religious works), **then as a consequence Christ died as a mere gratuity** (= for nothing; to no purpose).

20. **Therefore many of the Jews** (or: Judeans) **read this notice** (title), **because the place where Jesus was crucified** (hung on or suspended from a pole) **was near the city, and that which stood written was in Hebrew, Latin** (the Roman language) **[and] in Greek** (or: the Hellenist language).

Pilate meant this to be read by all the educated world – not just the Judeans or citizens of Jerusalem. It was to be read by the elite Jews (the only ones who would have likely been able to read Hebrew), Roman citizens (the Latin version), and the common people of Judea, who would have possibly been able to read the common language of the Hellenized society of that day, Koine Greek. It is interesting that he did not write it in Aramaic, for the unlearned Judeans. All who saw Jesus on the cross were meant to know the reason why He was on the cross, and Who this person was. But most likely, Pilate was sending the Judean leadership a message: You have had me crucify your king. His prior dialogue with those Jews does not lead us to conclude that he was saying this in a vindictive way. In vs. 14 he had, in perhaps a neutral manner, said, "**Look at and consider your king.**" We read him being portrayed as serious, and even reflective, by our author.

21. **Then the chief priests of the Jews** (Judeans) **began and persisted in saying to Pilate, "Do not be writing 'The King of the Judeans,' but rather, 'That one said, "I am King of the Judeans."'"**
22. **Pilate considered and replied, "What I have written, I have written!"**

The religious leaders understood the point that Pilate had made by posting that title on Jesus' cross, and they did not want that message to be broadcast by the plaque. They wanted Jesus to be seen as a pretender, a false-messiah. They had not wanted a messiah to come and displace their authority and position. But Pilate stands firm, showing that there was intent in what he had written.

23. **Then the soldiers, while they crucified Jesus** (during the time Jesus was affixed to the stake, or was hung from a pole), **took His outer garments and made four shares** (or: parts) **– for** (or: to) **each soldier a share** (part) **– also the tunic** (inner garment). **Now the tunic was seamless, out of those [kinds] woven from above** (= the top) **on throughout the whole.**

Taking His inner garment would have left Him at least figuratively (if not completely) naked: the condition in which Adam and Eve found themselves, after having partaken of the tree that would bring death to them (Gen. 3). It was the first place where humanity sought self-righteousness (making aprons of fig leaves) to cover their shame and fear. Jesus has been brought back to the beginning of the story, in order to redeem all and remove the results of death. The death decision (embodied in exile from the Garden), which began humanity's wilderness journey, became the antidote and the cure – the Path to the Promised Land where the resurrected Garden (Rev. 22) does not have the tree which produced death.

It is only this Gospel that mentions that His garments were made into four shares, or parts (by representatives of the Empire). Four is often used to refer to the four directions, and thus this could be a SIGN pointing to the world-wide covering that this Event implies, where it is now possible for all humanity to respond to Paul's admonition: "**you folks must clothe yourselves with** (or: enter within and put on) **the Lord, Jesus Christ, and stop** (or: do not continue) **making forethought** (constructing provision; planning ahead; performing provident care) **into excessive desires of the flesh**" (Rom. 13:14).

This is also the only Gospel to note these facts about His tunic, that it was a "**seamless... whole.**" This may speak to both His life, as being a "seamless whole," or to the entire story, from Adam... to Adam (1 Cor. 15:45-49), as being "**woven from above, on throughout the whole.**" The phrase "from above" harks back to Jesus speaking of being "born from above" (3:7, above), and suggests that Jesus' whole life had been "woven" by the Father, doing His will "throughout" His whole life.

We view it as significant that His garments (the outward presentation as well as the personal protection of a person) went to representatives of the Empire (almost like the kingdom passing on to ethnic groups that would one day produce its fruit). The four soldiers had something of His mantle. In what may be considered to be a distortion (note that 1 Cor. 1:13 proclaims: "**Christ has been parted and remains divided into fragments!**"), Rome would later be an outward representation of Christ. Perhaps the dividing of His garments to be worn by embodiments of violence was a foreshadowing of the warning that Jesus gave, about:

> "**ones that are habitually coming to you folks in clothing belonging to sheep** (= disguised as sheep; pretending to have the covering or appearance of sheep), **yet inside they are ravenous, savage wolves**" (Mat. 7:15).

Kaplan astutely points us to Jn. 16:2,

> "**an hour is progressively coming with the result that everyone in the process of killing you folks off may imagine** (suppose; hold the opinion of; think) [himself] **to be proceeding in presenting** (bearing forward) **an offering of sacred service to, and for, God.**"

24. **Therefore they said to one another, "We should not tear** (split; rend) **it, but rather let us cast** (or: draw) **lots concerning it, to decide whose it will be," so that the Scripture could** (or: would) **be fulfilled – the one saying,**

> "**They divide** (or: divided) **up My garments among themselves, and on My vesture** (apparel with beauty, being more or less stately and costly) **they cast [the] lot.**" [Ps. 22:18]

Indeed, the soldiers then did these things.

So our author sees what they did as a fulfilling of this Psalm. The Psalm has been "cast alongside" (which is the definition of a "parable") this that was experienced by Jesus. Threads from the tapestry of Israel's history are woven into the life (and garments) of Jesus.

25. **Now His mother, the sister of His mother** (= His aunt), **Mary the [wife] of Clopas, and Mary the Magdalene had been and remained standing beside the cross** (torture stake/pole) **of Jesus.**

These folks, and "**the disciple whom He was habitually loving and accepting**" (vs. 26), act out the scene that Paul describes, in the literal translation of Rom. 12:1,

> "**Consequently, brothers, I am repeatedly calling you folks alongside to advise, exhort, implore and encourage you, through God's compassions to stand your bodies alongside** (or: to set or place your bodies beside) **[the] Well-pleasing, Set-apart** (Holy; Different-from-the-usual), **Living Sacrifice by God** (or: in God; for God; to God; **with God**), **[this being] your sacred service which pertains to thought, reason and communication** (or: your reasoned and rational service; the logical and Word-based service from you folks; or: = temple service)."

26. **Jesus, therefore, seeing and perceiving [His] mother – and the disciple whom He was habitually loving and accepting, standing by** (or: in their presence) **– He says to His mother, "Woman** (or: Dear lady; Madam), **look at and consider your son.**"

Once again we encounter this unnamed disciple. Now the first layer of what Jesus says to His mother seems to be the passing on His own relationship to her to this anonymous disciple. She would no longer know Him according to His flesh (2 Cor. 5:16). But also recall what Jesus said in Mat. 12:50,

"You see, whoever may be doing the will, intent, purpose and desire of My Father – the One within and in union with [the] heavens (or: in the midst of [the] atmospheres) **– that very person is My brother and sister and mother."**

In the realm of the atmospheres (the kingdom of the heavens, as Matthew likes to term it) all relationships are blended into One. And everyone can function in every relationship. On this disciple, see Jn. 13:23; 18:15-16; 20:2; 21:7, 20-24.

27. **Next, He says to the disciple, "Look at and consider your mother." So from that hour the disciple took her into** (or: unto) **his own home** (or: place; things).

This disciple had become the son of Jesus' mother – for followers of Christ, there was a new creation in which all relationships were new. Paul put it this way, in regard to Jesus:

"those whom He foreknew (whom He knows from previous intimate experience), **He also marked out beforehand** (determined, defined and designed in advance) **[as] copies** (joint-forms) **of the image** (material likeness; portrait; form) **of His Son** (or: He previously divided, separated and bounded conformed patterns from the image/form of His Son) **into the [situation for] Him to be** (or: to continually exist being) **the Firstborn among, within the center of, and in union with many brothers** (= a vast family from the same womb; Gal. 4:26)!" (Rom. 8:29).

As Jesus was a representative of Israel, Mary, who had produced the Christ, had become a symbol of the Jerusalem which is above, **"who is** (or: which particular one continues being) **our mother"** (Gal 4:26), i.e., the mother of "the body of Christ." *Cf* Rev. 12:1-6

28. **After this, Jesus, having seen and knowing** (being aware) **that already He** (or: it) **has been brought to the purposed goal, His** (or: its) **destiny – and now remains completed, finished and perfected [for; as] all humanity** (or: [in] all things) **– in order that the Scripture could be finished** (would be at once ended; should be brought to its purposed and destined goal and perfected), **He now says, "I am thirsty."**

In this verse, we have some ambiguity since the text does not have an expressed subject for the third person, perfect, passive verb, "**has been brought to the purposed goal [and] destiny, and now remains completed, finished and perfected.**" When this is the case, we must supply an appropriate pronoun (in this case, either "**He**," or, "**it**"). Either of these readings makes sense, and we can see that both are true. He has been brought to the purposed goal, His destiny (etc.), or "it" has. Now "it" could refer to God's "plan of the ages," or, the Mosaic age, or the old covenant, or the old creation (Israel as a nation, together with its purpose), the story of the first Adam, or the focal point of Adam's story. It also could simply refer to His death on the cross. It is probably all of these implications.

Lending currency to the reading "**He**" is what He said in Lu. 13:32b,

"**I continue throwing out demons** (Hellenistic concept and term: = animistic influences) **and finishing off** (or: completing) **healings today and tomorrow, and then on the third day I am proceeding in being brought to the purposed goal and destiny** (or: I am progressively being finished and made fully functional)."

But supporting both readings is what Jesus says in vs. 30, below, "**It has been finished**," which is the exact, same verb form as is used here in vs. 28, but here He is not speaking but rather is "**knowing** (being aware)." So in this verse, both readings can be contemplated with benefit toward perceiving what He had seen, and thus was knowing.

The word "**all**" (*panta*) can function either as a masculine singular, "**all humanity**," or as a neuter plural, "all things." The KJV, and other translations, render it as the subject of the verb "has been brought to the purposed goal (etc.)," but the problem with this is that for "all" to be in the nominative case (which is the case form, i.e., spelling, for being the subject of a clause) it must be plural, and yet the verb is singular, so there is no agreement in number, as must be the case for "all" to be the subject of a singular verb.

Therefore, we must read "all" as being in the accusative case (note: the spelling, *panta*, fits nominative plural, or accusative singular or plural – sounds confusing, but this is the way it is). To read sensibly in English, we must insert a preposition that makes sense to the context of the sentence. On offer are the options "for; as; in," as can be seen in the rendering of the verse. So what does this mean? It means that the point in the story has been reached where He, or it, has been finished, completed and perfected "**for all humanity**," or, "**in all things**." Or, that He has been finished and perfected "**as all humanity**" – i.e., as humanity's representative; as Adam, or as Adam's redemptive counterpart (1 Cor. 15:45).

Moving on, we now have the subordinate clause, "**in order that the Scripture could be finished** (would be at once ended; should be brought to its purposed and destined goal and perfected)." Now this is the same verb that we just discussed, but it is in a different tense. So what Scripture does our author have in view here? Is this clause pointing backwards in the verse, toward what has just been said, or forward, to what Jesus will now say? The grammar is ambiguous: it can be read either way. His statement "**He now says, 'I am thirsty',**" can stand alone, not referring either to what came before, or directly to what follows. So, as with all ambiguities in ancient writings, we suggest that this subordinate clause be read both ways:

a) The use of the same verb in both the main and the subordinate clauses ("finished, etc.") lends currency to reading the subordinate as saying that the Scripture (i.e., the OT), which was primarily Israel's story along with the predictions of the coming of their Messiah, had come to their destined end, in Jesus, as being the Messiah. This finds an echo is Rom. 10:4,

"**for you see, Christ [is] an end of Law** (or: for Christ [is] Law's goal and destiny; for [the] Anointing [is] termination from [the Torah]; for Christ [was the] final act of [the] Law) **[leading] into the Way pointed out in fair and equitable dealings, and rightwised [covenant] relationships of justice in eschatological liberation, to, for and in everyone habitually trusting and believing**

(or: because Christ [entering] into the pointed-out Way – in everyone normally exercising faith with conviction, and with each person remaining loyal – [is; brings] Law's climax)."
This is saying that Christ coming and dying completes part 1 of the story and the end of the 1st creation (meaning, Israel). Or as Paul would also say:

"**for you folks are not under Law** (or: do not exist being subject to [Torah] or custom), **but rather under Grace** (or: the Act which produced happiness, which was granted as a favor)" (Rom. 6:14),

or: "**the original things** (the beginning [situations]; the archaic and primitive [arrangements]) **passed by** (or: went to the side)" (2 Cor. 5:17).

b) Reading the subordinate clause as pointing to what Jesus says ties it to the next verse, which would then be an allusion to Pss. 22:15 and 69:21. This fits nicely with viewing these verses in the frame of our proposed "lived-out parable," in which our author ties Israel's writings to what is happening to Jesus in this Event that can be viewed as the turning point of all history. But the reading suggested in a) seems to hold much greater depth of meanings.

Just as Jesus had been the Ideal Shepherd, and was now a slaughtered Sheep, likewise where we saw Him offering water to the Samaritan woman, and at the feast (7:37, above) offering a drink to everyone, in His dying He has poured everything out, and is Himself (as Humanity) thirsty. Even so, even when dead, there was still water within His body (vs. 34, below).

29. **Now a vessel** (container) **full of cheap sour wine** (a common, inexpensive vinegary wine, with a sharp flavor, that was a popular thirst-quenching drink) **was lying [close by]. Therefore, putting a sponge, full of the vinegary wine, around a hyssop stalk, they brought it to His mouth.**

Jesus' beginning SIGN was to turn water into "**fine, ideal wine**" (2:7-10, above), and He is ending His life by being offered "**cheap sour wine**." This verse echoes Ps. 69:21, "And so they gave gall, as my food, and unto my thirst they gave me vinegar to drink." It is also significant that most texts indicate that they used "**a hyssop stalk**," which is also mentioned in conjunction with what, under the Law, was "**initiated** (innovated; inaugurated; or: dedicated).... **by** (and: under) **Moses to and for all the People, taking the blood of calves and he-goats, with water, scarlet wool and hyssop, he sprinkled both the scroll and all the People**" (Heb. 9:18, 19). At Israel's first Passover, it was used to touch the lintel and the two jambs of the portal of each family's house with the blood of the Passover lamb (Ex. 12:22). We also find its use in Lev. 14:4-52; this plant was a part of rites for cleansing lepers – a disease of the flesh. The symbolism from these OT ceremonies, now associated Jesus' death as Israel, is hard to miss in this word **hyssop**, which is only used in this Gospel. Our author has presented another important SIGN.

30. **Then, when Jesus received the cheap sour wine, He said, "It has been finished** (or: It has been brought to its goal and end), **and now stands complete** (having been accomplished, perfected, ended and now is at its destiny)!" – **and so, bowing [His] head, He transferred the Spirit** (or: committed [His] spirit and life-force; or: gave over and surrendered to the side the Breath-effect). [cf Lu. 13:32]

The Vine (Jn. 15) had been fully pruned, and now hung naked (no leaves or fruit) upon its support. Support is needed for grapevines to keep the new shoots and fruit off the ground. If the fruit is in contact with the soil (earth), it will likely rot. A support gives a larger area of the vine access to sunlight and air. It actually lives and produces in the heaven (atmosphere). But Spring would soon arrive, with new shoots and a new crop of grapes that would bear the Fruit of the Spirit of the Vine. There would no longer be the cheap sour wine, but New Wine, in New Wineskins, which He would,

> "**drink from out of this product** (yield; offspring) **of the grapevine, [in] that day [that He would] habitually drink with folks in union with [His] Father's reign – when it [would be] new in kind, quality and character**" (Mat. 26:29, adjusted).

Our author does not focus on some of the other things that Jesus said, while on the cross, but rather brings the lived-out parable to the climax of its downward journey. The work of Christ has been finished; His fruit has been crushed, and the New Wine will begin to flow out into the New Wineskins. We see this as being the reason for the author saying that, "**He transferred the Spirit**" – to the New Containers (His apprentices, and the rest of humanity). This is the same verb that was used about Judah (Judas) transferring Jesus to the Judean authorities, to be "pruned." (Jn. 18:5; Lu. 22:48; etc.)

Jesus used the perfect tense of the verb, "It has been brought to its goal and end," and since this tense signifies that the completed action continues in its completed state, His work "**now stands complete** (having been accomplished, perfected, ended and now is at its destiny)." What He did next can also be rendered:

> a) He committed [His] spirit and life-force;
> b) He gave over, and surrendered to the side, the Breath-effect.

Lu. 23:46 records His last words differently, emphasizing His relationship with the Father, and then simply recording his death:

> "**'O Father... into Your hands I am now setting aside My spirit** (or: I proceed committing My Breath-effect and life-force)!'** [Ps. 31:5]
> **Now upon saying this, He out-spirited** (or: breathed out; expired)."

Mat. 27:46 focuses on another aspect of His death, as does Mk. 15:34. Both of these record Jesus as only making an enigmatic statement, or question, speaking Aramaic, and soon after giving out a loud cry, and releasing the Spirit/spirit. As we see, with our present author, what is emphasized is that the work and the story (of the first Adam, and of Israel) have come to a close. The author of Heb. 10:1-14 (following the descriptions of Jesus doing the work of the High Priest, on the Day of Atonement, in Heb. 9) casts the act of Christ on the cross (and His work following the resurrection) in terms of the old covenant sacrificial cultus, instructing us in Heb. 10:14,

> "**For you see, by and in ONE offering He has perfected** (brought to the goal; matured; completed; finished; brought to their purposed destiny) – **on into the whole length** (or: extended or stretched into the unbroken continuance) – **those folks being one after another set-apart**

(separated; made sacred and holy; [*p46* reads: restored back up again into the original state and condition; rescued back and delivered again; made healthy and whole again])."

Before speaking of "ONE offering" – in contrast to the MANY offerings proscribed by the Law – Heb. 9:26 had declared:

> "**Yet now** (at this time), **once, upon a conjunction** (a joined destiny; a bringing of [two] ends together ["denoting the joining of two age-times" – E.W. Bullinger]) **of the ages, He has been and remains manifested** (has been brought to light and continues visible) **into a displacement of the failure** (from the error, sin and deviation from the target) **through the sacrifice of Himself** (or: through His sacrifice; or: by means of the sacrificial altar-offering which was Himself)." [*cf* Rom. 6:9-10]

Then, in Heb. 10, he goes on and gives more explanation of this Event, using temple terminology to describe the new, post-resurrection situation with us being the new temple, and admonishes us:

> 19. **Therefore, having freedom, openness and boldness of speech which comes from being citizens, brothers** (folks from the same womb), **with a view to the Entrance of the set-apart places** (or: into the Pathway-into the midst, pertaining to the Holiest Place, which is the separated ones and which pertains to the sacred folks) – **within and in union with the blood of Jesus;**
> 20. **a Way** (Path; Road) **which was done anew** (or: which He innovates and makes new in species, character or mode, within and in the midst) **for us and in us, recently slain and yet living, through the veil that is His flesh** (or: which way through the veil He did anew for us – that is, His flesh (= His body): recently slain, and now living) – [*cf* Jn. 14:6; Rev. 5:6]
> 21. **along with a Great Priest [enthroned] upon God's House** (or: the house from God) –
> 22. **we can be continuously and progressively approaching with a true heart in union with full-assurance from the completed act of faithfulness** (or: centered within [the] full-carrying from [His] loyalty and fidelity), **the hearts having been sprinkled from a misery-gushed consciousness of what is evil or unserviceable** (or: a joint-knowledge full of annoying labor; a conscience in a bad condition), **and then the body having been bathed in and by clean water.** *Cf* Rom. 10:4 and Jn. 17:4; also, a possible allusion to Dan. 9:24.

Paul, in 1 Thes. 5:10, speaks of Jesus as:

> "**the One dying concerning and on behalf of us** (or: = while encompassing our [situation]; [other MSS: over our {condition}]), **to the end that whether we can or would exist being continuously awake** (attentively watching) **or continuously falling asleep** [note: a metaphor for "being alive or being dead"], **we can at the same time be alive** (or: live) **together with Him** (= share His life)."

31. **Then the Judeans** (= Judean leaders) – **since it was [the] Preparation – made petition of Pilate to the end that their** [i.e., of those crucified] **legs could at once be broken and they could soon be lifted off and carried away, so that the bodies would not remain upon the cross** (torture stake; upright suspension pole) **on** (or: within) **the sabbath, for the day of THAT sabbath was a great one.**

This is religion; this is idolatry: it was OK to murder an innocent man, but we cannot have anything that will taint or break our religious rules. Our religion reigns supreme. This was especially the case when that particular "something" would be seen as profaning the biggest religious holy day of the year! This was not just an ordinary sabbath, it was a sabbath because it was one of the main annual Feast days: the commemoration of Passover, which celebrated their nation's historic release from slavery in Egypt. It was not even necessarily the weekly sabbath. In Jn. 20:1 we read, "**Now on one of the sabbaths**…"

The idea of breaking their legs was so that they could not use them for support, while on the cross, and the weight of their own bodies would suffocate them. Thus, on that same day they could be removed from the crosses.

32. The soldiers therefore came (or: went) **and indeed broke the legs of the first one, and of the other one who was crucified with Him.**

33. Yet coming upon Jesus, as they saw and perceived Him being already having died, they did not break His legs,

34. but rather, one of the soldiers pierced (jabbed; punctured) **His side through the rib cage with the head of a javelin** (or: spear), **and at once** (straightway; immediately) **blood and water came out** (or: went straight out).

None of the synoptic Gospels record the details of vss. 31-34, nor of vss. 35-37, below. As vs. 37 reports, our author viewed that as the fulfillment of Israel's Scripture. In the Unveiling that was given to John, reference was made to this having happened:

> "**He is continuously** (or: presently; repeatedly; habitually; progressively) **coming with the clouds, and every eye will progressively discern and perceive** (or: continue recognizing; or: repeatedly see) **Him, even whichever of you folks pierced** (or: pierce) **Him…**" (Rev. 1:7)

The fact that "**blood and water came out**" may be pointing back to Jn. 3:5,

> "**unless anyone may** (or: someone would) **be born forth from out of water and spirit** (or: – as well as Breath-effect and attitude –) **he continues being unable** (remains having no power) **to enter into God's realm.**"

This theme may be what was spoken of in 1 Jn. 5:6, 8, and so we will quote from our commentary on those verses:

> 6. **This is the One at one point coming through water and blood and breath** (or: spirit; Breath-effect), **Jesus Christ. Not within the water alone** (or: not in only water), **but rather within the water and within the blood** (or: in union with water and in union with blood; [other MSS add: and within spirit; note: figure of a human birth, or natural lineage]), **and then there is the breath – that which is continuing to give evidence** (or: and the Spirit {Breath-effect} continuously exists being the One repeatedly testifying), **because the breath is** (or: Spirit or Breath-effect exists being) **the Truth and Reality!**
>
>> (or: and the spirit is the One {or: one} continuously witnessing that the Spirit is The Truth! or: the breath is that which constantly gives testimony that the Breath-effect is reality…)

It has been recognized that the idea of "**coming through**" signifies the way in which He came, but here the word "**spirit**" would align with the incarnation story in Lu. 1:35, as well as the report of the Holy Spirit coming upon Him at His baptism. In this next clause I rendered *pneuma* first as simply "**breath**" since it seems to correlate to the preceding "**water and blood**" as being with them in a natural birth. But the parenthetical renderings may give us another picture to consider. The Spirit of God within the believers, and among the community, continuously gives evidence of the presence of the new Reality into which they have been birthed. It is the Spirit of the risen Jesus, the Truth and the Life. The Spirit of God (God's Reality and Truth) bears witness for Itself through the revelation of the Messiah that has been given to us, imparted as "the anointing."

As to my rendering *pneuma* as "**breath**" the second time, the breath means that there is life, and this reaches all the way back to Gen. 2:7, the giving of life to the first Adam, and then traces the story of humanity to the last Adam (the corporate Christ; the Second Humanity) in 1 Cor. 15:44-49 where Paul also reaffirms God's purpose of creating humanity: to bear His image (vs. 49). We are corporately this new Humanity (Eph. 2:25 – Jew plus Gentile as "one"), and then individually we follow Paul's admonition as a member of this new Humanity.

> 7. **Because there are three constantly testifying** (or: … that three progressively give evidence; or: seeing that the normal witness bearers exist being three):

8. **the breath** (or: spirit; Breath-effect) **and the water and the blood, and these three are [coming; proceeding] into the midst of the One** (or: exist [leading] into one [reality]; are existing into the one thing; or: = are in unison; or: = are in agreement, or are for one thing).

Were it standing by itself, this pronouncement (unfortunately divided into two verses) could present us with an enigma. But it is a continuation of vs. 6, whose subject is Jesus, the Messiah who came by means of water and blood (= natural birth) and breath. Or, taken figuratively, came through immersion (baptism) and the blood of His cross, and now through the agency of His Spirit. Taken either way, each bears testimony and gives evidence to the historical Jesus being the Messiah, God's Anointed, and the breath of His words (in His teaching and speaking to people) brought Life (*cf* Jn. 6:63). His life and His words are constantly testifying of God's love for humanity. The second part of the message here (vs. 8) shows that these three aspects that compose the Second Human are, or exist being, "**into the midst of the One.**" I have suggested two secondary verbs, "**[coming; proceeding]**," since the preposition *eis* is a preposition of movement into the midst of something. These three elements of the Last Adam come into the midst of God (**the One**) to compose the Messiah.

The "**blood and water**" coming from His side, here in vs. 34, has been viewed as a symbol of birth: first of Eve from the side of Adam, and now as the called-out communities that were given birth through the death of Christ.

But also, both **water** and **blood** were ingredients for cleansing, in the Law, so this may also be pointing to another aspect of the work of the cross. And then, the pouring out of the elements of His Life speak to His placing His soul (remember: "the soul is in the blood") over us, and giving us "the water" of His Life.

35. **Now the man having seen [this] has borne witness** (given testimony), **and his witness is true, and that one has seen and knows that he is normally speaking true, so that you folks, also, can yourselves keep on loyally trusting and believing** [other MSS: can come to trust and believe], *Cf* Jn. 20:21; 21:24
36. **for these things came to be** (occurred; happened) **so that the Scripture could be fulfilled,**
    "A bone belonging to Him will not proceed in being worn down, crushed or broken,"
    [Ps. 34:20; Ex. 12:46; Nu. 9:12]
37. **and again, a different Scripture says,**
    "They will proceed seeing, catching sight, and perceiving into Whom they deeply pierce forth (or: lance from out of a stabbing).**"** [Zech. 12:10]

We may also have allusions to Ps. 22:16b-17 in these verses:
    "They pierced (or: gouged) my hands and feet, I counted all my bones" (LXX).

38. **Now after these things, Joseph from Arimathea – being a disciple of Jesus, yet being one having been hidden because of the fear of the Judeans** (= religious Judean authorities) – **made petition of Pilate, to the end that he could lift up and carry away the body of Jesus. And so Pilate turned upon [him] and gave permission. Therefore they** [other MSS: he] **came** (or: went) **and carried away His body.**

Lu. 23:50-51 gives us more details about Joseph, that he:
    "**a leader who was a member of the Council** (= the Sanhedrin); **a virtuous** (or: good) **and just** (fair; equitable; rightwised) **grown man – this man was not one having put [a vote] down together** (= concurring; consenting) **with their wish** (will; intent; purpose) **nor [was endorsing their] performance** (= action; what they committed)…"
Recall 12:42, above,

"**Just the same, however, many of the rulers also** (or: many, even from among the chiefs and ruling class) **believed and placed their trust into Him, but still, because of the Pharisees, they did not begin confessing** (= openly avowing their faith) **or keep on speaking in agreement – so that they would not become ones cut off from** (separated away from) **the synagogue.**"

Had no one asked for the body of Jesus, it likely would have been taken to Gehenna, but as we will see in vs. 41, it was taken to a Garden. Joseph wanted to honor Jesus. Recall Mat. 23:29 where Jesus pointed out that it was the custom of the scribes and Pharisees to do this:

"**you are repeatedly building the tombs** (sepulchers) **of the prophets, and are constantly adorning and decorating the memorial grave monuments of just and rightwised folks.**"

Our next verse, below, shows the extent to which these Jews desired to honor the Prophet (1:21b, above).

39. **Moreover, Nicodemus also came – the one coming to Him by night, at the first – bringing a mixture** [other MSS: roll, or, package] **of myrrh and aloes, roughly 75 to 100 pounds [of it].**

Bringing Nicodemus back into the story adds an element of closure. Recall that he was "**the teacher of Israel**" (Jn. 3:10). These hidden disciples are representatives of the Jewish People (two witnesses), in our parable. It was the System (the corrupt leadership) that had rejected Jesus. His disciples and the earliest Christian "church" were Jewish followers of Jesus, and throughout the writings that compose the NT we find both roots and branches that are founded in, and stem from, Israel's story and writings (cf Rom. 11:16-34). Cf 7:50-51, above.

40. **They then took the body of Jesus and bound** (or: tied) **it in** (or: with) **swaths of linen bandages, along with spices and aromatic oils – according as is the custom for** (or: with; among) **the Jews** (or: Judeans) **to normally prepare [one] for burial.** [cf the burial of Asa, 2 Chron. 16:14]

Such care and respect were involved, and our author includes these details regarding "**the body**." Recall that the Logos had become flesh. He had been the last, and final, Word of the old covenant; He had embodied their Scriptures. They were now honoring the One as they had traditionally honored the other. But both the body of Jesus, and the "body of Moses" (the Law; Torah), had to be buried and to await resurrection. God's Breath-effect would resurrect both, in due time.

41. **Now within the area where He was crucified** (suspended from a pole/stake) **there was a garden, and within the garden an unused memorial tomb within which, as yet, no one had been placed.**

Our lived-out parable is coming to a close as He is returned to a Garden – apparently a different garden, just as the New Jerusalem is a different Garden than the one in Eden (or, at least that Garden had been transformed, as we see in Rev. 22). This was a new burial place, and it would be like no other. He was the first one to be put there, but as we have seen elsewhere, He took all Israel, and all of Adam, there with Him. Instead of this being a "Mount" of Transfiguration, this was to be a "Tomb" of Transformation. He experienced both the heights and the depths of His creation, and He redeemed it all. Cf Lu.13:19

42. **Therefore, on account of the Preparation pertaining to the Jews' [Feast; festival; high sabbath], they placed Jesus there, because the memorial tomb was nearby.**

The Preparation turned out to be for a new exodus into a new Promised Land: a New Creation that was the Kingdom of the Atmospheres (Heavens), here upon the New Earth (Rev. 21:1). He was prepared by Joseph and Nicodemus for a Resurrection into a New Life – and He would bring us with Him!

We will end this chapter by quoting verses from Isa. 53, following the LXX:

4. **This Person constantly carries and repeatedly bears our failures** (mistakes; deviations; errors; sins; occasions of missing the target), **and He continues grieved** (or: He is repeatedly pained and experiences sorrow) **concerning us, and yet we, ourselves, consider Him to be** (continue existing) **within the midst of trouble** (or: hard, distressful labor; bodily exertion), **and in the midst of calamity from a beating** (in union with [the] blow; centered in a plague; [some MSS add: under, or by, God]), **and in the midst of ill-treatment in an ugly situation.**

5. **Yet** (or: Now; But) **He was wounded and damaged through, and because of, our failures** (mistakes; sins; deviations; errors; failures to hit the target), **and He was weakened and made sick** (ill; infirm) **through, and because of, our acts of lawlessness: child-training and discipline, which had a view to our peace and joining, [came] upon Him; by, in and with His bruise we, ourselves, were suddenly and miraculously healed.**

6. **All we, like sheep, have wandered astray – humanity has strayed in, with and by his own road** (path; way) **– and so [the] LORD** (= Yahweh) **transmitted Him to our failures**
    (entrusted Him with our errors; granted Him for our deviations; committed Him to be associated with our missing of the Target; surrendered Him for our sins; handed Him over to another's hands by our mistakes).

7. **Yet He did not open His mouth because of** (or through) **the [occasion] to have been ill-treated in an ugly situation: just as a sheep is led upon a slaughtering** (or: like a sheep, He was led onto [the] slaughter), **and as** (or: like) **a lamb [that is] set in position against the person shearing it [is] without a voice** (mute; voiceless; = silent), **in like manner He continues not to open up His mouth.**

8. **Within the midst of the low status and the experience of being abased and humiliated, His justice and equity** (or: the opportunity for a fair trial; or: the chance or ability to divide, separate and make decisions; or: the judging) **was lifted up and taken away. So who will continue fully taking over the lead of His generation** (or: will proceed conducting a thorough narration to recount His generation), **because His life is now being taken up, away from the earth** (or: taken away from the Land)? **From** (= on account of) **the acts of lawlessness of my** (or: My [?]) **people, He was led into** (or: unto; to) **death.**

9. **And so I will continue giving and entrusting** (or: proceed appointing, assigning or surrendering) **the useless, unprofitable and unsound people** (the bad, malicious, unserviceable folks) **in the place of and corresponding to** (or: instead of; in exchange for) **His burial, and the rich folks in place of and corresponding to** (or: instead of; in exchange for) **His death, because He committed and produced no lawlessness** (neither practiced nor built that which is without a law) **– nor yet [was there] bait, fraud, guile, treachery or deceit within His mouth.**

10. **So [the] Lord** (= Yahweh), **from desire, continued intending and purposing to cleanse and purify Him from the blow** (the beating; the calamity; the plague). **If you folks would** (or: can) **offer, for failure** (or: concerning error and deviation), **your soul will continue seeing and perceiving a long-lived Seed**
    [with other MSS: Should you people at some point give your inner life (person and consciousness) around sin, or concerning a mistake, it (or: He) will continue seeing a long-lived offspring].

11. **And yet with desire [the] Lord kept on purposing to take away from the trouble** (or: hard, distressful labor; bodily exertion) **of His soul and then to point out and demonstrate Light by, and in, Him, and then to shape and mold with** (or: by) **the Understanding. And so He himself will continue taking and bearing-up** (or: keep on bringing-back [from them] so as to carry-up) **their failures** (deviations; errors; mistakes; sins) **[in order] to bring eschatological deliverance and turn folks in the right direction** (or: to institute the Way pointed out; to demonstrate fairness and equity; to establish righted relationships) **in and by a Just One** (or: [the] Fair Person; [the] One who is pointed in the right direction) **– the One continuously slaving well for and among [the] Many** (or: within many people; by many [groups]).

12. Because of this, He himself will continue inheriting [the] Many and will keep on causing [the] Many to inherit, and thus will progressively divide the spoils of the strong folks, because His soul was transmitted into (or: delivered unto and committed to; surrendered and entrusted into the midst of) **death and He was considered and viewed** (or: counted and reckoned as being) **among the lawless folks. So He, Himself, took up and carried the failures** (deviations; errors sins; etc.) **of [the] Many, and through these acts of lawlessness** (or: because of the constructs that were without a law, and the additions that had no law) **He was transmitted, entrusted, committed, delivered, surrendered, handed over and given to [our] side.** (JM)

Chapter 20

1. Now on one of the sabbaths [note: Passover was one sabbath, and the seventh day of the week was another sabbath], **Mary the Magdalene is progressively coming early into the memorial tomb [area] – there yet being darkness** (or: dimness) **– and begins seeing and observing the stone, [already] having been lifted off and moved from the [opening of the] memorial tomb.**

I have not followed the convention of rendering the Greek word "**one**" as "first," and have not added "day" to the text, which is not in the MSS. Furthermore, I have not rendered the plural noun "**sabbaths**" as "week." The *Concordant Literal New Testament* also renders the phrase as I have it. The traditional renderings may be due to a desire to distance a Christian document from a Jewish concept of "sabbath." As indicated in the note inserted to my translation, as others have suggested, there may have been two sabbaths within the week of the crucifixion. We do not want to "strain at a gnat" with the rendering, but at the same time we do not want to gloss-over something that our author intended to communicate. Mary comes to the tomb early in the morning: "**there yet being darkness** (or: dimness)." And she did this "**on one of the sabbaths**" (a literal rendering of the Greek). Since Passover (the "other" sabbath, that week) was already past, this sabbath (where she is coming to the tomb) would have been early on the Last Day of the week (= our Saturday morning). The idea of a "Last Day" is significant in eschatology, and this Gospel is a Gospel of SIGNS.

The word *sabbath* is a transliteration into Greek from the Hebrew *sabbath*, and it means to cease, to rest, or a ceasing from work. The important thing to gain from all this is that Jesus was resurrected into a sabbath, for He had completed all His work. The writer of Hebrews picks up this theme in Heb. 3:11b, when quoting Ps. 95:7-11, which speaks about Israel wandering in the desert prior to entering into the Promised Land (a figure of a return to Paradise, the Garden in the LXX; recall Jesus' words in Lu. 23:43, "Today you will be with Me in Paradise" – i.e., the Garden). This passage in Heb. 3 speaks in terms of entering into rest (a figure for keeping sabbath), "**Now since** (or: if) **they shall proceed entering into My rest**…" The journey of humanity is from the Garden to the Garden. From the place of goodness, ease, well-being and rest, to a place of goodness, ease, well-being and Rest. We suggest reading Heb. 3 and 4, which allude to that time in Israel's history of their wandering in the wilderness, and then bring that theme into the new covenant, and the new Paradise, the New Sabbath. Heb. 4:4 refers to "**a certain place concerning the seventh, thus, 'And God rested in the seventh day**…'" Then, still in Heb. 4:

7. **again, He is determining a certain day, "Today!" In David He is saying, after so long a time, just as it has been said before,**
'**Today, if you would hear His voice, you would not be hardening your hearts.**' [Ps. 95:7-8]
8. **For you see, if Joshua caused them to rest, He would not after these things have continued speaking concerning another "Day."**
9. **Consequently, a keeping of a sabbath** (a state of rest) **is being left remaining for** (or: to; in; with) **God's people,**
10. **for the person entering into His rest also caused himself to rest from his own works** (actions; deeds), **just as God [did] from His own.**

11. **We should at once with diligence hasten, then, to enter into this rest** (or: that ceasing down [from work]; completely stopping), **so that one would not fall in the same example** (or: result of a pattern) **of incompliance** (or: stubbornness; disobedience; lack of conviction; [p46 reads: lack of faith and trust]).

We suggest that this is why it is important to note that the word "**sabbath**" was used in this verse.

The **darkness** (of the Law; of death) was still in process of fading away, and in the dimness, she "**begins seeing and observing the stone, [already] having been lifted off and moved from the [opening of the] memorial tomb.**" By first Light, on that SABBATH, the Resurrection was already history. In this Gospel, the Woman (Mary standing as a figure for the Bride of Christ, the called-out people; *cf* Eph. 5:29-32) was the first to see, and then to proclaim, that something unusual had happened.

2. **She therefore begins running** (or: racing) **and progressively going toward Simon Peter – and toward the** (or: that) **other disciple for whom Jesus was continuing feeling friendly affection and showing devotion – and [upon arriving] she is then saying to them, "They lifted up and carried the Lord** (or: the Master) **out of the memorial tomb, and we have not seen nor do we know where they put Him!"** [note: she says "we;" *cf* "the other Mary" in Matt. 28:1; also Mark 16:1 and Lu. 24:10]
3. **Peter and the** (or: that) **other disciple then went out, and were progressively coming into the memorial tomb [area].**

These two, Peter and "**the** (or: that) **other disciple,**" will be the central characters of His original twelve, in the rest of this Gospel. Our author uses a different verb (*phileō*) to describe Jesus' actions and feelings for this other disciple: "**for whom Jesus was continuing feeling friendly affection and showing devotion.**" Although Peter will be one of the leaders among the initial called-out folks, this other person was held in high regard by Jesus.

Mary misunderstood what happened – like so many others, down through the centuries. So the three of them (we see Mary there, again, in vs. 11, below) return to the tomb to check out her story.

4. **Now the two had been running** (or: racing) **alike** (the same; thus: together), **and yet the other disciple raced more quickly before Peter, and he came first into the memorial tomb [area],**
5. **and then, upon stooping down alongside, is seeing and continuing observing the swathing strips of linen bandages** (or: winding sheets) **still lying [there], though he did not enter.**

Mary is described as running, in vs. 2; now these two are running – quite understandably. Why is it important that "**the other disciple raced more quickly before Peter**"? Mary had seen the stone rolled away, but did not further check-out the tomb. The other disciple arrives at the tomb area before Peter and stoops down in order to see inside, but he did not enter. However, he observed "**the swathing strips of linen bandages** (or: winding sheets)." Our author is presenting a slow development of grasping the situation, among these three people. Why did he not enter? Did both he and Mary not wish to be ritually defiled (by being in a tomb), since they were still within the Feast of Unleavened Bread (Deut. 16:3)? Or was it significant that one of these witnesses did not go into what had passed (2 Cor. 5:17), and remained outside of the death-realm (the old covenant that was taken to the grave and buried in *sheol/hades*) as a witness in the New Day?

6. **Then Simon Peter, progressively following him, is now coming and he enters into the memorial tomb and continues intently gazing at the bandages** (strips of linen) **still lying [there],**
7. **also the handkerchief** (face-cloth; napkin) **– which had been upon His head – not lying with the linen bandages, but rather having been separately rolled** (or: folded) **in one place apart.**

Nothing would hold Peter back, he immediately entered, and was then followed by "**the other disciple**" (vs. 8). Recall that he had followed Jesus to the house of Annas (18:15, above), along with his buddy, "**the other disciple**" who was known by the chief priest. Peter is shown to be the leader of the pack, the point man. We find him leading disciples to return to their former life-way (fishing), in 21:3, below. But then he was the one that the risen Jesus instructed to feed His lambs and His sheep (21:15-16). He was also the first to take the Good News to the Gentiles (Acts 10).

It is interesting that there seem to be no words spoken, between them. It had to sink in slowly.

Why is it noted that "**the handkerchief** (face-cloth; napkin) – **which had been upon His head – [was] not lying with the linen bandages, but rather having been separately rolled** (or: folded) **in one place apart**"? Does this suggest action by a living person? Was this a SIGN that the Head was for a time separated from (in **one place apart** – 13:36, above) the rest of the (corporate) body?

8. **Then, therefore, the other disciple – the one coming first into the memorial tomb [area] – also entered, and saw with perception, and believed** (faithed-it; trusted; experienced faith).

Our author notes that "**the other disciple believed.**" He is the first one who is recorded as "faithing-in, trusting and experiencing faith." Nothing is said about Peter, here.

9. **You see, they had not seen and did not as yet discern** (perceive; know) **the Scripture that it is necessary for** (binding upon) **Him to rise up** (to stand up; to arise) **forth from out of the midst of dead ones.**

Peter, by the time of Acts 2:27, had later remembered Ps. 16:10,
> "For You will not leave My soul in *sheol* (*hades*; = the realm of the dead); neither will You allow Your Set-apart (Holy; Sacred) One to see (= experience) corruption (thorough ruin, rot and decay)."

As an aside: notice that *sheol/hades* was considered to be a place where bodies "rot and decay."

There is also Ps. 49:15, "But God will redeem my soul from the hand (= control) of *sheol* (*hades*), for He will TAKE me." Similarly is Hos. 13:14,
> "From the grip of the unseen (*sheol/hades*) I shall ransom them; from death I shall redeem them. Where are your plagues, Death? Where is your sting, Unseen (*sheol/hades*)?" (CVOT; parentheses added)

10. **Therefore the disciples went off** (or: came away) **again, toward themselves** (face-to-face with themselves; or: = to their own places and things; or: = met together, privately).

They did not join the group. They did not stay with Mary. Did they need to, by themselves, process what they had seen?

11. **Now Mary had taken a stand outside, facing the memorial tomb, and still stood there, continuously weeping and expressing strong inner emotions. As, then, she was continuing to weep, she stooped alongside [it] to peer into the tomb,**

Emotion had overcome her... where could she go, to deal with all that had transpired? She had "**taken a stand.**" Finally, she stooped alongside the tomb and through her tears, she peered in. Perhaps she is being held in place, to encounter the glory. Perhaps our author sets her as a third witness that looks into the realm of the past (the death realm of the Law – *cf* Rom. 7:9-11), pondering the symbology.

12. **and continues intently gazing at and carefully observing** (watching) **two agents** (or: messengers) **in brilliant, shining white** (as being in a bright light), **remaining sitting down – one toward the head, and one toward the feet – where the body of Jesus had been lying.**

[note the picture of this setting: within this set-apart chamber, the place where He had been lying corresponds to the ark of the covenant, with His blood on the mercy seat; the two agents are at the positions of the cherubim, at each end, sitting on the top of the ark]

The men had not experienced this encounter. She is the one who has "the divine appointment." We do not all experience the same things. Still being deeply moved, she "**continues intently gazing at and carefully observing** (watching) **two agents** (or: messengers)." If we saw two agents in brilliant, shining white, "**remaining sitting down**," we would probably continue observing, as well! As stated in the note that is attached to the text of this verse, the symbolism that can be seen in this setting is fascinating.

God met with Moses above the Mercy Seat, "between the cherubim" (Ex. 25:22). He meets with us in the death of Christ, and then in what follows. But this is more than a vision; there is interaction...

13. **And they are now saying to her, "Woman** (or: Dear lady; or: O married one), **why do you continue weeping?** [A*, D & others add: Whom are you presently seeking?]**" She says to them, "They took away my Lord** (or: Master; or: owner; the one having authority over me; or: my legal guardian and master of my house), **and I have not seen nor know where they put Him."**

They question her emotions, and the action that expresses them, in order to illicit a response from her. Notice that she does not fall on her face, but simply answers their question.

14. **Upon saying these things, she was suddenly turned around** (or: felt impelled to turn [and look]) **into the midst of** (or: unto) **the things behind [her] and continues intently gazing then carefully observing** (watching) **Jesus standing [there] – and she has not perceived, to be aware that it is Jesus.**

Notice the passive voice: something has acted upon her, for "**she was suddenly turned around**." On offer is a possible variation for the passive voice, "she felt impelled to turn." Either way, the Spirit was acting upon or influencing her. She [looks] into the midst of the situation that she now faces, and as in vs. 12, above, she "**continues intently gazing then carefully observing** (watching) **Jesus standing [there]**," but she has not perceived Who it is. He had left the grave clothes (wrapping) behind, in the tomb, so He must now be wearing something different. In 21:4, below, when Jesus is on the shore, the disciples did not recognize Him. Why not? Was it just that they had absolutely no expectation of seeing Him again? Or, did He actually now look different than when He had been with them before? Mk. 16:12 relates:

> "**Yet after these things, He was displayed in clear light and manifested – in a different form – to two of their group, when they continued walking along, being on their way journeying into [the] country**."

Did that occasion correspond to the incident on the Road to Emmaus, in Lu. 24:13-31, where they do not recognize Him until "their eyes were opened"? But back to our story...

15. **Jesus now says to her, "Woman** (or: Dear lady; or: O wife), **why do you continue weeping? Whom are you continuing to look for** (or: presently seeking)**?" That one, supposing** (or: imagining; thinking) **that He is the gardener, then says to Him, "Sir, if you yourself removed and carried Him away, tell me where you put Him, and I myself shall lift Him up and bear Him away."**

Jesus asks her the same question that was posed by the two agents who were within the tomb, but then He asks who it is that she is presently seeking. Why did He not directly identify Himself to her? Did she need time to overcome her emotions, and so He wanted to engage her mind? She answers Him by saying the same thing that she had said to Peter, and the "other" disciple (vs. 2, above). So she has obviously not changed her thinking – even after seeing the two agents "**in brilliant, shining white (as being in a bright light)**" – and in such an unusual setting! She had been "**supposing** (or: imagining;

thinking) **that He is the gardener**." Well, we might say that in one sense, she was right – He was the One who took care of the Garden. She thinks that Jesus is still dead, and wants to carry away His body from wherever He had been taken. What was her motive for wanting to do this? Was she wanting to hold on to the past, or just have His body in a place where she could visit it from time to time (as most everyone does who loses a loved one).

16. **Jesus then says to her, "Miriam** [other MSS: Mary]**!" Now, at once twisting herself about, spinning and springing to [Him]** (or: being [inwardly] turned), **that one** (= she) **is exclaiming to Him, in Hebrew, "Rabboni!" – which is normally translated and interpreted, "O Teacher** [D reads: My lord (or: master), my teacher]**!"**

Observe that it is her name – or else the way He said her name – that opened her ears and her eyes and brought recognition. If those that had been close to Him did not recognize Him, how could those outside of His close circle ever recognize Him? In Lu. 24:13ff. the risen Jesus was with the two disciples, talking with them as they walked along, and then entering for a meal with them, before "**their eyes were at once fully opened wide, and they experienced full recognition of Him**."

Consider the question of the kids (young goats) in the parable in Mat. 25:44, "When did we see You…?" He was now to be seen in even the least ones of His brothers (vs. 45). He had passed into another realm, but not one that was far away. He had entered our atmospheres, and people. So here, Miriam (Mary) whirled about and sprung on Him, in delighted surprise…

17. **Jesus then says to her, "Stop holding** (or: Do not continue hanging on and clinging to) **Me, for I have not yet stepped back up again so as to be ascended toward** (or: to; face to face with) **the** [other MSS: My] **Father. Now be going on your way toward** (or: to) **My brothers** (family, from the same womb; or: = fellow members), **and say to them [that I said], 'I am progressively stepping back up again** (or: now ascending) **toward My Father – even the Father of you folks – and My God: even [the] God of you people** [note: this would be Yahweh]**!'"**

He did not tell her not to touch Him (as, with the KJV), but to stop hanging on Him and clinging to Him. Apparently the transition back to the realm from which He had been sent had not yet been completed. We are not given any explanation about this. Perhaps it was simply that He was anxious to again see His Father's face, as He had before the incarnation – when, at the beginning of all this He was still face-to-face with the God (Jn. 1:1). Let the Spirit speak to you on this. When specifics are not specified, it is usually an invitation to ask the Lord about our questions.

Whatever the case, He had a mission for her – in which she would be the first to have seen the resurrected Jesus. She was to tell the rest of the Family that He was off to see their Dad.

18. **Miriam** [other MSS: Mary] **the Magdalene is progressively coming, repeatedly announcing** (reporting; giving the news; spreading the message) **to the disciples, "I have seen the Lord** (Master)**!" – and [that] He said these things to her.**

Can you picture her excitement? She is "**repeatedly announcing**" that she has seen the Lord, and then she functions as His prophet, giving them His message.

19. **Then, it being late in that day** (or: evening on that day) **– on one of the sabbaths – and the doors having been shut and locked** (or: barred) **where the disciples were gathered together, because of the fear of the Judeans** (= the Judean religious authorities), **Jesus came and suddenly stepped into the midst** (or: came into the midst and stood {or: took a stand}) **and is then saying to them, "Peace, from the Joining,** [or: = Shalom] **to you folks** (or, in our idiom: Hi)**!"**

Take note of the same phrase as in vs. 1, "**on one of the sabbaths**." What day it was seems to have been important to our author – as discussed, above.

Observe that the disciples had locked themselves apart, "**because of the fear of the Judeans** (= the Judean religious authorities)." We see, in the book of Acts, how Saul wanted to stamp out this movement. Most likely the disciples realized that the Judean elites would not stop with just killing Jesus, but would come after them, next. Their **fear** does not hold Jesus back from coming to them. Just as He suddenly disappeared, in Lu. 24:31, here He "**came and suddenly stepped into the midst** (or: came into the midst and stood {or: took a stand})." Notice the ways in which the second verb can be rendered: "stepped; stood; took a stand." Putting these together gives us a more detailed picture. The idea expressed in "took a stand" implies purpose, and a message: I'm here; I have arisen like I said I would: I am in charge and have taken control of heaven and of earth.

And now look at what He said to them: "**Peace, from the Joining,** [or: = Shalom] **to you folks** (or, in our idiom: Hi)." He repeats this (vs. 21, below), probably to overcome a possible stunned reaction within the disciples. He will say this to them, again, at His next visit (vs. 26). The coming of the Lord to us is to bring His peace and joining to us. This would also bring to their minds that He had spoken to them about their receiving His peace and joining, before (Jn. 14:27). My suggestion in correlating this greeting with our common saying, "Hi," is to convey the thought that He might have said this with a smile, and that He might have said it quietly – to help in overcoming their shock. But maybe not. He might have shouted it (He did have a sense of humor – and maybe this is why He said it again, more seriously (?) in vs. 21). Dan Kaplan reminded me of 1 Tim. 1:11 where Paul spoke of,

> "**the good news of** (or: the message of goodness and ease pertaining to) **the glory, reputation and assumed appearance of The Happy God.**"

20. **And upon saying this, He also pointed out** (or: shows) **His hands and side to them. Therefore, upon seeing** (or: at perceiving) **the Lord, the disciples rejoiced.**

So now He displayed the convincing evidence, and they let out a shout (or, laughed and wept at the same time – can we imagine the scene?). Our author does not present quite the same reaction that Mary had displayed – but, of course, they were men... (?) Actually, we do not know, and so we can only imagine.

21. **Then Jesus again said to them, "Peace** (or: Harmony and prosperity [= Shalom], from the Joining,) **to and for you folks! Correspondingly** (or: Accordingly; On the same level; In the same sphere; In line with) **as the Father has sent Me forth with a mission and as an Emissary** (Representative), **I Myself also am progressively** (or: repeatedly; or: one after another) **sending** (dispatching) **you folks."**

This is a heavy statement and commission that He gave to them. I say this because of the semantic range of the compound conjunction, "**Correspondingly as** (etc.)." He was sending, dispatching, THEM "**correspondingly as** the Father had sent [Him]." As an extension of Himself (termed by Paul as, "His body") they, through the Message (Logos) that they would spread, and the works of the Father that they would do, THEY (and then down through the centuries, WE) would be dispatched to bring His Salvation to the aggregate of humanity. Now let us consider the semantic range of *kata*, the first part of this conjunction:

> a) Accordingly as – in full accord with His work on the cross, and then His resurrection;
> b) On the same level as – it would be a work of God: "**God was existing within Christ** (God was and continued being centered in, and in union with [the] Anointed One) **progressively and completely transforming [the] aggregate of humanity** (or: world) **to be other [than it is]** (etc.)" (2 Cor. 5:19);
> c) In the same sphere as – in the sphere of the Spirit and the atmospheres (the heavens);
> d) In line with as – for the same purpose: the deliverance, salvation and rescue of humanity.

They, and we, are a continuation of the work of Christ. Acts 1:1 speaks "**concerning everything** (or: about all [the] things) **which Jesus both BEGAN to continuously do** (or: started to progressively make, construct and produce)..." Obad. 1:21 made a spectacular prophecy:

"Saviors (Deliverers) will come up in Mount Zion... and the kingdom (reign) will become Yahweh's." *Cf* Heb. 12:22-24

And Paul instructs us in 1 Cor. 3:9,

"**For we are God's fellow-workers** (or: we are co-workers of, and from, God, and are people who work together with God; we exist being workings-together who belong to God, synergies of God; attending deeds which are God)..."

No wonder Paul admonished folks to,

"**walk [your path]** (= behave; = live your life) **worthily pertaining to** (or: in a manner suitable to the value of) **the calling and invitation in regard to which you folks are called** (or: from which you were summoned)" (Eph. 4:1b).

The whole NT is full of the glory in which we are called to participate with Christ, being in a common existence with Him, as Paul said in 1 Cor. 1:9,

"**God [is] full of faith, trustworthy, loyal and faithful – through Whom you folks were called** (summoned) **into a common being of and existence from** (or: partnership, participation, fellowship, sharing and communion with) **His Son, Jesus Christ, our Lord.**"

The author of Heb. 3:1 says it this way:

"**Wherefore** (From which situation), **O set-apart and sacred brothers** (= consecrated fellow members from the same womb) – **common-holders** (partners; sharing possessors; joint-participants; associates; partaking members) **of an imposed-heavenly calling...**"

Jesus had quoted Isa. 61:1-2a as referring to Himself, in Lu. 4:16-21. This would also, therefore, apply to those that he was now sending forth. Isa. 61:2b has been rendered "a day of vengeance of our God, to comfort all who mourn," in the common translations. The LXX can give a different picture, since in the Greek the idea of vengeance is not necessarily there, and this extreme end of the semantic range of the word does not really fit what is said before it, or the context of what follows, in 61:3. The opposite end of this word's range of meaning is "restitution that is in the opposite position; a restitution, instead; a return, in its place; an award of being in the opposite position." One neutral meaning, from Liddell and Scott, is "a giving back, in turn." Also: "a repayment." From one of the prefixed prepositions of the word (*anti-apo-dosis*), the sense of "*apo-*" would give the reading "a giving away, instead (or: in its place)." My rendering of Isa. 61:2b is: "... **to call** (or: summon) **an accepted year of [the] LORD** (or: [Yahweh's] acceptable year) **and Day of Restitution in place of [what has been]** (or: a day which is a giving back, in turn; a day of an award of being in the opposite position; etc.) **to comfort, aid, encourage** (be the Paraclete to) **all the folks that are mourning.**" Note that this verse follows a proclamation of goodness, ease and well-being... healing... giving back sight to the blind, and what follows vs. 2 is,

"**glory instead of** (or: in place of -- *anti*) **ashes, an anointing of a good frame of mind** (an attitude of well-being; a disposition of ease) **in** (to; for) **the folks that are mourning; a corresponding** (or: commensurate) **garment of glory** (a good reputation and an assumed appearance) **instead of** (in place of -- *anti*) **a spirit of indifference** (or: an attitude of weariness). **And so they will continue being called 'generations of the Way pointed out** (or: from eschatological deliverance into covenant inclusion): **a result of [the] LORD'S planting into the midst of glory** (an assumed appearance which calls forth praise)" (vs. 3). *Cf* Isa. 11:1-5; Mat. 28:18

So we are now His emissaries and representatives, just as Jesus was. This is a serious call. In 17:18, above, He said to the Father,

"**Correspondingly** (or: Just; In the sphere; On the level) **as You sent Me into the System** (world of religious and political dominance; human aggregate) **as an Emissary, I Myself also send**

them forth as emissaries (representatives) **into the prevailing, organized system of the human aggregate.**"

22. **And after saying this, He suddenly blows on, and says to, them** (or: He breathes within [them], so as to inflate them [note: same verb as used in Gen. 2:7, LXX], and is saying to them), **"Receive a set-apart spirit!** (or: Get [the] Holy Spirit!; Take the Sacred Breath-effect!; or: Receive a sacred attitude).

He had just said that He was sending them correspondingly as the Father had sent Him. Recall what we read in 3:34, above,

> "**He Whom God sends forth with a mission** (dispatches as an Emissary and Representative) **habitually is speaking the gush-effects from God** (the results of the flows of God; God's declarations or sayings), **for God is habitually** (or: continuously) **giving the Spirit** (Breath; or: Attitude) **[and] not from out of a measure** (= not by a measured portion or limit; = without measure and without limitation)."

As the note in the text explains, this is a re-enactment of Gen. 2:7; it is a continuation of this lived-out parable that portrays Resurrection Life of the New Creation coming into the Body of the Second Humanity, the eschatos (last; final) Adam that will have its being in the reign (or: kingdom; realm) of the atmospheres (heavens). This was a prophecy of what would happen on the Day of Pentecost (Acts 2:1-4). His words are imparting both a directive and an empowerment. The rendering, "Take the Sacred Breath-effect," simply tells them to breathe-in the Spirit of the Christ-Life. It is like the new-born child, from above, taking its first breath in its new atmosphere. Since a person's spirit can also speak of that person's attitude, we can read this as saying, "Receive the Attitude of Christ."

Now they were being prepared for a mission – to carry on His work in the world. Receiving the set-apart Breath-effect was setting them apart for what He would lead them to do. The effect of His Breath was an anointing of them, which would fully happen in less than 50 days. Later, Paul would show how this was to be multiplied and passed on through the generations:

> "**And whatever you hear** (or: heard) **from my side through many witnesses, at once place** (or: set) **these things to the side for people full of faith** (or: deposit and commit these things, in trust for safekeeping, to trustworthy and loyal people; inculcate these things in reliable humans) – **whosoever will be competent** (or: adequately qualified) **to also teach others** (or: different folks)" (2 Tim. 2:2).

With this anointing and commissioning, what He said next would be the result of having received His Breath within them…

23. "**If you folks should send away** (dismiss; allow to depart; forgive; pardon; divorce; let go) **the mistakes** (sins; errors; failures; deviations) **of certain ones, they have been sent away for them** (or: have been and remain pardoned in them; let go for them; have been dismissed or divorced by them). **If you would continue holding fast and controlling** (or: should keep on grasping and exercising strength; or: can restrain, hinder, hold back) **those of certain ones, they have been and continue being held fast and controlled** (seized; grasped; restrained)."

Here He is explaining one aspect of what was meant by the commission to rule creation, in Gen. 1:26. He gave them authority in regard to "**the mistakes** (sins; errors; failures; deviations) **of certain ones**" – i.e., in regard to the folks with whom they are in relationship. He lays out two options, in this particular example:

> a) **If you folks should send away** (dismiss; allow to depart; forgive; pardon; divorce; let go) **the mistakes** (sins; etc.), **they have been sent away for them**,"
> > or: they have been and remain pardoned in them;
> > or: they have been let go for them;

351

or: they have been dismissed or divorced by them.

Take time to consider the semantic range of the verb "**send away**," in the parenthetical expansion that immediately follows this first rendering. Also consider the function of the pronoun "**them**," which is in the dative case, and thus on offer are the potential prepositions "for, in, or by." All of these renderings mean that those "certain folks" that encounter Christ's representatives can be released (rescued; saved) from the mistakes and sins that yet clung to them with negative effects upon their lives. They could be set free from the effects of their deviations from the Path and from the results of their errors and failures. What good news! But what does the second half of the verse mean?

> b) "**If you would continue holding fast and controlling** (or: should keep on grasping and exercising strength; or: can restrain, hinder, hold back) **those of certain ones, they have been and continue being held fast and controlled** (seized; grasped; restrained)."

What would it mean to "control, seize, grasp or restrain" someone's "**mistakes** (sins; errors; failures; deviations)"? Parents do this with children who are still under their supervision. Teachers have traditionally been able to do this, as well, by one means or another. Trainers do this for their trainees as they are learning new skills. We suggest that Christ's Spirit, dwelling within us and with Whom we are joined in union, empowers us to lovingly perform as paracletes to assist those who are making mistakes, etc. He used apocalyptic language to say the same thing, in Mat. 16:19,

> "**I will continue giving to you the keys** [note: = means of locking or unlocking] **which have their origin and source in the reign and activities of the heavens**
>> (or: which pertain to and have the characteristics of the kingdom of the heavens; or: which belong to the sovereignty from the atmospheres; or, as a genitive of apposition: the keys which are the sovereign influences of the heavens). **And so, whatever you can** (or: may; should; would) **bind upon the earth will continue being [something] having been bound, and still remaining bound, within the midst of the heavens** (or: in union with the atmospheres). **Also, whatever you can** (or: may; should; would) **loose upon the earth will continue being [something] having been loosed** (unbound; untied), **and remaining free of bonds, within the midst of the heavens** (or: in union with the atmospheres)." *Cf* Mat. 18:18

24. **Now Thomas – one from among the twelve, the one normally called, "Twin** (Didymus)**" – was not with them when Jesus came.**
25. **Consequently the other disciples kept telling him, "We have seen the Lord** (Master)**!" Yet he said to them, "Unless I can see and perceive the mark** (impression; print; exact replica) **of the blow of the nails** (spikes) **within His hands, and can thrust my finger into the impression** (or: mark) **of the nails and thrust my hand into His side, I can in no way** (or: I will by no means) **trust or believe."**

In our lived-out parable, Thomas stands for all of the rest of humanity that did not see the Christ Event; we all have trouble believing such a story – until the risen Christ reveals Himself to us. Kaplan has pointed out that what Jesus did for Thomas (vs. 27, below) was an example of His, and now our, mission – which He described in vs. 23, above. Thomas' lack of belief (vs. 25) was a missing of the goal. Jesus' visitation sent-away Thomas' unbelief and lack of faith. Jesus restrained and controlled his unbelief so that his eyes could be opened into the state of believing.

26. **And then, after eight days, His disciples** (students; apprentices) **were again indoors** (or: inside), **Thomas also with them. The door having been shut and locked** (bolted), **and being yet that way, Jesus is progressively coming, and then suddenly steps into the midst, and says, "Peace** [or: = Shalom] **of a Joining to, for and among you folks!"**

Why does our author mention "**eight days**"? In gematria, the number 8 signifies a new beginning. This may suggest the beginning of the New Creation. They were in the transition period between the ending of the old age and the beginning of the new one: the Age of the Messiah, in which we have eonian Life.

Notice their location: within a room with the door shut and locked. Once again, Jesus comes into their fear-ridden environment and announces, "**Peace of a Joining to, for and among you folks!**" His Breath-effect having been given to them (vs. 22, above), they were now joined as one body, having One Spirit, and One Life (Eph. 4:4-6). We are reminded, here, of Col. 1:20,

> "**THROUGH Him at once to transfer the all** (the whole; = all of existential creation), **away from a certain state to the level of another which is quite different**
>> (or: to change all things, bringing movement away from being down; to reconcile all things; to change everything from estrangement and alienation to friendship and harmony and move all), **INTO Him – making** (constructing; forming; creating) **Peace** (harmonious Joining) **through the blood of His cross** (execution stake/pole): **through Him, whether the things upon the earth** (or: land) **or the things within the atmospheres and heavens!**"

The coming of Peace, and a Joining, may be an allusion to the prophecy in Isa. 9:6-7,

> "**Because, you see, a disciplined and instructed young Child was** (or: is) **born to** (for; among) **us, and a Son was** (or: is) **given to** (for; among) **us, Whose beginning** (or: the rule and sovereignty of Whom) **came to be** (or: is birthed into existence) **upon His shoulder, and His Name is normally called 'Messenger** (or: Agent) **of Great Purpose, Counsel and Design. You see, it follows that I will bring Peace and a Joining upon the original and beginning people** (or: the rulers and sovereigns), **and Health by** (or: in; for; with; to) **Him** [with other MSS: His Name is repeatedly called Agent of Great Purpose (etc.), Wonderful Counsellor, Strong God, Authority from out of Being, Beginner and Ruler of Peace from the Joining, Father of the presently Impending Age]. **His beginning** (or: Rule and Sovereignty) **is great, and of His Peace and Joining there is no boundary or limit upon 'the throne of David,' that is to say, His reign** (kingship and sovereign influence or activity), **to set it up and keep it straight, and then to take hold of it and support it in union with the result of a decision** (centered in the effect of an evaluation and a judging) **and within rightwising** (a turning in the right direction) **of the Way pointed out, and eschatological deliverance of covenant participation – from now** (the present time) **and on into the midst of the Age** [of Messiah]. **The Zeal** (ferment of Spirit; ardent desire) **of the LORD of Hosts will progressively produce** (do; construct; perform; create) **these things**" (LXX, JM).

27. **Next, He is saying to Thomas, "Bring your finger here** (to this place) **and see** (or: perceive) **My hands; and bring your hand and thrust [it] into My side, and do not continue becoming unbelieving** (or: stop becoming without trust), **but to the contrary, believing** (trusting and faithful)**!**"

Notice the personal attention – and the knowing of someone's personal needs: "**Bring your finger here and see My hands; and bring your hand and thrust [it] into My side.**" He could be seen, and touched. He was not just a "spirit." He was the New Humanity. This all would have also been a witness for the rest of the folks gathered there. His message to them all was that they should be "**believing** (trusting and faithful)**!**"

28. **Thomas decidedly replies, and said to Him, "O my Lord** (or: Owner) **and my God!**" (or: "O my Master!," and, "O my God!"; or: = "My [Yahweh]!... even, my God!")

Thomas' eyes were now open, and He saw who Jesus was, and pronounces Him accordingly. This calls to mind 1 Tim. 1:17,

> "**So, to [the] King of The Ages** (or: eons; indefinite time periods), **to [the] incorruptible** (undecayable; unspoilable), **invisible** (unseen; not-able-to be seen) **One, to [the] only God** [some MSS add: wise; so: only wise God], **[be] honor** (value; worth) **and glory** (reputation which calls forth praise), **on into the ages** (or: indefinite time periods) **of the ages. It is so** (Amen)**!**
>> (or: Now in and by the King to Whom belongs the ages – in and by the imperishable, invisible [and] only One – in and by God [is] honor and glory, [leading] into the [most important] eons of the eons. So it is!)"

Thomas' acclamation calls to mind Pss. 73:25-26; 91:2; 118:28.

29. Jesus then says to him, "Because you have seen Me, you have trusted and believed! (or: ?) **Happy and blessed [are] those trusting and believing, although not also seeing or perceiving."**

Jesus' first reply to Thomas can be read either as a statement – perhaps with irony – or, it can be read as a question – like, "Really, because you have seen Me you are now trusting and believing?" Either reading leads us to the contrast of the next pronouncement. As Paul said in 2 Cor. 5:7,

> **"for we are habitually walking about** (= living our lives) **through faithfulness and trust** (or: faith; [His] loyalty) **not through perception of the appearance of external form."**

Then Peter reminds us,

> **"Whom not seeing** (or: perceiving), **you folks are continuously loving and accepting** (or: experiencing the urge for reunion); **into Whom at the present moment you folks are not constantly looking, yet are habitually believing** (or: continuously placing [your] trust and loyalty). **You folks are repeatedly rejoicing and being very happy in indescribable** (or: incapable of being spoken out) **joy which also exists having been made glorious**
>> (or: by unspeakable and glorified joy; in joy [that is] inexpressible and has made a notable reputation; with joy that is glorious beyond words, and which is filled with imagination and good opinion)" (1 Pet. 1:8).

30. To be sure (Indeed), **then, Jesus also performed** (made; did) **many other SIGNS in the sight and presence of the disciples – which things are not written within this scroll.**

Although not designated as such, the post-resurrection visitations were definitely SIGNS.

31. Yet these things have been written to the end that you folks can (or: may; would) **continue trusting and keep on believing** [other MSS: should come to trust and believe] **that** (or: should progressively be faithful, because) **Jesus is the Christ** (Anointed One), **God's Son** (or: the Son of The God and from God), **and so that in continually trusting, believing and being loyal, you can continuously hold** (would progressively have) **Life** [other MSS: eonian life (or: life from, and in the realm of, the Age; age-lasting life)] **within, in the midst of, in union with, and centered in, His Name.**

The whole point of relating the story, SIGNS and saying of Jesus was so that humanity could "**continuously hold Life.**" It was not written so that we might go one place, instead of another. "**His Name**" is a symbol for Him, His role as Messiah and the incarnated Logos, His character, His authority (from out of His Being) and for the new identity that we now have by being joined to Him (the Vine). We are now Him, in this world, as Paul declared:

> **"I was crucified together with Christ** [= the Messiah], **and thus it remains** (or: I have been jointly put on the execution stake in [the] Anointed One, and continue in this state)**... yet I continue living! [It is] no longer I, but it is Christ continuously living and alive within me!** (or: in the midst of, and in union with, me). **Now that which I, at the present moment, continue living within flesh** (= a physical body), **I am constantly living within [His] faithfulness – in and by that [faithfulness] which is the Son of God** (or: in union with the trust and confidence that is from God's Son; [with other MSS: in the faith and fidelity belonging to God and Christ]), **the One loving me and giving Himself over to another for the sake of me** (or: even transmitting Himself, over my [situation and condition]; or: also passing Himself along for me; committing and transferring Himself over me)" (Gal. 2:20).

As seen in the alternate rendering of the verb "**hold,**" this (like all life) is a progressive "having" of Life, as we branches continue growing and producing His Fruit. The remaining in the Vine happens as we are "**continually trusting, believing and being loyal**" – which is a function enabled by the Spirit of the Vine which is drawn up into, and through, us (in botany this process is called transpiration). It is also a process of transformation as we focus on the Lord's glory (2 Cor. 3:18), and as we are caused to be,

> "**turning [our] eyes away from other things and fixing them** (or: looking away) **into Jesus, the Inaugurator** (First Leader; Prime Author) **and Perfecter** (Finisher; the Bringer-to-maturity and fruition; He who purposes and accomplishes the destiny) **of the faith, trust, confidence and loyal allegiance**" (Heb. 12:2a).

We have an Epilogue, in the next chapter, which moves the story beyond the "lived-out" Two Gardens Parable, and which will point to the future of God's reign which Jesus established within His followers, and that they would take to the rest of the world, in the years to come, later to be expanded in the following centuries. We will find that the Epilogue is also filled with symbolism.

Chapter 21

1. **After these things, Jesus at one point manifested Himself** (or: displays and discloses Himself; causes Himself to be seen in clear light) **again to the disciples, upon [the shore] of Lake** (or: the Sea of) **Tiberias. Now He manifested** (or: manifests) **in this way:**
2. **Simon Peter, Thomas – the one normally being called "the Twin"** (Didymus), **Nathaniel – the one from Cana of the Galilee [area], the [sons] of Zebedee and two others of His disciples, had been continuing being together, in the same place.**

It is interesting that the setting of this manifestation of the risen Jesus is not in Jerusalem, but in Galilee. The disciples had gone home. The name Lake Tiberias is the Roman designation, while the popular name was "the Sea of Galilee." According to Mat. 4:15, this was considered to be a Gentile territory. Mat. 28:10 (and Mk. 16:7 is similar) records Jesus telling the two women,

> "**Stop fearing** (or: Do not continue being made to fear). **Continue leading the way and bring things under control as you go. Immediately report back to My brothers** (folks from the same womb; = family) **so that they would go off unto the Galilee [district] – and there** (in that area) **they will repeatedly see Me.**"

In Mat. 28:19, Jesus instruct the disciples: "**while going on your way, instruct and make disciples** (at some point enlist students and apprentices) **of all the ethnic multitudes** (the pagans; the Gentiles; the nations; the non-Israelites)…" By including this encounter with Jesus by the Sea of Tiberias, perhaps our author is pointing toward the mission to the Gentiles, rather than focusing on the later happenings in Jerusalem, which Acts will record through Luke.

Luke's Gospel ended with the disciples being sent back into Jerusalem, to wait for the Day of Pentecost, and then the book of Acts takes up their activities as being based from that city. Here, in vs. 19, below, He simply tells Peter to follow Him (after, in vs. 18, signifying the kind of death that Peter would first live, and then finally experience). In contrast to Luke's Gospel, our author makes no mention of Jerusalem or of a directive to go there. The disclosure of Himself to them in Jerusalem (Lu.24:36) has Him asking them for food, and they give Him some fish to eat. In vs. 9, below, He has cooked fish on the fire, as they disembark with their load of fish. This Epilogue has a different emphasis, and a different story to tell.

This episode will involve six disciples: Peter, Thomas, Jacob (James) and John (those were "**the [sons] of Zebedee**") and "**two others of His disciples**." Did our author have a reason for not naming these "two others"? We conclude that one of these two is highlighted by Peter, in vs. 20, when he focuses on "**the disciple whom Jesus was loving and accepting, who also leaned back upon His chest during supper.**" We will consider this man again, below, and will also note that this same person is tagged by this same description, in vs. 7a, below. Why are Peter and this unnamed disciple the main characters of this story – other than Jesus, of course? They were the same two that were involved in the discovery of the empty tomb (20:1-9, above). Tradition has assumed this "other" disciple to be the author of this Gospel, and this may well be the case. But take note that while tradition has John as being the author,

355

John is "named" here, through the name of his father, Zebedee. So John would not logically be one of those two termed "**others of His disciples**."

3. **Simon Peter is then saying to them, "I am under way** (departing; going off) **to continue my habit of fishing!" They are then saying to him, "As for us, we are also coming together with you!" So out they went and stepped straight into the boat** (or: and immediately boarded the ship). **But during** (or: within) **that night, they caught nothing.**

In this period, following Jesus' resurrection, Peter had returned to his former life as a fisherman. But recall that Jesus had called him to be "a fisher of men" (Mat. 4:19). Their old occupation had been work that was done in the night – before the coming of the Day.

4. **Now already, with [the] progressive birthing of morning coming to be, Jesus [comes] into the seashore** (or: unto the beach) **[and] stands [there]. The disciples, however** (or: of course), **had not clearly seen or perceived, so as to know that it is Jesus.**

As with Mary, at the tomb, they could not yet "**clearly see or perceive**," and therefore they did not know that Jesus had suddenly come to stand on the shore. He has come to meet them as they had returned, briefly, to the "sea of humanity" – here figured by the activities of their former life. The resurrected Jesus now faces the aggregate of humanity (the sea), and His disciples who had been toiling in the darkness, while passing over the darkness of the waters (a picture of humanity, and of the first creation). He has taken a stand, and is watching over them, as a Father over His children, at the dawning of the new creation…

5. **Jesus then says to them, "Lads** (or: Fellows), **are you not holding anything eatable** (or: Boys, do you have nothing, such as fish, to add to your bread)**?" They considered, and replied to Him, "No."**
6. **So He said to them, "You men cast the net into the areas at the right of the boat... and you will be finding [some]." Therefore, they cast [it], and were no longer having the strength to draw** (or: drag; tug) **it away from the great number of fish** (or: because of the multitude of the fishes).

Notice that the question which He asks in vs. 5 is posed with a negative conclusion. He could probably tell that their boat was not riding low from the weight of a catch, or that they were not coming in dragging the net behind them. Either way, or by His discernment, He knew that they had nothing.

Obviously, they did not recognize His voice. They were behaving as if they were not His sheep. In asking them if their boat is "**holding anything eatable**," this could be an allusion to His feeding the multitudes with bread and fish – a time when they had nothing to offer the multitudes. Now, they have found that their own efforts, and their old way of life, were fruitless. They need His Word to direct them. His instructions would cause them to cast their nets in **the right places** in order to have a huge catch of people from the sea of humanity. When they obeyed His directions, they would have success – so much so that they would not of their own strength be able to handle all whom they were dragging into the kingdom. This incident was another SIGN. In the way that this occurrence is described, we suspect that our author has 12:32, above, in mind: they were figuratively dragging the whole aggregate of the sea unto Jesus, in their net. We will observe the idea of fullness, or the whole, in the gematria of vs. 11, below. Jesus used them to bring in a "**great number, a multitude.**" This would be the character of their ministries. It is when we are being led by the Spirit (Rom. 8:14) that we are living in the realm of His reign, and this is where, when we seek, we will "**be finding**" (Mat. 7:7). This is both the secret, and a key, of His kingdom.

7. **Then, that disciple whom Jesus was loving says to Peter, "It is the Lord** (or: He is the Master)!**" On hearing that it is the Lord, Simon Peter at once put on his fisherman's shirt** (an outer garment),

tucking it under his girdle – for he was stripped for work (partially clad; naked, i.e., not having the "outer garment" on) – **and threw himself** (plunged) **into the lake** (or: sea).

It is this special, no-name disciple to whom it is revealed that "**It is the Lord.**" When Peter hears this, he abandons the fish and prepares to go to be with the Lord. He does not even wait for the boat to come to shore. Is his dawning his outer garment an allusion to Adam and Eve clothing themselves with fig leaves? Is our author saying that Peter had cast off the mantle of his call, but now he wants to distance himself from that decision and seeks to hide among the aggregate of humanity as his first parent hid among the trees in Eden? Was this a recognition that he had failed to believe, and to be faithful? Is the author saying that Peter is now ready to "**throw himself**" into the work of the Lord?

8. **Yet the other disciples came in the** [Concordant text adds: other] **little boat – for they were not far from land, in fact, about three hundred feet** (two hundred cubits) **away – progressively dragging in the net of fish** (or: which had the fishes).

We do not know how far the first boat was from shore, when Peter plunged into the water, but assuming that each boat had one end of the net, Peter would have had a ways to swim in order to reach the shore. Did he not want to be one of the first to greet Jesus, when the boat that he was in reached land? Endeavoring to recreate the scene through our imagination adds depth to understanding why these little details are in the text, but not explained. Such was the character of most of Jesus' parables. We must, of course, hold our mental constructions lightly, but the Spirit can use our ponderings to enlighten our minds and hearts.

9. **Then, as they stepped off** (disembarked) **onto land, they continued staring** (looking) **at a charcoal fire lying there with cooked fish** (food fish) **still lying upon [it], and bread.**

What were they thinking, as they "**continued staring**"? The first thought may have been, "Where did He get the fish?" But then their memories would go to the feeding of bread and fish to five thousand men, plus women and children (Mat. 14:15-21), following which Jesus sent the disciples off to sea, in a boat, and Jesus was left to send the multitudes home and then ascended into a mountain (vss. 22-23). Now Jesus offers them breakfast (vs. 12, below). That feeding in Mat. 14 was at the end of the day (a figure of the last part of the old age and of the old covenant). Here it is at the beginning of a new Day (a figure of the new age and the new covenant), and the fish are fresh, while in the Matthew account they would have been dried (it was a desert place). And now they had an abundance of food to share with others.

10. **Jesus is then saying to them, "Bring away some of the fish** (food fish) **which you just now caught."**

They would continue cooking, for a charcoal fire on the beach would only cook a few fish at a time, and those six men would have had a great hunger, after a whole night of toiling. Nights (or days) of hard toil usually produce a good appetite. They had first followed their human thinking, which led to weariness and no success. Peter, Jacob (James) and John had experienced a similar night just before the day that Jesus called them to follow Him (Lu. 5:5). Following Jesus' directions to once again "launch out into the deep" produced similar results then (vss. 6-9) as seen here. We also observe that Peter had a corresponding reaction at that point (Lu. 5:8) where he said,

> "**Now Simon Peter seeing [this], fell down at the knees of Jesus, while saying, "Go out, away from me, O Sir** (or: Lord), **because I am a man with the qualities of an outcast** (a man characterized by failure; a missing-the-target male; a sinful man; an adult male full of error, deviations and mistakes)!"

Was it recollection of this incident that caused Peter to plunge into the sea, here?

We also observe that at this point of our story Jesus used the work of the disciples, as well as what He had brought to breakfast, so the meal was a joint effort, but one that was directed by Jesus. Fellowship meals would be integral to the called-out communities, as they were one-after-another established through the witness of the sent-forth folks.

11. **Simon Peter therefore went back** (or: stepped up) **and dragged ashore** (onto land) **the net, filled and distended with one hundred fifty-three large** (or: big) **fish. And yet, [with there] being so many of them, the net was not split** (torn; rent).

A.E. Harvey suggests that the number 153 is arrived at by adding all the consecutive numbers from 1 to 17. This number is 10 + 7, and he points out that, "ten and seven were each numbers signifying a perfect whole. By such reasoning, 153 could have been understood to stand as a symbol for the whole of something (the whole of mankind, or the whole of the church)" (*The New English Bible Companion to the New Testament*, Oxford University Press, 1970 p 393). We realize that other interpretations could be assigned to this enigmatic number, but as noted above, 12:32 spoke of dragging **all** of **humanity** to Christ, so we feel that Harvey may have been on the right track.

It is also significant that when fishing for men is done under the direction of Jesus, our **nets** will **not** have **splits**. We suggest that **the net** is a metaphor for the work of Jesus through the called-out, covenant communities. Kaplan sees the net as the Logos of the Good News. That these were all "**large fish**" suggests that there will be substance and a "weight" of glory in those who are drug to Jesus. We could also see how principalities and powers of society would be subdued and brought to the obedience of Christ. Kaplan views this picture as an allusion to Gen. 1:26, where it speak of humans exercising "dominion" – over the "fish" (those of the "sea" of humanity). Recall how Paul described himself as having been "apprehended" by Christ (Phil. 3:12), and we saw that described in Acts 9.

12. **Jesus says to them, "Come folks! Have breakfast!" Now not one of the disciples was daring to inquire of Him, "You... who are You?" – having seen to perceive and so being aware and knowing that it is the Lord** (or: He is the Master).

The fact that our author states that they were not "**daring to inquire of Him, 'You... who are You?'**" suggests their initial uncertainty about who He was, but had come to the awestruck and bewildered conclusion of who He was from "**having seen to perceive and so being aware and knowing that it is the Lord** (or: He is the Master)." Notice that they are not described as falling on their faces, and He once again takes the position of being their attending Servant, having fixed breakfast for them. No "Halleluiah Chorus," no suggestion of praise or worship in this scene. They seem to have been in shock...

13. **Jesus is then coming and proceeds taking the bread, and likewise the fish, and continues presently giving [it] to them.**

Jesus is not recorded as giving them any explanation. It is as though He expects them to assume that His appearance to them is something normal, being nothing out of the ordinary. He is thoughtful of their need for sustenance, and functions as a caring Host. Bread and fish – the ordinary fare of the day. No wine or candles; He is welcoming them to His home. He provides traditional Judean hospitality.

Many interpreters want to see this as pointing to the ritual that institutional Christianity came to practice as being "the Lord's Supper," or, "the Eucharist," that is something magical, or at least, spiritually significant. We do think that this pointed both directions: back to the table fellowship (ordinary meals) that He had experienced with them, and with others who hosted Him, during His previous ministry while yet being under the old covenant, and at the same time pointing ahead, to the table fellowship (ordinary meals) that the called-out covenant communities would host – until this practice degenerated into a ceremony of a spot of grape juice (or, wine) and a cracker. The main idea that Jesus' actions were picturing was that of loving hospitality – not dissimilar to "foot washing." It speaks to caring for the needs of others – on all levels of our existence, here.

14. **Now this [is] already [the] third [time** (situation) **in which] Jesus was manifested** (was displayed in clear light) **to** (or: for; among) **the disciples [after; since] being raised up from out of the midst of dead folks.**

The author's specification that this was a/[the] "**third [time** (situation)**]**" can be taken in many directions, but we will suggest the pattern set by the Tabernacle, and then the Temple: the first time would have correlated to the "out court" where the ordinary Israelite could enter for the ritual sacrifices; the second time would correlate to the "holy place" that could only be accessed by the priests, and spoke of His body, or covenant communities, being "the Light of the world" (Acts 2:3-4; Rev. 1:20b); and this third time correlating to the "holy of holies" (the "third heaven") of God's manifested Presence, to where He had been "**raised up from out of the midst of dead folks**" (Eph. 2:6; Heb. 12:22-24). This is the place where (on the third major Feast of Israel: Tabernacles) in the Day of Atonement He entered the "heavenly" Temple (US) and sprinkled our hearts with His Life (Heb. chapter 9, and 10:19-22). Kaplan points us to Paul coming a "third time" to Corinth, and citing the Torah, in 1 Cor. 13:1,

> "**I am habitually coming to you folks – this third time, now!**
>> '**Upon [the] mouth of two witnesses – and of three – every effect of a flow** (gush-effect; matter; declaration; saying) **will continue being made to stand.**'" [Deut. 19:15]

15. **Then, when they had finished breakfast, Jesus says to Simon Peter, "Simon of John** [other MSS: Jonah], **are you continuously loving Me** (accepting Me without restriction; fully giving Yourself to Me; urging toward union with Me) **more than these things** (or: = more than you love these folks; or: more than these folks love Me; or: more than these fish)?"
He [Peter] says to Him, "Yes, Lord (Master), **You, Yourself, have seen and know that I am fond of** (or: like) **You and am Your friend."**

The rest of this "third time/occasion" is given to an intimate, possibly private (possibly public), conversation between Jesus and Peter, where Jesus interviews Peter about Peter's relationship with Jesus. There is no discussion about faith or belief, or even loyalty. No, it is all about "**loving Jesus.**" This can take us back to Jn. 5:42 and then, especially, 8:42,

> "**If God were your Father, you would have been, and continued, loving and urging toward union with** (or: progressively giving yourselves fully to) **Me.**"

The format of Jesus' questions to Peter, and then Jesus' instruction, following each of Peter's answers, can be seen in 14:15, above,

> "**If you folks are habitually loving and accepting Me** (or, as a subjunctive: would continue seeking union with, and fully giving yourselves to, Me), **you folks WILL continue observing** [other MSS, subjunctive: you folks can or should observe (or: note and keep watch over; guard and preserve; keep in view; hold in custody); other MSS, the imperative: Keep in view and take note of] **My implanted goals** (impartations of the finished product within; inward directives; interior purposes)."

Jesus seems to be wanting Peter to take an assessment of where his heart is. He presumes that Peter loves Him, but He is asking Peter to prioritize his values: are you loving Me:

> a) more than you love these folks?
> b) more than these folks love Me?
> c) more than these fish – i.e., more than the life of a fisherman?

Peter neither answers His question(s), nor does he respond in the same sphere as Jesus' question. We need not try to psychoanalyze Peter, by his response. Perhaps he had never thought on the level that Jesus was now addressing him. Perhaps he was not ready to make the commitment that was implicated by Jesus' question. Remember, our author is not simply presenting a biography of Peter's spiritual or ethical development; his readers (and WE) are being addressed in this entire interview. This is a teaching point. The question being asked is: Are you Jesus' disciple?

Jesus does not berate Peter. He simply accepts Peter's response, and then imparts a directive to him and implants in him His goal for him. It is as though Jesus said, "Well, if you like Me, and if I am your Friend, then..."

He [Jesus] says to him, "As a herdsman, be habitually feeding (or: grazing) **and tending My young lambs!"**

Jesus is revealing to Peter (and to his listeners/readers) that now Peter is to be a "good shepherd." It is early on, in this new age, so all those who would come under Peter's care would be "**young lambs**." But more than this, He is reminding Peter of what He had previously instructed:
> "**allow the young children to come toward Me, for you see, the reign and kingdom of the heavens** (or: = the sovereignty of this atmosphere) **belongs to and is comprised of such folks as these**" (Mat. 19:14).

Back then, Jesus may have been referring to children that are literally young, or metaphorically, to those folks that were new to the kingdom. And of what was this shepherding to consist? Teaching them to have fantastic spiritual experiences? No. "**Feeding** (or: graze) **and tend**" them. Paul found the folks at Corinth as being rich in spiritual experiences and abilities, and yet, in 1 Cor. 3, he said:
> "**And yet I myself, brothers, was not able to speak to you folks as to spiritual people** (= having the effect of the Breath; led by the Spirit/Attitude), **but to the contrary as to fleshly folks** (= people of flesh, being focused thereon; = as "natural" people, unaffected by the Breath/Spirit) – **as to infants in Christ** (or: babies/adolescents in Anointing). **I gave you folks milk to drink, not solid food**..." (vss. 1-2a).

In Heb. 5 a similar admonition is given:
> 12. **For also, being indebted** (or: obligated) **to be teachers, because of the time [gone by], you again have a need of someone to be teaching you folks the elementary things** (or: fundamental principles; rudiments and rules) **of the beginning of the brief spoken words** (or: which are the principle of the short thoughts; concerning the Beginning, from the little messages) **of and from God, and so you have become folks having need of milk, and not solid food.**
> 13. **For everyone partaking** (sharing in) **milk [is] untried** (inexperienced) **pertaining to [the] WORD of the Way pointed out** (from the message of fair and equitable dealing or an idea about rightwised relationships; also: = in regard to the idea of, and the reason derived from, covenant membership), **for he is a babe** (a non-speaking infant, or one who is still childish and unfit to bear weapons).

Such "**young lambs**" need to be fed the "**WORD of the Way pointed out**," once they stop nursing. Kaplan points out that Jesus said, "**My young lambs**," above, and "**My sheep**," below: the point being that they are HIS, and do not belong to "people." They do not belong to any human System or religious organization – they are His body.

16. **Again, a second [time], He continues, saying to him, "Simon of John** [or: Jonah], **are you continuously loving Me** (is your whole being progressively driving toward accepting union with Me)**?"** **He [Peter] says to Him, "Yes, Lord** (Master), **You, Yourself, have seen and know that I am fond of** (or: like) **You and am Your friend."**

How long did Jesus wait, before asking this second question? There is no way to know, but this time it is a shorter question. Peter's answer is the same – he still did not say, "I continue loving You and am progressively driving toward accepting union with You." Was Peter missing the point, or was his mind still in a daze? Was there fear of such deep commitment? Nonetheless, Peter remains constant in his affirmation of friendship.

He [Jesus] says to him, "Constantly shepherd (herd for grazing; = lead, protect, care for, nourish) **My sheep** [other MSS: small sheep]!"

The critical texts have "**sheep**" here, rather than "**young lambs**" as in the previous verse. Peter's responsibility is for the entire flock. Everyone needs food, care and protection. The verb that Jesus used here is more general and refers to all the duties of a **shepherd**. Here, leadership, protection and rescue (Lu. 15:4-5), as well as provision of food, expand Peter's calling.

17. **"Simon of John** [or: Jonah]**," He continues, a third [time] saying to him, "Do you like Me and are you habitually My friend, having fondness and affection for Me?"**

This third question meets Peter on the level of Peter's confession. We observe, below, that Peter was grieved that Jesus had here used the more general word of friendship, fondness and affection, instead of referring to *agapē* as He had in the previous two questions. God will come down to our level to meet us where we are.

Peter was made to grieve and be sad and sorry, because He said to him, the third [time], "Are you habitually My friend, liking and having fondness and affection for Me?" So he said to Him, "O Lord, You, Yourself, have seen and know all things and all humans. YOU continue knowing by progressive intimate experience and insight that I like You and continue as a friend with affection and fondness for You."

Peter could only respond from where he was.

Jesus says to him, "As a herdsman, be habitually feeding (or: grazing) **and tending My sheep** [other MSS: small sheep]!

Jesus ends this triad with the same instructions as He had with the first one. We wonder if this group of three questions-responses-directives are meant to correspond to this third manifestation of Himself to them (vs. 14, above). Does this set a pattern for us? Can we discern the Blueprint? Will He repeatedly raise inner questions to keep us focused on "the main things"? Will He repeatedly direct our attentions to the lambs and the sheep? Most of us can answer in the affirmative to these rhetorical questions. He does. Kaplan has observed how gently Jesus dealt with Peter as He draws him back to his calling. This personal attention would have been healing and restorative to Peter, demonstrating full acceptance of Peter as He brings him back on track, affirming his calling and establishing his position in the called-out communities. This was a time of transition for Peter.

18. **"Most assuredly** (Amen, amen) **I say to you** [note: singular; = Peter], **when you were younger, you used to clothe and gird yourself, and you habitually walked around where you were consecutively setting your will** (intending; purposing). **Yet whenever you may grow old and decrepit, you will proceed stretching out your hands, and another will continue clothing and girding you, and will proceed carrying you where you are not intending** (willing)."

We find it interesting that, in the records left to us, Peter is the only disciple who received a personal prophecy concerning his older years. But, as we perceive to be the case of this entire episode, this is very likely meant to be a word for most of us. Kaplan notes that it pointed Peter to a cruciform life (Mat. 16:24-25), a death to the old Adam "self" that he (and WE) will walk out. When Peter "**was younger**" can refer to the early days of following Jesus, but Jesus is pointing to when he would be an elder in the called-out communities. Now Peter would follow God's will, not his own, which would be a "death" that Peter would live. Following the Pattern (Blueprint) that Jesus lived out would insure for Peter that he would be a true shepherd, and not a hireling.

19. Now He said this showing by a SIGN (or: signifying) **by what sort of death he [Peter] will continue bringing glory** (a manifestation which calls forth praise, recognition, and a good reputation) **to God** (or: will proceed to present an assumed appearance for, and with, God). **And after saying this, He continues in saying to him, "Continue following Me!"**

Jesus' prophecy for Peter was a SIGN. He was telling Peter that he would be faithful to the end of his life, and then his death would be a manifestation of God's glory, just as the death of Jesus was. The verb **"bring glory to"** or "present an assumed appearance for, and with" is ambiguous, and thus on offer are the variations on the theme and semantic range of the idea of "glory." We surmise that the core idea of Jesus' statement is that Peter's mode of death will manifest God's presence just as Jesus' death had done. Folks will see God in the incident. What a personal destiny to have! And THAT is what it will mean for Peter to continue following Jesus. But also, regardless of knowing that an unwanted mode of death may await him, the Lord still imparts Peter's destiny as being that of continuously following Jesus. Following involves watching and observing where He is going, and this equates to being led by His Spirit (Rom. 8:14).

20. But Peter, being turned around, continues looking at the disciple progressively following along behind – [the one] whom Jesus was loving and accepting, who also leaned back upon His chest during supper and said to Him, "O Lord, who is the one transferring, committing and giving You over?"
21. Peter, therefore, seeing and perceiving this one, says to Jesus, "Lord (Master), **now** (or: but) **what [of] this man?"**

We get the picture, from vs. 20a, that Jesus and Peter must have been walking as they were talking, for Peter turns back and is "**looking at the disciple progressively following along behind**." Then our author gives an expanded description of to whom Peter is referring, in vs. 21. It is our same "no-name" disciple that is brought back into this episode. What is the purpose of Peter's question? Is he wondering if this other disciple will have a similar end as the one which Jesus had prophesied about Peter? How Jesus answers him, in the next verse, seems to show that this was how Jesus took his question. It is human nature to want to know about other people, and to compare their lives to ours.

22. Jesus then says to him, "If I am intending (willing; purposing) **him to continue remaining until I am progressively coming** (or: from time-to-time coming and going), **what [is it] to you** (or: what [effect comes] toward you)? **As for you, you be habitually following Me!"**

Here is the point of this exchange, and it is instruction for all of us who would wonder about other people's lives: "**What [is it] to you** (or: what [effect comes] toward you)?" Jesus gave Peter an ambiguous response: "**If I am intending** (willing; purposing)…" The message to our author's listeners, and to us, is, "**be habitually following [Jesus]**."

Observe the ambiguity of the present tense (continual, repeated or progressive action) of the verb, which means either "to come" or "to go" (*erchomai*). As to what Jesus might have meant, consider Rev. 2:1, where He referred to Himself as, "**the One continuously walking about within the midst of the seven golden lampstands** (i.e., called-out communities – Rev. 1:20b)." In the letters to these communities (Rev. 2 and 3), He spoke of visiting them with correction or judgment, as needed.

Jesus used the emphatic personal pronoun, when addressing Peter: "**As for you, you**…" This entire dialogue is meant for all who heard this Gospel, and for all who would read it. We all have our own paths to walk, and lives to live, and we should keep our eyes upon Christ, not on others (2 Cor. 12:10). Do we love Him, and are we progressively urging toward greater union with Him? Or, are we even His friends? Then perform as shepherds (or, as Paul would say, "Be paracletes") and care for His flocks. Feed them; nourish them; heal them; protect them; teach them; rescue them; lead them.

23. Then this word (saying; message; idea) **went forth unto** (or: into the midst of) **the brothers** (= fellow believers; members of the group) – **that that disciple continues not dying off. Yet Jesus did not say to him that he continues not dying off, but rather, "If I am intending** (willing; purposing) **him to continue remaining until I am progressively coming, what [is it; effect comes] to you?"**

We observe that, within the very immediate context, Jesus' words were misunderstood or taken to mean more than was said. We still read many extraneous things into the ancient texts. Kaplan observed the repeated emphasis on what Jesus "intends, wills and purposes" (vss. 18, 19, 22 and 23). One consideration, regarding the identity of this unnamed disciple, is that in Mk. 10:35-39, Jesus was addressing both sons of Zebedee (James and John), in which vs. 39 prophesies that they BOTH,

"**will progressively drink the cup which I, Myself, am now progressively drinking, and you will also be progressively immersed in** (or: baptized with) **the immersion** (baptism) **which I, Myself, am now progressively being immersed, unto saturation** (baptized)."

James would be martyred (Acts 12:2). We have no certain record about John.

24. This is the disciple: even the one constantly witnessing and testifying about these things, even the one writing these things – and we have seen and know that his witness (testimony) **is true** (genuine; real).

There is even ambiguity with this "explanatory" statement. It has been assumed that our author is referring to himself being "the disciple that Jesus was loving," but our author can be indicating that this "other disciple" also wrote these things that our present author is recording, and even expanding upon. Notice how he states this: "**And we have seen and know that his witness** (testimony) **is true**" – speaking about this disciple in the third person, as if of someone else. This being said, we notice that Jesus often spoke of Himself in the third person. It must not be of great importance, since our author remains anonymous, just as he speaks anonymously about this particular disciple. Keep in mind that Luke opened his Gospel, saying,

1. **Since it is admittedly true – and considering – that many people put their hand to and undertook to compile, collate and compose** (or: arrange back again and rehearse) **by** (or: for) **themselves a narrative that leads throughout the matters and facts** (the results and effects of events, practices, business, affairs and what has been done) **concerning the things having been brought to full measure** (or: having been fully accomplished) **among us,**
2. **just and correspondingly as the original** (the from [the] beginning) **eyewitnesses** (= personal examiners) **and assistants** (deputies and subordinates – "under-rowers," or, those under orders) **of the Word** (message; idea; Logos; Reason; thought; patterned flow, conveyance and transfer of Meaning-bearing Information) **gave, and transmit, [them] over to us** (or: pass along, commended and commit [them] among us),
3. **it seems [necessary; important; a good idea] also for** (or: to) **me – having followed alongside and accompanied closely from the earlier period – to write…**

Unfortunately, most of what those "many people" wrote is now lost to us. But this does not stop the scholars from such endeavors as the "Q theory" (source theory) involved with the Synoptic Gospels. And… it does not prevent others of us from having suspicions about the authorship of our present Gospel which we have been studying, and observing. :) Enjoy reading, and listening. It is full of Life.

25. Now there are also many other things which Jesus did (performed; made; created; produced), **which things – if ever it could be progressively written, one by one** (= in full detail) – **I am imagining** (or: continue evaluating and supposing) **that not even the organized System** (world; society at large; arranged order; cosmos) **itself will [be able] to contain the scrolls being constantly written.**

We have a bit of rhetorical hyperbole in this statement, but his point is well made. It affirms to us that what has been included in the Gospel had purpose with a view to the story that our author has presented for us. It had a "beginning," but the end of this particular story is open-ended, and anticipates another beginning, inviting us to step through the Door and into the New Creation of which other NT writers will "begin" to write. Kaplan observes that Christ's life is a living book, and throughout the centuries people have continued writing about Him (this present book included). What was included in this Gospel was not just "history," or even a biography of Jesus. It has a story to tell, and elements from the life and teachings of Jesus have been used to present this story. This Epilogue gives us a succinct summary: Love Jesus, follow Him, and care for others. It is about this life, not the "after-life." In this, it continues ever relevant and contemporary – it applies throughout the ages, for you see, "**Jesus Christ [is] the same yesterday and today and on into the ages**" (Heb. 13:8).

AFTERWORD

When meditating on the role played by Judah (Judas), and then the frequent, ambiguous references to "**the disciple whom Jesus was loving and accepting**," and "**that 'other' disciple**," Jesus' words in the Sermon on the Mount came to mind. We read in Mat. 5:44-47a,

> "**Be constantly loving your enemies** (urging toward reunion with, and accepting as persons standing on the same ground, those folks hostile to you; [comment: this could have applied to the Romans, as well as to personal enemies]), **and be habitually praying goodness over the people continuously persecuting you** (constantly thinking and speaking on behalf of the folks repeatedly pursuing you to have ease and well-being) **so that** (or: By this manner; This is how) **you folks can be birthed** (may and would come to be) **sons of your Father – the One within [the] atmospheres and in union with [the] heavens – because He is repeatedly making His sun to rise back up again upon bad** (evil; wicked; worthless) **folks as well as [upon] good** (virtuous) **folks, and He is habitually sending rain upon fair and equitable people** (those in right relationship; those within the Way pointed out; just ones; rightwised ones) **as well as [upon] unfair and inequitable people** (those not in right relationship; those not in the Way pointed out; unjust folks). **You see, if you should happen to love, accept, give yourself to, and participate with the ones constantly loving you folks, what wage or reward do you continue holding** (or: having)**?... And further, if you folks should only greet and welcomely embrace your brothers, what are you continuing to do [that is] excessive or extraordinary?**"

Would not Jesus have modeled this attitude and behavior for His disciples? At the end of His life, Luke records Jesus' dying words on the cross:

> "**O Father, let it flow away in them** (or: send it away for them; forgive them), **for they have not seen, so they do not know or perceive, what they are now doing**" (Lu. 23:34).

But what about the man whom He knew (6:64, above) would give Him over to the Judean authorities? Would not Jesus have been continuously loving, accepting and urging toward union with Judah (Judas)? And might that also be why our "author" never names that disciple?

The Epistle of Barnabas

An Expanded Translation by Jonathan Mitchell

INTRODUCTION

The Epistle of Barnabas is a Greek general letter (or: essay) that has been divided into twenty-one chapters, preserved in the 4th century Codex Sinaiticus where it appears at the end of the New Testament, following the book of Revelation. It is traditionally ascribed to Barnabas who is mentioned in the Acts of the Apostles, although current scholarship ascribes it to another Apostolic Father of the same name. A form of the Epistle, 850 lines long, is noted in the Latin list of canonical works in the 6th century Codex Claromontanus. The author uses symbolic exegesis that is similar to that of Paul in Gal. 4:21-31, and to that of Philo of Alexandria. "[It] is a good early example of what became the dominant method of interpreting the Bible in the early and medieval church" (*The Apostolic Fathers*, 2nd Ed., translated by J.B. Lightfoot and J.R. Harmer, Edited and Revised by Michael W. Holmes, Baker Book House, 1994 pp 159-60). Internal evidence (16:3-4, below) places the time of the writing to pre-AD 70, post-AD 70, or at least before Hadrian rebuilt Jerusalem in AD 132-35. John Dominic Crossan places the date as prior to the end of the 1st century AD (*The Cross That Spoke* p 121). John A.T. Robinson (*Redating the New Testament*, Westminster Press, 1976 p 352) sets the date as circa AD 75.

The reader of this letter will observe the author's educated familiarity with the Hebrew Scriptures (OT), since the entire work is filled with quotes of, or allusions to, those Scriptures. Scholars lean toward an early date of the writing from the fact that there are no quotes from the New Testament – it is an original work. My own conclusions are that it was a Jewish author who assumed that his audiences would be familiar with the Hebrew Scriptures (perhaps a Jewish called-out, covenant community). It was first quoted by Clement of Alexandria. The style of teaching may reflect what is suggested by Lu. 24:27,

"**And so, beginning from Moses, and then from all the prophets, He continued to fully interpret and explain to** (or: for) **them the things pertaining to** (or: the references about) **Himself within all the Scriptures.**"

BARNABAS

Chapter 1

1. **Be continuously rejoicing** (or: = Greetings), **O sons and daughters, centered in** (in union with) **[the] Name of [the] Lord – the One unrestrictedly accepting us, unambiguously driving toward reunion with us, fully Self-giving to us, and unconditionally loving us – centered in** (in union with) **peace-of-the-joining!**

2. **Indeed, from the results of God's just deed** (or: the effects of God's rightwising act of setting things right, in the Way pointed-out) **continuously being great and rich unto you folks** (into your midst), **on behalf of which – and on the level of an extreme degree – I continually enjoy pleasure and make merry at your happy** (or: blessed) **and inwardly glorious breath-effects** (or: esteemed spirits). **In this way, you have received and now continue to sustain and apprehend engrafted** (or: implanted) **grace and favor of, and from, the spiritual gift!**

3. **Because of this I share the joy in myself – even more – repeatedly** (or: continuously) **expecting to be delivered** (rescued; kept safe; made whole), **because I truly continue seeing within you folks** (or: among you folks) **a spirit** (or: [the] Breath-effect) **having been poured out** (or: forth) **upon you from the rich Fountain of** (or: spring from) **[the] Lord** [= Christ or Yahweh]. **Thus** (or: In this way), **upon – from**

you folks – your appearance, [which was] much desired by me, struck me with overwhelming awe and amazement.

4. Therefore, having been persuaded and convinced of this and sharing knowledge within myself (being conscious in myself; inwardly knowing from having perceived), that after saying much among you folks, I continue knowing (am progressively versed in [the fact]) that [the] Lord [= Christ or Yahweh] journeyed with me on the Path of eschatological deliverance (within the Road of the Way pointed-out; centered in the Way of rightwised relationships and justice; in union with the Path of being turned in the right direction and covenant participation). And so I continue wholly constrained and compelled with compressed necessity – even I, myself – unto this: to continuously love and unconditionally accept you folks with a drive toward reunion [with you] – over and above my own soul (life; person) – because great trust (faith; faithfulness) and love (unrestricted acceptance, with the urge for union) is continuing settled down to dwell within, and among, you folks, based upon expectation from, and which is, His Life – considering this, therefore,

5. that if it should continue being an object of care for me, concerning you folks, at some point to impart (or: transfer; sharing a communication) something from the part from which I received, because that will come to be unto a reward for me (or: it will exist in me for a reward), for having rendered helpful service and assistance to such spirits. I am eager and diligent to send a little [something] (or: along the line of a small [teaching]) to you folks, to the end that along with the trust possessed by you folks (or: by means of the faith from, and pertaining to, you folks) you would (could) continue having (holding; possessing) complete, finished, mature and perfected knowledge (intimate, personal insight that is based upon experience).

6. Therefore, there are three results from [the] Lord's appearance (or: effects of what seems to be from [the] Lord; results of the thinking and opinion of [the] Lord; effects of [the] imagination which is [the] Lord):
a) expectation from Living (expectation which is Life); a start (beginning) and a goal (completion; finishing; ending) from our trust (of our faith and loyalty; which is faithfulness);
b) also, eschatological deliverance into the Way pointed-out, in rightwised relationships of covenant participation – which is a beginning and goal (end) of evaluating and deciding (judging; a separating off) to make things right;
c) and then, love (unambiguous acceptance; urge for reunion) [experienced in] joy and exultation: a witness (evidence; a testimony) of eschatological deliverance in rightwised existence in the Way pointed out.

7. For you see, the Sovereign Master made known to (for; in) us, through the prophets, the things having passed by, as well as those things having stood within the midst and are now here, and then giving to us firstfruits of a taste (flavor) of, and about, things progressively being about to be – which continuing in seeing these things severally (according to each one; one thing after another) operating and inwardly working, just as He said, we continue obligated (we ought repeatedly), [being] richer and higher, to progressively bear forward and approach face-to-face in the respectful reverence of Him (or: by His pious fear).

8. Now I, myself, not as a teacher (instructor), but rather as one from among you folks, will progressively indicate and suggest (or: fully point out and show) a few things through which, in the midst of the present circumstances, you folks will increasingly be caused to have a good attitude and a healthful frame of mind.

Chapter 2

1. To go on, with days continuing in being misery-gushed (worthless; unprofitable; harmful; malicious; painful; evil), and yet The Active Worker, Himself, continuously having the right from out

of Being (constantly holding the privilege and authority), **we ought, owe it, and continue indebted, to, for and in ourselves – while continually staying focused** (holding ourselves toward, with attentive care and devotion) **to be progressively seeking out the effects of [the] Lord's Rightful Act**
(the results of [the] Lord's Act of Justice; or: the just-effects from [the] Lord; the results of righting and equity, in relation to [the] Lord; the effects of rectification, which are [the] Lord).

2. **Accordingly then, [the] aids and assistants from our faithfulness** (or: Consequently, then, helpers of our trust and faith) **are Reverent Respect** (or: Fear) **and Remaining-under-to-give-support** (or: Patient Endurance), **and the allies for us** (or: the fellow-contestants with us; the people constantly fighting at our side; the confederates in and among us) **[are] Holding-strong-feelings-at-a-distance** (or: Waiting-long before rushing with passion; Long-suffering) **and Inner Strength** (Discipline; Control of the self).

3. **So with these things continually remaining purely, face-to-face with [the] Lord** (or: Then from these things constantly dwelling sincerely, with a view to [the] Lord) – **Wisdom, Understanding** (the ability to make things flow together), **Skill** (Mastery in knowing and acquaintance; Scientific insight), **Intimate, experiential Knowledge – they are continuously caused to celebrate together in them from being caused to keep on having a good, corporate attitude with joined, healthy frames of mind, with them.**

4. **For you see, He has set in clear Light, so that it remains manifested to us** (for us; among us; in us), **through all the folks with Light ahead of time** (the prophets), **that He continues desiring neither sacrifices, nor whole burnt offerings nor a bearing-forward of approach presents** (or: oblations; general offerings), **saying, at one time, indeed,**

5. **"[The] LORD is now** (or: continues) **saying,**
'What, to or for Me, [are] a plethora of your sacrifices (or: [the] mass and abundance of the sacrifices from you folks)**? I am full of whole burnt offerings, and I do not continue desiring fat of sheep** (or: from lambs) **and blood of** (or: from) **bulls and goats – not even if you folks would repeatedly come to be seen by Me! For who sought out or required these thing from your hands? You people will not continue to set foot on or tread My temple court. If you should continue bringing an offering of the finest wheat flour, it is worthless, useless and ineffective.'"** [Isa. 1:11-13, LXX]

6. **Incense continues being disgusting to Me** (an abomination and a detestable thing for Me) **– [and] your new moon [feasts].** [Lightfoot, from other MSS adds: These things therefore He annulled (abolished), in order that the new law of our Lord], **Jesus Christ, being far away from** (without; = free of) **a yoke of compulsion and obligation, would continue having a bearing-forward [that is] not man-made** (an approach- present [that is] not human-formed, human-created or humanistic).

7. **And now, again, He continues saying to them,**
"As for Me, I did not at any point implant a finished goal in (impart an inner directive to; set an inner destiny among; invest as an end in view for) **your fathers – when progressively journeying forth out of the Land of Egypt – to bear-forward** (bring an approach present) **to** (for) **Me the effects of whole burnt offerings and sacrifices.** [Jer. 7:22-23, LXX]
8. **"To the contrary, this I implanted as the goal in them** (imparted as the inner directive to them; set for the inner destiny among them; gave as the end in view for them):
'Let each of you folks continue to bear no grudge or malice against his associate (near one; neighbor), **in ugliness and bad form** (or: badness) **within the midst of his own heart – as well as not habitually loving or accepting a false oath.'"** [Zech. 8:17, LXX]

9. **Consequently, we – [since] not being without understanding – continue obliged** (are constantly indebted; habitually ought) **to keep on taking notice, and thus constantly perceive the mind-set, the intention and the disposition of the goodness** (moral excellence) **of our Father, that He is continually speaking to, and in, us, desiring, willing and intending us to be habitually seeking how we should keep on approaching Him, drawing near to be face-to-face with Him – not repeatedly wandering or being led astray, like them.**

10. **To us, then, thus He continues saying,**
"A sacrifice to and for [the] Lord [is] a heart having been crushed, broken in pieces and remaining torn and shattered: a sweet fragrance to the Lord (in the Lord; for the Lord). **A heart continuously highly-esteeming and bringing glory to the One having made it."** [cf Ps. 51:17]

Consequently, O brothers (folks from the same womb), **we continue obliged** (are constantly indebted; habitually ought) **to continually make careful inquiry concerning** (or: thoroughly investigate about and pay strict attention with regard to; display consummate execution round about) **our deliverance (the salvation pertaining to us; the health and wholeness from among us), to the end that the misery-gushed person or situation** (the useless, laborsome, unprofitable, pain-flowing, malevolent person or situation) **may not slip into the midst from the side, producing a straying** (wandering) **among us** (within us; in the midst of us), **[and thus] would fling us out** (or: sling us from the midst), **away from our Life.**

Chapter 3

1. **Then He continues saying to them** (progressively lays it out toward them), **again, concerning these things:**

> **"To what end are you folks habitually fasting for Me,"** says [the] LORD, **"so that your voice is to be heard, today, in an outcry** (or: in the midst of, and in union with, crying)**? This is not the fast that I, Myself, laid out** (selected; or: choose) **– not a person repeatedly bringing down and abasing his soul** (habitually bowing low and humbling or humiliating himself)**,"** says [the] LORD.

2. **"Not even though you folks should at some point bend your neck as a hoop or a ring and then would put on** (clothes yourselves in) **sackcloth and would spread ashes under yourselves** (= make ashes your bed) **– not even in this way will you folks proceed in calling a fast [that is] acceptable** (or: a received fast)**."** [Isa. 58:4-5, LXX]

3. **Now** (But; Yet) **He continues laying it out toward us** (or: is still saying to us)**:**
"Look and consider (Behold; See) **this fast which I, Myself, have chosen,"** says [the] LORD. **"Progressively loose, and one-after-another untie, every band** (fetter; joined deal; conspiracy) **of injustice. Progressively fully-untie and dissolve intricate knots of violent contracts or forced agreements** (or: keep on untying the tightened cords of forcible effects of covenants). **Continually send away** (or: off), **in a release from captivity, people having been shattered and now continuing broken and then one-after-another tear in pieces every unjust writing or contract. Habitually break your bread with** (or: to; for) **[the] hungry, and should you see a naked person, at once clothe [him or her]. Habitually bring unsheltered, homeless people into your house, and should you see a humble** (or: oppressed; deprived; of-no-account; lowly; afflicted) **person, you will not overlook** (disregard; despise; disdain; neglect) **him or her – neither [shall anyone] among the household [or] from your seed** (offspring). [cf Mat. 25:35-36]

4. **"At that time** (or: Then; Next) **your Light will progressively be caused to break forth early, and your healing will progressively spring up** (or: grow again; rise above the horizon; dawn) **quickly, and the eschatological deliverance** (rightwising into the Way pointed out in equitable

relationships of covenant participation for justice) **will continuously and progressively journey forth in front of you, and the glory of God will continually environ you** (or: the assumed appearance from God will habitually surround you in a set and equipped arrangement; the manifestation from God, while calling forth praise, will progressively wrap you and cover you).

5. **"Then you will cry out, and God will continually listen and fully hear you. While you are still speaking, He will proceed in saying, 'Look and consider: I am here, at [your] side!' – if you would at some point separate, remove and take away [the] yoke from you, as well as [the] pointing of the finger** (or: scornful gesture) **and [the] effect of the flow of muttering complaint** (or: a spoken word of murmuring), **and then, from the midst of your soul** (inner being) **would give your bread to, and for, [the] hungry and would show compassion and extend mercy to [the] lowered and abased soul** (or: a person having been humbled)." [Isa. 58:6-10, LXX]

6. **Unto this end, therefore, O brothers** (folks from the same womb; = fellow believers), **in [His] seeing beforehand [that] the People – whom He had prepared and made ready in union with Beloved One** (centered within the midst of the Person having been accepted and now remaining unambiguously Loved, and who is from Him), **as in [that which is] unmixed, unshattered, simple and pure – will progressively trust, be habitually faithful to, and continue believing the** (or: This) **Long-suffering One** (the One that puts rushing emotion and wrath far away from Him; the One who waits long before rushing with passion), **He showed in advance, and in clear Light, to us** (manifested for us, ahead of time; revealed in us, and among us, beforehand) **concerning all humans, and about all things, to the end that we would not, like foreigners** (or: as incomers), **crash on** (or: shipwreck and break into pieces in; be wrecked by) **their Law** (or: the custom of those folks).

Chapter 4

1. **It continues binding and necessary for us, therefore, while investigating deeply and carefully** (to an added great extent) **concerning the present [events and situations], to continuously and progressively search out** (fully seek, investigate and scrutinize) **the things continuing able** (progressively having power) **to keep on delivering us** (to progressively save us; to continue making us whole and healthy). **We should, therefore, at once fully flee and completely take refuge from all the works** (activities; deeds) **of the lawlessness, lest the works of** (or: from; which are) **the lawlessness may take us down and seize us. Furthermore, we should hate the error and abhor the straying** (wandering) **of the present season** (from this now fitting situation), **to the end that we would continue being accepted** (received with a drive toward union in unambiguous love) **into that which is progressively** (or: continuously) **about to be.**

2. **We should not at any point give our own soul** (or: self) **relaxation from custody, so that it proceeds to have from its being** (or: continues to possess a privilege) **to repeatedly** (or: constantly) **run together** (associate or be in league) **with deviating, missing-the-goal people and misery-gushed** (or: harmful; painful; malicious; unprofitable) **people; at no time should we** (or: lest, perhaps, we would) **be made like them.**

3. **The last** (final) **trap-stick of the trap** (snare) **has drawn near and is now at hand** (close enough to touch; in effect), **concerning which it has been written, just as Enoch says, "You see unto this purpose the Master has cut short the seasons** (fitting situations; fertile moments) **and the days, so that His beloved and accepted one can hurry and would arrive upon the enjoyment and possession of the allotted inheritance."** [cf Mat. 24:22]

4. **Now thus says also the prophet:**

"Ten reigns (or: kingdoms) **will one-after-another** (or: one-beside-another) **reign upon the Land** (or: region; earth; ground) **and then following [them] a little king will rise up from the midst who will proceed in subjugating three of the kings under one."** [Dan. 7:24]

5. **Similarly** (In like manner), **Daniel speaks concerning him** (or: the same):
"**And I saw the fourth little wild animal – evil** (pain-causing; unserviceable; causing toilsome labor) **and strong, even more dangerous** (cruel; harsh; intractable) **than all the little wild animals of** (or: from) **the sea** [Lightfoot reads: earth; land] **– and how** (or: even as) **from out of it rose up ten horns, and how** (or: even as) **it brought low** (humbled; abased) **under one, three of the great horns."** [Dan. 7:7, 8]

6. **Therefore, you folks continue obliged** (or: progressively ought) **to understand** (to make things flow together and comprehend). **But still** (or: Now yet) **also this: I am proceeding in requesting of** (or: continue to entreat) **you folks – as continuing being one of you** (of your [community]; from among you people), **and yet constantly loving and accepting** (urging toward reunion with) **you all, in a special and particular way, more than my own soul** (above myself) **– now** (at the present time; as things now stand) **to constantly pay attention to and take care of yourselves** (hold-toward, focus on and guard one another) **and not to liken yourselves to** (or: be like) **certain folks [who], in piling error upon error** (heaping up with the sins, accumulating with the mistakes and adding to the failures) **among you, [are] repeatedly saying that their covenant** (arrangement) **[is; should be] also ours. Ours, indeed!** (or: Ours, in fact, [it is].) **But to the contrary, those folks, when already receiving [it] from Moses, in [the] end** (or: finally) **lost it in this way** (or: thus loosed it away and destroyed it, on into a final act):

7. **You see, the Writing** (Scripture) **continues saying,**
"**And then Moses continued being in the midst of** (or: on) **the mountain, continuing in fasting [for] forty days and forty nights, and he received** (took in hand) **the covenant** (arrangement) **from the LORD** (= Yahweh) **– stone tablets having been written by the finger of the LORD's hand."** [Ex. 31:18; 34:28]

8. **However, in** (or: by; when) **turning back upon the idols, they destroyed and lost it. For [the] Lord says, thus:**
"**Moses, Moses, at once descend** (walk down) **without delay** (or: quickly), **because your people, whom you led and brought out of the land of Egypt, act lawlessly** (behave without a custom or culture)." [Ex. 32:7; Deut. 9:12]
Then Moses understood (made it flow together), **and threw the two tablet out of his hands. And so their covenant** (arrangement) **was broken together, into pieces, to the end that the [covenant; arrangement] of, from, and which is, the Beloved Jesus would be sealed down within our heart – in expectation of His faithfulness!**

9. **Now though I am presently wishing to continue writing many things, not as a teacher, but rather as is fitting and continues suitable for a person continually loving and accepting with a drive toward union, not to fall short or lag behind from that which we continue having: I, your off-scoured, wiped-off filth and scum, am filled with zeal, making every effort to continue writing, on account of which, we should constantly pay attention, take care, hold-toward, focus on and be on guard within the midst of these last days, for it follows that the whole time of our trust, faith, loyalty and faithfulness will proceed in profiting** (continue benefitting) **us nothing** (not in one thing), **unless now – within this lawless season** (or: in the fertile moment that is apart from law or custom), **and in** (or: with; by) **an imminent** (progressively about to exist) **bait-stick of a trap, as is fitting and continues suitable for** (with; in) **sons of God – we continue standing in an opposing position** (or: we habitually stand on the opposite side to lend a hand) **so that the dark or obscure person or situation would** (or: can) **not at any point have an entrance at the side** (an opportunity of stealthily slipping in).

10. **We should at once flee away from all emptiness and futility; we should fully abhor** (hate to the end; completely detest) **the works and deeds of the misery-gushed road** (the worthless and unserviceable path). **When privately entering in, to retire into your own homes, do not separate yourselves as though living alone, as if being folks having already been made right, just, guiltless, fair, equitable and set in righted relationships. But rather, upon the very gathering together, you folks should seek together and inquire about the common, continuing mutual interest and advantage** (the corporate ongoing profitable work; the public common good; the general common-welfare).

11. **You see, the Writing** (Scripture) **continues saying:**
"**Alas** (Tragic will be the case) **[for] those [who are] intelligent in** (by; for) **themselves, and [are] educated, knowing folks – in their own eyes**" [Isa. 5:21]
We should come to be spiritual folks! We should come to be a finished temple (a mature, completed inner sanctuary that embodies the goal) **in God** (for God; with God; by God)! **From as much is** (exists) **within and among you folks, we should meditate on, study, practice and cultivate the reverent respect** (scruple; fear) **of, from, and which is God, and we should strive, as in the public games, to constantly watch over in order to guard, observe, keep and maintain His implanted goals** (imparted inner directives; centered destinies) – **to the end that we would have a good attitude and a healthy frame of mind, within and in union with the effects of His just Act** (in union with the results of the Right Deed that is Him).

12. **The LORD** (= Yahweh, or Christ) **will continue evaluating, repeatedly make decisions about, and keep on judging, the cosmos** (the aggregate of humanity; the world of religion, economics, culture and government; the domination System) **impartially: each person will receive just as he or she did** (according as he or she produced)**: if it should be good and virtuous** [Lightfoot's text adds: his {right deeds; just actions} shall go before him in the way; -- *brackets, mine*]**, but if misery-gushed** (worthless; pain-causing; unprofitable)**, his reward** (recompense; wage) **from the misery-gushed-ness** (the worthlessness; the unprofitability; the caused pain) **is before [him].**

13. **See that, lest – as called people, [then becoming] folks resting upon [this] – we may proceed in falling asleep to our deviations** (or: with our mistakes; by our sins; in our mistakes)**, and then the "misery-gushing chief"** (or: the worthless ruler) – **the person at some point receiving authority** (the right; the privilege of his being, or from his existing)**, in regard to us** (or: against us) – **may force us away from the reign** (sovereign activities and influences; kingdom) **of, and from, [the] Lord,**

14. **Yet still, my brothers, think about and consider this, also. When you folks are seeing that after so many signs and wonders had occurred** (happened) **in Israel, and yet, as follows: they were abandoned** (left down within the midst of [their situation])**, we should constantly pay attention and take care** (hold-toward, focus on and guard)**, lest we would be found, as it has been written:**
"**Many [were] called, yet few [were] picked out and chosen.**" [*cf* 1 Sam. 18:8b; Isa. 41:9b; Mat. 22:14]

Chapter 5

1. **It follows that unto this end the Lord remained under, giving support and enduring, to at one point give over** (deliver; commit; transmit; pass on) **the Flesh unto a downfall** (into the midst of the sphere of complete withering, decay and ruin)**, to the end that we would be cleansed and purified by the flowing away of the deviations** (in the release from the errors and mistakes; with the divorce from the sins) **which exists in** (continues being in union with; is in the midst of) **the blood, from the effect of His sprinkling** (or: His blood, which is the result of sprinkling; the blood of the effect of the sprinkling of Him).

2. **You see, it has been, and now remains, written concerning Him which, on the one hand, [is] toward Israel, which, on the other hand, [is] toward, and face-to-face with, us, and it says it this way:**
"**He was wounded and traumatized on account of** (through) **the lawless acts from us** (or: with a view to our conducts which were lawless), **and He had been made weak on account of the deviations from us** (through the times of our missing the target; with a view to the errors and mistakes among us); **in His bruise** (with and by His stripe), **we ourselves were suddenly, at one point, healed. As a sheep, He was at one point led upon a slaughter, and as a lamb without a voice** (or: silent) **before the one continuing in shearing it.**" [Isa. 53:5, 7]

3. **Are we not then constantly obliged** (continually owing it) **to be continuously offering extreme thanks** (showing exceeding gratitude for the goodness of [His] grace) **to, for and in the Lord** (= Christ or Yahweh)? **Because He has both made known the things having come to be present to, within, and for us** (or: the having come and now remaining beside us and with us), **and has made us wise in union with the things having stood within the midst** (centered in the present things), **and so unto the things continuing about to be** (presently imminent) **we are not folks void of intelligence** (people without understanding from being able to make things flow together).

4. **Now the Writing** (Scripture) **continues saying,**
"**Not unjustly are nets normally stretched and spread out** (deployed) **for birds.**" [Prov. 1:17; comment: a subtle reference to the Roman eagles?]
This is saying (This means) **that a person will justly progressively lose himself or rightly destroy himself, who, continuing in possessing** (habitually holding or having) **experiential insight and intimate knowledge of a Way of eschatological deliverance** (a Path from being turned into the Way pointed out, with rightwised relationships in covenant participation in [the] Road of justice and equity), **progressively encloses himself away** (shuts himself off) **into a way** (path; road) **of darkness.** [cf chapter 20, below]

5. **But still, also this, my brothers** (folks from the same womb; = fellow believers): **Since the Lord** [= Christ] **remained under and endures suffering concerning our souls, [though] continuing being Lord of all the aggregate of humanity** (the domination System; the world of religion, culture, economy and government; the cosmos) – **the One to whom** (or: for Whom; concerning, or with a view to, Whom; into Whom; with Whom; about Whom) **God said, from the foundations** (or: casting down) **of an ordered System** ([an] aggregate of humanity; a world of culture, religion, economy and government), "**We should make** (form; produce; construct; create) **humanity, according to** (corresponding to; to the level of; in the sphere of; along the line of) **our image and likeness,**" [Gen. 1:26] **How then, did He endure and remain under to suffer under [the] hand of humans? You folks must learn!**

6. **The prophets** (The folks with light ahead of time), **from continually having His grace** (or: while habitually holding the favor from Him), **prophesied with a view to Him** (or: proclaimed Light, ahead of time, into the midst of Him). **Yet He Himself remained under for support, and endured, to the end that He would idle-down** (render discharged, unemployed and useless; make barren; cause to cease the activity of; or: abolish) **the Death and would point out, demonstrate and display the resurrection from out of the midst of dead people, so that it remains necessary for Him at one point to be set in clear Light and manifested in Flesh,**
7. **to the end that He could give away or award** (or: give back; pay off; reward) **the Promise to** (or: in; among; with regard to; for) **the fathers, and He, Himself, while preparing, equipping and making ready the New** (new in kind and character) **People in Himself** (or: for Himself; unto Himself; with Himself), **He being upon the Land** (or: earth) **could and would display and point out that, in making** (from producing; while creating) **the resurrection, He Himself will be progressively evaluating, deciding about and judging.**

8. **Although continuously teaching Israel a conclusion** (an end; a termination), **and after constantly doing** (performing; creating; producing) **so many wonders and signs, He kept on proclaiming and preaching – and He continued dearly** (exceedingly) **loving and accepting him, urging toward reunion with him.**

9. **Now when He chose His own sent-forth folks – those continuing about to progressively preach and proclaim His message of goodness, ease and well-being – [they] were being** (existing) **lawless people, above all failure** (error; deviation; sin), **so that He could point out** (exhibit; demonstrate), **"that he did not come to call just and righteous folks, but to the contrary, outcasts** (sinners; folks in error; deviators; people that were failures)." [Mat. 9:13]
[Lightfoot's text adds: then He manifested Himself to be the Son of God (or: God's Son).]

10. **So then, if He had not been manifested** (made visible; shown in clear light) **in union with Flesh** (within flesh), **how were the people saved** (rescued; made whole; delivered) **by** (or: while) **looking at Him** (or: while seeing or in beholding Him), **when it is not to be, when being about to continue looking at the sun [and] not continuing strong to look face to face into its rays – a work of His hands being continuously there** (or: present), **and under-originating [it]?** [*cf* Nu. 21:8b, 9b; Jn. 3:14, 15; 12:32; Lu. 9:56]

11. **So accordingly the Son of God came into this, in union with Flesh** (within flesh; in a flesh [system]), **to the end that He would bring up to a head** (or: sum up) **the completion** (the final act; the finished product) **of the sins** (deviations; failures; mistakes) **in and for** (or: BY) **those centered in death that were, in union with death, pursuing and persecuting His prophets** (those with light ahead of time).

12. **Thus accordingly, He remained under and patiently endured into the midst of this, for you see, God continues saying [that] the blow of His flesh that [came] from them:**
"When they would strike (beat) **their shepherd, at that time the sheep of the flock will be progressively lost."** [Zech. 13:7; Mat. 26:31]

13. **Now He Himself set His will and intent in this way: to suffer! For you see, it continued binding and necessary that He would suffer upon a tree** (wooden pole or beam), **for the person prophesying said about Him:**
"Spare My soul (person; self) **from [the] sword,"** [Ps. 22:20]
And further,
"Drive pierce and drive nails through My flesh, because synagogues (congregations) **of misery-gushed folks stood up upon Me"** [Ps. 22:16; 86:14]

14. **And then again, He says:**
"Look and consider! I have placed, and so it continues set, My back unto a scourging, and the cheeks into the effects of a slap and a blow. Yet I set my face as a firm rock." [Isa. 50:6, 7; Ps. 129:3; Ezk. 3:8]

Chapter 6

1. **Now when He produced** (made; created; formed) **the implanted, finished goal** (the imparted inner directive; the inner destiny; the investment as an end in view), **what does He go on saying?**
> **"Who is normally making evaluations and decisions for Me** (or: Who is continually judging with Me; Who is now judging Me)**? Let him stand against Me** (resist Me; be opposed to Me; stand on the opposite side to assist, with Me). **Or, who is the person habitually deciding what**

is right for Me (or: repeatedly making things right to Me; or: continually doing things justly, by Me)? **Let him draw near to the Lord's Child** (or: by the Servant from [Yahweh]).

2.   **Tragic is the fate for you folks** (Woe to you people), **because you people will all, as wool, progressively grow old, and a moth will gradually eat you down."** [Isa. 50:8-9, LXX]

And then, again, the prophet continues saying, given that He was, as a hard, strong stone (or: a powerful, weighty piece of rock), **placed for and set unto crushing** (with a view to breaking [something] together, into pieces),

"**Look and consider! I will proceed in-setting into the foundation of Zion a very precious** (expensive), **selected** (choice and picked out; chosen) **Stone – a prime Foundation Stone** (or: a top, extreme Cornerstone) **invested** (imbued) **with honor, respect, as well as with great worth and value."** [Isa. 28:16]

3. **So then he continues saying,**
    "**And the person who will continue setting** (be habitually placing) **expectation upon Him will continue living on into the Age [of Messiah]."** [Ps. 9:18]

Is our expectation (or: expectant hope), **then, upon a stone** (or: a rock)? **May it not come to be** (Certainly not)! **Nevertheless, since [the] Lord set His flesh in strength, it follows that He continues saying,**

"**And so He set** (placed) **Me as a hard, solid rock."** [Isa. 50:7]

4. **Now again the prophet continues saying,**
    "**A stone which the people building the House rejected as unworthy and unfit, in this way came to be Head** (was birthed [the] Source) **of the Corner."** [Ps. 118:22; Isa. 28:16; 1 Pet. 2:7]]

Then again he goes on saying,
    "**This One is** (or: This exists being) **the great and wonderful Day which the LORD** (= Yahweh) **made** (produced; created; formed)." [Ps. 118:24; note: therefore, Christ IS the Day]

5. I – myself [being] an off-scouring from your love – **am now writing straightforwardly** (more simply and frankly) **to you folks, so that you can make things flow together and understand:**

6. **So what, then, is the prophet again saying?**
    "**A continuously misery-gushed synagogue surrounded Me** (or: A gathering together of worthless, pain-inducing people held a circle around Me); **they encompassed me like bees [swarming] a honeycomb."** [Ps. 22:12; 118:12]

And,
    "**Upon my garment they cast a lot** (= gambled)." [Ps. 22:18]

7. **Therefore, being about to be set in clear Light and manifested, and then to proceed suffering, in His flesh** (or: in union with the Flesh that pertained to, and belonged to, Him) – **the suffering shown beforehand** – it follows that the prophet continues saying upon Israel,
    "**Tragic will it be** (Alas; Woe) **to, for and in their soul, because they have deliberated and now determine a misery-gushed** (worthless; painful; malicious) **resolve against themselves** (or: in accord with themselves; along the line of themselves), **at one point saying, 'We should bind this 'just one,' because he continues being an inconvenient hindrance for us** (an annoying difficulty to us).'" [Isa. 3:9, 10; LXX]

8. **What does the other prophet, Moses, continue saying to them?**
    "**Look and consider! These things [the] LORD** (= Yahweh) **God continues saying, 'You folks at once enter into the midst of the Good Land** (the virtuous, well-born territory), **which [the] LORD** (= Yahweh) **affirmed with an oath to** (or: for) **Abraham and Isaac and Jacob, and**

then you people at once fully enjoy the allotment as heirs, possessing it – a Land continuously flowing in streams of milk and honey.'" [Ex. 33:1-3]

9. **But what does the Knowledge** (the intimate, experiential Insight; the *Gnosis*) **continue saying?** You folks at once learn! It continues saying, **"In one blow, put your expectation upon Jesus, the One repeatedly about to be set in clear Light and manifested among you folks** (or: within you; by you people; to you folks), **in union with Flesh** (centered in flesh; within flesh)."

"You see, humanity is, and continues being, dirt (soil; earth), **continuously experiencing and suffering; for he came to exist** (was birthed) **from the forming of Adam from the face of the earth** (ground; Land)

(or: for it happened from the formation of the Land {or: earth}, which is the countenance and presence of Adam)." [Gen. 3:19]

10. **What, then, does He continue saying** (or: What does He now mean),

"Into the midst of the Good Land (the virtuous, well-born territory), **a land** (territory) **continuously flowing in streams of milk and honey"?** [Ex. 33:3]

Our [Yahweh] [is] a Word of goodness, ease and well-being (or: The LORD {= Yahweh} [is] blessed and well thought-of by us), **brothers, at one point placing** (setting; establishing) **within the midst of us the wisdom and mind** (intelligence; understanding; disposition) **of, and from, His hidden things** (or the secret things that are Him). **You see, the prophet continues speaking a parable** (something cast alongside for comparison) **from [the] Lord** (or: concerning [Yahweh]): **who will progressively direct his mind to think carefully about, imagine, perceive, consider and then comprehend except a wise person, even one progressively skilled** (versed; proficient; prudent) **and constantly loving** (accepting and urging toward union with) **his or her LORD** (= Yahweh, or Christ).

11. **Therefore, since making us new again, in kind and character – another hammered-out image and model with patterned, archetypal content, as of little children – to progressively hold the soul; as if, at this point already His, forming and molding us again**

(or: as to continuously possess the inner life of children, as if by now already forming and creating us back up, from Him)!

12. **You see, the Writing** (Scripture) **continues saying, concerning us, just as it continues saying to the Son** (or: by the Son; for the Son; with the Son; in the Son),

"We should form (make; construct; produce; create) **the human according to an image and according to a likeness of Us, and then they should be heading** (ruling) **the little wild animals of the land** (earth; territory) **and the flying critters of the sky** (atmosphere), **as well as the fishes of the sea."**

And then, **upon seeing the beautiful, fine and ideal result of our form** (or: effect of the form of us), **[the] Lord said,**

"You people be caused to progressively grow (continuously increase) **and be repeatedly caused to multiply** (continuously swarm), **and then be caused to progressively fill and complete the earth** (land; territory)." [Gen. 1:26, 28]

These things [He said] to (or: face to face with) **the Son** (or: These [words] refer to the Son).

13. **Now again I will continue completely pointing out to you** (or: I will proceed fully displaying for you) **how He** [another MS reads: the Lord] **continues speaking to** (or: face to face with; in reference to) **us: He produced** (made; formed; created; built) **a second formation** (creation; molding), **upon** (or: at; added to) **last [days; times; folks]. Now [the] Lord continues saying,**

"Look and consider (See)! **I am progressively** (or: repeatedly; habitually) **producing** (making; forming; building; creating; doing) **the last things as the first things."** [*cf* Mk. 10:31; Rev. 21:5]

In reference to this, then, the prophet proclaimed,

"You folks at once enter into the midst of a Land continuously flowing in streams of milk and honey, and then you people at once correspondingly function as its owners (perform on the level as its masters and lords)." [*cf* Ex. 33:3]

14. **Observe, then: we ourselves have been created** (formed) **again, and now continue being a new creation** (formation), **just as, in a different prophet, He again continues saying,**
    "Look and consider, [the] LORD (= Yahweh) **continues saying, 'I will pull and draw out from** (breathe out of) **these folks'** – that is, from those whom the Spirit (Breath-effect) of, and from, **[the] LORD foresaw** (or: saw beforehand) – **'the stony hearts, and then I will inset** (or: put within) **[them hearts] of flesh,"** [Ezk. 11:19]
because He Himself was about to be manifested (set in clear Light) **in union with Flesh** (within the midst of flesh; centered in flesh) **and also to continuously take permanent residence** (be "housed-down" to continuously dwell and abide) **within and among us** (in union with us; centered in us).
15. **You see, our heart** (or: the heart of us) **[is] a set-apart** (sacred) **temple** (inner sanctuary; holy place and holy-of-holies), **the habitation** (the abode; the permanent dwelling-place) **for the LORD** (= Yahweh, or Christ).

16. **For [the] Lord again continues saying,**
    "Then within what will I continue being seen by (or: be made to appear to, or with) **the LORD** (= Yahweh), **my God, and will I continue having an assumed appearance** (will I progressively be given a manifestation which calls forth praise and be glorified; will I continue being given a good reputation)**?"**
He continues saying,
    "I will repeatedly speak forth the same word (message; thought; idea; information) **to, for, by and with You, in the midst of a called-out congregation of my brothers; then I will continue singing to, for, by and with You, again in the midst of a called-out community of set-apart** (sacred; holy) **folks."** [Ps. 22:22; 42:2]
So accordingly we ourselves are (continue being) **they whom He at one point brought into the midst of the Good Land!**

17. **What, then, [is; = means] the milk and the honey? Because the child is first kept alive by honey, and then next by milk. Thus, then, also we ourselves, being continuously made and kept alive in, by and with the trust from** (or: the faith of; the faithfulness which is) **the Promise, and then by** (with; in) **the** *Logos* (Word; Idea; thought; conveyance of patterned Information; message), **will continue living… continuously functioning as complete owners of the earth** (or: habitually performing accordingly as lords, with regard to the Land).

18. **Now as we previously said, above, "And so let them progressively grow** (continuously increase) **and repeatedly multiply** (continuously swarm) **and then continuously regulate** (govern) **fish or birds** (flying creatures) **of the sky," it follows that we ought to understand** (comprehend) **that "to regulate** (govern)**" is** (= means) **"privilege from out of being** (right; authority)**," so that the person who is imposing an arranged order or adds dispositions would function as a lord** (can perform as a master or owner). [*cf* Gen. 1:26, 28]

19. **Therefore, if this now is not presently happening** (occurring; coming to birth or existing), **until when** (at what time)**? When even we ourselves will proceed being made complete and fully developed** (or: being matured, finished and brought to the goal)**: to become heirs of the Lord's covenant** (possessors and enjoyers of the arrangement of, from, and which is, [the] Lord). [*cf* Gal. 4:1-7; Eph. 4:12-13]

1. **So accordingly, you folks continue intellectually perceiving** (understanding with your mind), **O children of a healthy frame of mind and a good attitude, that our beautiful** (fine; ideal; sound) **Lord has in advance shown everything in clear Light, to the end that we could and would intimately and experientially know** (have insight), **in Whom** (for Whom; to Whom; with Whom; by Whom), **we continue with an obliged duty** (or: are habitually under obligation; ought constantly) **to continuously offer praise – repeatedly expressing the goodness, ease and well-being of grace and favor, while constantly giving thanks in accord with** (down from; in line with; in correspondence to) **all things!**

2. **Since, therefore, the Son of God – while continuously being Lord** (Master; Owner) **and continuously being about to continue evaluating, repeatedly deciding about and habitually judging living folks and dead folks – suffered, to the end that His blow** (wound) **would give Life to us** (could create Life for us and make us live), **we should at once trust** (can faith-it in confident belief and loyalty) **that the Son of God was not being able** (could not continue) **to progressively suffer, except on account of** (with a view to) **us!**

3. **But also, when crucified He was given vinegar** (or: sour wine) **and bile to drink. You folks at once listen and hear... how, concerning this, the priests of the temple have been shown** (revealed; become visible) **in their true character. The imparted inner directive** (set implanted destiny; given end in view) **having been written [is]:**
    "'Whoever would not fast (i.e., observe) **the fast will proceed being rooted out and destroyed in** (or: by) **death,' [the] Lord implanted as a directive** (set as an end in view)." [Lev. 23:29]
Given that, also, He Himself was about to bear forward to offer the vessel of the Breath-effect (Spirit) **as a sacrifice concerning our failures and deviations** (mistakes; errors; sins) **to the end that the type – the one being birthed** (coming to be) **on Isaac when being held close and entangled upon the altar of burnt offering – would be brought to its goal and fulfilled** (be carried out and completed; be accomplished; come to its destined end).

4. **What, then, is it saying in [the book of] the prophet?**
    "And so, they must eat from the goat which is normally being offered in (or: at; during) **the fast over** (on behalf of) **all of the deviations** (failures; sins; mistakes; times of missing the target)." [cf Lev. 6:25-30; 10:16-17]
You folks keep on paying close attention and holding this to yourselves:
    "And so the priests alone must eat all the unwashed entrails (gut; bowel) **with vinegar** (or: sour wine)." [cf Lev. 1:13; 16:7ff]

5. **Why** (Toward what end)**?**
    "In as much as (Since) **you folks continue about to give bile with vinegar to Me to drink, when being about to bear forward and offer My flesh over** (on behalf of) **deviations** (failures; sins; mistakes; times of missing the target) **of My new people. You folks, yourselves, must eat it alone, while the people continues fasting and lamenting** (mourning), **in sackcloth [and] on ashes,"**
So that He could point out and exhibit that it continues binding and necessary for Him to proceed suffering under (by) **them.**

6. **You folks keep on paying close attention and holding this to yourselves, which He implanted as the end in view** (imparted as an inner directive; set with as the goal)**:**
    "You folks take two goats, fine (ideal; sound) **and alike, and then bring them close and offer [them] and the priest must take the one into the midst of a whole burnt offering, over** (on behalf of) **deviations** (errors; mistakes; sins; times of missing the goal)." [Lev. 16:7-9]

7. But what will they proceed doing with the other one?
    "He proceeds saying (declaring) a down-prayer (a corresponding prayer; an imposed-sphere, accorded prayer) upon that one." [Lev. 16:28]
You folks keep on paying close attention and holding this to yourselves, how the type of Jesus is shown in clear Light and made apparent.

8, "And then all you folks proceed spiting upon it and then keep on goading it so as to stab and pierce it, and place a scarlet wool thread around its head, and so, in this manner, you folks must impel (cast) it on into a desert or wilderness." [Lev. 16:10]
So when it would happen in this way, the person lifting up and ennobling (or: bearing; carrying) the goat continues leading it into the desert or wilderness, and then he takes off (removes) the wool thread and he continues by placing it upon a bush or shrub – the one normally being called Rachia [note: possibly a thorn-hedge, a briar, or a species of blackberry bush]: whereof, also, we are normally accustomed to eat the buds or blossoms (or: chew on the shoots or offspring) when finding them in the field or countryside. Accordingly, from only the fruits of the Rachia is it sweet and pleasant.

9. What, then, is this (does this mean)? You folks keep on paying close attention and holding this to yourselves:
    "On the one hand, the One [is] upon the altar; yet on the other hand, that One [is] the one [receiving] the laid-on-down-prayer (or: the imposed-sphere prayer; the added corresponding prayer; the accorded prayer),"
and for that reason, the One [receiving] the accorded, corresponding, imposed down-prayer is being the One having been given the Victor's wreath. Inasmuch as (or: When; Since) they will one-after-another be (or: will continue) seeing Him continuing in having the full-length (reaching the feet) scarlet robe around the flesh, then on that Day they will also repeatedly say,
    "Is not this he whom we ourselves then, upon setting at naught (in finding worthless; when scorning; while disdaining), crucified (impaled and suspended on a stake), also stabbing (piercing) and spitting on [him]? This one was truly being the one then progressively laying himself out to be (repeated saying himself to be) [the] Son of God!" [Mat. 27:27-28]

10. Come now, you say, How [is] that one like [the other]? In this view, and in this respect [are] the goats alike: "fine (ideal; beautiful; sound); equal" – so that when they would see Him, at that time [He would be like] [the] goat. Accordingly then, you must look, see and perceive the type and pattern of Jesus: one Who was being about to proceed suffering.

11. Now why [is it] that they normally (habitually) place the wool in the midst of the thorn-plant? It is a type and pattern of Jesus placing Himself in the called-out community (or: setting Himself with, and for, the called-out congregation), so that whoever may wish, or would intend, to take up and carry the scarlet wool, it continues binding and necessary for him to experience as well as to suffer many things, on account of the thorn-plant being of a fearful nature – and yet through pressured hardship, oppression or affliction to gain mastery of it. Thus He continues saying,
    "Those continuously wanting or progressively intending at some point to see Me and at some point to grasp and take hold of My reign (kingdom; sovereign influence) continue under obligation and necessity to receive Me (or: take hold of Me) through repeated pressing of having it hard (continual oppressing and afflicting; habitual squeezing and troubling) and repeated experiencing as well as periodic suffering." [cf Acts 14:22]

1. **Now what are you folks normally thinking or assuming [this] type and pattern to be, [where] it had been imparted as an inner directive to** (or: had been implanted and then continued as a goal for) **Israel that those men – within and among whom are full-grown sins** (completed failures; finished deviations; perfect errors; entire mistakes) **– are to repeatedly lead toward and offer a heifer, and after slaughtering [it] to continue completely burning [it] up. And next, children are habitually to take up the ashes and to cast [them] into a container, and then continue to twist the scarlet wool upon a tree** (or: put it around, and on, a stick, pole or stake)**? Look, see and perceive the type of the cross! And then the scarlet wool and the hyssop – and in this way the children are habitually to sprinkle the people, one by one, so that they would be cleansed and purified, away from the mistakes** (deviation; errors; failures to hit the target; sins).

2. **You folks are continuing to notice and consider, and are progressively perceiving with the mind, how, in frank simplicity, He progressively lays this out to you** (or: how He continues speaking to you in plainness)**: The calf is Jesus; the folks deviating and missing the target** (the sinners) **[are] the men proceeding in leading [it; Him] forward as an offering, those bearing Him face-to-face, upon the slaughter. So then, the glory** (the manifestation which calls forth praise; the reputation; the assumed appearance) **[is] no longer men; no longer from, or belonging to, deviating folks** (those missing the target).

    (or: After this, [it is] no more men [who offer]; the glory [is] no more of, from among, or pertaining to, sinners.)

3. **The children progressively sprinkling [are] the folks bringing to us, and proclaiming for and among us, the message of goodness, ease and well-being** (the Good News)**: the flowing away of the sins** (the liberation from the deviations; the divorce from mistakes and errors; the sending-away of failures to hit the goal) **and the cleansing** (purifying) **of the heart – to and among whom, being twelve, unto a witness of and from the tribes because twelve [were] the tribes of Israel, He gave from the message of goodness and wholeness, the right, from out of Being, into the [situation] to be constantly and progressively making public proclamation as heralds** (or: He gave the Gospel's privilege and the authority of Good News, with a view unto habitual preaching)**!**

4. **But on account of what** (or: Now why) **[were] three children the ones normally sprinkling? Unto a witness of** (or: testimony to) **Abraham, Isaac and Jacob, because these men [were] great in God** (important to God; mighty by God).

5. **Now in that the wool [is] upon the tree** (stake; pole)**, that [signifies that; means] the reign** (sovereign influence and activities; kingdom) **of Jesus [is] upon the tree** (stake; pole; = the cross)**, and that those placing expectation upon Him will continue living on into the midst of the Age [of Messiah].**

6. **But on account of what** (or: Now why) **[are] the wool and the hyssop together, at the same time? Because in His reign** (in union with His sovereign activities; centered in His kingdom) **misery-gushed** (worthless; unserviceable; pain-causing) **and soiled** (dirty) **days will continue being healed and progressively made whole** (keep on being saved; constantly be kept safe; repeatedly delivered)**, in which we ourselves will continue being healed and progressively made whole** (keep on being saved; constantly be kept safe; repeatedly delivered) **– and because the person continually feeling pain or hardship, [in the] flesh, progressively heals through the soil** (dirt; or: uncleanness; foulness) **of** (or: from) **the hyssop.**

7. **And so through this thus coming to be** (happening; occurring; being birthed)**, it is to** (for; with; in) **us, on the one hand, clearly seen** (apparent; evident; visible)**, yet on the other hand, to** (for; with;

among) **them, [it is] dark and obscure – because they did not listen to** (hear and obey) **[the] Voice of [the] Lord** ([the] Lord's voice; [the] Voice, which was [the] Lord).

Chapter 9

1. **It follows that He repeatedly lays it out** (or: For you see, He continues saying), **again, concerning the ears, how He circumcised our heart. [The] LORD repeatedly lays it out** (continues saying) **within the prophet,**
> **"They paid attention and fully listened to Me, unto** (as far as) **a hearing of** (from) **[the] ear."**
> [Ps. 18:44]

And again He is saying,
> **"'Those at a distance, being far off, will progressively** (or: repeatedly) **hear for** (or: in) **themselves, with an ability to hear** (or: in a report; by listening; for hearing obedience)**: they will come to know by experience what I do** (or: did; make; produced; form; constructed; create; created).' 'And so, you folks should circumcise your hearts,' [the] LORD continues saying."** [Isa. 33:13; Jer. 4:4]

2. **And again He repeatedly lays it out** (or: continues saying),
> **"Hear, O Israel, because [the] LORD** (= Yahweh), **your God, is now laying this out** (repeatedly says this)." [Deut. 6:6; Isa. 44:1; Jer. 7:2-3; 10:2; Ezk. 6:6]

Also again, the Breath-effect (Spirit) **of [the] Lord** (= Yahweh?) **continues giving Light ahead of time** (prophesying),
> **"Who is the person constantly wanting** (progressively intending) **that he or she might live on into the Age [of Messiah]? He or she must listen and hear with an ability to hear** (or: in a report; by listening; for hearing obedience) **from the Voice of My Child** (or: Servant)!" [Ps. 34:12; Isa. 50:10]

3. **Then again He repeatedly lays it out** (or: continues saying),
> **"Hear, O heaven** (sky; atmosphere), **and give ear, O earth** (Land; soil), **because [the] LORD** (= Yahweh) **spoke these things for a testimony** (as a witness; [inserting] evidence and proof)." [Isa. 1:2]

And yet again He keeps saying,
> **"You folks must listen, hear and pay attention to a Word of [the] LORD** (a message from [Yahweh]; [the] *Logos*, which is the Lord), **[you] rulers of this people."** [Isa. 1:10]

Next He again keeps saying,
> **"You folks must listen, hear and pay attention, O children: continual crying of a voice in the wilderness** (or: repeated crying out, from a voice within the midst of, and centered in, the desert!)." [Isa. 40:3]

Accordingly then, He circumcised our abilities to hear, to the end that in hearing a Word (a message; patterned information; a thought; an idea) **we could, and would, trust, believe, faith-it and be loyal.**

4. **And yet, in contrast, the circumcision upon which they had been convinced and persuaded, and now continue confident, has been rendered useless and unemployed** (completely idled-down, made barren and abolished)! **For you see, He had said not to produce** (give birth to; bring into being) **a circumcision of, from, or which pertains to, flesh. However, they walked to the side [of the path]** (deviated; transgressed), **because a misery-gushed agent** (a worthless, disadvantageous, harmful, malicious messenger; a person with a bad message) **played the "wise man" and, with clever device, deluded** (or: beguiled) **them.**

5. **He continues to lay it out for them** (progressively says to them) **– [and] here I am finding an implanted end in view** (imparted goal; inner directive):

"You people should not sow seed upon thorny plants (or, as present tense: not continue sowing among thorn-bushes); **you people must at some point be circumcised by your LORD [Yahweh]** (or: in your Lord [Christ]; for your Lord)." [Jer. 4:3, 4]

And so, what does it continue saying?

"You folks must be circumcised [in] your heart, and so you will not progressively stiffen (keep on hardening) your neck." [Deut. 10:16]

At once receive, again,

"'Look, and consider,' [the] LORD (= Yahweh) **continues saying: 'All the ethnic multitudes** (the nations; the non-Israelite; the pagans) **[have] an uncircumcised foreskin, but this People** [i.e., Israel] **[has] an uncircumcision of [the] heart** (from [the] heart).'" [Jer. 9:26]

6. **However, you folks will keep on saying, "In spite of that, indeed** (or: And yet, surely) **the People have been circumcised for a seal!" However, so also** (or: Nevertheless, even so) **[have] every Syrian and Arabian, and even the priests of the idols! Consequently then, those people are belonging to their covenant** (or: continuously exist from the midst of their arrangement)**! Even more than that, the Egyptians also are in union with [the] Circumcision** (or: exist centered in circumcision).

7. **Therefore, O children of Love** (or: from reunion-oriented Acceptance), **you must continue learning abundantly about all people** (or: you must progressively learn, concerning the abundance of all things), **because Abraham – [the] first one giving circumcision – in union with a Breath-effect** (or: centered in [the] Spirit) **was seeing ahead unto Jesus. He circumcised [people] upon receiving results of an appearance of three letters** (or: the effects of an opinion, which are three letters).

8. **You see, it continues saying,**

"And Abraham circumcised eighteen and three hundred men from out of his household." [cf Gen. 14:14; 17:23]

What knowledge and insight is being given in it (or: to him; by him; with it)**? Learn! Because the eighteen [were] first, and then, after making an interval, he continues in saying three hundred. [In] the 18, I** (= 10), **H** (= 8), **you have IHSOUS [Jesus]. Now because the cross, in the T** (the first letter of the Greek work for 300), **was continuing about to possess** (have; hold) **the grace and favor, He also goes on to say the three hundred. Therefore, indeed, he** (= Abraham) **manifested** (revealed; showed) **Jesus in the two letters** (IH) **and the cross** (execution stake) **in the one** (T).

9. **He** (= Abraham) **had seen, and then continued knowing the One placing** (setting) **the innate, inborn, natural gift of the teaching** [other MSS: covenant; arrangement] **within us. No one learned a more genuine** *Logos* (legitimate Word; reliable patterned-message; thought belonging to the Race and Family). **But I have seen, and now know, that you folks are worthy** (exist of equal value).

Chapter 10

1. **But in that Moses said,**

"You people will not continue to eat swine (pig; hog)**, nor eagle** (or: vulture), **nor hawk, nor raven** (or: crow), **nor all fish which do not have scales on them,"** [Lev. 11:7ff; Deut. 14:8ff] **he laid hold of** (took; or: received) **three results of an appearance** (or: effects from an opinion, or how it seemed) **within the understanding** (in union with [his] faculty of intelligence which could make things flow together).

2. **And furthermore** (or: So finally) **he said to them in Deuteronomy,**

"And so I will progressively fully-place, set-throughout and establish through the midst, My effects of what is right and in the Way that I point with a view to this People (or: I will keep on establishing, face-to-face with this People, the results of the things, from Me, that are just)." [Deut. 4:10, 13]

Consequently, then, God's implanted goal (the imparted end in view, from God; the inner directive, which is God) **is not [about; concerning] the thing not to crunch on or to chew, but you see, Moses spoke in union with [the] Spirit** (or: centered in the midst of Spirit; within the midst of a Breath-effect).

3. **He mentioned the swine with this intent [and] He continues affirming:**
"**You will not continue being joined to such people** (or: caused to adhere with folks of this kind) **– anyone who continues being like pigs** (as swine), **that is, whenever they are in luxury and are given to pleasure, they completely escape notice of, and forget, the Lord. Yet when they continue lacking, being in need or in poverty, they keep on fully noticing, recognizing, acknowledging and experientially knowing the Lord. And so, just as the pig does not see or know the owner, or master, whenever it normally crunches and chews [its food], yet when it continues hungry it repeatedly cries out** (squeals), **then upon receiving again, it continues silent** (or: and then with receiving, it continues silent, again)."

4. "**Neither will you continue eating the eagle** (or: vulture), **nor the hawk, nor the kite, nor the raven** (or: crow)." [Lev. 11:14]
He continues affirming,
"**Under no circumstances will you continue being joined to, or be caused to adhere to, nor continue being made like such people** (people of this kind) **– anyone who has not seen, and so does not know how to continue providing** (or: procure) **the food and provision for themselves through hard labor and sweat.**"
But to the contrary, as also, in their lawlessness, they continually seize, snatch away and steal the things belonging to another person (they repeatedly plunder), **and then they continue lying in wait and watching upon, as if in sincere harmlessness** (inviolate, unmixed purity), **while constantly walking around** (= living their lives) **and continually looking around for whom they will proceed in stripping** (ripping off), **on account of this insatiable greed** (desire to overreach so as to take advantage and have more; inordinate desire for wealth) **– just as, also, these birds alone continue procuring no food or nourishment for them, but instead, while continuously sitting idle and without work: it keeps on searching and seeking out how it can eat down [the] flesh** (or: meat) **belonging to** (or: from) **another – [these] are continuously being folks diseased by** (pestilential in and with) **their misery-gushed worthlessness** (malicious baseness; unsound condition).

5. **Also, He continues affirming,**
"**You will not continue eating sea-eel** (or: lamprey) **nor octopus, nor cuttlefish** (or: squid)." [Lev. 11:10-12]
He is saying [that] in no way will you be progressively made like such people (folks of this kind) **by being habitually joined to and caused to adhere to those who continue being utterly irreverent** (profane; without proper awe toward God) **on unto an end** (into [their] final performance), **and being folks who were already separated, evaluated and are now judged in the Death** (by the Death; to, and with, the Death) **– just as, also, these fish, alone imposed with a negative wish** (or: having an added down-prayer; fully prayed against), **habitually swim within the midst of the Deep** (or: deep [water]), **not swimming up on the surface and diving down or being suspended, as the remaining ones** (the rest of them), **but instead in the muck and mud down under the depth of the sea it will continue settled and dwelling.**

6. **But also,**
"**You will not at any point eat the rabbit** (hare)." [Lev. 11:6]
Toward what end (Why)? **He continues affirming, "You are in no way to at any point come to be a corrupter of children** (a pedophile), **neither proceed being made like such people** (folks of this kind), **because the rabbit keeps on gaining more anuses** (or: having more voiding of excrement) **each year, for as many years as it continues living, it continues having just so many orifices** (= it has as many openings, or anuses, as years)."

382

7.   **"But neither will you at any point eat the hyena."** [Lev. 11:27]
He continues affirming,

"You are in no way to at any point come be an adulterer nor a seducer, neither proceed being made like such people (folks of this kind)**."**
Toward what end (Why)? Because this living being (= person) **continues changing [its] nature, year by year, and so repeatedly coming to be, at one time, male, yet, at another time, female!**

8.   **"But further, He ideally abhors** (beautifully regards with ill-will) **the weasel."**
He continues saying,

"In no way at any point be made to exist like this, of what sort we repeatedly hear of women repeatedly producing (practicing; constructing; creating; doing) **lawlessness with their mouth."**
For it follows that this living creature (= person) **is constantly conceiving, being pregnant and bringing forth by** (with; in) **the mouth!**

9.   **Indeed, Moses, upon receiving results of an appearance of three letters** (or: the effects of an opinion, which are three letters; or: = three precepts), **thus spoke in [the] Spirit** (centered in and in union with a Breath-effect) **concerning the foods. But they, according to the over-desires** (strong passions and added rushing emotions) **of, and from, the flesh, kept on receiving [them] on face value** (or: face to face), **as though being about [actually] eating food!**

10.   **Now David continued receiving intimate knowledge and insight of the results of an appearance of these three letters** (or: the effects of an opinion, which are these three letters [or: = precepts]), **and so he continues saying,**

"Blessed and happy [is] a man who does not travel (journey on; pass from one place to another) **in counsel from impious and profane folks"**
– just as also the fishes progressively make their way (pass from place to place) **within darkness, into the depths; just as the folks continually appearing or pretending to be fearing the LORD** (= Yahweh), **as** (or: like) **the swine, continue failing to hit the target** (keep on making mistakes; constantly deviate into error; progressively sin) **–**

"and do not sit upon [the] seat of diseased and pestilential folks," [Ps. 1:1]
– just as the birds constantly perch with a view to a seizure and a snatching away.

You folks continue completely holding (or: holding maturely) **also [the teaching] concerning foods.**

11.   **Again, Moses continues saying,**
"You folks will continue eating everything [with a] dividing hoof and normally chewing the cud." [Lev. 11:3]
What is he saying? That the one continuously receiving the food and nourishment has seen, and thus knows, the One continually feeding and nourishing him, and upon Him, being habitually rested and refreshed, he normally seems (appears) **to continue being in a healthy frame of mind, and with a good attitude. He spoke well** (fitly; beautifully), **while seeing and perceiving** (or: in observing and considering) **the implanted goal** (the imparted destiny; the inner directive). **What, then, does he continue saying?**

"You folks continue being joined, glued and caused to adhere with the people continuously respectfully reverencing the LORD (= Yahweh, or Christ), **with those constantly meditating on, thinking about, studying and paying careful attention to the result of the distinct contrast of the gush-effect** (or: the effect of the difference from the result of the flow of what was spoken) **[that] you folks received in the midst of [your] heart, with the folks habitually speaking** (telling; discussing) **and maintaining** (guarding; preserving; watching over) **the effects of the rightwising, rightful, just deed of, and which is, [the] Lord, and the**

results of the equity and righted relationships from [the] Lord, with those seeing and knowing that the focused meditation and attentive study is a work (action) of a good attitude with a healthy frame of mind, as well as continually ruminating (progressively chewing over again) the *Logos* (Word; thought; idea; patterned information; message; reason) of, and which is, [the] Lord."

Now what [is] this "dividing hoof"? That the just (righted; fair; equitable; aligned-with-the-pointed-out-Way) person continues walking about (= living his or her life) in this domination System (world of religion, culture, economics and government) and yet continually receives from out of The set-apart and sacred Age [of Messiah]. You folks are constantly seeing how Moses beautifully established the Law (set the custom; placed the instruction; or: functioned as a law-giver).

12. Nevertheless, how and in what way [is it possible] for those folks to at some point direct their minds (use their intellect to conceive) or to make things flow together (understand) these things? Now we, ourselves, while rightly perceiving the implanted goals (imparted destinies; inner directives), continue speaking as the Lord (or: the LORD) willed and intends. On account of these things, He circumcised (or: circumcises) our ears and hearts, to the end that we could make these things flow together and understand them.

Chapter 11

1. Now let us seek, investigate and enquire whether it was a care to the LORD (a concern for [Yahweh]; of interest with the LORD) to set in clear Light and make visible and disclosed beforehand concerning the water and concerning the cross (execution stake). Indeed, concerning the water, it has been, and now stands, written upon (in reference to) Israel: how they will continue by no means accepting or receiving to themselves the effect of the immersion (baptism) which continues bringing (bearing; carrying) a flowing-away of (a release, a divorce and a dismissal from) failures to hit the target (mistakes; sins; errors; deviations)! But to the contrary, they will continue erecting a building for themselves! (or: In contrast, they will keep on constructing and establishing [the substitute] among themselves, and by themselves.)

2. You see, the prophet continues saying,
"Be amazed and removed from your place, O heaven (atmosphere; sky)! And let the earth (or: the Land) shudder and quake even more, at this! And that is because this People did two worthless, misery-gushed things: ME! The Fountain (or: Spring) of Life, they abandoned (left down within the midst), and then they dug for themselves a pit of death (or: dug out among themselves a cistern from death; prepared by themselves a hole that is death)!" [Jer. 2:12, 13]

3. "Is Sinai, My set-apart (sacred) mountain, a desolate rock in the wilderness? You see, you folks will progressively be as when a nest has been taken away from young (fledgling) birds." [Isa. 16:1f]

4. Then, again, the prophet continues saying,
"I Myself will continue going from one place to another (or: will keep on journeying on) in front of you, in your presence, and I will make level and even [the] mountains and I will continue crushing and breaking in pieces bronze or copper gates (or: two-winged doors), and I will repeatedly disjoint-together (shatter; burst) bars made of iron. Then I will proceed giving to (or: for) you treasures [that are] dark (or: obscure treasures), hidden (concealed) [and] invisible (or: unseen) – to the end that you folks can come to know by experience (or: would gain insight) that I, Myself, [am the] LORD (=Yahweh) God!" [Isa. 45:2, 3]

Also,
"You will proceed in settling down and continue dwelling as a permanent resident in the midst of a high cave (or: centered in a den or place of refuge) of a strong Rock." [Isa. 33:16a]

384

5. **And then,**

"**His water [is] faithful** (dependable; reliable; or: full of trust, faith and conviction). **You folks will continue seeing [the] King, with an assumed appearance** (with a manifestation which calls forth praise; with glory and a good reputation), **and your soul** (the inner being of you folks) **will continue caring for, meditating on, heeding, paying attention to, and studying [the] respectful reverence from [the] LORD** [= Yahweh or Christ] (or: a fear which is [Yahweh]; a respect from [the] Lord)."

6. **And further, in another prophet, He continues saying,**

"**And thus, he will continue existing, being like the Tree [that] has been planted beside the divided-out paths of the Waters** (or: outlets of water through [the orchard]; or: rivulets of the waters that pass through), – **[which will give** (yield; = produce) **its Fruit in its season** (or: fitting situation) **and] whose [leaf] will not proceed in falling off** (slipping away; flow from [it]). **And so, everything that he should continue doing** (or: all things – however much he can make or produce) **will proceed to be thoroughly prospered** (continuously led down an easy path, or along a good road)!" [cf Ps. 1:3; brackets reading from LXX, cf vs. 8, below]

7. "**Not thus [for] the profane and irreverent folks who lack awe and respect for God – no, not thus [is their] way! Rather, in contrast, [they are] like the dust or chaff which the wind habitually tosses out and scatters away from the face** (= surface) **of the ground** (or: land; earth). **Through this** (or: Therefore) **the profane and irreverent people will not continue standing up** (or: proceed to take a stand again; or: repeatedly arise) **in the midst of an evaluation** (a sifting and separating for a decision; a judging), **nor yet folks who normally fall short of the goal** (miss the target; fail; err) **within a counsel** (or: determination) **of folks who are just, equitable and in accord with the way pointed out. Because [the] Lord** (= Yahweh), **by intimate experience and insight, constantly knows the path** (way; road) **of the just, equitable and rightwised folks who live in the way pointed out. And yet, the path** (way; road) **of the profane and irreverent people will progressively lose and destroy itself** (of itself repeatedly come to ruin)." [Ps. 1:4-6, LXX]

8. **You folks normally notice and perceive how He defined and explained the water and the cross at the same time and on the same basis, for you see, this is [what] He proceeds laying out** (or: continues saying):

"**Happy and blessed are the people [who], having placed [their] expectation upon the cross, step down and descend into the midst of the Water,**"
because, indeed, He continues saying, "**the reward** (recompense; wage), '**in its season** (or: fitting situation; fertile moment),'" and then goes on saying, "**I will continue progressively repaying** (giving back; recompensing; giving away)," **But now He continues saying,**

"**the leaves will not proceed in falling off** (slipping away; flow from [it])." [Ps. 1:3]
He is saying (= meaning) **this: that every result of the flow** (gush-effect; or: saying; that which flows or falls) **which will continue going** (or: coming) **forth, from out of you folks, through your mouth, in Trust and Love** (in union with faith and acceptance; centered in faithfulness and an urge toward reunion) **will continue being with a view to** (will constantly exist unto) **a turning-around and an expectation for many people** (or: a conversion and a return, as well as expectant hope, in many folks; or: a turning-upon in order to pay attention, and then expectation, with many and by many).

9. **Then again, a different prophet continues saying,**

"**So the Land [which] continued belonging to Jacob** (or: the soil and earth [that] was progressively existing from, and was pertaining to, Jacob) **continues being praised beyond all that territory** (or: alongside of and in the presence of all the earth)." [cf Zeph. 3:19]

This is what he is saying: He continuously glorifies (progressively gives a good reputation to; repeatedly creates a manifestation which calls forth praise for; keeps on giving an assumed appearance in) **the vessel of His Spirit** (the container of His Breath-effect; the instrument or utensil from the Spirit).

10. **What does he continue saying afterward?**
     "And there was (continued being) **a river, continually drawing** (unsheathing; pulling; dragging) **from out of the right hand, and forth from it continued growing up** (was stepping up, growing back and mounting again) **beautiful, well-formed trees, and whoever will continue eating from out of them will continue living on into the midst of the Age [of Messiah]."** [cf Ezk. 47:12; Rev. 22:2]

11. **He keeps on saying this because we ourselves, indeed, keep on, one after another, stepping down and descending into the Water fully loaded with deviations** (from failures to hit the target, sins, errors, mistakes) **and pollution** (and from filth and defilement; dirt; uncleanness), **and then we, one after another, keep on stepping back up** (continue ascending again), **progressively bearing fruit in union with the Spirit** (centered in the Breath-effect), **while continuing in having, holding, and possessing [it]. Also:**
     "Whoever will continue eating for these, will continue living on into the midst of the (or: that) **Age [of Messiah]."**
     He keeps on saying (and meaning) **this:**
     "Whoever," He continues saying,
     "will continue listening and hearing (or, as a subjunctive: can or would listen and hear) **these sayings** (proclamations) **that are being repeatedly spoken and sounded out, and then would trust and be faithful** (or: believe and faith-it), **will go on living – on into the midst of the** (or: that) **Age [of Messiah]."**

Chapter 12

1. **Likewise** (Similarly; In like manner), **He continues defining and progressively explains again, concerning** (about) **the cross – in another prophet, continuing in saying,**
     "And so when will these things be joined together at the goal (be mutually accomplished; be consummated in a common end; be brought to their joint-destiny)**? [The] LORD** (or: Lord; Master) **proceeds saying: 'When a tree would at some point trickle** (pour down; stream; drop) **blood."** [cf 4 Ezra 4:33; 5:5]
     Again, you continue possessing [that teaching] concerning the cross (stake) **and the One continuing about to be crucified** (impaled; suspended).

2. **Now He continues saying, again, in Moses, when war was continuously being waged, and battles were repeatedly fought against Israel, by the other tribes** (races; nations), **and so that He might remind them, during the battling and waging of war, that through** (or: in the course of) **their deviations** (failures to hit the goal; mistakes; errors; sins) **they would at some point be given over into death. The Spirit** (Breath-effect) **continued saying into the heart of Moses that he should make** (form; construct) **a type** (mark from a blow; pattern; hammered image) **of [the] cross and of the One being about to suffer. He continued saying that should they not** (or: unless they) **place expectation upon it** (or: Him), **war will continue being waged [against them] on into the Age [of Messiah]. Therefore Moses progressively placed** (or: stacked) **one weapon upon another within the middle of the fight** (or: proceeded putting one spear on the midst of [his] fist), **and then being placed on a high place and standing higher than all [the] people, he stretched out his hands, and in this way Israel was again victorious. And then, whenever he let, or put, [them] down** (or: lowered [them]), **they continued being put to death.** [Ex. 17:8-13]

3. **Toward what end** (Why)? **So that they would come to know that a person continues without power** (unable) **to at any point be delivered** (rescued; made whole; healed; kept safe; saved) **unless they would place** (or: set) **[their] expectation** (or: expectant hope) **upon Him.**

4. **And again, in a different prophet, He continues saying,**
> **"The whole day long I have stretched out and spread forth My hands toward an unpersuaded, unconvinced, uncompliant, and thus, disobedient People – even those continually speaking against and repeatedly contradicting My pointed-out** Path (My just Road; a Right Way, which is Me)." [Isa. 65:2; comment: spread out hands may symbolize crucifixion, in the author's context]

5. **Again Moses proceeds building** (crafting; constructing; creating; producing) **a type of** (or: hammered image and pattern with reference to) **Jesus, because it continues binding and necessary for Him to proceed to suffer, and that He Himself – whom they continued supposing to have destroyed – will one-after-another continue producing life in a sign** (or: centered in a pointing denotation) **for those of Israel who continue falling. You see, [the] LORD made every snake to bite them, and then they died off – inasmuch as The Deviation and Transgression** [Lightfoot text adds: of Eve was through a snake] **– through their deviation and transgression, they will one-after-another** (or: progressively) **be given over into death's compression** (or: entrusted unto a squeezing pressure from death; or: delivered into the midst of an affliction of death).

6. **In the end, though, even Moses himself, after implanting the goal** (imparting this intended end; giving an inner directive),
> **"There will not continue being for you folks neither a molten and cast image, nor a graven or carved image, into being a god for or among you people,"** [Lev. 26:1; Deut. 27:15]
he himself proceeded making (constructing; producing) **one so that he could display a type and point out a pattern of Jesus** (show a model in a hammered image, with reference to Jesus). **Therefore, Moses proceeded progressively making** (producing) **a copper snake** (or: a bronze serpent), **continues in setting [it] conspicuously** (placing it gloriously, with honor and splendor; setting it in a seemly and apparent way), **and then progressively calls the People for** (or: by; with; in) **a proclamation.**

7. **Then, upon coming upon that very place, they make request of Moses, that he would hold** (bear; carry) **up an urgent petition** (prayer request to meet a need) **concerning them – concerning their healing. So Moses said to them,**
> **"Whenever any of you folks may be bitten,"** he went on saying, **"he must come** (or: go) **on to the serpent** (snake; viper) **– the one lying** (pressed; placed) **upon the tree** (stake; wooden pole) **– and in trusting and while faithing-it** (believing) **he must at once expect** (or: have expectation) **that it, being dead, continues able** (keeps on having power) **to make alive** (to produce life), **and immediately he will be healed** (made whole; saved; delivered). **So in this way, thus, they performed** (they did)," [Nu. 21:4-8; Jn. 3:14-15]
So again you folks continue having, also in these things, the glory of Jesus (the manifestation which calls forth praise, in the assumed appearance, of Jesus), **because all [are] in union with Him** (or: that all things [exist] within the midst of Him; because all [is] centered in Him) **and [proceeds] into the midst of Him.** [cf Rom. 11:36]

8. **So why does Moses, being a prophet** (existing as one having light ahead of time), **again continue speaking about Joshua** (in Greek = Jesus), **son of Nun, when putting on him this name** [cf Nu. 13:16], **that all the People should hear, and listen to, [him] alone? Because the Father [made/makes] all things clear, evident and apparent concerning the Son, Jesus.**
9. **Therefore Moses continues saying to Joshua, son of Nun, when setting this name, when he sent him [as] a spy of the Land,**

"Take a scroll into your hands and write what [the] LORD is saying, that the Son of God will cut out from the roots all the house of Amalek, upon [the] last of the days." [cf Ex. 17:4]

10. **See again Jesus – not a son from humanity** (or: a son of a human), **but rather, a Son of, or from, God – now being set in clear Light** (being caused to be seen; being made visible; being manifested; being presented in view) **in a type** (for a pattern; by a model; with a beaten image) **in flesh** (centered in flesh; in union with flesh), **since therefore they continued about to say that "Christ is [the] Son of David"** (or: a descendant of David), **David himself prophesies, when fearing and yet understanding the straying and wandering** (or: the delusion and deception) **of the folks deviating** (from the people failing to hit the target; concerning sinners; which are the ones making mistakes and errors):
> "[The] LORD (= Yahweh) **said to my Lord** (Master), **"Be continuously sitting from out of** (or: = at) **My right-hand [parts] until I should place** (or: put) **Your alienated ones** (or: folks filled with hate and hostility; enemies) **a footstool of Your feet."** [Ps. 110:1; Mat. 22:44]

11. **And again, Isaiah continues speaking in this way,**
> "[The] LORD (= Yahweh) **said to my Anointed Master** (or: for my Christ, the Lord) – **from Whom, from His right hand, I prevail and am strong to rule – [that the] ethnic multitudes** (nations; pagans; Gentiles) **are to hear, listen and obey** (= act appropriately), **before Him, in His presence, and so, I will continue breaking through [the] strength of kings."** [cf Isa. 45:1]

See how David continues calling Him Lord (Master), **and is not saying, "son."**

Chapter 13

1. **Now we should see whether this people or the first** (or: former [People]) **continues enjoying and possessing the allotted inheritance, and whether the covenant [is] unto us, or unto them** (or: if the arrangement had reference to us, or to them).

2. **You folks listen and hear, then, what the Writing** (Scripture) **continues saying concerning the People:**
> "Now Isaac kept on making a request (was repeatedly asking [God]) concerning Rebecca, his wife, because she continued being infertile (barren) – and then she conceived (became pregnant)! And then (or: Next) Rebecca went out to inquire (seek information and learn) from beside [the] LORD (or: at the side of [Yahweh]), and [the] LORD said to her, 'Two nations (ethnic groups) [are] within your belly, and two peoples within your uterus (womb), and thus, a people will progressively hold above and continue excelling over [the other] people, and then the greater (= the elder) will continue performing as a slave to the lesser (smaller; fewer; = younger).'" [Gen. 25:21-23]

3. **You folks continue making it your obligation** (or: You continuously ought) **to keep on discerning, perceiving and progressively understanding who Isaac [represents] and who Rebecca [represents], and thus upon whose case He has pointed out and demonstrated that this people [is] greater than that one.**

4. **And then, in another prophecy, Jacob continues saying, more clearly** (in a way that is easier to see; more evidently), **to Joseph, his son, by saying,**
> "Look, and consider, [the] LORD (= Yahweh) **did not deprive me of your face** (or: from your presence)! **Bring your sons toward me** (or: face-to-face with me) **to the end** (for the purpose) **that I will proceed in speaking words of goodness, ease and well-being for** (or: will be blessing) **them."** [Gen. 48:11, 9]

5. **And so he brought forward Ephraim and Manasseh, desiring and intending that Manasseh would be blessed** (spoken well upon), **because he was older – for you see, Joseph brought him forward unto the right hand of his father, Jacob. Now Jacob saw in, and by, the Spirit** (Breath-

effect) **a type and a pattern of the afterward** (in between; middle) **people. And so what does it continue saying?**

> **"And then Jacob made** (did) **his hands crossways and placed the right one upon the dead of Ephraim, the second and newer one, and then he blessed** (spoke words of goodness, ease and well-being upon) **him. Then Joseph said to Jacob, 'Change** (or: Transfer) **your right hand to [be] upon the head of Manasseh, because he is my firstborn son.' And yet Jacob said to Joseph, 'I see and know, child, I see and know. But rather, the greater** (= older) **will continue performing as a slave to the lesser** (smaller; fewer; = younger). **Even yet, this one also will continue being blessed.'"** [cf Gen. 48:14-19]

6. **You folks look at, see and consider upon which ones [it is that] He has placed and set this people to be** (to continue existing) **first, and thus [the] heir** (enjoyer of the allotted inheritance) **of the covenant** (arrangement).

7. **Since, then, it is still mentioned and called to attention through Abraham, we continue receiving in full and possessing from the perfection** (the intended goal; the completion; the final phase) **of our personal knowledge and insight. What, then, does He continue saying in Abraham** (or: to Abraham; with the case of Abraham; for Abraham)**? That only with trusting and faithing and being loyal was he placed, set and established into the midst of eschatological deliverance** (being turned unto the right direction of the Way pointed out, with rightwised relationships of the justice and fairness of covenant participation)**:**

> **"Look and consider! I set** (placed; established) **you, Abraham: a father of ethnic multitudes** (nations) **of folks constantly trusting God** (habitually being faithful to God; progressively believing by God; repeatedly faithing, in God; continuing loyal, for God), **even though uncircumcised!"** [cf Gen. 15:6; 17:5; Rom. 4:11ff]

Chapter 14

1. **Yes, indeed. Nevertheless, let us see whether the covenant** (arrangement) **– one which He swore to the fathers, to give to the People – whether He [actually] has given [it]. He has given it! Yet they themselves** (or: those folks) **did not come to be worthy to receive [it], on account of their deviations** (sins; failures to hit the target; errors; mistakes).

2. **You see, the prophet continues saying,**

> **"And Moses was continuing in fasting, within Mount Sinai, forty days and forty nights, so as to receive the covenant of and from [the] LORD** (or: [Yahweh's] arrangement) **toward** (or: with a view to) **the People. And thus, Moses received the two tablets – the ones having been written in Spirit by** (with) **the finger of the LORD's hand – from the presence of [the] LORD** (or: at the side of [the] LORD). **And so, upon receiving [them], Moses began bringing [them] down, to give [them] to the People.**

3. > **"And then [the] LORD said to Moses, 'O Moses! Moses! Descend quickly, because your People, whom you led out from the Land of Egypt, are without a law, and act lawlessly! And then Moses made things flow together, perceived and understood that they had again made** (formed; constructed) **for themselves the results of casting metal, and so he hurled** (cast) **the tablets of the covenant** (arrangement) **of, and from, [the] LORD, and they were at once broken in pieces!"** [cf Ex. 24:18; 31:18; 32:7-8, 19]

4. **Now how did WE, ourselves, receive [it]? Learn! Moses, being an attending aid, received [it]. But the LORD** (or: Lord; Master) **gave [it] to, and for, US – unto a people of an inheritance** (or: with a view to [being the] people of [His] inheritance; into the midst of a people which are enjoyers of an allotment) **– by staying behind, patiently enduring, and remaining under to give support, on account of US!**

5. **Now He was set in clear Light and caused to be seen** (made visible and thus publicly known; manifested) **so that THOSE folks would be caused to reach the end with regard to the sins** (or: be finished with the failures to hit the target; be brought to the goal by [their] deviations; be caused to reach the end of the course, so as to receive the fulfillment for the errors), **and yet WE, ourselves, would receive the inheritance** (allotment enjoyment) **of [the] Lord's covenant** (or: the arrangement from [the] Master; the covenant which is [the] Lord), **through Jesus, who was made ready and prepared unto this, to the end that, by He Himself appearing – already by having consumed our heart in, by and with death and by paying back for the lawlessness from the straying deception** (the error of wandering), **by releasing and liberating and setting [us] free from out of the Darkness – it was fully arranged and established within and among us: an arrangement** (a covenant) **by [the]** *Logos,* **with a Word of patterned information, and in a Message that transferred the conveyance of reasoned Meaning!**

6. **For you see, it has been, and now stands, written how the Father implanted a goal** (imparted an end in view; gave an inner directive): **after releasing, liberating and setting us free from out of the midst of the Darkness, to prepare and make ready a set-apart** (sacred; holy) **people in Himself** (with Himself; for Himself; to Himself).

7. **Therefore the prophet continues saying,**
    "I [the] LORD (= Yahweh), **your God, have called You in eschatological deliverance** (centered in the Way pointed out; in union with rightwised relationships of the justice of covenant participation), **and I will continue being strong so as to prevail from Your hand, and I will continually give** (progressively impart to) **You inner strength. So I have given You for a covenant** (unto an arrangement) **of Family** (pertaining to [the] race; from [the] species; which are kindred), **for a Light of [the] ethnic multitudes** (nations; Gentiles); **to open up the eyes of blind people and then to bring out of chains folks having been bound, and out of a house of guarding** (or: from a prison house) **those constantly sitting within Darkness."** [Isa. 42:6-7]
    We continue knowing, then, by intimate experience, from where we were released, liberated and set free.

8. **Again, the prophet continues saying,**
    "Look and consider! I have placed (set and established) **You for a Light of ethnic multitudes** (nations; Gentiles), **with a view for You to be for deliverance** (salvation; rescue; safety; healing; wholeness) **as far as [the] farthest part** (last point) **of the earth – thus continues saying [the] LORD, the One repeatedly releasing, progressively liberating and habitually setting you free: God."** [Isa. 49:6, 7]

9. **And again the prophet continues saying,**
    "[The] Spirit (or: A Breath-effect) **of [the] LORD [is] upon Me, for which purpose He anointed Me to bring and announce a message of goodness, ease and well-being: to humble, unimportant people of low status – grace and favor. He sent Me off to heal the folks with the heart having been crushed and continuing broken in pieces; to make public proclamation of release, a letting-go and a sending-off to captives, and a recovery of sight to blind folks; to summon** (call) **a received and acceptable year of, or from, [the] LORD** (=Yahweh) **and a day of reward and recompense** (paying back); **to call to My side for aid, encouragement and comfort all the people continuously sad, repeatedly sorrowful or presently mourning."** [Isa. 61:1, 2; Mat. 5:3]

1. **Then yet, also, concerning the sabbath, it has been written within the ten Words** (Thoughts; Ideas; Messages; Patterned Information; Transferred Conveyance of Reasoned Meaning) **in which He spoke face-to-face with Moses, within Mount Sinai:**

> **"And so, you people set-apart as sacred** (holy) **the sabbath** (rest) **of, and from, [the] LORD** (= Yahweh) **with** (or: by) **clean hands and with** (or: by) **a clean heart!"** [Ex. 20:8; Deut. 5:12; Ps. 24:4]

2. **And in a different place He goes on saying,**

> **"If My sons would guard, keep watch over and maintain the sabbath** (rest), **then** (at that point) **I will continue applying** (setting added; fully placing) **My mercy upon them."** [Ex. 31:13-17; Jer. 17:24; Isa. 56:2ff]

3. **He proceeds speaking [of] the sabbath within a beginning of the creation:**

> **"And God made** (formed; produced) **the works of His hands within six days, and next brought the goal together** (finished-and-ended-together; jointly-completed the project; closed-together the final act; consummated the finished product) **within the midst of** (or: centered in) **the seventh day, and then He completely stopped and rested down within it** (or: gave complete rest centered in it; ceased along the line of, and in union with, it), **and so He set it apart."** [Gen. 2:2, 3]

4. **Progressively hold toward and pay attention, children, to what He is saying:**

> **"He brought the goal together** (finished-and-ended-together; jointly-completed the project; closed-together the final act; consummated the finished product) **within six days!"**

THIS He continues saying: that within six thousand years [the] LORD (= Yahweh) **will progressively bring to the goal together** (finish-and-end-together; jointly-complete the project of; close the final act of; consummate the finished production of) **the joining together of all things** (the corporate, finished production of all; the whole, together), **for you see, the Day beside Him** (or: with Him; by Him) **shows by a sign** (signifies; indicates as a mark) **a thousand years. Now He Himself continues testifying** (progressively witnesses) **to me, repeatedly saying:**

> **"Look and consider! A Day of, or from, [the] LORD will continue being as a thousand years!"** [cf 2 Pet. 3:8]

Consequently, children, within six days, that is, within the six thousand years, the joining together of all things (the corporate, finished production of all; the whole, together) **will progressively be brought to the goal together** (finished-and-ended-together; jointly-completed; closed for the final act; consummated with the finished production).

5. **THIS He repeatedly says:**

> **"And then He completely stopped and rested down within** (or: gave complete rest centered in; ceased along the line of, and in union,) **within the midst of** (or: centered in) **the seventh day."**

When coming, His Son will proceed causing the season (or: situation) **of the lawless** (or: the lawless person) **to be progressively idle and useless** (to continue being discharged and out of work), **and He will proceed evaluating and deciding about** (or: continue judging) **those without awe of God** (the irreverent), **and then He will progressively change the sun and the moon and the stars.** [comment: a reference to Gen. 37:9-10; thus, in this figure, Israel being changed]

At that time He will continue beautifully giving complete rest and will proceed to ideally stop within that sphere – within the seventh Day!

6. **In the end, though, He continues saying,**

> **"You folks will set it apart with** (or: by) **clean hands and with** (or: by) **a clean heart."** [Ex. 31:12ff]

In all [these] things we have been deceived and led astray if, then, now anyone – even though being clean in the heart – continues able (with power) to set apart a day which God has [already] set apart!

>[comment: no human decision or work can set anything apart, or consecrate it; this is all God's decision and God's work; we only enter into His work, as the next verse explains]

7. **Look, then, and take note! Then, in now being folks continuing in completely resting beautifully** (habitually having fully stopped in an ideal way), **we will continue setting it apart while we will continue able** (having power) **– ourselves at one point having been set right**

>(being made just; being eschatologically delivered and turned in the right direction; being put in rightwised relationships of covenant participation) **and while taking away from the Promise** (obtaining, recovering, and receiving-off-from the Promise) **[and] NO LONGER constantly being of** (or: belonging to) **the lawlessness** (existing from that which is lawless), **but with ALL humans** (people) **HAVING BEEN BIRTHED ANEW, and now existing new, and with all things having now come to be new, by [the] Lord, while we will continue with power and ability to progressively set it apart, with we ourselves first being set apart!** [cf Rev. 21:5; 2 Cor. 5:17]

8. **In the end, though, He continues saying to them,**

>**"Your new moons and the sabbaths I cannot continue holding up to** (keep on tolerating, enduring, putting up with, bearing, accepting or standing)**."** [Isa. 1:13]

You folks see how He keeps on saying,

>**"The sabbaths [are] not acceptable to Me, but in contrast** (or: rather) **the one I have made** (constructed; produced; formed) **in which, when fully stopping the whole and completely resting all things, I will continue progressively making** (creating; forming; constructing; producing) **a beginning of an eighth Day, which is a beginning of another aggregate of Humanity** (or: another ordered and arranged System; or: another world)**."**

9. **On account of this, also, we continue bringing, and leading, the eighth Day into a good attitude and a healthy frame of mind, centered in** (or: in union with) **which also Jesus rose back up from out of the midst of dead folks, and then, after being set in clear Light** (manifested; made to appear publicly), **He stepped up into an atmosphere** (or: He ascended into heaven).

Chapter 16

1. **Now yet also, I will proceed telling you folks concerning the sanctuary of the temple** (shrine; = the holy place and the holy of holies), **seeing that these miserable** (distressed; wretched) **men, being continuously deceived and led astray, place their expectation** (or: placed expectant hope) **into the building, as being a House of God, and not upon their God – the One making** (forming; producing) **them!**

>[note: the aorist tenses of this passage can be rendered in English as either simple present tenses, or as simple past tenses (the aorist is characterized as an "indefinite" or "fact" tense, or one that gives a point of time "snapshot" of the action); if read as present, then this passage may indicate a pre-AD 70 date as the period of the letter's origin; if read as past, then it would indicate a post-AD 70 date]

2. **You see, almost like the ethnic multitudes** (the nations; the pagans; the Gentiles), **they officiate** (or: officiated) **as priests and consecrate** (or: consecrated) **Him within the sanctuary** (centered in the shrine; in union with the holy place). **In contrast, how is [the] Lord then speaking of proceeding in idling it down to be useless** (making it unemployed; discharging it as barren; abolishing it; nullifying it)**? You folks must learn.**

>**"Who measured the sky** (heaven; atmosphere) **with a span, or the earth with a hand? [Is it] not I, Myself?" [the] LORD continues saying. "The sky** (atmosphere; heaven) **[is] a throne for Me, but the earth [is] a footstool of My feet. What sort of house will you folks proceed building for Me, or what [is] a place of My stopping and resting?"** [cf Isa. 40:12; 66:1]

You folks have come to know by experience that their hope and expectation [is/was] groundless and fruitless.

3. In the end, though, He again continues saying,

"Look and consider! The people at some point pulling the sanctuary of this temple (= holy place and holy of holies) down will themselves be progressively building it (or: will keep on building it as a house)."

4. It is progressively happening (occurring; coming to be; birthing itself). You see, because of the [situation for] them to go to war, it is (or: was) pulled down by the hated people (or: hostile forces; = Gentiles?). Now even the very servants (or: subordinates) from among the hated people (or: hostile forces; = Gentiles?) will progressively rebuild (or: will continue building [it] up again).

5. And so it was shown in clear Light (or: is caused to be seen; made visible; made to appear; manifested): the sanctuary of the temple of Israel (Israel's shrine: the holy place) is to be progressively given over [comment: note the present infinitive], for the Writing (Scripture) continues saying,

"And so [the] LORD (= Yahweh) will proceed handing over the sheep of the pasture and the sheep-fold, even their tower, into complete destruction and ruin."

And thus it comes to be (or: it happened) according to what [the] LORD spoke. [comment: note the aorist infinitive: either in the present, or in the past]

6. Now we should inquire whether there is a sanctuary of the temple (shrine and holy place) of God. There is! Wherever He Himself continues saying to continue producing and to keep on calving (or: to progressively create and to continue knitting together; to keep on doing and to repeatedly adjust)! For you see, it has been, and now continues, written:

"And there will continue being, during the bringing of the ends of the goal (consummation; joint-accomplishing and concluding) of the week together, [that] a sanctuary (shrine; holy place and holy of holies) of, and from, God will progressively be formed gloriously (built as a House in a manifestation of praise and in an assumed appearance) upon the Name of [the] Lord." [Dan. 9:24]

7. Therefore, I continue finding that there is (there continues being) a sanctuary of the temple. How, then, will it be progressively formed (built as a House) upon the Name of [the] Lord? You folks must learn! Before the [situation for] us to continue trusting (faithing in loyalty) in, and by, God, the settled dwelling place of our heart continued being subject to ruin, decay and corruption (perishable) and without strength (weak; feeble) – truly (really) like a sanctuary (shrine) being built by hand that continues being full (or: filled), indeed, with idolatry – and continued being a house of demons (from animistic influences; [note: a Hellenistic concept and term from animistic religions]) through the [situation or tendencies] to keep on doing as much as continued being contrary, and in a position opposed, to God.

8. Yet, it will continue being built upon the Name of [the] Lord. Now hold yourselves toward this and pay attention: that the sanctuary (temple shrine; holy places) of the Lord is being built gloriously (in a manifestation which calls forth praise; with an assumed appearance). How? You must learn! In and by receiving the flowing away of failures to hit the target (the divorce from sins and release from mistakes; the liberation from deviations), and with placing expectation upon the Name, we were birthed to be new people (or: we have come to be new folks), from the midst of a beginning: people formed and created again from a state of disorder and wildness and framed to be founded and established! Because of this, in union with our settled habitation (centered in our permanent dwelling place), God truly and really continues permanently dwelling and living His life within us (centered in us; in union with us; in our midst)!

9. How? The *Logos* of His faithfulness (or: His Word from the Trust; The patterned Information which is His Faith; The Conveyance of the Message of His loyalty); His calling of and from the Promise (or:

the calling which is His promise); **the wisdom of the results from the Way pointed out** (the effects of being turned in the right direction and placed in rightwised relationships of covenant participation); **the imparted goals** (implanted destinies; inner directives) **of, and from, the teaching; He Himself continuously giving Light ahead of time** (prophesying) **within us; He Himself continuously dwelling within** (in union with and centered in) **us, as His permanent abode, while continuously opening up in us, to us, and for us – the ones having been enslaved in the Death** (with and by the Death) **– the Gate of the sanctuary** (the Door of the temple shrine, or, holy place), **which is a Mouth, [and then] in giving to us, and by granting for us, a change of mind** (perspective; way of thinking; attitude), **He progressively leads and brings us into the incorruptible** (into the midst of the imperishable) **sanctuary of the temple which cannot be ruined.**

10. **It follows that the person continually desiring and intending to be delivered** (made whole; rescued; saved; kept safe) **CONTINUES LOOKING not unto the human** (or: to mankind), **BUT RATHER unto the ONE within him** (in union with and centered in him) **– [Who is] continuously abiding** (being permanently settled down to live) **and constantly speaking upon him – while REPEATEDLY BEING AMAZED at the thing never** (not even at any time) **heard: neither the gush-effects** (results from the flow; things spoken) **of** (from; with regard to) **patterned information being laid out** (thoughts, ideas or a message being spoken) **from the mouth, nor yet [what] he at some time fully desired to continue hearing! THIS is** (continually exists being) **a spiritual sanctuary of the temple** (a set-apart, sacred and holy place or sphere having the quality, character and essence of a Breath-effect) **being continuously built** (progressively erected as a House) **in, by, with and for the Lord!**

Chapter 17

1. **In so far as I was being in union with ability and simplicity** (centered in power and frankness) **to explain and clarify to, and for, you folks, my soul, in my full, rushing passion, continues expectantly hoping that I have not left aside** (omitted) **anything pertaining** (relating) **unto deliverance** (salvation; rescue; wholeness; safety; healing).

2. **You see, if I continue writing to you folks concerning the things continuing in standing within the present** (the now), **or of imminent things** (things progressively about to be), **under no circumstances could you folks direct your minds so as to perceive or understand through the thing normally** (or: presently; habitually) **lying** (or: stored; situated) **within the midst of** (or: centered in) **parables** (illustrations cast at the side). **These things [are] indeed thus** (this way).

Chapter 18

1. **Now let us change our steps and pass on, even upon a different intimate, experiential knowledge** (or: insight; *gnosis*) **and teaching. There continue being two roads** (paths; ways) **of teaching** (instruction; training) **and privilege from out of Being** (or: right from authority) [*cf Didache* chapters 1-5] **– the one of the Light, and the one of the Darkness. Now [the] differences of the two roads** (paths; ways) **[are] much** (abundant). **You see, upon which, on the one hand, there continue being folks having been stationed** (placed and arranged) **[that are] God's agents that bring Light to the path, and guide with Light** (or: folks with the Message who bear the Light) **from God. Yet on the other hand [is the road or path] upon which [are] agents of, and folks with the message from, the adversary** (opponent; or, traditionally, *satan*).

2. **And so, on the one hand, is the Lord – from [the] ages, on into the midst of the Age [of Messiah] – yet on the other hand, [is] the ruler of the present** (now) **season** (or: situation) **of the lawlessness.**

Chapter 19

1. **Therefore, the Road** (Path; Way) **of the Light is THIS: should someone continue wanting, keep on intending and be repeatedly willing to progressively journey [the] Route and make one's way on to the Place** (or: region; position; space; location; occasion) **marked out and determined** (bounded, fixed and appointed), **he or she should urge on industriously, with eager haste, in** (with; for; to; by) **his or her works** (deeds; actions). **Consequently, the knowledge and insight being given to, for and in us, with a view to progressively walking about** (= living our lives) **within it, is such as** (or: like) **this:**

2. **You will continue urging toward reunion with, and will be progressively loving the One producing** (forming; creating; making) **you. You will be made to keep on revering and to continue respecting** (or: fearing) **the One fashioning and shaping you. You will continue giving a good reputation to** (glorifying; having a positive opinion of; producing a manifestation which calls forth praise to) **the One releasing you out of death. You will continue being single** (without folds; simple; noncomplex; open; sincere; guileless; straightforward) **in the heart, and yet wealthy in spirit and with Breath-effect. You will not continue being closely joined or glued or united with the folks habitually traveling in a road** (or: way) **of death** (or: a path from Death). **You will continue hating** (regarding with ill-will) **everything that is not pleasing to God or satisfying for God. You will continue hating** (regarding with ill-will) **all judging from a low position** (hypercriticism; hair-splitting legalistic nit-picking; pedantic behavior; or, a later meaning: hypocrisy). **You should by no means abandon** (leave down within the midst) **implanted goals from [the] Lord** (imparted, purposed-ends which pertain to [the] Lord; inner directives of, and from, [the] Master).

   [note: most of the verbs in this chapter are in the future indicative (a durative tense), not in the imperative; thus these are promises, not commands]

3. **You will not keep on lifting** (exalting; elevating) **yourself up high, but you will continue being humble-minded in relation to all things** (oriented toward the lowly, with respect to all people). **You will not keep on lifting or taking up glory** (a reputation; credit; an appearance; a presumption; something imagined) **upon yourself. You will not continue taking or receiving a misery-gushed resolution** (a worthless design; an unsound decision; a bad plan) **against your associate** (neighbor; near one). **You will not keep on giving arrogance, insolent boldness or rashness to your soul.**

4. **You will not continue being sexually promiscuous, prostituting yourself, being unfaithful** (fornicating) **or participate in idolatry. You will not keep on committing adultery. You will not continue abusing or molesting children. Under no circumstances should the** *Logos* (Word; conveyance of the Message; patterned Information; Thought; Idea) **of, or from, God go forth from any folks centered in what is not lifted from having been down** (in union with uncleanness, defilement or un-lifted down-ness or contrariness; or: come out of any people within the midst of worthless waste or impureness [such as decayed flesh]). **You will not continue receiving the face** (showing favoritism or making a difference between people; using a double standard) **to reprove or correct someone, upon the result of a fall to the side** (on the effect of a false step or a stumbling aside; at an offense or a trespass). **You will continue being gentle and considerate. You will keep on being quiet, tranquil and at rest! You will habitually tremble with awe at the words** (*logoi*; conveyances of information; messages; thoughts; ideas) **which you heard. You will not continue remembering anything ugly, of bad quality, or as it ought not to be, about your brother** (or: bearing a grudge about the one from the same Womb as you).

5. **Under no circumstance should you be two-souled** (double-minded; undecided; wavering; doubting) **whether a thing will proceed being** (something will continue existing), **or not. "Under no circumstance should you take the Name of [the] LORD** (= Yahweh) **on a meaningless, useless, fruitless or unprofitable [matter or situation]."** [Ex. 20:7] **You will progressively urge toward reunion with your associate** (continuously accept your neighbor; habitually love the one near you) **over**

(or: more than) **your soul! You will not proceed** (or: keep on) **killing a child, in abortion** (or: in corruption, damage or deterioration), **nor even, again, after being born, kill it off. Under no circumstance should you remove, or take away, your hand from your son or your daughter, but to the contrary, you will, from [their] youth, progressively teach respect of God** (or: reverential fear, from God).

6. **"Under no circumstance should you come to be progressively rushing upon** (continuously overly-passionate about; constantly having strong impulse toward or over-desire for) **the things of, or belonging to, your associate** (neighbor; person near you)" [Ex. 20:17]. **Under no circumstance should you come to be a person who has more than another** (or: someone with more than his or her share; greedy; or: one who defrauds for the sake of gain). **Neither will you, from out of your soul, continue joined to, or glued with, proud or haughty people, or with folks of high cultic position, but in contrast, you will continue being turned back to engage with lowly folks and to be involved with just folks. You will continue receiving, accepting and welcoming the results of experiences** (the effects from inner operations and implanted workings) **repeatedly walking together with you** (or: constantly happening to you) **as good, fair and virtuous, from having seen, and thus knowing, that apart from God nothing comes to be** (or: that not even one thing is happening or transpiring without God).

7. **You will not continue being with divided-knowing or existing from a divided will** (or: decision), **nor [being] of a double tongue** (or: from deceit). **You will habitually station** (set; place) **under, to give submissive support to masters** (for owners; among lords; with employers), **as a copy of God** (a type and pattern from God; a beaten image, which reflects God): **centered in shame and respectful fear** (in union with modesty and respect). **Under no circumstance in bitterness set upon** (give instructions or orders centered in harshness or animosity to) **your slave or female servant – for those folks continually place expectation** (or: expectant hope) **upon the same God – lest in some way they will proceed not caused to fear or respect the God [that is] upon both parties, because He did not come to call with respect of persons** (corresponding to surface presentation; according to a face; with regard to reputation), **but to the contrary, [to call] upon those whom the Spirit prepared** (or: whom the Breath-effect made ready).

8. **You will progressively have common being and existence with your associate in all things** (or: will continue sharing, fellowshipping and being in alliance with your neighbor), **and so you will not continue saying things to continue being your own. For since you folks continue being partners of a common existence** (sharers of common being) **within the incorruptible and imperishable, how much more within the corruptible and perishable? You will not continue being talkative or quick to speak, for it follows that the mouth [is] a snare of death** (or: a trap from death, and which is death). **So far as you continue able and with power, you will progressively be clean and consistent over [situations; areas] of your soul** (or: will continue pure, on behalf of your inner person).

9. **"Do not continue becoming on the one hand a person constantly stretching out the hands to repeatedly receive** (or: take), **yet on the other hand a person constantly pulling back and drawing the hands together toward the [situation for] giving."** [Sirach (Ecclesiasticus) 4:31] **You will continue urging toward reunion with, and habitually accept with constant love – as an apple of your eye – all people continuing in speaking the** *Logos* **from [the] Lord to you** (or: constantly proclaiming the Word of [the] Lord for you; repeatedly telling the patterned Information of the Message with you).

10. **Night and day you will continue remembering** (calling to mind, thinking about, giving careful consideration to and mentioning) **a day of examining, deciding about, or judging** (or: a deciding day), **and so daily keep on seeking out and searching for the faces** (= personal presence) **of the set-apart folks. Or, through a word** (or: by means of a thought or a conveyance of patterned information), **after**

continuing tired and weary from laboring and then progressively journeying on into the midst of release from your failures (mistakes; failures to hit the target), **you will not keep on hesitating from [receiving] a reward from an ideal Recompenser** (a beautiful One who gives away something instead; a fine Rewarder; an ideal One who gives back, in return or replacement).

[note: in the second half of the verse, the text may be defective; Lightfoot reads: "Thou shall not hesitate to give, neither shalt thou murmur when giving, but thou shalt know who is the good paymaster of thy reward."]

11. **You will continue guarding, watching over and taking care of that which you take to your side, neither adding nor taking away. You will constantly hate the misery-gushed** (the unsound; the painful; the unprofitable; the bad condition; the unserviceable), **on unto maturity** (into the midst of [the] final act; unto an end; unto a finished product). **You will continually decide justly and in accord with the Way pointed out** (or: You will repeatedly evaluate from a rightwised paradigm; You will habitually be judging fairly and from being in covenant).

12. **You will not continue making an effect of tearing apart** (a result of splitting; a division; a schism), **but you will keep on joining and progressively bringing or making peace, while constantly bringing together those continually fighting, quarreling or disputing. You will go on making grateful acknowledgements upon your failures to hit the target** (or: admitting and giving thanks upon your mistakes, errors and sins; speaking from sameness with a view to your deviations). **You will not continue approaching upon a thought, word or act with a view toward having goodness, ease or well-being** (or: come to prayer) **in a misery-gushed** (unsound; unserviceable; painful; bad-conditioned) **conscience.**

THIS is, and continues being, the Road (Path; Way) **of the Light!**

Chapter 20

1. **Now the road** (path; way) **of the dark and murky is** (continues being) **crooked** (bent; winding) **and filled with** (or: full of; thoroughly characterized by) **negative prayers** (down-oriented wishes; curses). **It is** (continues being) **a road** (path; way) **of death for an unspecified period of time** (or: of life-long death; or: which is death with regard to the Age [of Messiah]; or: from death characterized by this age), **together with corresponding retribution** (or: accompanied by compensating help on the side of, and with aid for, those who have been attacked or have suffered injury), **within** (or: on) **which are, and continue being, the things constantly loosing-away of** (or: repeatedly destroying; progressive losing from) **their soul: idolatry; arrogant boldness** (rash insolence; recklessness); **pride of ability** (exaltation or haughtiness of power); **judging from a low position** (hyper-criticism; hair-splitting legalistic nit-picking; pedantic behavior); **double-heartedness** (duplicity); **adultery; murder; seizure** (snatching-away; plunder; rape); **conceit** (or: over-display); **sorcery** (magic art); **desire for advantage so as to gain more; a lack of reverence of, and a lack of respect for, God** (or: without fear from God).

2. **[Such folks are] pursuers and persecutors of good and virtuous people; [they are] haters of truth and reality – folks constantly accepting what is false, and habitually loving a lie** (or: [the] Lie), **while not continuing on to experientially know a reward from the Way pointed out** (a recompense from eschatological deliverance and being pointed in the right direction; a compensation which is justice in rightwised, covenantal relationships), **while not continually joining themselves to [the] good, being glued into virtue, or associating with a well-born person; no deciding for right or justice** (no interpreting within the Way pointed out; no evaluating with rightwisedness; no judging by the right Path).

[They are] not habitually holding themselves toward, nor paying attention to, nor being concerned about (= ignoring) **widow and orphan; not continuing awake and watchful unto God's reverence and respect** (or: a reverent fear from God), **but rather** (but to the contrary) **[watchful] upon the misery-**

gushed and useless (the bad condition and unserviceable), **from whom gentleness** (mildness; meekness) **and patient remaining-under, to give support, [are] distant** (or: aloof) **and far away. [They are] constantly accepting and loving empty and meaningless things** (vain, worthless and "nothing" things), **while habitually pursuing the effect of repayment** (the result of a rendering in return), **[yet] not normally being merciful to** (doing acts of mercy for) **[the] destitute and impoverished. [They are] not normally working hard or toiling on behalf of a person that is oppressed, weary and born-down from toil, or a situation that is worn out or oppressed, [and yet are] easily inclined, and prone, in negative talking** (or: slander; gossip; down-saying), **yet not normally knowing the person making** (or: fabricating; producing) **them. [They are] murderers of children; decayers and corruptors of a result of a molding of God** (or: ruiners of God's formed image), **folks continually turning away from the person in need, while constantly oppressing the distressed** (squeezed; troubled; restricted and afflicted) **person. [They are] paracletes of rich folks** (lawyers, advocates, aids and encouragers of wealthy people); **unjust judges of poor folks; folks missing the mark** (deviating; failing; erring; sinning) **in all things!**

Chapter 21

1. **Therefore, after progressively learning the effects of the Way pointed out** (the results of what is right and just; the effects of relationships that are turned in the right direction) **from the LORD** (= Yahweh; or: which are the Lord [= Christ]; or: the Lord's Way-effects and Path-results), **it is, and continues being, beautiful, fine and ideal to habitually walk about** (= constantly live one's life) **centered in them** (in union with them) – **as many as have been written, [above]. For it follows that the person habitually doing** (continually performing; constantly producing) **these things will progressively be esteemed within God's reign**

> (or: will repeatedly be given an assumed appearance in the sovereign activities of God; will constantly be given a manifestation which calls forth praise, within the midst of the kingdom of God; will progressively be given a good reputation, in union with the sovereign influence from God).

The person constantly choosing (repeatedly selecting) **those [other] things will keep on mutually destroying himself, along with his works** (or: will progressively lose himself, together with the deeds from him). **Through this one [is] resurrection** (a standing back up, again); **through that one [is] a result of a corresponding giving back in repayment**

> (or: On account of this [is] resurrection; on account of this [is] an effect of a reward, or a requital).

2. **I repeatedly ask those continuing in having a higher station** (or: constantly holding [position or power] above [others])**: if you folks continue receiving any advice or counsel of good intention from me** (or: of virtuous motive and purpose from me), **continue holding with yourselves those unto whom you folks can perform the ideal** (or: habitually keep among you those in the midst of whom you folks would yourselves cultivate the beauty; keep on possessing with yourselves the fine, unto which you folks should work) – **do not leave [them] out, or leave [this] undone.**

3. **The LORD** (= Yahweh; or: the Lord [=Christ]) **[is] near** (close enough to touch, and available), **and the reward which is Him** (or: and so [is] His reward, or the wages from Him). [Isa. 40:10; Rev. 22:12]

4. **Yet also, I keep on asking of you folks: progressively come to be good custom-setters** (virtuous placers of normal patterns; excellent lawgivers) **among yourselves. You continue remaining faithful advisors and trusted counselors of yourselves: eliminate all judging from a low position** (hyper-criticism; hair-splitting legalistic nit-picking; pedantic behavior) **from among you folks.**

5. **Now may God, the One constantly functioning as** (or: being; performing as) **Lord and Master of all the aggregate of humanity and of all the ordered system** (or: from all the arranged universe), **give to you folks wisdom, understanding, skill from being versed in knowing how, insight and intimate,**

experiential knowledge of the effects of His Way that has been pointed out (the results of what is right and just from Him; the effects of relationships that are turned in the right direction, which is Him), **[and] patience** (remaining under [situations] in order to give support).

6. **So continue coming to be folks instructed and taught by God, constantly seeking out what [the] Lord continually seeks, or desires, from you folks, and then keep on doing** (progressively produce; habitually perform) **to the end that you folks would be found in union with a day from a deciding** (or: centered in a day of evaluation; resident within [the] Day, which is judging).

7. **Now if there continues being any remembrance of good** (or: from [the] excellent; which is virtue), **you folks call me to mind** (remember me) **when taking thought of, studying, attending, exercising or practicing these things, so that also the full-rushing passion and complete desire – as well as the wakeful care – can lead unto, and would reach into, something good and excellent. I continue asking you folks, begging a favor!**

8. **So long as the beautiful, ideal vessel** (= the body) **continues being with you folks, do not leave even one of them out, or leave even one of them undone, but further, embracingly**
    (in holding together with accompanying maintenance; with keeping [things; yourselves] from falling apart; with sequestering)
keep on seeking and searching out these very things and progressively make complete (make full; fill up; fulfill) **every implanted goal** (impartation of the finished product, within; internal directive), **for it follows that He is worthy** (or: for you see, this is of equal value and comparable worth).

9. **Because of this, I was more eager to write [to you], from what I was made able, unto** (with a view to) **the [situation for] you to be in a healthy frame of mind, with a good attitude. O children of love** (or: from the drive toward accepted reunion, which is from the full giving of Self to you) **and of peace from the Joining, you folks are being progressively delivered** (repeatedly rescued and kept safe; continuously saved; habitually made whole).

The LORD of the glory and of all grace
    (The Master of the manifestation which calls forth praise and of every favor; The Owner, from this assumed appearance and entire act producing happiness; [= Yahweh] who has the good reputation as well as every grace)
[is] with your [corporate] spirit
    (or: [is] in the company of, in the presence of, and [is] with the spirit of you folks; [continues being] on the side of the breath-effect from you folks)!

Lightning Source UK Ltd.
Milton Keynes UK
UKHW050641121020
371437UK00003B/85